THE NORTHERN DYNASTIES KINGSHIP AND STATECRAFT IN CHIMOR

A Symposium at Dumbarton Oaks
12TH AND 13TH OCTOBER 1985

Maria Rostworowski de Diez Canseco
and Michael E. Moseley, *Organizers*

Michael E. Moseley and
Alana Cordy-Collins, *Editors*

Dumbarton Oaks Research Library and Collection
Washington, D.C.

Library of Congress Cataloging-in-Publication Data

The Northern dynasties : kingship and statecraft in Chimor / Michael
  E. Moseley and Alana Cordy-Collins, editors.
     p.   cm.
    "A symposium at Dumbarton Oaks, 12th and 13th October 1985."
    Includes bibliographical references.
    ISBN 0-88402-180-7
    1. Chimu Indians—Politics and government—Congresses. 2. Chimu
Indians—Antiquities—Congresses. 3. Chan Chan Site (Peru)—
Congresses. 4. Peru—Antiquities—Congresses. I. Moseley,
Michael Edward. II. Cordy-Collins, Alana. III. Dumbarton Oaks.
F3430.1.C46N67   1990
985 .16—dc20   89-23336

Contents

Contents

Contents

Preface

ARCHAEOLOGY IS THE PRINCIPAL INVESTIGATORY METHOD for interpreting Pre-Hispanic culture in the New World largely because most of the New World cultures lacked alphabetic writing systems and left few written records. For the late Pre-Conquest cultures, however, there exist written records from the early Colonial period that speak of indigenous life. Some of these texts are the eye-witness accounts of the conquerors themselves, others are histories written by Spaniard and Indian alike to record the old ways (to speak of the gods and ancestors, and divine and secular deeds), still others are administrative records arising from litigations, disputes, and governmental regulations concerning the Indians. These documents complement in important ways evidence coming from excavation, and they can make possible a much fuller reconstruction of indigenous culture.

The difficulty comes with attempts to make firm concordances between the ethnohistorical and archaeological records. Close concordances are seldom achieved because the two records offer different, and sometimes conflictive, kinds of information. They also inform on different aspects of culture, and their interpretation is based on different methodologies. The interface of ethnohistory and archaeology remains one of the principal challenges confronting the investigator of late Pre-Hispanic cultures.

Ethnohistory can be used most successfully when it functions as an independent witness and as a check against archaeology; the reverse can equally be true. Archaeology produces information of a different kind about a culture. It is not simply that ethnohistory gives myth while archaeology provides fact, but ethnohistory and archaeology produce different kinds of facts. Through the accretion of bits of data, excavation presents broad pictures of a culture; it can tell about a city's growth and shrinkage, of its subsistence base, of its wealth. But it cannot tell about social and religious ideology with the same specificity as written records. A historical source may describe a political reality or a religious belief, and the archaeological record reveals its physical manifestations on the ground. Where historical sources may date an event by year, month, reign, or dynasty, the excavated record excels at revealing sequence. Written history can tell of events and actions, and archaeology can show the effects of those events and actions.

Many of these thoughts were on Michael Moseley's mind when he began to consider organizing a Dumbarton Oaks symposium for the fall of 1985. Because there had been so many recent advances made by archaeologists and ethnohistorians working along Peru's North Coast in the late period, he wanted to see what kind of concordances could in fact be made between text and excavated feature. Was there sufficient architectural or archaeological evidence to test the validity of the Naymlap legend, for example? Working with María Rostworowski de Diez Canseco and members of the Senior Fellows committee for Pre-Columbian Studies, he shaped the symposium to explore articulations in the archaeological and ethnohistorical records of kingship and rule in Chimor. Moseley and Rostworowski put a particular focus on the historical realities of royal succession in Chimor, and on the organizational principles of statecraft of the northern dynasties.

Moseley and Rostworowski co-chaired the meeting, which was held on October 12–13, 1985, following which Moseley began to gather the papers for publication. The essay by James B. Richardson, III, Mark A. McConaughy, Allison Heaps de Peña, and Elena B. Décima Zamecnik was added at this time because it brings in the northern frontier, which had not been represented at the meeting. As happens with so many large and complex works being brought together by busy people, the volume was long in coming together. In 1987 Alana Cordy-Collins gave it the needed push when she joined Moseley as co-editor of the book.

Most of the papers in this volume look at the art, architectural, and archaeological remains at Chan Chan and related sites to see if and how the excavated data, and especially the monuments, reflect events that may be described in early Colonial texts. Other papers focus more fully on the written sources themselves to inform views of Chimor society. Together, the monuments and the texts are analyzed for what they reveal about Chimu statecraft and views of kingship. Neither corpus can reveal a complete picture in isolation, but jointly they can present an integrated overview of the northern dynasties.

Elizabeth Hill Boone
Dumbarton Oaks

Structure and History in the Dynastic Lore of Chimor

MICHAEL E. MOSELEY
UNIVERSITY OF FLORIDA

INTRODUCTION

ENCOMPASSING SOME ONE THOUSAND KILOMETERS of Pacific coastland, Chimor is the second largest native polity to arise in South America that can be documented both ethnohistorically and archaeologically. Growth in this documentation is contributing to the emergence of a multilinear perspective on the evolution of Andean civilization. This viewpoint sees the vast Andean Cordillera as encompassing contrasting environmental conditions that fostered divergent ways of making a living, which, in turn, underlay distinctive trends in long-term development. Tropical forest adaptations prevailed in the equatorial north where the mountain range is low, narrow, and well watered. To the south, however, conditions change from more Amazonian to typically Andean as the Cordillera becomes significantly higher, wider, and drier. Here environmental variability supported two very different but closely juxtaposed adaptations. One was upland, characterized by mountain agropastoralism. The other was coastal, with people relying on irrigated desert valleys and marine resources. At its height, Chimor encompassed two-thirds of all land ever irrigated along the Pacific desert and, by inference, two-thirds of the coastal population. From a multilinear evolutionary perspective, the ancient kingdom is the culmination of the coastal trajectory of development that began when people first settled the Pacific desert. In many ways comprehending the long course of littoral evolution depends on our still-limited understanding of Chimor.

Residing at the metropolis of Chan Chan, the royalty of Chimor bitterly contested Inca territorial ambitions. Yet, the coastal polity fell to the Cuzco imperium around A.D. 1470 and, during ensuing generations, witnessed its own dismemberment under Inca rule. With Spanish contact and conquest came the first New World pandemics, which ravaged the coastal populations, completing the social disintegration of the once powerful kingdom.

As a result of prior political and demographic collapse, those Europeans who took an interest in the old kingdom encountered only truncated expressions of its institutions and fragmentary accounts of the royal dynasties that had forged Chimor into the continent's penultimate empire. Because of differences in language and worldview, what native people said about their life and history could vary from what the Spanish thought they said. Furthermore, the corpus of information available from coastal informants was artificially restricted by the Colonial legal policy of accepting the situation under Inca rule as the *terminus post quem,* and this fact curtailed Spanish inquiry into pre-Inca conditions. As a result, there are but two major categories of written information about Chimor: Colonial administrative and judicial records, and accounts of indigenous oral traditions. The former are much more numerous than the latter, which include only four fragmentary discussions of the coastal dynasties.

The documentary data for Chimor are often ambiguous and therefore subject to more than one interpretation. Ethnography offers interpretative insights; however, the applicability of ethnographic analogy to Chimor is constrained because this ancient empire occupied what is still the most productive region of the entire arid Andean coast. After the Spanish Conquest, the disproportionately high concentration of resources fostered intensive colonialism and capitalism. Today, the northern irrigated valleys are managed by large, mechanized agro-industrial complexes feeding export markets, and fishing has been similarly commercialized to supply international demands. Conditions that make this particular region of coast the fulcrum of the modern Peruvian economy are clearly relevant to understanding why Chimor developed into the continent's second-largest historically documented empire. Yet, because the industrialized coast lacks uninterrupted ethnic and demographic continuities with the Colonial and prehistoric past, this lack limits the role of ethnographic analogy as an instrument for illuminating earlier societies of the littoral desert.

THE SYMPOSIUM

There are only two primary sources of information about Chimor: the written works left by the Colonial occupation and the physical works left by the kingdom itself. While the former are unimposing, the latter are daunting for their abundance, size, and complexity. Scholars have long recognized that neither source of information can be deciphered adequately without reference to the other. Developing cross-references and exploring interpretative checks and balances are methodological themes underlying the symposium papers that follow.

One purpose of the symposium was to examine possible archaeological and ethnohistorical concordances that would be useful for distinguishing what might be the incidences and institutions of true history from the reflexive, potentially distorted pseudo-history of the royal dynasties that held sway on the North Coast during the millennium preceding Pizarro's arrival. To this end, Alan Kolata and I composed a "position" paper, "Myth and History on the North Coast of Peru: Steps to an Archaeological Concordat," which was circulated to the participants. The intent was to provide a set of target issues that could be responded to or elaborated upon, thereby focusing the symposium. I draw upon sections of the position paper in this introductory essay, into which I also incorporate additional issues elicited during the symposium.

The position paper proceeded from the premise that any interpretation of ethnohistorical material potentially subject to archaeological negation can be treated as a testable hypothesis. Disproving hypotheses can often be unequivocal, whereas their archaeological proof is frequently confined to circumstantial evidence that may be supportive, but ultimately equivocal. Constraints on testing propositions derived from ethnohistory are addressed directly in the contributions by Christopher Donnan and Izumi Shimada and indirectly in other papers. The position that all interpretations that can be framed as hypotheses should be tested was accepted by the participating archaeologists. However, when dealing specifically with oral traditions, this position was questioned by several of the contributing ethnohistorians. The paper by Patricia Netherly articulates the situation. She argues that Andean people conceive of time in a present and non-present framework, which expresses social distance or hierarchy, and, when specific events such as the founding of a dynasty or its devastation by a flood are described in a narrative, their purpose is to make a structural statement rather than give an account of actual events. This may well be true. Yet, who is to know unless the indigenous narratives are given archaeological scrutiny? Fortunately, the situation that Netherly describes is itself a hypothesis with testable implications as to the dearth of identifiable content in oral narratives of Chimor. With this in mind, my introductory essay explores the content of desert dynastic lore. It concludes that both history and structure are to be found, with the latter providing the cipher for decoding the former.

THE ORAL TRADITIONS

In saying that the oral traditions describe *dynasties,* the word itself predisposes us to think in terms of linear, historical chronology. However, R. T. Zuidema cogently points out in his paper that, in an Andean context, the term must be understood as one relating to kinship, kin terms, and kin obligations that were integrated with and regulated by the indigenous annual calendar. Moreover, concepts about kin, time, and the past involved the use of human mummies that were curated, carried about, dressed up, and displayed for ritual and political use. Beyond these problems, the oral traditions of Chimor are admittedly the most difficult of ethnohistorical sources to deal with due to their limited number, fragmentary nature, and lack of detail. Yet, the stories are of exceptional importance because these are the only accounts we have of what potentially might be pre-Inca history. Contained in four written sources, the oral traditions discuss pre-Inca events, individuals, institutions, and places relating to two imperia. One is the Taycanamo dynasty, comprising the rulers of Chimor. The other is the Naymlap dynasty of Lambayeque that Chimor came to incorporate. Salient features of the stories warrant brief recounting.

A purported history of the imperial heartland of Chimor is contained in the fragmentary first chapter of the *Anonymous History of Trujillo* (1604; published by Vargas Ugarte 1936: 232–233; and translated by Rowe 1948: 29–30 and by Kosok 1965: 74). Arriving by balsa watercraft, a man called Taycanamo settles in the lower Moche Valley, saying he was sent from over the sea to govern this land. His son Guacricaur conquers leaders of the valley. In turn, his son Ñançenpinco completes the upstream consolidation of the valley, then initiates the first stage of external expansion, extending the imperial frontiers to the Rio Santa in the south and the Rio Jequetepeque in the north. After this expansion there are some five to seven unnamed *caciques* or rulers up to Minchançaman, who is either the sixth or seventh of the *caciques,* or the next successor. He conquers the coast from the Rio Chillon to the Rio Tumbez in a second stage of imperial expansion. In turn, this ruler is conquered by an Inca lord called Topa Yapanqui and taken to Cuzco. An apparently "distant" son of Minchançaman, living in the province of Huara with his mother, is then installed by the Inca to govern. Thereafter, named and unnamed successors persist into the Colonial period to the time the anonymous account was written.

Indirectly relating to the Taycanamo story is a brief account of Chimor's conquest and administration of the Jequetepeque Valley written by Antonio de la Calancha (1638: 546–547; translated by Means 1931: 56–57). The valley is said to have been subdued by a military leader called Pacatnamu who was installed as the first provincial governor and who built an administrative center that came to bear his name. Pacatnamu's incorporation of Jequetepeque would presumably cross-tie to the first stage of Chimor's external expansion, and the administrative center he built is apparently that of Farfan, discussed in Geoffrey Conrad's paper.

There are two apparently independent accounts of the Naymlap dynasty. The more detailed is by Miguel Cabello Balboa in the 1586 *Miscelánea Antarctica* (1951; summarized and commented upon by Means 1931: 51–53; Rowe 1948: 37–39; Kosok 1965: 73; and Netherly n.d.: 302–307, among others). A briefer version appeared in 1782 by Justo Modesto de Rubiños y Andrade (1936). Reaching the Lambayeque coast with a flotilla of balsas, a man called Naymlap arrives with his wife, a green stone idol, and a very large entourage, including a retinue of some forty officials. He establishes a settlement at a place called Chot, thought to be the ruins known today as Chotuna. A senior son Cium has twelve sons, many of whom supposedly found other important Lambayeque settlements. A succession of twelve named rulers begun by Naymlap ends with the ruler Fempellec, who is tempted by a sorceress to move the founder's green stone idol. This brings on thirty days of disastrous rains and disruptive flooding followed by famine and pestilence. The potentate's vassals rise up and cast Fempellec into the sea. After an interregnum of unknown duration, Chimor conquers the region and holds it through a succession of three named governors before the land is, in turn, conquered by the Inca. The incorporation of Lambayeque by Chimor would presumably cross-tie to the second stage of imperial expansion in the Taycanamo dynastic account.

While acknowledging potential mytho-poetic content, a measure of historicity was ascribed to these scant accounts by scholars such as Philip Ainsworth Means (1931), John Rowe (1948), and Paul Kosok (1965), all of whom used the narratives to estimate the antiquity of the coastal dynasties. Kosok's efforts are particularly noteworthy because he cross-correlated events mentioned in the two imperial successions and surveyed the archaeological sites that are mentioned. He viewed the Naymlap story as relating to a confederated polity, while the Taycanamo tradition pertained to a centralized conquest state. This interpretation remains viable. In estimating the antiquity of the two dynasties, Kosok and his predecessors pursued the premise that if the accounts were complete and reflected unilineal successions of rulers, then by working back from the time of the Inca conquest an average duration of reign could be calculated for each earlier ruler down to the lineage founder. This is a logical procedure, and, indeed, it is the one by which Inca chronology is calibrated. However, its applicability to Chimor is now questionable on ethnohistorical grounds. María Rostworowski points out in her paper that succession among the lords of the North Coast was from brother to brother, and only after exhausting positions in the senior generation was rule passed to the following generation. Furthermore, she is joined by Netherly and Zuidema in arguing for duality of rule and diarchy, rather than monarchy, as the pervasive structure of power on the coast and elsewhere in the Andes. These considerations would certainly reduce the number of potential generations spanned by the imperial narratives and imply that the dynasties were either established very recently, or that any historical content is truncated or absent. Such implications are best assessed archaeologically. As in the position paper, I will employ what is known about the Moche Valley and Chan Chan, the capital of Chimor, as a basis for cross-tying the regional archaeological record pertaining to potential events, institutions, and individuals mentioned in the oral traditions.

However, it is useful first to review the salient features of the archaeological setting that Chimor embraced.

THE SETTING

The oral traditions relate to times, places, and remains in the prehistoric record that are now often referred to as *Chimu*. This general term is sometimes treated as synonymous with Chimor and its people. Yet, technically the latter refers to a polity and the former to a rather loosely defined style of remains. The polity encompassed substantial ethnic diversity, and many archaeological remains within Chimor are not Chimu but local in style. Because the term *Chimu* subsumes a great deal of regional and local variation, it is subject to subdivision. Archaeological materials particularly pertinent to the Taycanamo story are those associated with Chan Chan, and they define a style called "Imperial Chimu." In the Lambayeque region, remains relevant to the Naymlap account are associated with a style called "Sican." Due in part to the nature of coastal irrigation agriculture, a number of imposing monuments are pertinent to northern dynastic lore.

The South American Cordillera is low, narrow, and well watered in Ecuador. Along the Pacific watershed, tropical conditions rapidly give way to typically arid Andean conditions as the mountains rise to the south, and the ranges become progressively higher and drier. South of the Rio Tumbez there is normally no significant annual precipitation at elevations below 1,500 m, and the Andean coastlands comprise the driest New World desert. Here, torrential rainfall occurs only in association with rare but recurrent El Niño-Southern Oscillation (ENSO) events. During such events precipitation varies from one coastal valley to another. Statistically, however, there is more rainfall in the north than south and much more rainfall at lower elevations than higher ones (Waylen and Caviedes 1986). Torrential downpours on the unvegetated desert landscape can result in disastrous flooding. Therefore, if there is any validity to the legend of Fempellec's flood in the Naymlap narrative, it should pertain to the consequences of El Niño rainfall (Moseley 1987).

Rivers crossing the desert coast provide the source for irrigation agriculture, and rivers tend to become shorter, steeper, and carry less highland runoff as the Cordillera gains in altitude. There is a concomitant narrowing of the continental shelf and coastal plain, and, south of the Rio Viru, mountains arise directly out of the sea (see Shimada, fig. 1, this volume). Chimor encompassed two-thirds of the coastal Andean population because it held the greatest potentials for irrigation agriculture. These include a majority of the largest desert drainages and most of the arable coastal plain. Both are more abundant in the northern region discussed in the Naymlap narrative than in the southern area where Taycanamo reputedly settled. To overcome irregularities in the distribution of runoff and arable terrain, canals must transport water from drainages where it is abundant to drainages where land is abundant. Topographic constraints on constructing such intervalley canals increase to the south as the Cordillera becomes higher and pushes into the sea.

The Lambayeque Valley Complex

Kosok (1965) recognized that the largest intervalley canal networks built in the past lay in the north. He called the very biggest of these the "Lambayeque Valley Complex." Canals united the upper La Leche, Lambayeque, and Zaña Valleys and accounted for one-third of all irrigated land on the coast (see Shimada, fig. 2, this volume). Commensurate with its exceptional economic potentials, this vast agricultural system holds ruins that are exceptional in size and number. Fortunately, this volume benefits from two perspectives on the Lambayeque area. One is Donnan's focus upon the Chotuna-Chornancap architectural complex as a likely candidate for Naymlap's court. The other is Shimada's regional overview and broad assessment of the oral traditions.

Sorting out the Lambayeque monuments for the purposes of this symposium begins with the metropolis of Pampa Grande. This was the preeminent site on the North Coast during Moche Phase V times. There is general agreement that the city was the short-lived capital of a major northern polity and that the rise and fall of Pampa Grande was associated with far-reaching changes that are still poorly understood. This monument anchors the regional chronology and overview that Shimada develops in his paper. The demise of the Moche capital is associated with that of Moche-style arts and the emergence of the new Sican tradition. Sican art integrates features carried over from earlier times, local innovations, and more distant influences associated with the Middle Horizon polity based at Huari in the highlands more than 800 km to the south. Shimada divides Sican into Early, Middle, and Late phases and correlates these with the largest integrated suite of radiocarbon assays currently available for the northern coast. He notes that some stylistic attributes associated with Huari influence appear in Early Sican, but they then persist much longer in the Lambayeque region than they do in their southern area of origin. Therefore, dating based purely upon style will be misleading if ages for attributes in the south are applied to their northern expressions.

After the fall of Pampa Grande, the Lambayeque Complex did not see the rise of a regional center of comparable magnitude until Middle Sican times, A.D. 900–1100. During this period, the central sector of La Leche Valley became a major seat of power expressed at the Sican Precinct of Batan Grande, a sprawling complex of enormous mounds, ancillary structures, and cemeteries housing thousands of interments. Shimada characterizes the precinct as the capital of a Vatican-like religious polity that promoted ideological and social unity while fostering regional economic intensification, commerce, and exchange. Copper artifacts, called *naipes,* served as a standard medium of exchange and may have been traded in Ecuador for Spondylus shell. The Sican Precinct saw rather abrupt and dramatic abandonment when many of the major structures were deliberately burned and the region was inundated by flood-waters of exceptional magnitude. During Late Sican times a new power center arose at the monumental complex of El Purgatorio, situated near the juncture of the La Leche and Lambayeque Valleys. Later, Imperial Chimu and Inca occupations seem to be associated more with the use of existing settlements than with the building of new cities.

There are many other imposing sites in the Lambayeque Complex than those inferred to be capitals of ancient polities. One of these is the Chotuna-Chornancap Complex, which is situated some 5 km in from the coast between the La Leche and Lambayeque drainages. Naymlap supposedly built two courts, one for himself and one for his principal wife. In this volume, Donnan argues that Chotuna was probably the founder's court, and Chornancap was the court of his consort. After initial construction that Donnan dates around A.D. 750, there was a long period of use before much of the monumental architecture at Chotuna was destroyed by large-scale flooding thought to date around A.D. 1100. After some lapse of time, construction was initiated again, and the site continued in use through the Imperial Chimu and Inca occupations.

It is useful to touch upon some points of potential articulation between local events that Donnan detects at this monument and regional ones that Shimada proposes in his overview of the Lambayeque Valley Complex. Correlating the signatures of El Niño flooding within and between valleys rests upon circumstantial evidence. However, if the episode of destructive flooding evident at Chotuna is associated with the same episode of El Niño flooding that inundated Batan Grande, then this event cross-ties the two complexes along with certain shared artistic and architectural attributes. If the same flood inundated both complexes, then the initial use of Chotuna and Chornancap extended through Middle Sican times. This center would, therefore, be contemporary with the political flowering of the Sican Precinct at Batan Grande. Although the precinct was abandoned at the end of the Middle Sican phase, most all of the standing architecture visible at the Chotuna-Chornancap Complex would have been erected in Late Sican times. If the assumptions underlying these articulations are generally correct, then several suggestions may help clarify the situation in the Lambayeque Valley Complex relative to the Naymlap legend. First, the Chotuna-Chornancap Complex could represent the shrine of a dynastic founder, but the Sican Precinct would represent the capital of a polity potentially associated with his cult. In a sense this reasoning brings us back to Kosok's (1965) original suggestion that the Lambayeque lore bespeaks a more confederated than centralized rule. Second, forming testable expectations about the historicity of dynastic lore is affected not only by the differences between shrine center and political center, but also by the differences in preservation. At the Sican Precinct, Shimada works with relatively well-preserved remains that are potentially contemporaneous with the reign of Naymlap's heirs. Yet, at Chotuna and Chornancap, such remains were largely destroyed, and Donnan must work back from later transformations of the complex to infer its original nature. Long ago, Kosok (1965) made it clear that sorting out legendary fictions and archaeological facts in the vast Lambayeque Valley Complex involves many problems. Yet, the challenge is a rewarding one because it forces interdisciplinary discussion and debate between ethnohistorians and archaeologists. Let me now turn to a smaller North Coast setting with which I am more familiar.

THE MOCHE VALLEY

At the end of the Moche Phase IV occupation, more or less coincident with the onset of the Middle Horizon, the Moche Valley landscape, if not much of the adjacent coast, was resculpted by a dramatic episode of erosion and deposition. The duration of this episode is not clear. Rainfall and destructive flooding associated with El Niño activity are implicated, and more than one El Niño event may have been involved. The scale of erosion suggests that the impact of flooding may have been exacerbated by prior tectonic activity that destabilized local drainages. This episode of large-scale environmental alteration produced a fundamental change in patterns of archaeological preservation. Earlier remains are in very poor condition, and surviving monuments are mainly limited to large, solid platform mounds. Later remains are well preserved, and monuments are dominated by high, freestanding mud brick walls rather than mounds alone. This change is evident in the overview of architectural development that William Conklin presents in this volume.

Ethnohistorical sources indicate that coastal lords resided in walled compounds with spacious, open courts and facilities for entertaining their counterparts and receiving their subjects (Netherly n.d.). After the onset of good preservation around A.D. 500, vast rectangular enclosures, with high adobe walls and an interior mortuary mound, are the dominant and salient features of Chimor's imperial heartland. Built more or less sequentially over the course of a millennium, twelve of these palatial structures still stand and graphically commemorate the rise and fall of the desert empire. The first was erected at Galindo, a Moche Phase V city in the valley neck. The last major enclosure was built under Inca aegis at Chiquitoy Viejo, astride the main road leading to Chan Chan from the Rio Chicama. At the imperial nexus itself there were no fewer than ten of these architectural marvels, including the largest and the most elaborate.

Chan Chan is the archaeological type site for the Imperial Chimu style of art and architecture, which is distinct from other Chimu expressions on the North Coast, such as Sican in the Lambayeque region. Hallmarks of the imperial style express continuities and discontinuities with the more distant past. At the old Moche capital of Huaca del Sol and Huaca de la Luna, the latter preserves traces of high adobe enclosing walls. This suggests local origins for the later enclosures at Galindo and Chan Chan. At the latter, imperial compounds contain small U-shaped office buildings called *audiencias*. This distinct architectural form is an outgrowth of much earlier U-shaped ceremonial centers that Conklin addresses in his contribution. Maritime themes are prominent in imperial iconography and dominate adobe friezes, which are restricted to the most prestigious buildings at Chan Chan. As Donna McClelland demonstrates in her paper, this iconography arose as part of the ideological and cultural adjustments triggered by the episode of radical landscape alteration at the end of Moche Phase IV. These adjustments included abandonment of the old capital at Sol and Luna, the rise of Galindo as the major local center, and the founding of a new political capital at Pampa Grande in the Lambayeque region. Thereafter, Lambayeque remained politically prominent and powerful until conquered by Chimor some 800 years later.

Chan Chan

The Taycanamo narrative lists some nine to eleven pre-Inca rulers, depending upon how unnamed potentates are counted. At Chan Chan there are nine to eleven monumental enclosures or related structures that can be interpreted as palaces associated with kingly rule, depending upon how certain of the earliest edifices are categorized. This situation led me to presume there was a one king-one compound association when I began working at the metropolis. With improved chronological controls on urban growth and with more refined ethnohistorical models of Andean statecraft, more viable interpretations can be considered after briefly reviewing the composition and growth of the metropole.

The builders of Chan Chan used construction material and architecture to distinguish the class and occupation of residents. The urban majority was craft and technical personnel who resided and worked in quarters composed of small irregular rooms and courts of cane-wall construction that John Topic describes in his article. Excavation of these structures and analysis of associated ceramics provide one set of chronological monitors of the city's growth (J. Topic 1982, n.d.; J. Topic and Moseley 1983). In contrast, the urban minority consisted of elites, lords, and rulers, who lived and worked in detached enclosures of mud brick and who carried out activities atop platform mounds of similar construction. Adobe architecture provides the other major set of monitors of the city's development. Because the buildings dominating Chan Chan are extremely complex, architectural seriations have, expectably, varied in detail. Drawing principally upon changes in brick form, the building order that Alan Kolata (n.d., 1982) developed and employs in his paper is acceptable to most symposium participants. However, Raffael Cavallaro (n.d.) has recently proposed a somewhat different construction sequence based upon integrated seriations of (a) bricks, (b) U-shaped buildings called *audiencias,* (c) mortuary platforms, and (d) entry courts. The building order that Alan Kolata employs in his paper agrees with that of Cavallaro in general terms of early, middle, and late phases of construction. Both sequences envisage sets of two enclosures as sharing close construction dates, and for middle-phase construction both see the Gran Chimu and Laberinto enclosures as the bridging pair between earlier and later sets of compounds. The sequences differ as to which structure within a pair is earlier or later. Cavallaro points out that the four enclosures erected last are extremely similar. Therefore, construction order is very difficult to discriminate on the basis of architectural attributes alone, and here he differs with Kolata as to which set of structures was built last. The reason architectural seriations have varied in detail may, in part, relate to Cavallaro's cogent argument that the structural ordering of the great enclosures was governed by principles of duality and moiety organization. Therefore, instead of sequential building, pairs of enclosures may have been under more or less concurrent construction.

Except for the partially built Squier enclosure, which was not completed, sequencing based upon adobe architecture is in general agreement with the construction order of elite compounds inferred from excavations in lower-class quarters of cane-wall construction. The excavated ceramics and artifacts provide an independent means for ordering the last sets of enclosures to be erected. Derived from monumental architecture, the sample of radiocarbon dates from Chan Chan is small and not internally consistent. J. Topic sees these as supporting somewhat later dates for occupation phases than does Kolata. Potential cross-ties between Chan Chan and radiocarbon-dated remains in the Lambayeque region seem late, whereas ties to dated Imperial Chimu remains in the Jequetepeque region are consistent with the early phases of long duration envisaged by J. Topic, Kolata, and Cavallaro.

In addition to large compounds, there are some thirty small adobe enclosures known as intermediate architecture (Klymyshyn 1982). Of irregular internal organization, these compounds contain *audiencias* and elite storage facilities, but otherwise lack attributes of the so-called monumental enclosures. The latter have external walls two or more stories high that enclose areas many times larger than a football field. The majority of the roofed floorspace is occupied by warehousing facilities for elite goods. Access and movement were controlled by *audiencias,* which were occasionally built over dedicatory burials and often ornamented with friezes. Friezes are all but exclusively associated with the monumental enclosures, as are mounds known as burial platforms. In most of the cases, the outside walls of enclosures were built first. Internal architecture was then added, and the funerary platform was erected last. During initial use, remodeling could and did transpire. At a certain key point, however, the use pattern changed, and the monuments were "frozen." All internal construction terminated. Other structures could be later annexed to or removed from the exterior. Yet, after interior construction ceased, the internal architecture was simply maintained. The time span between construction onset and termination was significantly longer for early enclosures than for later ones.

Some Moche Phase ceramics have been found within the 6 km² urban core in superficial and buried context; however, all standing adobe architecture is of Chimu affiliation. Chimu monumental buildings were first erected near the coast in the southeastern quadrant of the city, perhaps around A.D. 850 or 900. Surviving early structures include the poorly preserved Higo platform that may once have had enclosing walls and several large compounds that were later buried. The city subsequently expanded west and inland but, after A.D. 1300, reversed course and grew back upon itself toward the coast. In the course of half a millennium, the monumental enclosures evolved from early compounds of variable form to later ones of standardized form. Early enclosures of nonrepetitive form include Chayhuac as well as Uhle and Tello. The latter two are architectural composites of multiple sectors erected at different intervals that overlapped building activity at other enclosures and monuments. Uhle had four sectors with administrative architecture. The eastern two were apparently erected before A.D. 1100, and their western counterparts were not completed until a century or so later. After termination of the two composite compounds, the six remaining monumental enclosures completed at Chan Chan followed repetitive canons of internal organization, as discussed in the contribution by Kolata. Called *ciudadelas,* these marvelous monuments were built in the following sets: Laberinto and Gran Chimu, Velarde and Bandelier, and Rivero and Tschudi. Tschudi is dated last on the basis of excavated ceramics and other remains banked against or adjacent to its exterior wall (J. Topic 1982) and on the basis of interior excavations that yielded Chimu-Inca ceramics (Narváez n.d.).

Each *ciudadela* and earlier enclosure, with the exception of Tello, are associated with a burial platform that can be identified as an ancestral shrine. As Cavallaro (n.d.) points out, the platform associated with Laberinto was built late, long after *ciudadela* construction had terminated. The mortuary structures must have contained an inordinate amount of precious metal because they were commercially mined by the Spanish. This left most structures in very poor condition, but it is reasonable to presume that they housed imperial mummies. The platforms are associated with a "shrine complex" of distinctive remains that include abundant Spondylus and Conus shells, llama bones, bones of human juveniles (apparently young females), and exceptional concentrations of elite goods. To judge from the later, better-preserved examples, each platform contained a large, T-shaped central cell, flanked by smaller rectangular cells in which items of the shrine complex were deposited. Conrad (1982) investigated the platforms and concluded that the large central cell most likely contained the corpse of the ruler who commissioned construction of the associated enclosure. Yet, as Zuidema's paper points out, corpses were ritually manipulated for many ends. Therefore, the central platform cell may best be understood as the special repository for an ancestral mummy associated with construction and use of the enclosing compound.

In many cases, a smaller platform with a number of T-shaped cells was built later and annexed to the principal mortuary mound. The annexes are thought to have housed corpses of particularly prominent heirs of the ancestral mummy. Calculating the number of regents that a palace enclosure may have served depends upon the status ascribed to the corpses in the burial platform annexes. Initially, I took these to be important lords of *panaca*-like royal lineages whose kingly ancestor was enshrined in the main platform. However, the corpses could equally well be those of kings and reflect a succession of potentates. I see the latter interpretation as providing a better fit with current ethnohistorical models of imperial rule in the Andes. It would also be more in line with early monumental enclosures that saw multigenerational use and construction, such as Uhle. Thus, for the purposes of this essay, I will treat the monumental palaces as imperial offices, each of which may have served a succession of regents claiming descent from a common ancestor.

Identifying numbers of kings or regents strains the specificity of the archaeological record. Yet, acknowledging an association of the city's monumental enclosures with the dynamics of rule opens historical questions and interpretations of interest. I certainly concur with Conklin's observation, in this volume, that this ancient capital physically resembles no other of antiquity or modern times. There is no prominent central mall, no singular place or edifice that bespeaks imperial unity or symbolizes political integration. For Conklin, the architectural image that the city evokes is one of a concatenation of high-walled museums, each ritually displaying, storing, and warehousing imperial relics. Yet, the shift from early "museums" of variable organization to later ones of repetitive form certainly reflects increasing formalization and growing standardization in the curation of the empire. Much of this transpired gradually; however, there were epochs of marked change in both monumental architecture and the composition of the city's crafts personnel, which the papers by Kolata and J. Topic tie to external political events. In particular, the Uhle compound and the Velarde *ciudadela* are thought to be associated with foreign conquests. Therefore, it is instructive to review potential links between the ethnohistorical and archaeological records pertaining to events, institutions, and individuals that shaped Chimor.

EVENTS

Except for a "thirty-day" deluge in Lambayeque lore, all narrative accounts of regional events with potential archaeological expression are political in nature and entail territorial expansions of imperial networks. The largest and latest Pre-Hispanic episode of expansion was the Inca domination of the North Coast. Earlier and smaller episodes include the Tumbez to Chillon "second-stage" expansion of Chimor, preceded by the "first-stage" Jequetepeque to Santa incorporation, and the still earlier Moche Valley stage of consolidation. Finally, in the Lambayeque Valley, the arrival of Naymlap and his entourage is portrayed as an event entailing the arrival of a new elite and a new political order.

Inca Incorporation

The Inca portrayed themselves to the Spanish as harbingers of civilization who transformed barbarian populations into cultured societies by introducing the decimal system, ordered land tenure, and other refined institutions. Susan Ramírez scrutinizes such claims for the North Coast and finds them wanting. I find this perfectly reasonable. Chimor was the largest, most powerful adversary that Tahuantinsuyu, the Inca Empire, ever confronted. Propaganda to the contrary, the Inca mission on the coast was not that of building civilization, but rather of systematically undermining it.

The oral traditions of Chimor say nothing about Inca conquest and incorporation of the North Coast that is at odds with the archaeological record. In part, this is because they say little about the situation at all, other than supplying names associated with this last era of Pre-Hispanic rule. The Taycanamo account mentions that Chimor was partitioned into holdings governed by local lords approved by the Inca and that the rule of Taycanamo's heirs had been reduced to the confines of the Moche Valley when the Spanish arrived. The archaeological record indicates that no *ciudadelas* were erected at Chan Chan after it fell; however, a late monumental enclosure replete with burial platform was erected under Inca aegis at

Chiquitoy Viejo on the south side of the Rio Chicama (Conrad 1977). Intended to monitor movement, this administrative center sat directly astride the main thoroughfare to Chan Chan and can be interpreted as lending considerable credence to the destructuring of coastal rule described by the Taycanamo narrative.

Ethnohistorical information about the Inca regnum comes principally from Colonial administrative and judiciary records and from the oral traditions pertaining to Cuzco itself. Drawing on these sources, the papers by Rostworowski, Ramírez, and Netherly all demonstrate that rule on the North Coast was administered by local lords when the Spanish arrived. Presumably, this reflects an Inca policy of accentuating local government at the expense of Chimor's former hegemony. Netherly goes on to argue, however, that the independent potentates of Chimor had formerly exercised power through the same sort of hierarchic structure. Indeed, the enclosures composing Chan Chan's intermediate architecture probably housed lower-level lords. If this were the case, then the Inca simply co-opted the extant structure of government and emphasized its tendencies toward fission by increasing the autonomy of local lords loyal to Cuzco.

The political dismemberment of the coastal state was certainly not uncontested, as Rostworowski's article makes clear. After the initial incorporation of the desert polity into Tahuantinsuyu, the paramount lord of Chimor rebelled. Among other things, this led to his execution and to the permanent disarming of the coastal populace by their highland overlords. Another important consequence of the failed uprising was the physical dispersal of the rebel's subjects and their forced resettlement in distant provinces of the Inca realm as isolated colonies called *mitmaqs*. Many, if not most, of the monumental enclosures at Chan Chan were, in part, burned upon abandonment or shortly thereafter, and these conflagrations may well pertain to the era of Inca subjugation. One reported aspect of the Inca's *mitmaq* colonization policy was the removal of metalworkers and their resettlement at Cuzco. The rapid mass exodus of Chan Chan's artisans and craft personnel is a dramatic and well-defined archaeological event described in J. Topic's paper.

Without enumerating further ethnohistorical and archaeological linkages, I believe we can reasonably conclude that the Colonial documentary sources pertaining to the incorporation of Chimor by Tahuantinsuyu are not entirely without verifiable historical content. Such content certainly reflects the fact that coastal incorporation was relatively recent (ca. A.D. 1460–1470), that the region was under Inca rule when the Spanish arrived, and that there is a good deal of ethnohistorical documentation relating to this era. Nonetheless, I see nothing in this situation that implies that the oral narrations discussing pre-Inca times on the coast are qualitatively different and necessarily lack historical content.

Late Expansion of Chimor

Following political consolidation of the Moche Valley, the Taycanamo narrative frames the multivalley expansion of Chimor in terms of two stages, as discussed by Theresa Topic in her paper. The first, under the aegis of Ñançenpinco, reached from Jequetepeque to Santa, and the second stage, ascribed to Minchançaman, reached from the Rio Tumbez in the north to near the Rio Chillon in the south. Archaeological information pertinent to the later stage indicates that territorial annexation was indeed bilateral and that growth to the north and south was more or less concurrent. In this volume, the paper by James Richardson and his associates leaves no doubt as to the very late incorporation of the Tumbez region in the far north. Culturally, this was quite important because it terminated a long process of wresting the far north from the Ecuadoran sphere of Amazonian influence and bringing it into the Andean fold. This complicated process was initiated in Moche times and then may have intensified under the aegis of the Middle Sican polity at Batan Grande before culminating with Imperial Chimu domination.

In the south, there is rather thinner archaeological evidence of Imperial Chimu intrusion, particularly below Paramonga and into the Chillon drainage. This could be the product of an extremely late and very short-lived occupation, as Carol Mackey and Ulana Klymyshyn discuss. Their paper argues that the second stage of southern expansion can be subdivided into at least three phases that spanned multiple generations. The first phase comprised the Nepeña and Casma Valleys. In the latter drainage, excavations by these authors at the Imperial Chimu administrative center of Manchan suggest that it correlates with the Velarde *ciudadela* at Chan Chan. This suggestion would imply that Chimor's second stage of southern expansion began well before Minchançaman could have lived. Thus, while the last of Chan Chan's independent rulers might have pushed Chimor's southern frontier to the Rio Chillon, many of the intervening valleys had been previously incorporated.

Much the same can be said for northward expansion. Both Kolata and J. Topic associate *ciudadela* Velarde with a period of major changes in the capital, and each suggests that this reflects conquest of the Lambayeque region. This was the largest and most populous irrigation complex of the entire arid coast, and its annexation certainly had far-reaching consequences. Shimada's paper discusses radiocarbon assays, indicating that Lambayeque was not incorporated before A.D. 1350. The year A.D. 1370 is suggested by Donnan on the basis of his excavations at Chotuna. Both he and Shimada see the onset of Inca domination around A.D. 1460–1470. Thus, rule of the region by Chan Chan's potentates would have spanned more than a single generation. There is no conflict here with Cabello Balboa's account of three Imperial Chimu governors reigning in Lambayeque prior to its incorporation by Tahuantinsuyu; however, it does again indicate that Chimor's second stage of expansion had greater time depth than the Taycanamo narrative indicates.

Except for the number of generations involved, the archaeological record largely agrees with the oral traditions. Indeed, there would be no disagreement had the narrative simply said Minchançaman "governed" versus "conquered" from the Tumbez to the Chillon. When the problem becomes one of wording, I am not certain that we can tell if the situation reflects what native informants said or what Spanish authors thought they said.

Early Expansion of Chimor

Similar agreements and disagreements surround the first stage of territorial expansion. As reviewed in Conrad's paper, the northern frontier in Jequetepeque is well established by excavations at the Imperial Chimu administrative center of Farfan, which dates around A.D. 1200 and correlates with the Uhle enclosure at Chan Chan. A comparable center has not been found in the Santa drainage. However, Donald Collier (1955) excavated one in the Viru Valley, and this complex, V-124, also correlates with the Uhle enclosure (Andrews 1974; see also Mackey and Klymyshyn, this volume). It is significant that Farfan and V-124 exhibit closer architectural similarities to Chan Chan than do later administrative centers, such as Manchan, associated with the second stage of expansion.

Theresa Topic's discussion of fortifications makes it clear that both the consolidation of the Moche Valley and the first stage of multivalley expansion entailed a number of phases and spanned more than a single generation. Therefore, Ñançenpinco may have pushed the imperial frontiers to Jequetepeque and to Santa, but conquest of the entire region was an agglutinative process initiated by earlier rulers. Here again what the Taycanamo narrative portrays as a single conquest event is a composite of smaller annexation events, and what is implied to have transpired in a single lifetime took place over multiple generations. What we seem to be seeing is not so much myth as it is compressed history. Yet, T. Topic convincingly points out that we may also be looking at a threefold classificatory system expressing relatedness of subject peoples to the ruling dynasty. In such a system, those most closely related to the sovereigns of Chan Chan would be the people brought into the imperial fold with the conquest and consolidation of the Moche Valley, and those most distantly related would be the populations of the second stage of multivalley expansion. Here I see no reason to presume that the Taycanamo narrative does not have both historical and structural content.

Michael E. Moseley

The Naymlap Arrival

Both Taycanamo and Naymlap reach their new homelands by sea. Whereas the former is alone, the latter is said to have been accompanied by a large entourage of lords and other followers. This allows Naymlap's arrival to be assessed as an event entailing the ascendancy of a new, if not exogenous, elite that established its base at Chot and then radiated to other Lambayeque centers. As Donnan (this volume) argues, such a hypothesis could be negated if the Chotuna-Chornancap Complex, the presumed site of Chot, exhibited a long occupation reaching back to a pre-Moche era and thus beyond a reasonable time depth for the narrative. However, the Complex is a *sui generis* monument founded well after the collapse of the Moche polity at Pampa Grande. On the basis of iconographic evidence, Donnan suggests a founding date of about A.D. 750, whereas Shimada sees the architecture as exhibiting Middle Sican affiliations. Both authors agree, however, that the initial phase of occupation continued up to about A.D. 1100 before flooding destroyed much of the settlement and interrupted use of the monument.

The arrival story states that third generation heirs and members of Naymlap's court settled at other sites in the region. The spread of a new elite could be negated if the occupation of Chotuna was not coincident with significant changes elsewhere in the Lambayeque area. Shimada's paper carefully scrutinizes cultural continuities and discontinuities between the Early Sican (A.D. 700–900) and Middle Sican (A.D. 900–1050/1100) phases of regional occupation. Although continuities are strong, Middle Sican was clearly a dramatic time when old traditions were restructured, and a new order emerged in ideology, art, and architecture. Shimada cautions that the inception of this new order cannot, as yet, be identified with the intrusion of a well-defined foreign elite securely traced to a specific outside point of origin, such as coastal Ecuador or elsewhere. Exploring local origins, this investigator suggests Naymlap might represent the prophet or charismatic leader of a successful revitalization movement and thus the culture hero remembered for initiating changes that flowered with the distinctive new order of Middle Sican culture.

If the archaeological record does not categorically negate potential historical realities surrounding the founding of the Naymlap dynasty, does it provide any insights for deciphering fact from fiction in the narrative? Perhaps arrival by sea of dynastic founders must remain a mythical motif for separating special origins if we cannot identify specific foreign connections for Naymlap or Taycanamo. Yet, historical authenticity here is much more plausible than in the Inca origin myth, where the dynastic founder Manco Capac emerges via special creation from a cave or the waters of Lake Titicaca. If, for argument's sake, we were to agree that the founding of

Chot, specifically the Chotuna-Chornancap Complex, was associated with a regent called Naymlap—be he of local or foreign origin—and if this regent was commemorated in Middle Sican iconography by the so-called Sican Lord figures, then we would be in a position to say that the northern narrative is a truncated portrayal of a complex event. This presumes that Chotuna was founded about A.D. 750, and that the new order represented by Middle Sican first flourished about A.D. 900. In this case, seminal events spanning a century and a half of archaeological time would be portrayed in terms of three imperial generations.

The Fempellec Flood

According to Lambayeque oral traditions, a thirty-day deluge with ensuing flooding, famine, and social unrest brought the reign of Fempellec and the Naymlap dynasty to an end. This would certainly be myth if catastrophic flooding never occurred on the desert coast. However, the 1982–83 El Niño perturbation of normal ocean-atmosphere conditions was a trenchant reminder that rare but recurrent cataclysmic floods are an expectable historical feature of the Andean desert. Indeed, the climatological ice core record from the Quelccaya glacier south of Cuzco leaves no doubt that ENSO events frequently struck the Cordillera during the last one and a half millennia (Thompson et al. 1985). El Niño events generally last about eighteen months. However, the glacial ice records occasional perturbations lasting a decade or more, and the dates of these episodes are summarized in the paper by Richardson and his associates.

The ending of a former era by catastrophic flooding is certainly a motif common to myths from around the world. Because of this, several symposium discussants argued that Fempellec's flood can only be construed as fictive. This may be. Yet, the flood also constitutes a testable hypothesis subject to archaeological negation, as the papers by Donnan and Shimada admirably demonstrate. If there were not a significant ice core anomaly dating around A.D. 1100, if the Chotuna-Chornancap Complex (the site Naymlap presumably founded) were not destroyed by flooding about this time, if Batan Grande and other Lambayeque or North Coast settlements lacked evidence of contemporary inundation, and if Middle Sican iconography (which potentially portrays dynastic insignia) were not also purged at this date, then we would be in a much better position to negate the narrative rather than to support it with circumstantial evidence.

I concur with Shimada's observation that the basic problem may have less to do with Fempellec's flood being fictive than with identifying to which of the many past El Niño events it might refer. Because of the increased scale of erosional and depositional alteration, it is archaeologically easier to detect large magnitude ENSO events than smaller perturbations. There is considerable variation in El Niño rainfall between one valley and another (Waylen and Caviedes 1986). Therefore, regional correlations of flood events must be approached with caution. Correlations between scale of alteration and ENSO magnitude are affected by tectonic activity because the effects of an El Niño event will be much more severe for a landscape that has previously experienced a strong earthquake than for a landscape that has not experienced seismic disturbance. Refining cross-ties to the Quelccaya ice core sequence should clarify the variables underlying episodes of exceptional landscape alteration. In order of decreasing magnitude, Moche Valley data suggest that epochs of exceptional alteration transpired within a century or so of 500 B.C., around A.D. 500 with the end of Moche Phase IV, and again at about A.D. 1100. Erosional signatures of what I judge to be potentially smaller El Niño events during Moche Phase V are evident at Galindo, Pacatnamu, and Pampa Grande. The paper by Richardson et al. reviews the ice core dates for major events transpiring during Chimu times. Thus, there is a wealth of potential referents for the Fempellec incident. However, if the Naymlap dynasty was either physically associated with Chotuna or given iconographic expression in Middle Sican arts, then the flood narrative would in all probability refer to the episode of exceptional alteration that transpired around A.D. 1100.

Let me conclude with four observations. First, Fempellec's flood cannot be demonstrated as fictive on the basis of current archaeological evidence. Second, I do not doubt that El Niño events of greater intensity or length than the 1982–83 perturbation can trigger the fall of governments because they destroy the irrigation systems that feed the desert populace. Third, the limitations of archaeological evidence do not allow me to disagree with Zuidema's (this volume) observation that the story of Fempellec's flood served as a temporal reference to a particular time of a specific month in the indigenous yearly calendar. Indeed, I would be surprised if the indigenous calendar did not associate ENSO activity with a particular time of the year. After all, the contemporary name for these events is derived from their association with the Christmas season and the coming of the Christ child, El Niño. And, fourth, I am not convinced that, because it may have served in a calendrical capacity or because flood motifs are common to the lore of many societies, the Fempellec story necessarily lacks historic reality. It seems to me that this might be akin to saying the Fourth of July is without historical basis because it is a major holiday and because most modern nations have independence-day motifs.

INSTITUTIONS

Deciphering the content of desert dynastic lore must be guided by an understanding of certain institutions of northern statecraft. Administrative and legal documents, complemented by the archaeological record, provide most of the relevant information on these matters. After briefly reviewing institutional aspects of political organization in Chimor, I will return to the oral traditions and the individual figures that they discuss.

Territorial Organization

The flow of water united and divided indigenous populations into discrete hierarchical groups, each under its own lords and leaders. On the coast, these groups were called *parcialidades,* or "parts of a whole," by the Spanish who understood little of the ranking of the parts or what made them a whole. At the broadest level, hydrology distinguished and generated tension between uplanders living where rain fell and lowlanders receiving only runoff. Competition and cooperation among these populations are explored in the papers by Ramírez and Rostworowski. The latter argues that coast-highland frontiers were dynamic, shifting upstream or downstream as the pendulum of political power swung between littoral and mountain polities. During the reign of Chimor, lowland control pushed upstream, but this was reversed during Inca times, and the Lords of Cuzco set new boundaries at lower elevations (Netherly n.d.). Explored in the paper by Ramírez are other changes that the Inca might have imposed upon coastal land tenure that clearly include dissolving the holdings of Chimor among its component *parcialidades.*

Given the importance of water, it is reasonable that the initial territorial ambition of Taycanamo's heirs was to extend their frontiers up the Rio Moche. To gain control over the valley neck and narrows was to gain control of the intakes of the major coastal canals. The archaeological evidence of fortification patterns reviewed by T. Topic indicates that consolidation of the lower drainage was indeed the first order of imperial expansion. Yet, the story of upstream expansion may also be a metaphor expressing political concern with wresting water rights from highland sources. Rostworowski and Netherly demonstrate that rivers mediated territorial divisions on the coast and that valleys were first split along river courses on a left-bank vs. right-bank basis. Each valley half was, in turn, further partitioned along canal courses with different *parcialidades* holding different lands. Insofar as irrigation systems are hierarchical structures, the ranking of *parcialidades* was likely intertwined with the land tenure system. Cultivated land abandoned in antiquity is characterized by large, integrated field systems worked on a cooperative basis, much as the northern irrigated valleys are managed today. Hierarchical organization of irrigated terrain and dependent populations was certainly an ancient coastal tradition that has graphic archaeological expression in settlement patterns and sites ranked by size and scope of monumental construction.

In arguing for the dual organization of Chimor, Netherly posits that the Rio Moche divided the old empire into asymmetrical halves characterized by small valleys to the south and large ones to the north. Litigation records leave no doubt that the valley itself was so split when the Spanish arrived. The use of rivers as primary dividers appears to have fostered intervalley bonds between populations on the north side of one drainage and those on the south side of the adjacent drainage. These linkages were, no doubt, important in the development of the largest of the canal systems—those moving water from one drainage to another, such as the imposing La Cumbre Canal. More than 70 km in length, this channel was designed to draw water from the south bank of the Rio Chicama and distribute it above Chan Chan on the north side of the Moche Valley. Ramírez discusses another such tie between the Zaña and Jequetepeque Rivers. Here, canals from each drainage were brought to within a short distance of juncture and then diverted down slope, rather than joined, and the separation of irrigated terrain was marked with stone piles (Eling 1977). This is an apt reminder that what was technically feasible was not always politically obtainable.

Dual Organization

When the Spanish arrived, they found individual *parcialidades* to be under the rule of a hierarchy of lords. They called the most important lord the *cacique principal* and the next the *segunda persona*. As discussed in Netherly's contribution, these terms are now understood to reflect a pattern of dual rule involving moieties that were further subdivided into two, four, or even more sections, each under a lesser lord. Duality and quadripartition of rule on the coast are thought to have been pervasive and long-standing by Rostworowski and the other ethnohistorians contributing to this volume. There is consensus that dual organization was asymmetrical, and powers were unevenly divided. Primary and secondary moieties differed insofar as the former could draw upon labor and resources of the latter, but not vice versa. Below the quadripartite level, indigenous organization was probably decimally based, according to Netherly. Zuidema reminds us that this numerical concept was quite important in the Otuzco region, upstream from Chan Chan, where he says there were ten *huarancas* (ten groups of one thousand families each). Decimal organization is one of the gifts of civilization that the Inca claimed to have brought to their subject populations, but Ramírez finds little evidence that it was imposed upon Chimor.

The textual and archaeological expressions of duality and quadripartition of rule are sometimes difficult to recognize or are equivocal in nature. For example, Netherly suggests that the named rulers in the Taycanamo narrative represent one imperial moiety and the unnamed rulers another. However, other symposium participants see the narrative as too vague to support this interpretation. Most participants expect Chan Chan to reflect asymmetrical dual organization. But recognizing such organization is hindered by a lack of archaeological models defining the physical expressions of co-regencies on the coast. From an architect's perspective, Conklin sees the metropolis as rather unorganized and quite unlike other capital cities. He finds no single architectural focus uniting the city, such as an imperial mall. Nor is there a central thoroughfare like the Avenue of the Dead at Teotihuacan in Mexico. If the imperial nexus of Chimor is physically unlike other capitals in its lack of a dominating symbol of integration, then we must ask whether this was by chance or by design. Perhaps, at the apex of state rule structured by asymmetrical dual organizations, the political parts were considered more important than the imperial whole. Such a notion might lie behind Conklin's observation that the city's architectural image is that of an amalgam of museum-like edifices with towering walls enclosing the symbols of royalty. I see the metropolis as exhibiting somewhat greater organization and integration than Conklin does. Yet, these are certainly not bold expressions. A very long "city wall" demarcates the northern, inland extent of the capital. However, this great wall is only half the height of *ciudadela* walls. There is a large open area in the heart of the city (see Kolata, fig. 9, this volume). It is not formally delimited as a plaza by walls or by an enclosing structure. Rather, it is simply defined by where palaces were not built. The central plaza may well have served the city as a whole, but its architectural image is that of a void.

If we are to probe for structural expressions of diarchy, rather than monarchy, then we need to look for patterned replication and patterned division reflecting co-regencies. Replication is most likely reflected by *ciudadelas* and monumental enclosures, and division by an east-west pairing of palaces around the central plaza. The eastern sector of the city houses all major platform mounds and many of the largest enclosures. Both Netherly (this volume) and Raffael Cavallaro (n.d.) argue that the arrangement of platforms and palaces reflects a dominant eastern and complementary western moiety. Accepting this proposition, I believe that spatial organization at Chan Chan may also relate to indigenous notions about rivers as the mediators of territorial organization. The Rio Moche reaches the sea along a course flowing from north–northeast to south–southwest. With fifteen degrees of tolerance, this is the long axis of all major enclosures and monumental structures at Chan Chan. This orientation reaches beyond the city. In the surrounding countryside, it is the preferential course placement for canals and fields where topographic constraints can be overridden. This is also the preferred axis of state-built *audiencia* sites outside the capital. Within the city this axis was established at an early date as an open line of sight that separated Uhle in the east from Tello in the west. This sight line runs through the city's central plaza, which is bounded on both sides by *ciudadela* pairs. It is intruded upon by the unfinished Squier enclosure, but, otherwise, it splits the monumental architecture into eastern and western complexes that represent the moieties envisaged by both Netherly and Cavallaro.

Let me tie together aspects of the foregoing discussion with a speculative scenario that presumes moiety organization and dual rule. First, Taycanamo's named and unnamed heirs used the lower course of the Moche River as a spatial axis for territorial organization. Land and conquests to the north of the river were affiliated with one kin group, the western moiety. Terrain and expansion to the south were affiliated with the eastern kin group. Symbolic of water, the river axis was employed in laying out canals and fields. It was also employed in organizing architectural and urban space. This was an old tradition insofar as Huacas El Sol and La Luna share the same orientation as the Chan Chan monuments. At the latter capital, this axis oriented individual compounds and also segregated them into the residential groups of eastern and western co-regents. To the degree that earlier palatial enclosures remained in use as new ones were added, the monumental architecture points to growing numbers of imperial offices and royal lineages at the apex of rule. Rapid construction of the last four *ciudadelas* is compatible with the rise and formalization of quadripartition. This process could reflect fission within moieties, junior lineages achieving the status of senior ones, or the incorporation of outside lineages. Yet, throughout the process, the *cacique principal* resided in the east, and this moiety was associated with the largest *huaca* platforms of the city and their religious cults. The *segunda persona* resided in the west, and this moiety did not build large religious structures. Initially, as Cavallaro (n.d.) points out, dual organization was markedly asymmetrical. The western palaces lacked royal burial platforms and were smaller than their eastern counterparts. This changed dramatically after Laberinto and Gran Chimu were completed. Size differences between *ciudadela* pairs reversed in the case of western Velarde and eastern Bandelier. More importantly, burial platforms were now built for the ancestral cult of the *segunda persona.* At this time, burial platforms were even annexed to the exterior of older eastern palaces such as Laberinto and Squier. This striking decrease in asymmetry that characterizes the last four palaces appears to correlate with the far-reaching urban and economic reordering of the capital that the papers by Kolata and J. Topic ascribe to incorporation of the Lambayeque Valley Complex. This reordering, in turn, suggests that the benefits of this northern conquest accrued largely to the western moiety and brought it into closer parity with the kin groups of the *cacique principal*. This scenario builds upon admittedly speculative propositions that place Chan Chan squarely into the fold of Andean duality. Here I must caution that the imperial capital is not unlike a vast architectural Rorschach test, and less may have been built into it by design than we now read into it by imagination.

Administration

On the coast, administrative hierarchies probably arose in a coevolutionary process with irrigation agriculture. Ethnohistorical sources demonstrate that the primary concern of these hierarchies was organizing and scheduling labor and overseeing the circulation of the fruits of this labor. Zuidema points out that the annual calendar was of such vital importance to the administration that its twelve-month count could override the decimal system and structure concepts about genealogical time, such as in the twelve generations of the Naymlap dynasty.

Increasing formalization of hierarchical rule at Chan Chan finds graphic expression in the evolution of monumental enclosures along with their associated *audiencias* and warehousing facilities, as Kolata's paper documents. Another tier of Chimor's nobility is thought to have resided in the smaller enclosures constituting the city's intermediate architecture. The lower status of this architecture is called out by its lack of friezes and, more particularly, by the absence of burial platforms. These enclosures became much more numerous as monumental enclosures evolved into *ciudadelas* and as the latter, in turn, became more standardized. Thus, as the apex of the bureaucracy became more rigid, the base expanded.

Provincial administration also changed through time. The first stage of territorial expansion beyond the imperial heartland is marked by two Imperial Chimu administrative centers—Farfan in the north and V–124 in the south. Both have *audiencias* that are duplicates of those at the capital in the Uhle enclosure, but, more importantly, both have structures that can be identified as burial platforms. This suggests to me a system of administration by "viceroyalty." A very different policy prevailed later when the Casma drainage was incorporated. As Mackey and Klymyshyn point out, local sites—and presumably local lords—were co-opted into an administrative hierarchy under the imperial center of Manchan. Unlike its earlier counterparts, this government complex has no burial platform, and its *audiencias* are not duplicates, but variants of those at the capital. My impression is that we are again witnessing expansion in the lower levels of the administrative hierarchy, while the upper levels were purged of rural viceroyalty. This could well relate to concurrent transformations at the apex of imperial rule involving the ascendancy of Chan Chan's western moiety and a concentration of all major emblems of rule within the confines of the capital.

Taxation

It is reasonable to suppose that kingship and government in Chimor were supported by a "taxation" system that required people to work for the state, and that such work was directed by the administrative hierarchy. More people probably rendered agricultural labor than any other type of government work. However, there is archaeological evidence of two other categories of service. One entailed working on construction projects, and, for unskilled laborers drawn from the farming populace, this was probably a seasonal or part-time obligation of males. The other type of service was rendered by skilled artisans of both sexes and by technical personnel. Working on a full-time basis, these people were attached to the courts of lords and dynastic rulers and were state supported.

In the Moche Valley, prehistoric construction was characterized by a phenomenon called *segmentation*. To erect adobe walls and brick platforms, or to dig canals, projects were subdivided into repetitive, modular construction units, each executed by a different work party. Huacas El Sol and La Luna were built of bricks bearing makers' marks, each mark presumably identifying a particular group of adobe producers. Each construction segment in these *huacas* was generally built of bricks with only one maker's mark, and adjacent segments had bricks with different marks. I interpreted this as a system of labor tax (Moseley 1975). "Communities" were the unit of taxation, and levies entailed completing a particular segment of a construction project. For El Sol and La Luna, this was a "multitask" tax that began with the production of bricks and culminated with their being mortared into position. Gary Urton (1988) reports an analogous ethnographic situation at Pacariqtambo in which the church courtyard is segmented and the construction and maintenance of each section are the responsibility of a different *ayllu* kin group.

Although characterized by segmentation, construction at Galindo and Chan Chan did not employ marked adobes; however, their use persisted in the Lambayeque region and is discussed by Shimada. Significantly, the disposition pattern for Sican architecture is one of bricks with different marks occurring in the same segments or units of construction. This suggests greater organizational complexity and, I would suspect, greater task specialization, with some groups being identified as brick producers and others as masons.

Without marked bricks we cannot tell if a similar situation prevailed at Chan Chan. However, viewing segmentation as a signature of labor taxation is very important for understanding the city. This is a metropolis of vast size dominated by numerous great monuments. Yet, at its height, the capital may have held no more than some 36,000 people (J. Topic and Moseley 1983). The marked disparity between physical size and population size simply reflects the fact that Chan Chan was not built by its resident populace. Rather, it was erected by a nonresident work force mobilized by organizational principles that still persist among traditional communities such as Pacariqtambo. In the position paper, Kolata and I concluded that the "taxation system left the capital's resident population free to specialize exclusively in the concerns of state administration or in direct villein service to the ruling dynasties." To varying degrees, similar situations must have characterized Chan Chan's satellite administrative centers, such as Farfan and Manchan, as well as independent centers, such as Chotuna and Batan Grande.

Reciprocity

Reciprocity and expectations that for something rendered something is to be returned are widespread among traditional Andean populations. Between people of similar status what is returned is expected to be equal in kind or value to what was rendered. In the context of Chimor's imperial government and hierarchical administration, however, reciprocity was certainly asymmetrical, with commoners giving more than they received. It is likely that laborers expected to be fed while working on government projects. Archaeologically, this is reflected by a remarkable prevalence of numerous small serving bowls at Quebrada del Osso, a state-built architectural complex erected to oversee construction of the La Cumbre Canal (Keatinge 1974, 1975, n.d.). However, I suspect that many of the commoners were fed from gourd bowls, not ceramic ones. Expectations of receiving drink, and *chicha* beer in particular, must have permeated all tiers of society. Libation vessels, stirrup-spout forms of Imperial Chimu, and double-spout forms of Middle Sican received great elaboration as emblems of ethnic affiliation and status. The documentation of large-scale brewing activity at Manchan is discussed by Mackey and Klymyshyn, and there is no question that *chicha* was vital in satisfying obligations of hospitality.

Reciprocal obligations among high-ranking lords are discussed by Rostworowski. She notes that when the *curaca* of the Mala Valley called upon the nearby *curaca* of Coayllo for the temporary loan of laborers, the latter were granted temporary use of certain farmlands as compensation. The Inca may have undermined coastal civilization by ceding certain water rights to highlanders. For the Lambayeque region, Rostworowski reviews complaints to Spanish officials by local lords, such as the *principal* of the "Deer Hunters" and the *principal* of the "Cooks," that they had to "pay tribute" to highland rulers for water to irrigate coastal fields. It is not clear in all cases if such "tribute" was in the form of labor, access to farmlands, foodstuffs, or manufactured goods.

Manufactured goods, particularly those in the realm of the fine arts, were certainly critical to the nobility in satisfying obligations among themselves. Exquisite objects of personal adornment and masterful emblems of high status are dramatic aspects of Chimor's archaeological record. I would posit that artistic goods were ranked by value and circulated appropriate to status in the hierarchy of lords and nobles, with items of precious metal restricted to the most prestigious of individuals. In the absence of currency or a standard medium of exchange, such as Middle Sican *naipes,* fine art was the "coin of the realm" among the northern dynasties. As J. Topic's paper demonstrates, artisans were accorded very special status. Elevated above commoners, craft personnel had the privilege of wearing earspools—albeit wooden plugs—and the privilege of residing adjacent to the nobility whom they served as favored retainers.

Coincident with the construction and use of *ciudadela* Velarde, there was a dramatic increase in the number of artisans residing at Chan Chan. J. Topic proposes that this probably reflects the conquest of Lambayeque and a forced resettlement of craft personnel from that region at the capital. If this was the case, the rulers of Chimor must have sought to monopolize the production of valued goods, such as objects of precious metal and fine textiles. By resettling Chan Chan's metalsmiths and other craft personnel in the Cuzco environs, the Inca later perpetuated the practice. Put in contemporary economic parlance, it could be said that, stripped of the coin of the realm, or more correctly the imperial "mint," financing a revolt would have been difficult for the Lords of Chimor.

Economic Specialization

Whereas Andean mountain folk were subsistence generalists who performed many different tasks, their coastal counterparts were specialists. Historical sources tell us that specialization began at the level of carbohydrate and protein production, with rigid distinctions between farmers and fisherfolk. The two groups spoke separate dialects, lived in separate communities, married among themselves, and served their own lords. Specialization permeated higher orders of coastal production and organization as well. Indeed, to judge from the Naymlap narrative, lords of royal courts bore imperial titles designating specialized crafts, such as "master of feathered cloth production," or specialized activities. Fonga Sigde, who scattered shell dust where his sovereign would walk, is an example of the latter. Dust of ground Spondylus shell was carefully placed in a small, stone-lined basin in front of the kingly burial platforms at Chan Chan. Brought from the warm waters of Ecuador, these exotic shells were extremely sacred to the elite of Chimor, and prodigious quantities of whole, cut, and burned valves were deposited in and around royal mortuary structures. Examining Middle Sican iconographic representations of divers retrieving these mollusks, the paper by Alana Cordy-Collins develops the hypothesis that Fonga Sigde was the title of a Sican imperial office responsible for Spondylus procurement. Supporting such a hypothesis, J. Topic argues that the thousands of craft personnel at Chan Chan were organized as *parcialidades,* each with its own hierarchy of administrative lords.

There certainly appears to be a good articulation between ethnohistorical and archaeological sources relating to specialists in the fine arts of Chimor. However, maintaining kingdoms and running empires require cadres of other technicians, such as accountants, about which we still know very little. It would be ludicrous to presume that the imposing monuments of Chimor and its antecedent polities were erected without professionals akin to architects and engineers. A technical study of the great intervalley La Cumbre Canal with its sophisticated channel design supports the proposition that such works were in the hands of technical personnel akin to hydrological engineers (Ortloff et al. 1982). Drawing on ethnohistorical sources, Rostworowski identifies three categories of specialists from Chimor that the Inca resettled as *mitmaq* colonies: metalsmiths, fishermen, and water management specialists. She notes that important canals in distant South Coast valleys were or still are called "la Mochica," a name associated with people from the Rio Moche region. Here it is worth remembering that the very largest canal systems ever erected in the continent were those within the realm of Chimor. Removing the critical technical personnel responsible for building and maintaining the vast irrigation networks would have undercut the coastal subsistence economy and thereby have facilitated Inca dismemberment of Chimor.

Huaca Hostage

Adobe friezes constitute a remarkable, yet enigmatic, archaeological linkage between the presumed royal courts of Naymlap and Taycanamo. At each nexus, there is a single structure ornamented with multiple yellow-painted panels of repetitive design depicting a double-headed serpent or "dragon" surrounded by a standard set of anthropomorphic and zoomorphic figures. The frieze structures are the entry court of Huaca Gloria at Chotuna and of Huaca Dragon, a structural outlier at Chan Chan. The serpent friezes are illustrated and analyzed in Donnan's paper on the Chotuna-Dragon connection. There is little question that the panels depict a single, complex iconographic theme, thus far known only from structures at the two dynastic centers.

The symposium position paper postulated that this unusual cross-tie between capitals reflected the institution of "*huaca* hostage" (Moseley and Kolata n.d.). The argument held that—as with the Inca who believed their founder, Manco Capac, had turned into a stone that they venerated—many Andean groups traced their ancestry to sacred bodies, such as stones, statues, stelae, or mummies. Therefore, capturing such *huacas* and holding them hostage would place their venerators in bondage and promote proper subordinate behavior. At Cuzco, compulsory preservation of sacred objects from subject provinces is well documented (Rowe 1968). The practice is evident at Tihuanacu as well (Chávez 1976) and has been inferred for Chavin (Lathrap 1985).

The proposition that the rulers of Chimor engaged in a similar practice was based on the premise that the presence of sacred ancestral bodies is identified by the "shrine complex" of unusual remains found in association with imperial burial structures. Along with friezes, this complex occurs in two very different spatial contexts. Within Chan Chan, it is present only in association with monumental enclosures and platform structures related to kingly rule. The other context of occurrence is outside the urban core at three peripheral, but important, structures. These structures were erected at different times adjacent to the capital, but not within the sacred central precinct that housed both the living and dead potentates of Chimor. Near the coast, the westernmost is called Calavario de los Incas and has not been excavated. The other two structures, Huacas Taycanamo and Dragon, are situated inland and to the east of the great north wall of the capital. The former was built at a time contemporary with Chan Chan's earliest imperial enclosures, and the bricks used in the latter are the same form as those employed in erecting *ciudadela* Velarde. Both of the outlying platforms exhibit architectural canons that are very different from those of Chan Chan, and both are ornamented with friezes iconographically and technologically alien to the maritime wall art of the capital. Indeed, other than being built of locally produced adobes, the structures are basically foreign to the city. Given this background and the similarity of the Chotuna and Dragon serpent friezes, Kolata and I went on to ". . . hypothesize that this outlying structure at Chan Chan housed the primary cult object of the Naymlap dynasty—either an ancestral mummy, Naymlap's green stone idol, or some other object or objects—and that Huaca Dragon was erected in commemoration of the Lambayeque conquest" (Moseley and Kolata n.d.: 14). The earlier Taycanamo and Calavario structures were similarly interpreted as ritual repositories for sacred objects acquired in prior conquests.

Drawing upon his excavations at Chotuna, Donnan takes this interpretation to task with considerable justification. First, it is apparent that if Naymlap's court was once ornamented with friezes emblematic of his dynasty, then the A.D. 1100 flood removed all trace of such artwork. Therefore, the extant serpent friezes at Huaca Gloria would date after the collapse of the dynasty if the flood is that of Fempellec. The excavator points out that, while other friezes at Chotuna were technically and artistically well made, the serpent panels were executed in a vague or abstract manner, implying that the artisans at Huaca Gloria were unfamiliar with the iconography. There is no such vagueness with the Dragon panels, and Donnan posits that the iconography in question appeared first at Chan Chan and then later at Chotuna, prior to Chimor's conquest of the region. He suggests that this may reflect a south to north movement of ideas with iconographic origins potentially lying between the Rios Nepeña and Supe where double-headed serpents are depicted on press-molded ceramics of Middle Horizon Epoch 3 stylistic affiliation.

This is certainly a viable hypothesis, if not the best interpretation, of the Chotuna-Dragon connection. There are but two observations that I can offer in defense of the original *huaca* hostage proposition. First, after their appearance in Moche iconography, double-headed serpents or dragons become a relatively common motif in Middle as well as Late Sican arts. Dragon heads appear on libation vessels depicting the Sican Lord, an iconographic candidate for Naymlap discussed by Shimada (this volume, fig. 14), and they are represented on such vessels after the Sican Lord has been purged from the Lambayeque tradition. However, serpent heads do not figure in Imperial Chimu iconography. Second, if such lords and serpents were indeed emblems of a political era that ended abruptly, then, generations later, archaistic revival of the bygone iconography—for whatever reason—might initially entail vague or inept renditions of the subject matter.

Although the Chotuna-Dragon connection is far from clear, I believe that it bespeaks a highly orchestrated imperial manipulation of exogenous power symbols. If Huaca Dragon is not an iconographic statement about the conquest of Lambayeque, and if Donnan is correct, then the heirs of Taycanamo encountered these powerful symbols in the south, used them once on an outlying shrine complex at Chan Chan, and then exported them north where they came to bedeck Naymlap's ancestral shrine.

INDIVIDUALS

If there is a reasonable degree of iconographic, archaeological, and ethnohistorical concordance relating to the nature and sequence of regional events, as well as the institutional contours of native statecraft, then there are no a priori grounds for dismissing inquiry into the potential historical realities of the named and numbered figures mentioned in the dynastic traditions. The fundamental problem, of course, is the lack of narrative detail essential for teasing such identities out of the archaeological record.

Names

Most named figures in the northern oral traditions are not assigned distinguishing deeds that might facilitate their archaeological identification. This leaves very few names open to assessment, and we have already seen that some purported deeds, such as Chimor's two stages of expansion, are aggregates of events that transpired over multiple generations. The position paper held that, ". . . if the royal successions are truncated in the oral traditions, then those individuals surviving in name may be composite characters who appropriated by design, or by the vagaries of the oral transmission of history, the qualities, accomplishments, and reputations of earlier monarchs. This problem of merging of royal identities is probably more acute for the earlier rulers in a succession, those closest to the putative founders of a dynastic line, than for the more recent sovereigns who, in some cases, ruled within memory of people able to give testimony to the Spanish chroniclers" (Moseley and Kolata n.d.: 16).

Turning to the Naymlap narrative, there are many names, but what might be identifiable deeds or events are associated only with the first, third, and last generations. If we accept the circumstantial evidence both for Chotuna as the royal court and for Sican Lord iconography as commemorating the patriarch, then there is more potential reality to Naymlap than to other Andean dynastic founders. Heirs and lords of the third generation reportedly settled at other con.plexes, and Kosok (1965: 73) proposed that five named individuals could be linked to known archaeological complexes, such as Llapchillulli with Jayanca and Cala with Tucume. Little is currently known about when these sites were first occupied, therefore their temporal compatibility with the narrative has yet to be resolved. Yet, just because the sites are real does not make their named lords either real or fictitious. If we read the third generation as representing the radiation of a new elite or, more broadly, as the inception of a new cultural order, then the rise of the Sican Precinct and the political flowering of the Lambayeque region during Middle Sican times lend credence to the oral traditions.

Fempellec, the last imperial heir, performs no outstanding acts himself other than being in power when catastrophic flooding leads to his end and to that of the dynasty. The documentation of large-scale flooding around A.D. 1100 has been discussed. Events potentially associated with the end of dynastic rule and the rejection of the former political order are described by Shimada. He reports dramatic evidence of widespread, large-scale conflagration of Middle Sican *huacas* at the time of their abandonment. This was followed close in time by flooding and the abrupt rejection of the once prestigious Sican Lord imagery. In turn, these events were followed by the rise of a new regional power center at El Purgatorio, one of the most impressive complexes of monumental architecture in the Cordillera. Although none of this makes Fempellec tangible per se, there is no question that the Middle Sican cultural and political order came to an abrupt and violent end. To my way of thinking, all of this makes the tale about the end of the dynasty, if not the execution of the last royal heir, historically plausible. Yet, as Zuidema's paper points out, water symbolism—such as arrival by sea and destruction by flood—has potentially widespread associations with the rise and fall of primordial polities in the Andes. Here it is intriguing that lore seems not to mention fire with the fall of polities because, as Shimada points out, fire then flooding is associated with the collapse of the

Moche polity based at Pampa Grande as well as at its later counterpart at the Sican Precinct.

Perhaps because he was not the member of a dynastic succession, the Chimu nobleman, "General" Pacatnamu, is our very best case for the individual historical reality of a native figure based on the confluence of ethnohistorical and archaeological evidence. In Calancha's (1638) account of pre-Inca life in the Jequetepeque Valley, Chimor's conquest of the region is attributed to General Pacatnamu, who is said to have founded an administrative center from which he ruled as governor. If Conrad's contribution to this volume is correct, then we have in hand at the site of Farfan both the imperial settlement this noble built and the burial platform that was his mausoleum.

With respect to the royal succession that Pacatnamu served, there are but four named kings with distinguishing human actions. Taycanamo's main feat is founding the dynasty, about which we are told rather little. He is a shadowy character compared to Naymlap. Other than arriving alone by watercraft—reputedly sent by a great lord from afar—this figure pursues a markedly mundane career. There is no account of him building a court or monument. We are told of no great deeds, nor even mythical ones, such as turning into a sacred stone. Thus, Taycanamo lacks the heroic qualities generally ascribed to founding ancestors. Given the power and prestige of Chimor, this dearth of embellishment is remarkable. It does not make Taycanamo real, but someone real did beget the dynasty.

Consolidating the Moche Valley is said to have gone on under the succeeding heir, Guacricaur, who was followed by Ñançenpinco, purported conqueror from Jequetepeque to Santa. The latter ruler may have resided in the Uhle enclosure, as will be discussed below. However, in assessing events of territorial consolidation and expansion associated with these two figures, I have previously pointed out that Chimor's growth was incremental and spanned several centuries, not just two lifetimes. This does not invalidate the existence of the two named rulers, but it does imply that there were others as well. The same can be said of Minchançaman, who reputedly conquered from Tumbez to the Chillon. While these may have been the frontiers to which his rule was pushed, they were reached by building on prior conquests. With the defeat of Chimor, Minchançaman was carried off to Cuzco. By inference, if this was a historical figure, his imperial quarters might have been *ciudadela* Tschudi.

Of the four named figures just discussed, Ñançenpinco offers the greatest potential for archaeological dissection, which is rather speculative but quite intriguing. If this name is legitimately associated only with the maximum frontiers of first-stage expansion, then it should designate the reign that witnessed the exploits of General Pacatnamu, the incorporation of Jequete-peque as an important economic province, and the construction of Farfan, which was modeled in accordance with the imperial architectural canons of Chan Chan. The architecture of Farfan and its *audiencias* cross-tie to the southwestern sector of the Uhle enclosure (Keatinge and Conrad 1983; Conrad, this volume). This suggests a possible association of the figure of Ñançenpinco and the Uhle compound. As we have seen, Uhle is a compos-ite of four segregated structural complexes, each serving potentially differ-ent administrative regimes at potentially different times. The interior archi-tecture in the two eastern complexes exhibits extensive erosional damage that I associate with the A.D. 1100 flood event, whereas their western counterparts—which lack such erosional damage—are later and the south-western sector was operational around A.D. 1200 to judge by associated radiocarbon dates. As previously noted, I consider the early monumental enclosures at Chan Chan imperial offices that witnessed long use spanning many generations. *Audiencia* types within the eastern sectors of Uhle do not occur outside of the Moche Valley. However, an *audiencia* type of the north-western sector appears at V-124, the Imperial Chimu administrative center in the Viru Valley, while certain types of the southwestern sector were established farther afield in the Chicama Valley and by Pacatnamu at Farfan. This pattern of occurrence suggests that the four architectural complexes of Uhle were associated with successively larger imperial domains. Therefore, if the name of Ñançenpinco is truly associated with Uhle, then the physical evidence implies that this dynastic entity represents a merging of royal identities with the appropriation of prior political accomplishments in the character of said king. In short, the corrective insights of the archaeological record allow Ñançenpinco to be understood as a composite figure in the dynastic narrative. His name can be legitimately associated with the maxi-mum political frontiers of first-stage imperial expansion and, by inference, with the last of the four administrative quadrants in Uhle. Yet, Ñançen-pinco as the title of a king would have to subsume important political conquests, actions, and monuments of his predecessors. Alternatively, Ñançenpinco as the title of a kingly office would subsume at least four reigns of conquering lords commemorated in the quadrants of Uhle and by the widening webwork of rural administrative centers culminating with Farfan.

Others of Chan Chan's early enclosures and monuments that are of a composite nature or saw long construction and use may well be physical expressions of similar composite reigns. Here the archaeological data strongly suggest that the legendary history of the royal dynasty of Chimor was manipulated by compressing true chronology and by merging multiple royal identities, as Conrad's paper brings out. If this was the case, then the fragmentary dynastic narrative left to us must be viewed as a highly truncated version of imperial history.

Numbers

Compressing genealogical time and imperial history is something of a less obvious problem in the Naymlap narrative. In part, this is because the "interregnum" following the overthrow of Fempellec is of unspecified length. If Lambayeque was incorporated by Chimor around A.D. 1370 and if Fempellec's demise was associated with the A.D. 1100 flood, then the interregnum would have spanned slightly under three centuries, which seems sufficient to accommodate the construction and political flowering of El Purgatorio during Late Sican times. Naymlap's dynasty reputedly spans twelve successive generations. If we equate the founding of the dynasty with the A.D. 750 opening date that Donnan assigns to Chotuna on the basis of stylistic considerations and the closing date with A.D. 1100 flooding, then the narrational generations would average just under thirty years each. While not untenable, these would be rather long reigns, suggesting that regents may have been deleted from the account. Alternatively, if we see the early architecture at Chotuna as Middle Sican in affiliation, as Shimada does, and Naymlap's dynasty as correlating with this phase of the Sican tradition, then twelve generations spanning some two hundred years are not implausible.

In contrast, the Taycanamo roster is obviously very short on potentates if the earliest monumental construction at Chan Chan did not predate the founding of the dynasty. Truncation of dynastic history and elimination of the names and deeds of rulers are implicated by the archaeological record. Nonetheless, there are intriguing correlations between the number of potentates that survive in the dynastic tradition and the number of surviving monuments at the imperial capital. There are nine to eleven pre-Inca rulers, depending upon how unnamed figures in the narrative are counted. Chan Chan has some nine to eleven dominant structures potentially associated with kingly rule, depending on how complexes such as Tello and Higo are categorized. I do not think this is coincidence. Rather, I believe that royal monuments were both preserved and eliminated from the imperial landscape, just as kings' names and mummies were subject to selective retention or rejection. Evidence for this comes from Uhle, the composite compound of the composite figure Ñançenpinco. Around A.D. 1100, administrative architecture in the two eastern sectors of the compound was severely damaged by intense rainfall and flooding and was not subsequently rebuilt. However, the present exterior compound wall enclosing these sectors was built, or rebuilt, after the catastrophic event, as were the two western architectural complexes. If the early eastern structures had not been selectively enclosed and thereby physically protected, they would not have survived later urban renewal and the erection of new monuments, which was particularly intense in the southeastern quadrant of the city. Chayhuac is another early compound that suffered flood damage and was subsequently preserved by building a new enclosure wall abutted to the old. Catastrophic flooding certainly afforded a provident occasion for deciding which past monuments would be protected or rebuilt and which would be allowed to fall into ruin or to be leveled for new structures. This selective maintenance of pre-flood monuments greatly truncated the early end of the archaeological record. Correspondingly, I would suspect that truncation is most acute at the early end of the dynastic narrative and that all named figures here are titles of composite characters or office titles held by a succession of characters.

Ancestral monuments were also clearly eliminated with studied deliberation. In the southeastern quadrant of the city, excavations by J. Topic (J. Topic n.d.; J. Topic and Moseley 1983) identified traces of two early monumental enclosures erected before flooding and maintained after the event. In size, one was perhaps on the order of *ciudadela* Rivero, and the other was smaller. Significantly, both were purposely razed and systematically filled in during later phases of urban occupation. No monument was built atop or near the larger, whereas the smaller was eliminated for the construction of *ciudadela* Tschudi. Perhaps later canons of physical symmetry dictated by duality or quadripartition called for eliminating past enclosures when new ones were erected. Whatever the case, it is dramatically evident that some monuments were carefully preserved, while others were artificially erased from the imperial landscape. In so doing, the nobility of Chimor redefined its own dynastic history, deciding which royal predecessors and commemorative monuments would be perpetuated in memory and vista and which would be permitted to fade into the obscurity of the unremembered past, their identities forgotten or merged into composite figures of more heroic stature.

If we see the sovereigns of Chimor compressing genealogical depth, eliminating past regents, and erasing their monuments, what does this imply about the number of figures that do survive as named or unnamed entities in oral traditions? Here structural principles may come into play. I would speculate that once a maturing dynasty attained genealogical depth of ten or twelve lords—reckoned by duality or by whatever means—lesser figures were regularly dropped from mention to keep the imperial rosters in balance with Andean structural predilections for decimal or calendrical counts. In this vein, Conrad aptly describes the Chimu as having an Orwellian "memory hole" that allowed the present to expurgate the past. Here, I would simply propose that this was a formally structured memory hole predictively patterned by dual, decimal, and duodecimal organization.

If this is the case, then such structural principles provide the predictive ciphers for decoding the historical content of oral traditions. In theory, they would call for the compacting of mature dynastic traditions. This would not alter historical content in terms of sequence or order, but it would compress many small events into a few large ones. Ultimately, incremental conquests would be merged into perhaps no fewer than two great episodes of expansion, one associated with each moiety. Similarly, the reigns of many lords would be compressed into ten or twelve titled positions representing composite characters and thus, essentially, offices historically occupied by a number of lords.

CONCLUSIONS

This volume brings together many different perspectives on articulations of ethnohistorical and archaeological sources. There is unanimity of opinion that, when pursued jointly, both are of fundamental importance in eliciting native institutions of statecraft and structural principles. For Chimor and its subject polities, the primary documentary sources for these institutions and principles are Colonial legal and administrative records. These sources are quite abundant in comparison with the four Spanish accounts of native oral traditions discussing pre-Inca times and the once powerful dynasties that reigned on the North Coast. The position paper for the symposium concluded that there was a favorable articulation between aspects of the oral narrations and the archaeological record. "This concordance includes important basic agreement about the nature and relative order of major regional events, such as the establishment of political centers, distinct episodes of conquest, and the occurrence of a devastating natural catastrophe. Evaluated against the archaeological evidence, the oral traditions emerge as highly compressed statements about seminal events, institutions, and individuals that profoundly affected the course of social history on the North Coast of Peru. The fundamental problem with interpreting these traditions lies less with the authenticity of what is mentioned than with the deliberate truncation of what was preserved through vigorous indigenous historical revisionism" (Moseley and Kolata n.d.: 21). Yet, this was not a foregone conclusion. The following papers demonstrate a broad range of views as to whether or not concordance is possible, artificially imposed, or objectively demonstrated.

In this essay I have drawn upon the archaeological record to probe another possible concordance, that of structural and historical interpretation of oral traditions. In Andean studies, the differences between structural and historical positions may be more apparent than real because each tends to proceed largely from a priori judgments. However, it is also possible to use the content and events of oral narratives to frame interpretive positions in terms of testable archaeological hypotheses, as many of the following papers do. If the purpose of dynastic traditions was only to make structural statements, then I would expect a far less favorable concordance between the oral narrations and the archaeological record than the one that emerged with this symposium. Alternatively, I believe that the concordance may show us how Andean structural predilections can provide a critical key for deciphering the historical content of dynastic traditions. Approached from the combined perspectives of archaeology, iconography, history, and indigenous social structure, the native narratives lose a measure of their intractability and thereby lead us to a deeper, richer appreciation of the great Andean empires.

Ultimately, the oral traditions of the northern desert dynasties are all that are left to us of the structural and historical expressions of the continent's penultimate native empire. Chasing legends and validating imperial lore are certainly not our primary business. Still, reexamining the traditions every so often is very important because the nature of Andean research is changing and reassessment brings forth new insights and new hypotheses for investigation. In this essay, I have perhaps strayed toward the side of history rather than of myth. Yet, after long dealing with faceless processes and impersonal institutions of the past, it seems both refreshing and challenging to think in terms of potentially real people, royal offices, and rare events that names such as Pacatnamu, Ñançenpinco, and Fempellec conjure up for consideration.

BIBLIOGRAPHY

ANDREWS, ANTHONY P.
> 1974   The U-shaped Structures at Chan Chan, Peru. *Journal of Field Archaeology* 1 (3/4): 241–264.

CABELLO BALBOA, MIGUEL
> [1586]   *Miscelánea antarctica.*
> 1951   Instituto de Etnología, Universidad Nacional Mayor de San Marcos, Lima.

CALANCHA, ANTONIO DE LA
> 1638   *Crónica moralizada del Ordén de San Augustín en el Perú con sucesos egenplares en esta monarquía.* Pedro Lacavalleria, Barcelona.

CAVALLARO, RAFFAEL
> n.d.   Architectural Analysis and Dual Organization at Chan Chan. Paper presented at the 46th International Congress of Americanists, Amsterdam, July 1988.

CHÁVEZ, SERGIO JORGE
> 1976   The Arapa and Thunderbolt Stelae: A Case of Stylistic Identity with Implications for Pucara Influence in the Area of Tiahuanaco. *Ñawpa Pacha* 13: 3–26.

COLLIER, DONALD
> 1955   *Cultural Chronology and Change as Reflected in the Ceramics of the Virú Valley, Peru. Fieldiana: Anthropology* 43. Field Museum of Natural History, Chicago.

CONRAD, GEOFFREY W.
> 1977   Chiquitoy Viejo: An Inca Administrative Center in the Chicama Valley, Peru. *Journal of Field Archaeology* 4(1): 1–18.
> 1982   The Burial Platforms of Chan Chan: Some Social and Political Implications. In *Chan Chan: Andean Desert City* (Michael E. Moseley and Kent C. Day, eds.): 87–117. University of New Mexico Press, Albuquerque.

ELING, JR., HERBERT J.
> 1977   Interpretaciones preliminares del sistema de riego antiguo de Talambo en el valle de Jequetepeque, Perú. *III Congreso Peruano, El Hombre y la Cultura Andina (1977): Actas y trabajos* (Ramiro Matos M., ed.) 2: 401–419. Lima.

KEATINGE, RICHARD W.
> 1974   Chimu Rural Administrative Centers in the Moche Valley, Peru. *World Archaeology* 6: 66–82.
> 1975   Urban Settlement Systems and Rural Sustaining Communities: An Example from Chan Chan's Hinterland. *Journal of Field Archaeology* 2 (3): 215–227.
> n.d.   Chimu Ceramics from the Moche Valley Peru: A Computer Application to Seriation. Ph.D. dissertation, Department of Anthropology, Harvard University, 1973.

Keatinge, Richard W., and Geoffrey W. Conrad
    1983   Imperialist Expansion in Peruvian Prehistory: Chimu Administration of a Conquered Territory. *Journal of Field Archaeology* 10(3): 255–283.

Klymyshyn, Alexandra M. Ulana
    1982   Elite Compounds in Chan Chan. In *Chan Chan: Andean Desert City* (Michael E. Moseley and Kent C. Day, eds.): 119–143. University of New Mexico Press, Albuquerque.

Kolata, Alan L.
    1982   Chronology and Settlement Growth at Chan Chan. In *Chan Chan: Andean Desert City* (Michael E. Moseley and Kent C. Day, eds.): 67–85. University of New Mexico Press, Alburquerque.
    n.d.   Chan Chan: The Form of the City in Time. Ph.D. dissertation, Department of Anthropology, Harvard University, 1978.

Kosok, Paul
    1965   *Life, Land and Water in Ancient Peru.* Long Island University Press, New York.

Lathrap, Donald
    1985   Jaws: The Control of Power in the Early Nuclear American Ceremonial Center. In *Early Ceremonial Architecture in the Andes* (Christopher B. Donnan, ed.): 241–268. Dumbarton Oaks, Washington, D.C.

Means, Philip A.
    1931   *Ancient Civilizations of the Andes.* Charles Scribner's Sons, New York.

Moseley, Michael E.
    1975   Prehistoric Principles of Labor Organization in the Moche Valley, Peru. *American Antiquity* 40 (2): 191–196.
    1987   Punctuated Equilibrium: Searching the Ancient Record for El Niño. *Quarterly Review of Archaeology* 8(3): 7–10.

Moseley, Michael E., and Alan L. Kolata
    n.d.   Myth and History on the North Coast of Peru: Steps to an Archaeological Concordat. Paper prepared for the Dumbarton Oaks symposium The Northern Dynasties, October 1985.

Narváez V., Luis Alfredo
    n.d.   Excavaciones en el Palacio Tschudi: Nuevos datos e impresiones sobre la historia de Chan Chan. *Andean Past.* (In press)

Netherly, Patricia J.
    1984   The Management of Late Andean Irrigation Systems on the North Coast of Peru. *American Antiquity* 49 (2): 227–254.
    n.d.   Local Level Lords on the North Coast of Peru. Ph.D. dissertation, Department of Anthropology, Cornell University, 1977.

Ortloff, Charles R., Michael E. Moseley, and Robert A. Feldman
    1982   Hydraulic Engineering Aspects of the Chimu Chicama-Moche Intervalley Canal. *American Antiquity* 47(3): 572–595.

ROWE, JOHN HOWLAND
    1948   The Kingdom of Chimor. *Acta Americana* 6(1–2): 26–59. Mexico City.
    1968   What Kind of a Settlement was Inca Cuzco? *Ñawpa Pacha* 5: 59–76.

RUBIÑOS Y ANDRADE, JUSTO MODESTO DE
    [1782] Sucesión cronológica: ó serie historical de los curas de Mórrope y
    1936   Pacora en la Provincia de Lambayeque del Obispado de Truxillo del Peru . . . (Carlos A. Romero, ed.). "Un manuscrito interesante . . ." *Revista Histórica* 10(3): 289–363. Lima.

THOMPSON, LONNIE G., E. MOSLEY-THOMPSON, J. F. BOLZAN, and B. R. KOCI
    1985   A 1500-Year Record of Tropical Precipitation in Ice Cores from the Quelccaya Ice Cap, Peru. *Science* 229: 971–973.

TOPIC, JOHN R.
    1982   Lower-Class Social and Economic Organization at Chan Chan. In *Chan Chan: Andean Desert City* (Michael E. Moseley and Kent C. Day, eds.): 145–175. University of New Mexico Press, Albuquerque.
    n.d.   The Lower Class at Chan Chan: A Qualitative Approach. Ph.D. dissertation, Department of Anthropology, Harvard University, 1977.

TOPIC, JOHN R., and MICHAEL E. MOSELEY
    1983   Chan Chan: A Case Study of Urban Change in Peru. *Ñawpa Pacha* 21: 153–182.

URTON, GARY
    1988   La arquitectura publica como texto social: La historia de un muro de adobe en Pacariqtambo, Peru (1915–1985). *Revista Andina* 6 (1): 225–261. Cuzco.

VARGAS UGARTE, RUBÉN
    1936   La fecha de la fundación de Trujillo. *Revista Histórica* 10: 229–239. Lima.

WAYLEN, PETER R., and CÉSAR N. CAVIEDES
    1986   El Niño and Annual Floods on the North Peruvian Littoral. *Journal of Hydrology* 89: 141–156.

Architecture of the Chimu: Memory, Function, and Image

WILLIAM J CONKLIN

FIELD MUSEUM OF NATURAL HISTORY

THE VAST ARCHITECTURAL RUINS of the northern coast of Peru constitute the primary evidence for the existence as well as for the power of the northern empires of ancient Peru. This volume of papers concentrates on a correlation of the fragmentary literary evidence concerning those northern empires with that architectural and related archaeological evidence. The architectural evidence should provide geographic and chronological scale and should suggest the organizational principles and broad value systems of those empires; however, the architectural evidence is wordless and can provide no names and no stories.

Ethnographic accounts record only a few remote references to North Coast imperial architecture, yet an analysis of the massive architectural evidence is obviously critical in any determination of larger societal interpretations of the nature of those empires. That analysis must, of course, be based upon a study of the extensive walls and mounds that remain. But it is possible that even after the architectural forms have been identified archaeologically, the original significance of those forms may remain unknown.

What are the methods of research that can lead to the discovery of the significance or meaning of architectural forms? How can one tackle in an orderly way the subject of "what did the architecture mean?" This difficult and problematic question is, however, the *only* question if one is after knowledge of what was in the builders' minds, rather than simply what was in the ground. The anthropological question arising from archaeological analysis of architecture must be, literally, "What did they have in mind?"

Analysis can begin with a trial formula that seems to be applicable to other known architecture. This formula suggests that meaning in architecture can be considered one part *memory,* one part *use,* and one part *image.* That is, if one were to ask a proud builder about his own recent construction—a question such as "Why did you make the walls so high?"—he might well answer something like "We always make the walls high; it keeps the robbers out, and besides, it impresses the neighbors." Thus the tripartite presence of memory, function, and image are the balancing components of architectural meaning. To some degree, the data on the architectural forms of the northern dynasties can provide us with access to all three aspects of architectural meaning.

Memory

The power of architectural forms tends to be remembered longer than the specifics of their iconography. Consider the architectural forms of the capital city of the United States. Washington, D.C., is dominated by the gigantic cosmic dome of the Capitol, a dome whose original Middle-Eastern meaning is forgotten, but a form that nevertheless makes a statement about the United States as a worldly and powerful nation. Down the Mall from the dome stands a huge obelisk, an architectural form invented in Egypt to commemorate a tyrannical pharaoh, but astonishingly co-opted by the early Americans to commemorate the founder of their democracy. Nevertheless, the Washington Monument makes quite clear the nation's belief in its own direct connection to the heavens above. So, evidently the power of architectural forms can continue for thousands of years, even though the specifics of their meaning change.

The documents of the northern empire seem to record Chimu memories of people and events. Interestingly enough, we also know something about Chimu memories of architectural form because we know something of the architectural precedents that must have made up their memories. As a measure of their memory, we can note Chimu respect for ancient *huacas* by observing the presence or absence of Chimu burials therein. We can examine the early architectural traditions of the Moche Valley prior to the rise of the Chimu and explore architectural forms that continued to hold power even though their meaning shifted over time.

Function

Function in architecture is, unfortunately, never an exact correlative of form, though one can certainly deduce by flow and fit analyses something about the use of architectural forms. Flow analysis (activity A occurred before activity B because A is closer to the entrance; or, activity C involved high security because it has a tightly controlled access) can sometimes provide a sequence that we can match against a model. Fit analysis (activity B probably involved few people because it is a tiny space) can be a check on the scale of the model. In the architectural analysis of an archaeological ruin, the original functional use of a space sometimes can be suggested by fragments of remaining ancient artifacts, sometimes by ethnographic parallel, or sometimes by mental testing with logical models of human activity. In such testing, though, we always must bear in mind that the architectural form of a given space has only a loose relation to its function.

Understanding the planning and organization evident in the typical arrangements of the interrelated spaces of the *ciudadelas* of Chan Chan, for example, clearly requires the creation of a model of human activity—one that can explain, approximately at least, the patterns of the spaces. There are today virtually no traces of artifacts left in the ruins to suggest their former use, and there are no comparable compounds still in use today to suggest to us an ancient use. However, several models for the ancient functional activities of the *ciudadelas* have been proposed and a new model will be proposed for consideration here. A *ciudadela* compound at the site of Pacatnamu will be examined, and aspects of an activity model for that compound will be considered.

Image

As used here, the word *image* refers not to a technical record such as a photograph or drawing, but to that which remains in the mind of the viewer after he has turned away from the actual scene. Image refers to that interpreted and censored record remaining after vision itself has been completed. Image is both more and less than a photographic record and involves a memory of associated emotions and impressions as well as a memory of form. This remaining image very likely is closer to being a record of the meaning than it is to the actual architecture. If our ultimate interest is in the mental construct of that original viewer, then the record of his images may be as important as the adobe remains themselves.

The Chimu actually left many images of their architecture. Many Chimu ceramics portray temple mounds with superstructures. However, the Chimu left no images of mounds in the denuded form in which they appear today, that is, without superstructures. Models of Chimu houses and courts exist. Yet, the Chimu left no images of what archaeologists now call their capital—Chan Chan, the urban complex that appears to have been their most impressive construction. This Chimu choice of what to portray and what not to portray must be considered an important clue to the meanings once associated with their architecture.

CHIMU ARCHITECTURAL MEMORIES

An examination of the possible meanings of Chimu architecture can begin with a review of pre-Chimu architecture, which logically must have constituted the architectural memories of the Chimu. Amongst the early Chimu, it seems probable that at least the elite would have been familiar with the Moche V cities of Galindo and probably also Pampa Grande, both of which immediately preceded the Chimu.

Pampa Grande in the Lambayeque River drainage is geographically distant from the Moche Valley, but its ceramics are indistinguishable from coeval ceramics of the Moche Valley. Its architecture, however, is distinct (Haas 1985). Architecture is, after all, a far less portable art than ceramics. The inertia of architecture provides resistance to the waves of fashion, creating a slower cycle of change than that characterizing ceramics.

The city of Galindo was contemporary with Pampa Grande but was constructed in the Moche Valley. Galindo has Moche V ceramics and architecture, which, though not particularly impressive, provide important clues concerning the transition between Moche and Chimu cultures. Chan Chan, not surprisingly, seems more closely related to Galindo than it does to Pampa Grande. Perhaps the architecture most prominent in the Chimu consciousness, though, was not Galindo, the latest construction in the Moche Valley, but the somewhat earlier Huaca del Sol—still today the largest construction in the valley.

The very ancient *huaca* mounds in the Moche Valley also must have formed a background architectural consciousness for the Chimu. The Moche Valley is littered with very early architectural mounds that were most likely still revered *huacas* in Moche and Chimu times. Both the Moche and Chimu cultures probably derived their architectural memories from these local Moche Valley mounds, though Moche ceramic and textile traditions (Conklin 1979) seem to have come from the adjacent valley sites of Gallinazo and Salinar. A brief chronological review of the Moche Valley *huacas* can help us understand the early power of that Moche Valley architectural tradition, and perhaps provide misty glimpses of the nameless ancient Moche Valley empires that preceded Moche, Chimu, and Sican.

INITIAL PERIOD AND EARLY HORIZON HUACAS IN THE MOCHE VALLEY

Menacucho

Far up the Moche Valley is an awesome mound complex called Menacucho (Fig. 1), constructed in part of stone walls with fill, and in part of cylindrical and conical adobes. The construction variety suggests a long evolution. The *huaca* occupies the middle ground between the mountains behind to the east, and the river and valley in front to the west. Construction probably dates to the Initial Period. The corners of the main mound were not constructed square but were rounded, unlike any other known building in the valley. It is a two-part *huaca* in which the smaller, north-facing mound is probably older, and the larger, west-facing mound later. Both parts have U-shaped forms on top of rectangular basal mounds. Chimu burials exist in the ground to the north of the *huaca,* indicating its continued respect in Chimu times 2,000 years or more after its construction.

Fig. 1 Menacucho, an early mound complex in the Moche Valley. The large mound has round corners and appears to have had a U-shaped form.

Puente Serrano

Not as far up the Moche Valley and on the north side of the river is the mound complex of Puente Serrano (Fig. 2). Robert Feldman (personal communication, 1980) reports the presence of Salinar ceramics. Construction is of stone walls with fill, with some cylindrical adobes and some highly irregular short, square adobes. Some exterior stucco still exists. The *huaca* has massing somewhat like Sechin Alto in the Casma Valley, with a central, high rectangular stepped mound and side wing mounds. It is also similar in form to Huaca Los Reyes in the Moche Valley. Puente Serrano's wings embrace a grand view of a mountain peak up valley. Compound walls are associated with the rear portions of the mounds. Burial grounds of undetermined age exist to the north.

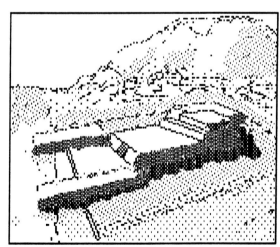

Fig. 2 Puente Serrano, an early mound complex on the north side of the Moche Valley.

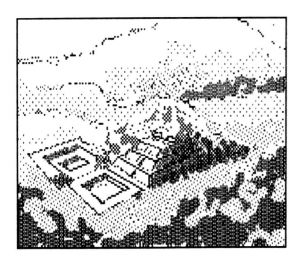

Fig. 3   Huaca de Los Chinos, an early mound complex on the south side of the Moche Valley (see also Kosok 1965: 92).

Los Chinos

On the south side of the Moche Valley is Los Chinos, another ancient *huaca* mound (Fig.3) and also a two-part composition (Kosok 1965). Topographically, it is like the others: it occupies an intermediate position in the landscape, mediating between the water below and the mountain above. One of the mounds is terraced and oriented to the east. It is constructed of stone and has occasional Chavin sherds (Robert Feldman, personal communication, 1980). The larger mound, seemingly later, is U-shaped and faces north. The U shape surrounds a square courtyard and overlooks a second square courtyard beyond. The U mound faces directly toward a symmetrical three-part mountaintop to the north. This visual conversation and implied relationship between the man-made mountain and the actual mountain perhaps invoked the transfer of power to the *huaca*. Burial grounds exist to the north.

Los Reyes

Huaca Los Reyes of the Caballo Muerto group of early *huacas* (Fig.4) is located still further down river in the Moche Valley. It is the best-preserved and hence most easily analyzed Moche Valley Early Horizon *huaca* (Conklin 1985). Even during its final stage, which must have approached Moche times, the earliest *huaca* mound (probably Initial Period) was still preserved, an indication of the amazing longevity of *huaca* power. The siting of Los Reyes, however, differs radically from the previously discussed *huacas*. It was constructed on an open plain; and though it opens to a mountain view, it has a *quebrada* at its back, not a mountain. It does not have the sense of being a mediating form constructed between mountain and river as do the

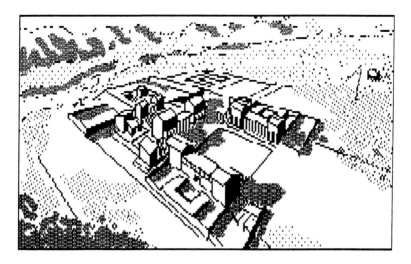

Fig. 4   Huaca Los Reyes, an Initial Period and Early Horizon mound complex on the north side of the Moche Valley. Diagrammatic reconstruction drawing.

others discussed. No associated burial grounds have been noted either, but a simple rectangular pyramid mound, which may have formed a two-part composition with Los Reyes, exists east and north of the main complex.

The first of Los Reyes' sequential U-shaped *huacas* faced up river and toward the view of Cerro Galindo. But later stages, which enclosed the composition with encircling courtyard walls, cut off that view. Furthermore, little U-shaped *huacas* were built inside courtyards and had no views at all. These *huacas* were oriented in a variety of directions. The power of the U form at Los Reyes clearly outlasted the specifics of its early meaning.

In a previous study of Los Reyes, I interpreted these little U-shaped *huacas* in courtyards as cult centers subsidiary to the main cult (Conklin 1985), but their activity model could equally well be that of administration with religious overtones. With either interpretation, the architecture clearly speaks to us about a society that was developing specialization and subdivision and one in which religious monuments had, in part, lost their direct relation to landscape.

EARLY INTERMEDIATE PERIOD MOCHE HUACAS

Missing from the architectural record are Moche Valley mounds that can be clearly attributed to the early phases of the Moche ceramic sequence. Michael E. Moseley (1983) has suggested that this may be due partially to environmental destruction. Also, it is possible that the inner cores of later *huacas* are actually early and date to this period. Or perhaps there was something of a hiatus in the Moche Valley mound tradition and none was built during early Moche times.

Huaca del Sol and Huaca de la Luna

The early stages of construction and evolution of Huaca del Sol and Huaca de la Luna are not well understood, but their final paired relationship in Moche IV provides clues to the meaning of Moche Valley architecture in general (Fig. 5). This pairing has been stressed by Theresa Topic (1982), who found at Huaca de la Luna evidence of elite residences, a walled compound, and exotic murals. On the other hand, giant El Sol was built on the site of ordinary residential constructions and must have been rebuilt many times. T. Topic (1982) found Huaca del Sol had massive use and occupation, and there is extensive evidence in El Sol of non-elite Chimu burials (Conklin and Versteylen 1978). The dichotomy of forms and use certainly suggests a memory of the frequent pairing of the old Moche Valley *huacas.*

During early Chimu times, at the end of the Middle Horizon and the beginning of the Late Intermediate Period, Huaca del Sol must have been reasonably well preserved and still sacred. The major destruction of El Sol occurred during Colonial times when the Rio Moche was diverted to "mine" the mound hydraulically in a large-scale looting operation. Though El Sol's original form remains uncertain, its impressive grandeur is unquestioned. The composition of El Sol and La Luna as two dialectical mounds occurs with the visible presence of the river in front and the mountain behind. These Early Intermediate Period *huacas* are, then, more conservative in their placement than was the earlier Los Reyes.

Observing the Chimu use of U-shaped forms, one logically could argue that there must have been highly influential U-shaped *huacas* in existence during the hundreds of years of Moche rule that preceded the Chimu, though none as yet has been identified. This reasoning would argue, then, that the most important Moche *huaca,* as well as the more ancient valley *huacas,* must have been U-shaped. Perhaps the ground compaction patterns caused by the original form of El Sol can someday be used to detect its original form.

Galindo

As previously noted, the late Moche site of Galindo is rather unimpressive. If one can see an evolution from the cosmos-connecting mounds that the early Moche Valley centers created in the Initial Period, a secularization in Los Reyes during the Early Horizon, and a grandiose but conservative expression of the tradition in El Sol and La Luna, then Galindo seems anticlimactic (Fig.6). Only small pyramid mounds exist there, the largest of which has an attached forecourt, a surrounding wall, and a very flat access

Fig. 5 Aerial photograph showing Huaca del Sol and Huaca de la Luna as paired mounds at the base of the mountain. Photograph by Shippee-Johnson, 1931, neg. no. 334910, courtesy of the Department of Library Services, American Museum of Natural History.

Fig. 6 Aerial photographs of the Moche V city of Galindo showing the extent and variety of the wall forms used in the city. Photograph by Shippee Johnson, 1931, courtesy of the Department of Library Services, American Museum of Natural History.

ramp. But none of these constructions is impressive, as Garth Bawden has noted (1982), and none of the mounds has any discernible relation to mountains, rivers, or views. With its mild statement of *huacas* and religious structures, the Galindo forms speak of decline in religious power and a rise in civil complexity (Bawden 1982). The vast plan of Galindo has a variety and complexity of compounds and urban forms that make it seem like a true city—a major change from the monumental, *huaca*-dominated early religious sites of the Moche Valley.

But it is the walls of Galindo that are of great interest, not the pyramids. Enclosing walls are seen as protective elements constructed around the *huacas* of Los Reyes, but such enclosing walls exist at Galindo without any *huacas* inside. Instead, most walls enclose courtyards with steps, benches, and secondary rooms. Activities unrelated to *huacas* have become worth protecting. One walled compound encloses a stadium-like form. Most others contain a variety of open and closed rooms and courts. This proliferation of walled compounds in Galindo seems to indicate that many new societal forms were evolving and were worth definition and protection.

Linear walls at Galindo are also varied and complex. For example, there are walls that are city-scaled and seem to separate classes; walls that cross valleys, suggesting a dam-like, hydraulic role; walls that parallel the watercourse like linear dikes; and walls that form terrace edges.

One might see this change as a wall obsession. Such then were the rich memories of the Moche Valley architectural tradition that were inherited by the Chimu. The Moche Valley contains neither architecture that could possibly be attributed to Huari, nor architecture that could be attributed specifically to the Middle Horizon by the presence of Huari materials. The unique Middle Horizon interments found on a platform of Huaca del Sol by Max Uhle (1913) attest as easily to El Sol's own continuing power at that time as they do to the power of the Huari Empire.

Pampa Grande

No researcher, aware of the modest Galindo built within sight of mighty El Sol, has really explained the revolution that must have occurred with the postulated transfer of power away from El Sol and the Moche Valley to Pampa Grande in the Lambayeque Valley. Possibly, Galindo and Pampa Grande were symbiotic or paired. One might see them as a precursor of the Chan Chan/Pacatnamu association discussed later.

Pampa Grande (Shimada 1978; Haas 1985) is clearly a large and complex city of the same culture and time period as Galindo. Walled rooms and compounds at Pampa Grande also form the major texture of the city. Sunken courts, though present in the Moche Valley as early as Huaca Los Reyes, have a frequency and elaboration in Pampa Grande that make them seem new in the Moche architectural vocabulary. Pampa Grande differs profoundly from Galindo, however, in having at its center Huaca Grande, a colossal pyramid (one-third the bulk of the Empire State Building) situated with its back to Cerro Pampa Grande, the mountain behind. The front is open to a view across the Chancay River toward distant mountain peaks (see Kosok 1965: 159, figs. 23, 24). Also in the foreground of this *huaca* are two irrigation canals, probably controlled by the city.

Because of the height of the mound and the consequent length of the access ramp, the ramp itself achieves architectural prominence and development. The form of the ramp includes a portion that crosses the face of the mound diagonally. The checkpoints along the access ramp and the roofed and elaborated intermediate platforms make clear that access had become a primary ritual. The access ramp had, itself, become a *huaca*. The mound does not have flanking wings and shows no evidence of having U-shaped structures. It does, however, have an associated smaller mound, and its position in the cosmic landscape strictly follows the early Moche Valley precedents.

Such then are the highlights from the rich architectural heritage of the Moche and Lambayeque Valleys. If the Chimu are the direct descendants of the Moche hegemony, then it might be expected that the last architecture that could be identified as Moche would have been the only memory for Chimu architecture. But architecture, unlike ceramics, does not break easily, it endures. As a result, Chimu architecture in the Moche Valley certainly shows a remembrance of Galindo, and a memory of visits to Pampa Grande, but it also shows a strong remembrance of the early Moche Valley forms.

CHIMU ARCHITECTURAL IMAGES

The meaning of the architecture of the Chimu dynasty can be discerned in part by examination of the Chimu's own images of their architecture. No ceramic or woven images can be identified with specific monuments, but we do have many generalized representations of architecture in Moche, Moche-Huari, and Chimu ceramics, metals, and textiles.

Pots with images of *huaca* mounds sometimes show mighty deities posed seated atop the mounds (Fig. 7). If the relationship I have postulated between the early Moche Valley *huaca* mounds and their corresponding mountains is correct, then these pots suggest the transference of the powers of the deity to the *huaca* itself. But chroniclers' descriptions of the Chimu religion suggest that the mountains themselves in Chimu times were still the primary seat of power. From Fr. Pablo Arriaga comes considerable evidence of Chimu mountain worship. "They also worship and reverence the high hills and mountains and huge stones. They have names for them and numerous fables about their changes and metamorphoses, saying they were once men

Fig. 7 Ceramic image of a deity sitting on a throne at the top of a pyramid mound. Water bottle from Departamento La Libertad (Viru Valley), Peru. Photograph by Hillel Burger, courtesy of the Peabody Museum, Harvard University.

who have been changed to stone" (Arriaga 1969: 23–25). The architectural mounds must borrow power from the sacred mountains by way of the deity.

Pacatnamu textiles may contribute understanding to the character of the *huaca*-top superstructures, which must have formed the climactic visual impression of the architecture (Conklin 1979). Textiles from a late Moche burial (Fig. 8) from beneath a Chimu *huaca* at Pacatnamu in the Jequetepeque Valley suggest the importance of the superstructures in late Moche times. Both gable roofs and lean-to gable roofs are represented, and each has rows of ornaments added at the skyline. Such ornaments are also often found on the superstructure represented in Moche mound ceramics (Fig. 9).

There are also many images of Chimu construction. Chimu architectural ceramics often portray lean-to gable roofs appearing above scenes of important activity. One-way, lean-to structures are usually interpreted as domestic, and are seen in many house models from Chancay, a local culture whose art, textiles, and technology show strong Chimu influence (Fig. 10). Probably the actual form of the basic roof is a one-way pitched design, but when special activities were housed, or special meaning was required, then a frontal porch was added. For greatest emphasis, roof ornaments were added, in a tradition related to the way that war clubs, stepped frets, and strombus monsters were added to Moche roof lines.

Fig. 8 Textile fragment from a late Moche burial found at Pacatnamu and excavated by Ubbelohde-Doering. Several of the textile fragments from the burial illustrate architecture.

Fig. 9 Moche ceramic representation of a superstructure on top of a mound with a ramp represented in spiral form. Probably most religious mounds (*huacas*) in the Moche culture carried such superstructures (after Donnan 1976: fig. 60).

Fig. 10   Textile model of a Chancay house with figures (after Conklin and Benson, 1981: 122).

Fig. 11   Ceramic model of Chimu temple front. Brüning Museum, Lambayeque.   Photograph courtesy of Margaret Hoyt.

Fig. 12 Chimu textile from Chiquitoy Viejo in the Amano Museum. The figure is portrayed on a small platform in front of a temple porch that has a diamond-patterned roof and side wings (after Conklin and Benson 1981: 57).

Fig. 13   Chimu textile showing weavers and their loom in front of a Chimu temple that has broom-like roof combs. Private collection.

One Sican ceramic depicts what appears to be a temple front (Fig. 11). It has an elaborate roof comb with a three-part form, supported by a pair of entrance columns. Another Chimu image of architecture is a wooden temple model (Donnan 1975), which has round columns, a decorated platform, and high walls. Though the model has no existing roof, the presence of sewing holes in the wooden substructure suggests that the roof may have been a textile structure.

A Chimu textile (Fig. 12) in the Museo Amano collection, which Dr. Amano said has a Chiquitoy Viejo provenance (Yoshitaro Amano, personal communication, 1976), portrays a mythological figure with associated characters and a loom in front of a Chimu temple. The main figure stands on a small platform in front of the temple porch. There is a diamond-patterned frontal roof, and the temple has side wings, also with diamond-patterned roofs.

Another textile fragment (Fig. 13) contains a similar, but clearer temple scene. Though the textile's provenance is unknown, the structure is technically identical to many identified Chimu textiles. The main temple front has an elaborate three-part roof comb like the ceramic representations, but with greater detail. The roof comb in the textile has miniature bristles or straws projecting vertically above the decorative accessory band. It is probable that the actual roof comb of the building was similarly constructed of reeds on a larger scale.

Beneath the main temple roof is the porch, with diagonal patterning like that in the Amano textile (Fig. 12). Perhaps the diagonal patterning represents plaiting. This front porch (Fig. 13) is held up by Y columns, as are the side wings of the temple. These side wings also have roof combs and project forward toward the viewer in a U-shaped form.

In front of the temple is a scene of weavers and a vertical X-type loom with bars. The tapestry being woven is clearly represented, as are bobbins with various colored yarns below. Two weavers work at the loom, one on either side. A child stands behind the weaver on the right. The axial relationship between the temple and the loom provides symbolic evidence of a deep relationship between weaving and architecture in Chimu culture.

Also of great interest is the seemingly happy mood portrayed, inasmuch as it is quite possibly an actual image of life in front of a Chimu temple. The open-mouthed posture of the bird casually perched on the loom with the cats portrayed below suggests the cat-calls between felines and yard birds. The Chimu ceramic shown beside the weavers can be readily identified as a Chimu burial type with Lambayeque associations (Bennett 1939: fig. 20g) and suggests that the weaving scene may portray the weaving of a burial textile. So the images of architecture that Chimu society created for itself and for posterity include temples on mounds, elaborate temple tops, courts, houses, and associated activity. But of great importance is the fact that the society apparently left no images at all of Chan Chan—no painting, no textile, no pot. Therefore, it is not possible to analyze their image of Chan Chan, but it is possible to analyze the patterns of the reality of Chan Chan.

CHIMU ARCHITECTURAL FUNCTIONS

The formal concepts of the architecture created at Pacatnamu and Chan Chan during the years of the Chimu dynasty certainly demonstrate Moche and pre-Moche memories. But Chimu construction also resulted from new activity patterns and astonishing new image goals.

Chan Chan

Thanks to Michael Moseley and his associates (Moseley and Day 1982), Chan Chan is one of the most thoroughly and imaginatively studied ruins in Peru. Nevertheless, its architectural meaning remains somewhat elusive. The repetitive form of the compounds creates a pattern of urbanization unlike any other in the entire world. Hence the analyst lacks explanatory analogies or metaphors. The individual compounds have been called appropriately *ciudadelas,* that is, citadels or little cities. Nonetheless, Chan Chan's cluster of citadels with associated infill construction does not quite connote the activity model that characterizes the Western concept of *city.*

There is little about the plan of Chan Chan as a whole that speaks of singularity or of a unified state (Fig. 14). There is no common plaza to represent that city or state, no main street, no common water supply, and, most astonishing of all, no common defense. Chan Chan has no surrounding wall at all equal to the scale of the individual compound walls within. If the individual *ciudadela* walls are read as defensive forms, then they were clearly not built to defend Chan Chan as a capital against an outside force, but each must have been built as either actual or symbolic defense against the others.

The parts of Chan Chan seem to be far more important than the whole. Michael Moseley (personal communication, 1980) has pointed out, however, that the pyramid mound called Huaca Obispo, located on the northern edge of Chan Chan, is associated with wall remains that might be interpreted as parts of city boundary walls. Although no detailed plan of Obispo has been attempted, its scale is impressive, and the ruins suggest that a north-facing ramp might have existed that would have provided the *huaca* with an orientation toward the Cerro Cabras in the distance and toward irrigation canals in the middle ground. Huaca Obispo, although thought to have been constructed quite late in the evolution of Chan Chan (Topic and Moseley 1983), seems to have the traditional orientations and relationships of Moche Valley *huacas*. It may have been a central *huaca* for Chan Chan and would therefore provide evidence of Chan Chan actually having had some form of central focus.

Fig. 14 Aerial photograph of central Chan Chan showing both the non-hierarchical patterning of the major compounds and the commonality of their orientation. (Photograph by Shippee Johnson, neg. no. 334879, courtesy of the Department of Library Services, American Museum of Natural History.

The *ciudadela* walls were the most impressive architectural statement the Chimu made and present an architectural image and scale that had no precedent in the Moche Valley. Although compounds were highly developed in Galindo, they were richly varied, and the scale of their walls in all cases suggests function: the thickness and height seem related to security or other functionally definable purposes. The forms of the walls at Galindo seem not to have been determined by either memory or image.

In Chan Chan, the traditional Moche Valley relationship of scale between boundary wall and *huaca* is reversed. The surrounding walls of the Chan Chan compounds are gigantic, while the U-shaped forms that dominated most Moche Valley sacred sites are scaled like furniture in Chan Chan. The U-shaped forms in the Chan Chan compounds have entirely lost their once consistent orientation and powerful relation to landscape.

In Chan Chan, the height and thickness of the surrounding compound walls vastly exceed any conceivable security threat. Though the walls have some precedent in Moche architectural traditions (i.e., they have a memory base and the walls have security as a functional excuse), the explanation of their scale lies in their intention as expressions of power and in their role as creators of an image.

The position of wall openings also is critical to the meaning of the compounds. The great peripheral walls of the compounds at Chan Chan have openings only on the north, whereas Galindo's walls had openings in all directions. The walled compounds at Chan Chan seem to have superseded all ordinary human functions and to have become fundamentally related to the cosmos. Like the great *huacas* of the Moche Valley that preceded them, the walls of Chan Chan have become architecture used as intercession between human beings and their larger mythological environment. The once-secular security wall became powerful and sacred, while the once sacred U mounds were domesticated.

Alan Kolata's (1982) brick sequence and *audiencia* analyses have ingeniously provided a likely chronology for the compounds. The survey and publication of the plans of Chan Chan (Moseley and Mackey 1974) have permitted creative activity model analysis by Kent Day (1982), Geoffrey Conrad (1981), and others. Their proposed activity models focus on redistribution and administration by sequential rulers who were eventually regally buried.

Attractive as that activity model is, there remains a series of problematic concerns in attempting to reconcile that model with the architectural evidence at Chan Chan. Based on that evidence, it is difficult to support specifics of empire administration or control. For example, water was not controlled at the site as it probably was in Pampa Grande. Shipping and transportation could not have been controlled from within the blinders of the compound walls. Agriculture seems to have been controlled in segments from local compounds whose architectural form was similar to the Chan Chan compound, but smaller (Keatinge and Conrad 1983).

Redistribution—that is, bringing materials and products in, sorting, and carrying them out again—is an activity pattern that emphasizes access, as in a contemporary Andean market plaza. The Chan Chan compounds' access limitations are extraordinary. In fact, the plans of the compounds with their restricted and devious routes seem to be explicitly anti-access. The redistribution model also clearly would be supported by the discovery of "leftovers" in storage areas, permitting the identification of products and processes; but none has been found. Such absence suggests that whatever was stored was easily and completely removed. Removable artifacts seem to be more likely candidates for the storage rooms than are grain or other foods.

Nor does the detailed architectural patterning seem to support the idea of Chan Chan as the unified empire capital. The largest-scale design unit seems to be the compound. Certainly Chan Chan has the construction area of an empire capital, but it does not seem to have the city-scale patterns that would be expected of such a hypothesized capital. The rigorously organized plans inside the compounds contrast radically with the patterns outside the compounds, indicating that those in power inside a compound did not control the outside, not even at the entrance to the compound. Where specific activities outside the compound can be deduced from the archaeological evidence (Topic and Moseley 1983: fig.26), the pattern distribution of that activity does not indicate centralized activity, but rather piecemeal, compound-related activity. This contrast between the whole of Chan Chan and its parts and the contrast between the inside of the compound and the outside seem to suggest that perhaps the compounds represent a group of princely strongholds rather than a unified empire or capital city, more like Embassy Row in Northwest Washington, D.C., than the Mall, more like Florence than Rome.

One part of the activity model for Chan Chan already noted (i.e., the sponsorship, collection, display storage, and burial of art on a vast scale), however, does indeed fit the archaeological evidence. Tremendous quantities of art have been discovered at the ruins of Chan Chan. During Colonial times the ruins were, in fact, referred to as "gold mines."

What then is the operational terminology of a facility that houses this quantity of art and range of art activities? *Mausoleum* is a term that comes to mind, but that clearly does not include the activity of collection and display that occurred prior to burial. *Art school* might be suggested. This would come closer to implying the activity that the circulation, courtyards, and service facilities imply. The activity model most closely fitting the forms of the architectural evidence, it seems, is that of a *museum* (Fig.15). That is, each of the enclosures can be understood best as a vast personal museum in

Fig. 15 Pattern of niches in a Chan Chan wall. The niches seem to have been designed more for display of art objects than for simple storage (after Holstein 1927: fig. 24).

which the collector/owner reigned, defended, administered, and was eventually laid to rest.

The apparent long-term institutional life associated with the compound forms, involving occasional additions and rebuilding, also fits well into the growth-of-collections museum model. It is the private collections activity that, paralleling a decline in religious power, must have become the dominant activity of the Chimu Empire. This activity called for the new forms of Chan Chan: the separate fortress walls surrounding each of the sequential and competitive collections with their vast art storage and display facilities and their token religious structures. Princely collecting had reversed the old architectural images of great mounds and small walls and had created new architectural forms in the service of the new activities.

Pacatnamu

Although the site of Pacatnamu bears no topographic similarity to either the Moche Valley or the site of Pampa Grande, the cosmic planning principles relating the Pacatnamu architecture to the landscape are deeply related to those of the Moche Valley architectural tradition (Fig. 16). The ruins are dominated by numerous pyramidal mounds, virtually all of which (52 out of 53) have the same orientation, facing toward the mountains like obedient supplicants. Many of the pyramids have ramps. To the north of the site are mountains, Cerros de Catalina, which seem to be the specific landscape focus of all of the pyramidal mounds. Straight-line land markings, like those on the Pampa de Nasca, also converge on a focus in front of the mountains. This cosmic landscape of Pacatnamu's architecture and its moun-

Fig. 16 Aerial photograph of Pacatnamu in the Lambayeque Valley showing the generally even patterning of the *huaca* mounds, their common orientation, and the slightly dominant central mound called Huaca 1. Photograph courtesy of the Servicio Aerofotográfico Nacional, Lima, 1943.

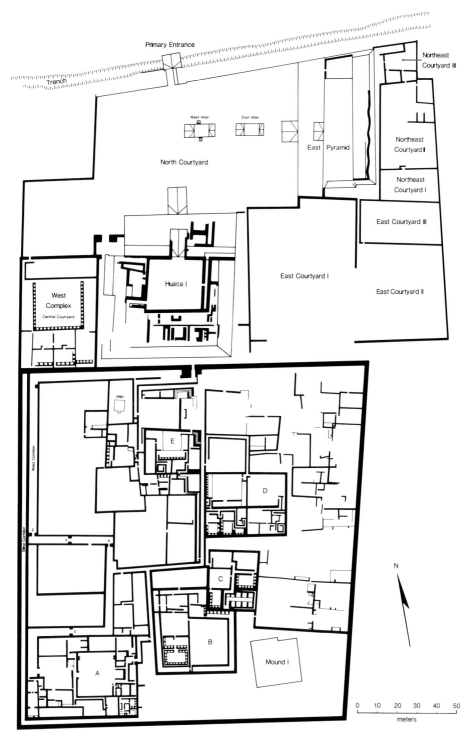

Fig. 17 Plan of Huaca 1, Pacatnamu (after Donnan and Cock 1986: fig. 2).

tains seems literally to suggest that a mountain deity was the focus of the religion of the site. Recently, from a different point of view and based essentially on the variety of its artifacts, Pacatnamu has been considered a religious site—specifically a pilgrimage center (Keatinge and Conrad 1983).

The one exception to the north-facing *huacas* is a mound at the ocean end of the Pacatnamu peninsula. This *huaca*, no. 38 (Hecker and Hecker 1982: Gesamtansicht) has a U-shaped form and faces west toward the ocean. Thus, as an architectural form, apparently it makes reference to forms more ancient than those of the other *huacas*. This *huaca* is located at a logical beginning point for the evolutionary development of a gradually expanding, fan-shaped plan for Pacatnamu. It is possible that this is an early Pacatnamu *huaca*, and its form may have been modeled from ancient U-shaped Moche Valley *huacas* or from Huaca del Sol, which also might have been U-shaped with a sea orientation.

With the Moche V graves found by Heinrich Ubbelohde-Doering (1967) near Pacatnamu's Chimu pyramid mounds, Pacatnamu must be considered as direct a descendant of Moche traditions as is Chan Chan itself. In fact, the formal elements of the architecture at Pacatnamu—the pyramids, the walls around the pyramids, and the imposing public impression given by the *huacas*—are more directly related to Moche Valley architectural memories than is Chan Chan. Also the activity patterns that best seem to fit the plans at Pacatnamu differ considerably from those of Chan Chan.

The plans of Huaca 1 (Fig. 17), the largest and central pyramid mound at Pacatnamu, and its associated facilities are fascinating to consider. The pyramid mound with its entrance plaza and staged north-facing ramp clearly seems to have been influenced by Pampa Grande. To the east of the main mound, a sunken courtyard of comparable size exists (East Courtyard 1). On the top of the main mound there is a very small, room-sized version of the familiar U-shaped forms from Moche Valley history. The rectangular walled compound behind the pyramid has a single north-facing entrance and thus is typologically like the Chan Chan compounds. But the mound and compound have a unified access system that distinguishes them from structures at either Pampa Grande or Chan Chan.

This access route seems to begin in the frontal plaza on the north side of Huaca 1, goes through an introductory sequence of courts around to the back of the mound, and finally enters the associated restricted-access compounds to the south. The activity pattern thus suggested is that of the palace, with the public ceremonial front and the palatial rear quarters. The private and protected rear quarters have circuitous circulation.

Of special interest in the Pacatnamu Huaca 1 plans are the detailed interior patterns, especially in the subcompounds (i.e., the compounds contained within the enclosing wall). An important clue to interpretation lies in the plan of one central subcompound (D in Fig. 17), which has thick walls and a most unusual bipartite plan. The entrance into the subcompound is from the north, but is designed to provide access to two equal courts. The court on the west is embellished with niches as an entrance statement, and then that route leads on to rear quarters that contain many niches. The court on the east, equal in size, does not contain niches, but instead contains a curious labyrinthine pattern of thin walls. Two possible paths lead through this maze, with both routes eventually arriving at the same inner maze. The maze court on the east and the niche court on the west are essentially equal but for their special inner wall forms. Examination of other subcompounds suggests that many of them also clearly belong to either the "niche type" or the "maze type." Within the whole of the south compound of Huaca 1, there are three subcompounds that have niches, and three that have mazes. The apparent symbiotic dualism may be explicable by a functional activity model, but the labyrinth is difficult to imagine as other than a visual and psychological form. Even the niches seem arranged more for display than for storage. The dualism of the maze and the niche seems to permeate the meaning of the architecture of Pacatnamu's Huaca 1.

CONCLUSIONS

This volume's primary concerns—the written tales of the heroes traveling up and down the northern Andean coast carrying the power of empire with them—are believable because architectural evidence records the transfer of tradition over a vast geographical scale and over millennia of time. In fact, the architectural evidence for those empire connections vastly exceeds the suggestive scope of those few remaining words.

But the architecture articulates the detailed relationships of the parts of those empires. The architectural traditions of the northern dynasties of ancien Peru (Moche, Chimu, Sican) were clearly built upon the age-old architec:ural craditions of the Moche Valley. Although no literary reference to this radition exists, each of the empires appears to have had an architectural memory of that origin.

Moche architectural history, in turn, evolved directly from earlier Moche Valley Initial Period and Early Horizon precedents, and continued until the Moche V period. At that time, a form of radical secularization seems to have occurred with the decline of the power of the *huaca* and the rise of a more secular city, as we have seen in the site analysis of Galindo.

Chimu architecture continued that secularization with the local construction of each of the Chan Chan *ciudadelas* being in spirit bureaucratic, art oriented, and competitive. As wealth accumulated in Chimu times, it would appear that a succession of powerful acquisitors at Chan Chan built a series of heavily walled, vast, private "museums." However, some forms at Chan Chan continued to retain religious power even though their relation to land and sky seems remote.

The architecture at Pacatnamu, on the other hand, clearly seems to have retained the meaning of the mound forms. Perhaps a religious center of this complex coastal Chimu society was at Pacatnamu, where the architecture forms a more traditional relation with the cosmos. The superstructures on Chimu mounds such as those at Pacatnamu can be seen in ceramics and textiles that show memories of Moche precedents but have newly invented, elaborate roof combs.

Sican, the northern Chimu cultural area, with its great pyramidal *huacas* at El Purgatorio, Pampa Grande, and Batan Grande, has no early local northern precedents for such *huaca* construction and appears to have remembered its Moche Valley origins more clearly than did the southern Chimu. In Sican culture, the mounds were built in resonance with the sacred mountains and had wings that embraced the view as in the old Early Horizon days.

There is interesting evidence that religion of the northern dynasties may have been organized with some form of balanced dualism. The architecture, in part, supports such an interpretation. The old Moche Valley *huacas* were usually in two parts, but not as two equals. Usually one *huaca* seems to have been the old temple, and one the new.

Michael Moseley (this volume) has proposed for consideration the very interesting idea that there is a possible pairing of the *ciudadelas* of Chan Chan. He suggests that this might be explained as a political restatement by the Chimu of the duality of the north and south Moche River banks and their related political organizations. The earlier architecture, however, would not seem to provide precedent for that interpretation. The early Moche Valley *huacas* were not organized as dialectical pairs on opposite sides of the river. The absence of such an organizing principle in the ancient traditions of the valley makes such Chan Chan planning appear to have been a Chimu innovation.

Raffael Cavallaro (n.d.) has developed a carefully analyzed chronological sequence in which the compounds are built as pairs. But the two parts of the pairs do not seem to illustrate the consistent architectural relationships that one would expect from consciously planned pairing. If site plans can be scanned for evidence of the form of societal power, then both Chan Chan and Pacatnamu must be read as plans that show a cluster of ruling-class compounds that, among themselves, show little evidence of hierarchical ordering. These cluster-of-power Chimu architectural statements seem parallel to the cluster of princely towers in San Gimignano and in other Italian medieval hill towns. Both Galindo and the later northern Batan Grande, however, have a central dominant *huaca* and hence have site plans that can be read as evidence of a single-focus society.

Based on a study of the distribution and character of its portable artifacts—pottery, textiles, and metalwork—the Chimu culture appears to have existed on a vast scale and to have been quite unified. The distribution of its art styles, technologies, and portable artifacts extends almost as far south of the Moche Valley as north. The distribution of its architectural traditions, however, was not as symmetrical. The northern portions of Chimu influence relied heavily upon the Moche mound tradition for expressions of centralized power, but at the southern end of Chimu influence, only modest pyramids were built in the Moche Valley style, such as those in the Chancay Valley.

The architectural traditions of this inclusive definition of Late Intermediate period Chimu culture, from far north to far south, come from the memories of the Moche Valley tradition, not from Chan Chan, its presumed Late Intermediate period focus. The architectural influence of the Chan Chan image and style was literally nil. Outside of its local administrative centers, no *ciudadelitas* were ever built. No recreations of *ciudadela* forms appear ever to have been constructed in pottery, in metalwork, or in textiles. No single capital building or urban form at any site seems to have symbolized or summarized the whole empire. Perhaps an answer to the problem of the architectural expression of imperial unity lies in some large-scale, symbiotic dualism unifying the special purpose, cluster-formed sites of Chan Chan and Pacatnamu, whose architecture we continue to study.

BIBLIOGRAPHY

ARRIAGA, PABLO JOSEPH DE
   1969   *The Extirpation of Idolatry in Peru.* University of Kentucky Press, Lexington.

BAWDEN, GARTH
   1982   Galindo: A Study in Cultural Transition during the Middle Horizon. In *Chan Chan: Andean Desert City* (Michael E. Moseley and Kent C. Day, eds.): 285–320. University of New Mexico Press, Albuquerque.

BENNETT, WENDELL C.
   1939   *Archaeology of the North Coast of Peru.* Anthropological Papers of the American Museum of Natural History 37(1). New York.

CAVALLARO, RAFFAEL
   n.d.   Architectural Analysis and Dual Organization at Chan Chan. Paper presented at the 46th International Congress of Americanists, Amsterdam, July 1988.

CONKLIN, WILLIAM J
   1974   An Introduction to South American Archaeological Textiles with Emphasis on Materials and Techniques of Peruvian Tapestry. In *Archaeological Textiles* (Patricia L. Fiske, ed): 17–30. The Textile Museum, Washington, D.C.
   1979   Moche Textile Structures. In *The Junius B. Bird Pre-Columbian Textile Conference* (Ann P. Rowe, Elizabeth P. Benson, Anne-Louise Schaffer, eds.): 165–184. The Textile Museum and Dumbarton Oaks, Washington, D.C.
   1985   The Architecture of Huaca Los Reyes. In *Early Ceremonial Architecture of the Andes* (Christopher B. Donnan, ed.): 139–164. Dumbarton Oaks, Washington, D.C.

CONKLIN, WILLIAM J, and ELIZABETH P. BENSON
   1981   *Museums of the Andes.* Henry A. LaFarge, editorial director. Newsweek, Inc. & Kodansha Ltd., Tokyo.

CONKLIN, WILLIAM J, and EDUARDO VERSTEYLEN
   1978   Textiles from a Pyramid of the Sun Burial. In *Ancient Burial Patterns of the Moche Valley, Peru* (Christopher B. Donnan and Carol J. Mackey, eds.): 384–398. University of Texas Press, Austin.

CONRAD, GEOFFREY W.
   1981   Cultural Materialism, Split Inheritance, and the Expansion of Ancient Peruvian Empires. *American Antiquity* 46 (1): 3–28.

DAY, KENT C.
   1982   Ciudadelas: Their Form and Function. In *Chan Chan: Andean Desert City* (Michael E. Moseley and Kent C. Day, eds.): 55–66. University of New Mexico Press, Albuquerque.

DONNAN, CHRISTOPHER B.
   1975   An Ancient Peruvian Architectural Model. *The Masterkey* 49 (1): 20–29. Southwest Museum, Los Angeles.

1976   *Moche Art and Iconography*. U.C.L.A. Latin American Center Publication, University of California at Los Angeles.

DONNAN, CHRISTOPHER B., and GUILLERMO A. COCK, eds.
1986   *The Pacatnamu Papers, Volume 1*. Museum of Cultural History, University of California, Los Angeles.

HAAS, JONATHAN
1985   Excavations on Huaca Grande: An Initial View of the Elite on Pampa Grande, Peru. *Journal of Field Archaeology* 12(4): 391–409.

HECKER, GIESELA, and WOLFGANG HECKER
1982   *Pacatnamu, Vorspanische Stadt in Nordperu*. Verlag C. H. Beck, Munich.

HOLSTEIN, OTTO
1927   Chan Chan, Capital of Great Chimu. *Geographical Review* 27: 36–61.

KEATINGE, RICHARD W., and GEOFFREY W. CONRAD
1983   Imperialist Expansion in Peruvian Prehistory: Chimu Administration of a Conquered Territory. *Journal of Field Archaeology* 10(3): 255–283.

KOLATA, ALAN L.
1982   Chronology and Settlement Growth at Chan Chan. In *Chan Chan: Andean Desert City* (Michael E. Moseley and Kent C. Day, eds.): 67–85. University of New Mexico Press, Albuquerque.

KOSOK, PAUL
1965   *Life, Land and Water in Ancient Peru*. Long Island University Press, New York.

MOSELEY, MICHAEL E.
1983   Patterns of Settlement and Preservation in the Viru and Moche Valleys. In *Prehistoric Settlement Patterns* (Evon Z. Vogt and Richard Levanthal, eds.): 423–442. University of New Mexico Press, Albuquerque.

MOSELEY, MICHAEL E., and KENT C. DAY, eds.
1982   *Chan Chan: Andean Desert City*. University of New Mexico Press, Albuquerque.

MOSELEY, MICHAEL E., and CAROL MACKEY
1974   *Twenty-four Architectural Plans of Chan Chan, Peru*. Peabody Museum Press, Cambridge.

SHIMADA, IZUMI
1978   Economy of a Prehistoric Urban Context: Commodity and Labor Flow at Moche V Pampa Grande, Peru. *American Antiquity* 43(4): 569–592.

TOPIC, JOHN R., and MICHAEL E. MOSELEY
1983   Chan Chan: A Case Study of Urban Change in Peru. *Ñawpa Pacha* 21: 153–182.

TOPIC, THERESA LANGE
1982   The Early Intermediate Period and Its Legacy. In *Chan Chan: Andean Desert City* (Michael E. Moseley and Kent C. Day, eds.): 255–284. University of New Mexico Press, Albuquerque.

William J Conklin

UBBELOHDE-DOERING, HEINRICH
1967   *On the Royal Highways of the Inca.* Praeger, New York.
UHLE, MAX
1913   Die Ruinen von Moche. *Journal de la Société des Américanistes de Paris* 10: 95–117.

A Maritime Passage from Moche to Chimu

DONNA McCLELLAND

UNIVERSITY OF CALIFORNIA AT LOS ANGELES

L ONG BEFORE THE KINGDOM OF CHIMOR dominated Peru's fertile North Coast, the Moche people conquered these same rich river valleys. They bequeathed a cultural legacy to the Chimu people that is evident in the art. Iconographic analysis of the rich artistic heritage from both cultures provides a unique and abundant resource that sheds light on the transition from Moche to Chimu. Unlike architecture, which was subject to reconstruction during later occupations, and oral traditions, which were subject to changes through retelling (Conrad, this volume) and to selective documentation by the Spanish chroniclers, ceramic art provides an original, unaltered record of a mythical world filled with supernatural figures and rituals. If we accept the premise that ancient societies encoded into their art and mythology changes taking place in their real world, then iconographic analysis might reveal these real-life changes. It is my position that such an investigation can help clarify the cultural transition from late Moche to Chimu times, as well as the foundations of Chimu culture.

Marine iconography predominates in Chimu art. For example, in a study of fifty-three "Chimu"[1] friezes, Madeleine Fang (n.d.: 42) suggested that they all depict a marine motif. Fifty of these are located in Chan Chan, the heartland of imperial Chimu.[2] In contrast, Moche murals (Bonavia 1985: 47) are not centered around a marine theme. The dominant maritime theme of Chimu art, as opposed to the more terrestrial orientation of Moche art, suggests a discontinuity between the two traditions.

In a chronological study of North Coast ceramics, Rafael Larco Hoyle (1948) seriated Moche ceramics into five phases, based primarily on vessel and spout form. He further differentiated Moche ceramics from Chimu.

---

[1] Fang included a frieze from the Nepeña Valley and two from the Lambayeque Valley at Chotuna (Donnan, this volume). She did not distinguish between Sican (Shimada, this volume) and Imperial Chimu.

[2] The friezes are located in eight of the *ciudadelas* at Chan Chan: Uhle, Laberinto, Gran Chimu, Velarde, Bandelier, Rivero, Tschudi, and Squier. Velarde contains a room adorned with a frieze featuring tule boats and marine animals on three walls (Fang n.d.: 20).

Yet, the acceptance of a rigid division between Moche Phase V and Chimu may be misleading. Our Moche iconographic research at U.C.L.A. demonstrates that a major shift to maritime activity occurs in Moche art between Phases IV and V, foreshadowing the maritime emphasis of Chimu art. Thus, the most significant break in the North Coast artistic tradition seems to have occurred between Moche IV and V rather than between Moche V and Chimu.

Fineline drawings on pottery provide the best iconographic resource to trace the evolution of Moche ceramic art. The overwhelming majority of Moche ceramics in museums and collections was produced during Phase IV. This is understandable inasmuch as the Moche people expanded their territory to its maximum and occupied the greatest number of sites during Phase IV. There are significantly fewer Moche V sites. One of the problems that hindered earlier iconographic studies of the Moche-Chimu transition was the small available sample of Moche V bottles with fineline drawings. Before we undertook our research, there were even fewer—less than two dozen—roll-out drawings from these bottles, and most drawings were incomplete. Consequently, any observations about the relationship between Moche and Chimu art had to be based on a comparison of Chimu art with the more numerous fineline drawings from earlier Moche phases; changes within Moche mythology from the early phases to the terminal phase simply could not be taken into account.

This iconographic study is based on a sample[3] of more than 700 Moche IV bottles with fineline drawings. These were compared with a sample of 303 Moche V bottles with fineline drawings, many of which surfaced in recent years.[4] We added 119 roll-out drawings from Moche V bottles[5] to the small number previously available. Roll-out drawings are essential to the study of Moche V iconography because the elaborate ornamentation used during this phase makes it difficult to distinguish the subject from the background filler elements. For clarity, the repetitious geometric background elements were omitted from the roll-out drawings illustrated in this article.

ICONOGRAPHIC EVIDENCE OF THE MARITIME SHIFT

Moche fineline drawings provide a detailed pictorial account of the Moche mythical world as well as a rich resource to document the maritime shift between Phases IV and V. Less than one-fourth of the Phase IV drawings

---

[3] The Moche sample used in this study is Christopher Donnan's photographic archive of Moche art. Carol Mackey's Chimu photographic archive provided a large sample of Chimu art.

[4] Fifty-two of those bottles that surfaced recently are reputedly from the site of Huaca Moro in the Jequetepeque Valley.

[5] These roll-out drawings were prepared by the author using photographs by Christopher B. Donnan.

relate to maritime activity. In marked contrast, more than one-half of the Phase V fineline drawings portray this activity. Furthermore, more than one-third of the nonmarine subjects in Phase IV are not portrayed in Phase V.

Moche fineline drawings illustrate a small number of themes (Donnan 1978: 158) that focus on an activity or event such as a goblet ritual in the Presentation Theme (Donnan 1975), hunting in the Deer Hunting Theme (Donnan 1982: 235), and an important interment in the Burial Theme (Donnan and McClelland 1979). Larco Hoyle's seriation of stirrup-spout bottles makes it possible to trace a theme through the five phases. Some themes and deities appearing in earlier phases occur in Phase V, demonstrating the underlying continuity of the Moche mythical world; however, in Phase V the introduction of new marine themes and deities, the participation of these new marine-related deities in themes that originated before Phase V, and the overwhelming presence of marine activity demonstrate an increasing maritime focus.

The Tule Boat Theme illustrates this dramatic maritime shift between Phase IV and Phase V. Fourteen vessels with fineline drawings of tule boats are known from Phases I through IV; of these, eleven are from Phase IV. These bottles comprise less than 2 percent of the Phase IV fineline drawing sample. In contrast, tule boats are painted on sixty-three Phase V bottles— more than 20 percent of the bottles from this phase—a remarkable incidence. Equally notable are the changes in the tule boats, the boatmen, and their activities in Phase V.[6]

In earlier phases, tule boat scenes feature fishing: a standing boatman catches a large fish on a line (Fig. 1). In many cases both the boatman and the fish have supernatural attributes. Although two boatmen are drawn on opposite sides of the bottle chamber, their similarity suggests that only one deity is actually being portrayed. The fishing ritual typical of Phase IV tule boat scenes is rarely portrayed in Phase V.

Phase V tule boats differ greatly from those of Phase IV. They appear to be larger and have a lower deck or cargo hold capable of transporting people (Fig. 2). The drawings suggest that some tule boats actually used during Phase V could carry numerous individuals as well as cargo. The sea as a highway for transporting people and goods is a new concept in Moche art.

Two new boatmen command the tule boats in Phase V (Fig. 3). They differ not only from Phase IV boatmen but from one another in their apparel and activities. One boatman wears a short shirt and loin cloth and is encircled with war clubs and shields. He usually paddles his boat in a kneeling position. The other boatman wears a long shirt and an elaborate headdress and is surrounded by rays. He sits rather than kneels in his boat. Some

[6] A previous study of tule boats by Alana Cordy-Collins (n.d.) supplied an iconographic framework for a review of this theme.

Fig. 1 *left and opposite* Supernatural figures fishing from a tule boat on a Moche IV stirrup-spout bottle. Private collection, La Jolla, California. Photograph by Christopher Donnan; roll-out drawing by the author.

vessels have the same boatman on both sides. When it is the rayed boatman, the tule boat is abstracted into a crescent form (Cordy-Collins 1977) emphasizing the mythical nature of this new tule boatman (Fig. 4).

Not only do the boats, the deities, and their activities in the tule boat theme change dramatically in Phase V, but the two new boatmen appear in Phase V drawings of some themes from earlier phases. This appearance frequently adds a marine element to a previously nonmarine theme, emphasizing both the mythical importance of the two boatmen and the maritime shift. For example, these deities are the central figures in a Phase V version of the Presentation Theme (Donnan 1975) where they stand in a lean-to structure (Fig. 5).

One of them also appears in the Burial Theme (Donnan and McClelland 1979), a new Phase V theme that portrays the ceremonial burial of an important personage (Fig. 6). Many figures dressed like one of the new boat deities attend the graveside rites. One also appears on the opposite side of the bottle in a ceremonial conch shell exchange. Inasmuch as the conch shell, *Strombus galeatus,* is native to Ecuador, this association with the boatman deity suggests that the conch shell was being transported by tule boats during Phase V; however, this is not shown in any drawing. Although the *Spondylus princeps* shell is also native to Ecuador and is widely portrayed in

Fig. 2   Detail of a drawing on a Moche V stirrup-spout bottle showing a supernatural boatman transporting prisoners and jars. Private collection, Buenos Aires.

Fig. 3   *left and opposite* The Tule Boat Theme on a Moche V stirrup-spout bottle. The rayed boatman is on the left, and the paddling boatman is on the right. Private collection, Lima. Photograph by Christopher Donnan; roll-out drawing by the author.

Fig. 4 *left and opposite* The Tule Boat
Theme on a Moche V stirrup-spout
bottle. The boat becomes a crescent
when the rayed boatman is painted on
both sides of the chamber. Private collection, Lima. Photograph by Christopher Donnan; roll-out drawing by
the author.

Chimu art, it is never illustrated in Moche art. The sudden appearance of
representations of the Spondylus shell in Lambayeque-Chimu art (Middle
Sican) is discussed by Alana Cordy-Collins in this volume.

The new Tule Boat Theme appears with at least two other Moche scenes
in a spiral formation on the bottle in Figure 7. At the bottom of the spiral,
inanimate objects, including a tule boat, come to life and capture humans
(Lyon 1981). Continuing up the spiral, an anthropomorphized feline warrior sits in a tule boat behind the boats of the two new boatmen. They
navigate toward a lean-to structure, the site of a ritual presentation of goblets. At the top of the spiral behind the lean-to structure, figures dressed like
the rayed boatman duplicate this ritual.

The paddling boatman deity appears in another theme from earlier
phases, the Confrontation Theme (McClelland n.d.), which features a ritual
fight with crescent-bladed knives (*tumis*) between supernatural figures and
anthropomorphized marine deities.[7] Although the theme can be found as
early as Phase III, its incidence also peaks with the maritime shift in Phase V.

---

[7] One interpretation of this theme is suggested in a 17th-century Spanish document by
Marmolejo, who recorded native religious practices (Rostworowski 1975: 344). In one account
from coastal Peru, the sun and moon battle nightly with demons or marine monsters deep in
the ocean before rising each morning.

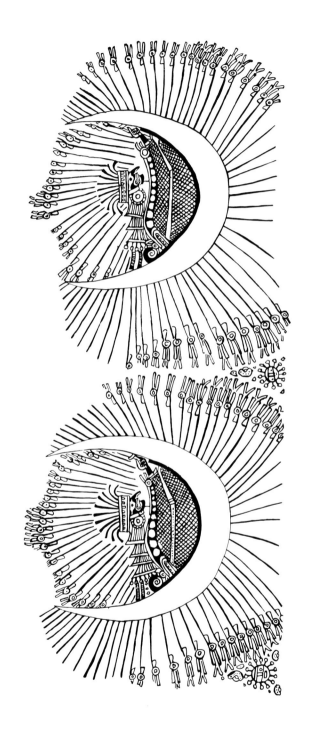

83

Fig. 5 *left and opposite* Anthropomorphized inanimate objects surround a lean-to
structure in which the two new Phase V
boatmen participate in the ritual presentation of goblets. Moche V stirrup-spout bottle. Private collection, Los Angeles. Photograph by Christopher Donnan; roll-out
drawing by the author.

On a Moche V bottle (Fig. 8) the paddling boatman deity struggles in this
fight against a fanged supernatural figure. He is easily identified by his attire
and the clubs and shields encircling his head and shoulders. His paddle has
become an elongated fish, and he fights with it instead of a *tumi*. On the
opposite side of the bottle an anthropomorphized crab deity also fights a
fanged supernatural figure. This drawing suggests that the boatman is taking sides with the anthropomorphized marine deities in this ancient battle
because he is fighting in place of one of them.

Both the new Tule Boat Theme and the Confrontation Theme appear on
the same Phase V bottle in Figure 9. On one side of the bottle the paddling
boatman deity propels his boat; on the opposite side two deities from the
Confrontation Theme struggle. It is not clear whether the Moche artist
meant simply to juxtapose the two themes or whether he meant to show the
tule boatman deity rowing to help the marine deity in his fight.

The more frequent appearance of marine deities in Phase V drawings
documents the maritime shift in Moche mythology. In addition, a new
marine deity, the Anthropomorphized Wave, is introduced in Phase V. This
deity is prominent in the Confrontation Theme. The Anthropomorphized
Wave is particularly important in tracing a Moche-Chimu continuum; it
occurs so often in Chimu art that it is a common signifier of that style. In

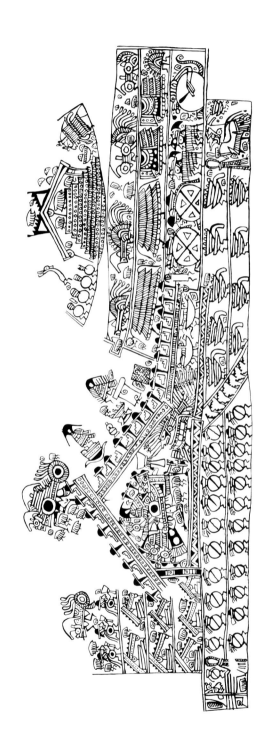

Fig. 6 *left and opposite* The Burial Theme on a Moche V stirrup-spout bottle. An anthropomorphized warrior is painted on the bottom of the bottle. Collection of Herbert Lucas, Brentwood, California. Photograph by Robert Wollard; roll-out drawing by the author.

Moche art the wave is formed by an arching band, filled with fish, and outlined with spiral wave designs. Either an upside-down human head (Fig. 9) or human body (Fig. 10) is attached to the band to anthropomorphize it. The Chimu Anthropomorphized Wave (Fig. 11) is similar to the Moche depiction in Figure 10 in which only the head is attached to the wave. The deity on the Chimu piece has been modeled in clay and decorated with low relief designs (Fig. 11). On the left side of the bottle, the hair juts up in a wedge from the wave's upside-down head. This bottle demonstrates that the Chimu artist fully understood the Moche concept of the Anthropomorphized Wave. In Figure 12, a Moche V bottle shows interconnecting representations of the head and arching band, a common form in Chimu art. A row of them can be seen curving above a tule boat on the chamber of a Lambayeque-Chimu bottle (Fig. 13). The bottles in Figures 11 and 13 are from the Lambayeque Valley and are commonly called Lambayeque-Chimu.[8] The interconnecting Anthropomorphized Waves are also on a frieze in the Uhle enclosure at Chan Chan (Fang n.d.: figs. 9a, b), suggesting widespread distribution. The Uhle enclosure is one of the early structures (Moseley, this volume), thus documenting an early maritime presence

[8] Izumi Shimada (this volume) differentiates Lambayeque-Chimu with his Sican sequence.

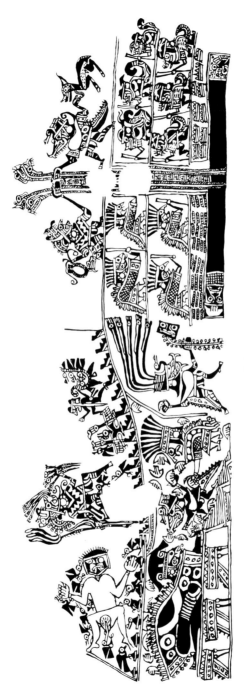

Fig. 7 *left and opposite* The Animated Objects Scene, the Tule Boat Theme, and the Presentation Theme spiral up the chamber of a Moche V spout-and-handle bottle. Private collection, Los Angeles. Photograph by Christopher Donnan; roll-out drawing by the author.

in Imperial Chimu art. Clearly, this maritime figure represents a link between the art of Moche V and Chimu.

The mythical world of the Moche records a major iconographic shift to maritime activity between Phase IV and Phase V. An explanation for this shift may be found in events surrounding the real world of the Moche.

THE ARCHAEOLOGICAL RECORD

At the same time as the maritime shift in Moche iconography, the archaeological record indicates that major changes were occurring in the North Coast environment and in Moche society.

Environmental Factors

Recent investigations of geological and climatic activity (Moseley et al. 1983; Nials et al. 1979; Thompson et al. 1985) on the North Coast indicate that two recurring forces drastically alter the landscape: uplifting of the continental margin with resulting downcutting by the rivers and catastrophic flooding from episodic El Niño currents. Either force can severely damage the irrigation systems within a valley. If the Moche canal systems had been severely damaged or destroyed, then their agricultural base would have been devastated and the ocean resources could have provided relief. On the other hand, El Niño greatly reduces sea life, and the ocean could not have provided a bountiful food resource. If a major El Niño was responsible for the changes between Moche IV and V, then one would not expect the Moche to feature fishing in Phase V fineline drawings.

Moche occupation of the North Coast was greatly disrupted between Phases IV and V. Many Phase IV sites were abandoned. This desertion is

Fig. 8 *left and opposite* The Confrontation Theme on a Moche V stirrup-spout bottle. Two wrinkled-face supernatural figures fight the tule boatman and an anthropomorphized crab. The boatman's paddle becomes a fish that he wields as a weapon. On the right, the anthropomorphized crab fights with his pincers. Private collection, Lima. Photograph by Christopher Donnan; roll-out drawing by the author.

very evident in the southern area, most notably at the site of Huaca del Sol and Huaca de la Luna in the Moche Valley, the center of the Moche kingdom. The site was continuously occupied from Phase I through Phase IV. Its extensive Phase IV occupation makes its abandonment during Phase V quite significant. Excavation at Huaca del Sol and Huaca de la Luna in 1972 revealed widespread flooding of the site at the end of Phase IV. Moche IV tombs had been constructed in a large mud brick platform between Huaca del Sol and Huaca de la Luna, where whole mud bricks had been removed to form a rectangular pit. In contrast, the small circular pits of the later, tightly flexed, early Chimu burials on the same platform appear to be broken out of solidified mud bricks, suggesting the platform was flooded with enough water to melt the bricks and fuse them together during the time between the Moche IV burials and the early Chimu burials (Donnan and Mackey 1978: 241).

The Quelccaya ice cap in the southern Andes provides additional evidence of major flooding on the North Coast (Thompson et al. 1985). Ice cores from the glacier can be used to identify major periods of rainfall caused by El Niños on the North Coast. One such period around A.D. 570 might be associated with the end of Phase IV. Extensive flooding of the site could easily account for the abandonment of Huaca del Sol and Huaca de la Luna.

During Phase V, large inland sites were established at the necks of the river valleys, relatively far from the ocean. Phase V occupation of the Moche Valley was centered at Galindo, about 20 km inland, and a major site was established at Pampa Grande in the Lambayeque Valley, approximately 40 km from the ocean. These sites would have provided refuge from the flood plains of the river valleys; however, the movement inland to the neck of the river valleys might have been an attempt to reestablish and/or control the irrigation systems (Shimada, this volume). The intensity of Phase V occupation of the Lambayeque Valley and the size of Pampa Grande leads Izumi Shimada to consider the Lambayeque Valley the center of the Moche kingdom during this phase.

Widespread flooding, devastating the North Coast at the end of Phase IV, could explain the abandonment of Huacas Sol and Luna and the reorganization of Moche occupation in Phase V. This disruption may have forced them to modify their mythical world to handle these overwhelming circumstances of nature. The appearance of new marine deities, the new tule boatmen and the anthropomorphized wave, documents these changes. If the ocean either contributed to this stressful period or alleviated it, then the ocean and its marine deities may have acquired enlarged and new mythical roles. This would explain the maritime shift in Moche art from Phase IV to Phase V. Further, the maritime shift in Phase V continued into Imperial Chimu mythology as seen in Chimu art.

Societal Factors

Archaeological excavations in the Moche Valley support an uninterrupted transition from Moche to Chimu culture. Settlement patterns, architecture, and the structure of society seem to have changed very little from Moche to Chimu times. Theresa Topic (1982: 280) has argued that Moche and Chimu societies were structurally similar, based on a comparison of architecture and settlement patterns. Alan Kolata (1982: 71) sees an "equivalency in brick types" between the Moche V site of Galindo and the earliest Chan Chan structures. The similarity in layout of the largest rectangular enclosure at Galindo and the major rectangular compounds at Chan Chan has led Geoffrey Conrad (n.d.) to suggest that the Galindo enclosure was a Moche antecedent for the Chimu *ciudadelas*. In a study of settlement patterns in the Moche Valley, Carol Mackey (1982: 322) concluded that Chimu urbanism developed locally. She traced its evolution from Salinar and Gallinazo settlements to those of Moche. She contended that all elements of urbanism were established by Moche times and that Chan Chan was the culmination of the development of urbanism in the Moche Valley.

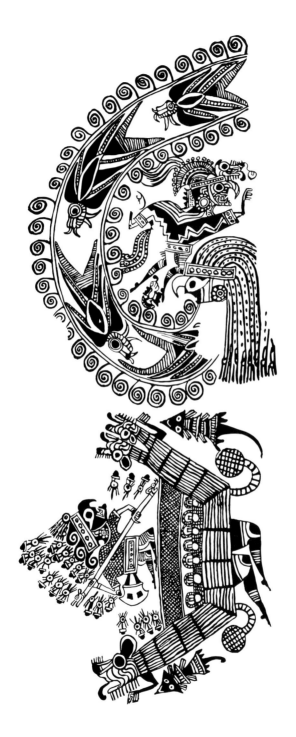

Fig. 9 The paddling boatman, from the Tule Boat Theme, appears on one side of a Moche V stirrup-spout bottle. On the opposite side, the Anthropomorphized Wave overpowers a wrinkled-face supernatural figure. Private collection, Lima.

Fig. 10 *left and opposite* The Confrontation Theme on a Moche V stirrup-spout bottle. On the left, the Anthropomorphized Wave overturns a wrinkled-face supernatural figure. Private collection, Lima. Photograph by Christopher Donnan; roll-out drawing by the author.

Huari Influence

The Huari state has been described as a religious (Menzel 1964: 67) and as a militaristic (Willey 1953: 420; Collier 1955: 136) state that spread from the southern highlands of Peru across the entire Andean area. The long-standing conjecture about its influence on the North Coast has somewhat obscured the relationship between the Moche and Chimu cultures by tending to reinforce the concept of a division between them.

Our sample of Moche V bottles displaying Huari ceramic traits supports Dorothy Menzel's (1964, 1977) dating of Moche V to the Middle Horizon. Although Huari ceramics are rarely found on the North Coast (Collier 1955: 185; Mackey 1982: 325), a cache containing both pure Moche V and Huari ceramics was reported by Christopher Donnan (1973: 134, pl. 7) in the Santa Valley.[9] The cache contained a Moche V stirrup-spout bottle with fineline decoration and two pure Huari pod-shaped jars decorated with polychrome paint. Two vessels in the cache were particularly interesting, because they were Moche attempts to copy the pod-shaped Huari jars. Although the artists reproduced the Huari pod-shaped form and polychrome paint, they painted simple Moche designs on the jars.

[9] Eleven ceramic vessels comprised the cache.

Fig. 11 The Anthropomorphized Wave on a Lambayeque-Chimu bottle. Museo Brüning de Lamba-yeque. Photograph by Donald McClelland.

Fig. 12 *left and opposite* Interconnecting Anthropomorphized Waves encircle a Moche V stirrup-spout bottle (spout not original). Private collection, Buenos Aires. Photograph by Christopher Donnan; roll-out drawing by the author.

Fig. 13 Modeled boatmen straddle a tule boat on top of a Lambayeque-Chimu bottle. Another tule boat is rendered in low relief under an arch of interconnecting Anthropomorphized Waves. Museo Brüning de Lambayeque. Photograph by Donald McClelland.

Fig. 14 *left and opposite* Crayfish warriors are painted with red and white slip on a Moche V stirrup-spout bottle. Collection of Oscar Rodríguez Razzeto, Chepen, Peru. Photograph by Christopher Donnan; roll-out drawing by the author.

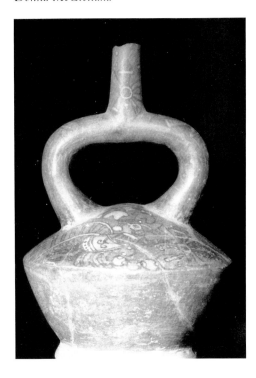

Fig. 15 *left and opposite* Crayfish warriors are painted with polychrome slip on a Moche V stirrup-spout bottle. Collection of Oscar Rodríguez Razzeto, Chepen, Peru. Photograph by Christopher Donnan; roll-out drawing by the author.

There are Phase V bottles in which Moche ceramicists seem to have experimented with Huari ceramic techniques, resulting in interesting combinations of Huari double-spout-and-bridge bottles painted with conventional Moche red and white slip paint, and Moche stirrup-spout bottles decorated with fineline drawings rendered in Huari polychrome slip paint. Although the Moche experimented with Huari ceramic technology, they continued to paint Moche motifs on the bottles. Two Moche V bottles show how difficult it can be to recognize Moche "fineline drawings" when they are painted in polychrome slip paint. In Figure 14, Moche anthropomorphized crayfish warriors are painted on a Phase V stirrup-spout bottle with Moche red and white slip. These same crayfish warriors were painted on another Moche V stirrup-spout bottle using Huari polychrome technique (Fig. 15). John Rowe described one of these Moche/Huari combinations in 1942. On that double-spout-and-bridge bottle, the Moche artist also used polychrome slip to paint Moche figures.[10] Recently, another double-spout-and-bridge bottle was recovered with these same Moche figures painted on it, but using traditional Moche bichrome slip.

[10] Two Moche figures were painted on opposite sides of the chamber, lying across a stepped dais, and holding "sticks." One is a supernatural deity, and the other is an anthropomorphized iguana. The background is filled with beans.

Although there is evidence of Huari influence on the North Coast, Huari iconography is not centered around a maritime theme (Menzel 1977: 35; see also Shimada, this volume) and thus does not provide an explanation for the Moche iconographic maritime shift. Furthermore, the similarity of Moche and Chimu iconography suggests that Huari influence was not sufficient to interrupt the North Coast artistic tradition.

SUMMARY

A number of simple elements from Moche art may be identified in Chimu art; for example, small modeled figures, such as monkeys, perched on the spouts of Chimu stirrup-spout bottles can be traced back to Moche V stirrup-spout bottles (Figs. 10, 14). A much more complex continuum can be traced from Moche V fineline drawings of the Tule Boat Theme to maritime art of Chimu as has been demonstrated in this essay.

Our greatly expanded sample of fineline drawings from Moche V, the terminal phase, has provided an invaluable resource for tracing the iconographic transition from Moche to Chimu. The content of North Coast art shifted strongly to maritime activity between Moche IV and V, rather than between Moche V and Chimu, indicating that the maritime motif, which permeates Chimu art, evolved from Moche V. The maritime shift is documented by the increased incidence of marine-related drawings, the introduction of marine elements into previously nonmarine themes, the expanded roles of the marine deities, and new marine deities.

The introduction of the Anthropomorphized Wave deity in Phase V is notable because of its frequency in Chimu art. Both the maritime shift and the Anthropomorphized Wave represent an iconographic continuity between Moche V and Chimu art and demonstrate the evolution of the North Coast artistic tradition.

Although our evidence for a break between Moche Phase IV and Phase V is mainly iconographic, it is interesting that a great corresponding change also takes place in the archaeological record. Severe flooding is evident on the North Coast during this time as well as major reorganization of the Moche occupation of the North Coast. Recent North Coast excavations of Moche V sites demonstrate that many Chimu antecedents were present in Phase V sites paralleling the findings in the art.

Although Huari ceramics are found on the North Coast, the similarity in content between Moche V and Chimu art suggests that Huari influence was apparently insufficient to perturb the North Coast artistic tradition.

The shift in content within the Moche mythical world of Phase V may signify a religious reorientation brought about by the increased importance of the ocean in their real world. If the ocean played a major role during a period of upheaval, then the ocean and its deities may have acquired a significant position in the mythical world that led to the maritime shift in Moche iconography and the continuing importance of maritime motifs in Chimu art.

The new tule boatmen launch into Phase V mythology on ocean-going craft. Their dramatic arrival signals a new Moche view of the ocean as a travel route on which two maritime deities ply their course, carrying cargo and sometimes prisoners. Whereas the ocean was associated with ritual fishing in the earlier phases, it now presents an avenue of trade and commerce. This may presage the importation of Spondylus shells from Ecuador that were so important in Imperial Chimu ceremonies (Cordy-Collins, this volume). I am not suggesting that the boatmen can be related to either of the stories of the dynastic founders, Naymlap or Taycanamo (Moseley, this volume); however, in view of the maritime shift between Phases IV and V, and the maritime orientation of Chimu art, I do not find it surprising that their stories each begin with their arrival from the sea.

Donna McClelland

BIBLIOGRAPHY

BONAVIA, DUCCIO
  1985   *Mural Painting in Ancient Peru* (Patricia J. Lyon, trans. and ed.). Indiana University Press, Bloomington.

COLLIER, DONALD
  1955   *Cultural Chronology and Change as Reflected in the Ceramics of the Virú Valley, Peru. Fieldiana: Anthropology* 43. Field Museum of Natural History, Chicago.

CONRAD, GEOFFREY W.
  n.d.   Burial Platforms and Related Structures on the North Coast of Peru: Some Social and Political Implications. Ph.D. dissertation, Department of Anthropology, Harvard University, 1974.

CORDY-COLLINS, ALANA
  1977   The Moon is a Boat!: A Study in Iconographic Methodology. In *Pre-Columbian Art History: Selected Readings* (Alana Cordy-Collins and Jean Stern, eds.): 421–434. Peek Publications, Palo Alto, Calif.
  n.d.   The Tule Boat Theme in Moche Art: A Problem in Ancient Peruvian Iconography. M.A. thesis, Institute of Archaeology, University of California, Los Angeles, 1972.

DONNAN, CHRISTOPHER B.
  1973   *Moche Occupation of the Santa Valley, Peru*. University of California Press, Berkeley.
  1975   The Thematic Approach to Moche Iconography. *Journal of Latin American Lore* 1(2): 147–162.
  1978   *Moche Art of Peru*. Museum of Cultural History, University of California, Los Angeles.
  1982   La caza del venado en el arte Mochica. *Revista del Museo Nacional* 46: 235–251. Lima.

DONNAN, CHRISTOPHER B., and CAROL J. MACKEY
  1978   *Ancient Burial Patterns of the Moche Valley, Peru*. University of Texas Press, Austin.

DONNAN, CHRISTOPHER B., and DONNA McCLELLAND
  1979   *The Burial Theme in Moche Iconography*. Studies in Pre-Columbian Art & Archaeology 21. Dumbarton Oaks, Washington, D.C.

FANG, MADELEINE WEIHSIEN
  n.d.   The Marine Theme of Chimu Friezes. M.A. thesis, Department of Anthropology, University of California, Los Angeles, 1975.

KOLATA, ALAN L.
  1982   Chronology and Settlement Growth at Chan Chan. In *Chan Chan: Andean Desert City* (Michael E. Moseley and Kent C. Day, eds.): 67–85. University of New Mexico Press, Albuquerque.

Larco Hoyle, Rafael

    1948   *Cronología arqueología del norte del Peru.* Biblioteca del Museo de Arqueología "Rafael Larco Herrera," Hacienda Chiclín, Trujillo. Sociedad Geográfica Americana, Buenos Aires.

Lyon, Patricia J.

    1981   Arqueología y mitología: La escena de "Los Objetos Animados" y el tema de "El Alzamiento de los objetos." *Scripta Etnológica* 6: 105–108. Buenos Aires.

Mackey, Carol J.

    1982   The Middle Horizon as Viewed from the Moche Valley. In *Chan Chan: Andean Desert City* (Michael E. Moseley and Kent C. Day, eds.): 321–331. University of New Mexico Press, Albuquerque.

McClelland, Donna D.

    n.d.   The Cache from Huaca Moro: Moche V Fineline Bottles. Unpublished manuscript.

Menzel, Dorothy

    1964   Style and Time in the Middle Horizon. *Ñawpa Pacha* 2: 1–106. Berkeley.

    1977   *The Archaeology of Ancient Peru and the Work of Max Uhle.* R. H. Lowie Museum of Anthropology, University of California, Berkeley.

Moseley, Michael E., Robert A. Feldman, Charles R. Ortloff, and Alfredo Narvaez

    1983   Principles of Agrarian Collapse in the Cordillera Negra, Peru. *Annals of Carnegie Museum* 52(13): 299–327. Carnegie Museum of Natural History, Pittsburgh.

Nials, Fred L., Eric E. Deeds, Michael E. Moseley, Shelia G. Pozorski, Thomas G. Pozorski, and Robert A. Feldman

    1979   El Niño: The Catastrophic Flooding of Coastal Peru. *Bulletin of the Field Museum of Natural History* 50(7): 4–14 (Part I); 50(8): 4–10 (Part II). Chicago.

Rostworowski de Diez Canseco, María

    1975   Pescadores, artesanos y mercaderes costeños en el Perú prehispánico. *Revista del Museo Nacional* 41: 311–349. Lima.

Rowe, John Howland

    1942   A New Pottery Style from the Department of Piura, Peru. *Notes on Middle American Archaeology and Ethnology* 1(8): 30–34. Carnegie Institution of Washington, Division of Historical Research, Cambridge.

Thompson, Lonnie G., E. Moseley-Thompson, J. F. Bolzan, and B. R. Koci

    1985   A 1500-Year Record of Tropical Precipitation in Ice Cores from the Quelccaya Ice Cap, Peru. *Science* 229: 971–973.

Topic, Theresa Lange

    1982   The Early Intermediate Period and Its Legacy. In *Chan Chan: Andean Desert City* (Michael E. Moseley and Kent C. Day, eds.): 255–284. University of New Mexico Press, Albuquerque.

Donna McClelland

WILLEY, GORDON R.

1953   *Prehistoric Settlement Patterns in the Virú Valley, Peru.* Bureau of American Ethnology, Bulletin 155. Smithsonian Institution, Washington, D.C.

The Urban Concept of Chan Chan

ALAN L. KOLATA

THE UNIVERSITY OF CHICAGO

INTRODUCTION

THIS IS AN INQUIRY CONCERNING the determinants of city form and the evolution in form of one city in particular. Chan Chan was the royal capital of the Kingdom of Chimor, an expansive imperial power that incorporated into its realm most of the northern and central coasts of Peru between A.D. 1000 and 1450.

This essay will explore the urban concept of Chan Chan and the forces that underlay its transformations. By urban concept I mean that set of structural attributes pertaining to the morphology, function, and sociological meaning of the city, which is shaped by the interaction of its principal institutions. With respect to Chan Chan, I will be concerned here primarily with its fundamental political and economic structures. In order to understand Chan Chan and the sociological and symbolic meaning that the city held for the people of Chimor, we must first review the empirical data concerning the city's various architectural ensembles: their nature, functions, and patterns of growth.

CHRONOLOGY AND ARCHITECTURAL SEQUENCE AT CHAN CHAN

Architectural Definitions

The ancient city walls of Chan Chan encompass more than 20 km^2, with a 6 km^2 urban nucleus of monumental architecture dominated by large, high-walled enclosures built of adobe. Eleven of the twelve largest structures in Chan Chan are monumental enclosures with elaborate interior architectural features (Fig. 1). These enclosures, referred to here as *ciudadelas,* are interpreted as sequentially built palaces that housed the Chimor dynasty. This dynasty may have been structured by fundamental Andean moiety and *ayllu*-like lineage divisions (Netherly n.d., 1984, this volume). The monumental enclosures evolved from early compounds of variable form to six

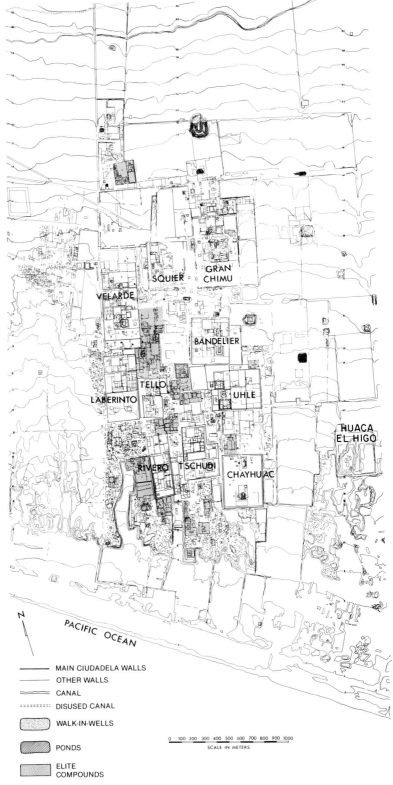

VELARDE

SQUIER

GRAN CHIMU

BANDELIER

TELLO

LABERINTO

UHLE

HUACA EL HIGO

RIVERO   TSCHUDI

CHAYHUAC

N

PACIFIC OCEAN

——— MAIN CIUDADELA WALLS

——— OTHER WALLS

≈≈≈ CANAL

::::::: DISUSED CANAL

WALK-IN-WELLS

PONDS

ELITE COMPOUNDS

0   100 200 300 400 500 600 700 800 900 1000
SCALE IN METERS

Fig. 1   General plan of Chan Chan.

late *ciudadelas* of relatively standardized layout with repetitive internal architecture (Kolata 1982; Conklin, this volume).

Nine palace enclosures contain three distinct types of interior structures analyzable in quantitative terms: (a) *audiencias,* representing elite administrative offices, (b) storerooms, which housed the portable wealth of the Chimor dynasty, and (c) walk-in wells, the sole source of potable water in the city. Each *ciudadela* is also associated with a royal burial platform.

Massive looting has largely destroyed the earlier burial structures. However, each platform constructed during and after *ciudadela* Bandelier retains remnants of a single, central, disproportionately large T-shaped tomb, surrounded by ranks of subsidiary cist tombs. The heavily looted burial structures in Velarde and Gran Chimu were probably of a similar character. This architectural pattern, which links each of the six late *ciudadelas* with one distinctively conceived burial platform, has been interpreted as direct evidence for a socio-political pattern that identified one king exclusively with one palace. This interpretation envisions the sequentially built *ciudadelas* as reflections of a succession of rulers who each built separate quarters that initially served as a palace administrative center and ultimately as a royal mausoleum maintained after the king's death by a kin-related corporate body (see Conrad n.d., 1982 for a full development of this hypothesis).

More irregular versions of *audiencias,* storerooms, and walk-in-wells, although not burial platforms, occur in smaller adobe-walled enclosures termed *intermediate architecture.* These smaller enclosures are interpreted as residences of the minor nobility and state functionaries of Chimor (Klymyshyn n.d., 1982). A third type of architecture, small irregular agglutinated rooms (SIAR), has neither *audiencias* nor storeroom complexes. Extensive areas of SIAR, with a combined minimum of 25,000 individual rooms, housed the majority of the urban population. Most SIAR inhabitants were engaged in elite craft production, particularly metallurgy, for the nobility of Chimor (J. Topic n.d., 1982, this volume; Topic and Moseley 1983).

Architectural History

The architectural history of Chan Chan can be calibrated by quantitative analysis of mud brick dimensions, which changed systematically through time (Kolata n.d., 1982). Figure 2 correlates the palace sequence with my general relative and absolute phase chronology for Chan Chan. Figures 3–9 illustrate graphically the sequential development of the twelve largest structures within the city. SIAR architecture did not employ mud brick in significant, datable numbers. Therefore, cross-dating these structures to the palaces is somewhat conjectural, although inferences based on radiocarbon dates and physical associations can be drawn. These inferences on the growth of SIAR, drawn from the work of John Topic (n.d., this volume; Topic and Moseley 1983), are reflected in Figures 3–9.

ABSOLUTE CHRONOLOGY	PHASE CHRONOLOGY	PALACE SEQUENCE
years A.D. 1400 - 1470	Late Chimu 2	Rivero Tschudi
1300 - 1400	Late Chimu 1	Bandelier Velarde
1200 - 1300	Middle Chimu	Squier Gran Chimu
1100 - 1200	Early Chimu 2	Laberinto Tello
900 - 1100	Early Chimu 1	Uhle Chayhuac

Fig. 2   Relative and absolute phase chronology for Chan Chan. The dates and phases indicate primary occupancy.

Construction activity at Chan Chan began in the southeast sector of the city (Huaca Higo and *ciudadela* Chayhuac: Fig. 3). The city first expanded inland to the north (*ciudadela* Uhle east: Fig. 4; *ciudadela* Uhle west: Fig. 5), and then to the west (*ciudadelas* Tello and Laberinto: Fig. 6). After the construction of *ciudadela* Laberinto, the entire northern terminus of Chan Chan was delimited by the erection of *ciudadela* Gran Chimu (the largest palace enclosure) and its satellite architecture (Fig. 7). The city then grew back upon itself south and coastward in successive steps (*ciudadela* Squier, Velarde, Bandelier: Fig. 8; and then Tschudi and Rivero: Fig. 9). During the construction of the last two palaces, substantial portions of the old southern city core were razed to accommodate the new buildings.

URBAN GROWTH AND HYDROLOGICAL REGIME[1]

Although in this essay I will focus principally on the social and institutional developments that shaped the city of Chan Chan through time, it is

[1] This segment of the essay was written in collaboration with Michael E. Moseley. It represents a joint effort to synthesize the data pertaining to the relationship between the evolution of Chan Chan's sustaining irrigation system/hydrological regime and changing architectural patterning in the city. The research underlying this interpretation was supported by National Science Foundation grants BNS76-25438 and BNS77-24901 to Michael E. Moseley, Principal Investigator. Additional support for aspects of the research was provided by a Thaw Fellowship from Harvard University to Alan L. Kolata.

Fig. 3–9   Phases of urban growth at Chan Chan (after Kolata 1983; Topic and Moseley 1983).

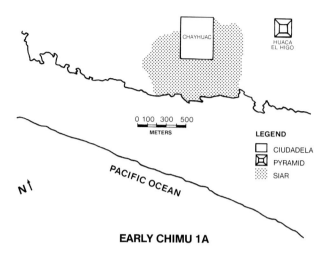

Fig. 3

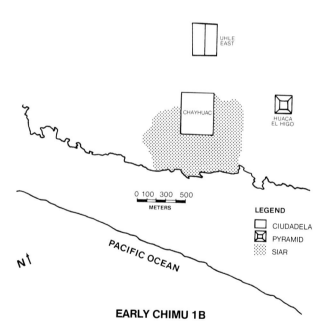

Fig. 4

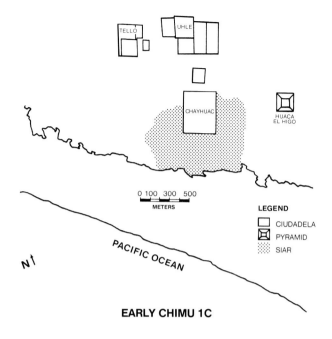

EARLY CHIMU 1C

Fig. 5

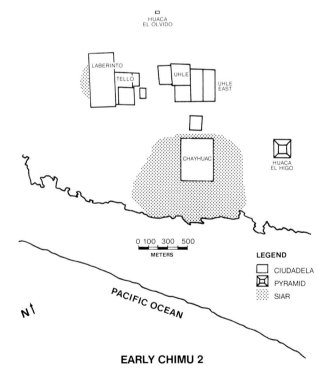

EARLY CHIMU 2

Fig. 6

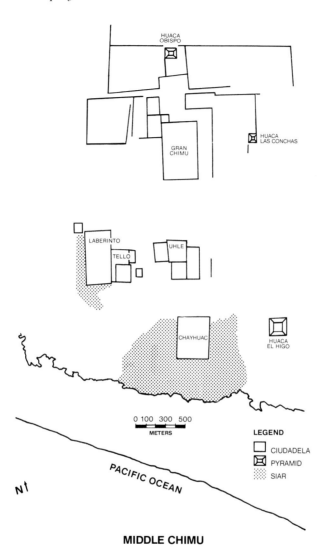

Fig. 7

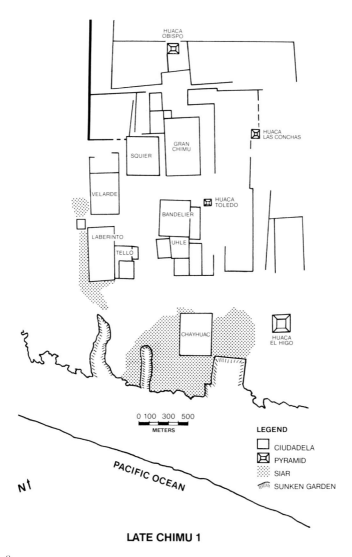

LATE CHIMU 1

Fig. 8

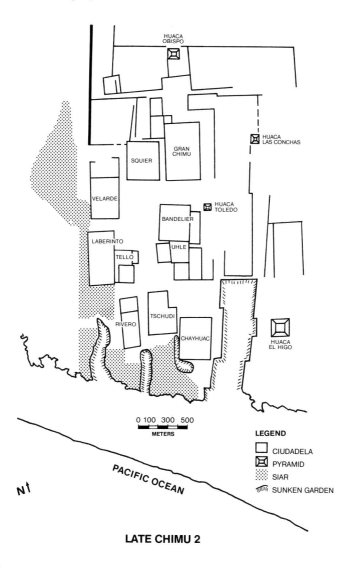

LATE CHIMU 2

Fig. 9

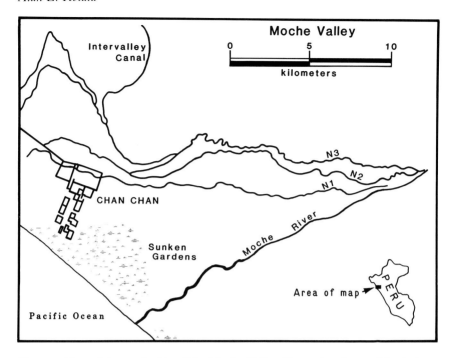

Fig. 10 Map of the north side of the Moche Valley illustrating the spatial relationship between Chan Chan and its principal irrigation canals.

essential to outline briefly the role of historical developments in the human-altered hydrological regime that directly affected the physical growth of Chan Chan.

Hydrological History

The first palace enclosures at Chan Chan were erected near the beach, behind a seacliff cut through coarse alluvium and interbedded sands that form a plain, Pampa Esperanza, extending inland for some 8 km. East of Huaca Higo, the ground surface, consisting of coarse sands, is lower, and is associated with high water table conditions that extend diagonally inland toward the Moche River, which lies 8 km southeast of the city.

The Moche River is fed by runoff from highland rains and is the only source of fresh water in the region. River flow is markedly seasonal, ranging from 10 to 34 m³/sec. during January to May, but in subsequent months dropping to 0 to 4 m³/sec. (Moseley and Deeds 1982; Ortloff et al. 1982: 587). The local water table, fed by the river, also has a seasonal high and low cycle, peaking between June and September, well after the river has crested. During eight months of the year, all river discharge is absorbed by intensive

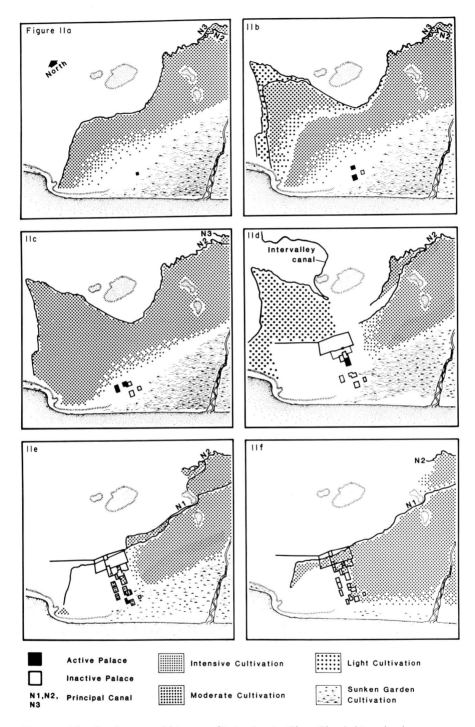

Fig. 11   The developmental history of irrigation in Chan Chan's hinterland correlated with architectural developments in the city.

irrigation agriculture, which, north of the river, was sustained at different times by three primary canals, designated N1, N2, and N3, respectively, from lowest to highest (Fig. 10).

When Chan Chan was founded, Pampa Esperanza was irrigated by an extension of the N3 canal (Fig. 11a). The irrigation system was expanded north and west in several stages before being destroyed by a cataclysmic episode of torrential rains and flash flooding spawned by a major El Niño event (Fig. 11b). This event has been dated by archaeological evidence (substantial water-borne destruction of architecture and canals; massive silt deposition) to around A.D. 1100 (Nials et al. 1979; Moseley et al. 1981; Moseley, this volume).

The reconstructed canal system, initiated contemporaneously with the western sector of *ciudadela* Uhle, was fed by the N2 primary canal (Fig. 11c). However, from its inception, this canal delivered little water to the western plain. Ultimately, atrophy of the N2 stimulated construction of an inter-valley canal more than 70 km long that was designed to resupply the system with water from an adjacent valley to the north (Ortloff et al. 1982; Pozorski and Pozorski 1982; Farrington 1983).

Rather than channeling water via a relatively short course directly to the fields west of the city, the intervalley junction with the dry N2 canal was placed centrally above Chan Chan. This entailed the seemingly disproportionate cost of building a much longer canal (Fig. 11d; Ortloff et al. 1982: 574). While the intervalley canal was under construction and Pampa Esperanza left unirrigated, the city expanded inland. During the time of *ciudadela* Gran Chimu, vast tracts of formerly cultivated land were incorporated into the urban landscape with construction of Chan Chan's great north wall. North and west of the wall, feeder canals were laid out for supply by the intervalley canal. The atrophied N2, no longer able to supply Pampa Esperanza, was now intended to provide water only for fields east of the city (Fig. 11d).

However, the intervalley canal, planned as the keystone of the revitalized water distribution system, was never completed (Ortloff et al. 1982; Kus 1984). Irrigation resumed later, but in a largely symbolic fashion during, or shortly before, the time of *ciudadela* Tschudi (Fig. 11e) when the N1, built to replace the N2, was cut through the city wall in order to irrigate the interiors of several palace enclosures selectively, and one small area west of the city. Recut at slightly lower elevation than the prehistoric N1, the modern N1 continues to support farming in the northern portion of Chan Chan's ruins (Fig. 11f).

The development of sunken-garden farming, an option available to the farmer hampered by a lack of surface water, is known in less detail. Sunken gardens are created by excavating plant surfaces to a level at which natural ground moisture sustains plant growth (Parsons and Psuty 1975; Knapp

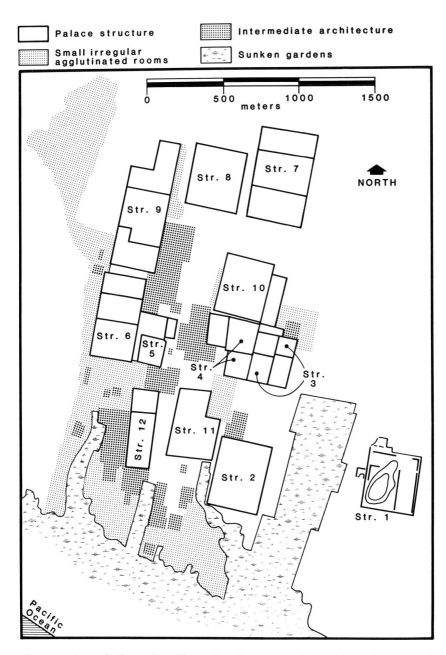

Legend:
- Palace structure
- Intermediate architecture
- Small irregular agglutinated rooms
- Sunken gardens

Scale: 0 — 500 — 1000 — 1500 meters

NORTH

Str. 8
Str. 7
Str. 9
Str. 10
Str. 6
Str. 5
Str. 4
Str. 3
Str. 12
Str. 11
Str. 2
Str. 1

Pacific Ocean

Fig. 12   Map of Chan Chan illustrating the spatial relationship of the city with massive sunken gardens.

1982; Smith 1983). When Chan Chan was founded, such gardens extended inland at least 4 km to the center of the valley. After flooding disrupted the canal systems, gardens began to intrude upon the southeast sector of the city in increasing numbers and size. By the time of *ciudadelas* Tschudi and Rivero, massive "royal gardens" were being cut through the thick alluvium behind the seacliff, representing vast labor expenditures (Fig. 12). Moseley and I interpret this emphasis upon labor-intensive gardens during the later stages of Chan Chan's occupation as an expectable response to the decreasing availability of irrigated land caused by the contracting canal system.

Michael Moseley et al. (1983) postulate that the contraction of irrigation, reflected in the progressively diminishing delivery capacity of the N2 canal and its replacement by the N1 canal, was a mechanical response to ongoing tectonic uplift of the coastal watershed. They argue that as the landscape undergoes vertical displacement, the river downcuts its course in equilibrium response, gradually choking off and eventually stranding canal intakes. Tectonic uplift also has the effect of lowering the water table with respect to the land surface. Early sunken-garden remnants, located 4 km inland in the Moche Valley, are today 10–12 m above the ground water level, and thus are completely nonfunctional. The vast royal gardens at Chan Chan are still farmed, but only by means of pump irrigation because, even adjacent to the coast, the water table is more than 1 m below its terminal Pre-Hispanic level.

Irrigation and Urban Growth

The architectural growth of Chan Chan was linked to the hydrological regime of the coast by its wells. When the city was founded, the aquifer supplying fresh water to Chan Chan was charged by upslope irrigation on the Pampa Esperanza. Expansion of the irrigation system presumably maintained an artificially high water table and mitigated the water table's seasonal low cycle, allowing relatively shallow wells to support inland urban expansion.

When dwindling water supplies from the post-flood N2 canal prompted construction of the intervalley canal, a significant element of the design, as noted above, was placement of the channel juncture centrally above Chan Chan, requiring an exceptionally long canal to complete the linkage. We infer that this costly feature was incorporated into the new system so that runoff and seepage from irrigation would continue to recharge the city's aquifer. When intervalley water never materialized, the inland terrain enclosed by the great north wall during the time of *ciudadela* Gran Chimu could not sustain human settlement except by means of extremely deep wells. In Gran Chimu, these walk-in wells reached their maximum operable depth, estimated at greater than 15 m.

The subsequent decline in the water table generated by the combined effects of lack of irrigation and general tectonic uplift halted inland urban expansion. More important, this worsening condition forced the city to grow successively back upon itself toward the coast where declining ground water was more accessible in shallow wells. The loss of high water table conditions was not without social cost: extensive areas of extant architecture had to be razed to accommodate new, near-coast buildings, such as *ciudadelas* Tschudi and Rivero.

In effect, the deterioration of a sensitive, human-altered hydrological regime forced the architects of Chan Chan to cannibalize their own city to accommodate new construction schemes. When the abandoned N2 canal was finally replaced by the N1, this new primary canal ran at too low an elevation and reached too little of Pampa Esperanza for reactivated irrigation to recharge the urban aquifer significantly. At this point several palace interiors were selectively irrigated by means of long canals with relatively low delivery capacity. The indigenous rationale for irrigating the palace interiors selectively at this time remains elusive. But this apparently symbolic use of water graphically illustrates the role of a changing hydrological regime in shaping the form of the city.

ARCHITECTURAL TRENDS AT CHAN CHAN

Implicit in the foregoing account of patterning in the architectural history of Chan Chan are a number of developmental trends in the architecture at the settlement. The evolution of specific architectural elements in the city carries implied information about the social formations that conditioned that evolution. Specifically, the function of architecture is a product of particular economic and political institutions. If this is true, formal variation in the architecture at Chan Chan, when ordered in proper sequence, will yield valuable clues toward understanding changes in the economic and political organization of Chimu society.

Monumental Architecture

There are six major attributes of the palaces at Chan Chan that exhibit systematic formal change throughout the history of the city: (a) the overall design of the *ciudadela* itself, (b) annexes, (c) access patterns, (d) *audiencias,* (e) storerooms, and (f) burial platforms. By systematic formal change I mean simply that these six architectural attributes did not vary randomly, independent of each other, but rather in concert in response to changes in the social formations of the Chimu state.

First I will document the nature of the formal change in each of these six attributes, as well as the concurrent and dependent configuration of intermediate and SIAR architecture as a whole. Then I will present a general model that explains the cause of these architectural changes in terms of the development of specific historical events and social institutions in the organization of the Kingdom of Chimor.

Ciudadela Design and Annexes

During what I have termed the Early Chimu 1 Phase of Chan Chan (ca. A.D. 900–1100; Fig. 2), the design of the palace was noncomplex, consisting of a simple though exceptionally large rectangle (Chayhuac), or an apparently ad hoc collection of such rectangles (Uhle, Tello). In many respects, Burr Cartwright Brundage's (1967: 80) characterization of the imperial palaces of Cuzco also applies to these *ciudadelas:* "the palace proper generally resembled on an exaggerated scale its model, the traditional stone-walled Peruvian farm enclosure called the *cancha.*"

The architecture within these palaces exhibits no overall concern for internal ordering beyond a general north-south orientation. In both Chayhuac and Uhle, the bulk of the internal space is devoid of architecture although the structures that are present occur in dense, well-defined nodes (enclosed on at least three sides by substantial adobe walls). In Tello, on the other hand, the interior architecture is more evenly distributed, occupies a much higher percentage of internal space, and includes distinctive structures rarely found in Chayhuac or Uhle: relatively small, elevated platforms that at one time were probably surmounted by superstructures made of perishable materials. But this is not surprising for, as noted elsewhere, Tello was not functionally equivalent to the other *ciudadelas* of Chan Chan (Klymyshyn n.d.; Kolata n.d., 1982). This enclosure was probably intended as a residence of an expanding class of bureaucrats who were involved in managing the state. It is this heavily residential function that imparts a distinctive look to Tello.

Uhle and Tello were begun during the Early Chimu 1 Phase of Chan Chan: Uhle in 1B, Tello in 1C (Figs. 4, 5). In this early phase, protracted occupation and reworking of these two enclosures is directly perceivable architecturally in that they were built in separate stages of construction: Uhle in perhaps as many as four separate stages, and Tello in at least two— north and south. It is at this time that the concept of *ciudadela* annexes first appears. Uhle possesses two annexes: a largely vacant enclosure appended to its west side and a partially destroyed northern annex, again consisting of an apparently vacant enclosure that extended more than 300 m to the north of Uhle's northern wall. Although not generally recognized, a northern annex that Tello also possesses controls access to its single entrance. But this annex is very small and, unlike Uhle's, contains a number of apparently residential structures (again, elevated platforms). Given the primary evidence for multiple stages of construction in Uhle and in its mortuary platform complexes, this palace enclosure may have had an occupation that spanned as much as two hundred years (ca. A.D. 1000–1200).

Fig. 13   Aerial photograph of the Laberinto palace compound at Chan Chan illustrating the standardized tripartite division of interior space characteristic of the later *ciudadelas*.

With the construction of Laberinto in the Early Chimu 2 Phase (ca. A.D. 1100–1200), the interior design of the *ciudadelas* was changed radically. From this time and throughout the subsequent history of the city, each *ciudadela* was organized with a tripartite distribution of internal space (Fig. 13): a northern sector, provided with a large entry court and smaller courts flanked by a variety of structures; a central sector, provided with a second entry court and similar smaller courts, flanking structures, and generally a burial platform; and a southern sector devoid of permanent adobe architecture, but frequently containing walk-in-wells and a congeries of domestic structures built of perishable materials.

One structural correlate of this change in the organization of interior architecture was that *audiencia* courts and banks of storerooms were now consistently linked in the overall design scheme, a development that was foreshadowed in the symmetrical array of storerooms and *audiencias* of Uhle's late southwestern sector. Specifically, from this time on, *audiencia* courts either contain storage facilities or are situated along access routes to storerooms. In addition, a secondary association of *audiencia* courts with other key circulation "break points" (placing *audiencias* near *ciudadela* entrances, or on access routes to burial platforms) also began to develop.

Moseley (1975: 222) notes that these "*audiencia* courts are frequently laid out in a hierarchical manner so that access to one U-shaped structure is controlled by other *audiencias*. This connotes a ranking of the structures, and, by inference, ranking of the occupying individuals and the functions they performed." The exact nature of the functions performed by the *audiencia* occupants remains uncertain, although the context of the structures suggests that they were involved in some type of administrative or supervisory activities.

After Laberinto, the subsequent six *ciudadelas* retain the tripartite organization and tight structural association between *audiencia* courts and storage units. In fact, the only subsequent change in overall enclosure design was an increasing emphasis on the construction of annexes. Gran Chimu (A.D. 1150–1300), the largest enclosure, illustrates this trend: it contains an extremely elaborate northern annex equipped with high-status architecture heavily decorated with friezes—*audiencia* structures, storerooms, spacious courts, huge elevated platforms—and several largely vacant western annexes.

The following palaces, although reduced in scale, continue to integrate well-planned northern annexes with substantial architecture into the overall design: Velarde, Bandelier, and Tschudi. Rivero, the final enclosure, reflects the culmination of this trend toward incorporation of structurally autonomous annexes into a preconceived plan; here, three annexes, north, south, and east, containing dense internal architecture, become subsidiary wings of the enclosure (Fig. 14).

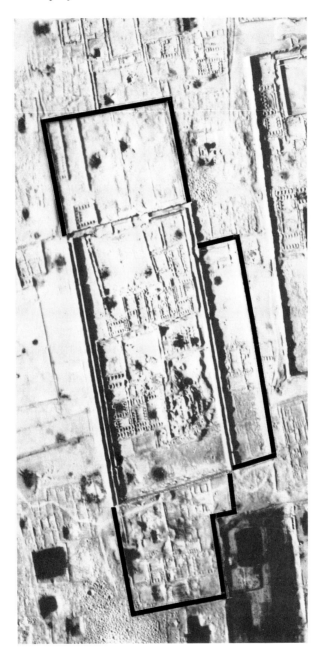

Fig. 14   Aerial photograph of *ciudadela* Rivero, with its three formal annexes outlined for emphasis. Photograph courtesy of the Servicio Aeronautico Nacional, Peru.

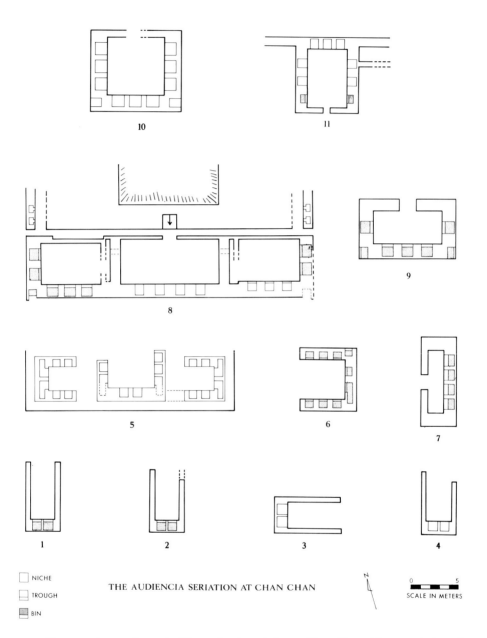

THE AUDIENCIA SERIATION AT CHAN CHAN

NICHE
TROUGH
BIN

SCALE IN METERS
0   5

Fig. 15 *above and opposite* The *audiencia* seriation at Chan Chan. The association of *audiencias* to *ciudadelas* is: 1–4 = Uhle (East); 5–9 = Uhle (West); 10, 11 = Tello; 12–15 = Laberinto; 16 = Gran Chimu; 17, 18 = Velarde; 19, 20 = Bandelier, Tschudi, Rivero.

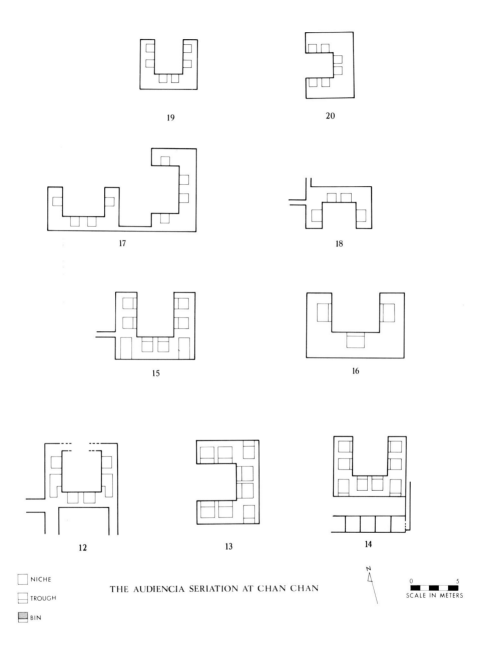

NICHE
TROUGH
BIN

THE AUDIENCIA SERIATION AT CHAN CHAN

SCALE IN METERS

Audiencia Form and Context

Audiencias, like *ciudadelas,* changed in form through time. And as it was for *ciudadelas,* this change was characterized by increasing standardization (Fig. 15). The earliest *audiencias* are found in Uhle in a variety of forms: only three of twenty-two structures are identical. Initially these *audiencias* were constructed only in *ciudadelas* or in state administrative sites in the surrounding rural hinterland and subject valleys. During Middle Chimu times, specifically at Gran Chimu, *audiencias* began to appear in the palace annexes. By Late Chimu 2 (A.D. 1400–1470), these structures occur not only in the enclosures themselves and their annexes (Tschudi and Rivero), but also in the more complex units of intermediate architecture (the "high" or "intermediate architecture" as defined by Klymyshyn n.d., 1982) that cluster around these two late palaces. The *audiencias* of this last politically independent phase of Chan Chan were exclusively of the "standard," six-niched variety.

Aside from increasing standardization in the form of *audiencias,* it is clear as well that the architectural context of *audiencias* varied through time. As noted above, the general context of *audiencias* in Chan Chan varied from being restricted to *ciudadelas* (Early Chimu 1–Early Chimu 2) to occurring in *ciudadelas* and their annexes (Middle Chimu) and finally to appearing in *ciudadelas,* annexes, and intermediate architecture (Late Chimu 2).

The specific context of *audiencias* within *ciudadelas* also changes through time. As we have seen, the close association between *audiencias* and storage facilities that developed in Laberinto represents one such change in specific architectural context. After Laberinto, this association is retained, but the distribution of *audiencias* between the two sectors of the *ciudadelas* containing these structures—north and central—begins to vary in a constant and uniform fashion.

Moseley (1975: 221–222) has suggested that

> [within] the compounds there are more U-shaped structures in the north than central sectors. The average ratio for the two areas is about 5:1, which implies the northern areas of the enclosures were the most active. . . . Yet there is an inverse relationship between numbers of *audiencias* in the north and central sectors of the compounds and numbers of storage facilities in these areas. This implies the U-shaped structures were more than simple accounting stations.

However, this statement is not accurate for the earlier *ciudadelas* and presents a misleading portrait of the relationship between *audiencias* and palace compounds. Tabulation of the data makes this abundantly clear.

As indicated in Table 1, it is only with Bandelier (after ca. A.D. 1350) that there are more *audiencias* in northern than central sectors. However, given

TABLE 1. AUDIENCIA DISTRIBUTION IN *CIUDADELAS*

Ciudadela	Date Range (A.D.)	Units of Association in *Ciudadela*		
		North	Central	North Annex
Rivero	1450–1500	10	1	0
Tschudi	1400–1450	12	5	2
Bandelier	1350–1400	6	2	0
Velarde	1300–1350	2	4	6
Gran Chimu	1150–1300	0	8	1
Laberinto	1100–1200	5	8	1
Uhle	1000–1200	Northeast: 8	Northwest: 7	South: 7

the large number of *audiencias* in Velarde's northern annex, I would argue that, if *audiencias* are viewed as the locus of administration, the shift toward a greater intensity of administrative activity in the northern sectors of palaces actually occurred at this time (the beginning of Late Chimu I, ca. A.D. 1300). Prior to this time, the relationship between numbers of *audiencias* in north and central sectors and numbers of storerooms in these areas is not as neat (inverse) as Moseley portrayed it; although in the early enclosures there are more storerooms in the central than northern sectors (as in the late enclosures), there are also more *audiencias*.

In relative terms, the degree of administrative activity in palace sectors expressed as the ratio of *audiencias* to storerooms may be summarized as follows. In Uhle, the four preserved sectors have about an equal degree of activity, although the ratio of activity is somewhat more intense in the northwest sector (recall, however, that the four sectors of Uhle were built sequentially). In Laberinto, Gran Chimu, and Velarde, the use intensity of the central sectors is clearly greater than that of the nothern sectors (although, again, if Velarde's north annex *audiencias* are included, the measure of its use intensity reverses, and its northern area becomes the locus of greater administrative activity). In Bandelier and Tschudi, the transition to a greater use intensity in the northern sector is complete; in these two enclosures the ratio of activity of northern relative to central sectors is nearly equivalent. With Rivero, the locus of administrative action becomes almost exclusively centered in its northern sector.

Thus, the actual relationship between *audiencia* distribution and *ciudadela* sectors was one of flux. Through time, the locus of administrative activity within palaces shifted from an equal spatial distribution, to an initial emphasis on central sectors, to a clear preference and ultimately almost exclusive focus on the northern sectors.

Beginning with Late Chimu I (ca. A.D. 1300), there was a trend toward an inverse gradient of (administrative) use intensity in *ciudadela* design. That is, from this time, in spatial terms along a path from north to south in the palace enclosures, the public activity of administration was directed away from the central sector toward the northern sector and annex. This implies that, through time, penetration of the central sector was being increasingly restricted and that, as access was reduced, this sector was becoming an exceptionally private space.

Storeroom Complexes

Structures in Chan Chan have been identified functionally as storerooms "on the basis of form, high inconvenient thresholds and a lack of association with domestic debris of any kind" (Day n.d.: 254). Storerooms in palaces remained relatively uniform in morphology and context throughout the city's history (see Day n.d. for a detailed description). In the earliest enclosures—Chayhuac and Uhle—rows of adjacent storerooms cluster around the burial platforms and, in the case of Uhle, around the *audiencia* courts. In later palaces (from Laberinto on), repetitive banks of storerooms occur in well-defined contexts in both northern and central sectors, although a greater number of these rooms were constructed in the central sectors.

Many of the palace storerooms seem to be stamped from the same mold: they possessed gabled roofs, characteristic high thresholds, and a similar compact size (about 2 m × 2.5 m × 2 m). Yet there is considerable dimensional variation, particularly in the earlier *ciudadelas:* Uhle, Laberinto, Gran Chimu, and Velarde contain a wider range of storeroom sizes (including one much larger than the "standard size" cited above) than the subsequent enclosures, Bandelier, Tschudi, and Rivero. Like its architectural counterpart, the *audiencia,* it appears that the storerooms in Chan Chan were also subject to increasing standardization through time.

Unfortunately, there has not been an extensive program of testing and clearing storerooms in Chan Chan (Day, n.d., who excavated most of the storerooms in *ciudadelas,* concentrated his efforts on Rivero), and therefore the significance of dimensional variation in these structures is unknown. It is possible that storerooms of different sizes contained different kinds of valued goods. Given this lack of excavation information, I can document nonimpressionistically change in only one attribute of palace storerooms: gross quantity of storage space. The calculated combined floor space of storage areas (m²) in each *ciudadela* is compiled in the graph in Figure 16.

From the patterning in this graph, it is immediately clear that there are two general orders of magnitude in storage area floor space: those enclosures with less than 3,000 m² and those with greater than 6,000 m². Specifically, the three earliest *ciudadelas* each contain storage facilities of essentially equal total area: Chayhuac has around 2,200 m², while in Uhle and Tello the figure rises to 3,000 m². In the three subsequent palaces, Laberinto, Gran

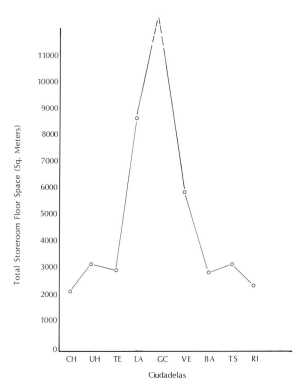

Fig. 16   Graph of storeroom floor space in palace enclosures of Chan Chan.

Chimu, and Velarde, storage area jumps to the second order of magnitude
(greater than 6,000 m²).

Laberinto witnessed the most precipitous increase in storage space: from
3,000 m² in Uhle to nearly 9,000 m², or a gain of 300 percent. It is interesting
to note that this remarkable surge in space devoted to storage was accompanied by reorganization of the *ciudadela* into the tripartite interior design. In
Gran Chimu the trend toward increased storage space continued. As indicated by the open-end on the graph, the total floor space of storerooms in
Gran Chimu is unknown. The central sector of this enclosure is badly
preserved, and many of its presumptive storerooms have been obliterated.
However, measurements on the more intact northern sector revealed a
storage area of 9,850 m² for this sector alone. Therefore I estimate conserva-
tively that the total for Gran Chimu exceeded 11,000 m².

In Velarde there was a reversal of the trend. Here space tied up in storage
plummets from the peak in Gran Chimu to about 6,000 m². Although this is
still a considerable amount of space, it is a substantial reduction from the

levels attained earlier in either Laberinto or Gran Chimu. The final three palaces (Bandelier, Tschudi, Rivero) exhibit a continued reduction in store-room floor space, reverting to the first order of magnitude (less than 3,000 m²). In this final period of development in the city, the end of Late Chimu 1 through Late Chimu 2, the scale of the palace enclosure diminished consider-ably and steadily until Rivero, the last and smallest enclosure. In tandem with this reduction in the size of the palaces was a marked decline in the total storage space.

If gross storage space can be construed as an approximate indicator of wealth (that is, level of production), consecutive variations in that space shown by each palace enclosure can be used as a relative index of economic productivity. Change in this index then could be tied to, and perhaps ex-plained by events in the political history of Chan Chan, events that deter-mined changes in the quantity or kind of goods that were valued, produced, and stored. I will, in fact, use implication derived from this assumption as partial support for my general model of social change at Chan Chan.

Burial Platforms

Developmental trends in the form of the burial platforms and their enclos-ing courts have been discussed at some length by Geoffrey Conrad (n.d., 1982). Here I will point out only the most important aspects of these trends.

Burial platforms in monumental architecture occur throughout the his-tory of Chan Chan. Conrad (n.d.) has convincingly demonstrated that these burial platforms served as the royal tombs of the kings of Chimor. In life, the *ciudadelas* were the palaces and administrative seats of these kings. In death, the burial platforms, the last structures built within the palace enclo-sures, became the focal point of the deceased kings' estate: a sacred sepulchre and monument to the divine ruler.

Conrad (1982: 103) argues that the death of the king occasioned "a series of complex funerary rituals extending over a considerable period of time." One of these rituals entailed construction of additions to the original plat-form in which parts of the king's burial ceremony were repeated: tomb chambers in the additions were equipped with offerings of gold and silver objects, lavish textiles, woodcarvings, and apparently a new set of sacrificial victims, presumably chosen from the royal house.

From this kind of physical evidence, employing analogy from the Inca state, Conrad goes on to suggest that the disposition of the deceased king's estate was governed by a principle of "split inheritance." In accordance with split inheritance, the principal heir acceded to the throne and state office, but the disposable wealth of the king's estate was bequeathed to a corporation consisting of his other consanguineal descendants. "These secondary heirs managed their ancestor's property in his memory . . . cared for his mummy and maintained his cult. The new ruler was forced to acquire his own wealth by levying additional taxes in the existing provinces of the empire or by enlarging his domain through new conquests" (Conrad 1982: 107).

I agree with Conrad's functional interpretations of Chan Chan's burial platforms. His sophisticated reconstruction of the interlocking set of social institutions that underlay construction and maintenance of these royal tombs, however, remains speculative and will require independent confirmation. As Conrad (1982: 115) indicates, the complex social institutions governing access to the throne and disposition of the king's estate were "probably incompletely developed during the early part of Chan Chan's history" and became codified only gradually.

The two earliest burial platforms in the city (Chayhuac and Uhle) bear evidence of substantial remodeling (apart from the structural additions just discussed). They are contained in enclosures that were very likely the palaces of more than a single king. Laberinto lacks a burial platform altogether. I am not convinced that the small, isolated burial structure (Huaca Avispas) in proximity to this palace's northwest corner, which was built much later than the palace itself, represents a "retroactive memorial" to a long-deceased king who had once lived in Laberinto as suggested by Conrad (1982). Gran Chimu contains a burial platform, but here again there is direct evidence for protracted construction on both the palace enclosure and the burial platform itself (Kolata n.d.). I have estimated that the primary occupation of Gran Chimu spanned some one hundred fifty years, and in this time there was certainly more than a single king who ruled from and was buried in this *ciudadela*.

Beginning with Velarde, however, the remaining four palaces were each built and occupied over a period of approximately fifty years, or potentially within the lifetime of a single king. Each of these enclosures possesses a burial platform with well-defined structural additions but no evidence for repeated and extensive remodeling. Therefore, I believe that the full development of the pattern of royal succession (perhaps governed by split inheritance) occurred during the first half of Late Chimu I (A.D. 1300–1350) and was first made manifest archaeologically in the layout of *ciudadela* Velarde. For the last one hundred fifty years of the kingdom's history, then (A.D. 1350–1500), the palaces (Velarde, Bandelier, Tschudi, and Rivero) were expressly built for and occupied by a single king.

Intermediate Architecture and SIAR

The intermediate architecture and SIAR of Chan Chan developed as a result of specific social needs and grew in response to particular political events. Certainly both types of architecture (and the people who inhabited them) were present throughout the history of the city. The earliest units of

SIAR clustered to the east of *ciudadela* Chayhuac, while the earliest intermediate architecture appeared between Chayhuac and Uhle and immediately
east of Tello, both developing early in the Early Chimu 1 Phase (A.D. 900–
1100). A certain portion of this architecture evolved as a natural result of
internal population growth. But, in great part, I have shown that the
growth of intermediate architecture and SIAR was episodic, occurring in
two temporally bounded bursts of construction activity: (a) during Early
Chimu 2 (A.D. 1100–1200) and (b) from Late Chimu 1 through Late Chimu
2 (A.D. 1300–1470).

The evolution of intermediate architecture, in particular, was marked by
periods of relative quietude punctuated by remarkable episodes exhibiting a
greatly accelerated rate of construction. The prime example of this kind of
architectural evolution is the arc of intermediate architecture to the south
and west of Tschudi and Rivero. These units, forming a substantial percentage of the total universe of intermediate architecture, were built essentially
all at once between about A.D. 1400 and 1470 (Late Chimu 2). The SIAR
were also subject to this abrupt, episodic type of architectural evolution;
however, SIAR seem to have been somewhat more stable than was intermediate architecture in that, during periods of expansion, their rate of growth
generally was not as precipitous as the intermediate architecture.

Finally, it is crucial to note that the two episodes of frenetic construction
activity in intermediate architecture and SIAR appear to have coincided
with the two major episodes of Chimu military expansionism related by the
oral traditions condensed in the Anonymous History of Trujillo: the first
with Ñançenpinco's initial conquests from Santa to Zaña at sometime before A.D. 1200, and the second with the subjugation of the great
Lambayeque Valley complex around A.D. 1350–1370. In this case, as I will
make explicit, the coincidence of these two resulted from a causal rather
than a casual relationship.

ARCHITECTURAL CHANGE AND SOCIAL HISTORY

What were the causes of the architectural changes at Chan Chan, and
what was their social significance for the people of Chimor? In general, how
do we make sense out of these changes?

I have made the claim that the specific architectural attributes of the
ciudadelas, as well as the intermediate architecture and SIAR as a whole,
varied systematically (that is, in a dependent and interconnected fashion) in
response to changes in social formations of the Chimu state. I am now
prepared to maintain specifically that two closely related social phenomena
were primarily responsible for these systematic architectural changes: (a) the
economic consequences of institutionalized military expansionism and (b)
the political consequences of increasing distance between the king and his

subjects, or, more generally, heightened status differentiation within the governing hierarchy.

The changes in the form of Chan Chan that I have documented can be explained most economically and completely by reference to these two phenomena. For the sake of analysis I will describe the particular effects of each of these phenomena on the form of the city separately, but because they were related features of the same process of social change in Chimor, I will also illustrate the connections between them. The results of this analysis will be a synthesis of the foregoing data on patterns of growth at Chan Chan and a general model of the political and economic forces that brought form to the city.

Military Expansionism

The effects of military expansionism on the form of Chan Chan were most acutely registered in intermediate and SIAR architecture, and in the storage complexes of the *ciudadelas*. As we have seen, during the Early Chimu I Phase (A.D. 900–1100), small concentrations of SIAR, and to a lesser extent intermediate architecture, clustered around Chayhuac and to the south of Uhle. At this time, the economic emphasis of the state was placed on developing and expanding the local irrigation network into a viable life-support system for the city, presumably to a point well beyond simple autarchy. That is, agricultural surplus from the immediate hinterland formed the wealth of the nascent state.

However, at some point around A.D. 1100, Chan Chan and its productive rural hinterland experienced a catastrophic episode of El Niño-induced flooding that effectively destroyed the sustaining network of irrigation canals on the pampas to the north of the city (Moseley, this volume; Nials et al. 1979: 4–14). Not surprisingly, this disaster forced a reorientation of the state's extractive economy, and it is at this time that we see evidence for the first phase of Chimu military expansion recorded in the dynastic chronicles. (See Table 2 for a graphic representation of the suggested correlation of dynasties and conquest events on the North Coast of Peru implied here.)

We have identified this initial phase of conquest with the reign of Ñançenpinco, the third ruler of Chimor, which spanned the period between A.D. 1150 and 1200 (Moseley and Kolata n.d.). At this time, the prime source of economic stimulus shifted from parochial exploitation of local resources to a parasitic extraction of foreign resources. Extensive revenues in the form of taxes levied in the five valleys subjugated by Ñançenpinco flowed to the capital. This new wealth was directly reflected architecturally at Chan Chan in the construction of Tello and its annexes and various small units of intermediate architecture and, at a somewhat later date, in the

TABLE 2. A SUGGESTED CORRELATION OF DYNASTIES AND RECONSTRUCTED HISTORICAL EVENTS ON THE NORTH COAST OF PERU.

A.D.	Major Regional Events	Lambayeque Valley Sequence		Jequetepeque Valley Sequence
		King List	Local Events/ Architecture	
	Spanish Conquest	Xecfuinpisan	Spanish Administration	Spanish Administration
1500	Inca Conquest of Coast	Fallenpisan Cipromarca Chullumpisan Llempisan	Inca Administration	Inca Administration
		Oxa		
1400		Palesmassa		
		Pongmassa	Chimu Conquest of Lambayeque	
1300	Phase II of Chimu Conquest		Late Phase: Chornancap	
		?		
1200	Phase I of Chimu Conquest			Farfan Established: Seat of Administration for Chimu Governor "General Pacatnamu"
1100	Great Chimu Flood	Fempellec Acunta	Flooding in Lambayeque: Batan Grande Complex	
		Lanipatcum		
		Llamecoll		
1000		Mulumuslan		
		Nofan-Nech	Middle Phase: Chotuna/Chornancap	
		Allascunto		
900		Cuntipallec		
		Mascuy		
		Llapchilulli-Cala		
800		Cuntipullec-Nor-Escuñain		
		Cium and Zolsdon	Early Phase: Chotuna/Batan Grande	
700		Naymlap and Ceterni		
			Pampa Grande: Moche V Capital	

Chan Chan/Moche Valley   Viru/Casma Valley Sequence

King List	Architectural Sequence		Viru/Casma Valley	A.D.
	Effective Abandonment: Chan Chan		Spanish Administration	
	Chiquitoy Viejo: Chicama		Inca Administration	1500
Minchançaman	Rivero			
	Tschudi			
	Bandelier			1400
	Velarde	Huaca Dragon		
?			Manchan Established: Casma Valley	1300
	Squier			
Ñançenpinco	Gran Chimu	Huaca Calavario	V-124A Established: Viru Valley	1200
	Laberinto			1100
	Tello			1000
Guaricuar	Uhle			
Tacaynamo	Chayhuac			900
	Huaca Higo	Huaca Tacaynamo		800
				700
	Galindo (Moche V)			

137

quantum leap in storage space allocated in *ciudadela* Laberinto. Tello and the less-imposing intermediate architecture were built to accommodate high-status members of the expanding bureaucracy that was formed to manage the economic and political affairs of the newly gained provinces. The impressive number of storerooms in Laberinto were built to accommodate the massive influx of portable wealth, probably in the form of high-status goods such as fancy textiles, precious metals, and the like, that was being extracted in tribute from the conquered provinces.

At the time Laberinto was occupied (ca. A.D. 1150–1200), the lords of Chimor were actively engaged in restoring Chan Chan's damaged local system of intensive irrigated agriculture. But, as has been demonstrated elsewhere (Ortloff et al. 1982), this attempt, which took the remarkable form of cutting the massive La Cumbre, or intervalley canal, ultimately ended in failure, and the irrigation system never again reached the peak of efficiency gained in Early Chimu 1 times. In fact, current evidence indicates that by about A.D. 1400 (Late Chimu 2), the local irrigation system had all but atrophied.

The second great campaign of military expansion, the conquest of Lambayeque, began between A.D. 1300 and 1370 (Late Chimu 1 phase). With the annexation of this great province, new wealth again began to flow to the capital, and again conquest triggered a new, even more vigorous program of construction activity in the city. In Late Chimu 1 (A.D. 1300–1400), Velarde and then Bandelier were built. But more important, for the second time, SIAR and intermediate architecture began to expand rapidly, particularly around the Velarde palace compound (J. Topic 1982, this volume). This expansion continued and intensified during Late Chimu 2. It was during this phase that the SIAR attained its maximum expanse (J. Topic n.d.), and more than 65 percent of all intermediate architecture was constructed (Klymyshyn n.d., 1982; Kolata n.d., 1982).

Unlike the first burst of construction activity after Early Chimu 2, the second surge, during Late Chimu 1–2, did not include a radical expansion of storage space in palaces. In fact, as indicated in Figure 16, the total area occupied by storerooms decreased. But this does not necessarily signal a massive decline in economic productivity.

First, it should be noted that there was a redistribution of storage space at this time. That is, the increase in intermediate architecture, much of which contained storeroom complexes, may have compensated for the decline in palace storage space. Moreover, I would suggest that after the annexation of Lambayeque, there was a reorientation of the state economy that involved a change in emphasis on the types of goods being stored in the palace enclosures. Specifically, after Late Chimu 1, the items stored in the *ciudadelas* were exclusively high-status goods: textiles, gold, silver, and the like— particularly those gained from the provinces of Lambayeque where metalworking was a long and well-established tradition (J. Topic n.d., this volume; Topic and Moseley 1983; Shimada, this volume).

Prior to this time, as I have noted, palace storerooms show considerable dimensional variability. Although there is no direct evidence, I think it plausible that the contents of these storerooms also varied considerably. Before the conquest of Lambayeque, variation in storeroom size in the enclosures implies that some of the larger storerooms they contained were used for bulk storage, perhaps for agricultural produce, while the smaller storerooms were reserved for high-status goods. After this time (A.D. 1300–1350), palace storerooms became smaller and increasingly standardized in dimensions. By inference I would argue that the contents of these storerooms also became standardized; that these uniformly sized storerooms now contained exclusively precious, elite commodities.

As I see it, the economy of Early Chimu Chan Chan was based on exploitation of local agrarian resources. With the conquests of Early Chimu 2, a "dual economy" that drew revenue from both local and foreign sources was instituted. The wealth of this dual economy, consisting of both agricultural surplus and portable, elite items, was deposited in the newly expanded storage facilities of the great enclosures. However, by the Late Chimu 2 Phase, one aspect of that dual economy, the local irrigation system that had provided agricultural surplus, atrophied from the combined effects of severe local tectonic uplift and the early El Niño flooding (Moseley et al. 1983; Ortloff et al. 1982). It appears that after the failure of the intervalley canal to reactivate the destroyed network of irrigated fields, the Chimu made no further serious attempts to restore or expand permanently the local agricultural landscape. I would contend that the annexation of Lambayeque in Late Chimu 1 marked the beginning of a trend toward increased reliance on revenue extracted from foreign provinces—an economic reliance that came to be expressed architecturally in palace storeroom size, contents, and decreased variability.

In short, changes in the essential character and emphasis of the Chimu state economy were reflected in the architecture of Chan Chan. These changes, in turn, describe a trend that, in the light of specific historical events (the initiation of extra-valley conquest in Early Chimu 2, El Niño devastation, tectonic uplift of the agrarian landscape) makes eminent sense: initial dependence on the local agrarian economy, to initiation of the dual economy [a mixed agrarian and tribute-based economy], to ultimate reliance on economic stimulus through extraction of foreign resources. In a sense this progression, paralleled in the architecture of Chan Chan, is a compact paradigm for the social history of Chimor. At the focal point of this progressive change in state economy, a change that continuously altered the shape of the city, was an intensifying emphasis on military expansion as a prime source of revenue.

Social Differentiation

The second social force transforming the urban landscape through time was increasing status differentiation within the ruling hierarchy. Specifically, I believe it is possible to infer from certain modifications in the architecture of Chan Chan that there were two important and complementary changes in the political structure of Chimor: (a) the person of the king became increasingly distinguished in status and authority from the other members of the ruling elite and (b) the class of the ruling elite itself greatly expanded and became increasingly complex over time. These changes in status relationships, essentially a restructuring of the governing hierarchy, substantially altered the form of the monumental architecture: palaces and their annexes.

There were several modifications to the palace enclosure and its interior architecture (*audiencias,* storerooms, burial platforms, and patterns of access) that directly reflect heightened "social distance" between the king and his subjects. Perhaps the clearest of these is the change in the internal design of the palace to a sectorial, tripartite form, accompanied by the gradual redistribution of administrative structures within these sectors.

As we have seen, through time, the central sectors of the enclosures became increasingly insulated from the administrative activities associated with *audiencia* courts. As the public activity of administration was progressively removed to the northern sector and annex of the *ciudadelas,* the central sector became an increasingly private space, fitted only with one or two large *audiencia* courts, storerooms, and, ultimately, a burial platform. The central sector was almost certainly the specific locus of residence for the king and perhaps for principal court attendants and a harem as well. (An analogous identification of specific royal residence may be seen in Inca palaces where the king's quarters were located towards the "back of the enclosure" [Brundage 1967: 80].)

The increasingly physical isolation of the central section—the king's residence—from public activities was a direct spatial expression and symbol of increased social differentiation between the king and his subjects. In fact, the physical boundary that was being drawn between the central sector and the rest of the palace enclosure resulted from the evolution of a very specific institution: divine kingship.

We know that divine kingship was a prominent feature of Chimor on the eve of its conquest by the Inca (Rowe 1948). But when did this institution appear? Was it a characteristic of Chimu social organization from the beginning? I believe that the architectural evidence from Chan Chan shows that divine kingship was not a fixed and permanent feature of the political structure of Chimor, but rather only gradually evolved as the principal institution around which the political system came to be organized. Furthermore, this same evidence suggests that the concept of divine kingship crystallized relatively late, at some point after the subjugation of Lambayeque around A.D. 1350–1370. It was at this time that access to the central sector was severely restricted. It finally had become inviolate to the public, it was the locus of the sacred. It was at this time that the pattern of "one king-one palace-one burial platform," perhaps reflecting the principle of royal succession by split inheritance, became manifest in the architecture.

Prior to the Lambayeque conquest, palaces were less standardized in overall design and interior architecture. Several appear to have housed more than one king and were occupied for a number of generations (Moseley and Kolata n.d.). All had administrative structures more evenly distributed throughout the enclosure. These patterns imply that effective political power was also more evenly distributed at this time, or at least had not yet been focused as sharply in the person of the king.

Expansion of the ruling hierarchy seems to have occurred episodically after major campaigns of imperial conquest. Clearly, annexation of foreign provinces opened up increasing numbers of managerial positions. Not surprisingly then, construction of residences for these new bureaucrats (the presumed tenants of intermediate architecture) also increased substantially after each episode of conquest.

In addition, the gradual development of elaborate northern annexes to the palaces, annexes incorporated as wings of *ciudadelas,* and the more imposing units of "high" intermediate architecture, all point to progressive status differentiation within this growing elite class of managers. The Chimu solution to this complexity was to develop a clearly articulated political hierarchy in which each position was ascribed distinct obligations, privileges, status, and authority. These positions were probably hereditary, and vertical movement in the hierarchy was rare. Likewise, these positions enjoyed specific rights of residence: in late Chan Chan, the nobles of highest rank and authority probably resided in the elaborate northern annexes of the palace enclosures (present in Gran Chimu, Velarde, Tschudi, and Rivero) and there engaged directly in the daily administrative duties most closely affecting the king. Nobles of lesser rank and with fewer responsibilities were housed in various kinds of intermediate architecture, again arranged in a hierarchy determined by ascribed position.

I think it now is clear that both military expansionism and heightened status differentiation were among the prime determinants of change in the form of Chan Chan; the former, in particular, was responsible for change in the configuration of SIAR and intermediate architecture, while the latter altered the form and distribution of activities in the palaces and their annexes. These two social phenomena were interrelated in that economic expansion brought on by military conquest created new positions of authority that were located in an increasingly complex hierarchy of political power.

Furthermore, the specific evolution of divine kingship, perhaps with the attendant principle of royal succession by split inheritance, was accompanied by an emerging ideology of conquest. That is, by the time the institution of divine kingship had fully developed in Late Chimu 1, military conquest had become both a prerogative and an obligation of the king. Conquest itself was justified by appeal to religious ideology. It was a sacred function of the divine ruler. Although sanctioned by religion, the underlying impetus to military expansion was economic. By the time divine kingship had fully evolved, the local agrarian economy had contracted severely, never fully recovering from the devastating impact of tectonic uplift and El Niño flooding. The transition to emphasis on an extractive tribute economy was complete. It is perhaps not simple coincidence that the institution of divine kingship finally appeared at a time when significant growth in the state economy had become dependent upon annexation and taxing of foreign provinces.

DEVELOPMENTAL TRENDS: AN OVERVIEW

The changes in the form of Chan Chan are an architectural document of the origins, expansion, and ultimate contraction of the Chimu state and the empire it controlled. Trends in the development of the architecture draw a portrait of bureaucratic state organization forming gradually, but becoming increasingly complex, and subject to episodic reformation through time. The principal force underlying growth in the size and complexity of the state was change in the economy, particularly that caused by military expansion.

The focal point of the state economy was the *ciudadela*. It was the residence of the royal dynasty, the seat of government, and the locus for the storage and redistribution of the kingdom's wealth. Through time, the *ciudadelas* and the structures they contained became increasingly standardized in form and function. This standardization was a reflection of the gradual growth in political and economic power vested in the king and his lineage that culminated in the emergence of the institution of divine kingship.

The development of intermediate architecture and SIAR was directly dependent on growth in the state economy; the varying economic and political fortunes of the kings of Chan Chan, ruling from their *ciudadelas,* determined the size and configuration of this architecture. The *ciudadela* and its supporting architecture were linked in a system of growth. This system was shaped primarily by forces in the political economy. Change in the state economy occasioned change in the political structure that managed this economy. Thus, through time, the urban concept of Chan Chan assumed different forms.

BIBLIOGRAPHY

BRUNDAGE, BURR CARTWRIGHT
  1967   *Lords of Cuzco.* University of Oklahoma Press, Norman.

CONRAD, GEOFFREY W.
  1982   The Burial Platforms of Chan Chan: Some Social and Political Implica-
         tions. In *Chan Chan: Andean Desert City* (Michael E. Moseley and Kent
         C. Day, eds.): 87–117. University of New Mexico Press, Albuquerque.
  n.d.   Burial Platforms and Related Structures on the North Coast of Peru:
         Some Social and Political Implications. Ph.D. dissertation, Depart-
         ment of Anthropology, Harvard University, 1974.

DAY, KENT
  n.d.   Architecture of Ciudadela Rivero, Chan Chan, Peru. Ph.D. disserta-
         tion, Department of Anthropology, Harvard University, 1973.

FARRINGTON, IAN S.
  1983   The Design and Function of the Intervalley Canal: Comments on a
         Paper by Ortloff, Moseley, and Feldman. *American Antiquity* 48(2):
         360–375.

KLYMYSHYN, ALEXANDRA M. ULANA
  1982   Elite Compounds in Chan Chan. In *Chan Chan: Andean Desert City*
         (Michael E. Moseley and Kent C. Day, eds.): 119–143. University of
         New Mexico Press, Albuquerque.
  n.d.   Intermediate Architecture in Chan Chan, Peru. Ph.D. dissertation,
         Department of Anthropology, Harvard University, 1976.

KNAPP, GREGORY
  1982   Prehistoric Flood Management on the Peruvian Coast: Reinterpreting
         the "Sunken Fields" of Chilca. *American Antiquity* 47(1): 144–154.

KOLATA, ALAN L.
  1982   Chronology and Settlement Growth at Chan Chan. In *Chan Chan:
         Andean Desert City* (Michael E. Moseley and Kent C. Day, eds.): 67–
         85. University of New Mexico Press, Albuquerque.
  n.d.   Chan Chan: The Form of the City in Time. Ph.D. dissertation, Depart-
         ment of Anthropology, Harvard University, 1978.

KUS, JAMES S.
  1984   The Chicama-Moche Canal: Failure or Success? An Alternative Expla-
         nation for an Incomplete Canal. *American Antiquity* 49(2): 408–415.

MOSELEY, MICHAEL E.
  1975   Chan Chan: Andean Alternative of the Pre-Industrial City? *Science* 187:
         219–225.

MOSELEY, MICHAEL E., and ERIC E. DEEDS
  1982   The Land in Front of Chan Chan: Agrarian Expansion, Reform and
         Collapse in the Moche Valley. In *Chan Chan: Andean Desert City* (Mi-
         chael E. Moseley and Kent C. Day, eds.): 25–53. University of New
         Mexico Press, Albuquerque.

MOSELEY, MICHAEL E., ROBERT FELDMAN, and CHARLES ORTLOFF
    1981   Living with Crisis: Human Perceptions of Process and Time. In *Biotic Crises in Ecological and Evolutionary Time* (Mathew Nitiecki, ed.): 231–267. Academic Press, New York.

MOSELEY, MICHAEL E., ROBERT FELDMAN, CHARLES ORTLOFF, and ALFREDO NARVAEZ
    1983   Principles of Agrarian Collapse in the Cordillera Negra, Peru. *Annals of Carnegie Museum* 52: 299–327.

MOSELEY, MICHAEL E., and ALAN L. KOLATA
    n.d.   Myth and History on the North Coast of Peru: Steps to an Archaeological Concordat. Paper prepared for the Dumbarton Oaks symposium The Northern Dynasties, October 1985.

NETHERLY, PATRICIA J.
    1984   The Management of Late Andean Irrigation Systems on the North Coast of Peru. *American Antiquity* 49(2): 227–254.
    n.d.   Local Level Lords on the North Coast of Peru. Ph.D. dissertation, Department of Anthropology, Cornell University, 1977.

NIALS, FRED, ERIC DEEDS, MICHAEL E. MOSELEY, SHELIA POZORSKI, THOMAS POZORSKI, and ROBERT FELDMAN
    1979   El Niño: The Catastrophic Flooding of Coastal Peru. *Field Museum of Natural History Bulletin,* Part I, 50(8): 4–10.

ORTLOFF, CHARLES R., MICHAEL E. MOSELEY, and ROBERT FELDMAN
    1982   Hydraulic Engineering Aspects of the Chimu Chicama-Moche Intervalley Canal. *American Antiquity* 47(3): 572–595.

PARSONS, JEFFREY R., and NORBERT PSUTY
    1975   Sunken Fields and Prehispanic Subsistence on the Peruvian Coast. *American Antiquity* 40(3): 259–282.

POZORSKI, THOMAS, and SHELIA POZORSKI
    1982   Reassessing the Chicama-Moche Intervalley Canal: Comments on Hydraulic Engineering Aspects of the Chimu Chicama-Moche Intervalley Canal. *American Antiquity* 47(4): 851–868.

ROWE, JOHN H.
    1948   The Kingdom of Chimor. *Acta Americana* 6(1–2): 26–59.

SMITH, RICHARD T.
    1983   Making a Meal out of Mahames: A Reply to Knapp's Prehistoric Flood Management on the Peruvian Coast. *American Antiquity* 48(1): 147–149.

TOPIC, JOHN R.
    1982   Lower-Class Social and Economic Organization at Chan Chan. In *Chan Chan: Andean Desert City* (Michael E. Moseley and Kent C. Day, eds.): 145–175. University of New Mexico Press, Albuquerque.
    n.d.   The Lower Class at Chan Chan: A Qualitative Approach. Ph.D. dissertation, Department of Anthroplogy, Harvard University, 1977.

TOPIC, JOHN R., and MICHAEL E. MOSELEY
    1983   Chan Chan: A Case Study of Urban Change in Peru. *Ñawpa Pacha* 21: 153–182.

Craft Production in the Kingdom of Chimor

JOHN R. TOPIC

TRENT UNIVERSITY

INTRODUCTION

IN THIS PAPER I WILL DISCUSS craft production in Imperial Chimor. I will compare these activities at Chan Chan with provincial centers of more local importance. Furthermore, I will suggest a reconstruction of historic events, evaluate the nature and role of social institutions, and analyze the congruity of ethnohistoric and archaeological data.

Background

When I initiated archaeological work at Chan Chan in 1969, I began to study the lower-class areas and only tested two small houses. It was somewhat of a surprise to find evidence of craft activities in what were assumed to be the houses of the more impoverished inhabitants of the city. I interpreted these craft activities, which included some metalworking and spindle-whorl manufacture, as "cottage industries" (J. Topic n.d.a); I assumed that materials were provided to the artisans by some more centralized organization and that the artisans were remunerated on a per-piece basis. When major excavations were carried out in 1972–73 in these areas, it became clear that craft production was the major focus of the lower-class occupation. By that time however, it did not seem so surprising to find artisans in the lower-class areas, and excavations were designed to eluci-

I am grateful to Michael Moseley and Carol Mackey, directors of the Chan Chan-Moche Valley Project, for the opportunity to work at Chan Chan. In addition to support from that project, my fieldwork was partially supported by a National Science Foundation Graduate Fellowship and Dissertation grant, by Ford Foundation grants administered by the Peabody Museum, and by a grant from the Committee on Latin American Studies of Harvard University. Some illustrations were prepared through the financial assistance of the Social Sciences and Humanities Research Council of Canada. In addition to comments by the symposium participants, this paper has benefited from conversations and communications with Warwick Bray, Sarah Brooks, Eric Deeds, Jerry Moore, Barbara Price, and William Sanders; none of these colleagues, however, had the opportunity to comment directly on the final draft of this paper and cannot be held responsible for any misinterpretations in the paper.

date the organization of craft production by examining different archaeological contexts possibly representative of family residences, workshops,
retainer housing, and so forth.

By 1975, the analysis was complete, and an interpretation of the organization of craft production had already emerged (Moseley 1975). This interpretation stressed that Chan Chan artisans worked full time at their crafts; that
the crafts were organized in a hierarchical guild-like manner; that the artisans were likely endogamous, which would result in caste-like kin groups;
that some artisans were directly attached to the royal court; and that the state
was heavily involved in the major crafts of weaving and metalworking (J.
Topic n.d.b, 1980, 1982).

While these interpretations were being formulated, much more detailed
analyses of North Coast ethnohistory were being carried out independently.
Although María Rostworowski had earlier (1961) noted differences between
highland and coastal inheritance rules, the foundation of a distinctive coastal
ethnohistory was laid down in 1970 when she published "Mercaderes de
Chincha." It was only in 1975, however, that this new coastal perspective
was extended to the artisans of the North Coast (Rostworowski 1975,
1977a, 1977b). Rostworowski not only emphasized the different roles that
occupational specialization played on the coast and in the highlands, but also
interpreted the organization of the coastal artisans in a manner similar to
that indicated by the archaeological evidence. At the same time that excavations were going on at Chan Chan, Patricia Netherly (n.d.) was conducting
archival research to locate information specific to the North Coast. Her
dissertation is the most complete source for the ethnohistory of the North
Coast, and moreover, it begins the process of comparing ethnohistoric and
archaeological information. More recently, Susan Ramírez (1982) has taken
up the problem of occupational specialists.

Although the archaeological and ethnohistoric studies were contemporaneous, they were largely independent of each other. This conference provided the first opportunity in which the archaeologists and ethnohistorians
were all together. Our consensus is that there is a great degree of congru-
ence between the archaeological data on craft production from Chan Chan
and the ethnohistoric information on occupational specialization on the
North Coast, but most importantly, that each set of data contributes pieces
of the puzzle lacking in the other set.

In the following sections of this paper, I will compare the ethnohistoric
interpretation to the interpretation of archaeological information from Chan
Chan. Comparisons also will be made to recently excavated provincial sites.
These comparisons reinforce the earlier interpretation of the importance of
craft production at Chan Chan and, indeed, underscore the pivotal role that
craft production played at the uppermost level of the political hierarchy
during late Chimu times.

THE ETHNOHISTORIC INFORMATION

Before briefly summarizing the ethnohistoric information, it is useful to examine its limitations. It is important to point out, especially for non-Andeanists, that much of the recent work is based on judicial and administrative documents and not chronicles. Much of this documentation also is contemporaneous with or predates the first *reducciones*[1] carried out by González de Cuenca in 1566–67 and predates the later massive Toledan *reducciones*. As Barbara Price (1980) notes, this type of documentation is the best source for detailed economic information. Indeed, Chimu ethnohistory provides excellent data from the early Colonial period on local economic organization.

The coverage of local areas is not uniform, however. The best documentation is from the valleys north of Moche, while the southern provinces of the Chimu Kingdom are less well known (Mackey and Klymyshyn n.d.: 21, this volume). There is also the problem that during the early Colonial period the Spanish neither understood the indigenous system nor commanded the local languages well enough to probe the intricacies of the system (Ramírez 1982: 131). Few people on the North Coast spoke Quechua, the indigenous language most familiar to the Spanish during the period; instead the coastal population in the Chimu heartland spoke three distinct, but probably related, dialects (Netherly n.d.). It was not until the 1550s that a few Spaniards learned these dialects (Rabinowitz 1983: 262).

By the time the Spanish were able to communicate effectively with the North Coast people, the Kingdom of Chimor had been subject to foreign domination for almost four generations. Three of these generations lived under highland rule, during which time the Inca had systematically subdivided large political units and eliminated the highest levels of organization (Netherly 1984: 230; Rostworowski 1961; J. Rowe 1948). The fourth generation witnessed the massive depopulation associated with the Spanish invasion. Nathan Wachtel (1977, 1984) has eloquently described the effects of the Spanish invasion on the highland populations as a process of destructuration (i.e., the survival of partial ancient structures outside the context of a coherent whole). Netherly (1984: 230) has pointed out that the loss of population on the coast was even greater than in the highlands (as much as 80–90 percent by 1567) and that the combination of Inca political policy and depopulation resulted in the preservation of only the middle levels of the organizational hierarchy.

Despite these limitations, many aspects of the organization of artisans are

[1] *Reducciones* were settlements resulting from the Colonial policy of concentrating dispersed populations into a relatively few Spanish-style towns. The *reducciones* were meant to facilitate the control of the population, the collection of tribute, and the catechization of the native population. The relocation involved in the *reducción* mixed different social groups (*parcialidades, huarangas, pachacas,* etc.) together, often removing these groups to new towns far from their ancestral lands.

clear. Occupational specialization was a major organizational principle on the North Coast. The artisans were grouped into social units or *parcialidades* by specialty and were forbidden to change profession. At this lowest level the artisans were probably also united by kinship ties (Netherly 1984: 231; Rostworowski 1977b: 245). Netherly (n.d.: chap. 6) has noted that these social units were grouped into larger, hierarchically arranged groups with their own headmen (*mandones*) and even lords (*principales*) who were themselves artisans. Rostworowski (1977a: 177; 1977b: 244) has likened these hierarchical groups of artisans to guilds. Artisans contributed only the products of their specialties to the state and were exempt from other labor services (Rostworowski 1977b: 246; Ramírez 1982: 125; Netherly n.d.: chap. 6).

Middle-level polities included a wide range of occupational specialists (Netherly n.d., 1984; Ramírez 1982: 125). Although varying considerably in size, these middle-level polities were small enough that a single large valley, such as Chicama, could accommodate two within its coastal plain (Netherly 1984, this volume). Some occupational specialists were artisans, but the vast majority were farmers and fishermen. Some artisans were attached directly to the lords' courts, while others lived in separate villages (Netherly n.d.; Ramírez 1982: 126). As Netherly, especially, has shown (n.d.; Rostworowski 1983, this volume), occupational specialization as a principal of organization co-existed with the principal of duality. A middle-level polity was divided into moieties, each with its own lord, and the moieties were further subdivided by quadripartition. The result was that a middle-level polity consisted of a ranked set of *parcialidades* and lords.

Much of the exchange of specialized products took place through redistribution supervised by the lords or the state, but some goods were simply bartered through local exchange networks (Netherly n.d.: 252). In some cases, the occupational specialists themselves traveled to nearby towns to sell their products (Ramírez 1982: 128); however, some goods were circulated by exchange specialists, although the exact role of these exchange specialists is not clear (Netherly n.d.: chap. 6; Ramírez 1982; Rostworowski 1977a, 1977b). It seems likely, though, that the lords and the state were heavily involved in the exchange of metal goods and fancy textiles and that this involvement extended to procuring raw materials such as alpaca wool and metal ores from the highlands (Netherly n.d.: 253, 264–269).

As we will see, there is a general agreement between the archaeological and ethnohistoric information relating to occupational specialization in general and craft production in particular. The basic question, however, concerns the extent to which ethnohistoric descriptions of middle-level polities apply in detail to the highest level of political organization, which is represented at Chan Chan.

CHAN CHAN

Dating

The archaeological evidence for craft production at Chan Chan is mainly confined to the late phases at the site (J. Topic n.d.b; Topic and Moseley 1985). Both the initiation and termination of craft production seem to have taken place within relatively short time spans.

Of these two events, the initiation of craft production as a major activity is the more difficult to date. Stratigraphic excavations have documented a five-part ceramic sequence at Chan Chan[2] (Topic and Moseley 1985: fig. 4). Before the beginning of Phase 4, evidence for craft production is sparse. In terms of metalworking, for example, only two copper wires can be dated to Phase 3; by the beginning of Phase 5, however, some evidence of metal-working occurs in most excavations. Similarly, Ann Rowe's (1984) seriation of Chimu textiles suggests that large-scale weaving of fine cloth dates to the late occupation of Chan Chan. These data indicate that the initiation of craft production on a very large scale occurred during Phase 4. Tentatively this event has been correlated with the occupation of *ciudadela* Velarde, which may have been as early as A.D. 1300–1350 (Kolata, this volume) or as late as A.D. 1350–1375 (Topic and Moseley 1985: table 1).

It is difficult to trace the development of craft activity at Chan Chan. The tools used in metalworking and weaving, the two major craft activities, are valuable and can be expected to have been reused over a long period of time. Moreover, Phase 4 ceramic material is relatively rare in unmixed collections. Inasmuch as it is thought that Phase 4 spanned only about two generations, it is likely that there was a major reorientation of the economic activities of a large proportion of Chan Chan's population during a relatively brief time period.

The magnitude of the change can be illustrated by noting that during Phase 5 there were perhaps as many as 12,000 full-time adult artisans (male and female) at Chan Chan. Extrapolating back to Phase 4, the number might have been as many as 7,300 (Topic and Moseley 1985). This is an incredibly large number of artisans specialized in the technologically complex fields of weaving and metalworking. Where did they all come from? It is not easy to believe that so many specialists could have developed out of the existing population of Chan Chan within a generation, nor does changing occupations fit well with the ethnohistoric data. I hypothesized several years ago (J. Topic n.d.b) that these artisans were imported from conquered territories, and specifically that metalworkers might have been imported

[2] The ceramic phases have estimated dates as follows: Phase 1 (A.D. 850–1000), Phase 2 (A.D. 1000–1100), Phase 3 (A.D. 1100–1350), Phase 4 (A.D. 1350–1400), Phase 5 (A.D. 1400–1470) (Topic and Moseley 1985: table 1).

from Lambayeque. Although the timing of the influx of craftsmen fits well with the conquest of Lambayeque, the hypothesis was based on scanty evidence from Wendell Bennett's (1939) excavations. More recent excavations in the Lambayeque area have neither confirmed nor disputed this hypothesis, and more work is needed on this point. For reasons outlined later, however, I still feel that we can provisionally accept the interpretation that the conquest of Lambayeque resulted in a major reorganization at Chan Chan (cf. Kolata, this volume).

In contrast, the termination of craft activity at Chan Chan is very clear-cut. The evidence indicates that the artisans abandoned the site suddenly, en masse. This general abandonment probably correlates to the Inca conquest of the Chimu and the removal of skilled craftsmen to Cuzco and other Inca cities (J. Rowe 1948: 11; Rostworowski 1977b, this volume). It is interesting that textiles, rather than metal objects, provide the best evidence for this dispersal of craftsmen. Anne Rowe (1984: 122–125, 185–186), for example, has been able to show that large quantities of Chimu cloth occur on the South Coast during the Late Horizon, although it is not clear whether this results from the Inca moving artisans or only their products.

The Organization of Chan Chan's Artisans

An exceptional record from one moment in time allows a detailed interpretation of the organization of craft activities at Chan Chan. In addition to leaving pots still on the hearth and storage jars lined up against the walls of small rooms, the artisans abandoned ingots on the floors of houses (Fig. 1), hammers and other tools in workplaces (Figs. 2, 3), storage bins full of cotton waiting to be spun, and unfinished textiles (Figs. 3, 4).

Fig. 1 Four copper ingots wrapped in a piece of cloth and left on the floor of Complex 1, room J (cf. Fig. 6).

Fig. 2 An anvil found in the *barrio* south of *ciudadela* Laberinto. This is one of six metalworking stones (five anvils and one hammer) found together in a cache pit dug into a floor and sealed over with plaster.

Fig. 3 *below*. Weaving implements and cloth fragments in a bin in Complex 1, room D (cf. Fig. 2). Materials found in this bin included seven heddles, four weaving swords, five spindles, a large wooden needle, three balls of wool yarn, a slit tapestry fragment, about one hundred copper and shell beads wrapped in a cloth fragment, pieces of mother-of-pearl inlay, and fragments of copper.

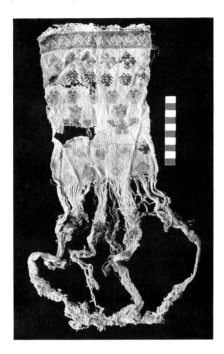

Fig. 4 An unfinished supplementary weft textile found in the retainer area west of *ciudadela* Laberinto.

The quantity of materials abandoned, though large, represents only a portion of the total inventory present just prior to abandonment, but the contextual associations of what was left behind are ideal. Despite this excellent context, it is likely that the artisans abandoned their belongings selectively. It is also likely that the Inca selectively looted materials and products. The lack of evidence for gold and silver metallurgy or for the finest weaving and feathercloth in the archaeological record, for example, can be easily ascribed to the selective removal of this evidence by both the conquered and the conquerors. Still, the archaeological record, which I have described more completely elsewhere (J. Topic n.d.b), abundantly documents the major orientations of occupational specialists at Chan Chan.

Occupational specialists at Chan Chan occupied three distinct types of areas, which can be called here *barrios,* retainer areas, and caravansaries (Fig. 5). Each of these will be discussed in turn.

The bulk of the population lived in four *barrios.* During Phase 5 these areas housed an estimated 26,400 persons, of whom about 10,500 would have been adult craft specialists. The four *barrios* are largely distinguished by the presence of separate cemeteries that, following the ethnohistoric information (Netherly n.d.), may indicate the presence of four *parcialidades.* Again following ethnohistoric data (Netherly, this volume), the presence of

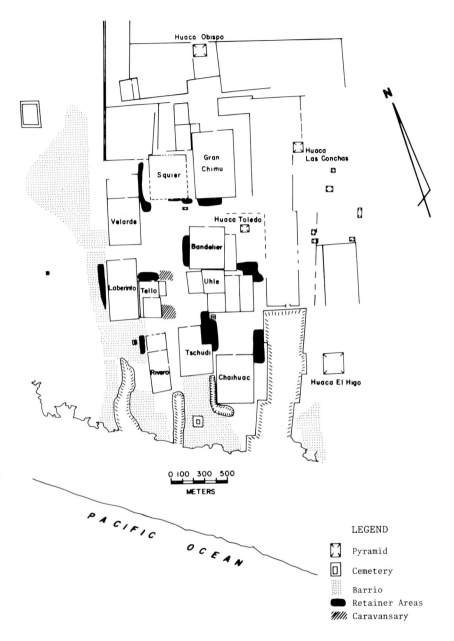

Fig. 5   Chan Chan, with the locations of *barrios*, retainer areas, and caravansaries indicated.

Fig. 6 Architectural complexes, located in the *barrio* south of *ciudadela* Laberinto, containing work areas, kitchens, and small-scale storage facilities.

four *barrios* may indicate that these *parcialidades* were part of a ranked system of moieties.

Within each *barrio* the artisans were housed in single-family domestic units with kitchens, storage areas, work space, and domestic animals (Fig. 6). Most houses contained evidence of both metalworking and the weaving of elaborate textiles, suggesting that both the adult males and females were artisans. The fact that almost all the ingots, together with generally crude hammers, were found in *barrio* houses suggests that the preliminary fabrication of sheet metal was a major activity. The houses themselves were grouped into blocks in two manners: some blocks were formed by adding on extra rooms to an existing core, suggesting that as families grew, they enlarged and subdivided their houses; in the other form (Fig. 6), the boundaries of the block remained stable, but space fluctuated from one household to another by the remodeling of doorways. Both types of blocks suggest that there was a close relationship between neighboring families.

Interspersed among the houses were workshops (Fig. 6, Complex 3; Fig. 7) and administrative areas (Fig. 8). Administrative activities are indi-

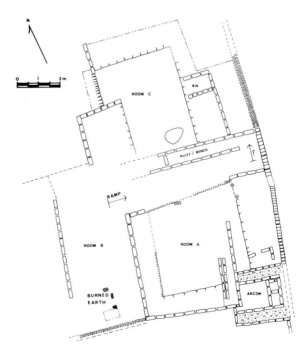

Fig. 7 A workshop, located in the *barrio* west of *ciudadela* Laberinto, which specialized in remelting copper scrap into ingots.

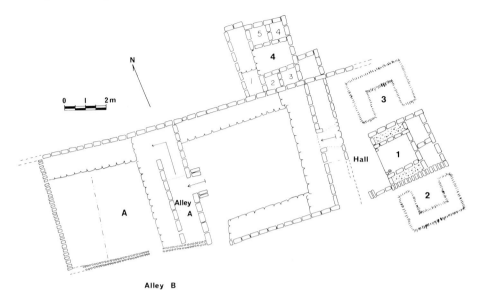

Fig. 8   An administrative facility located near the workshop shown in Fig. 7.

cated by the presence of an *arcón,* a three-sided structure with bins, similar to the more elaborate *audiencia.* These *arcones* are intimately associated with craft production, either being full of raw material, such as cotton, or else filled with tools and partially finished products. In the first case (Fig. 8), the administrative structure may have served to move raw materials to the artisans and to remove the finished products. The second case, however, occurs in workshops (Fig. 6, Complex 3; Fig. 7), probably indicating that some artisans supervised other artisans, and on the access routes to wells (Fig. 9), probably indicating that artisans performed other administrative services within their *barrios.* These indications of artisan/ supervisors conform to the ethnohistoric evidence of artisan/*mandones.* Elite compounds interspersed in *barrio* areas may have housed *principales* (Klymyshyn n.d.).

Workshops were specialized spaces but did not necessarily specialize in one product. The two excavated workshops had *arcones* as well as special benches. Reginaldo de Lizárraga ([1603–06?] 1909: 490–491) provides a description of metalworking from Tumbez, on the far northern coast but still within Chimu territory, in which the worker lay lengthwise on a bench about 20 cm high with his head and arms extending beyond the end of the bench; these workers specialized in making *chaquira* (small beads), and the prone position might have been favored because it brought the workers' eyes closer to the work. Girolamo Benzoni ([1565] 1967: 62–63), in con-

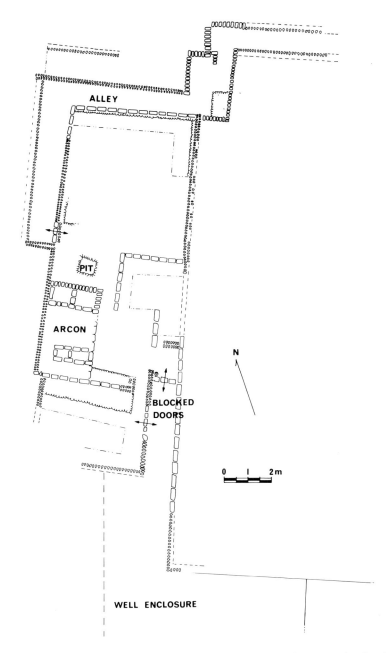

Fig. 9 An *arcón* located on the access route to a well in the *barrio* south of *ciudadela* Laberinto.

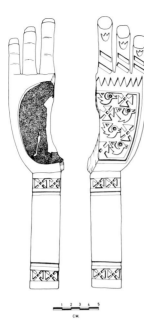

Fig. 10 Front and back views of an elaborately carved wooden hand. Low-relief areas are originally inlaid with copper and an object, probably a mirror, was once set into the palm with bitumen.

trast, provides an illustration of a metalworker from the Quito area sitting on a bench with the work between his feet. In a famous Moche weaving scene, which Christopher Donnan (1976: 131) has interpreted as showing the manufacture of ceremonially important headdresses, the weavers seem to be depicted as sitting on long, roofed benches.

One workshop (Fig. 6, Complex 3) probably concentrated on woodworking, but there is also some evidence there for spinning, weaving, and metalworking. It may be that this shop specialized in inlay. A carved wooden hand elaborately inlaid with copper (Fig. 10) was found there, thus suggesting that both metal and woodworkers plied their trades under a common roof. Furthermore, weaving activities also took place in the shop. The other shop (Fig. 7) concentrated on the melting of metal. Some small lumps of copper may represent prills,[3] but for the most part workers in this shop probably remelted scrap copper into ingots. Crucible fragments were found in the shop, and a *tuyere* (blowtube for creating draft) was found nearby; this last was made of pottery with copper inclusions in the paste and might have been manufactured in the shop itself. Other tools suggest that metal was worked as well as melted in the shop.

Retainer areas have evidence of the same mixture of weaving and metal-

---

[3] Prills are the small droplets or pellets of copper or arsenical copper bronze that formed within a slag matrix during smelting. After smelting, the slag matrix was crushed with large grinding stones to extract the prills. The prills were then remelted to form ingots.

working activity, but the organization is very different. The best evidence for the retainer areas comes from rooms set atop platforms adjacent to *ciudadelas* Velarde, Bandelier, and Squier. The retainer areas differ from the *barrios* in being elevated on artificially constructed platforms and in having different kitchen arrangements. The Velarde retainer area, for example, had a very large kitchen area extending over at least three rooms (Fig. 11). This

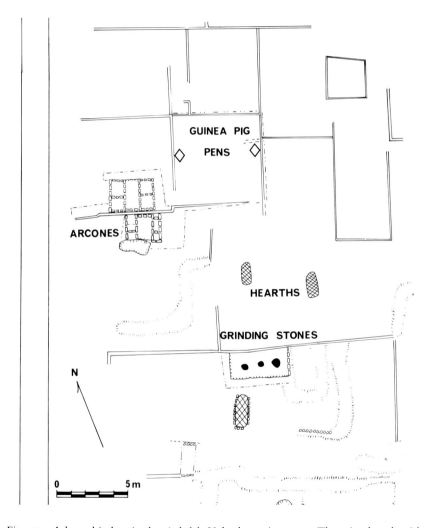

Fig. 11   A large kitchen in the *ciudadela* Velarde retainer area. There is a bench with places for three grinding stones, three hearths, and storage areas in two *arcones*. Two guinea pig pens were also located in the kitchen area.

kitchen had two hearths in one room and another in an adjacent room. There were also spaces for three grinding stones, and the kitchen area included two *arcones*. The presence of this large kitchen area, and the absence of evidence in it for *chicha* production, indicates a different social arrangement from that in the *barrios;* the entire retainer area can be considered a single household, at least in terms of food preparation.

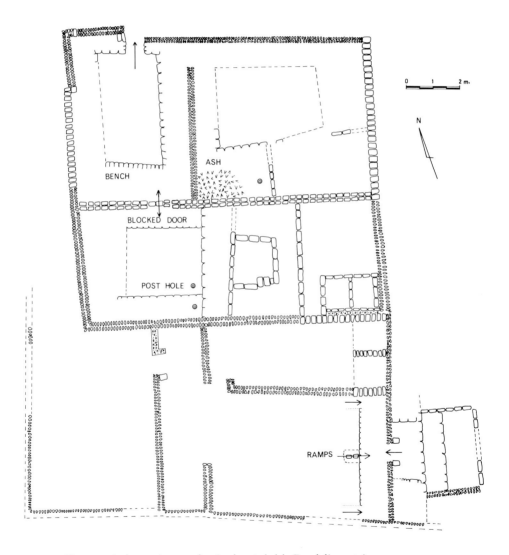

Fig. 12   A domestic complex in the *ciudadela* Bandelier retainer area.

Excavations in the Bandelier retainer area provide additional information on housing. There we excavated almost an entire house (Fig. 12). This house was about the same size as a *barrio* house, but the floors were nicely plastered, rooms were more regularly arranged, and numerous benches were built into the most easily accessible rooms. Significantly, we were unable to locate any kitchen facilities in this house.

In terms of craft production, there is a suggestion that preliminary work, such as the beating out of sheet metal and the spinning of yarn, was less important in these areas and that finishing work was more important. All indications are that the people housed in these areas were of a higher status than those in the *barrios*. The close association with *ciudadelas* and the difference in food preparation facilities permit the interpretation that these people were attached to the lords' households. By the time of the abandonment of the site, there may have been as many as three thousand retainers (Topic and Moseley 1985).

The two caravansaries were located in the center of the site at the terminus of the transportation network. The one most intensively studied (Fig. 13) had a communal kitchen, large corral-like rooms, a platform filled with llama burials, and rooms with multiple sleeping benches (Fig. 14). The other caravansary appears to be similar. They were capable of housing about six hundred people. The fact that there were two communal kitchens and two platforms filled with llama burials again suggests the dual organization discussed by Netherly (n.d., this volume). The caravansaries undoubtedly housed exchange specialists. Some artifactual evidence suggests exchange with the sierra or beyond. Along with other exotic goods, it is likely that two essential raw materials, alpaca wool and metal ingots, were brought into Chan Chan by caravan. There is ample evidence that Chimu trade routes, though not actual Chimu control, extended to the metal-rich Quiruvilca region at the headwaters of the Rio Moche at this time (J. Topic and T. Topic 1985). Alpaca wool was brought into the site in pre-spun and pre-dyed skeins, probably from the Department of Ancash or further south (T. Topic et al. 1987). The relationship between these specialists and the Chimu state is unclear, though it must have been a close one.[4]

[4] Miguel Cornejo and Segundo Vásquez (personal communication, 1986) have recently excavated an area at Chan Chan in which fish were salted and dried. Inasmuch as salted fish was, and still is, a major coastal commodity traded into the highlands, the fish-processing area may be related to the evidence for exchange specialists in the caravansaries. Although neither the exchange specialists nor the fish processors are craftsmen in the strict sense of the term, it is appropriate to mention them in this paper for two reasons: they provide further archaeological evidence for the occupational specialization of coastal populations that the ethnohistorians stress, and their activities can be viewed as supportive of craft production at Chan Chan.

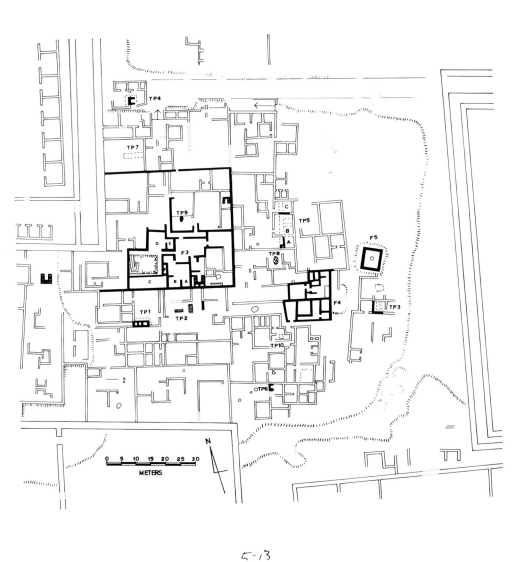

Fig. 13   One of the two caravansaries at Chan Chan. Excavated areas are indicated by solid walls. Note the controlled well access (located bewteen C and D). The artificial platform with llama burials is labeled F5.

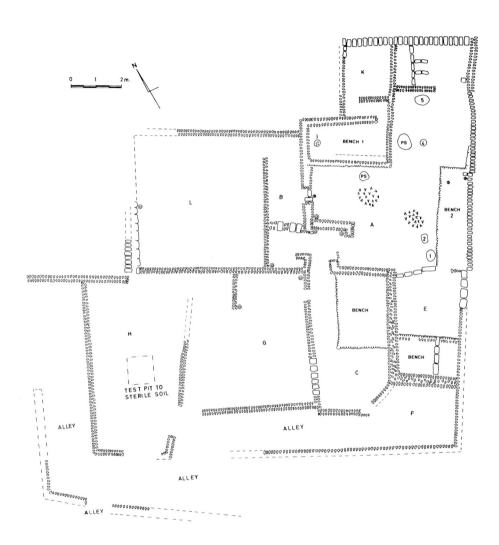

Fig. 14   A living area within the caravansary.

Discussion

The organization of Chan Chan's artisans as reconstructed from the archaeological data is similar to what would be expected from the ethnohistoric information. Both major principles of organization are evident—duality and occupational specialization. There are artisans attached to lords' households as well as those organized in their own *parcialidades*. These *parcialidades* may have had their own *mandones* and even lords, and the *mandones*, at least, were probably artisans. The presence of *mandones* in the shops suggests a guild-like structure of master-apprentices. A number of lines of evidence, including storage facilities and diet (J. Topic n.d.b, 1982; Pozorski 1982) indicate that the artisans contributed only the products of their specialties to the state. These same lines of evidence suggest that most exchange was based on redistribution supervised by the lords or the state. Certainly, too, there were long-distance exchange specialists, probably also supervised closely by the lords and the state.

The evidence provided by the caravansaries at Chan Chan for exchange specialists is perhaps as clear-cut as one could hope for in an archaeological context. It is impossible to tell, however, whether these specialists were merchants, allowed to trade for their own profit, or whether their role was restricted to the management of caravans under the direct control of the lords. The context of these caravansaries, surrounded by elite and monumental architecture in the center of the site, certainly suggests a close association with the elite. Similarly, the exotic material in this area indicates that exchange networks extended at least into the highlands, but these caravansaries also may have served as termini for coastwise exchange. The architecture in these areas lacks any familial connotation and indicates that the exchange specialists were transients rather than permanent residents of the city; in this sense, they can be considered outsiders, but whether they were coastal people, highlanders, or both cannot be determined. Because of the importance of the commodities brought into the capital by the exchange specialists, I find it somewhat surprising that they were not permanently based within the city where they could be more easily monitored and controlled by the elite.

The mixture of artisans at Chan Chan is also somewhat surprising. From the ethnohistoric information, I have the impression that each occupational specialty was associated with its own *parcialidad*. At Chan Chan, however, there was a clear association of distinct specialties (e.g., woodworkers, metalworkers, and weavers) within individual shops, blocks, and *barrios*, which suggests that they were members of the same *parcialidad*. This difference may indicate that artisans at Chan Chan were reorganized by the state; if so, this reorganization was probably a late event and may indicate changing state economic strategies. In any case, the horizontal integration of specialists allows for more immediate cooperation between them to produce compound products such as the copper-inlaid carved-wood hand (with mirror?) (Fig. 10), and pieces of clothing that combine feathers, metal, and cloth (e.g., A. Rowe 1984: figs. 156, 168, 169, and pl. 24). Additionally, horizontal integration allowed for direct contact between woodworkers, who probably made many weaving and spinning tools, and the weavers and spinners who used them. Horizontal integration is, in fact, the most logical manner of organizing craft production both to produce complex elite products and for the efficient large-scale production of utilitarian products.

Finally, the scale of craft production at Chan Chan must be commented upon. The ethnohistoric information indicates that middle-level polities incorporated a number of different occupational specialists, including artisans, but that farmers and fishermen were in the majority; such a polity can be considered self-sufficient. Chan Chan, however, had a tremendous concentration of artisans and cannot be considered self-sufficient. Although it was definitely sustained by rural food producers, the sustaining area need not have been large; the Moche Valley itself probably could have provided the major support for the artisan population with some input from the adjacent Chicama and Viru Valleys. Even when considered within this wider sustaining area, craft production at Chan Chan goes far beyond any level of production required for self-sufficiency. It is clear that these artisans were not serving a local market only.

Similarly, craft production at Chan Chan was not oriented toward supplying only the demands of the elite. While production for elite demand undoubtedly was important, that demand probably could have been met by the retainers. *Barrio* production was oriented toward a larger group of consumers. Metal production in these areas emphasized small utilitarian or ornamental items in copper or arsenical copper bronze. Both the material and its size are significant. Although copper was available on the coast, arsenical copper alloys were imported from highland mines about three days' journey away (Lechtman 1976; J. Topic and T. Topic 1983: fig. 8.2) and almost all late Chimu artifacts are arsenical copper bronze (Lechtman 1979: table 1). Perhaps because the metal had to be shipped in, small objects, such as needles, were more typically produced than large objects. Although some large "digging stick points" have been found at Chan Chan, Lechtman (1979: 21–22) considers these to be "depositories" of metal rather than functional artifacts. In a context in which essential raw materials must be imported from some distance, it would make economic sense to use these materials sparingly and add value to the raw material by labor-intensive processing.

Weaving seems to follow the same pattern as metalworking. Rowe (1984: 32) suggests that two styles, the Pelican Style and the Plain Crescent Headdress Style, might be substantially contemporaneous, the former being favored by the elite, with the latter being produced in larger quantity for wider consumption and export. Support for her observation comes from the fact that the Pelican Style occurs in an elite burial platform, while all the identifiable textile fragments from the *barrios* were executed in the Toothed Crescent Headdress Style (A. Rowe 1984: 32, 105), which is closely related to the Plain Crescent Headdress Style. In that case, *barrio* weavers, like the metalworkers, were oriented toward a large group of consumers. Even these barrio textiles, however, used large quantities of camelid fibers, probably alpaca wool. The uniformity of spin direction and the degree of twist, the narrow range of colors used, and the form in which the yarn is found provide good evidence that the alpaca yarn was brought into Chan Chan in pre-spun and pre-dyed skeins from the highlands of Ancash or further south (A. Rowe 1984: 25; J. Topic n.d.b, 1982; T. Topic et al. 1987). The wool, however, was used only for decorative elements. Some of the *barrio* textiles used wool supplementary wefts to create designs; A. Rowe (1984: 26) has observed that this is a very economical use of the alpaca fiber. Other textiles employ much more wool to produce tapestry bands and panels, but these were commonly appliqued as decorative elements on a cotton ground cloth.

Craft production at Chan Chan differs in several respects from that described ethnohistorically for the middle-level polities. It is larger in scale, both absolutely and proportionately, but more important, it is qualitatively different; the major emphasis of the city is on craft production. This can be seen easily in the large areas devoted to artisan housing and shops. It is also clear that long-distance exchange functioned to supply raw materials and to circulate finished products. Less obvious, perhaps, is the way in which the monumental architecture at Chan Chan was affected by this intensive level of production. As Netherly (1984: 247) has noted, a centralized state bureaucracy was not necessary for the management of rural production in valleys under Chimu control, yet many archaeologists have interpreted the monumental architecture at Chan Chan as evidence for a strongly developed bureaucracy in Chimu society (see especially Day 1982a: 64–65; 1982b: 349). My view is that the bureaucratic aspects of the late monumental architecture, specifically storage and its administration, were closely related to the craft orientation of the city. In support of this interpretation, I have previously (J. Topic n.d.b; Topic and Moseley 1985) outlined the changes that occurred in the bureaucratic aspects of the late monumental architecture coincident with the establishment and expansion of craft production at Chan Chan.

PROVINCIAL CRAFT SPECIALISTS

Recent excavations have documented the presence of craft specialists in the Chimu provinces. Although provincial craft production was highly organized, it differed in magnitude and organization from that at the capital.

I will briefly summarize the provincial information before discussing these differences.

The Northern Provinces

In a series of publications, Izumi Shimada (n.d., 1978, 1982, 1985; Shimada et al. 1982, 1983) has documented a long metallurgical tradition extending from Moche V to the Spanish Conquest in the Lambayeque area. Current evidence (Shimada 1985) suggests that this metallurgical tradition flourished during the Middle Sican Phase (A.D. 900–1100), which saw the initiation of large-scale smelting, great concentrations of metal artifacts in tombs, and possible trade in metal objects over wide areas of Peru and Ecuador. Under the Chimu (A.D. 1350–1470), at least some aspects of this tradition continued.

The best evidence of Chimu-controlled production comes from Cerro de los Cementerios in the Batan Grande region. Chimu control of these smelting operations is attested to by a U-shaped structure set atop a T-shaped platform mound. This structure was associated with four small storage bins that may have held ingots (Shimada et al. 1982, 1983). It is clear that large-scale smelting went on at this site and that the smelting activities took place within a cluster of individual workshops (ibid.). The smelting resulted in prills in a slag matrix, and these prills had to be extracted by crushing the matrix; this extraction process also took place in the workshops. Other aspects of the metallurgical process are not yet clear. The prills had to be remelted into ingots before the metal could be worked into artifacts. This process has not yet been well documented (Shimada et al. 1982: 956). Inverted urns filled with charcoal may have been used to roast ores before smelting (ibid.: 957) or as annealing braziers (Shimada et al. 1983: 45). The prills and ingots tested were shown to contain arsenic (Shimada et al. 1982: 957), and Shimada (1985: 372–374) has discussed several possible ways in which arsenic ores may have been obtained and added to the local, non-arsenical copper ores.

Considerable evidence for metalworking was found by Donnan (personal communication, 1985; this volume [Chotuna]) at Huaca Chotuna, also in the Lambayeque area. There the artisans were housed in a large compound, and the evidence for metalworking again spans several centuries (A.D. 900–1600). There is a brief break in the Huaca Chotuna sequence at about A.D. 1300, and it is tempting to correlate this break with the Chimu conquest of the area; however, the Chimu conquest seems to have taken place slightly later (Donnan, this volume [Naymlap]) and metal production continued, indeed expanded, under Chimu domination (Donnan, personal communication, 1985). The products included needles, tweezers, and personal ornaments. It is quite possible that the prills worked at Chotuna were smelted at Batan Grande, providing evidence of an intraregional exchange network;

certainly there is no evidence for smelting at Chotuna. The metalworkers at Chotuna may provide a good example of artisans attached to the court of an important local lord.

The major ceremonial center of Pacatnamu continued to be occupied after the Chimu conquest of the Jequetepeque Valley. Both before and after the Chimu conquest, the main focus of craft production appears to be weaving, and there was an emphasis on miniature textiles (Bruce 1986a, 1986b; Keatinge 1978). The presence of miniature tunics with horizontal neck and arm openings is an interesting similarity between the Pacatnamu textiles and those of the central coast (Bruce 1986a: 103; 1986b), and Keatinge (1978) has pointed out iconographic similarities between the Pacatnamu textiles and textiles from Pachacamac, a major ceremonial center on the central coast. Both the production and consumption of miniature textiles at Pacatnamu seem to have taken place within a highly ceremonial context: the textiles were some of the offerings associated with the dedicatory burials of young females (Bruce 1986b: 192), while the actual weaving of the miniatures may have been one of the ritual activities that took place at the site (Donnan 1986). Bruce (1986b: 193) notes that the alpaca yarn used in the miniatures is quite similar to the wool yarn used at Chan Chan and may have come from the same highland source.

Although other provincial Chimu centers north of the Moche Valley such as Farfan (Conrad, this volume) and Chiquitoy Viejo have been excavated recently, little evidence of craft production has been reported yet. It may be that artisan areas so far have not been found at these sites or that no artisans were attached to these courts.

The Southern Provinces

South of the Moche Valley, the most important work has centered on the Chimu occupation of the Casma Valley. As part of the project directed by Carol Mackey and A. M. Ulana Klymyshyn, Jerry Moore excavated evidence for craft production at Manchan, an intrusive center, and Laguna II, a co-opted center. In both cases, the evidence was found in cane-walled structures outside the elite compounds, a context more similar to the *barrios* at Chan Chan than to the probable retainer areas at either Chan Chan or Chotuna. Moore (1981) estimates the total population of the cane structures at Manchan between 280 and 420. There is evidence there for metalworking, textile production, and large-scale *chicha* brewing (Mackey and Klymyshyn n.d.: 9–10; this volume). Metal ores are apparently available in the valley and were smelted into prills, although the smelting site has not yet been discovered. As well as producing elaborate textiles in Chimu, Casma, and mixed Casma-Chimu styles, artisans spun alpaca wool into yarn (Mackey and Klymyshyn n.d.: 9, 25; this volume); this is the only well-documented case of the spinning of alpaca wool on the coast, and it may be a reflection of Casma's closeness to the highland sources of wool. The importance of *chicha* to the maintenance of reciprocal relations between the lords and their subjects is repeatedly mentioned in the ethnohistoric data (Netherly n.d.), but Casma provides the first archaeological documentation for large-scale *chicha* brewing on the coast (Moore 1981). It appears that *chicha* production expanded greatly under Chimu domination at Laguna II, but there is as yet no evidence for metalworking or weaving from the Chimu occupation at that site (Mackey and Klymyshyn n.d.: 15–16).

Moore (n.d.a, n.d.b, n.d.c, personal communication, 1985) has kindly provided some preliminary results from Manchan. Much as at Chan Chan, Moore finds that activities that should be carried out by separate *parcialidades* are mixed together within single households, and this leads him to question whether full-time specialists were present. Although *chicha* was brewed in relatively large quantities, Moore (n.d.a) calculates that the direct evidence in at least one house indicates only enough *chicha* for 25–50 person/days of consumption, and, moreover, that house also contained some evidence for fishing, agriculture, woodworking, and weaving. Comparative data on five houses (Moore n.d.c) indicate that one had evidence exclusively of weaving and all had some evidence for weaving. Evidence of metallurgical production was restricted to a single house. All except one house also had some evidence for either fishing or farming as subsistence activities. While admitting that the data are somewhat uneven, Moore (n.d.b) suggests that these households were largely self-supporting, but also engaged in craft activities relating to a supra-household level of exchange. The evidence from Casma is extremely important, and because analysis is still ongoing, we can expect even more detailed results within a short time.

Discussion

Although the state was heavily involved in craft production and concentrated artisans at the capital, artisans also flourished in provincial centers under Chimu domination. Because much of the evidence from provincial centers is still preliminary, organizational details are still tentative. It is clear that the Chimu co-opted the smelting facilities in the north. In earlier times, these facilities were probably under the direct control of the Middle Sican state (Shimada 1985: 377) and were part of an integrated industry that included all stages of manufacture from mining to finished product. The results of Shimada's excavations suggest to me that the Chimu may have reduced this industry to a more restricted emphasis on only mining and smelting. Interestingly, the Inca, while terminating craft production at Chan Chan, may have reinstated integrated metallurgical activities at Cerro de los Cementerios (Shimada et al. 1983: 45). The data from Chotuna indicate that the Chimu did not interfere with artisans attached to the courts of local lords. Chotuna, however, probably did not consume all the metal produced at Cerro de los Cementerios; some must have been shipped to other metalworkers in the north, while part probably was redirected to Chan Chan. Generally, it seems that provincial centers lacked the degree of horizontal integration present at Chan Chan, where weavers, woodworkers, and metalworkers concentrated in one site all contributed their skills to the fabrication of complex artifacts. The data from Manchan, however, do indicate a greater variety of crafts and less specialization. It may well be that the textile industry at Manchan, which is still incompletely analyzed, was more important and more specialized than the metalworking industry (Mackey and Klymyshyn, this volume). Manchan also provides the best provincial evidence for interregional exchange of raw materials, at least in unspun camelid fibers; interregional exchange of partially processed raw materials (i.e., spun and dyed alpaca yarn) is demonstrated at Pacatnamu. The ceremonial context in which weaving activities took place at Pacatnamu appears unique within the sample of Chimu provincial sites discussed.

CONCLUSIONS

The most striking thing about Chimu craft production is its concentration in one center. Obviously, crafts continued to be practiced in the provinces, but on a much smaller scale than in the capital. Although, with the exception of Manchan, we have no population estimates, the relatively small size of the documented artisan areas at Chotuna (40 m × 60 m) and Cerro de los Cementerios (150 m × 200 m) suggests that the populations involved were in the same size range as those at Manchan. The provincial evidence fits well with Ramírez' (1982: 125) estimate that only 5–6 percent of the total population were skilled craftsmen.

The Chan Chan population does not fit well within that estimate. This discord suggests that at the highest level of integration, the state, the economic structure was quite distinct from local norms of organization. The economy of the capital was emphatically based on manufacturing rather than on agriculture. By implication, the highest levels of the Chimu elite based their power largely on control of craft production rather than agricultural production.

Mackey and Klymyshyn (this volume) recognize a similar distinction in their discussion of economic centralization and storage capacities; they note the low storage capacities at provincial centers and the great concentration of storage at Chan Chan. Kolata (this volume) notes that the floorspace devoted to storage fluctuated between about 2,000 and 3,000 m² in the latest three *ciudadelas;* assuming that only one of these *ciudadelas* was functioning at one time, the active storage space in the capital was about 2,500 m². The amount of active storage space at the capital is proportionately large, perhaps half of all known Chimu storage, but it is also probably far less than the storage capacity at a single small Incaic provincial center, such as Huamachuco (T. Topic and J. Topic 1984).

This simple comparison of Chimu and Inca storage capacities illustrates well a fundamental difference in Chimu and Inca state finance (Earle and D'Altroy 1982; D'Altroy and Earle 1985; Moseley 1985). Both economic systems relied on an agricultural base as well as on centrally organized craft production, but at the state level the Chimu relied much more heavily on the latter aspect. The smaller Chimu storage capacities reflect smaller volumes of higher value goods, while the Inca storage pattern allowed for larger volumes of staples.

There are some similarities between the Chimu system and northern Andean chiefdoms. In Ecuador, traders or *mindalaes* were at times monopolized by the largest chiefdom in an area, in Incaic Quito they were quartered in the center of the city near the palaces of the elite and often imported high-value raw materials rather than finished craft goods (Salomon 1978: 154–155; 1977–78: 236, 238). Colombian chiefs valued metalsmiths highly, seem to have exercised strict control over them, and even traded or leased them to other chiefs; these smiths were apparently much more mobile than their Chimu counterparts, however (Bray 1974: 46–47).

Although these economic systems are similar in some respects to the Chimu pattern, the best antecedent for the Chimu system is found on the Peruvian North Coast itself in polities such as Sicán. It is most likely that Chan Chan was reorganized after the conquest of Lambayeque and at that time adopted some aspects of Sicán organization as well as co-opting metallurgical production at Cerro de los Cementerios.

Only after the conquest of Lambayeque did the distinctive Chimu economy discussed in this paper appear. The earlier Chimu military expansions relied on a different economic base. In fact, there is little reason to believe that an economy based largely on artisan production is compatible with large-scale military expansion; that would require the broader logistical base so evident in Inca storage. Craft production at Chan Chan, however, did provide the Chimu elite with an effective means of maintaining their status vis-à-vis the provincial lords under peacetime conditions and, perhaps, of extending commercial relations or economic dependence beyond the area subdued by force.

BIBLIOGRAPHY

BENNETT, WENDELL C.

    1939   *Archaeology of the North Coast of Perú.* Anthropological Papers of the American Museum of Natural History 37 (1). New York.

BENZONI, M. GIROLAMO

    [1565] *Dell'Historie Del Mondo Nuovo* (Carlos Radicati Di Primeglio, trans.).
    1967   *Comentarios del Peru,* numero 5. Universidad de San Marcos, Lima.

BRAY, WARWICK

    1974   The Organization of the Metal Trade. In *El Dorado: The Gold of Ancient Colombia:* 41–54. Center for Inter-American Relations and The American Federation of Arts, New York.

BRUCE, SUSAN LEE

    1986a The Audiencia Room of the Huaca 1 Complex. In *The Pacatnamú Papers, Volume 1* (Christopher B. Donnan and Guillermo A. Cock, eds.): 95–108. Museum of Cultural History, University of California, Los Angeles.

    1986b Textile Miniatures from Pacatnamú, Peru. In *The Junius B. Bird Conference on Andean Textiles* (Ann Pollard Rowe, ed.): 183–204. The Textile Museum, Washington, D.C.

D'ALTROY, TERENCE N., and TIMOTHY K. EARLE

    1985   Staple Finance, Wealth Finance, and Storage in the Inka Political Economy. *Current Anthropology* 26: 187–206.

DAY, KENT C.

    1982a Ciudadelas: Their Form and Function. In *Chan Chan: Andean Desert City* (Michael E. Moseley and Kent C. Day, eds.): 55–66. University of New Mexico Press, Albuquerque.

    1982b Storage and Labor Services: A Production and Management Design for the Andean Area. In *Chan Chan: Andean Desert City* (Michael E. Moseley and Kent C. Day, eds.): 333–350. University of New Mexico Press, Albuquerque.

DONNAN, CHRISTOPHER B.

    1976   *Moche Art and Iconography.* U.C.L.A. Latin America Center Publications. University of California at Los Angeles.

    1986   An Elaborate Textile Fragment from the Major Quadrangle. In *The Pacatnamú Papers, Volume 1* (Christopher B. Donnan and Guillermo A. Cock, eds.): 109–116. Museum of Cultural History, University of California, Los Angeles.

EARLE, TIMOTHY, and TERENCE D'ALTROY

    1982   Storage Facilities and State Finance in the Upper Mantaro Valley, Perú. In *Contexts for Prehistoric Exchange* (Jonathan E. Ericson and Timothy K. Earle, eds.): 265–290. Academic Press, New York.

KEATINGE, RICHARD W.

    1978   The Pacatnamú Textiles. *Archaeology* 31(2): 30–41.

KLYMYSHYN, ALEXANDRA M. ULANA
    n.d.   Intermediate Architecture, Chan Chan, Peru. Ph.D. dissertation, Department of Anthropology, Harvard University, 1976.

LECHTMAN, HEATHER N.
    1976   A Metallurgical Site Survey in the Peruvian Andes. *Journal of Field Archaeology* 3: 1–42.
    1979   Issues in Andean Metallurgy. In *Pre-Columbian Metallurgy of South America* (Elizabeth P. Benson, ed.): 1–40. Dumbarton Oaks, Washington, D.C.

LIZÁRRAGA, FRAY REGINALDO DE
[1603–06?]   Descripción breve de toda la tierra del Perú, Tucumán, Río de la Plata,
    1909   y Chile. In *Historiadores de Indias* 2 (M. Serrano y Sanz, ed.): 485–660. Nueva Biblioteca de Autores Españoles 15 (Marcelino Menéndez y Pelayo, series director). Bailliére é Hijos, Madrid.

MACKEY, CAROL J., and ALEXANDRA M. ULANA KLYMYSHYN
    n.d.   Political Integration in Prehispanic Perú. Final Project Report to the National Science Foundation, 1981–82.

MOORE, JERRY
    1981   Chimu Socio-Economic Organization: Preliminary Data from Manchan, Casma Valley, Peru. *Ñawpa Pacha* 19: 115–128. The Institute of Andean Studies, Berkeley.
    n.d.a   Technology, Social Context, and Archaeological Correlates of Prehistoric Maize *chicha* Production in Perú.
    n.d.b   Lower Class Residences at Manchan. Paper presented at the 24th Annual Meeting of the Institute of Andean Studies, Berkeley, 1983.
    n.d.c   Political and Economic Integration of the Lower Class: Archaeological Investigations at Manchan, Casma Valley, Perú. Paper presented at the 83rd Annual Meeting of the American Anthropological Association, Denver, 1984.

MOSELEY, MICHAEL E.
    1975   Chan Chan: Andean Alternative of the Pre-Industrial City. *Science* 187: 219–225.
    1985   Comment on "Staple Finance, Wealth Finance, and Storage in the Inka Political Economy" by Terence N. D'Altroy and Timothy K. Earle. *Current Anthropology* 26(2): 199–200.

NETHERLY, PATRICIA
    1984   The Management of Late Andean Irrigation Systems on the North Coast of Peru. *American Antiquity* 49(2): 227–254.
    n.d.   Local Level Lords on the North Coast of Peru. Ph.D. dissertation, Department of Anthropology, Cornell University, 1977.

POZORSKI, SHELIA
    1982   Subsistence Systems in the Chimú State. In *Chan Chan: Andean Desert City* (Michael E. Moseley and Kent C. Day, eds): 177–196. University of New Mexico Press, Albuquerque.

PRICE, BARBARA
  1980   The Truth Is Not in Accounts but in Account Books: On the Epistemological Status of History. In *Beyond the Myths of Culture: Essays in Cultural Materialism*. Academic Press, New York.

RABINOWITZ, JOEL
  1983   La Lengua Pescadora: The Lost Dialect of Chimu Fishermen. In *Investigations of the Andean Past: Papers from the First Annual Northeast Conference on Andean Archaeology and Ethnohistory* (Daniel H. Sandweiss, ed.): 243–267. Latin American Studies Program, Cornell University.

RAMÍREZ HORTON, SUSAN
  1982   Retainers of the Lords or Merchants: A Case of Mistaken Identity? In *El hombre y su ambiente en los Andes centrales* (Luís Millones and Hiroyasu Tomoeda, eds.): 123–136. Senri Ethnological Studies 10. Museo Nacional de Etnología, Osaka.

ROSTWOROWSKI DE DIEZ CANSECO, MARÍA
  1961   *Curacas y sucesiones: Costa norte*. Imprenta Minerva, Lima.
  1970   Mercaderes del valle de Chincha en la época prehispánica: Un documento y unos comentarios. *Revista Española de Antropología Americana* 5: 135–178. Madrid.
  1975   Pescadores, artisanos, y mercaderes costeños en el Perú prehispánico. *Revista del Museo Nacional* 41: 311–349. Lima.
  1977a Coastal Fishermen, Merchants, and Artisans in Pre-Hispanic Perú. In *The Sea in the Pre-Columbian World* (Elizabeth P. Benson, ed.): 167–186. Dumbarton Oaks, Washington, D.C.
  1977b *Etnia y sociedad: Costa peruana prehispánica*. Historia Andina 4. Instituto de Estudios Peruanos, Lima.
  1983   *Estructuras andinas del poder. Ideología religiosa y política*. Historia Andina 10. Instituto de Estudios Peruanos, Lima.

ROWE, ANNE POLLARD
  1984   *Costumes and Featherwork of the Lords of Chimor: Textiles from Perú's North Coast*. The Textile Museum, Washington, D.C.

ROWE, JOHN HOWLAND
  1948   The Kingdom of Chimor. *Acta Americana* 6 (1–2): 26–59. Mexico City.

SALOMON, FRANK
  1977–78 Pochteca and Mindalá: A Comparison of Long-Distance Traders in Ecuador and Mesoamerica. *Journal of the Steward Anthropological Society* 9(1/2): 231–246.
  1978   *Ethnic Lords of Quito in the Age of the Incas: The Political Economy of North Andean Chiefdoms*. Latin American Studies Program Dissertation Series Number 77, Cornell University.

SHIMADA, IZUMI
  1978   Economy of a Prehistoric Urban Context: Commodity and Labor Flow at Moche V Pampa Grande, Peru. *American Antiquity* 43(4): 569–592.

1982   Horizontal Archipelago and Coast-Highland Interaction in North Peru. In *El hombre y su ambiente en los Andes centrales* (Luís Millones and Hiroyasu Tomoeda, eds.): 137–210. Senri Ethnological Studies 10. National Museum of Ethnology, Osaka.

1985   Perception, Procurement and Management of Resources: Archaeological Perspective. In *Andean Ecology and Civilization* (Shozo Masuda, Izumi Shimada, and Craig Morris, eds.): 357–400. University of Tokyo Press, Tokyo.

n.d.   Socioeconomic Organization at Moche V Pampa Grande, Peru: Prelude to a Major Transformation. Ph.D. dissertation, Department of Anthropology, University of Arizona, 1976.

SHIMADA, IZUMI, STEPHEN M. EPSTEIN, and ALAN F. CRAIG

1982   Batan Grande: A Prehistoric Metallurgical Center in Peru. *Science* 216: 952–959.

1983   The Metallurgical Process in Ancient North Peru. *Archaeology* 36(5): 38–45.

TOPIC, JOHN R.

1980   Excavaciones en los barrios populares de Chanchan. *Chanchan: Metrópoli chimú* (Rogger Ravines, ed.): 267–282. Instituto de Estudios Peruanos, Lima.

1982   Lower-Class Social and Economic Organization at Chan Chan. In *Chan Chan: Andean Desert City* (Michael E. Moseley and Kent C. Day, eds.): 145–176. University of New Mexico Press, Albuquerque.

n.d.a   A Lower-Class Residential Area of Chan Chan: Initial Excavations. B.A. honors thesis, Harvard University, 1970.

n.d.b   The Lower Class at Chan Chan: A Qualitative Approach. Ph.D. dissertation, Department of Anthropology, Harvard University, 1977.

TOPIC, JOHN R., and MICHAEL E. MOSELEY

1985   Chan Chan: A Case Study of Urban Change in Peru. *Ñawpa Pacha* 21: 153–182.

TOPIC, JOHN R., and THERESA L. TOPIC

1983   Coast-Highland Relations in Northern Perú: Some Observations on Routes, Networks, and Scales of Interaction. In *Civilization in the Ancient Americas: Essays in Honor of Gordon R. Willey* (Richard M. Leventhal and Alan L. Kolata, eds.): 237–259). University of New Mexico and Peabody Museum Presses, Albuquerque and Cambridge.

1985   Coast-Highland Relations in Northern Perú: The Structure and Strategy of Interaction. In *Status, Structure and Stratification* (Marc Thompson, María Teresa García, and François J. Kense, eds.): 55–65. Chac Mool, University of Calgary.

TOPIC, THERESA LANGE., and JOHN R. TOPIC

1984   *Huamachuco Archaeological Project: Preliminary Report on the Third Season, June-August 1983.* Trent University Occasional Papers in Anthropology, Number 1. Department of Anthropology, Trent University, Peterborough.

John R. Topic

TOPIC, THERESA LANGE, THOMAS H. McGREEVY, and JOHN R. TOPIC

    1987   A Comment on the Breeding and Herding of Llamas and Alpacas on the North Coast of Peru. *American Antiquity* 52: 832–835.

WACHTEL, NATHAN

    1977   *The Vision of the Vanquished: The Spanish Conquest of Peru through Indian Eyes 1530–1570.* The Harvester Press, Sussex.

    1984   The Indian and the Spanish Conquest. In *The Cambridge History of Latin America* 1 (Leslie Bethell, ed.): 207–248. Cambridge University Press, Cambridge.

Territorial Expansion and the Kingdom of Chimor

THERESA LANGE TOPIC

TRENT UNIVERSITY

INTRODUCTION

T HE KINGDOM OF CHIMOR, between the years A.D. 900 and 1470, brought under its control a territory more extensive than that of any previous coastal society in prehistoric Peru. The limits of Chimu control are generally conceded to be Tumbez in the north and Chillon in the south, giving the Chimu Empire a coastwise extent of more than 1,000 km. The use of the term *empire* is appropriate here, because peoples of diverse cultural tradition, political complexity, and language were incorporated into this far-reaching polity.

This paper will examine the Chimu expansion, looking at the information available from ethnohistoric sources and the archaeological data that pertain to fortifications, military activity, and imposition of administration on subject territories. These are obviously two very different types of evidence. Alone, neither one allows a very satisfactory reconstruction of the expansion. A considerable amount of published and unpublished archaeological data have accumulated on the expansion, but many gaps remain.[1] The dating of particular constructions and events is often less precise than we would like. In addition, certain problems consistently occur in the interpretation of remains of prehistoric militarism (J. Topic and T. Topic 1987). The few available ethnohistoric sources on pre-Incaic Chimor must also be used cautiously. Are these accounts to be read as history, as myth, or as

---

[1] Most of the new information on Chimu fortifications presented in this chapter was gathered by the Prehistoric Fortifications Project between 1977 and 1980. This project was directed by John R. Topic and Theresa Lange Topic, and funded by the Social Sciences and Humanities Research Council of Canada and by the Committee on Research at Trent University. The project surveyed sierra fortifications in the headwaters of the Chicama, Moche, and Viru Valleys during the summers of 1977–79. In 1980, the project was based in Trujillo and investigated fortication features in the middle Moche Valley between altitudes of 200 and 1,200 m above sea level. Also during 1980, selected coastal fortifications between the Jequetepeque and Nepeña Valleys were surveyed. The assistance of the many Peruvians, Canadians, and Americans who worked on the project is gratefully acknowledged.

some other sort of information about the past? As will be shown, the ethnohistoric accounts refer to the Chimu expansion in terms of very specific events, individuals, and relationships. This specificity means that the expansion provides a good test case with which to assess the degree to which the accounts can be read as "true" history.

THE ETHNOHISTORIC SOURCES

Ethnohistoric information on the pre-Incaic Chimu Empire is limited. Patricia Netherly (this volume) draws a distinction between Spanish administrative and judicial records, which relate to the post-Conquest world but shed some light on pre-Incaic North Coast society, and oral traditions persisting from Chimu times and recorded after the Spanish Conquest. This latter group of accounts is of interest here, but they are few in number and make only passing mention of territorial expansion and military matters.

The Anonymous History of 1604 (Vargas Ugarte 1936: 232–233) is a very cryptic account of the Chimu dynasty, but it is invaluable because it focuses on the home valley of the dynasty and provides a list of rulers and their exploits. This source states that Taycanamo founded the dynasty, and that his son Guacricaur ". . adquiriendo mas señorio que su Padre fue ganando yndios y principales deste valle." The third ruler, Ñançenpinco, in turn conquered the Moche Valley up to the *cabezadas*[2] of the sierra, and extended his control along the coast south to Santa, and north to the Jequetepeque Valley. Six or seven rulers are left unnamed, and their achievements are not detailed. Minchançaman, the last independent Chimu ruler, is credited with conquering the area from Chillon in the south to Tumbez in the north. Minchançaman was conquered by the Inca Topa Yapanqui ". . . con mucha fuerza de armas y gente" (Vargas Ugarte 1936: 232).

Antonio de la Calancha ([1638–39] 1974) prepared a multivolume work that dealt primarily with the history of the Augustinian order in Peru, but included information on a wide variety of Incaic and pre-Incaic groups, places, and individuals. In his description of the Pacasmayo (or Jequetepeque) Valley (ibid.: 1225–1235), he attributes the conquest of the valley only to "Chimu Capac," a rich and powerful lord from Trujillo. A skilled "capitán" named Pacatnamu was entrusted with the subjugation of the new territory, and he was—after much difficult fighting—successful. He stayed on as governor and was remembered as a good one. The locale from which

---

[2] The term *cabezadas* has been variously translated as ". . . the upper part of the valley toward its mountain headwaters . . ." (Rowe 1946; note 2), and as ". . . the *cabezadas* (the beginnings) of the Sierra . . ." (Kosok 1965: 74). The *Vocabulario Andaluz* (1951) defines *cabezada* as "parte superior de un valle en pendiente rápida." In *Diccionario de autoridades* (1976) the term is discussed as follows: "Se llama en algunas partes la frente de las tierras de pan llevar, que están más levantadas que las otras. . . ." These definitions do not help us get a sense of how far inland the early conquest might have extended.

he administered the valley was supposedly called Pacatnamu, in his honor (a locale now identified as Farfan; see Conrad, this volume). Calancha does not specify who was responsible for the expansion from Tumbez to the southern border (which he sets at Paramonga). He states only that it was a Chimu ". . . Cacique . . . siendo de natural brioso, de ánimo alentado, i de coraçón anbicioso . . ." (ibid.: 1235).

Miguel Cabello Balboa ([1586] 1951: 327–330) gives us little direct information on the Chimu Empire before the Inca, but provides some useful information on the incorporation of the Lambayeque complex. According to his account, power in the Lambayeque dynasty passed from the founder Naymlap to his son Cium, and on through ten successors with no mention of conquest, intrigue, or any of the usual dynastic activities. The account implies that twelve sons of Cium colonized different parts of the valley complex, perhaps forming a secondary level of authority. The thirteenth ruler, Fempellec (". . . el último y mas desdichado de esta generación . . ."), was executed by his subjects. After an interval described only as "muchos días," Chimu Capac came with an invincible army and took control of the valleys. A governor was left in charge of Lambayeque, and his son and grandson succeeded him in that position. During the grandson's tenure news came of the Inca in Cajamarca.

Although the information in these accounts is very limited, it is sufficient for the construction of a very cursory outline of Chimu military history. The Anonymous History is the most complete, presenting as it does three events: (a) the consolidation of the Chimu heartland, (b) the conquest from Santa north to Jequetepeque, and (c) expansion to the maximum extent of the empire. The information in Calancha on the Jequetepeque Valley is one retelling of the second event, while Cabello Balboa's discussion of the Lambayeque dynasty provides a very minimal amount of information relating to the third. The Anonymous History links the first event to Guacricaur, the second to Ñançenpinco, and the third to Minchançaman. The other two sources neither corroborate nor contradict, as each identifies the Chimu ruler responsible for conquest only as "Chimo Capac"; this term translates roughly as "mighty Chimu" and is best understood as a title rather than a name. For the moment we will ignore the question of assigning individuals to events (but see Conrad, this volume, and Donnan, this volume [Naymlap]) and focus only on the archaeological evidence that might help to determine whether the conquest proceeded in this step-like fashion.

THE ARCHAEOLOGICAL DATA

There are a variety of methodological problems inherent in reconstructing Chimu military history from archaeological remains. Sites that served military functions tend to be difficult of access, unimpressive, and poorly preserved. Dating these sites is a problem. The Chimu ceramic sequence is still not as finely tuned as one might like, and the specialized assemblages from forts are difficult to tie into chronologies based on collections from other sorts of contexts. Most daunting is the macro-regional scale on which remains of the Chimu conquest need to be studied. A great deal of information is available on Chimu militarism, although the core area of the empire is overrepresented in comparison to the more peripheral valleys. This information does suggest that the Chimu expansion took place in three stages, and the following discussion considers each stage in turn.

Consolidation Stage

An early stage of the Moche Valley consolidation encompassing the founding of Chan Chan, construction of early compounds there, and definition of territory may have begun about A.D. 900 and continued to A.D. 1000 or 1050. This early phase of pre-urban development at Chan Chan is poorly dated and incompletely understood, inasmuch as later construction has destroyed or buried much of the area at the south end of the site that was in use at that time. The scale of occupation posited by John Topic and Michael Moseley (1985: fig. 23) for this phase is modest and on a scale that might be expected of lords of only local importance struggling to assert authority over a single medium-sized valley.

Fortification features that probably relate to this early stage of consolidation in the Moche Valley were surveyed by Fortifications Project personnel in 1977 and 1980. The two prominent hills that flank the valley neck, Cerro Galindo and Cerro Oreja, are two such features (see Fig. 1). Both hills were found to be fortified, and early Chimu ceramics were associated with the defensive construction. Cerro Oreja is a steep hill on the south side of the river whose peak lies 604 m above sea level; on a clear day the ocean, 17 km to the southwest, is visible, and a good view can be had 10 km upvalley to the point at which the river turns behind a hill. Projecting rock masses near the peak were modified into salient angles overlooking all directions except the east. The approach up the hill is from that direction, and it was heavily protected by small terraces overlooking the path. While these minor modifications of the hill probably date to this early phase, a massive structure on the peak and a cluster of thirty-five to forty barracks-like rooms north of and below the peak may well date later; reoccupation and illegal looting obscure the situation. The earlier ceramics fit broadly into Topic and Moseley's (1985: fig. 4a, b) Ceramics Phases 1 and 2 as defined at Chan Chan.

Across the river atop Cerro Galindo several clusters of rooms and platforms were built early in the Late Intermediate period. On the more gently sloping north flank two concentric parapets were built; the rest of the summit is defended only by cliffs. Access into the summit architecture was possible from either the west or east, and paths up the hill were not as

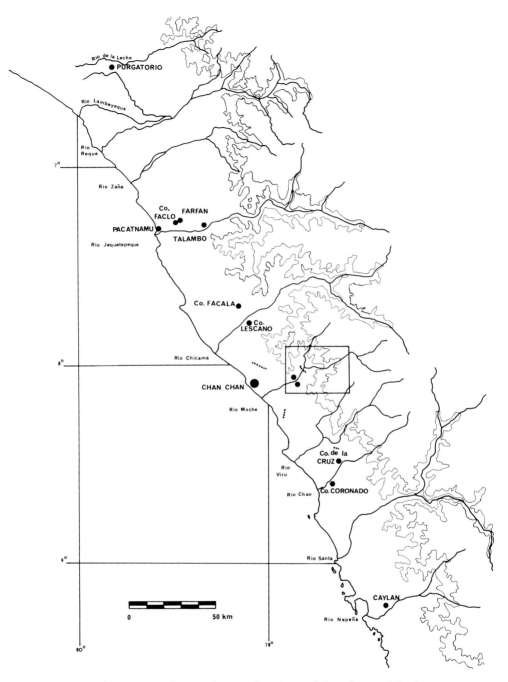

Fig. 1   Northern coast of Peru, showing locations of sites discussed in the text.
Walls in the Moche and Viru Valleys are represented by dotted lines. The 1,000- and
2,000-m contour intervals are shown. The area in the inset is shown at larger scale in
Fig. 2.

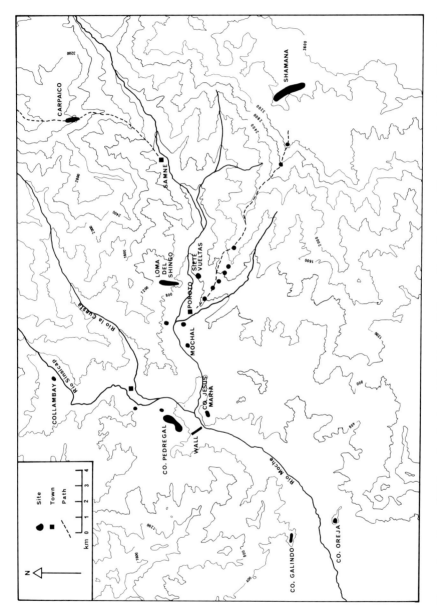

Fig. 2   Locations of Chimu sites in the middle Moche Valley and its tributaries. The two paths indicated by dashed lines lead to sierra centers of major importance during the Late Intermediate period.

tightly defended as they were at Cerro Oreja. Sherds included a high proportion of bowls, as well as heavy rims from either large bowls or *ollas*. There is relatively little ceramic and other refuse, and the site probably saw only brief use. J. Topic (personal communication, 1980) considers the ceramic assemblage to date slightly later than the early component from the Cerro Oreja fortifications.

Ten kilometers further inland at the juncture of the Rio de la Cuesta and Rio Moche, an occupation on the south slope of Cerro Pedregal may mark the furthest inland control by the early Chimu, at a strategic point where the valley bifurcates and two routes penetrate into the higher elevation midvalleys and the sierra (see Fig. 2). Remains of a wall 2–3 m wide run across the narrow floodplain of the river at this point; the wall cannot be traced far into modern fields and brush, but its trajectory strongly suggests that it would have run the 1-km distance from the steep rocky slopes of Cerro Pedregal on the north to the sheer face of Cerro Jesus Maria on the south side of the river. The wall must have been built before the consolidation stage of Chimu expansion; Chimu sherds consistent with early dating were embedded in sediments washed up behind the wall.

The wall lies at 325 m above sea level, in the transition zone between coastal and *chaupiyunga*[3] environmental zones. *Chaupiyunga* populations were politically independent in the Moche and Viru Valleys well into the Early Intermediate period, as shown by distinctive ceramic styles. Coastal pressure becomes evident by Moche III times, and the limit of actual control must have fluctuated until the end of the Middle Horizon. Consolidation phase control by the Chimu in the middle valley seems not to have moved much beyond the wall at the junction of the rivers. A wall of this sort must be understood as both a defensive construction and as a definition of territory; the line followed by the wall was a reminder to groups on both sides that a change in group affiliation occurred here. The wall and the ethnic division it represents would continue to be important even after midvalley groups were absorbed into the expanding Chimu Empire. The later Chimu built a fortress and settlement on Cerro Jesus Maria, and a lookout station atop Cerro Pedregal; this continued attention underscores the strategic importance of this sector of the valley.

Other walls in the Moche Valley may also have served to define space during this earliest Chimu phase. A massive construction on the north side of the Moche Valley known as the La Cumbre Wall runs 7.5 km southeast

---

[3] The *chaupiyunga* zone on the western slopes of the Andes corresponds to the midvalley stretches of most of the rivers draining into the Pacific. This zone is sunny and very warm, lying above the coastal floodplains, which are blanketed by fog from June to September. Agriculture in the *chaupiyunga* is normally dependent on irrigation, as precipitation is rare below 2,300 m above sea level. Netherly (1988: 264) sets elevational boundaries for the *chaupiyunga* ecozone at 800–1,200 m at 12° S. Lat. and 300–1,800 m at 9° S. Lat.

from Cerro Campana to the rocky slopes behind Cerro Cabras (Fig. 1); it is difficult to date the construction precisely, but it post-dates Moche Phase IV (Beck n.d.: 85–86). On the Pampa Salaverry on the south side of the valley, a shorter wall defines the southern edge of the valley (Fig. 1), but it cannot be dated (Beck n.d.: 68).

It is quite likely that during this early stage of consolidation at least parts of the neighboring Viru and Chicama Valleys would have become allied with and subject to the Moche Valley dynasty. As Netherly (personal communication, 1983) has pointed out, in a zone of closely spaced rivers like the Chicama-Moche-Viru area, the economic and social ties between groups on the southern side of one valley and the northern side of its southerly neighbor may be as strong as between groups on opposite sides of the same river. The "consolidation" stage of Chimu history may well have included rebuilding and strengthening of alliances with adjacent coastal populations who had, after all, only recently been linked to the Moche center at Huaca del Sol.

On the south side of the Chicama Valley is a fortified site, Cerro Lescano, with early Chimu pottery similar to that at Cerro Oreja, and with slingstones piled behind defensive walls. The site could be either an early fort or a place of refuge. While ceramic cross-ties at this early stage of Chimu development cannot be assumed to imply political control by Moche Valley lords, they do constitute evidence for close associations between the populations of the two valleys.

Construction was begun at a much larger place of refuge on the opposite side of the Rio Chicama at Cerro Facala, but this unfinished site probably dates somewhat later than Cerro Lescano.

In the Viru Valley early Chimu ceramics are associated with a series of walls and small structures built in the upper reaches of the Huacapongo drainage in a *quebrada* that allows access into the Chao Valley to the south. If the ceramic markers for this Chimu Phase 1 were more abundant, it might be possible to assign several other complexes combining walls and hilltop construction in this part of the Viru Valley to that phase.

This early round of consolidation clearly needs more study, but the information now available indicates that the major concerns were the demarcation of territory and defense. Links were probably reforged with groups and elites in the neighboring valleys, providing a political basis for future expansion.

The First Wave of Conquest

A second and more aggressive stage of expansion may date between about A.D. 1130 and 1200, in Early Phase 3 as defined by ceramic markers (Topic and Moseley 1985: 159). The best evidence for expansion comes from valleys to the north and south of the Chimu heartland.

The conquest of Chao certainly falls into this stage. In this small valley, two very suggestive pieces of evidence were encountered by the Fortifications Project in 1980. Cerro de la Cruz (Fig. 1) is a site of local tradition with non-Chimu ceramics, built well inland, just outside the zone of ancient irrigation and near an inland pass from the Viru Valley into Chao. Domestic structures were built on terraces ascending the flanks of a crescent-shaped hill (see aerial photograph in Kosok 1965: 184). The habitation area is protected by up to three concentric stone walls; the walls are provided in many places with parapets consisting of benches and breastworks. A dry moat forms an outer line of defense around part of the hill. Excavations carried out at the site by other workers produced dates of A.D. 720 ± 60 and A.D. 880 ± 70 (Cárdenas 1979); these dates indicate the earlier end of the occupation span. The Fortifications Project recovered evidence of a siege at the site, but no fighting. Outside the site's defensive walls and moats on the west and northwest are piles of rounded stones, selected for size (slightly smaller than fist-sized). Similar stonepiles elsewhere have been interpreted as ammunition for slingers (Topic and Topic 1987; T. Topic n.d.), but such piles are normally found within site boundaries, along the inside faces of defensive walls. The presence of stonepiles outside the site walls implies that a hostile force took up positions surrounding Cerro de la Cruz. A thin scattering of Chimu sherds across the site suggests that the invaders were Chimu who stockpiled ammunition outside the moat surrounding the site; the fact that the ammunition was never used implies that the invasion succeeded without a battle.

Although the Cerro de la Cruz siege cannot be dated, confirmation of the events outlined above and their date is provided by the construction of a Chimu fortification on Cerro Coronado, 10 km downstream but still 10 km from the ocean. Cerro Coronado consists of two peaks, a steep northeast one and a more gently sloping southwest one, with a saddle connecting the two. The summits are only 40–50 m above the valley floor, but even this slight elevation provides a good overview of the lower Chao Valley and the desert stretches to the north and south. The site is beside the modern Panamerican Highway and is well located to control traffic moving north and south. The defenses are constructed on the southwest peak, which has three concentric defensive walls with offset doorways and, at the summit, an artificially leveled platform. The walls are roughly faced stone with rubble fill, about 1.5 m high on the outer face. *Algorrobo* branches in the fill helped to consolidate the loose rubble. Along the inner face of the lowest defensive wall, quantities of fist-sized river cobbles were found on the ground, undoubtedly intended to serve as slingstones. There were numerous small stone-faced terraces on the flanks of both peaks, but there were no structures on them and very little domestic refuse was observed. The fort seems to have been in use for only a limited time. An organic sample from the site produced a radiocarbon date of A.D. 1130 ± 60 (Cárdenas 1979).

Information on the Chimu incorporation of the Santa Valley is not yet available. That valley contains a high concentration of defensive constructions (David Wilson 1983, and personal communication, 1980), but most date earlier in the sequence.

Expansion north into the Jequetepeque Valley occurred at roughly the same time as the expansion south into Chao. Richard Keatinge and Geoffrey Conrad (1983) have identified Farfan as the Chimu center constructed after the conquest of the valley, and Conrad (this volume) cites dates of A.D. 1155 ± 130 and 1250 ± 75 from early contexts in Compound II at that site. These dates are corroborated by comparable ceramics and similarly sized adobes from both the southwestern sector of *ciudadela* Uhle at Chan Chan and the small Chimu rural administrative center of El Milagro de San Jose.

There is good evidence for a battle having been fought in the Jequetepeque Valley at Talambo, a site of local tradition. This large site was constructed on the flanks of rocky hills at the valley neck, on the north side overlooking the river (see Fig. 1). The site may not have been the valley's dominant center; Keatinge and Conrad (1983: 259) suggest that political control was not highly centralized in the Jequetepeque Valley before the Chimu conquest, and that Talambo may have been only one of several centers in this hydrologically complex valley. A series of stone walls defend the very diverse architecture within the site boundaries at Talambo (see aerial photograph in Kosok 1965: 124–125). Several transects made by the Fortifications Project outside the main wall revealed an intriguing pattern of distribution of cobbles. Within the site boundary the cobbles were found only along the top of the innermost defensive wall at the very summit of the site. Outside the lower walls, many were found on the ground, in increasing frequencies up to 40 m out, then in decreasing frequencies out to 80 m. Many of the stones had apparently broken on impact with the ground or other obstacles. The size range of these stones is larger than for similar stones that have been called "slingstones" in other contexts, and it is interesting that the stones actually used traveled relatively short distances; it is possible that many or all of them were thrown rather than slung. Similar unsorted stones, possibly for throwing, were noted by Fortifications Project personnel atop walls at Pacatnamu and at Charcape in the same valley.

Talambo's location at the valley neck was an important one, overlooking the valley's water supply as well as the route eastward to Cajamarca in the sierra. The Chimu constructed a compound here at the westernmost end of the site, to serve as a minor administrative post subsidiary to Farfan (Keatinge and Conrad 1983: 258). Clearly the Chimu were interested in Pacatnamu also, the great ceremonial center built on a bluff overlooking the ocean. Farfan, however, was the seat of secular control of the valley after the Chimu conquest, and its location along the north-south coastal highway and close to the eastward link to Cajamarca demonstrates the Chimu concern with communication routes.

While Farfan itself apparently was not fortified, a small fort was constructed by the Chimu on Cerro Faclo, overlooking the site. A wall encloses the top of the hill, while short wall segments lower down on the ridges protect the top. An ample supply of slingstones was laid in here along wall interiors. Access to the hilltop is tightly controlled, but once the top is reached, a curious, wide road-like construction leads to the walled part of the summit, while running off a cliff in the other direction. This feature resembles a ceremonial parade ground, and it may have been used in some sort of display of military might to the locals. The fortifications on Cerro Faclo seem to have seen only a short term of use. The ceramics here may be somewhat later than those at Cerro Coronado, but both sites are Early Phase 3 constructions.

Probably contemporaneous with the Chimu expansion north to Jequetepeque and south to Chao is a major push upvalley in the Moche Valley itself. During Early Phase 3 (but perhaps beginning in late Phase 2, as indicated by the presence of some ring bases from ceramics of the latter period) Chimu control moved beyond the wall that had marked the limit of inland control during the earlier stage of valley consolidation. The Chimu boundary was re-established 10 km further up the Rio Moche. Along this narrow stretch of the river, remains of Chimu fortifications and fortified settlements are found atop many hills (see Fig. 2). Some sites, like Loma del Shingo (Melly Cava n.d.), have evidence for a considerable occupation and a variety of other activities. Other sites like Siete Vueltas lack intensive habitation debris and appear to have served strictly as fortifications.

There are several reasons why the Chimu would have considered it worthwhile to extend their hegemony 10 km further up the river. This move was costly to the Chimu, as evidenced by the substantial fortifications they were forced to build. One advantage to the Chimu of territorial expansion inland was the opportunity for more direct control of roads leading into the sierra. This is clear especially in the Moche Valley. Near the modern town of Poroto, the valley narrows considerably, and the river begins to climb much more quickly (see Fig. 2). Upriver from Poroto, the valley is very narrow, very rocky, and has little agricultural potential except in small scattered pockets. At Poroto, though, there is a good natural access route into the sierra, via a ridge with a relatively gradual slope averaging 11°. Here foot traffic and llama caravans in 13-km horizontal distance could climb from an elevation of 700 m above sea level to the Carabamba Plateau at 3,400 m above sea level. This ridge southeast of Poroto shows considerable evidence of use, and Late Intermediate period ceramics are common. Several Chimu forts and settlements are clustered at the foot of the ridge, and surface survey by the Fortifications Project in 1980 discovered a mix of Chimu, sierra, and local sherds on these sites. This route would have been the most direct one to the Quiruvilca area where J. Topic (this volume) suggests arsenical copper was produced for export to Chan Chan.

The equivalent access point to the sierra on the north side of the Rio Moche lies 12 km further upvalley, at the modern town of Samne. The Fortifications Project survey did not include the area lying between Poroto and Samne, but a "string" of forts was surveyed on the ridge above Samne, starting at 1,600 m above sea level and continuing up to the 4,000 m high altitude divide between the Chicama and Moche Valleys (Coupland n.d.). These forts were under local control and Chimu sherds were very sparse except at Carpaico; this site was located at 3,200 m above sea level and was the major Late Intermediate period center for the north bank of the Moche River in the Otuzco area.

Inasmuch as the Fortifications Project survey did not continue far up into the Sinsicap drainage, we lack archaeological evidence for the nature of interaction between Chimu and local groups there. This northern tributary of the Moche River drains a catchment basin that is effectively cut off to the north and east by the upper Rio Chicama (see Fig. 1); thus the Sinsicap Valley would have provided less direct access to sierra resources and to north-south communications routes than did the Moche Valley proper. Netherly (1988), though, presents interesting information on three coca fields at Collambay well up the Rio Sinsicap. Colonial documents indicate that the fields had belonged to Chimu rulers but were taken over by the Inca after the conquest of Chimor. During the Late Horizon the Collambay ethnic groups were subject to the *curaca* of Mochal in the middle Moche Valley. This *curaca* would certainly have owed allegiance to the Chimu once their control of the middle valley was consolidated in Phase 3. Under the Inca, however, as part of the imperial policy of alienating *chaupiyunga* groups and lands from coastal control, the *curaca* of Mochal was made subject to the *curaca* of Huamachuco, whose seat was a considerable distance to the east, in the sierra. Coca from the *chaupiyunga* areas of both the Sinsicap and Moche Valleys clearly had great value, and it is quite likely that control of these zones would have provided another powerful incentive for Chimu expansion upvalley.

The Early Phase 3 expansion inland then gave the Chimu control of the foot of important coast-sierra trade routes, eliminated *chaupiyunga* middle-men who may have been active in exchange, and gave the coastal lords control of prized coca fields. During Early Phase 3, the Chimu were powerful enough to absorb the local groups with little difficulty.

The Second Wave of Conquest

There is less information available on the Chimu expansion north of Jequetepeque and south of the Santa Valley. The Fortifications Project survey did not extend into these outer areas of the Chimu territory, and there has been no equivalent research by others focusing specifically on fortifications; however, other papers in this volume (Donnan, Mackey and Klymyshyn, Richardson et al., Shimada) supply considerable information that indirectly touches on the Chimu conquest in these more peripheral territories.

Carol Mackey and A. M. Ulana Klymyshyn (this volume) discuss the Chimu expansion into valleys south of Santa, and see the first two valleys, Nepeña and Casma, as being ones in which Chimu power and administration were fully expressed. They cite a date of A.D. 1305 ± 75 for the early construction at Manchan, which marks the Chimu presence in the Casma Valley. The site may have served as more than a local administrative center, though; it is larger and more complex than other centers with Chimu architecture. Mackey and Klymyshyn suggest that it may have been a regional capital for several of the coastal valleys in the southern sector of the Chimu Empire. Chimu architecture and ceramics do occur in the Nepeña Valley, where new construction in Chimu style took place alongside the local center at Caylan (Proulx 1973: 79), implying that the local elites were co-opted into participation in the Chimu realm. This site's lack of regional importance is suggested by its location well inland away from the north-south coastal highway, beside which Manchan is located.

Mackey and Klymyshyn view Chimu control of the Nepeña and Casma Valleys as "consolidated"; some Chimu control was exercised from Culebras to the Huaura Valley, but there was apparently little investment in administrative or defensive construction. Chimu influence in the form of ceramics and other artifacts occurs from the Chancay to Chillon Valleys (the southern limit of conquest according to the Anonymous History), but Mackey and Klymyshyn infer that the Chimu exercised little real political control this far south.

To the north, the Chimu conquest of the Lambayeque region took place during the fourteenth century. Izumi Shimada (this volume) dates the event after A.D. 1350, while Christopher Donnan (this volume) suggests a placement of A.D. 1370. Although there is considerable information available on the Lambayeque area, it is not the sort of information that allows us to say much about local defenses, the process of conquest itself, or the military and administrative aftermath of the Chimu takeover. Certainly though, the size, wealth, and complexity of the Lambayeque complex would have forced the Chimu to innovate considerably in their military and political dealings with this unit.

James Richardson et al. (this volume) discuss the Chimu expansion onto the far North Coast from Piura to Tumbez. This very late stage of conquest is characterized by the presence of imposed centers. The degree of political complexity in this area prior to the Chimu incursion seems to have been rather low, and new centers had to be constructed to house the Chimu victors.

THE CORRELATION OF ARCHAEOLOGICAL AND ETHNOHISTORIC INFORMATION

How much reliance then can be placed on the historical accuracy of ethnohistoric accounts that appear to document the Chimu expansion? Has the archaeological evidence confirmed or rejected the reliability of the accounts as history?

The Anonymous History, the most complete ethnohistoric source on the Chimu expansion, states that conquest occurred in three phases and credits a single ruler with each phase. The archaeological data outlined above corroborate the three-part conquest; coastal expansion apparently did proceed in three waves separated by a century or more.[4] It is not possible, however, that each phase of expansion was in the hands of a single individual, much less the individuals singled out by the account.

The consolidation of valley authority is relatively well documented by survey of fortifications, but there are no radiocarbon dates associated with early forts and walls, and we do not know how quickly this process of power building proceeded. The emergent Chimu dynasty must have used a variety of political, social, and military means to expand and secure its authority in the Moche Valley and in adjacent areas, and it is unlikely that this phase lasted only for the lifetime of Guacricaur. A rough estimate of A.D. 900–1050 is offered for this stage of military and political activity.

The second stage of expansion, the conquest from Santa to Jequetepeque, is attributed by the Anonymous History to Ñançenpinco. Dates from Chao and from Jequetepeque have suggested that this second stage took place between A.D. 1130 and 1200, and it is conceivable that it might have been carried out by one long-lived individual. Ñançenpinco, the third ruler, is not a likely candidate though, unless one assumes a late date for the founding of the Chimu dynasty, well after the founding of Chan Chan. There

---

[4] J. Topic (personal communication, 1988) suggests that the data may show a strategy of quick conquest, followed by more leisurely incorporation of conquered groups. Consolidation of the lower Moche Valley and annexation of the south bank of the Chicama Valley and the lower Viru Valley are shown by large forts with some time depth. The first round of conquest then involved rapid movement up the Moche Valley and quick expansion north to the Jequetepeque Valley and south to the Santa Valley; the quickness of this initial movement is demonstrated by incomplete fortifications or fortifications with very short periods of use. Consolidation of the new boundaries is shown by construction of more permanent settlements, some fortified (Loma del Shingo) and some unfortified (Farfan).

appears to be a century-long gap in the thirteenth century during which no major conquest took place.

The incorporation of Nepeña-Chillon and Zaña-Tumbez is similarly attributed to one individual, but here there is no concordance between the dynastic history and the archaeological reconstruction. These expansionist episodes were spread out over more than one lifetime. Dates from Casma indicate that the Chimu had begun construction of Manchan very early in the fourteenth century, while the Lambayeque annexation most likely occurred toward the end of that century, and the incorporation of Piura-Tumbez was later still. Moreover, Minchancaman, the last Chimu ruler, cannot have been responsible for the imperial expansion credited to him. If he had been carried off to Cuzco around 1470, he could not have annexed Lambayeque in 1370 or Casma in 1300. This last Chimu ruler, like the last Inca ruler, may have been engaged in military activity on the margins of his realm, but could not have done all that was said of him.

The Anonymous History then is quite possibly accurate in characterizing the expansion as episodic, with long intervals between campaigns. But even if we assume that the king list has historical validity, it is clear that the wrong rulers are given credit for various stages of the expansion. A certain amount of telescoping of events and misstatement of facts is evident in the account. We can write the account off as flawed and inaccurately transmitted, or we can probe a bit more deeply and see what other sorts of information are contained in it. As Netherly (1988) and others have long insisted, there are other levels of meaning to ethnohistorical accounts beyond historicity in the Western sense.

The accuracy of the pre-Incaic section of the Anonymous History account is suspect, but there is useful information in it about the way the Chimu viewed their political landscape. The territorial expansion is quite clearly incremental, but it may be worthwhile to consider the three stages of conquest as categories rather than campaigns. The consolidation stage defines the core of the empire. Special status and prestige must have accrued to members of lineages that participated in the foundation of the Chimu dynasty. By analogy to the Inca, we might expect this core group to have supplied much of the bureaucracy at Chan Chan, administrative posts in the provinces, and upper ranks in the army. The first wave of expansion encompassed groups that must have been quite similar to the core group in many ways, and well-known to them, but these groups would have been classed as outsiders. The territory included in the second round of conquest shows great political, geographical, and economical diversity; at first glance it is difficult to see how the very wealthy Lambayeque dynasty could be classed with the impoverished and backward valleys of the far north. In terms of degree of difference and social distance though, the Chimu clearly placed them in one category. Each of the three categories includes territory and people both to the south and north of Chan Chan, but each successive category encompasses more territory, more people, at greater distances, whose ties to Chimor were more recent.

A second point of interest in all three ethnohistoric accounts is that no mention is made of the sierra at all. The Chimu defined their political geography strictly in terms of the coast. Again, the archaeological record provides confirmation. Chimu control in the valleys from which we have information stops well before the sierra. In the Moche Valley, Chimu control extended 40 km inland, and there was a great effort to control routes that led into the sierra, but no evidence at all that the Chimu ever attempted to extend territorial control into the sierra. Cabello Balboa ([1586] 1951: 317) indicates that relations between Minchancaman and the ruler of Cajamarca were close enough that Minchancaman sent a trusted lieutenant with troops to aid in Cajamarca's defense against the Inca. Similar alliances must have been made with leaders of the many other polities in the sierra adjacent to Chimor, and it is quite possible that there was conflict from time to time. But the Chimu clearly regarded the sierra very differently from the coast—as an area not for conquest and as an area not worth mentioning in a dynastic history. This view of the sierra is consistent with earlier coastal attitudes; the climate and environment of the sierra, as well as the economic and social organization of highland groups, were so very different from the coastal experience that actual control of sierra territory was probably never a coastal ambition. Other mechanisms were available to acquire raw materials, finished goods, allies, and other desirable things from the sierra, and these other mechanisms were used.

A third interesting aspect of the account is the emphasis it places on militarism, which leads to the inference that militarism was an important component of Chimu statecraft. The archaeological data confirm this point, at least for early Chimu; there is evidence of battles fought, battles threatened, and fortifications quickly constructed in conquered areas during the pacification process. We cannot be sure of the degree to which alliances, treaties, marriages, and the like contributed to expansion of Chimu control; these nonmilitary means must have contributed significantly to expansion, but they are not the stuff of heroic legends. It is interesting that the Lambayeque dynastic account lacks any mention of militarism. We might infer from this that the Chimu were more aggressive than other North Coast polities, and that their success in creating a new web of social and political relations in the region owed much to this difference.

The few accounts of Chimor that come down to us from the Chimu themselves do not constitute a military history. They are silent, ambiguous, or incorrect on much that we want to know. But they do provide some understanding of how the Chimu defined their political and social landscape. Military activity had a role in Chimu imperial expansion but may have been superseded by other mechanisms in later stages of territorial increment. Later additions to the empire may have owed more to diplomacy, alliance, and a willingness of Andean groups to give allegiance to lords and regimes that were demonstrably successful. The ideological power of militarism remained great, though, and later stages of the expansion may be presented less truthfully than earlier stages in the dynastic accounts. Further archaeological research in valleys on the northern and southern peripheries of the empire will allow the testing of this hypothesis.

BIBLIOGRAPHY

BECK, COLLEEN
    n.d.   Ancient Roads on the North Coast of Peru. Ph.D. dissertation, Department of Anthropology, University of California, Berkeley, 1979.

CABELLO BALBOA, MIGUEL
    [1586]   *Miscelánea antártica*. Instituto de Etnología, Universidad Nacional
    1951   Mayor de San Marcos, Lima.

CALANCHA, ANTONIO DE LA
    1974   *Crónica moralizada*. Crónicas del Peru, Edición de Ignacio Prado Pastor, Lima.

CÁRDENAS MARTÍN, MERCEDES
    1979   A Chronology of the Use of Marine Resources in Ancient Peru. Stiftung Volkswagenwerk. Pontíficia Universidad Católica del Perú, Instituto Riva Aguero, Seminário de Arqueología.

COUPLAND, GARY
    n.d.   A Survey of Prehistoric Fortified Sites in the North Highlands of Peru. M.A. thesis, Department of Anthropology, Trent University, 1979.

KEATINGE, RICHARD W., and GEOFFREY W. CONRAD
    1983   Imperialist Expansion in Peruvian Prehistory: Chimu Administration of a Conquered Territory. *Journal of Field Archaeology* 10(3): 255–283.

KOSOK, PAUL
    1965   *Life, Land and Water in Ancient Peru*. Long Island University Press, New York.

MELLY CAVA, ALFREDO
    n.d.   Informe final de los trabajos realizados por el Proyecto Arqueológico "Loma del Shingo: Un sitio Chimu fortificado en el Valle de Moche." Tesis, Programa Academico de Ciencias Sociales, Universidad Nacional de Trujillo, 1983.

NETHERLY, PATRICIA
:   1988   From Event to Process: The Recovery of Late Andean Organizational Structure by Means of Spanish Colonial Written Records. In *An Overview of Peruvian Prehistory* (Richard W. Keatinge, ed.): 257–278. Cambridge University Press, Cambridge.

PROULX, DONALD
:   1973   *Archaeological Investigations in the Nepeña Valley, Peru*. Research Report 13, Department of Anthropology, University of Massachusetts, Amherst.

ROWE, JOHN H.
:   1948   The Kingdom of Chimor. *Acta Americana* 6(1–2): 26–59.

TOPIC, JOHN R., and MICHAEL E. MOSELEY
:   1985   Chan Chan: A Case Study of Urban Change in Peru. *Ñawpa Pacha* 21: 153–182.

TOPIC, JOHN R., and THERESA LANGE TOPIC
:   1987   The Archaeological Investigation of Andean Militarism: Some Cautionary Observations. In *The Origins and Development of the Andean State* (Jonathan Haas, Shelia Pozorski, and Thomas Pozorski, eds.): 47–55. Cambridge University Press, Cambridge.

TOPIC, THERESA LANGE
:   n.d.   The Middle Horizon in Northern Peru. Paper presented at the Dumbarton Oaks Round Table on Huari, May 1985.

VARGAS UGARTE, RUBÉN
:   1936   La fecha de la fundación de Trujillo. *Revista Histórica* 10: 229–239. Lima.

WILSON, DAVID
:   1983   The Origins and Development of Complex Prehispanic Society in the Lower Santa Valley, Peru: Implications for Theories of State Origins. *Journal of Anthropological Archaeology* 2: 209–276.

The Southern Frontier of the Chimu Empire

CAROL J. MACKEY

CALIFORNIA STATE UNIVERSITY, NORTHRIDGE

A. M. ULANA KLYMYSHYN

CENTRAL MICHIGAN UNIVERSITY

INTRODUCTION

U NTIL RECENTLY, there was little information on Chimu occupation outside of the central area of the empire (i.e., the Chicama, Moche, and Viru Valleys). Within the past ten years, several projects (Conrad, Donnan, and T. Topic, this volume) have investigated the Chimu occupation in the outlying areas of the empire. This has allowed for preliminary conclusions concerning Chimu policies of expansion and administration in these areas. In this paper, we focus on the results of our research in the southern part of the empire in order to propose certain general principles of Chimu policies of expansion and administration. These principles are based on a comparison of settlement patterns and other data in the southern part of the empire with similar data from the northern part. In proposing these principles, we attempt a correlation betwen the ethnohistoric information and the results of archaeological research, especially in reference to the chronology of Chimu expansion.

Ethnohistoric documents (Anonymous History of 1604 in Rowe 1948; Cabello Balboa [1586] 1951; Calancha 1638) provide information on the dynastic succession of the Chimu kings and on events related to the expansion of the empire. According to these documents, the Kingdom of Chimor expanded in two stages: after the consolidation of Chimu rule in the Moche

The research for this essay was funded by the National Science Foundation, the Center for Field Research, University of California: U.R.E.P., California State University in Northridge, and Central Michigan University. The illustrations were prepared by Genaro Barr Argomedo and the graphics departments of both C.S.U.N. and C.M.U. We would like to thank the students and volunteers who have helped with this project, in particular Jerry D. Moore, William Herrman, and Jean Wood. In conducting our research, we have benefited greatly from discussions with many of the colleagues represented in this volume.

Valley by Guacricaur, the first stage of expansion occurred during the reign of the founder's grandson, Ñançenpinco, and included the area north of the Moche Valley to the Zaña Valley and south to the Santa Valley. The second stage occurred during the reign of the last independent ruler, Minchan-çaman, and included the area north to Tumbez and south to the Chillon Valley (Fig. 1). In this paper we are concerned primarily with the second stage of expansion in the area south of the Santa Valley.

The archaeological evidence for the area south of the Santa Valley consists primarily of survey results; the amount and kind of information available for individual valleys vary greatly. Even though his survey focused more on the valleys closer to the capital, Paul Kosok (1960, 1965) discusses the entire southern part of the empire. The settlement typology proposed by Richard Schaedel (1951) was partially based on Chimu centers south of the Santa Valley. Prior to our work, the most intensive surveys in this part of the empire had been carried out in the Casma, Huaura, and Chancay Valleys (Cárdenas 1978; Collier 1962; Tello 1956; Thompson 1966, n.d.). More limited studies had been carried out by Lorenzo Samaniego (1973) and by Rosa Fung and Victor Pimentel (1973) in the Casma Valley and by Wendell Bennett (1939) in the Fortaleza Valley. In the remaining valleys, no work has been carried out since Kosok's survey.

Since 1979 we have been surveying Chimu administrative centers in the southern part of the Kingdom of Chimor, and excavating those in the Casma Valley (Mackey n.d.a; Mackey and Klymyshyn 1981, n.d.b; Moore 1981; Pozorski et al. 1983). Basing our discussion primarily on the results of these investigations, we begin this paper by presenting the evidence for a Chimu occupation in the Casma Valley. We then proceed to discussions of the chronology and policies of Chimu expansion as evidenced by the data from the southern part of the empire. We conclude with a comparison of the expansion and administrative policies in the northern and southern parts of the empire.

EVIDENCE FROM THE SOUTHERN PART OF THE EMPIRE

The Casma Valley is the southernmost valley with a well-developed network of Chimu settlements, which includes ten administrative centers and five villages. After the second stage of expansion, one of these administrative centers—Manchan—served as the regional capital of the southern part of the empire. Before discussing this network of Chimu settlements, we examine the differences between the pre-Chimu and Chimu settlement patterns and present the evidence used to identify the Chimu occupation.

Pre-Chimu Settlement Patterns

The ceramic style characteristic of the Casma Valley during the late Middle Horizon period (ca. A.D. 700–800) and the Late Intermediate period

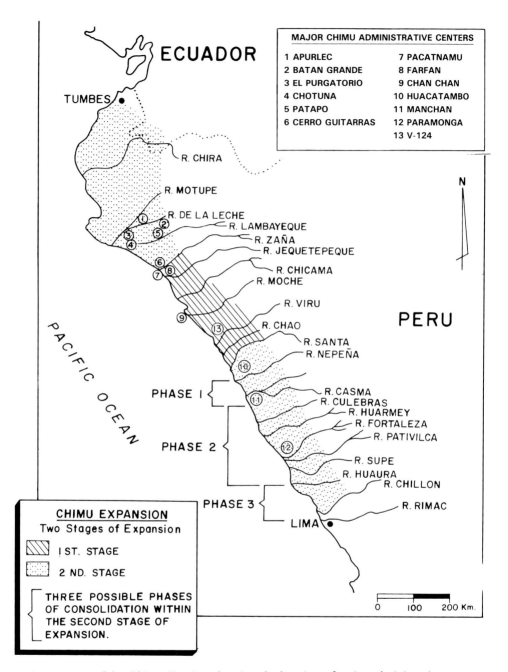

Fig. 1   Map of the Chimu Empire, showing the location of major administrative centers and indicating the areas conquered during the first and second stages of expansion, as well as three possible phases of political consolidation during the second stage of expansion in the southern part of the empire.

(LIP, ca. A.D. 800–1460) has been identified as "Casma Incised" (Tello 1956). Based on this local style, we have been able to distinguish two phases of the LIP: LIP I, which precedes the Chimu conquest, and LIP II, which follows the Chimu conquest. The largest pre-Chimu center associated with Casma Incised ceramics is El Purgatorio in the Casma Valley. Based on the distribution of Casma Incised ceramics (cf. Collier 1962; Daggett 1983) and the settlement pattern during LIP I, El Purgatorio may have been the center of a unified polity extending from the Chao to the Huarmey Valleys (Mackey and Klymyshyn n.d.b)[1]. In addition to El Purgatorio, seven LIP I settlements have been identified in the Casma Valley: six of these cluster close to the confluence of the two arms of the river, one is located close to the valley mouth, and one is found at the neck of the Sechin branch.

The changes the Chimu instituted when they occupied the valley affected settlement patterns and the exploitation of resources. These changes, however, were such that they did not completely disrupt the existing economic and political organization. Although the Chimu built their own structures at El Purgatorio, the major portion of the center did not continue in use. Rather than using an existing center, the Chimu preferred to build their own regional center—Manchan. Including El Purgatorio, the Chimu co-opted (i.e., continued to use) seven of the eight LIP I settlements; and they reocccupied four Middle Horizon settlements. In addition, including Manchan, they built three intrusive centers. Inasmuch as two of the intrusive centers and one of the reoccupied Middle Horizon settlements are located close to the valley mouth, it is evident that the Chimu intensified the exploitation of resources in this area.

Evidence for a Chimu Occupation

Both architectural and artifactual remains have been used to identify the Chimu occupation in the Casma Valley. The identification of these remains as Chimu is based on a comparison with similar remains from the capital, Chan Chan, and other administrative centers in the Moche Valley. The specific architectural features and artifacts used to identify the Chimu occupation at a given settlement depend on its rank in the settlement hierarchy.

Architectural features. In Chan Chan, as well as in other administrative centers in the Moche Valley, several architectural features have been linked with administrative activities. The pattern of association among these features consists of a court leading to a U-shaped structure or *audiencia,* which in turn controls access to storerooms (see also Kolata, this volume). The courts are characterized by at least one of the following features: baffled

[1] Since we finished this article, David Wilson proposed a polity extending from the Chicama to the Huarmey Valley, with El Purgatorio in Casma as the main center (Wilson 1988).

entries, pilasters, niches, benches, or ramps. The *audiencias* have been identified as both the places of work and the residences of administrators (Andrews 1974, n.d.). Similar patterns of architectural features have been found
in the Casma Valley, especially in Manchan.

In Manchan, several rooms have been designated *"audiencia* variants."
These occur in clusters of rooms that also include four or more contiguous
storerooms. In each cluster, the *audiencia* variant is architecturally different
from or located apart from the storerooms. The exterior walls of the
audiencia variants are generally preserved to a height of less than 1 m. Nonetheless, in the interior of one of these rooms we were able to excavate the
bases of niches in three walls and a raised floor with a small ramp. The fact
that the five *audiencia* variants in Manchan were more elaborately constructed than the surrounding architecture is evidenced by the fine plaster on
the walls and the thickness of the silt floors in the excavated ones. Though
these rooms do not have the same form and all of the characteristics of the
audiencias in Chan Chan, because of their location in the compounds and
their association with storerooms they are functionally equivalent to *audiencias.* It is for this reason that we refer to them as *audiencia* variants.

Two *audiencia* variants are located in a compound that shows other similarities to Chimu architecture in the Moche Valley. The entrance to this
compound is a baffled entry; corridors lead to two courts with benches,
niches, and ramps. From the second of these courts, a corridor leads to the
audiencia variants and then to the associated storerooms. Similar entries and/
or courts are found in at least four other compounds in Manchan, as well as
in other administrative centers used by the Chimu.

Ceramics. At some of the settlements (i.e., the five villages that have no
compounds), ceramics were more definitive in the identification of a Chimu
occupation than was the architecture. Chimu fine and course wares, as well
as domestic and nondomestic vessel forms, were found at both administrative centers and villages. Within each vessel-form category (*olla* [cooking
vessel], jar, *tinaja* [urn], plate, bowl, and neckless *olla*), Chimu rim shapes
identified in the Moche Valley (Keatinge n.d.; Mackey n.d.b; J. Topic 1982,
n.d.) have been found in the Casma Valley. In Manchan, 51 percent of the
olla rims, 100 percent of the jar rims, and 52 percent of the *tinaja* rims are
Chimu shapes. Of the local rim shapes that continued in use, most are
associated with food preparation (i.e., *ollas* and *tinajas*). The relatively high
frequency of Chimu rim shapes in Manchan may be due to its rank and
awaits comparison with lower-level centers. Nonetheless, it is evident that
even at co-opted lower-level centers, Chimu fineware replaced local fineware and that Chimu rim shapes replaced many of the local ones in the
domestic vessel-form categories. Not only are Chimu rim shapes and wares
represented, but the vessels were manufactured and decorated using Chimu
techniques and designs. Thus, it is quite clear that these are facsimiles—

perhaps made by using molds sent from Chan Chan—and not imitations of Chimu ceramics.

Textiles and Wood Artifacts. Most of the textiles in the excavated sample have been recovered from Manchan, and the majority of the finished textiles were associated with burials. These garments and shrouds include cotton textiles with painted decoration, textiles using both cotton and alpaca fibers with woven decoration, and feathercloth. Of the styles and techniques that have been identified, one is Chimu in both technique and decoration, whereas another combines local techniques with Chimu decoration. These two styles represent the majority of the excavated sample. The decorative motifs occurring most frequently are birds and fish, similar to those represented in various media in the Moche Valley. Other strong indicators of a Chimu presence are the Chimu hats and loincloths found in the high-status burials (Jill Mefford, personal communication, 1983).

Several carved wooden staffs and statues, which seem to have been indicators of high status within the administrative hierarchy, have been found in burial and nonburial contexts. All of these represent human figures, either the full body or just the face. The facial characteristics of these carved figures are similar to those found on carved figures in the Chimu capital and are like those represented on late Chimu ceramics.

These artifacts, combined with the presence of Chimu architectural features, indicate that the Chimu conquered the valley rather than just traded with the inhabitants or influenced them from afar. Certainly, the high-status goods and symbols of authority used by the elite were all made in a Chimu style. Furthermore, Chimu-style ceramics were used not only by the elite, but the commoners also used mainly Chimu-style ceramics in their daily activities. This daily use—more so than the evidence of the architecture and the other classes of artifacts—indicates a Chimu occupation long enough for the replacement of many of the local ceramics by Chimu wares.

Chimu Settlement Network in the Casma Valley

Valley Description. The Casma Valley consists of both the Casma River and its tributary, the Sechin. The valley measures approximately 5 km in width near the river's mouth and begins to narrow at about 5 km inland, beyond which point the arms measure less than 1–3 km in width. The alluvial plains of both rivers are bounded by relatively steep chains of Andean foothills that are not suitable for cultivation. The two arms of the river differ in the availability of both land and water. Of the two arms, the Sechin has a larger area of land available for cultivation, but its flow of water fluctuates more from year to year. The Casma arm, on the other hand, has a more dependable water supply, but less land available for cultivation. The two main areas of arable land are at the river's mouth and near the confluence of the two rivers (Kosok 1965; ONERN 1972; Thompson n.d.).

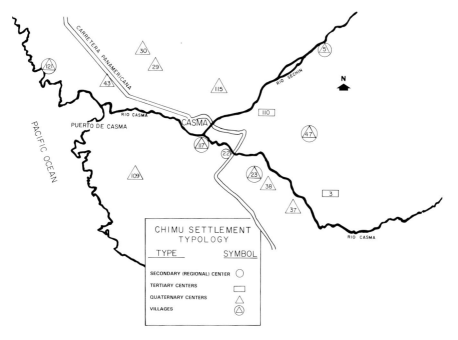

Fig. 2   Map of the Casma Valley, showing the location and typology of Chimu settlements.

Location of Centers within the Valley. Of the ten administrative centers and five villages used by the Chimu in the Casma Valley, five cluster around the valley mouth, nine are located close to the confluence of the two rivers, and one is at the neck of the Sechin branch (Fig. 2). Most of the settlements located at the confluence of the rivers are on the Casma branch. Of the three intrusive administrative centers, one (Fig. 2, no. 22) is located at the confluence of the rivers, and the other two (nos. 29, 43) are located close to the valley mouth. Of the four centers that were co-opted by the Chimu (Fig. 2, nos. 3, 30, 38, 110), three are close to the confluence and one at the valley mouth. The remaining three centers (Fig. 2, nos. 37, 109, 115) were reoccupied by the Chimu. Of these centers, one controls the raised fields close to the valley mouth and the other two are at the confluence.

Ranking of the Settlements. The difference between the two Chimu settlement types—administrative centers and villages—is that administrative centers contain adobe and/or stone compounds that have internal divisions consisting of rooms and courts. Based on the number of compounds, three hierarchical ranks of administrative centers have been identified in this valley. In reference to the settlement hierarchy for the entire empire, the intrusive center of Manchan (Fig. 2, no. 22) is a secondary or regional center with nine compounds. Two co-opted centers, Laguna II (no. 110) with five compounds and El Purgatorio (no. 3) with seven compounds, served as tertiary centers during the Chimu occupation. The other seven administrative centers are quaternary in rank with one or two compounds each. All centers have a domestic occupation, with the possible exception of El Purgatorio, where a domestic occupation has not yet been identified. Although Cahuacucho (no. 5) has so far been classified as a village, the ceramics and artifacts associated with the Chimu cemetery indicate at least a small elite occupation at the site. Therefore, Cahuacucho also might have been an administrative center, probably a quaternary one.

One of the major differences between Manchan and all lower-level Chimu centers in the valley is its size: Manchan covers an area of 63 ha, while the other centers appear to be less than 20 ha each. Without excavation it is not possible to define the full extent of the Chimu component at a given center. Our experience at Laguna II indicates that there is not necessarily a correlation between the site surface covered by Chimu ceramics and the actual area occupied by the Chimu. Furthermore, there does not seem to be any correlation between site size and number of compounds. Without excavation it is also not possible to correlate the size of the center or the number of compounds with population size. Most of the inhabitants lived in cane-walled structures, the walls of which are not always visible on the surface. Using the number of cane-walled structures visible on the surface, the population of Manchan has been estimated at less than two thousand.

Just as it is difficult to estimate population size, so it is difficult to determine the number of administrators at a given center. One possible measure that could be used is the number of *audiencias* or their variants at a given center. The use of this measure is, however, complicated by the fact that in addition to the *audiencia* variants, room clusters without *audiencia* variants have been identified as the residences of administrators in Manchan. It is difficult to ascertain the number of either architectural feature without excavation. Nevertheless, on the basis of surface remains, it does appear that the number of administrators in any of the centers was relatively low. In Manchan, we estimate fewer than ten; at the lower-level centers the number would have been even smaller.

In addition to differences in size and the numbers of compounds, the centers vary in storage capacity, burial patterns, and production. The only center in Casma with storage facilities is Manchan. This difference probably is related to Manchan's role as regional center in tribute collection, the transshipment of goods to the capital, and redistribution. Similarly, it appears to be the only center with separate burial structures. It should be noted, however, that these structures are not like the burial platforms in Chan Chan, but are separate compounds with subterranean tombs. So far, the only conclusive evidence for production also comes from the regional center. Evidence for the production of such commodities as *chicha,* copper artifacts, and textiles was found in the cane structures. One cane structure was a specialized copper workshop; even in the houses, however, these commodities were being produced for consumption above the household level (Moore n.d.) There is also evidence for stoneworking and woodworking, but the context and level of production for these crafts are not well defined. At Laguna II, a tertiary center, evidence has been found for *chicha* production above the household level, but as yet no evidence has been found for the production of other commodities at this level. Surface remains from all of the quaternary centers show evidence for the production of at least one of the commodities just mentioned. Unfortunately, it is not possible to tell from surface remains whether this production was for consumption on or above the household level.

Chronology and Nature of the Chimu Presence in the Southern Part of the Empire

According to ethnohistoric sources (Anonymous History of 1604 in Rowe 1948; Cabello Balboa [1586] 1951; Calancha 1638), the expansion of the Chimu Empire occurred in two stages after the consolidation of power in the Moche Valley; the Casma Valley was conquered in the second stage during the reign of the last king, Minchançaman. In this section, we present the data for a revised chronology of the Chimu occupation in the Casma Valley, and, on that basis, we reinterpret the current version of the chronology and nature of the Chimu presence in the southern part of the empire.

Results of Radiocarbon Assays and of the Ceramic Analysis. The revised chronology of the Chimu occupation in the Casma Valley is grounded both on absolute and relative dating methods, that is, carbon-14 assays and ceramic seriation. Of the seventeen radiocarbon assays, seven correlate well with the associated cultural material.[2] One of these dates has been recalibrated at A.D. 1305 (665 ± 75 BP); this sample (UGa-4316) came from the earliest compound in Manchan (Fig. 3, no. 1). The other acceptable results have been recalibrated between A.D. 1430 and 1650; these samples were associated with the artifacts from the final phases of the Chimu occupation, as well as from the Inca and the Colonial occupations.

The results of the ceramic analysis corroborate the results of the radiocarbon assays. Some of the Chimu rim shapes, especially from Manchan, are the same as rims that first appear in *ciudadela* Velarde in Chan Chan and continue in use through *ciudadelas* Rivero and Tschudi (the last of the monu-

---

[2] The other ten have been recalibrated at 950 B.C.–A.D. 1290 and A.D. 1510–1780. These results are not considered reliable, either because the samples were associated with late imperial Chimu ceramics or for stratigraphic reasons.

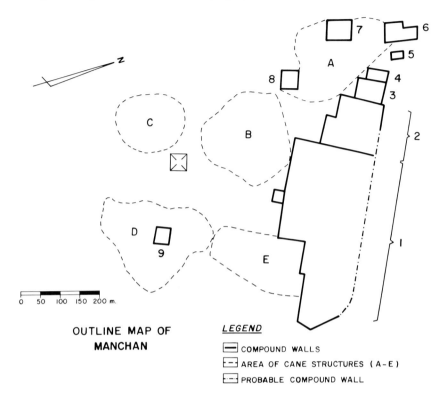

OUTLINE MAP OF
MANCHAN

LEGEND
COMPOUND WALLS
AREA OF CANE STRUCTURES (A-E)
PROBABLE COMPOUND WALL

Fig. 3   Schematic map of Manchan showing the location and outline of the compounds (1–8) and of the areas with cane-walled structures (A–E).

mental compounds to be constructed) (Keatinge n.d.; Mackey n.d.b; J. Topic 1982, n.d.).[3]

The radiocarbon assays and ceramic analysis indicate that the Chimu occupation of Manchan possibly correlated with *ciudadela* Velarde (the sixth of ten palace compounds to be constructed in Chan Chan). The dating of this *ciudadela* between A.D. 1300 and 1350 is discussed by several authors in this volume (Kolata, Moseley, and J. Topic). A correlation also is made between Velarde and the Chimu conquest of Lambayeque between 1360 and 1370 (Donnan, Shimada, and T. Topic, this volume). Without going into the evidence involved in these correlations and the associated question

[3] An additional relative dating technique that was attempted was the application of the brick seriation established for Chan Chan by Alan Kolata (1982, n.d.). We found, however, that the height: length ratios of the adobes from Manchan and other centers in the Casma and Nepeña Valleys do not conform to this seriation. Specifically, though most of the adobes from these valleys are similar in form to those from the early phase in Chan Chan, the artifacts correspond to the late phase.

of how many rulers can be associated with each palace compound, it is safe to say that the Chimu occupation in the Casma Valley may have started as early as 1305 and might be associated with *ciudadela* Velarde. The Chimu conquest of the Casma Valley may be earlier than the conquest of the Lambayeque area. More evidence is needed before any of these statements can be validated; however, the existing data indicate that the last king of Chimor could not have been responsible for all of these and other events attributed to him in the chronicles.

Growth of Manchan. The evidence for a long Chimu occupation of the Casma Valley is supported further by the evidence for several construction phases in Manchan. These construction phases are defined by both the architecture and the artifact content of the compounds. Manchan consists of nine compounds, four of which are agglutinated and five separated. The earliest compound to be built lies at the eastern end of the settlement (Fig. 3, no. 1). Abutments of the exterior walls of the agglutinated compounds indicate that the compounds were built from east to west with no interconnecting entries between them. Separated compounds are later, a judgment drawn from their location at the western end of the settlement, their orientation, and the architectural features found within them.

The earliest, and easternmost, compound (Fig. 3, no. 1) is the largest and shows some features not found in the others. The most prominent of these features are three terraces surrounded by high *tapia* walls on the hill at the east end of this compound. Incorporated within the compound are two mounds that appear to have been residential rather than ceremonial. Similar terraces and mounds are more characteristic of the pre-Chimu than the Chimu settlements in the valley; nonetheless, they are associated with Chimu ceramics. Three of the room clusters without *audiencia* variants that have been identified as residences of administrators but are not characteristic of Chimu architecture are found within this compound. The most elaborate of the architectural features in this compound is a large court located between the two mounds and containing sixty-five round solid-adobe columns that were painted red. Unlike the terraces and mounds, however, the columns appear to be a post-Chimu rather than a pre-Chimu feature on the basis of stratigraphy. Not surprisingly, this compound shows the most remodeling, which also indicates a longer span of use.

The other compounds in Manchan show an increase in Chimu architectural patterns. For example, in the three later agglutinated compounds (Fig. 3, nos. 2–4), the pattern of enclosing an *audiencia* variant and its associated storerooms in a separate court similar to those in Chan Chan is clearly established. All three later agglutinated compounds show an increased number of benches and ramps. The separated compounds, with the exception of no. 5, follow Chimu architectural patterns even more closely: all have baffled entries, interconnected courts leading to *audiencia* variants and/or store-rooms, courts with niches, and courts with benches and ramps. Internal access in the separated compounds is by means of corridors, which is not the case in the agglutinated compounds. Furthermore, the *audiencia* variants in compound no. 6 are the most similar to the U-shaped structures in Chan Chan, given their niches and a raised floor with an entry ramp.

Based on differences in architectural features and on wall abutments, we can define three major construction phases in Manchan. The first phase consists of just the largest agglutinated compound, no. 1. The second phase consists of three agglutinated compounds, nos. 2–4, plus one separated compound, no. 5. The third phase consists of four separated compounds, nos. 6–9. These three construction phases indicate that this regional center had a longer occupation than the reign of the last Chimu king mentioned in the chronicles, Minchançaman. More importantly, these three construction phases allow us to infer that the consolidation of Chimu power in this valley—as represented by the increased presence of Chimu architectural features in the regional center—probably became stronger over time.

Extent and Nature of the Chimu Network. The extent of the Chimu network in the Casma Valley also indicates that the Chimu take-over took place before the reign of Minchançaman. The Chimu structures at all ten administrative centers represent a large labor investment by the Chimu. The three intrusive centers (Fig. 2, nos. 22, 29, 43) contain a total of eleven compounds ranging in length from 30 to 270 m. At the two co-opted tertiary centers, the Chimu built a total of twelve compounds ranging from 40 to 140 m in length. An additional seven compounds were built at the quaternary centers, which were either co-opted or reoccupied. As mentioned previously, the nine compounds at Manchan represent three construction phases. This construction style seems to follow the pattern of sequential building of both monumental and elite compounds in Chan Chan. Thus, the compounds at the two tertiary centers probably also were built sequentially. The number of compounds built in the valley indicates not only an investment of labor, but also that this investment took place over time. Furthermore, the building of the intrusive centers and of Chimu compounds at the co-opted and reoccupied centers shows that the Chimu not only utilized an existing administrative network, but also expanded it. And finally, there is evidence that the Chimu intensified and expanded the area of cultivation within the valley, a situation indicated by the building of two intrusive centers (Fig. 2, nos. 29, 43) in an area that was not extensively used in pre-Chimu times. Evidence for this intensification also comes from the domestic architecture at Muenga (Fig. 2, no. 109), the center associated with raised fields and salt pans. Even though it is impossible to judge how much time would have been needed for these accomplishments, it seems clear that it would have been longer than the rule of a single monarch as reported by the chronicles.

Differences in Consolidation. The settlement pattern south of the Casma Valley varies considerably from that in the valleys between the Casma and the Lambayeque Valleys, all of which have networks of Chimu administrative centers. South of Casma, the valleys contain few if any administrative centers (Fig. 1), suggesting that the expansion into this area occurred in more than one phase and that the consolidation of power was different in different valleys. Though the Casma Valley was not the southern boundary of the empire, it was the southern limit of the consolidation of power. Paramonga, located in the Fortaleza Valley, is possibly a Chimu fortress, suggesting that the Fortaleza-Pativilca-Supe region could have been a buffer zone.

Based on the distribution of Chimu administrative centers from the Nepeña to the Chillon Valleys, it is evident that Chimu power was not consolidated to the same degree in all of the valleys in this region. Only Nepeña and Casma show evidence of a fully developed network of Chimu administrative centers. In the area between the Huarmey and Huaura Valleys, only three possible Chimu administrative centers have been identified, including Paramonga. No Chimu centers as yet have been found south of the Huaura Valley, though Chimu ceramics have been collected there (Collier 1962; Kosok 1965; Mackey and Klymyshyn n.d.b; Proulx 1968, 1973; Samaniego 1973; Schaedel 1951, 1966; Tello 1956; Thompson 1966, n.d.). Thus, the valleys incorporated during the *second* stage of expansion in the southern part of the empire can be divided into three groups: (a) those valleys where Chimu power had been consolidated (Nepeña through Casma); (b) those valleys where consolidation had been initiated but not completed (Culebras through Huaura); and (c) those valleys where no consolidation of Chimu power occurred (Chancay through Chillon) (Fig. 1). It should be noted that stages of expansion as defined by the chronicles and degrees of consolidation as indicated by settlement pattern data do not correspond. This discrepancy may indicate that the chronicle version is a compressed account. We propose that these groups correlate with three separate phases within the second stage of expansion.

The evidence just presented calls for a reinterpretation of the southern expansion as recorded in the chronicles. The data from the Casma Valley indicate a Chimu occupation that most probably occurred before Minchançaman's reign. The different settlement patterns in the valleys incorporated during the second stage of expansion point to the probability that the expansion took place in phases and that these valleys were differentially integrated into the empire. Thus, the conquests attributed to Minchançaman probably represent a composite version of the accomplishments of more than one ruler just as do those conquests attributed to Ñançenpinco (cf. Conrad and T. Topic, this volume).

When discussing policies of expansion, it is necessary to distinguish between the initial take-over of an area and the subsequent integration of the inhabitants and the territory into the imperial organization. According to the chronicles, the Chimu expanded their territorial control through conquest (Anonymous History in Rowe 1948; Cabello Balboa [1586] 1951; Calancha 1638). However, with the major exception of the results of the study done by John and Theresa Topic (see T. Topic, this volume), the archaeological data available on the initial take-over are too fragmentary to allow for a full discussion of this phase of Chimu expansion into any area. Thus, this discussion of policies of expansion focuses on the second point, that is, policies related to the subsequent integration of the provinces and to the nature of Chimu political and economic organization in these areas.

Much of the information on the political and economic organization of the empire has been derived from excavations in and around the Moche Valley. On this basis, three major principles of imperial organization have been identified: (a) the Chimu ruled through a hierarchy of administrators, most of whom were nobles; (b) there was a high degree of economic centralization; and (c) the main administrative activity was the control of resources (Moseley and Day 1982). A fourth principle—the integration of indigenous lords into the Chimu hierarchy—has been identified on the basis of ethnohistoric information (Netherly 1984, n.d., and this volume; Rostworowski, this volume). In discussing Chimu policies of expansion, we use a comparison of the information on Chimu political and economic organization derived from the sources just mentioned along with the results of our excavations in the Casma Valley.

Administrative Hierarchy

As in other early state societies, Chimu kings ruled through nobles who administered the empire and who were organized into hierarchical levels. Using primarily architectural evidence, several levels of administrators have been identified in the capital, Chan Chan: (a) administrators in the first level resided in the monumental compounds or royal palaces and were probably members of the dynasty; (b) administrators in the second level resided in elite compounds smaller than, but similar to, the royal palaces ("type A") and were nobles, though probably not members of the dynasty (judging by the proximity of type A elite compounds to the palaces, the tasks of second-level administrators were related to those in the first level); (c) administrators in the third level resided in smaller, less elaborate elite compounds ("type B") and were also nobles (based on the location of these compounds, the tasks of these administrators may have been related primarily to the supervision of craft production); and (d) administrators in the fourth level were associated with isolated U-shaped structures located among domestic structures and workshops (these administrators might not have been nobles). The tasks of fourth-level administrators were also related principally to the supervision of production (Klymyshyn 1982, 1987).

A comparison of the architecture in Manchan to that in Chan Chan shows that first-level administrators were not represented at the regional center. Like second- through fourth-level administrators in Chan Chan, their counterparts in Manchan were neither buried in burial platforms nor did they control anywhere near the amount of storage facilities controlled by the administrators in the imperial palaces. This absence of first-level administrators at a regional center is consistent with central place theory (cf. Christaller [1933] 1966, Loesch [1940] 1954). Third- and fourth-level administrators were probably present in Manchan, even though as yet they have not been associated with specific architectural features.

Chimu administrative centers also can be grouped into at least four hierarchical levels or ranks. Ideally, the characteristics of the different ranks, as well as the rank of a specific center, should be based on site size, architectural complexity, and the distribution of artifacts (cf. Isbell and Schreiber 1978; Johnson 1973, 1977; Wright 1977; Wright and Johnson 1975). All three criteria have been used in ranking those Chimu centers that have been excavated. For those centers not yet excavated, however, only architectural complexity can be determined with any degree of certainty by using surface indications of the type and number of compounds, the size and number of areas with domestic structures, and other architectural features.

Three ranks in the Chimu settlement hierarchy—primary, tertiary, and quaternary centers—are represented in the Moche Valley. An additional rank—secondary or regional center—has been identified in the provinces (Mackey and Klymyshyn n.d.a). This distribution indicates that administrators in the capital or primary center were responsible for administering both the empire as a whole and the region immediately around the capital. This region would have included the Moche and Chicama Valleys. Second-level administrators in the capital were probably responsible for the administration of this region, while the first-level administrators were responsible for the empire as a whole. Second-level administrators in the regional or secondary centers would have been responsible only for their own regions. Thus, the responsibilities of administrators on the same hierarchical level, whether in the capital or in a regional center, would have been similar. Furthermore, because tertiary and quaternary centers have been identified not only in the Moche and Casma Valleys, but in many other valleys as well (Mackey and Klymyshyn n.d.a), second-level administrators in both the primary and the secondary centers delegated more direct administrative tasks within their regions to administrators in the same lower ranks of the hierarchy, that is, third- and fourth-level administrators at tertiary and quaternary centers.

Economic Centralization

To date, most of the evidence for economic centralization in the Chimu Empire has come from the capital, Chan Chan. This evidence includes the size of the capital, storage capacity, and the nature of craft production. The results of recent research in the provinces enables us to verify the high degree of centralization indicated by these data.

One of the more striking differences between the capital and the southern regional center, Manchan, is size. Chan Chan, which covers an area of 2,000 ha, is more than thirty times the size of Manchan, which covers an area of 63 ha. Such a great disparity in size between primary and secondary centers is indicative of a highly centralized political and economic system. The difference in size is an indication of the channeling of a disproportionate amount of human and other resources into one center at least for its construction and maintenance. The channeling of resources in turn indicates the power of a single center to command this vast amount of resources.

The difference between Chan Chan and Manchan in storage capacity is similar to their difference in size. The enormous storage capacity of Chan Chan is demonstrated by the fact that more than 2,300 storerooms have been identified in the monumental compounds (Klymyshyn 1987; Kolata n.d., this volume). Outside of Chan Chan, storage facilities have been found only in secondary centers. However, fewer than fifty storerooms have been identified in Manchan, a figure well below 1 percent of the capital's storage capacity. This concentration of economic goods in the capital represents a classic redistributive system, in which all goods—not just elite goods—are being funneled into the primary center. Furthermore, this concentration obviously means that virtually all stored economic goods were under the control of the administrators in the capital.

There was a difference between Chan Chan and Manchan not only in storage capacity but also in the way in which the goods were stored. Although access to storerooms was highly restricted in the capital, it is interesting that Manchan has storerooms with both restricted and unrestricted access. The restricted storerooms were accessible through corridors and/or guarded by *audiencia* variants. The majority of the storerooms, however, had unrestricted access, that is, they were directly accessible from plazas, and were relatively large (Mackey 1987; Mackey and Klymyshyn n.d.b). It seems, then, that the majority of the storerooms in Manchan were not used for permanent storage, but rather for temporary storage in bulk of utilitarian goods and comestibles that were to be shipped to Chan Chan. Although the remaining storage capacity would be sufficient for satisfying immediate needs, it is not large enough for the storage of surplus goods. Thus, it seems that surplus products were stored primarily in the capital, including goods for emergencies such as those caused by El Niño episodes.

Further evidence for the economic centralization of the Chimu Empire comes from information on production. The crafts produced in Chan Chan were better in quality and greater in quantity than those produced in Manchan, even though production above the household level occurred in both centers. The data from Manchan indicate that textiles, *chicha,* and artifacts of copper, wood, and stone were being produced in non-elite domestic structures and—in the case of copper artifacts—also in workshops. Based on the raw materials, the spinning and weaving implements, and the finished pieces recovered from houses in which textiles had been produced, it is evident that both fine and plain textiles were produced at Manchan. Nevertheless, the other artifacts produced there were either not of the same craftsmanship as at Chan Chan (e.g., wooden staffs) or were utilitarian (e.g., copper needles). This indicates that the level of training and specialization of the craft producers in Manchan was lower than in Chan Chan. Furthermore, the copper used at Manchan was not of good quality, and there is no evidence for the working of any other metal or metal alloys; at Chan Chan, of course, the full range of ores and alloys would have been available. The range of raw materials for other crafts was similarly more limited at Manchan than at Chan Chan. The tools available to the craftsmen in Manchan were not of the same quality as those available in Chan Chan. And finally, the number of craft producers in Manchan was lower and so the quantity of goods that they could produce was also lower (cf. Moore 1981, n.d.; J. Topic 1981, n.d., and this volume).

There is also a difference in production between tertiary and quaternary centers in the Moche Valley and those in the Casma Valley. Surface remains in areas of domestic structures in the lower-level centers in the Casma Valley show evidence for the production of the same commodities as in Manchan. However, it is not possible to determine from surface remains whether production was only for household consumption or on a larger scale. This distribution is very different from that found in the Moche Valley where there is no evidence for either craft production or for permanent support populations at tertiary and quaternary centers.

The information on production and storage is indicative of at least some aspects of distribution in the empire. It is clear that the inhabitants of Manchan were not dependent on the capital for all craft products, but produced many of their own. Though some high-status goods, such as textiles, were produced in Manchan, probably most of the high-status goods were sent from Chan Chan. On this basis, it seems that very few (mostly elite) goods were coming into the Casma Valley. The goods that might have been sent out of the valley as tribute could have included cotton, agricultural products, and salt.

All of the evidence presented on the differences between Chan Chan and Manchan in site size, storage capacity, and production indicate a high degree of centralization. Though most of the evidence presented is related to the economic organization of the empire, it is also indicative of a similar degree of political centralization. For example, the high-status and other goods available to the lords of Manchan are both qualitatively and quantitatively poorer than those available to the first-level administrators in Chan Chan. This shows, of course, that not only was the economic power of the lords of Manchan weaker, but also that neither the symbols of the highest levels of social and political power nor the power itself were available to them. Thus, it appears that social, political, and economic power was centralized in the capital. A further indication of this political centralization is the relatively low number of administrators in Manchan and other centers in the Casma Valley as compared to the number of administrators in Chan Chan.

Resource Control

Based on the location of the tertiary and quaternary centers in the Moche and Chicama Valleys, it has been proposed that the main function of administrators at lower-level Chimu centers was the control of irrigation canals and of fields (Keatinge 1974, 1975; Kus 1980). Given the location of Chimu centers in the Casma Valley, this proposition seems to hold true in the provinces as well. The two major concentrations of Chimu administrative centers in the Casma Valley are in areas with the largest amount of arable land—above the confluence of the rivers and at the river mouth (Fig. 2). Since the secondary center (no. 22) and both of the tertiary centers (nos. 3 and 110) are located adjacent to the single largest concentration of arable land at the confluence, it seems clear that control of arable land was one of the main functions of Chimu administrators in this valley. Because the network of Chimu irrigation canals has not been identified completely in the valley (due partly to problems of preservation), it is not possible to determine the relationship between the location of the canals and the location of the centers. Nonetheless, more Chimu settlements are clustered on the Casma branch of the river, which has the more dependable water supply, so it seems that control of water was also important to the Chimu lords.

The information on settlement patterns in the Casma Valley indicates that control of resources may have been one of the main reasons for the Chimu take-over of this area. The Chimu intensified and expanded the utilization of resources in the area around the mouth of the river. Two of the settlements located close to the mouth of the river, nos. 43 and 109 in Figure 2, controlled more specialized resources. The former (no. 43) controlled marine as well as agricultural resources, while the latter (no. 109) controlled an extensive area of ridged fields and salt pans. Given the importance of these specialized resources and the expectation that more specialized resources would be controlled by higher-ranked administrators, it is odd that the centers in this area are quaternary rather than tertiary ones.

Incorporation of Indigenous Lords

One of the decisions that expanding societies have to make is whether to establish new administrative networks or to share power and use existing ones. The ethnohistoric evidence indicates that the Chimu shared power and used existing networks wherever possible (Netherly n.d.; Rostworowski 1961). This way is, of course, very efficient and effective for administering conquered provinces: not only do the indigenous lords know the area to be administered, but—even more importantly—they are not strangers to the local population. The work done in the Casma Valley corroborates the ethnohistoric evidence that the Chimu used existing administrative networks.

The Chimu policy of using existing networks of administrators is demonstrated by the co-opting of existing local administrative centers by the Chimu and the blending of Chimu and local styles, especially in architecture. Of the eight settlements in use immediately before the Chimu takeover, six continued in use during the Chimu occupation. This indicates that resettlement of the population was kept to a minimum, that local lords at existing centers were probably integrated into the Chimu network, and that the labor involved in building new settlements was also kept to a minimum. The tendency to minimize labor is further demonstrated by the reuse of Middle Horizon centers.

Of the six co-opted sites, four are administrative centers and two are villages. Of the co-opted administrative centers, only the two tertiary centers (nos. 3, 110) have compounds built by the Chimu; no new compounds were built at the two quaternary centers (nos. 30, 38). This further corroborates the incorporation of indigenous lords into the Chimu network; however, this also indicates that there might have been differences in incorporation at different levels of the administrative hierarchy. Nonetheless, the presence of Chimu-built compounds cannot be used as a conclusive indicator of the presence of Chimu rather than indigenous lords. The available data are simply insufficient to determine whether Chimu compounds were built to elevate the status of the indigenous lords or whether the newly built compounds simply indicate an increase in administrative personnel, whether local or Chimu.

The architecture in Manchan and the lower-level administrative centers shows a blending of local and Chimu styles and/or a continuation of local architectural styles. This refers to construction techniques as well as to architectural features. Not surprisingly, it is at the three intrusive Chimu centers that we find the closest adherence to Chimu architectural patterns. Nevertheless, of the compounds in the intrusive center, Manchan, the earlier agglutinated compounds have fewer Chimu features than the later separated compounds. This blending of local and Chimu styles indicates that local labor was being used in the construction and—more importantly—that the Chimu did not completely superimpose either their style or their power on the local people.

Like the architecture, the textiles show a blending of local and Chimu styles. Of the styles identified in Manchan, one shows all Chimu characteristics, one shows only local characteristics, and the third is a blend of both. The ceramics, however, do not indicate such a blending of styles. Local rim shapes and stylistic elements continue in use in the domestic-form categories along with Chimu rim shapes and stylistic elements. The local fineware, however, does seem to have been superseded by Chimu fineware.

The evidence for the integration of indigenous lords into the Chimu hierarchy indicates that the Chimu occupation of the valley did not result in a major disruption of existing socio-economic patterns. However, it is evident that some changes did occur. One of the most obvious changes is the relocation of people to the intrusive Chimu settlements and to the reoccupied Middle Horizon centers. The largest group of people was resettled in the regional center, where it is estimated that the population numbered less than two thousand inhabitants. The major change, of course, was the transfer of power from the local elite to the Chimu.

COMPARISON OF THE NORTHERN AND SOUTHERN PARTS OF THE EMPIRE

Though, in general, the principles of Chimu imperial organization discussed previously operated in both the northern and southern parts of the empire, there are variations between these two areas in the specific applications of these principles. In this section, we present the differences between these regions and discuss the variables that might have caused them. Our discussion is couched in a manner suggesting that differences in the applications of Chimu policies correlate primarily with the division between the areas north and south of the capital. This may, however, be more a reflection of the available data than of actual distinctions within the empire. For example, it should be remembered that not all areas of either the northern or the southern part of the empire were incorporated at the same time (Fig. 1). When it is both possible and applicable to do so, we also discuss the effect of chronological differences on Chimu policies.

Differences in Administrative Hierarchy

One of the more obvious differences between the northern and the southern parts of the empire is in the distribution and characteristics of large administrative centers (Fig. 1). For the first stage of expansion (i.e., between the Zaña and the Santa Valleys), a northern regional center has been identified—Farfan in the Jequetepeque Valley. The possible southern regional center during this stage of expansion is V-124 in the Viru Valley. However, V-124 differs significantly in size and number of compounds from both Manchan and Farfan (Collier 1955; Keatinge and Conrad 1983; Willey 1953). In the areas conquered during the second stage of expansion, every northern valley from the Zaña to the Motupe is dominated by a large Chimu center. In the region south of the Santa Valley, however, there is only one large center—Manchan.[4] Some of the northern centers, like Apurlec and Cerro Guitarras, are comparable to Manchan in size and number of compounds. On this basis, even though it is difficult to determine the rank of a center without excavation, several of these northern centers can be identified as probable regional centers (cf. Kosok 1965; Schaedel 1951, 1966).

If there were more regional centers north of the Moche Valley, then this area was divided into more administrative units on the secondary or regional level than was the southern part. However, Manchan would then have controlled a larger area than any of the northern centers. Given the available information, it is not possible to determine whether there are also more tertiary and quaternary centers in the northern area. The available information seems to indicate that there are few centers at these levels in the Jequetepeque Valley, but more in the Lambayeque region than in the south (Keatinge and Conrad 1983; Kosok 1965). The expectation, of course, is that a higher number of regional centers would correlate with a higher number of lower-level centers.

These differences in the distribution of Chimu centers are probably related, but it is difficult to determine what they really indicate about Chimu policies of expansion and administration in the provinces. The differences might well be correlated with both a larger area of arable land and a larger population in the northern valleys between Jequetepeque and Motupe than in the south. These differences between the two areas would have warranted a larger number of both administrative units and administrators in the north.

The distribution of Chimu centers north of the Zaña Valley indicates that this area was not all conquered at one time during the second stage of expansion. There is a sharp decline in the number of Chimu centers north of the Motupe Valley (cf. Richardson et al., this volume), which indicates that Chimu power was not as consolidated in this northernmost area of the

[4] Paramonga, in the Fortaleza Valley, may well have been a Chimu center; however, neither its size nor the date of occupation has been well established.

empire as it was farther to the south. Though the data do not allow for a detailed comparison, they do seem to indicate that the northern part of the empire might have been conquered in phases similar to those outlined previously for the southern part.

A general difference between the northern and southern parts of the empire is that at least some of the architectural features in the northern centers appear to follow Chimu patterns more closely than in the southern centers. The main evidence for this is the presence of a greater number of U-shaped structures or *audiencias* that more closely resemble those in Chan Chan. Though the U-shaped structure in V-124 closely resembles standard Chan Chan *audiencias* (Andrews 1974, n.d.), the U-shaped structures in Manchan are variants. In the north, the U-shaped structures in at least Farfan, Pacatnamu, Cerro Guitarras, and El Purgatorio are more similar in form to the U-shaped structures in Chan Chan.

Though other probable secondary centers have been identified from surface remains, large Chimu compounds have been excavated extensively only in Farfan and Manchan. The compounds in both centers resemble the elite rather than the monumental compounds in Chan Chan. However, Manchan and Farfan differ from each other in high-status burial patterns and thus possibly also in the status of the resident administrators. In Manchan the nobles were buried in subterranean chambers in separate burial compounds. In Farfan, on the other hand, one of the compounds contains a burial platform similar to those associated with royal burials in Chan Chan (Conrad 1982, n.d.; Keatinge and Conrad 1983; Mackey 1987; Mackey and Klymyshyn 1981, n.d.b). Similarly, the surface remains in V-124 indicate the presence of a small burial platform (Mackey n.d.a). As far as we know, Farfan and V-124 are the only secondary centers with burial platforms, signifying that the rank of one of the resident administrators (probably the "provincial governor") might have been higher than of administrators at other regional centers, including Manchan. If interment in a burial platform really was a perquisite of the royal family, at least three explanations can be proposed for this difference: (a) the status of the individuals interred in these burial platforms represents departures from Chimu policy; (b) the administrators in Farfan and in V-124 were granted royal status in return for services rendered to the crown; or (c) Chimu policy regarding the rank of provincial governors changed after the first stage of expansion, and governors during the second stage were no longer members of the royal family. Perhaps the excavation of other secondary centers will resolve this question.

Economic Centralization

A comparison of the northern and southern centers provides support for the statement made previously that the storage of economic goods was concentrated in the capital. Neither the surface remains at the unexcavated centers nor the excavations in Manchan and Farfan have revealed large numbers of storerooms. It seems, then, that with the exception of Chan Chan, Chimu centers had little or no storage capacity; none of the tertiary or quaternary centers showed any evidence of the presence of storerooms.

The storage capacities of the two excavated regional centers are roughly comparable; however, the two differ in the distribution and possibly the function of the storerooms.[5] In Farfan, all of the storerooms are similar to those in the capital in that access to them is restricted. As described previously, the access to many of the storerooms in Manchan is unrestricted; furthermore, the storerooms with unrestricted access are larger than those in Farfan. These differences may indicate that more of the storerooms in Manchan were used either for the bulk storage of comestibles or for the temporary storage of goods being shipped to Chan Chan from outlying lower-level centers. The fact that Farfan has only storerooms with restricted access may mean that the storage of elite goods was more important here than the storage of comestibles (cf. Keatinge and Conrad 1983). Another difference in storage between the two centers is the location of the storerooms. About half of the storerooms in Farfan are behind the burial platform, signifying that the goods stored in them were associated with funerary rites. This association between storerooms and burial platforms occurs in the two earliest compounds in the capital (Uhle and Chayhuac) and was discontinued before the second stage of expansion (Klymyshyn 1987). In Manchan, there is no association between storage and funerary structures. This difference between Farfan and Manchan probably can be attributed to the fact that the former was built during the first stage of expansion and the latter during the second stage.

Though the different areas of the empire are similar in the relative lack of storage facilities, they appear to differ in patterns of production. This difference is evidenced both by variations among centers of the same rank in the presence/absence of evidence for production and by variations in the type of goods being produced. Of the two excavated regional centers, Manchan shows evidence for production and the presence of a permanent support population, while Farfan does not (Keatinge and Conrad 1983). Unfortunately, there is no information on production at other possible regional centers. There is, however, evidence for production at the tertiary and quaternary centers in the Casma Valley, but not in the Moche, Chicama, and Jequetepeque Valleys (cf. Keatinge 1974, 1975; Keatinge and Conrad 1983; Keatinge and Day 1973). As mentioned before, production at Manchan was limited to utilitarian goods with the possible exception of fine textiles. This production differs from the Chimu occupation at Batan Grande (probably a tertiary or quaternary center), where high-status metal artifacts, as well as ingots for distribution to other centers, were produced (Shimada, this volume; Shimada et al. 1982). This difference between Manchan and Batan Grande, however, might reflect variations in the distribution of resources rather than in Chimu policies related to the centralization of production and of economic power.

Resource Control

In the Moche, Chicama, and Jequetepeque Valleys, administrative centers (except for the capital) are located where they can control irrigation canals and field systems. They are not, however, associated with domestic structures indicative of a resident support population. On the other hand, there is evidence for a resident support population at administrative centers in the Viru, Nepeña, and Casma Valleys. Thus, the lower-level lords in Moche, Chicama, and Jequetepeque were apparently controlling a *mita*-like labor force engaged in tasks associated with agricultural production. In contrast, the lords in the valleys farther south were controlling a resident or permanant population engaged not only in agricultural work, but probably also in other types of production. The inference this leads to is that the lower-level lords in the valleys to the south had a more permanent and direct association with their support populations than the lower-level lords in the Moche, Chicama, and Jequetepeque Valleys. This archaeologically based inference seems to contradict the information in the ethnohistoric sources from the Chicama Valley (cf. Netherly 1984, n.d., this volume). Obviously, more excavations are needed in order to clarify this discrepancy.

Incorporation of Indigenous Lords

Without excavation, it is difficult to assess the degree to which indigenous lords were integrated into the Chimu hierarchy. Nonetheless, the integration of indigenous lords in the northern part of the empire is demonstrated by the co-opting of existing centers. The co-opting of existing centers was one of the more consistent policies followed by the Chimu in both the northern and the southern parts of the empire. However, the ratio of co-opted to intrusive centers at different levels of the administrative hierarchy is not known. Nevertheless, the available data indicate that all of the co-opted centers are either tertiary or quaternary in rank, with the possible exception of Pacatnamu. In occupying a large existing center, such as Batan Grande or Chotuna, the Chimu rarely used the entire area of the co-opted center. Once the centers were co-opted, the Chimu generally remodeled the existing structures and built new compounds. From what we know of secondary centers, that is, Farfan and Manchan, it appears that secondary centers were intrusive and not co-opted. Given the importance of the Lambayeque region and the mention of the governors of this area in the chronicles (Cabello Balboa [1586] 1951), it can be predicted that an intrusive secondary center exists in this area; a possible candidate is Apurlec.

The other line of evidence used to determine whether indigenous lords were incorporated into the Chimu hierarchy is the presence/absence or degree of blending of local and Chimu styles. The only obvious indication for the blending of architectural styles in the north is the continuation of the local pattern of building a relatively high number of mounds at major centers. Beyond this, there is virtually no information on whether and to what extent the blending of Chimu and local styles observed in the south also occurred in the northern part of the empire. Without this information, it is not possible to compare the degree to which indigenous lords were incorporated in different parts of the empire.

In addition to the evidence for the incorporation of the indigenous lords, there is evidence that their autonomy was limited. This differs from the interpretation of the ethnohistoric information, which states that the indigenous lords maintained a high degree of autonomy under Chimu rule (Netherly 1984, n.d.). The evidence for the lack of autonomy is similar to the evidence for economic centralization in the empire. As mentioned previously, there is little evidence for the long-term storage of economic goods or for the production of high-status crafts outside of the capital, implying that the indigenous lords were limited in their economic and political power. Let us remember, though, that this limitation applied not only to the indigenous lords, but also to the Chimu nobles sent from the capital to administer the provinces.

CONCLUSIONS

According to the chronicles, the maximum extent of the Chimu Empire included Tumbez in the north and Carabayllo in the south. Within this area there is a high degree of variation in Chimu settlement patterns. In the southern part of the empire, the area with valley-wide networks of administrative centers extends only as far as the Casma Valley. In the valleys farther south only three possible Chimu administrative centers have been identified. North of the Moche Valley, the area with valley-wide networks of administrative centers extends only as far as the Motupe Valley. The valleys farther north contain few if any Chimu settlements (cf. Richardson et al., this volume). On the basis of this distribution of Chimu administrative centers, one can infer that Chimu power was not consolidated to the same degree in all areas of the empire and that the extent of the consolidated empire was probably from the Motupe Valley in the north to the Casma

Valley in the south. Although the process of consolidation was begun in the valleys farther north and south, apparently it was never completed.

The differences in settlement pattern also indicate that the conquest of these areas did not occur in just two episodes as indicated in the chronicles, but in a series of smaller territorial additions. According to the chronicles, the first stage of expansion and conquest is attributed to Ñançenpinco, the grandson of the founder of the dynasty, and the second to Minchançaman, the last independent Chimu ruler. There is evidence from the central part of the empire that the conquests attributed to Ñançenpinco occurred in several phases and over a longer time than a single reign (T. Topic, this volume). Though the evidence from the areas allegedly included in Minchançaman's conquests is not as definitive as from the part of the empire consolidated by Ñançenpinco, the known distribution of settlements in the valleys south of the Santa Valley points to the possibility that this southernmost part of the empire was conquered in three phases.

Perhaps the most important result of our research in the Casma Valley is the evidence that the Chimu take-over occurred earlier than previously indicated. The longer occupation is supported by evidence for three construction phases in Manchan, the high number of Chimu centers in the valley, the distribution of these centers throughout the valley, the number of compounds built by the Chimu, and the apparent expansion of cultivated land in the valley. Further evidence comes from Manchan in the form of a radiocarbon date recalibrated at A.D. 1305 and similarity to ceramics from Velarde in Chan Chan. All of these lines of evidence point to the conclusion that the Chimu presence in the Casma Valley represents a greater time depth than the reign of a single ruler. Thus, similar to his ancestor, Minchançaman should be viewed as a composite figure credited with the exploits of his predecessors and/or successors.

Based on a comparison of the evidence from the Moche Valley with similar evidence from the provinces, one of the overriding principles of Chimu policy was the centralization of economic and political power in the capital, Chan Chan. Architecturally this policy is reflected in the enormous disparity in size between Chan Chan and the secondary centers (e.g., Manchan and Farfan). The economic centralization of the empire is best seen in the differences between Chan Chan and the secondary centers in storage capacity and production. In both Manchan and Farfan, the storage capacity is a fraction of the storage capacity at the capital. Thus, almost all of the empire's wealth seems to have been channeled into the capital, and little was under the direct control of the provincial lords in secondary centers. To date, no storerooms have been located at any of the tertiary or quaternary centers. Of the two excavated secondary centers, only Manchan shows evidence of production. Apart from some fine textiles, most of the production is of utilitarian nature. The lower classes were not dependent upon Chan Chan for craft goods, but the nobles were dependent on Chan Chan for almost all high-status goods.

A second general principle of imperial expansion was controlling the provinces through an administrative hierarchy. Architecturally this hierarchy is reflected by centers of different administrative ranks within the empire. Based on a comparison of elite compounds in Chan Chan with the compounds at secondary centers, the status of administrators in the provinces is comparable to that of the administrators in the elite compounds. But just as not all nobles residing in elite compounds in Chan Chan had the same rank in the administrative hierarchy, so there were differences in rank among administrators in the provinces. Farfan and V-124 present possible exceptions to the general status of provincial administrators as nonroyal nobility because of the presence of burial platforms. The burial platforms might indicate that the administrators buried in them were related to the royal family. Regardless of status, one of the more surprising results of research in the provincial centers is that the empire was administered by very few functionaries.

The third policy of expansion supported by archaeological evidence from the Casma Valley and the valleys north of the Moche Valley is the integration of local indigenous lords into the Chimu hierarchy, as implied in the chronicles. The first line of evidence for this is the co-opting of existing centers by the Chimu at least at the tertiary and quaternary levels. Even at the intrusive secondary center, Manchan, there is evidence for the integration of indigenous lords. The compounds built during the first two phases of construction show a blending of local and Chimu architectural styles. More than half of the textiles found in this center show a blending of local weaving techniques with Chimu decorative motifs.

In general, Chimu policies do not seem to have been very disruptive to pre-existing settlement and economic patterns. Evidence for resettlement of the indigenous population shows that the Chimu did not resettle people to the same extent as did the Inca. The Chimu maintained the existing economic patterns and in some cases expanded resource utilization, indicating that economic motives played an important role in the empire's expansion. Economic reasons and the distribution of resources might also account for many of the differences between the northern and southern parts of the empire. One of these differences—the larger number of major Chimu centers in the north—may be related to both greater resources and a larger population in this area. A second difference—the apparent closer adherence to Chimu architectural patterns in the north—might also be related to the greater economic importance and hence closer control of this area.

BIBLIOGRAPHY

ANDREWS, ANTHONY P.
1974 The U-Shaped Structures at Chan Chan. *Journal of Field Archaeology* 1 (3/4): 241–264.
n.d. A Preliminary Study of U-Shaped Structures in Chan Chan and Vicinity, Peru. B.A. thesis, Department of Anthropology, Harvard University, 1972.

BENNETT, WENDELL C.
1939 *Archaeology of the North Coast of Peru.* Anthropological Papers of the American Museum of Natural History 37 (1). New York.

CABELLO BALBOA, MIGUEL
[1586] *Miscelánea antártica.* Universidad Nacional Mayor de San Marcos, 1951 Lima.

CALANCHA, ANTONIO DE LA
1638 *Crónica moralizada del Ordén de San Augustín en el Perú, con sucesos egenplares en esta monarquía.* Pedro Lacavalleria, Barcelona.

CÁRDENAS MARTÍN, MERCEDES
1978 *Columna cronológica para el valle de Huaura.* Instituto Riva-Aguero, Pontifica Universidad Católica del Perú, Lima.

CHRISTALLER, W.
[1933] *Central Places in Southern Germany* (C. W. Baskin, trans.). Prentice-1966 Hall, Englewood Cliffs, N.J.

COLLIER, DONALD
1955 *Cultural Chronology and Change as Reflected in the Ceramics of the Virú Valley, Peru. Fieldiana: Anthropology* 43. Field Museum of Natural History, Chicago.
1962 Archaeological Investigations in the Casma Valley, Peru. *Akten des 34. Internationalen Amerikanistenkongress, Wien, 1960:* 411–417.

CONRAD, GEOFFREY
1982 The Burial Platforms of Chan Chan: Some Social and Political Implications. In *Chan Chan: Andean Desert City* (Michael E. Moseley and Kent C. Day, eds.): 87–117. University of New Mexico Press, Albuquerque.
n.d. Burial Platforms and Related Structures on the North Coast of Peru: Some Social and Political Implications. Ph.D. dissertation, Department of Anthropology, Harvard University, 1974.

DAGGETT, RICHARD E.
1983 Megalithic Sites in the Nepeña Valley, Peru. In *Investigations of the Andean Past* (Daniel H. Sandweiss, ed.): 75–97. Cornell Latin American Studies Program, Ithaca.

FUNG PINEDA, ROSA, and VICTOR PIMENTEL G.
1973 Chankillo. *Revista del Museo Nacional* 39: 71–80.

ISBELL, WILLIAM H., and KATHARINA J. SCHREIBER
1978 Was Huari a State? *American Antiquity* 43(3): 372–389.

JOHNSON, GREGORY A.
>   1973   *Local Exchange and Early State Development in Southwestern Iran.* University of Michigan Museum of Anthropology, Anthropological Paper 51.
>   1977   Aspects of Regional Analysis in Archaeology. *Annual Review of Anthropology* 6: 479–508.

KEATINGE, RICHARD W.
>   1974   Chimu Rural Administrative Centers in the Moche Valley, Peru. *World Archaeology* 6: 66–82.
>   1975   Urban Settlement and Rural Sustaining Communities: An Example from Chan Chan's Hinterland. *Journal of Field Archaeology* 2(3): 215–227.
>   n.d.   Chimu Ceramics from the Moche Valley, Peru: A Computer Application to Seriation. Ph.D. dissertation, Department of Anthropology, Harvard University, 1973.

KEATINGE, RICHARD W., and GEOFFREY W. CONRAD
>   1983   Imperialist Expansion in Peruvian Prehistory: Chimu Administration of a Conquered Territory. *Journal of Field Archaeology* 10(3): 255–283.

KEATINGE, RICHARD W., and KENT C. DAY
>   1973   Socio-economic Organization of the Moche Valley, Peru, during the Chimu Occupation of Chan Chan. *Journal of Anthropological Research* 29(1):275–295.

KLYMYSHYN, ALEXANDRA M. ULANA
>   1982   Elite Compounds in Chan Chan. In *Chan Chan: Andean Desert City* (Michael E. Moseley and Kent C. Day, eds.): 119–143. University of New Mexico Press, Albuquerque.
>   1987   The Development of Chimu Administration in Chan Chan. In *Origins and Development of the Andean State* (J. Haas, T. and S. Pozorski, eds.): 97–110. Cambridge University Press, Cambridge.

KOLATA, ALAN L.
>   1982   Chronology and Settlement Growth at Chan Chan. In *Chan Chan: Andean Desert City* (Michael E. Moseley and Kent C. Day, eds.): 67–85. University of New Mexico Press, Albuquerque.
>   n.d.   Chan Chan: The Form of the City in Time. Ph.D. dissertation, Department of Anthropology, Harvard University, 1978.

KOSOK, PAUL
>   1960   El valle de Lambayeque. *Actas y trabajos del II Congreso Nacional de História del Perú (época pre-hispánica), 1958* 1: 49–67. Centro de Estudios Histórico-Militares del Perú, Lima.
>   1965   *Life, Land and Water in Ancient Peru.* Long Island University Press, New York.

KUS, JAMES S.
>   1980   La agricultura estatál en la costa norte de Perú. *America Indígena* 40(4): 713–729. Mexico City.

LOESCH, A.
[1940]   *The Economics of Location* (H. Woglom and W. F. Stolper, trans.). Yale
1954   University Press, New Haven.

MACKEY, CAROL J.
1987   Chimu Administration in the Provinces. In *Origins and Development of the Andean State* (J. Haas, T. and S. Pozorski, eds.): 121–129. Cambridge University Press.
n.d.a   *Archaeological Investigations in the Southern Part of the Chimu Empire.* English version of report submitted to the Instituto Nacional de Cultura, Lima, 1979.
n.d.b.   Ceramics from the Chimu Heartland: A Ceramic Seriation from the Moche and Chicama Valleys, Peru. Unpublished manuscript.

MACKEY, CAROL J., and ALEXANDRA M. ULANA KLYMYSHYN
1981   Construction and Labor Organization in the Chimu Empire. *Ñawpa Pacha* 19: 99–114.
n.d.a   A Preliminary Ranking of Chimu Sites. Paper presented at Annual Meeting of Institute of Andean Studies, Berkeley, 1980.
n.d.b   Political Integration in Prehispanic Peru. Final report to the National Science Foundation for 1981–82. Unpublished manuscript, 1983.

MOORE, JERRY D.
1981   Chimu Socio-Economic Organization: Preliminary Data from Manchan, Casma Valley, Peru. *Ñawpa Pacha* 19: 115–128.
n.d.   Household Economics and Political Integration: The Lower Class of the Chimu Empire. Ph.D. dissertation, Department of Anthropology, University of California, Santa Barbara, 1985.

MOSELEY, MICHAEL E., and KENT C. DAY, eds.
1982   *Chan Chan: Andean Desert City.* University of New Mexico Press, Albuquerque.

NETHERLY, PATRICIA J.
1984   The Management of Late Andean Irrigation Systems on the North Coast of Peru. *American Antiquity* 49(2): 227–254.
n.d.   *Local Level Lords on the North Coast of Peru.* Ph.D. dissertation, Department of Anthropology, Cornell University, 1977.

ONERN (Oficina Nacional de Evaluación de Recursos Naturales)
1972   *Inventário, evaluación y uso racionál de los recursos naturales de la costa: Valles de Casma, Culebras y Huarmey.* Lima.

POZORSKI, THOMAS, SHELIA POZORSKI, CAROL MACKEY, and ALEXANDRA M. ULANA KLYMYSHYN
1983   Pre-Hispanic Ridged Fields of the Casma Valley. *The Geographical Review* 73(4): 407–416.

PROUXL, DONALD
1968   *An Archaeological Survey of the Nepeña Valley, Peru.* Research Report Number 2, Department of Anthropology, University of Massachusetts, Amherst.

1973   *Archaeological Investigations in the Nepeña Valley, Peru.* Research Report Number 13, Department of Anthropology, University of Massachusetts, Amherst.

ROSTWOROWSKI DE DIEZ CANSECO, MARÍA
1961   *Curacas y sucesiones: Costa norte.* Imprenta Minerva, Lima.

ROWE, JOHN H.
1948   The Kingdom of Chimor. *Acta Americana* 6(1–2): 26–59.

SAMANIEGO, LORENZO
1973   *Los nuevos trabajos arqueológicos en Sechín, Casma, Perú.* Ediciones Larsen, Trujillo.

SCHAEDEL, RICHARD P.
1951   Major Ceremonial and Population Centers in Northern Peru. *Civilizations of Ancient America, Selected Papers of the 29th International Congress of Americanists:* 232–243. Chicago.
1966   Incipient Urbanization and Secularization in Tiahuanacoid Peru. *American Antiquity* 31(1): 338–344.

SHIMADA, IZUMI, STEPHEN M. EPSTEIN, and ALAN F. CRAIG
1982   Batan Grande: A Prehistoric Metallurgical Center in Peru. *Science* 216: 952–959.

TELLO, JULIO C.
1956   *Arqueología del Valle de Casma. Culturas: Chavín, Santa o Huaylas Yunga y Sub-Chimú.* Universidad Nacional de San Marcos, Lima.

THOMPSON, DONALD E.
1966   Archaeological Investigations in the Huarmey Valley, Peru. *XXXVI Congreso Internacional de Americanistas, Madrid, 1964* 1: 541–548.
n.d.   Architecture and Settlement Patterns in the Casma Valley, Peru. Ph.D. dissertation, Department of Anthropology, Harvard University, 1961.

TOPIC, JOHN R., JR.
1982   Lower-Class Social and Economic Organization in Chan Chan. In *Chan Chan: Andean Desert City* (Michael E. Moseley and Kent C. Day, eds.): 145–176. University of New Mexico Press, Albuquerque.
n.d.   The Lower Class at Chan Chan: A Qualitative Approach. Ph.D. dissertation, Department of Anthropology, Harvard University, 1977.

WILLEY, GORDON R.
1953   *Prehistoric Settlement Patterns in the Virú Valley, Northern Peru.* Bureau of American Ethnology, Bulletin 155. Smithsonian Institution, Washington, D.C.

WILSON, DAVID J.
1988   *Prehispanic Settlement Patterns in the Lower Santa Valley, Peru.* Smithsonian Institution, Washington, D.C.

WRIGHT, HENRY T.
1977   Recent Research on the Origin of the State. *Annual Review of Anthropology* 6: 379–397.

Carol J. Mackey and A. M. Ulana Klymyshyn

Wright, Henry T., and Gregory A. Johnson
    1975   Population, Exchange, and Early State Formation in South-Western
           Iran. *American Anthropologist* 77: 267–289.

Farfan, General Pacatnamu, and the Dynastic History of Chimor

GEOFFREY W. CONRAD

INDIANA UNIVERSITY

THE JEQUETEPEQUE VALLEY, some 100 km north of Chan Chan, is the third largest Peruvian coastal valley. In late prehistoric times it was an important Chimu province, part of a five-valley irrigation complex that formed the empire's northern breadbasket (Kosok 1965; Moseley 1983).

According to Antonio de la Calancha's (1638) chronicle, Jequetepeque was conquered and annexed by a Chimu military leader named Pacatnamu.[1] The king of Chimor rewarded "General Pacatnamu" for his victory by installing him as the first provincial governor of the valley. The general administered his province from a site that was built to serve as his capital and eventually came to bear his name (Calancha bk. 3, ch. 1, 1638: 546–547; Means 1931: 56–57).

Although presumably a nobleman, General Pacatnamu was not a member of the dynastic succession, and he is not mentioned in the list of Chimu rulers given in the Anonymous History of 1604 (Vargas Ugarte 1936: 232–233). In fact, as far as I know, he appears only in Calancha's account. Nonetheless, he represents the best case for the reality of a specific Pre-Columbian individual named in the native histories of Chimor. After a brief review of the archaeological data supporting that claim, I would like to consider what General Pacatnamu has to tell us, directly and indirectly, about the nature of Chimu dynastic history.

FARFAN AND GENERAL PACATNAMU

Archaeological investigations in the Jequetepeque Valley have identified the site of Farfan, rather than another site currently known as Pacatnamu, as the administrative center built for the general—that is, as the Chimu provincial capital of the valley. The evidence arguing that Farfan is the real

---

[1] Calancha (bk. 3, ch. 1, 1638: 546) says the name means "padre común, o padre de todos."

Pacatnamu has been presented in detail elsewhere (Keatinge and Conrad 1983), and I will give only a brief recapitulation here.

Farfan's topographic placement is consistent with the location of General Pacatnamu's palace as described in Calancha's (1638) account. Furthermore, architecture, ceramics, and other artifacts identify Farfan not just as an intrusive Chimu administrative center but as the largest such site in the valley. The ruins of Farfan consist of six large, rectilinear compounds built according to canons apparent in some of the monumental architecture of Chan Chan. In particular, the principal structure at Farfan, Compound II, shares many architectural details with the royal compounds of Chan Chan. Most notably, Compound II contains the following Chan Chan-like features: a main entrance in the form of a pilastered doorway adorned with carved wooden figures; access from the doorway to the rest of the compound via a walled entry court; banks of small, contiguous rooms that are thought to have served as storerooms; an *audiencia,* or three-sided structure with niched walls, in association with the largest group of "storerooms"; and a high-status funerary structure of the type known as a burial platform, located toward the rear of the compound.

Interestingly, the burial platform seems to have been used only once, for the funeral of a single high-status individual, and then to have been sealed off at a relatively early date in the occupation of Farfan. In fact, all of the major structures at the site were erected at the beginning of its Chimu occupation; subsequent work was confined to minor remodeling (Keatinge and Conrad 1983). The single early burst of construction undoubtedly reflects Chan Chan's desire for a highly active and visible imperial presence in the valley immediately after the conquest; as time went by and Jequetepeque became fully integrated into the empire, the need for such an obtrusive show of force declined, and no more large buildings were added to Farfan. Similarly, I suggest that the first chief official at the site was given a highly prestigious reward—the right to be interred in a burial platform—as a symbol of his own importance and of that of the newly conquered province to Chimor. Again, after a generation of Chimu rule, Jequetepeque was a well-established province, and the lords of Chan Chan did not feel the need for such conspicuous attention to the valley and its imperial supervisor.

All of the archaeological evidence is completely consistent with Calancha's account of a Chimu conqueror who was rewarded with the governorship of the valley and who established its provincial capital. This military and political leader built the site of Farfan, lived in Compound II, and was buried in its burial platform.[2] While his name may or may not have been

---

[2] Interestingly, Calancha (bk. 3, ch. 1, 1638: 547) says that only one building in General Pacatnamu's capital served as the palace of the governor, while all the rest were *huacas,* or ceremonial structures. This statement is congruent with the archaeological evidence from Farfan. Compound II appears to be functionally distinct from the other major constructions.

Pacatnamu, the figure described in Calancha's chronicle was a real, historical individual.

In addition to identifying General Pacatnamu as a real person, the archaeological data allow us to attach an approximate date to his life and to correlate it with the sequence of construction at Chan Chan. (Again, see Keatinge and Conrad 1983, for a more detailed exposition.) Ceramics from sealed contexts place the founding of Farfan in the early phase of Chimor's imperial history. Furthermore, Farfan was built with mud bricks of a type characteristic of the early phase of monumental architecture at Chan Chan. More precisely, the specific form of the *audiencia* crossdates Compound II at Farfan with the southwestern sector of Uhle, the second royal compound in the Chan Chan sequence, and with El Milagro de San Jose, a Chimu rural administrative center in the Moche Valley (Kolata n.d.; Keatinge and Conrad 1983). Radiocarbon dates of A.D. 1155 ± 130 and 1250 ± 75, obtained from early contexts in Compound II, are consistent with a date of A.D. 1195 ± 150 from the southwestern sector of Uhle and with assays of A.D. 1135 ± 80 and 1225 ± 80 from El Milagro de San Jose (Keatinge and Conrad 1983). All of these different lines of chronological evidence are consistent. They place General Pacatnamu's conquest of the Jequetepeque Valley and the founding of Farfan around A.D. 1200 (more accurately, somewhere between A.D. 1150 and 1250).

Likewise, the chronological data argue that when General Pacatnamu marched forth, he did so on behalf of a ruler who was living in the southwestern sector of the Uhle compound at Chan Chan. Accordingly, for a time around A.D. 1200, we now have one event and two individuals whose historical reality can be confirmed. The event is the Chimu conquest of the Jequetepeque Valley; the individuals are General Pacatnamu and an unnamed king in the southwestern sector of Uhle.

According to the Anonymous History, the Jequetepeque Valley was conquered during the reign of Ñançenpinco. The third monarch on the dynastic list, he is described as the first Chimu ruler to conquer territory outside the Moche Valley and is credited with subjugating the coast from Jequetepeque in the north to Santa in the south. When this account is combined with Calancha's, Ñançenpinco becomes the king who sent Pacatnamu forth and rewarded the general's victory with a governorship.

The archaeological data do provide a measure of support for the existence of a Chimu monarch named Ñançenpinco. An event attributed to him, the conquest of Jequetepeque, occurred during the reign of one of a still-undetermined number of kings who ruled Chimor from the southwestern sector of Uhle. As confirmation of an individual's historical reality, this evidence is certainly modest. Compared to General Pacatnamu, Ñançen-pinco remains a shadowy figure.

In fact, with Ñançenpinco tidy correlations between archaeological and ethnohistorical data begin to break down. Archaeological evidence places the conquest of·Jequetepeque around A.D. 1200, but it dates the founding of Chan Chan to A.D. 850 or 900 (Kolata 1982, n.d.). Accordingly, Ñan-çenpinco and the two rulers who precede him, Taycanamo and Guacricaur, need to be seen as composite figures. Certain deeds attributed to these early Chimu kings—the founding of the ruling dynasty (Taycanamo), political consolidation of the Moche Valley (Guacricaur), and the first major stage of imperial expansion (Ñançenpinco)—reflect actual historical phenomena; however, those events and processes took place over a span of roughly three centuries, not three generations (Mackey and Klymyshyn, this volume; T. Topic, this volume).

Apparently, the oral tradition recorded in the Anonymous History com-pressed the seminal events of Chimor's first three-hundred-odd years into the figures of three kings. The process was indeed one of compression: fictitious personages were not added to real individuals to expand the num-ber of kings. Instead, rulers were deleted from the actual historical succes-sion to create an official dynastic list. If we ask why, we are really asking two questions: why did the Chimu alter their account of the dynastic suc-cesssion, and why did they choose to do so by compressing it?

COSMOLOGY, SOCIAL STRUCTURE, AND THE DYNASTIC HISTORY OF CHIMOR

One potential answer, most thoroughly explored in the works of R. Tom Zuidema (1973, 1977, 1983, this volume, and elsewhere) is grounded in a structuralist theoretical perspective. According to Zuidema, the royal gene-alogies of Andean polities were not shaped by chronological progression of events and individuals, but by cosmologies and social structures. That is, an Andean dynastic list is not a historical document in the Western sense, but a presentation of a society's fundamental organizational principles. In this volume such reasoning underlies not only Zuidema's own paper, but also that of Patricia Netherly. All Andean historiography, Netherly claims, has a structural purpose, and even narrative accounts of real events are intended to make structural statements.

In the specific case of Chimor, the Anonymous History purports to list the heads of the ruling dynasty from its inception down to 1604. The founding father, Taycanamo, is said to have arrived from across the sea on a log raft typical of the area around the Gulf of Guayaquil. The narrative then traces the dynasty's fortunes through three distinct epochs: that of Chimor's existence as an independent polity, the era of Inca domination, and the first seventy years of Spanish rule. The number of rulers on the list is subject to various interpretations (e.g., Kosok 1965: 73–74; Rostworowski 1961: 54–57; Rowe 1948: 28–30, 39–41): there are nine named individuals and anywhere from ten to thirteen nameless ones (Table 1).

Interestingly, Zuidema himself (this volume) finds the Anonymous History too fragmentary to be of much use, and he concludes that it has no structural significance; however, Netherly (this volume) suggests that the Chimu king list is in fact a presentation of the structural principle of dual division. Considering only the Pre-Hispanic figures, Netherly sees the list as reflecting an upper moiety with some eight named rulers and a lower moiety with seven nameless ones.

While this interpretation is possible, there are many other equally plausible alternatives. For example, Netherly makes no distinction between the independent kings of Chimor and their descendants who served as provincial administrators under Inca domination. Yet there are good reasons to believe that the two groups should be separated for analytical purposes. The Anonymous History discusses the Inca conquest in more detail than any other event in Chimu history, with the possible exception of the founding of the dynasty. Furthermore, the narrative emphasizes that the Inca victory brought an imposed change in the Chimu leadership: the conquerors dethroned Minchançaman, the last independent king of Chimor, carried him off to Cuzco, and replaced him with one of his sons.

In view of these facts, I suggest that the Inca conquest is meant to be seen as a cataclysmic event marking the beginning of a new epoch of Chimu history, and that the Inca underlings need to be distinguished from the independent kings. That is, the Anonymous History should be read as listing four named rulers vs. five to seven nameless ones for the epoch of Chimu autonomy, four named figures and no anonymous ones for the era of Inca domination, and two named individuals and five or six nameless ones for the early Colonial period (Table 1). If this list is really concerned with stressing dual division through the presentation of an anonymous lower moiety, it does so very ineffectively.

Consider the number of rulers in each epoch. If the list is really a statement of organizational principles, rather than a historical narrative, the historically accurate number of rulers is irrelevant, and no concession should be made to it. The numbers on the list should have been chosen solely for the purpose of depicting structural principles. To portray dual division, it would have made the most sense to have an equal number of named and nameless rulers for the epoch of Chimu autonomy. Equal numbers would have emphasized pairing, and thus duality. Instead, the list presents us with four named rulers and five to seven nameless ones—numbers that do not seem to emphasize much of anything, except uncertainty and ambiguity.

TABLE 1. THE DYNASTIC SUCCESSION OF CHIMOR
(From the Anonymous History of 1604)

Epoch	Sequence of Rulers/Administrators in the Text*	Named Individuals	Unnamed Individuals	Ambiguities
	Don Antonio Chayguar			Is Antonio Chayguar the sixth Christian *cacique*, or did he follow the sixth?
Spanish Colonial	6 Christian *caciques*	2	5 or 6	
	Cajaçimçim/Don Martín (became Christian; changed name)			
Inca Domination	Cajaçimçim Ancocuyuch Guamanchumo Chumuncaur	4	0	
	Minchançaman 7 descendants of Guacricaur	4	5, 6, or 7	Did the author actually mean seven descendants of *Ñançenpinco*? If not, is Nançenpinco included in the unnamed descendants of Guacricaur?
Chimor as Autonomous Polity	Ñançenpinco Guacricaur			Is Minchançaman the seventh descendant, or did he follow the seventh?
	Taycanamo			

*Read up from earliest to latest.

The same argument applies even more dramatically to the Inca and Colonial periods. As it stands, the numbers of rulers seem to have been chosen with an eye to obscuring, rather than highlighting, the possible presence of two moieties.

Furthermore, what are we to make of the lack of unnamed rulers during the era of Inca domination? The lower moiety seems to have vanished. In view of the presumed importance of dual division in both Chimu and Inca society, this disappearance is highly surprising. In fact, it makes the "anonymous lower moiety" argument untenable for the period of Inca control.

All in all, given the problems, discrepancies, and inconsistencies that arise no matter how the rulers are grouped, I do not find the "anonymous lower moiety" interpretation compelling. Perhaps I should make clear that I am not attempting to deny the existence of moiety organization on the North Coast. What I am saying is that I am not convinced Chimu dynastic oral tradition is fundamentally a presentation of dual division. In truth, I cannot tell whether moiety organization is reflected in the Anonymous History at all.

Likewise, if one searches for underlying structural principles in the numbers of rulers, it soon becomes apparent that quite a few different numbers can be teased out of the list. I have been able to identify potential groupings of three, four, five, six, seven, eight, nine, ten, eleven, twelve, thirteen, fourteen, fifteen, nineteen, twenty, and twenty-one individuals; there are probably others as well. While all of these numbers are embedded in the narrative, there is no way to tell which, if any, of them are significant and which are accidental (cf. Hammel 1965).

Accordingly, I must agree with Zuidema's conclusion that the Chimu dynastic list has no structural significance. Here it might be useful to draw a distinction between significance in the sense of content and significance in the sense of purpose. As to whether the king list has any structural content—that is, whether it reflects dual division or other structural principles—I am skeptical but admit that the Anonymous History is too fragmentary to permit a definite answer. Because the very existence of structural content is in doubt, I am extremely reluctant to say that the *purpose* of the king list is to present organizational principles. In fact, I do not think the search for hidden structural significance is a particularly helpful approach to the Anonymous History. In my opinion, it diverts attention away from the most important purposes of the narrative.

STATECRAFT AND DYNASTIC HISTORY

Like all states, the Chimu Empire faced the need to mobilize its citizens, to induce them to participate in projects ranging from military campaigns to the construction of monuments and the farming of state fields. For me, this practical political problem provides the key to the most fruitful way of analyzing the Anonymous History, namely, as a piece of imperial propaganda that was continuously reworked to suit the purposes of the Chimu state. The events of the pre-Inca epoch described in the dynastic list are what has survived of an official, state-sanctioned history of Chimor. I suggest that the mixture of fact and fiction, the compression of chronological time and the truncation or elimination of certain kings are not only understandable, but expectable. They represent propagandistic manipulations designed to serve the specific goals of individual Chimu rulers.

There is an extensive sociological literature on propaganda. Definitions vary (e.g., Doob 1935: 71–90; Ellul 1965: 61–87), but all authorities agree that propaganda is fundamentally an attempt to mobilize individuals by influencing their attitudes (Doob 1935: 3–4, 31, 89; Ellul 1965: 30–31, 61). An essential characteristic of propaganda is that it is goal-oriented. Propaganda aims at producing results through action.

The propagandist, however, is not simply concerned with impelling people to perform some specific deed in the here and now. In fact, without proper long-term preparation such efforts stand a good chance of failing. Hence, a crucial objective is "to make [the individual] sensitive to some influence, to get him into condition for the time when he will effectively, and without delay or hesitation, participate in an action" (Ellul 1965: 30–31). The skillful propagandist aims to instill attitudes that will lead his audience to respond as desired in the future, no matter what its members are called upon to do.

The concern with both present action and preparation for an unforeseeable future means that an integrated propaganda campaign has three purposes: indoctrination, motivation, and justification. In the specific case of state propaganda, the type at issue here, indoctrination consists of the attempt to arouse favorable attitudes toward the state and its leaders, and therefore toward the projects proposed by those leaders. Successful indoctrination allows the state to motivate its citizens to participate in specific actions and also helps to provide convincing justifications for those actions and their consequences. In turn, projects in which people have participated willingly and whose results have been justified become part of the state's record of success, facilitating the task of indoctrination. In effective propaganda, indoctrination, motivation, and justification are mutually reinforcing goals.

An essential element of the entire process is the need to take control of history and rewrite it (Ellul 1965: 14). In the hands of the propagandist, the past is reshaped to create precedent for the present. An official, state-sanctioned history is at the same time a source of indoctrination, motivation, and justification. Accounts of heroic ancestry and past glories are intended to produce positive attitudes toward the state and its rulers. It is particularly helpful for the propagandist to claim or imply that the state's history has goals or purposes that were only partially fulfilled in the past, but which may be completed in the present. In this way motivation and justification for the state's projects are provided simultaneously.

While the rewriting of history to suit the ends of the state is an all too familiar characteristic of the twentieth century, it is certainly not a modern invention. The manipulation of history for propagandistic purposes has been noted for Sumer, Akkad, Assyria, and Babylonia (Finkelstein 1979), Vedic India (Sharma 1979), imperial China (Wright 1979), and Aztec Mexico (Conrad and Demarest 1984: 30–38), to name just a few ancient civilizations. In a particularly relevant example, Jacob Finkelstein (1979: 59–64) has discussed how ancient Mesopotamian king lists were reworked to serve state purposes.

Although such historical revisionism can be attempted by anyone, it is particularly easy for societies that, like the Chimu, lack written records. Margaret Mead (1979) has emphasized how readily the past can be transformed in nonliterate societies, where the remembering and transmission of historical knowledge is in the hands of a relatively small number of individuals.

> In fact, one of the significant characteristics of preliterate societies is the ease with which the past is edited and the record altered. . . . There are no books to burn, no chronicles to alter, no steles or carved stone records to tear down . . . in the absence of such comparisons, new customs may be very rapidly transmuted into ancient custom, and the young of each generation may be given a feeling of immutability, of the complete absence of change. . . . (Mead 1979: 28)

Herein lies one of the most striking differences between the structuralist approach to dynastic history and my own. The interpretation of dynastic history as a presentation of cosmology and social structure demands a static format to preserve the integrity of the metaphor. In contrast, the view of state-sanctioned history as goal-oriented propaganda predicts a more fluid situation. It expects that important symbols will be continuously manipulated in attempts to fulfill concrete needs, demands, and desires. As specific motives and purposes change, different elements can be emphasized, downplayed, ignored, added, or deleted. Details of the state's official version of its own history can be expected to change through time.

And yet, despite whatever manipulations are involved in any use of history as propaganda, we can expect a framework of essentially accurate facts to endure. Perhaps the single most widely held misconception about propaganda is that it is somehow concerned with getting people to swallow lies. In reality, effective propaganda is always grounded in truth. This principle has been recognized not only by all leading scholars of propaganda but by all of its most notorious modern practitioners as well (Ellul 1965: 52–61). Indeed, no less an authority than Dr. Joseph Goebbels, the Nazi Minister of Public Enlightenment and Propaganda, constantly insisted that the facts to be disseminated must be accurate. As Lenin put it, "In propaganda, truth pays off" (Ellul 1965: 53).

The adept propagandist prefers to confine falsehoods to the realm of intentions and interpretations, not facts (Ellul 1965: 53). Even then, indirect means of conveying false messages are preferable to direct ones. Outright lies are dangerous, unless there is no way of checking up on them. It is better to communicate untruths by omission—the suppression of undesirable facts (Ellul 1965: 56)—or through deliberately ambiguous statements (Mead 1979: 28). Even such "indirect lies" are most effective when they are embedded in a matrix of facts whose accuracy can be established or is at least taken for granted by the intended audience.

This brief review of the basic principles of effective propaganda implies that any dynastic history with propagandistic intent should have the following characteristics. It will attempt to serve the goals of indoctrination, motivation, and justification. Traced through time, it will exhibit a certain fluidity of detail; if seen at only one time, it will have to display definite potential for manipulation. Finally, it will have a general framework of "truths" that are accurate, or at least widely believed by its audience. Useful untruths will be set into this framework, preferably through omission and ambiguity.

THE CHIMU KING LIST AS PROPAGANDA

The Anonymous History records Chimu oral tradition, and its pre-Inca section is what remains of a late imperial account of Chimor's history. The surviving remnants are sketchy, and we cannot know everything that underlay the full version. Nonetheless, even in its woefully incomplete form, the account presented in the Anonymous History embodies every characteristic of the effective use of history as propaganda.

The king list aims to indoctrinate Chimu citizens by inducing them to see their rulers as heroic figures, superhuman beings whose decisions must be correct and whose orders must be followed. In addition to the overall sanctioning of Chimu history provided by this view of the state's leaders, the Anonymous History offers a justification for one specific historical event: the conquest of the empire's northern frontier. At the same time, the narrative contains motivation and justification for events that had not yet happened when Chimor fell—namely, further conquests in the north.

Certain elements of the Anonymous History can be shown to have been altered, and other details are subject to further manipulation. Nonetheless, the framework of Chimu history given in the king list is basically true.

Where demonstrable falsehoods occur, they tend to take the form of omissions, suppressions, and ambiguities, rather than the fabrication of events that never happened.

In the Anonymous History indoctrination—the attempt to create favorable attitudes toward the state, its leaders, and their projects—occurs through the legitimation of the ruling dynasty. The legitimating intent of the narrative is obvious and straightforward. The Anonymous History describes how a great lord sent the founding father, Taycanamo, across the sea to govern the Moche Valley. Possessed of powerful ritual paraphernalia and esoteric knowledge, Taycanamo is clearly portrayed as a superior being. Small wonder that the native inhabitants of the valley obeyed him and gave him their daughters to marry.

Historical revisionism through truncation and the creation of composite characters contributed to the legitimating effect of this tale. Dynastic oral history compressed the seminal events of Chimor's first three centuries into three generations, producing the heroic figures of Taycanamo, Guacricaur, and Ñançenpinco. Receiving credit for the deeds of a whole series of rulers did not merely enhance their own reputations; it turned them into Heroic Ancestors who aggrandized their entire dynasty and sanctioned its right to rule.[3]

Read as state propaganda, the surviving version of the dynastic succession also provides a justification for the conquest of Chimor's northern frontier, the region between Paita and Tumbez on the northernmost coast of Peru. Oral tradition atttributed this event to Minchançaman's reign. Archaeology places it very late in the independent history of Chimor, probably after A.D. 1400 (Richardson and Heaps de Peña n.d.; Richardson et al., this volume).

Recall that a great lord sent Taycanamo across the sea on a balsa raft. Whence precisely did the founder of the Chimu dynasty supposedly come? The Anonymous History disclaims exact knowledge but notes that "the balsa of logs is used on the coast of Payta and Tumbez, from which it is presumed that this Indian did not come from a very distant region" (translation by John H. Rowe [1948: 28]). That is, a detail given in the Anonymous History suggests that Taycanamo came from the Paita-Tumbez region. Hence, the legend implies that when Minchançaman conquered the northernmost Peruvian coast, he may not have been invading foreign territory. Instead, he may well have been simply reincorporating his ancestral homeland into his domain. In this light the Chimu conquest of Paita and Tumbez emerges as completely right and just—in reality, nothing more than a form of homecoming for the state's rulers.

And yet, in terms of what it can motivate and justify, the Anonymous

---

[3] Calancha (bk. 3, ch. 2, 1638: 554; see also Rowe 1948: 47) indicates that the Chimu nobility were believed to have been created separately from the commoners.

History is open-ended. The narrative never states unambiguously that Taycanamo came from far northern Peru; it only provides a detail that indicates he *might have*. However, that same detail—the balsa raft—was also typical of coastal Ecuador in late prehistoric times (Cordy-Collins, this volume; Estrada 1955; Lothrop 1932; Murphy 1941). If for no other reason than that it was the source of Spondylus shell, one of the most important ritual goods in Chimor (Cordy-Collins, this volume), coastal Ecuador would have been a very attractive target to the Chimu leadership.

All that was necessary was to find some "proof" that Taycanamo could not have come from far northern Peru. Any inconsistency, no matter how minor, between the oral tradition and actual conditions in the Paita-Tumbez region would have sufficed. Taycanamo's balsa raft would then have made coastal Ecuador the leading candidate for the ancestral homeland of the Chimu dynasty. In other words, the very same logic that legitimated the conquest of Tumbez would have vindicated an invasion of coastal Ecuador, had Chimor survived long enough to make one. The notion that the empire's expansion had not proceeded far enough was already implicit in the king list. Motivation and justification for further campaigns were built right into the Taycanamo legend.

If Chimu dynastic tradition serves the purposes of indoctrination, motivation, and justification, archaeological evidence also indicates that it is grounded in historical truth. Even in the Taycanamo legend, the section of the Anonymous History most closely approaching an outright lie, truth and falsehood are muddled. As Izumi Shimada (this volume) argues, Chimu culture exhibits strong northern influences. In that sense the claim of foreign origin is not completely baseless. Furthermore, by A.D. 1400 or so, the average Chimu citizen obviously had no way of proving that the founder of the dynasty had not arrived from across the sea on a balsa raft. (For that matter, neither do I.) Undoubtedly, the truth of the Taycanamo legend was simply taken for granted.

More importantly, as Carol Mackey and A. M. Ulana Klymyshyn (this volume) and Theresa Topic (this volume) have demonstrated, the outline of the Chimu expansion presented in the Anonymous History is essentially correct. Moreover, where it errs, it does so through omission and suppression. Again, the Chimu king list represents a compression of historical reality. Various early rulers—the exact number is unknown—have been edited out of the state's memory to create the official version of the dynastic succession.

There is good reason to believe that these manipulations were deliberate, for the reworking of the dynastic succession apparent in the written record is paralleled in the archaeology of Chan Chan. The capital city's earliest monumental constructions have been selectively preserved, altered, or destroyed (Moseley, this volume; Topic and Moseley 1983). Evidently the Chimu rulers tried to make the visible physical evidence consistent with the official account of their own origins. Truncations in the oral tradition were accompanied by a dramatic form of architectural "editing" in which the monuments associated with certain early rulers were deleted from the record.

A final feature of the Anonymous History is its purposeful ambiguity. As Mead (1978: 28) notes, the deliberate use of ambiguity "is a political skill that is well developed, and easily implemented when there are no written records of any kind. . . ." One of the greatest strengths of dynastic oral tradition as propaganda is the flexibility it gains from the adroit handling of ambiguity, and the Chimu king list is a perfect example. The anticipatory justification, or "pre-vindication," of the conquest of coastal Ecuador arises from the presence of the balsa raft, a symbol with an ambiguous geographical referent, in the Taycanamo legend.

Indoctrination, motivation, justification, a basic framework of truth incorporating useful omissions and ambiguities—the Anomymous History displays all the essential characteristics of the manipulation of history as propaganda. In its surviving form it legitimates the Chimu dynasty and provides a sanction for what was surely one of Chimor's last conquests. Yet it also serves as a standing invitation to further military campaigns. With the addition or deletion of a few minor details it could justify an attack on any part of the coastal Andean world. I cannot help but suspect that in General Pacatnamu's day the details of the Taycanamo legend hinted that the founding father of the Chimu dynasty might have come from the Jequetepeque-Zaña region.

CONCLUSIONS

The reintroduction of Pacatnamu brings me back to my starting point; I seem to have wandered rather far from the general. I began with the archaeological data that identify General Pacatnamu as a real historical individual and his supposed contemporary, the Chimu ruler Ñançenpinco, as a composite figure. Subsequently I examined the dynastic history of Chimor from two different perspectives, as an idealized presentation of a cosmological and social order and as a piece of imperial propaganda.

I find the latter approach more productive. To me, the oral traditions seem to deal with seminal events, institutions, and individuals in the history of Chimor. These elements are grounded in truth, but their presentation was continuously manipulated to serve the ambitions of the state and its rulers.

In the position paper that set the theme for this symposium, Michael Moseley and Alan Kolata (n.d.: 21–22) concluded that the

> . . . fundamental problem with interpreting these traditions lies
> less with the authenticity of what is mentioned than with the delib-

Geoffrey W. Conrad

erate truncation of what was preserved through vigorous indigenous historical revisionism.

I cannot help but agree. George Orwell would have said that the Chimu had a "Memory Hole." Fortunately, archaeology can help us to resurrect some of the people, places, and things who vanished down it.

BIBLIOGRAPHY

CALANCHA, ANTONIO DE LA

    1638   *Corónica moralizada del Orden de San Augustín en el Perú, con sucesos egenplares en esta monarquía.* Pedro Lacavalleria, Barcelona.

CONRAD, GEOFFREY W., and ARTHUR A. DEMAREST

    1984   *Religion and Empire: The Dynamics of Aztec and Inca Expansionism.* Cambridge University Press, Cambridge.

DOOB, LEONARD W.

    1935   *Propaganda: Its Psychology and Technique.* Henry Holt and Company, New York.

ELLUL, JACQUES

    1965   *Propaganda: The Formation of Men's Attitudes* (Konrad Kellen and Jean Lerner, trans.). Alfred A. Knopf, New York.

ESTRADA, EMILIO

    1955   Balsa and Dugout Navigation in Ecuador. *The American Neptune* 15(2): 142–149.

FINKELSTEIN, JACOB J.

    1979   Early Mesopotamia, 2500–1000 B.C. In *Propaganda and Communication in World History, Volume 1: The Symbolic Instrument in Early Times* (Harold D. Lasswell, Daniel Lerner, and Hans Speier, eds.): 50–110. University of Hawaii Press, Honolulu.

HAMMEL, EUGENE A.

    1965   Review of R. T. Zuidema, The Ceque System of Cuzco. *American Anthropologist* 67: 780–785.

KEATINGE, RICHARD W., and GEOFFREY W. CONRAD

    1983   Imperialist Expansion in Peruvian Prehistory: Chimu Administration of a Conquered Territory. *Journal of Field Archaeology* 10(3): 255–283.

KOLATA, ALAN L.

    1982   Chronology and Settlement Growth at Chan Chan. In *Chan Chan: Andean Desert City* (Michael E. Moseley and Kent C. Day, eds.): 67–85. University of New Mexico Press, Albuquerque.

    n.d.   Chan Chan: The Form of the City in Time. Ph.D. dissertation, Department of Anthropology, Harvard University, 1978.

Kosok, Paul
    1965   *Life, Land and Water in Ancient Peru.* Long Island University Press, New York.

Lothrop, Samuel K.
    1932   Aboriginal Navigation off the West Coast of South America. *Journal of the Royal Anthropological Institute* 62: 229–256. London.

Mead, Margaret
    1979   Continuities in Communication from Early Man to Modern Times. In *Propaganda and Communication in World History, Volume 1: The Symbolic Instrument in Early Times* (Harold D. Lasswell, Daniel Lerner, and Hans Speier, eds.): 21–49. University of Hawaii Press, Honolulu.

Means, Philip A.
    1931   *Ancient Civilizations of the Andes.* Charles Scribner's Sons, New York.

Moseley, Michael E.
    1983   Central Andean Civilization. In *Ancient South Americans* (Jesse D. Jennings, ed.): 179–239. W. H. Freeman and Company, San Francisco.

Moseley, Michael E., and Alan L. Kolata
    n.d.   Myth and History on the North Coast of Peru: Steps to an Archaeological Concordat. Paper prepared for the Dumbarton Oaks symposium The Northern Dynasties, October 1985.

Murphy, Robert Cushman
    1941   The Earliest Spanish Advances Southward from Panama along the West Coast of South America. *Hispanic American Historical Review* 21: 2–28.

Richardson, James B. III, and Allison Heaps de Peña
    n.d.   The Emergence of the State in the Chira Region of Northwest Peru. Paper presented at the 39th Annual Meeting of the Society for American Archaeology, Washington, D.C., May 1974.

Rostworowski de Diez Canseco, María
    1961   *Curacas y sucesiones: Costa norte.* Imprenta Minerva, Lima.

Rowe, John H.
    1948   The Kingdom of Chimor. *Acta Americana* 6 (1–2): 26–59.

Sharma, R.S.
    1979   Indian Civilization. In *Propaganda and Communication in World History, Volume 1: The Symbolic Instrument in Early Times* (Harold D. Lasswell, Daniel Lerner, and Hans Speier, eds.): 175–204. University of Hawaii Press, Honolulu.

Topic, John R., and Michael E. Moseley
    1983   Chan Chan: A Case Study of Urban Change in Peru. *Ñawpa Pacha* 21: 153–182.

Vargas Ugarte, Rubén
    1936   La fecha de la fundación de Trujillo. *Revista Histórica* 10: 229–239.

WRIGHT, ARTHUR F.

1979   Chinese Civilization. In *Propaganda and Communication in World History, Volume 1: The Symbolic Instrument in Early Times* (Harold D. Lasswell, Daniel Lerner, and Hans Speier, eds.): 220–256. University of Hawaii Press, Honolulu.

ZUIDEMA, R. TOM

1973   Kinship and Ancestorcult in Three Peruvian Communities: Hernández Príncipe's Account of 1622. *Bulletin de l'Institut Français d'Etudes Andines* 2(1): 16–33.

1977   Mito e historia en el antiguo Perú. *Allpanchis* 10: 15–32.

1983   Hierarchy and Space in Incaic Social Organization. *Ethnohistory* 30: 49–76.

An Assessment of the Validity of the Naymlap Dynasty

CHRISTOPHER B. DONNAN

UNIVERSITY OF CALIFORNIA AT LOS ANGELES

O NE OF THE MOST INTRIGUING of the ancient dynasties on the North Coast of Peru begins with a king named Naymlap who ruled the Lambayeque Valley centuries before European contact. Although some scholars have argued that the story of the Naymlap dynasty is mythical (e.g., Rowe 1948; Zuidema, this volume), it is entirely possible that it contains information about real people and places and describes events that actually occurred. In this paper, I will review the arguments for and against the validity of the Naymlap dynasty and assess the accounts of the dynasty in light of archaeological evidence that has recently been recovered.

The story of the Naymlap dynasty was first recorded by Miguel Cabello Balboa in 1586. In essence, the story is as follows:

> The people of Lambayeque say that in times so very ancient that they do not know how to express them, a man of much valor and quality came to that valley on a fleet of balsa rafts. His name was Naymlap. With him he brought many concubines and a chief wife named Ceterni. He also brought many people who followed him as their captain and leader. Among these people were forty officials, including Pita Zofi, Blower of the Shell Trumpet; Ninacola, Master of the Litter and Throne; Ninagintue, Royal Cellarer (he was in charge of the drink of that lord); Fonga Sigde, Preparer of

The author is grateful to Gloria S.A. of Lima and the National Geographic Society for their generous support of the fieldwork of Chotuna and Chornancap, and to the Instituto Nacional de Cultura for the necessary permits. The Museum of Cultural History at U.C.L.A provided administrative support for the research. The Museo Brüning in Lambayeque helped resolve many logistical problems while the fieldwork was ongoing and has, appropriately, become the permanent home for the Chotuna and Chornancap collections. John Rowe kindly provided me with copies of the Cabello Balboa manuscripts that are in the New York Public Library and the University Library of the University of Texas, Austin. Geraldine Clift was very helpful in providing comments on earlier versions of this report.

the Way (he scattered seashell dust where his lord was about to walk); Occhocalo, Royal Cook; Xam Muchec, Steward of the Face Paint; Ollopcopoc, Master of the Bath; and Llapchillulli, Purveyor of Feathercloth Garments. With this retinue, and with an infinite number of other officials and men of importance, Naymlap established a settlement and built his palace at Chot.

Naymlap also brought with him a green stone idol named Yampellec. This idol represented him, was named for him, and gave its name to the valley of Lambayeque.

Naymlap and his people lived for many years and had many children. Eventually he knew that the time of his death had arrived. In order that his vassals should not learn that death had jurisdiction over him, his immediate attendants buried him secretly in the same room where he had lived. They then proclaimed it throughout the land that he had taken wings and flown away.

The empire and power of Naymlap were left to his oldest son, Cium, who married a maiden named Zolzdoñi. By her and other concubines he had twelve sons, each of whom was father of a large family. After ruling many years, Cium placed himself in a subterranean vault and allowed himself to die so that posterity might regard him as immortal and divine.

Subsequently there were nine rulers in succession, followed by Fempellec, the last and most unfortunate member of the dynasty. He decided to move the idol that Naymlap had placed at Chot. After several unsuccessful attempts to do this, the devil appeared to him in the form of a beautiful woman. He slept with her and as soon as the union had been consummated the rains began to fall, a thing which had never been seen upon these plains. These floods lasted for thirty days, after which followed a year of much sterility and famine. Because the priests knew that their lord had committed this grave crime, they understood that it was punishment for his fault that his people were suffering with hunger, rain, and want. In order to take vengeance upon him, forgetful of the fidelity that is owed by vassals, they took him prisoner and, tying his feet and hands, threw him into the deep sea. With his death was ended the lineage of the native lords of the valley of Lambayeque, and the country surrounding remained without patron or native lord during many days.

Then a certain powerful tyrant called Chimu Capac came with an invincible army and possessed himself of these valleys, placing garrisons in them. In Lambayeque he placed a lord called Pongmassa, a native of Chimu. He died a peace-loving lord and left as his successor a son named Pallesmassa. He, in turn, was succeeded by his son, Oxa, and it was in his time that the Incas were passing through Cajamarca. Thus, Oxa was the first of his lineage to have news of the Inca lords. From this time foward the coast people began to live in constant dread of being conquered by the people from Cuzco.

Subsequently there were five successive rulers, followed by Pecfunpisan, in whose reign the Spaniards entered Peru. (adapted from a translation by Means 1931: 51–53)

In 1781, nearly two hundred years after the Naymlap story was recorded by Cabello Balboa, it was recorded for a second time by Father Justo Ru-biños y Andrade, the *cura* of the parish of Morrope. He apparently was unaware of the Cabello Balboa manuscript, and thus his account can be viewed as an independent recording of the Naymlap story.

The Rubiños y Andrade version is incomplete—it does not go beyond the reign of Naymlap's son Cium (spelled Suim by Rubiños y Andrade). Although there are details that occur in one version and not in the other, the essential elements of the story, including events, places, and individuals, are almost identical. The spelling of personal names frequently differs, but in nearly every case they are cognates.

In 1931 Philip A. Means analyzed Cabello Balboa's account of the Lam-bayeque dynasties, and treated both the Naymlap dynasty and the later one founded by the Chimu as history (Means 1931: 50–55). John H. Rowe, on the other hand, has stated that the early dynasties of the North Coast, and particularly the story of Naymlap,

> are partly explanations of monuments and customs whose origins have been forgotten, and partly just stories to entertain. To interpret them, we cannot go far wrong if we follow the principle that if a story explains the origin of a shrine or custom, or if the hero becomes a divinity or disappears instead of dying, then it belongs to the realm of legend. (Rowe 1948: 36)

Rowe goes on to state that

> Chot is almost certainly the ruin called Huaca Chotuna in modern times . . . the huaca of Sotenic is identfied by Brüning as the one now called Huaca de la Cruz . . . the native name of which he gives as Sioternic . . . The "palace" built by Cium (or Suim) was probably another huaca.
>
> The story as a whole, then, seems to be little more than an explanation of the origin of the inhabitants of the various districts of Lambayeque valley and of their monuments. . . . We may conclude then that the "Naymlap" story is pure legend. It may even be of relatively late origin. (1948: 38)

Although the Naymlap story may be legend, it seems inappropriate to dismiss it as such on the basis of Rowe's criteria. In many parts of the world there are monuments, shrines, and ceremonies the origins of which are derived from historical people or historical events. Therefore, a story cannot be dismissed as mythical for this reason.[1]

Some scholars who have analyzed the Naymlap story consider it to be a water myth or flood myth because Naymlap is said to have come from the water—the sea—and his dynasty ended with water—the thirty-day rain that brought about the death of Fempellec (e.g., Zuidema, this volume). Though it is interesting to consider the Naymlap story in this way, both Naymlap's arrival by boat and the Fempellec rain are events that could reasonably have taken place on the North Coast of Peru.

First, let us consider the arrival by boat. A new dynasty for the Lambayeque Valley could have begun either with someone local or with an outsider. Assuming that the founder was an outsider, there are only three avenues of entry: from the mountains to the east, from the coast to the north or south, or from the sea by boat. One means is just as probable as another, and arrival by boat is certainly not an unreasonable possibility. There is good archaeological and historical evidence for ocean-going vessels traveling along the west coast of South America from the Gulf of Guayaquil in the north to the Chincha Valley in the south (Edwards 1965; Rostworowski 1975; Cordy-Collins n.d., and this volume). Large tule boats containing multiple passengers and cargo are depicted in Phase V Moche iconography (Cordy-Collins n.d.; McClelland, this volume), and the large ocean-going balsa rafts that traveled the coast of Peru at the time of European contact may well have been in use since the Middle Horizon, if not earlier. Given this evidence, it is perfectly reasonable that the founder of a new dynasty in Lambayeque could have arrived by boat. Were the Naymlap story simply a water myth, why not have it begin with Naymlap issuing forth from the rivers that flow out of the Andean Cordillera, or coming with his people as drops of rain? If indeed he is to come from the sea, why not simply appear directly out of the ocean? Yet, the story tells us more about boats and the people getting off them, and where they came ashore, than it does about the ocean.

In considering the end of the Naymlap dynasty, we also find a series of events that are perfectly reasonable, given the natural conditions of the Peruvian North Coast. While this area normally receives little or no precipitation,

---

[1] American history is full of instances where the application of Rowe's criteria would lead to an entirely erroneous judgment. The naming of Pennsylvania after William Penn and Washington, D.C., after George Washington does not make these two individuals mythical. The same is true of assuming that if the story explains the origin of a custom, it is mythical. The celebration of Christmas and Thanksgiving are two obvious examples of customs that are based on real rather than mythical events.

periodically there are years of major rainfall that have a devastating impact on the population. The complex oceanographic and meteorological factors that create the rain are not well understood, but it is clear that this is a recurring phenomenon. The last occurrence of an El Niño, as these conditions are called, was in 1982–83. That year erratic rains saturated the normally parched landscape, and runoff transformed dry washes and ravines into torrential streams. Flash floods destroyed villages, cut road systems, and ruined many of the complex irrigation canal systems on which local agriculture depends. At the same time, warm sea currents, which are an integral part of El Niño conditions, upset the delicate marine ecosystem along the coast, thus greatly reducing the available maritime resources (Murphy 1926).

The immediate impact of El Niño conditions is always death and destruction, but the long-term effects are famine and great suffering. Re-establishing the food supply from farming depends upon the time-consuming process of rebuilding the damaged canal networks, and the fishing industry must await a gradual reconstruction of the normal marine food chain.

Given that El Niño conditions occur intermittently but relentlessly along the northern coast of Peru, we would expect that they also occurred in the Pre-Columbian past. Recent archaeological and geological evidence has confirmed the presence of such catastrophic events, as well as their effect on archaeological sites and ancient canal systems (Nials et al. 1979; Sandweiss et al. 1983; Shimada, this volume; Kolata 1982; Moseley and Deeds 1982; Moseley et al. 1983). In some instances, as will be discussed in detail later, El Niños that occurred in the Pre-Columbian past appear to have been of considerably greater magnitude that those in the historic period. This evidence indicates that an event such as the thirty-day rain of the Naymlap story is not at all impossible for the northern coast of Peru. On the contrary, it is not only possible, but expectable. Furthermore, one could assume that a major El Niño would have had exactly the consequences that are described in the Naymlap story. Such catastrophic conditions may well have precipitated the end of a dynastic reign, particularly if the local people had held their ruler responsible for the disaster.

Of course, the fact that El Niños occur intermittently does not confirm the validity of the Fempellec flood any more than the existence of ocean-going craft along the coast in ancient times verifies the story of Naymlap's arrival. They do, however, make such occurrences plausible and certainly underscore the importance of keeping an open mind to the possibility that part, if not all, of the story of the Naymlap dynasty is based on fact.

If the story is true, where and when did the events take place? As Means points out:

> The territory involved in this story is roughly coterminous with the modern department of Lambayeque. . . . It is not certain just what

> river is indicated by the name Faquisllanga in the legend, but it is
> probable that it designates the Lambayeque River. . . . (1931: 54)

In the lower part of the Lambayeque Valley there are two archaeological
sites that are thought to correspond to the Naymlap story (Fig. 1). The
larger of these, Chotuna, may well be Chot, where Naymlap is said to have
built his palace. The smaller site, Chornancap, is located approximately one
km west of Chotuna (Fig. 2). Because of its contemporaneity and proximity
to Chotuna, this might well have been where Naymlap built the palace for
his principal wife.

Until 1980 very little was known about Chotuna and Chornancap. Neither site had been systematically excavated or even accurately mapped, and
almost nothing was known about the ancient people who inhabited them.
Betwen 1980 and 1982 we conducted a total of ten months of archaeological
excavation at Chotuna and Chornancap.[2] As a result, we were able to
reconstruct the sequence of occupation at the two sites and assess the degree
to which the archaeological evidence corresponds to the story of the
Naymlap dynasty.

CHOTUNA AND CHORNANCAP

The site of Chotuna consists of a series of pyramids, palaces, and walled
enclosures scattered over an area of approximately 20 ha (Fig. 3). What is
visible today, however, is only a fraction of the architecture that once
characterized this important center. Deep accumulations of windblown
sand have buried much of the settlement, and some of the large dune formations may even obscure major pyramid and/or palace complexes. In some
areas of the site, wind and water erosion have scoured away important
architectural features, leaving only the slightest trace of what were major
constructions. As a result of the combination of erosion and inundation by
sand, it is extremely difficult to gauge the original size of the site or to assess
the functional relationship between individual structures. Nevertheless, excavation made it possible to map most of the visible architecture accurately
and to understand something of the development of the site through the
period of its occupation.

Chornancap, located approximately one km west of Chotuna, consists of
a single truncated pyramid, which is clearly T-shaped, with a central ramp
leading down from the summit at the center of the east side (Fig. 4). Windblown sand deposited on the north side of the *huaca* has preserved an extensive area of adobe architecture consisting of agglutinated rooms, corridors,
and open courtyards. The upper levels of architecture were often superim-

---

[2] The excavation was under my direction and involved students from the University of
California at Los Angeles and the Universidad Católica Santa María, Arequipa.

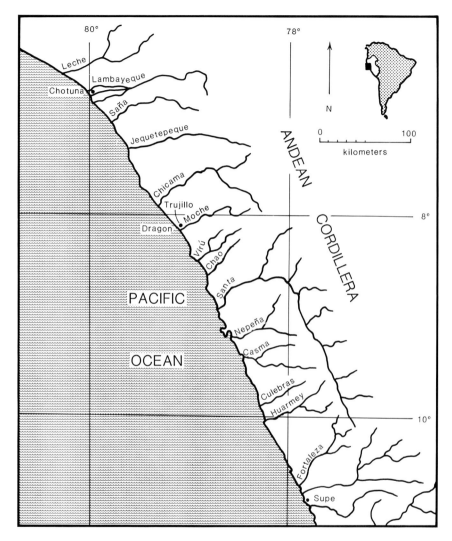

Fig. 1   Map of the northern coast of Peru.

posed over multiple layers of earlier construction, suggesting a long period of occupation with a complex sequence of rebuilding (Donnan 1984). Sur- rounding the *huaca* and its adjacent architecture are numerous low sand dunes, many of which contain occupational refuse and remnants of ancient architecture.

Excavation at Chotuna and Chornancap provided a chronological se-

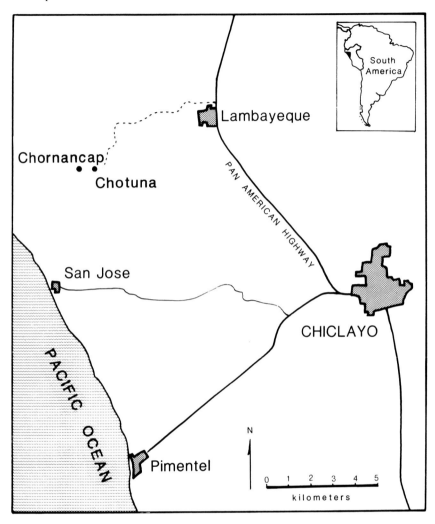

Fig. 2   Map of the lower Lambayeque Valley showing the location of Chotuna and Chornancap.

quence for the occupation of the two sites. This sequence, which consists of three successive phases (Fig. 5), is based primarily on the seriation of ceramics and mud bricks, stratigraphy, sequential architectural construction, and radiocarbon determinations. Presented here is an overview of the chronological sequence, focusing largely on mud brick seriation and ceramics whose forms and features are most characteristic of the phases and whose presence or absence is most useful for providing temporal identification.[3]

[3] A longer and much more detailed ceramic description is in preparation (Donnan n.d.).

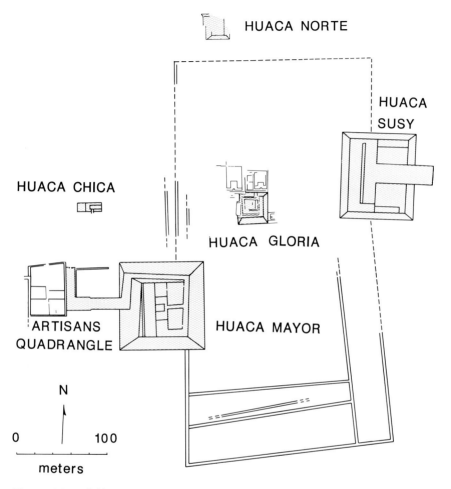

Fig. 3   Map of Chotuna.

Sufficient detail is provided so that other investigators working in the Lambayeque area will be able to assess the degree to which their ceramics and mud bricks correspond to those from Chotuna and Chornancap.

Early Phase

The Early Phase dates from approximately A.D. 750 to 1100. Early Phase material was found in the levels just above sterile soil, often close to the present water table. Stratigraphically, these were the lowest levels excavated, and the material they contain is presumed to represent the earliest occupation of the site. Early Phase mud bricks have a flat rectangular form (Fig. 5).

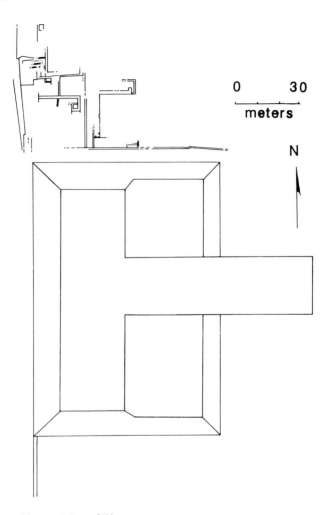

Fig. 4   Map of Chornancap.

Various features distinguish Early Phase ceramics from those of Middle/ Late Phase. Most notable is the complete absence of paddle-marked ceramics in the Early Phase assemblages. On the other hand, three-color decoration is present in the Early Phase ceramics but absent from the Middle/Late Phase assemblages. Tricolor decoration, consisting of red, white, and black slip, is found on flask-shaped bottles (Fig. 6a) and on ring-base plates (Fig. 6b).

Red on white slip-painted decoration is also characteristic of Early Phase ceramics and is particularly common on ring-base plates (Figs. 6c, 7a, b).

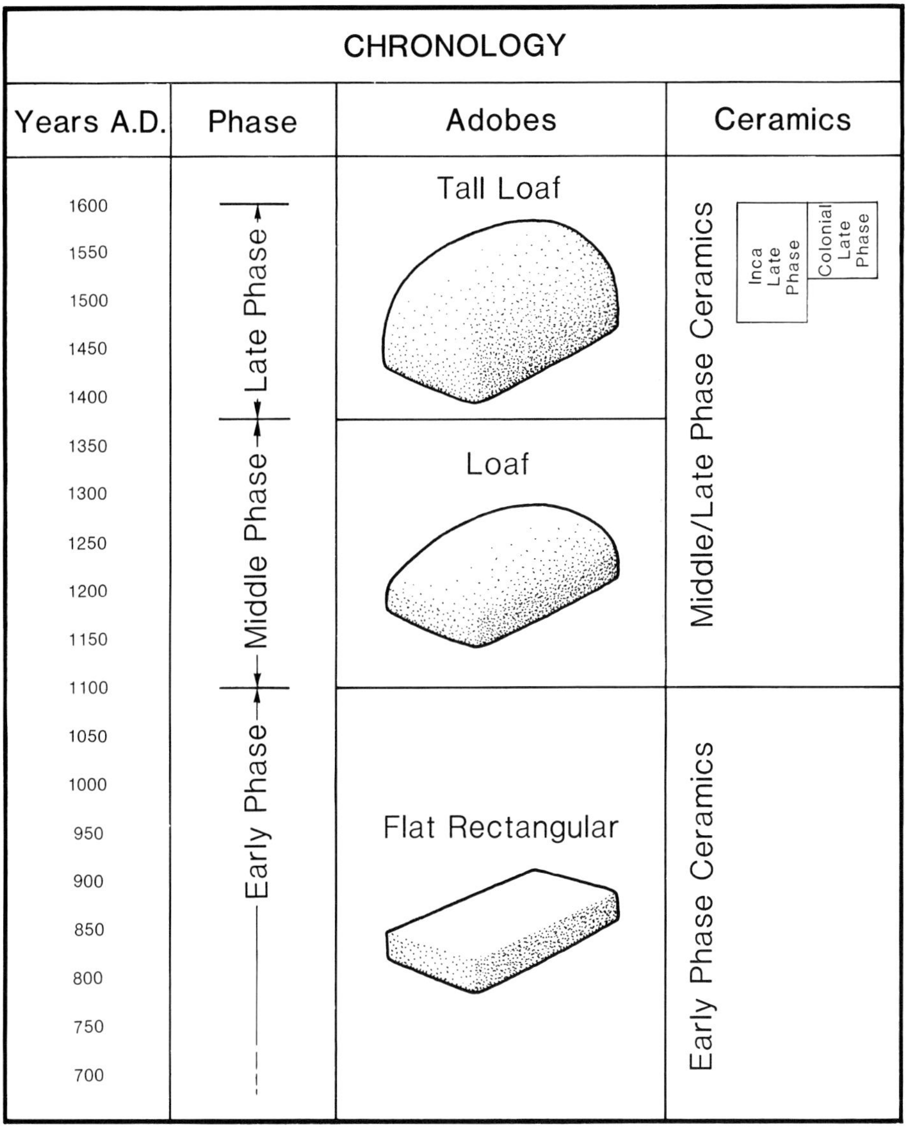

Fig. 5   Chronological chart.

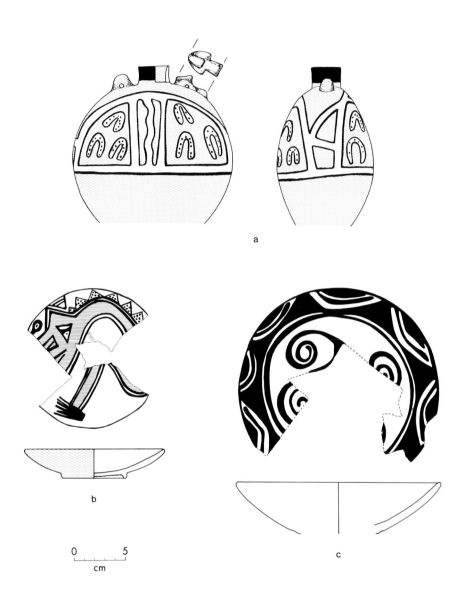

Fig. 6   Early Phase ceramics: (a) flask-shaped bottle; (b–c) ring-base plates.

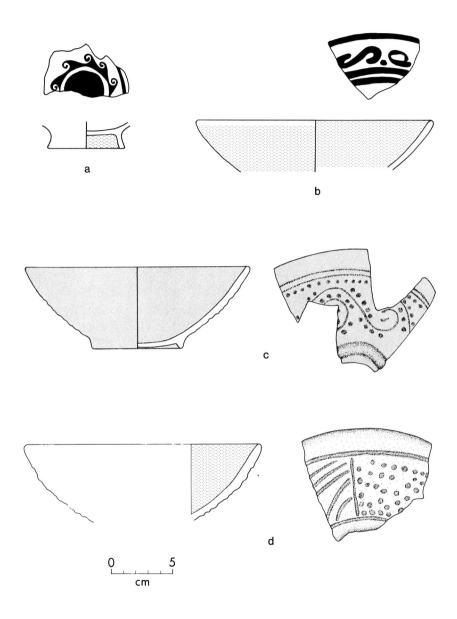

Fig. 7   Early Phase ring-base plates.

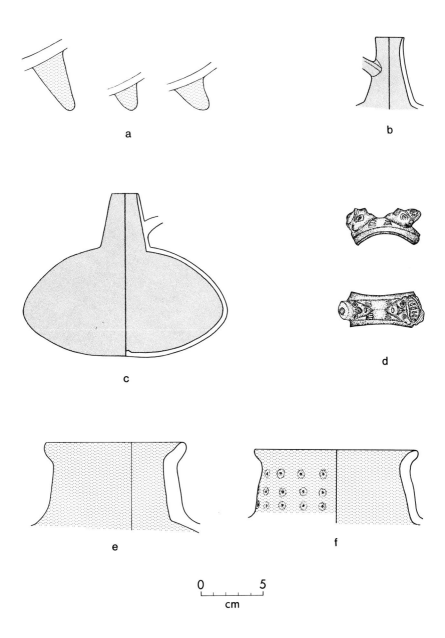

Fig. 8   Early Phase ceramics: (a) tripod legs; (b) bottle spout; (c) spout-and-handle bottle; (d) bottle handle; (e–f) jar necks.

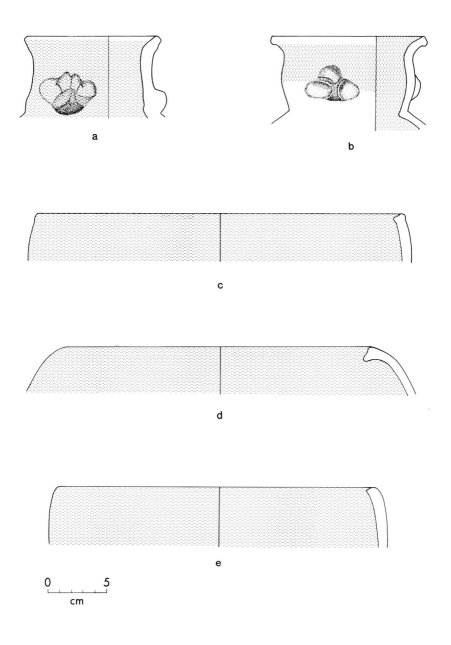

Fig. 9   Early Phase ceramics: (a–b) jar necks; (c–e) large vessel rims.

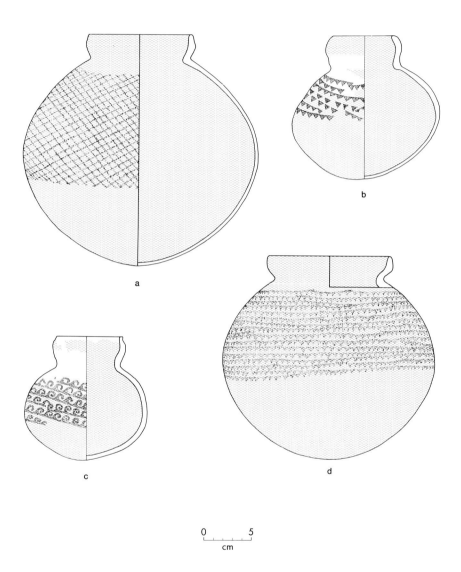

Fig. 10   Middle/Late Phase *ollas*.

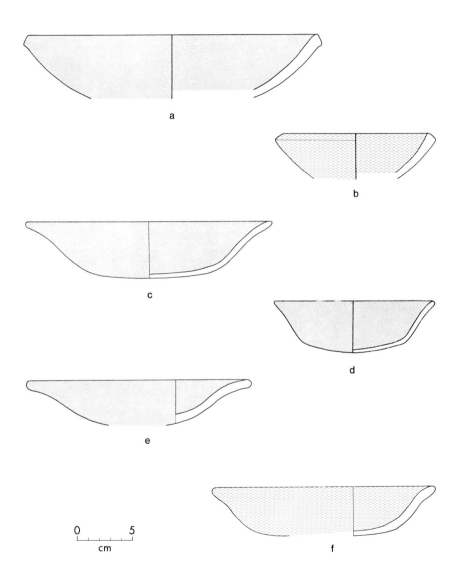

Fig. 11   Middle/Late Phase plates.

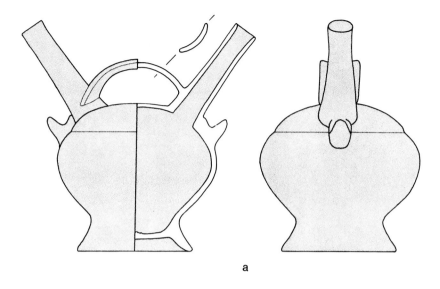

a

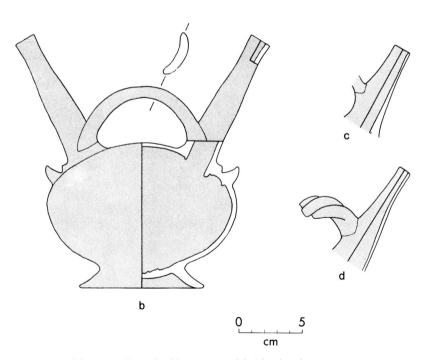

b

c

d

0   5

cm

Fig. 12   Middle/Late Phase double-spout-and-bridge bottles.

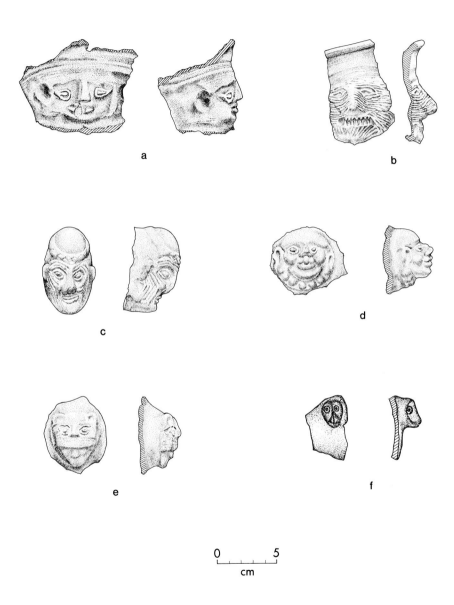

Fig. 13   Middle/Late Phase ceramics: (a–b) face neck jars; (c–f) lugs.

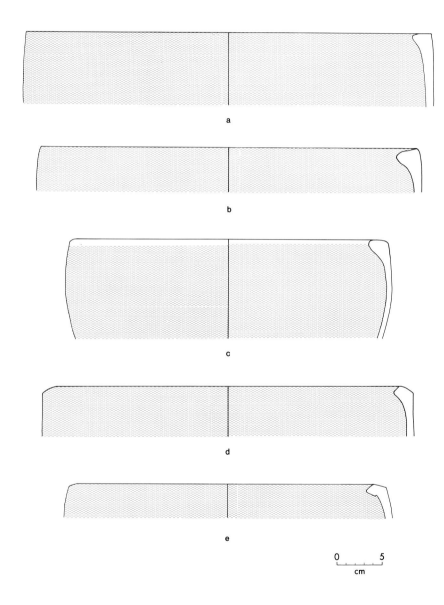

Fig. 14   Middle/Late Phase large vessel rims.

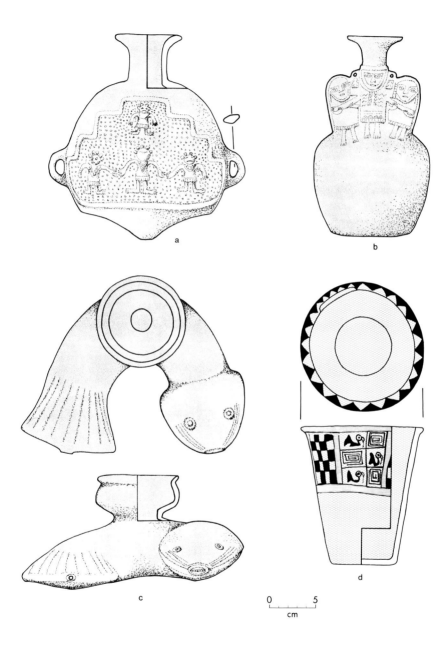

Fig. 15   Inca-influenced Late Phase ceramics: (a) aryballoid bottle; (b) bottle; (c) *paccha;* (d) kero-shaped goblet.

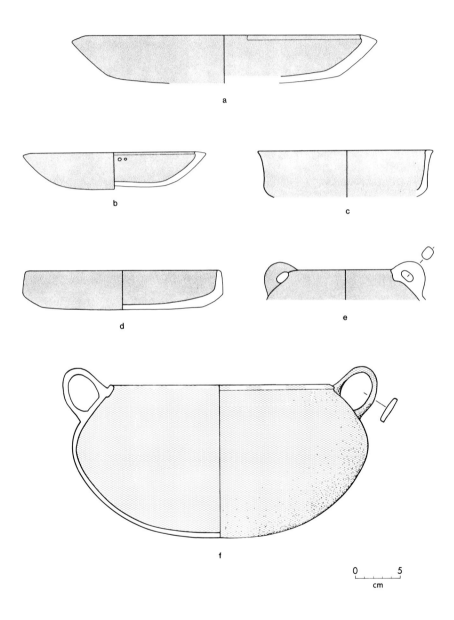

Fig. 16 Inca-influenced Late Phase ceramics: (a–b) hook-rim plates; (c) flaring-rim plate; (d) vertical-sided plate; (e–f) double-handled bowls.

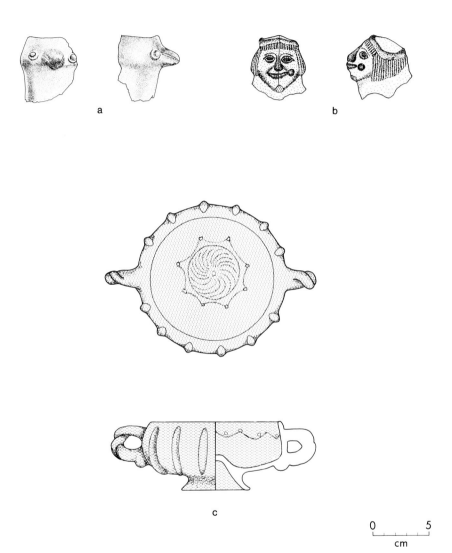

Fig. 17   Inca-influenced and European-influenced Late Phase ceramics: (a) jar neck with bird head; (b) human head with short-cropped hair; (c) pedestal base bowl with a gadrooned chamber.

Ring-base plates with press-molded decoration on their exterior surface are exclusive to Early Phase ceramics (Fig. 7c, d), as are tripod-base plates (Fig. 8a). Another vessel form found only in the Early Phase is a spout-and-handle bottle with an oblate chamber (Fig. 8b, c). Several fragments of the handle portion of these vessels suggest that the handles were narrow and sometimes had heads modeled on their upper surfaces (Fig. 8d). They were highly burnished and reduction fired.

One jar form is exclusively Early Phase. It has a characteristic neck that rises vertically from the chamber and flares abruptly at the rim (Fig. 8e, f). The vertical section of the neck generally has a slight bulge and often has a distinctive decoration on the outside, which resulted from having been pinched with either two or three fingers while the clay was still plastic (Fig. 9a, b). Finally, Early Phase ceramics include numerous large cooking and storage vessels (Fig. 9c, d, e). Generally these have simple rim profiles compared with those of Middle/Late Phase.

The Early Phase occupation was not identified at Chornancap; neither Early Phase ceramics nor flat rectanglular bricks were found there. It may be that this site was not yet occupied, although a more thorough excavation in the area could ultimately reveal an Early Phase component. Early Phase material was found in several locations at Chotuna, and various constructions can be attributed to this time.

Middle Phase

The Middle Phase dates from approximately A.D. 1100 to 1300. The mud bricks are loaf shaped, and through time they gradually increase in height (Fig. 5).

A new ceramic assemblage appears suddenly at the beginning of the Middle Phase and seems to replace the Early Phase ceramics. This new assemblage continues through the Late Phase without major changes, and in most instances it is not possible to make clear distinctions between the ceramics of Middle and Late Phases. In part, this is because very few ceramics were recovered from contexts that were exclusively Middle Phase, and thus the sample available to define the Middle Phase is very small. In addition, it is clear that Middle Phase and Late Phase ceramics are basically the same tradition that did not undergo substantial evolution during the centuries in which it was in use. The paste types, vessel forms, and decorative techniques appear to have been established at the beginning of the Middle Phase and to have persisted with only subtle changes throughout the Late Phase. Although changes must have occurred, it is not possible to identify these changes on the basis of our sample. Therefore, most of the Middle and Late Phase ceramics are combined in the descriptions that follow and are referred to as Middle/Late Phase ceramics.

Perhaps the most significant new feature of these ceramics is paddle marking, which is very common as a decorative feature (Fig. 10a–d). Tricolor decoration does not continue from Early Phase, and red on white slip is very rare.

Ring-base plates continue to be common, although they are no longer decorated with either press molding or polychrome slip paint. Instead, they are normally unpainted or given an overall application of white or red slip. Some examples are reduction fired. Several plate forms not seen in the Early Phase assemblages are present in Middle/Late Phase. These include plates with thick, flattened rims (Fig. 11a, b) and plates with a lyre-shaped cross section (Fig. 11c–f).

The double-spout-and-bridge bottles are characterized by high pedestal bases, long tapering spouts, and handles that are generally lenticular or ribbon shaped (Fig. 12a–c) in cross section. The handles on several examples have twisted, ropelike elements (Fig. 12d). Also included are face-neck jars with human faces (Fig. 13a, b) and numerous lugs in the form of human and animal heads (Fig. 13c–f). These latter were probably part of the chambers of large jars. The majority of the lugs were made in two-piece molds, although some were probably created with stamps. Finally, Middle/Late Phase ceramics include large cooking and storage vessels with rims that are distinct from those of Early Phase (Fig. 14a–e).

Middle Phase may have been the time of peak population density in the lower Lambayeque Valley. The majority of the monumental construction at Chotuna dates to this period. Chornancap was occupied at the time, and the *huaca* there was constructed during this era.

Late Phase

The Late Phase dates from approximately A.D. 1300 to 1600. The loaf-shaped form of the mud bricks used during the Middle Phase gradually evolved into a tall loaf shape characteristic of Late Phase (Fig. 5). Tall loaf-shaped bricks can be seen in construction at both Chotuna and Chornancap. In comparison to the earlier phases, there was less new construction undertaken, but most of the existing architecture was substantially remodeled at this time.

During the Late Phase, the Lambayeque Valley underwent three successive waves of foreign influence. The first of these was the result of the expansion of the Kingdom of Chimor. This kingdom, with its capital at Chan Chan in the Moche Valley, is thought to have conquered Lambayeque in approximately A.D. 1370. A century later (ca. 1470), the Lambayeque Valley was conquered by the Inca Empire. The Inca maintained their domination of the area until the arrival of the Spanish around 1530, at which time European influence began to affect the culture of the local people.

The basic ceramic tradition at Chotuna and Chornancap during Late Phase is the same as defined above for Middle Phase and given the term Middle/Late Phase. Added to this local ceramic tradition, however, are new characteristics that clearly resulted from outside influence. Although it is difficult to identify ceramic influence from the Kingdom of Chimor, both Inca and European influences are clearly discernible in certain vessel forms and decorative techniques.

Inca influence during the Late Phase brought several new vessel forms to the ceramic inventory: aryballoid bottles (Fig. 15a), bottles with flaring rims (Fig. 15b), *paccha* ceremonial vessels (Fig. 15c), kero-shaped goblets (Fig. 15d), hook-rim plates (Fig. 16a, b), flaring-rim plates (Fig. 16c), vertical-sided plates (Fig. 16d), and double-handled bowls (Fig 16e, f). There is also a new jar neck in the form of a bird head (Fig. 17a), and a new lug form, a human head with short-cropped hair (Fig. 17b).

European influence during the Late Phase included the application of green glaze to ceramic bottles and one new vessel form, a pedestal-base bowl with a gadrooned chamber (Fig. 17c). Most of the ceramics in use at Chotuna and Chornancap during the early Colonial period were the basic Middle/Late Phase ceramic assemblage, with some new forms that were the result of Inca influence. European influence at Chotuna and Chornancap is also reflected in the presence of glass beads, iron objects, and, in some burials, the shift from flexed to extended burial position.

DATING THE NAYMLAP DYNASTY

The chronological information provided in Cabello Balboa's account of the dynasties of the Lambayeque Valley supplies some interesting clues for dating the Naymlap dynasty. Clearly, the dynasty founded by Chimu Capac, with Pongmassa as the first ruler, was relatively late in the history of the valley. The third ruler of this dynasty, Oxa, must have reigned around A.D. 1470 because that was the time of the Inca conquest of the North Coast. Inasmuch as the ninth ruler of the dynasty, Pecfunpisan, was ruling when the Spanish entered Peru in 1528, we can confidently assign this dynasty to the later part of the Late Intermediate period and the Late Horizon, perhaps A.D. 1370 to 1530.

The earlier dynasty, beginning with Naymlap, is more difficult to assign to a chronological period. This is largely because Cabello Balboa's narrative is not specific about the length of time between the two dynasties. Means (1931: 54–56) suggests that the interregnum was contemporary with the time of Huari influence on the North Coast, thus making the Naymlap dynasty contemporary with the latter part of the Moche kingdom. Arbitrarily assigning an average reign of twenty-five years to each of the twelve rulers of the Naymlap dynasty, he suggests that the dynasty must have lasted about three hundred years, and that this occurred during the first six

centuries A.D. When Wendell Bennett conducted an archaeological reconnaissance of the Lambayeque Valley in 1936, he found little evidence of
Moche occupation and suggested that the Naymlap dynasty occurred during the early part of the Chimu domination of the North Coast rather than
during the Moche period (Bennett 1939: 120).

Between 1969 and 1979, however, substantial evidence of Moche occupation in the Lambayeque Valley was uncovered (Day 1971; Donnan 1972;
Shimada n.d., and this volume). Moreover, we began to recognize various
individuals and activities depicted in Moche art that correlated precisely
with the northern oral traditions existing at the time of the Spanish arrival.
These correlations suggested that the oral tradition of the Naymlap dynasty
might actually be referring to events that occurred as early as the Moche
domination of the North Coast (Donnan 1978: 86–101). Thus, it seemed
possible that Naymlap might have been a Moche king, and when we began
our excavations at Chotuna in 1980, we anticipated that we might find
evidence of a Moche occupation. During the three seasons of excavation
there, however, not one piece of diagnostic Moche ceramics was found.
Therefore, it is clear that if Chotuna is indeed Chot of the Naymlap story,
then Naymlap and his followers were not Moche.

What we did find at Chotuna, however, was a chronological sequence
that is perfectly compatible with the accounts of the Naymlap dynasty. In
assessing how the dynastic accounts fit the archaeological evidence, the
transition between the Early Phase and the Middle Phase occupation is the
key. This transition, which is thought to have occurred around A.D. 1100, is
the only clear break in what otherwise appears to be a continuous occupation by people maintaining their cultural traditions.

Much of the Early Phase architecture at Chotuna has been severely damaged by erosion, apparently due to massive flooding. While it is not possible
to date this flooding precisely, it appears to have occurred at or near the end
of the Early Phase occupation, and actually may have been responsible for
the end of this occupation.

In recent years there has been substantial independent evidence of a major
El Niño occurring about A.D. 1100 that had a dramatic impact on a large
part of the Andean area. For example, at Pacatnamu, located at the mouth of
the Jequetepeque Valley, approximately 85 km south of Chotuna, there is
evidence of a major El Niño at this time, which appears to have caused
abandonment of the site. As at Chotuna, the reoccupation of Pacatnamu
after A.D. 1100 involved an entirely new brick type and ceramic assemblage
(Donnan 1986: 22). There is also evidence of major flooding in the Moche
Valley at this time (Moseley and Deeds 1982; Moseley and Kolata n.d.). It
may be that the sudden abandonment of Poma, in the Batan Grande area of
the upper Lambayeque Valley, at about this time (Shimada and Elera 1983:
46; Shimada, this volume) was also related to a major El Niño. Moreover,

coring of the Quelccaya ice cap, located in the central sierra of Peru, has provided evidence of substantial El Niño activity dated between A.D. 1097 and 1109 (Thompson n.d.).

If the break between the Early and Middle Phase occupation at Chotuna is due to a major El Niño, it is tempting to correlate this with the flood of Fempellec that brought an end to the Naymlap dynasty. The implications of such a correlation are:

1. Naymlap and his followers were the first inhabitants of Chotuna.
2. Naymlap lived approximately A.D. 750.
3. The Early Phase architecture at Chotuna, utilizing flat rectangular bricks, was built during the reign of the Naymlap dynasty.
4. The people living at Chot during the Naymlap dynasty used Early Phase ceramics.
5. The flooding that ended the Naymlap dynasty effectively destroyed the cultural traditions of the people living at Chotuna and probably caused an abandonment of the site.
6. The flooding had a more severe impact on the local people than any subsequent El Niño that occurred until the arrival of Europeans in the sixteenth century.

The only apparent anomaly in such a correlation is that we found no evidence of an Early Phase occupation at Chornancap. If this site is where Naymlap built a palace for his wife Ceterni, it should have had an Early Phase occupation. Our excavations at Chornancap were not extensive, however, and as noted before, more thorough excavation in the area could ultimately reveal an Early Phase component. Alternatively, Chornancap may not have been the location of Ceterni's palace; it could have been one of the other *huacas* located in the lower Lambayeque Valley.[4]

It is also possible to correlate the Naymlap dynasty with the Middle Phase occupation at Chotuna and Chornancap. The implications of this correlation are:

1. Naymlap and his followers came to the lower Lambayeque Valley shortly after it had been devastated by a major El Niño.
2. Naymlap lived approximately A.D. 1150.
3. Much of the Middle Phase architecture at Chotuna and Chornancap, utilizing loaf-shaped bricks, was built during the reign of the Naymlap dynasty.
4. The basic Middle/Late Phase ceramic assemblage was introduced to the Lambayeque Valley by Naymlap and his followers.

[4] Heinrich (Enrique) Brüning felt that the most likely candidate was Huaca de la Cruz (Huaca Sotenic) located near the fishing village of San Jose (Brüning 1922).

5. The flood that ended the Naymlap dynasty with the reign of Fempellec was relatively mild by comparison to the one that immediately preceded Naymlap's arrival in Lambayeque. It did not leave any evidence in the archaeological record of a subsequent time of chaos, nor lead to an abandonment of Chotuna and Chornancap.
6. The friezes that decorate the Huaca Gloria complex at Chotuna (Donnan [Chotuna], this volume) and the murals at Chornancap (Donnan 1984) were probably created during the Naymlap dynasty.

In support of this second correlation is the fact that Chornancap has abundant evidence of a Middle Phase occupation and may not have been occupied before this time. The major weakness in this correlation is the lack of evidence for a major El Niño near the end of Middle Phase. While it is possible that the Fempellec flood was actually an El Niño of lesser magnitude, it seems more plausible that it was a major environmental perturbation—one that left a lasting, indelible impression on the folk memory of the people of Lambayeque and remained a vivid part of their oral traditions for more than five centuries. The fact that Chotuna clearly experienced such an event at the end of the Early Phase occupation provides such an excellent correlation between the archaeological evidence and the Naymlap story that it compels us to opt for equating the Naymlap dynasty with the Early Phase occupation. It is, however, important to realize that equating the Naymlap dynasty with the Middle Phase is also possible.

CONCLUSIONS

In conclusion, it must be stated that this report in no way should be seen as an effort to prove the validity of the Naymlap story. Given the present evidence, such proof is virtually impossible. It is also the case, however, that given the present evidence, it is impossible to demonstrate that the Naymlap story is mythical.

The excavation of Chotuna and Chornancap could have demonstrated that the Naymlap story did *not* take place at these sites. If, for example, neither site had been occupied until after the Inca conquest of the North Caost, then Naymlap, having ruled the Lambayeque Valley prior to the Inca, could not have been present at these sites. Alternatively, if the sites were built and occupied only during the Early Horizon, they would have been too early to correlate to the Naymlap story. The fact that the ancient occupation of Chotuna correlates with our expectation of when Naymlap and his descendants lived provides some support for the possible validity of the story. The flood that created a break in the occupation at about A.D. 1100 also offers a plausible correlation to the Fempellec flood that terminated the dynasty.

Christopher B. Donnan

While field archaeology is severely limited in its ability to confirm or deny the validity of myths, legends, and oral traditions, it nevertheless can provide important insights that can help in their analysis. Andeanists should be encouraged to frame hypotheses from the oral traditions that can be tested through field archaeology. They should also be cautious about accepting or rejecting the validity of these traditions until more evidence is available.

BIBLIOGRAPHY

BENNETT, WENDELL C.
  1939 *Archaeology of the North Coast of Peru.* Anthropological Papers of the American Museum of Natural History, 37(1). New York.

BRÜNING, ENRIQUE (HEINRICH)
  1922 *Estudios monográficos del Departamento de Lambayeque.* Tomo I: *Lambayeque.* Dionisio Mendoza, Chiclayo.

CABELLO BALBOA, MIGUEL
  [1586] *Miscelánia antártica.* Universidad Nacional Mayor de San Marcos,
  1951 Lima. (Manuscript copies are in the New York Public Library and the University Library of the University of Texas, Austin.)

CORDY-COLLINS, ALANA
  n.d. The Tule Boat Theme in Moche Art: A Problem in Ancient Peruvian Iconography. M.A. thesis, Institue of Archaeology, University of California at Los Angeles, 1972.

DAY, KENT C.
  1971 *Quarterly Report of Royal Ontario Museum Lambayeque Valley Expedition 1971.* Office of the Chief Archaeologist, Royal Ontario Museum, Toronto.

DONNAN, CHRISTOPHER B.
  1972 Moche-Huari Murals from Northern Peru. *Archaeology* 25(2): 85–95.
  1978 *Moche Art of Peru.* Museum of Cultural of History, University of California, Los Angeles.
  1984 Ancient Murals from Chornancap, Peru. *Archaeology* 37(3): 32–37.
  1986 Introduction. In *The Pacatnamú Papers, Volume I* (Christopher B. Donnan and Guillermo A. Cock, eds.): 19–26. Museum of Cultural History, University of California, Los Angeles.
  n.d. Excavations at Chotuna and Chornancap, Lambayeque Valley, Peru. Manuscript, Museum of Cultural History, University of California, Los Angeles.

EDWARDS, CLINTON
1965   *Aboriginal Watercraft of the Pacific Coast of South America.* Ibero-Americana 47. University of California Press, Berkeley.

KOLATA, ALAN
1982   Chronology and Settlement Growth at Chan Chan. In *Chan Chan: Andean Desert City* (Michael E. Moseley and Kent C. Day, eds.): 67–85. University of New Mexico Press, Albuquerque.

MEANS, PHILIP A.
1931   *Ancient Civilizations of the Andes.* Charles Scribner's Sons, New York.

MOSELEY, MICHAEL E., ROBERT A. FELDMAN, CHARLES R. ORTLOFF, and ALFREDO NARVAEZ
1983   Principles of Agrarian Collapse in the Cordillera Negra, Peru. *Annals of the Carnegie Museum* 52(13): 299–327. Carnegie Museum of Natural History, Pittsburgh.

MOSELEY, MICHAEL E., and ERIC C. DEEDS
1982   The Land in Front of Chan Chan: Agrarian Expansion, Reform, and Collapse in the Moche Valley. In *Chan Chan: Andean Desert City* (Michael E. Moseley and Kent C. Day, eds.): 25–54. University of New Mexico Press, Albuquerque.

MOSELEY, MICHAEL E., and ALAN L. KOLATA
n.d.   Myth and History on the North Coast of Peru: Steps to an Archaeological Concordant. Paper prepared for the Dumbarton Oaks symposium The Northern Dynasties, October 1985.

MURPHY, ROBERT C.
1926   Oceanic and Climatic Phenomena along the West Coast of South America during 1925. *Geographical Review* 16: 26–54. American Geographical Society, New York.

NIALS, FRED L., ERIC E. DEEDS, MICHAEL E. MOSELEY, SHELIA G. POZORSKI,
THOMAS G. POZORSKI, and ROBERT A. FELDMAN
1979   El Niño: The Catastrophic Flooding of Coastal Peru. *Bulletin of the Field Museum of Natural History* 50(7): 4–14 (Part I); 50(8): 4–10 (Part II). Chicago.

ROWE, JOHN HOWLAND
1948   The Kingdom of Chimor. *Acta Americana* 6(1–2): 26–59.

ROSTWOROWSKI DE DIEZ CANSECO, MARÍA
1975   Pescadores, artesanos y mercaderes costeños en el Perú prehispánico. *Revista del Museo Nacional* 41: 311–349. Lima.

RUBIÑOS Y ANDRADE, JUSTO MODESTO DE
[1781] Sucesión cronológica: ó serie historical de los curas de Mórrope y
1936   Pacora en la Provincia de Lambayeque del Obispado de Truxillo del Perú . . . Ed. Carlos A. Romero, "Un manuscrito interesant." *Revista Histórica* 10(3): 289–363. Lima.

Christopher B. Donnan

SANDWEISS, DANIEL H., HAROLD B. ROLLINS, and JAMES B. RICHARDSON III
  1983   Landscape Alteration and Prehistoric Human Occupation on the North
            Coast of Peru. *Annals of Carnegie Museum* 52: 277–298. Carnegie Mu-
            seum of Natural History, Pittsburgh.

SHIMADA, IZUMI
  n.d.   Socioeconomic Organization at Moche V Pampa Grande, Peru: Pre-
            lude to a Major Transformation. Ph.D. dissertation, Department of
            Anthropology, University of Arizona, 1976.

SHIMADA, IZUMI, and CARLOS ELERA
  1983   Batan Grande y la emergente complejidad cultural en el norte del Perú
            durante el Horizonte Medio: Datos y modelos. *Boletín del Museo
            Nacional de Antropología y Arqueología* 8: 41–47. Lima.

THOMPSON, LONNIE G.
  n.d.   Letter to Michael E. Moseley, October 16, 1985.

The Chotuna Friezes and the Chotuna-Dragon Connection

CHRISTOPHER B. DONNAN

UNIVERSITY OF CALIFORNIA AT LOS ANGELES

CHOTUNA IS A MAJOR ARCHAEOLOGICAL SITE located in the lower part of the Lambayeque Valley (figs. 1, 2 in Donnan [Naymlap], this volume). It is thought to have been associated with a legendary dynasty, founded by Naymlap, that ruled the valley centuries before European contact (Donnan: ibid.). In 1941 grave robbers uncovered two walls at Chotuna that were decorated with elaborate low-relief friezes. Because the friezes appeared to be remarkably similar to those at the site of Dragon, located in the Moche Valley approximately 180 km to the south, the relationship between Chotuna and Dragon has been the subject of much speculation during the past four decades (cf. Helsley n.d.; Iriarte n.d.; Kosok 1965; Schaedel 1966).

Between 1980 and 1982 we conducted an archaeological exploration of Chotuna,[1] and in the process relocated the friezes found in 1941. Extensive excavation in that area of the site revealed additional friezes, as well as the form of the architectural complex on which the friezes appeared. Thus, after more than forty years, we are now able to assess the similarities of the Chotuna and Dragon friezes and to understand better their relationship to the prehistory of northern Peru.

Our excavations indicate that friezes are not common at Chotuna. We found them only in the complex of rooms and courtyards on the north side of Huaca Gloria, a relatively small truncated pyramid near the center of the

The author is grateful to Gloria S.A. of Lima and the National Geographic Society for their generous support of the fieldwork at Chotuna, and to the Instituto Nacional de Cultura for the necessary permits. The Museum of Cultural History at U.C.L.A. provided the administrative support for the research. The Museo Brüning in Lambayeque helped resolve many logistical problems while the fieldwork was ongoing and has, appropriately, become the permanent home for the Chotuna collections. Geraldine Clift and Anne Helsley were very helpful in providing comments on earlier versions of this report.

[1] The excavation was under my direction and involved students from the University of California at Los Angeles and the Universidad Católica Santa María, Arequipa.

site (fig. 3 in Donnan [Naymlap], this volume). It was in this area that we located the friezes that had been discovered previously. As we cleared the deep windblown sand in which they were buried, we discovered that they decorated walls that formed the southwest corner of a large open courtyard, measuring approximately 26 m N–S by 16 m E–W (Figs. 1, 2). A central ramp led from the floor of the courtyard up to a raised bench along the south wall. In the middle of the bench was a trough, attached to an elaborate step that led through a doorway near the center of the south wall.

Flanking the step was a series of square columns that probably supported a roof. Each column originally consisted of a large hardwood beam, socketed vertically into the bench. The beam was wrapped with rope, which provided purchase for a thick coating of mud plaster. Four columns were found, but it is likely that there were originally six, two of which had been destroyed by grave robbers. Of the four columns that remained, two were undecorated and two had friezes on each of their four sides (Figs. 3–5). The front of the bench and the sides of the ramp that led up to it were also decorated with friezes, although only portions of them were preserved (Fig. 6).

Elaborate friezes completely covered the walls that formed the southern end of the courtyard. Those in the southwest corner were the ones found in 1941. Fortunately, shortly after their discovery, they were photographed by Julio Rondón, an amateur archaeologist living in the nearby city of Chiclayo. In 1944 two of Rondón's photographs were published by Alfred Kroeber (1944: pl. 33A, B). That same year Hans Horkheimer published two others (1944: figs. 5, 6). The photographs are extremely important because the friezes were largely destroyed by exposure to the elements after their original discovery.

A section of the friezes originally uncovered in 1941 was photographed by Richard Schaedel when he visited Chotuna sometime between 1948 and 1950 (Schaedel 1966: 456, pl. 28A).[2] This same section, immediately west of the doorway in the south wall, was re-excavated and photographed by Hermann Trimborn in 1972 (1979: 78–79, figs. 56–58). It was still relatively well preserved when we cleared the courtyard in 1980 (Fig. 7).

In the course of exposing these friezes, we found that there were friezes in the southeast corner of the courtyard that had not been excavated previously. They had been covered over with mud plaster by the ancient inhabitants of Chotuna and were subsequently buried by windblown sand.

---

[2] Schaedel also uncovered a portion of another frieze at this time and assumed that it was an additional section of the friezes found in 1941 (Schaedel 1966: 456, pl. 30). We relocated it in 1980, on the south wall of a small room at the northwest corner of the courtyard where the other friezes were found (Fig. 1). Whereas the friezes in the courtyard appear to have been painted with only yellow pigment, the frieze in this room has traces of red, black, and white pigment.

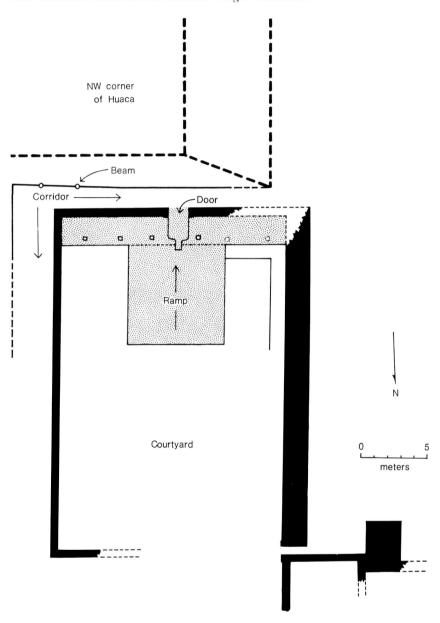

NW corner
of Huaca

Beam

Corridor

Door

Ramp

N

Courtyard

0   5

meters

Fig. 1   Map of the courtyard on the northwest corner of Huaca Gloria. The friezes decorate the southern portion of this courtyard.

Fig. 2   Reconstruction of the southern portion of the courtyard at Chotuna, viewed from the north.

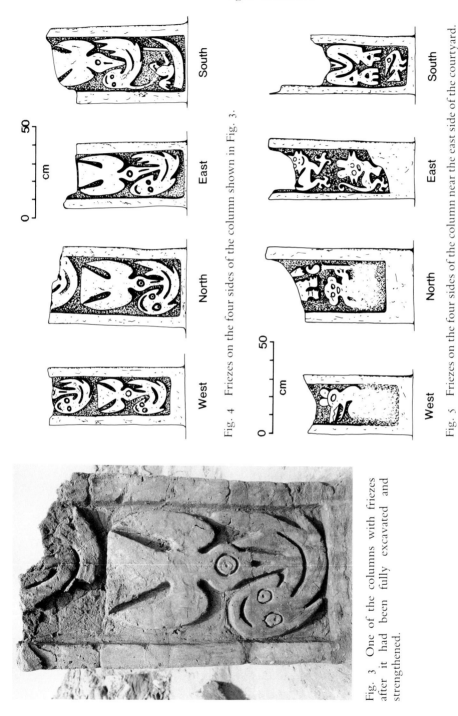

Fig. 4 Friezes on the four sides of the column shown in Fig. 3.

Fig. 5 Friezes on the four sides of the column near the east side of the courtyard.

Fig. 3 One of the columns with friezes after it had been fully excavated and strengthened.

279

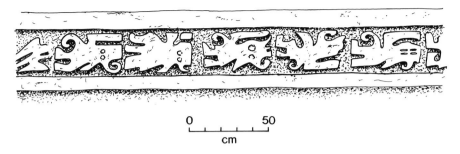

Fig. 6   Frieze on the front of the raised bench, east of the ramp.

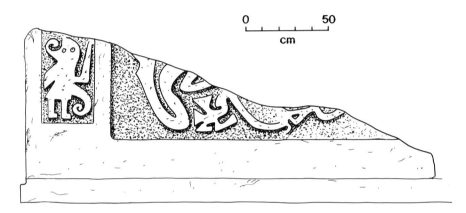

Fig. 7   Frieze on the south wall of the courtyard, west of the door.

Once the sand was excavated, careful removal of the later plaster revealed the original friezes (Figs. 8–10). Because the walls in the southeast corner were preserved to nearly their original height, we were able to reconstruct some of the framing panels that characterize the upper part of the frieze design.

By combining the information derived from our excavation of the courtyard with photographs taken of it in 1941, we were able to make a plausible reconstruction of its original appearance (Fig. 2). It must have been very impressive—nearly all vertical surfaces at the southern end were covered with elaborate friezes painted with yellow pigment. The changing angle of sunlight during the day would have played across the low-relief designs, alternately accentuating some and masking others.

Although the function of the courtyard is not clear, the focus is clearly toward the southern end. There the elevated bench, surrounded by the high, elaborately decorated walls, would have provided an ideal stage for the

Fig. 8   Southeast corner of the courtyard during the cleaning of the friezes.

Fig. 9 Frieze on the south wall of the courtyard, east of the door.

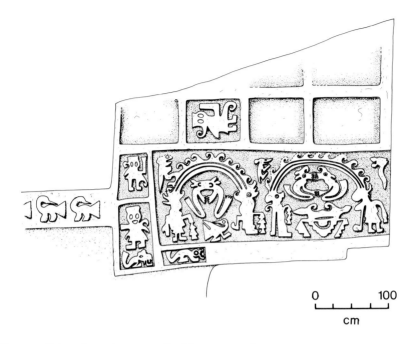

Fig. 10   Frieze from the east wall of the courtyard.

performance of activities that could be witnessed by numerous individuals in the courtyard below. The central ramp providing access to the elevated bench implies that some individuals were expected to move between that area and the floor of the courtyard. In contrast, the elaborate step and trough in the center of the bench seem altogether unsuited for recurring foot traffic. The overhanging lip around the top of the step and the carefully sculpted trough, which were constructed of adobe and mud plaster, would have been destroyed quickly if they had been walked on. Perhaps the step served simply as a raised platform—an individual could have reached the step through the door at the back, remained on the platform during a ceremony, and exited through the same doorway.

COMPARISONS WITH DRAGON

It is clear that the plan of this courtyard at Chotuna is not at all similar to the architecture of Dragon, the site with similar friezes located in the Moche Valley (fig. 1 in Donnan [Naymlap], this volume). Dragon consists of a large rectangular enclosure surrounding a truncated pyramid with an elaborate ramp that provides access to its summit (Fig. 11). Along three sides of the pyramid are large cell-like rooms. The friezes at Dragon cover the exterior of the walls enclosing the truncated pyramid, as well as the sides of

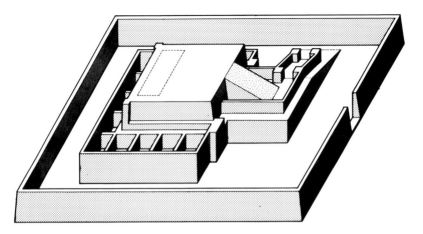

Fig. 11   Isometric reconstruction of Dragon, viewed from the northwest.

the pyramid and its ramp (Fig. 12). Thus, one could view some of the friezes from outside the compound without entering it. At Chotuna, on the other hand, the friezes were visible only to those who gained access to the court-yard, and within this structure they appear exclusively at the southern end—the other parts of the courtyard show no evidence of frieze decoration.

Furthermore, although most of the friezes on the walls of the courtyard at Chotuna are similar to those at Dragon, there are some important differ-ences. The friezes at Dragon consist of individual panels with arched double-headed serpents, each of which is framed by vertical panels depicting other figures (Fig. 13). In contrast, at Chotuna the arched double-headed serpents are repeated along the length of the wall without being separated by framing panels.

Although the same figures are shown at Chotuna and Dragon, the ones at Dragon are clearer and more consistent; those at Chotuna are often amorphous and exhibit considerable variation in the way they are de-picted. For example, at Dragon the double-headed serpent arch can be easily recognized—each of the two heads has its mouth open and appears to be biting a conical hat worn by an anthropomorphic figure standing below (Fig. 14 above). At Chotuna, the heads of the double-headed ser-pents are unclear and tend to blend into an amorphous form that in only a few cases resembles a standing figure (Fig. 14 below). Similarly, the paired animals beneath the serpent arches at Chotuna resemble their Dragon coun-terparts, but again important details have been omitted or left unclear. Beneath these animals on the Dragon friezes is a design element that consists of a crescent-shaped figure with two facing heads. This motif has been so simplified and abstracted in the Chotuna friezes that it no longer retains any animal characteristics.

Fig. 12   View of the friezes at Dragon. Portions of this structure and the friezes that decorate it have been reconstructed.

Fig. 13   Friezes at Dragon.

Realizing that the Chotuna friezes are often simplified and abstracted versions of elements depicted in the Dragon friezes, we can identify some of the other elements as derivations from Dragon prototypes. The amorphous shapes in the upper corners of the arched serpent panels at Chotuna (Fig. 14 below) are probably derived from the double-headed animal forms in the same location on the Dragon friezes (Fig. 14 above). Similarly, most of the figures in framing panels at Chotuna (Fig. 15 right) almost certainly are derived from the figures in framing panels at Dragon (Fig. 15 left). Repeatedly, motifs that are clearly depicted and instantly recognizable in the Dragon friezes are garbled at Chotuna and become undecipherable forms, as though the Chotuna artists did not truly understand what they were depicting. The inconsistency with which these Chotuna friezes are rendered underscores the impression that these motifs simply were not familiar to the artists.

In contrast, the design elements at Chotuna that have no counterpart at Dragon are quite clear and intelligible. These include all the friezes that decorate the columns: birds with fish in their beaks, a person in a tule boat, a sash-like object, and various anthropomorphic and zoomorphic figures (Figs. 4, 5). The same is true of the bird, fish, and animal forms scattered among the arched serpent motifs on the walls (Figs. 9, 10). In almost every

Fig. 14 Comparison of the principal motif in the friezes at Dragon *above* and Chotuna *below*.

Fig. 15   Comparison of the friezes in framing panels at Dragon *left* and Chotuna *right*.

case, if the object is not depicted at Dragon, its depiction at Chotuna is clear, intelligible, and executed with confidence. If it is similar to an object depicted at Dragon, it is garbled. This indicates that the garbling of the Dragon motifs is not the work of inept craftsmen who were unable to render designs clearly, but rather it is the work of skilled craftsmen who simply were not familiar with what they were illustrating. It also implies that they were copying from a pattern or model. The nature of this pattern or model is a question that will be considered near the end of this report. It should be noted at this point, however, that since the friezes at Dragon are so much clearer and more consistent than those at Chotuna, it seems virtually impossible that the Dragon friezes were copied from those at Chotuna. If the friezes at one site were derived from the other, those at Chotuna would have to have been derived from the ones at Dragon.

Our excavations at Chotuna indicate that the site was occupied from approximately A.D. 750 until the early part of the Colonial period, approximately A.D. 1600 (Donnan [Naymlap], this volume). The architecture with friezes is assigned to the Middle Phase of this occupation (approximately A.D. 1100 to 1350) on the basis of the form of mud bricks used to construct the walls on which the friezes occur. These bricks are loaf shaped and have a relatively low profile, a type that is characteristic of the Middle Phase.

Five radiocarbon determinations from Huaca Gloria help assess the absolute dating of the friezes. Four of these are from two wood beams inside the columns at the south end of the courtyard:

First beam:

1. UCR-1482 = A.D. 1200 ± 80 years (750 ± 80 BP) Wood from inside the column with seabird designs
2. UCLA 2346-A = A.D. 1250 ± 100 years (700 ± 100 BP) Wood from inside the column with seabird designs

Second beam:

3. Beta-12281 = A.D. 720 ± 60 years (1230 ± 60 BP) Wood from inside the undecorated column located second from the east side of the courtyard
4. Beta-14736 = A.D. 1090 ± 60 years (860 ± 60 BP) Wood from inside the undecorated column located second from the east side of the courtyard

The fifth radiocarbon determination is from a beam on the north side of Huaca Gloria (Fig. 1). This face of the *huaca* formed a corridor along the south side of the frieze-decorated courtyard and almost certainly would have been contemporary with it.

5. Beta-12280 = A.D. 1230 ± 50 years (720 ± 50 BP).[3]

Because the Middle Phase has been dated from A.D. 1100 to 1350 on the basis of other radiocarbon determinations from Chotuna and Chornancap (Donnan [Naymlap], this volume), it is likely that the third determination, Beta-12281, is aberrant and that the other four dates are accurate assessments of when the frieze-decorated courtyard was constructed, sometime between A.D. 1100 and 1250.

It is interesting to consider the iconography of the Chotuna friezes and to look for similar representations in the art of northern Peru. The motif of the

---

[3] Calibrated dates (Klein et al. 1982) are: (1) 1210, (2) 1300, (3) 760, (4) 1150, and (5) 1280.

double-headed serpent forming an arch to frame other motifs has a long tradition in the local iconography. It is found as early as Moche III, ca. A.D. 400 (Fig. 16). One Moche IV example, dating approximately A.D. 500, shows the double-headed serpent in a manner remarkably similar to the way it is depicted in the Chotuna friezes—it even has a human head in the jaws of each serpent (Fig. 17). In Moche representations, however, the serpent consistently frames one or more human figures who are shown in profile. It was not until Middle Horizon Epoch 3 (ca. A.D. 1100) that the double-headed serpent arch was used to frame a frontally depicted anthropomorphized figure and paired animals like those seen in the Chotuna and Dragon friezes. These were popular motifs at this time and often were depicted together in press-molded ceramics (Figs. 18, 19).

INTERPRETING THE CHOTUNA-DRAGON CONNECTION

When Kroeber and Horkheimer published Rondón's photographs of the Chotuna friezes in 1944, both noted that the designs were similar to the friezes at the site of Dragon. Other scholars have also commented on this similarity (Kubler 1962; Schaedel 1966; Iriarte n.d.; Trimborn 1979; Helsley n.d.). In 1959 Paul Kosok suggested that the Chotuna friezes date to his Middle Period (1000–1200) and that they might correspond to the reign of Naymlap and his followers (1959: 63).[4] He also argued that their similarity to the friezes at Dragon "may well indicate cultural interrelationships that must have been strong during the Middle Period" (1965: 91). Kosok did not, however, suggest what the nature of that interrelationship might have been.

Schaedel, who conducted the most thorough excavation at Dragon, felt that it dated to what he called Tiahuanacoid III/Moche (1966: 455). Presumably this would be roughly equivalent to Kosok's Middle Period. Schaedel felt that on the basis of architecture alone, "arguments are equally good for deriving the Chotuna temple from Dragon as vice versa" (ibid: 456). The ceramic evidence, however, suggested to Schaedel that the primary direction of influence was north to south rather than south to north. This direction was particularly evident with the increasing popularity of blackware and the introduction of paddle-marked ceramics in the Moche, Viru, and Chicama Valleys at this time—ceramic traits that are thought to have originated in the north and spread south. Although Schaedel alludes to the possibility that the Chotuna friezes relate to the Naymlap dynasty and Dragon ones relate to the later Taycanamo dynasty, he does not argue strongly for such a correlation.

---

[4] The story of the Naymlap dynasty correlates best with the Early Phase occupation of Chotuna (Donnan [Naymlap], this volume). Therefore, if the Naymlap dynasty actually existed, and lived at Chotuna, it is likely that this occurred prior to the creation of the friezes.

Fig. 16   Moche III fineline drawing of a double-headed serpent framing a standing figure.

Fig. 17   Moche IV fineline drawing of a double-headed serpent framing a standing figure. Note the human heads in the jaws of the serpent.

Fig. 18   Front and back views of a Middle Horizon Epoch 3 ceramic vessel with press-molded designs. One side (*left*) depicts the double-headed serpent arched over a standing human figure, while the other (*right*) shows the same serpent arched over paired animals. Photograph courtesy of the Lowie Museum of Anthropology, University of California, Berkeley.

Fig. 19   Press-molded design from a Middle Horizon Epoch 3 ceramic vessel. Note the similarity between these motifs and those on the Chotuna and Dragon friezes (drawing after Carrión Cachot 1959: fig. 29).

Most recently, Michael Moseley and Alan Kolata have suggested that the similarity between the Chotuna and Dragon friezes might have resulted from "*huaca* capture" by the people of Chan Chan, who conquered the Lambayeque Valley around A.D. 1370. They argue that the frieze-decorated structure at Chotuna "was the shrine of the Naymlap dynastic lineage at the time of Chimor's conquest of Lambayeque, and that the primary cult object from the shrine was removed to Chan Chan where it was housed in the Huaca Dragon, a platform mound built explicitly for this purpose" (Moseley and Kolata n.d.: 17–18). Dragon is thus thought to

> reflect a policy of "huaca hostage," or compulsory curation, in the imperial capital of sacred objects captured in the course of territorial conquest and held hostage for purposes of political coercion. . . . [This] implies that conquest was not simply a matter of acquiring land, labor, and artisans, but also entailed the acquisition of the sacred objects that were emblematic of and symbolically unified the subject nations and their ruling lineages. By physically holding such huacas hostage, the descendant corporate bodies were symbolically held hostage and thereby ritually and politically bound to the conquering nation. (Moseley and Kolata n.d.: 14–15)

Although this is a reasonable scenario in the absence of detailed information about the Chotuna friezes, the evidence recovered during our excavations makes such an explanation untenable. As demonstrated above, the friezes at Chotuna are garbled and nearly undecipherable, while the same motifs at Dragon are depicted clearly and are instantly recognizable. Thus it would have been impossible to derive the Dragon friezes from those at Chotuna. Furthermore, the Chotuna friezes were created during the Middle Phase of the site's occupation, estimated to date between A.D. 1100 and 1350. Iconographically they relate to Middle Horizon Epoch 3. Since it seems likely that Dragon is contemporary with the Chotuna friezes, they would both predate the conquest of the Lambayeque Valley by the Kingdom of Chimor, which took place approximately A.D. 1370.

The press-molded ceramics of the Middle Horizon Epoch 3 that are similar to the iconography of the Dragon and Chotuna friezes are most commonly found in the area between Supe and Nepeña (fig. 1 in Donnan [Naymlap], this volume).[5] Therefore, it may be that the stylistic influence moved from south to north along the coast. If so, this might partially account for the motifs being depicted clearly at Dragon but garbled further north—and further from the source—at Chotuna.

It is interesting to note that Middle Horizon Epoch 3 was a time when

---

[5] For illustrations of this type of ceramics, see Tello (1956) and Carrión Cachot (1959). For their attribution to Middle Horizon Epoch 3, see Menzel (1964 and 1977).

Fig. 20   Painted textile depicting the double-headed serpent arched over a human figure. Photograph courtesy of the Lowie Museum of Anthropology, University of California, Berkeley.

painted textiles were very popular on the central and northern coasts of Peru. Many of these textiles have complex iconography, including the depiction of double-headed serpent arches framing frontal human figures (Fig. 20). In the Andean area of South America, textiles often served as the medium by which complex iconography was diffused over great distances. Although it is highly speculative, we might consider the possibility that the Dragon motifs were copied on painted textiles that were then transported to Lambayeque and ultimately used as models from which the Chotuna friezes were copied. The blurring of detail that generally characterizes painted textiles may well have been the cause for the distortion of the Chotuna friezes—local artists, not understanding what they were depicting, resorted to slavishly copying the blurred images. Whatever the means of diffusion might have been, the inept rendering of the friezes at Chotuna suggests that the motifs were unfamiliar to the craftsmen who created them and that they were intrusive to the lower Lambayeque Valley.

After A.D. 1100, the tradition of decorating architecture with friezes continued to flourish in the Moche Valley and reached its greatest proliferation in the magnificent *ciudadelas* of Chan Chan. In the Lambayeque Valley, however, we have no evidence of later friezes. Those in the courtyard at Chotuna remain a seemingly isolated flowering of architectural embellishment. The reason for the sudden appearance and demise of this artistic form must await further archaeological investigation.

BIBLIOGRAPHY

CARRIÓN CACHOT, REBECA
   1959   *La religión en el antiguo Peru (norte y centro de la costa, periodo post-clásico).* Tipografía Peruana, S.A., Lima.

HELSLEY, ANNE MARIE
   n.d.   The Friezes of Huaca El Dragón: An Interpretation. M.A. thesis, Department of Anthropology, University of Texas, Austin, 1985.

HORKHEIMER, HANS
   1944   *Vistas arqueológicas del noroeste del Perú.* Instituto Arqueológico de la Universidad Nacional de Trujillo. Librería y Imprenta Moreno, Trujillo.

IRIARTE BRENNER, FRANCISCO E.
   n.d.   La huaca "El Dragón" y su restauración. Ph.D. dissertation, Universidad Nacional Mayor de San Marcos de Lima, 1969.

KLEIN, J., J. C. LERMAN, P. E. DAMON, AND E. K. RALPH
   1982   Calibration of Radiocarbon Dates: Tables Based on the Consensus Data of the Workshop on Calibrating the Radiocarbon Time Scale. *Radiocarbon* 24(2): 103–150.

KOSOK, PAUL
   1959   *Peru. Volume 1, Lima.* Lima.
   1965   *Life, Land and Water in Ancient Peru.* Long Island University Press, New York.

KROEBER, ALFRED L.
   1944   *Peruvian Archaeology in 1942.* Viking Fund Publication in Anthropology Number 4. The Viking Fund, New York.

KUBLER, GEORGE
   1962   *The Art and Architecture of Ancient America.* Pelican, Baltimore.

MENZEL, DOROTHY
   1964   Style and Time in the Middle Horizon. *Ñawpa Pacha* 2: 1–106. Berkeley.
   1977   *The Archaeology of Ancient Peru and the Work of Max Uhle.* R. H. Lowie Museum of Anthropology, University of California, Berkeley.

Christopher B. Donnan

MOSELEY, MICHAEL E., and ALAN L. KOLATA

    n.d.   Myth and History on the North Coast of Peru: Steps to an Archaeological Concordat. Paper prepared for the Dumbarton Oaks symposium The Northern Dynasties, October 1985.

SCHAEDEL, RICHARD P.

    1966   The Huaca "El Dragón." *Journal de la Société des Américanistes* 55(2): 383–496.

TELLO, JULIO C.

    1956   *Arqueología de Valle de Casma. Culturas: Chavín, Santa o Huaylas Yunga y Sub-Chimú.* Universidad Nacional Mayor de San Marcos, Lima.

TRIMBORN, HERMANN

    1979   *El reino de Lambayeque en el antiguo Perú.* Collectanea Instituti Anthropos 19. Haus Völker und Kulturen–Anthropos Institut, St. Augustin.

Cultural Continuities and Discontinuities on the Northern North Coast of Peru, Middle–Late Horizons

IZUMI SHIMADA

HARVARD UNIVERSITY

INTRODUCTION

MORE THAN HALF A CENTURY AGO, A. L. Kroeber (1930) recognized that the "Northern North Coast" of Peru, composed of the five contiguous river valleys of Motupe, La Leche, Lambayeque, Zaña, and Jequetepeque (Fig. 1), possessed architectural, linguistic, and environmental unity, along with characteristics significantly different from those of the coastal valleys on the southern half of the North Coast. Clarification of time depth, as well as of the factors and processes responsible for this cultural unity and idiosyncrasies, however, was long in coming.

A significant advance was made by Paul Kosok (1959, 1965; also see Schaedel 1951a, 1966a, b, 1972), who argued that the upper La Leche,

The data for this paper was collected during eleven field seasons between 1973 and 1986 in the Lambayeque region of the North Coast of Peru through the generous support of the following institutions: Canada Council, National Geographic Society, National Science Foundation, Harvard and Princeton Universities. I am grateful to the members of the Sican Archaeological Project for their assistance in fieldwork, sharing data, and stimulating discussions. In particular I thank Raffael Cavallaro, Kate Cleland, Miguel Cornejo, Alan Craig, Carlos Elera, Frances Hayashida, Alvaro Higueras, Susan Ramírez, and Brian Schaffield. In addition, Susan Bruce kindly allowed me to study her valuable comparative data from the Chotuna-Chornancap Complex. Dorothy Menzel has provided me with insightful comments on Middle Horizon ceramics. Richard P. Schaedel was generous in sharing his ideas and invaluable for deepening the level of analysis and broadening my perspective. I am also grateful to Alana Cordy-Collins, Kate Cleland, and Melody Shimada for their helpful substantive and editorial comments. I am solely responsible for any misunderstandings and errors that may be contained in this paper.

The following institutions generously gave permission to photograph collections and/or reproduce photos here: Museo Arqueológico Regional "Brüning" in Lambayeque (Figs. 10 and 14), Fundación Museo Amano in Lima (Fig. 13), the Royal Ontario Museum in Toronto (Fig. 16), and Servicio Aerofotográfico Nacional of Peru (Fig. 29). In addition, Figure 22 was modified from an original drawing by Hans Knapp and is reproduced here with his permission. Figure 26 was compiled from Susan Bruce's fieldnotes.

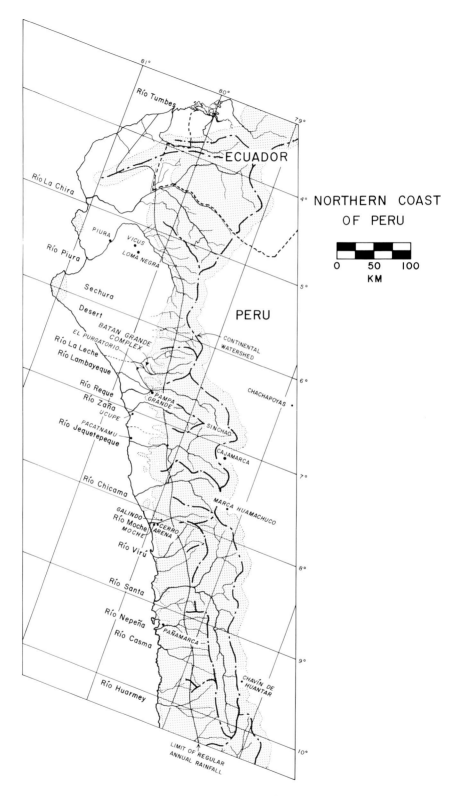

Fig. 1   Map of the North Coast of Peru showing the major sites mentioned in the text.

TABLE 1. CHRONOLOGICAL CORRELATION FOR NORTH PERU

YEAR	PERUVIAN REFERENT CHRONO ROWE & MENZEL 1967	CAJAMARCA BASIN REICHLEN & REICHLEN 1950	CAJAMARCA BASIN TERADA & MATSUMOTO 1985	LAMBAYEQUE SICAN ARCHAEOLOGICAL PROJECT	LAMBAYEQUE ZEVALLOS 1971 — LAMBAY TARDIO	LAMBAYEQUE ZEVALLOS 1971 — CHIMU/INCA REGIONAL	KOSOK 1959	MOCHE VALLEY MOSELEY 1982
1532 / 1476	LATE HORIZON	CAJAMARCA V	FINAL CAJAMARCA PHASE	SICAN INCA / SICAN CHIMU		CAJAMARCA; LAMBAYEQUE II ESTILO SERRANO COSTEÑO; TRICOLOR; CREMA ROJO; ROJO CREMA; SERIE CABALLITO	E	CHIMU INCA
	LATE INTERMEDIATE PERIOD AD 900–1476	CAJAMARCA IV	LATE CAJAMARCA PHASE	LATE SICAN B AD 1100–1350/75 A	LAMBAYEQUE MEDIO (FUSIONAL)		D	CHIMU
1000		CAJAMARCA III		MIDDLE SICAN AD 900–1100			C	
	MIDDLE HORIZON AD 550–900	CAJAMARCA II	MIDDLE CAJAMARCA PHASE B / A	EARLY SICAN AD 700/50–900		MOCHICOIDE (INFLUENCIA CACHACO SERRANA) LAMBAY I TRANSFORM	B	EARLY CHIMU — V
500		CAJAMARCA I	EARLY CAJAMARCA PHASE C / B / A	MOCHE V / IV	LAMBAYEQUE CLASICO	LAMBAYEQUE I	A	MOCHE IV
AD 0 / BC	EARLY INTERMEDIATE PERIOD 400 BC – AD 550	TORRECITAS–CHAVIN	INITIAL CAJAMARCA PHASE B / A	GALLINAZO-LIKE				MOCHE III
				SALINAR-LIKE / VICUS ?	LAMBAYEQUE PRECLASICO	TRANSITO MOCHICA; VICUS ?		MOCHE II / I
500			LAYZON PERIOD					GALLINAZO
	EARLY HORIZON 1400–400 BC		LATE HUACALOMA PERIOD	CUPISNIQUE-LIKE	LAMBAYEQUE TEMPRANO	CHAVIN BICROMO; POLICROMO; MONOCROMO (FORMATIVO)		SALINAR
1000			EARLY HUACALOMA PERIOD					CUPISNIQUE
1500	INITIAL PERIOD –2100 BC				LAMBAYEQUE PRECERAMICO			

CAJAMARCA TRADITION (TERADA & MATSUMOTO 1985)

Lambayeque, and Zaña Valleys were hydrologically and politically integrated into a single system[1] during the Lambayeque C period, ca. A.D. 1000–1200 (Table 1). This system, in turn, lay at the heart of what Kosok called the "Lambayeque Valley Complex" (Fig. 2) that encompassed an estimated third of the total population and cultivatable land on the Peruvian coast during its maximum extent in the Lambayeque C period (Kosok 1959; 1965: 147).

Kosok (1965: 178) felt, however, that, in spite of hydrological linkage and a kind of cultural unity within the valley complex, "politically there was probably more diversity than unity," and that the size and geographical variety of the complex contributed to this picture. He asserts that "it is improbable that Lambayeque rulers ever organized a state comprising the whole Lambayeque Complex" (ibid.: 80–81).

The data base for his opinion of regional political formation and organization was never adequately explained or published. However, it becomes evident when we realize that Kosok accepted as a reliable account of historical reality the legend of Naymlap and the Lambayeque dynasty as recorded by Miguel Cabello Balboa ([1586] 1951; cf. Rowe 1948; see Donnan [Naymlap], this volume, for a summary).

Using twenty-five years as the average reign of each ruler, Kosok (1965: 73, Table 2) arrived at a date of ca. A.D. 1025 for Naymlap's arrival in the Lambayeque Valley from Ecuador. Kosok (1959: 63–64) argued for the rapid conquest of local polities centered at Colluz and Mirador and the establishment of Chotuna as the center of the lower and middle Lambayeque Valley shortly after Naymlap's arrival. Further, he sees steady territorial expansion by Naymlap's descendants through conquests, with regional polities centered at the conquered or newly established settlements (by around A.D. 1075–1100) of Patapo or Cinto, Sipan-Collique, Jayanca, and Tucume forming "a kind of kinship-dominated federation of local 'states' " (Kosok 1965: 178; Fig. 2). The foundation for the above multi-valley polity, according to this view, was established by the grandsons of Naymlap.

Seemingly good correspondence between the names and locations of settlements specified by the legend and known archaeological sites, as well as a long list of successive rulers who descended from Naymlap, are factors that preconditioned his acceptance of the "legend" as "history based on facts." His scenario is, then, a history transcribed using modern anthropological terms and concepts.

---

[1] The Chancay-Reque River of the Lambayeque Valley has a large discharge volume, stable flow, and relatively high elevation (Kosok 1959; Portugal 1966). These features, together with the low, even gradient of the valley made the river the backbone of this macro-irrigation system.

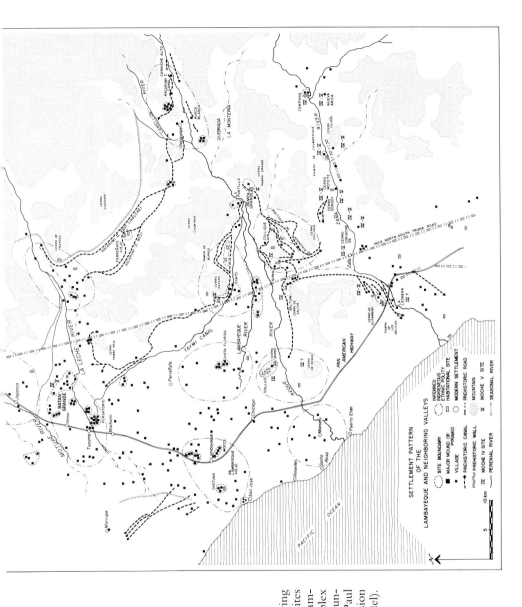

Fig. 2 Map showing major archaeological sites and features of the Lambayeque Valley Complex (revised version of an unpublished map by Paul Kosok in the possession of Richard P. Schaedel).

TABLE 2. KOSOK'S CHRONOLOGICAL RECONSTRUCTION OF THE NAYMLAP LEGEND
AND THE LAMBAYEQUE DYNASTIES (1965: 73, CHART III)

Date (A.D.)	Lambayeque	Chimu
1025	1. Naymlap and Ceterni	
1050	2. Cium and Zolsdoñi (sons)	
1075	3. Llapchillulli, Cala, Escuñain, (Jayanca) (Tucume) (Lambayeque) Nor, Cuntipullec, other sons (Patapo) (Collique) (to other parts)	
1100	4. Mascuy	
1125	5. Cuntipallec	
1150	6. Allascunto	
1175	7. Nofan-Nech	
1200	8. Mulumuslan	
1225	9. Llamecoll	1. Taycanamo—from north (Chimu Capac)
1250	10. Lamipatcum	2. Gaucricaur—conquers the entire Moche Valley
1275	11. Acunta	3. Ñançenpinco—conquers Pacasmayo to Santa (Empire of 6 valleys)
1300	12. Fempellec (killed) (30-day flood)	4. ?
		5. ?
		6. ?
		7. ?
1400		8. ?
		9. ?
1450		10. Minchançaman—controls 600 miles of coast. Conquered by Incas
1500		11. Chumun Caur—set up by Incas
		12. Guaman Chumu—Incas break up Chimu lands
1525		13. Ancocoyuch
		14. Chimu Cajaçimçim—baptized as Don Martin

Although not as explicitly or comprehensively as Kosok, many scholars from the days of Enrique (Heinrich) Brüning (1922) and Philip A. Means (1917, 1931) have speculated on such matters as the cultural and geographical origin of Naymlap and the timing of his arrival (e.g., Alva and Alva 1984; Carrión 1940; Donnan 1978; Kauffmann 1983; Rondón 1966).

Hermann Trimborn's (1979) treatment is notable in that the entire monograph was devoted to verifying the legend based on radiocarbon dates and the locations of major sites in Lambayeque such as Apurlec, El Purgatorio, and Chotuna. His study had a diachronic and regional perspective but was seriously weakened by a lack of methodological rigor in respect to architectural history and his use and interpretation of radiocarbon dates, as well as failure to consider other plausible hypotheses at various stages of his investigation. For example, as with various other investigators who preceded him, on the basis of a seemingly good correspondence between the legendary descriptions, on the one hand, and archaeological site names and locations, on the other, he accepted the site of Chotuna as the site of the Temple of Chot. According to the legend, the Temple was built by Naymlap on the bank of a major river near its mouth soon after his arrival. Our recent geomorphological and hydrological analysis of the lower Lambayeque Valley (Shimada et al. 1981: 434), however, shows that, contrary to popular belief, the solitary pyramid of Chornancap on the north bank of the partially sand-filled ancient course of the Lambayeque River corresponds better to the Temple of Chot mentioned in the legend than does Chotuna, which is further upstream and east of any ancient river. In other words, many earlier and recent toponymic studies do not provide an adequate empirical or documentary basis for accepting present toponyms as accurate indicators of indigenous locations.

More recent efforts to verify the legend archaeologically include the work of the Chotuna-Chornancap Project directed by Christopher B. Donnan (this volume) and the work of Walter Alva and Susana Meneses de Alva (1984). Among the three hypotheses briefly considered, Alva and Alva favor the view that figures depicted in the magnificent polychrome frieze at Ucupe in the lower Zaña Valley show the arrival of Naymlap and his entourage in Lambayeque.

These studies, taken as a whole, do not spell out adequately and explicitly (a) specific test implications and attendant methodology for field testing the legend, or the basis for (b) acceptance of the legend as a reliable chronicle of historical events and (c) rejection of other plausible hypotheses.

Concurrent with the studies discussed above, other researchers have pursued Lambayeque prehistory in a manner largely detached from the legend (e.g., Nolan n.d.; Schaedel 1951a, b, 1966a, b, 1978a, 1985a, b; Shimada 1982, 1985a, b). Richard Schaedel (1972: 25; 1985a) emphasizes the significance of El Purgatorio in the development of the above intervalley irrigation system and polity. He (1951a: 240; cf. Kroeber 1930: 75–76; Moseley 1982; Moseley and Deeds 1982) hypothesizes a clear relationship between valley size and political power, arguing that the small La Leche and Moche Valleys with their notable urban developments and massive constructions were the seats of political power over the large, adjacent, primarily agricultural Lambayeque and Chicama (breadbasket) Valleys, respectively. In essence, Schaedel sees the process of political centralization as largely coeval with the urbanization process and argues that El Purgatorio was the most highly urbanized center ("elite urban center") and the seat of a major political state on the North Coast during the period he designates "Middle Lambayeque" (A.D. 800–1200).

Through a chronological and distributional analysis of architectural features such as marked adobes, "chamber-and-fill," and "encased columnar" construction formats found in many of the monumental adobe constructions in the Lambayeque Valley Complex, I have argued (Shimada 1985a; Shimada and Cavallaro 1986, n.d.) that the unity Kroeber saw in the northern North Coast was due in part to cultural overlays and continuities between Moche V (A.D. 600–700) and Middle Sican (A.D. 900–1100; see Table 1). For example, Moche V sites in the Valley Complex, such as Pampa Grande, Sipan-Collique, Patapo (Cinto), and various *huacas* in the Batan Grande region, inevitably show a Middle Sican occupation. In fact, territorially speaking, the Complex was the "heartland" of both the Moche V and Middle Sican intervalley polities.

AIMS, APPROACHES, AND DATA SOURCES

The preceding introduces two contrasting perspectives on the late prehistory of the Lambayeque Valley Complex: (a) one that emphasizes a regional perspective and cultural continuities and sees archaeological and documentary data as two independent bodies of data, each of which must internally assess its reliability before venturing to comment on the other, and (b) one that is predicated on the implicit or explicit assumption of the historicity of the Naymlap legend, which, in turn, largely dictates archaeological research and perception of Lambayeque prehistory. The latter typically takes a topically focused, single-site orientation.

Test Implications

As already alluded to, the legend is not readily testable as there are too many ambiguities, such as the unspecified duration of each ruler and the interregnum that followed the thirty-day rains. Kosok (1965: 80) himself clearly recognized these difficulties and observed, "We have, at present, no way of testing the validity of the list of [Lambayeque dynastic] kings. They may have been altered in transmission from generation to generation. Indeed, the early parts may have even been forged in order to give ancient roots and traditions to the ruling houses" (see Netherly, this volume; Zuidema, this volume). For both the Chimu and Lambayeque dynastic lists, Kosok (1965: 80) thus concluded that "the more recent parts are probably closer to the truth." Schaedel (1985b: 463; Rowe 1948) echoes this sentiment by noting that "protohistoric relevance" in the Lambayeque region would begin ca. A.D. 1250.

Kosok's reconstruction is just one of numerous possible interpretations of the Naymlap legend; however, it is by far the most detailed reconstruction offered to date with specific references made to known archaeological facts and sites. In other words, though the legend cannot be directly tested, the Kosok reconstruction reifies the legend to the extent that partial verification is possible. Good correspondence or lack of it between the available archaeological data and parts of the legend should not be taken as support or refutation of the entire legend or related reconstruction.

As already noted, perhaps the most apparent and crucial test implication of Kosok's "model" (and, for that matter, other similar models), according to the conventional archaeological wisdom (cf. Hodder 1978, 1979 for cautionary notes), is that we would expect to find physical evidence of a full or partial "site-unit intrusion" (as opposed to "trait-unit intrusion" [Willey and Lathrap 1956]). This might be in the form of the abrupt appearance of a constellation of material, organizational and ideological traits, and features that earlier evolved in Ecuador, the inferred homeland of Naymlap—for example, a corporate or elite art style and architecture, around A.D. 1025 at the Chotuna-Chornancap complex, the inferred temple-place of Naymlap and Ceterni. This would be followed by rapid political ascendancy and territorial expansion of Naymlap's descendants. The expansion would be concentric and radiate out from the Chotuna-Chornancap complex, toward the perimeter of the Lambayeque Valley Complex, dating later the farther one moves out from the center. Local cultural tradition(s) as represented in ceramics, iconography, architecture, and settlement patterns should manifest corresponding changes to varying degrees and/or forms.

Clearly, a reconstruction as elaborate as Kosok's has numerous other test implications. Those just specified, however, would be enough to obtain a good grasp of whether the legend and any derivative reconstruction could be verified, verifiable, or even worth verifying archaeologically.

Archaeological Data

Admittedly, my personal interest is not archaeological verification of the Naymlap legend or his arrival in Lambayeque but rather elucidation of the conditions under which such an intrusion might have occurred, the incorporation of the inferred newcomers into regional geopolitics, and the long-term consequences of the intrusion. For example, after Naymlap's inferred arrival, what would have allowed for the rapid establishment of the new elite and political order?

However, given that the preceding test implications can be properly examined only if we have an adequate understanding of local chronologies and cultural traditions, it is essential that priority be given to the presentation of available archaeological data unbiased by the legend but pertinent to assessment of regional cultural continuities and discontinuities during the Middle to Late Horizons. In other words, among other prerequisites, adequate archaeological testing of the legend requires a diachronic (encompassing both the inferred pre- and post-Naymlap arrival periods) and regional (multi-site) perspective.

Specifically, this paper examines two categories of data: (a) ceramics and associated iconographies, and (b) settlement patterns and architectural materials, techniques, and forms. The point of such an examination is to identify major cultural changes and develop insights into the character, timing, factors, and forces that conditioned initiation and promotion of those changes. In regard to the latter category, we now know a good deal about the overall form, construction techniques, and materials of monumental corporate architecture of the area and period under consideration. Much the same can be said of the former category (ceramics and iconographies), particularly for Moche V to Late Sicán times. My data presentation is accompanied by discussion of how these two categories may relate to the major test implications just delineated.

The previous two categories are sensitive to different stimuli (e.g., changes in value systems, use or procurement of resources), and their responses may vary in rate and nature. The relevant data derive from eleven seasons of mapping, survey, and excavation at sixteen sites in the Lambayeque Valley Complex. These sites are of divergent character and span the years from about 1000 B.C. to A.D. 1532 (Table 3). Much of the relevant data comes from (a) the Moche V capital of Pampa Grande at the neck of the Lambayeque Valley, and (b) the Batan Grande region in the central La Leche Valley (Fig. 3). Fieldwork at Pampa Grande focused on a detailed, structural-functional study of inferred indigenous Moche V urbanism at the site. The Batan Grande work, which is an outgrowth of the Pampa Grande studies, emphasized an interdisciplinary approach and regional perspective and included among its aims elucidation of post-Moche V cultural history and dynamics in the Lambayeque region.

The backbone of the relative chronology for this region is provided by abundant diagnostic ceramics from secure contexts within a stratigraphic sequence that spans some 1,000 years (ca. A.D. 500?–1532; Table 1) at the residential-craft production site of Huaca del Pueblo Batan Grande (HPBG). This relative chronology is complemented by an absolute chronology based on thirty-one radiocarbon dates from firepits, smelting furnaces, structural

TABLE 3. CHARACTERIZATION OF SITES EXCAVATED BY THE SICAN ARCHAEOLOGICAL PROJECT

Site Name	Inferred/Documented Functions	Primary Occupation Periods
Huaca Cholope-Lucia	Cemetery/residence/ceremonial center	Early Horizon, Middle Horizon–Late Intermediate Period
Huaca Soledad	Cemetery/residence/ceremonial center	Early–Late Horizon
Sican Precinct (subsuming Huacas Botija, El Moscon, El Corte, La Merced, Oro, Rodillona, and Las Ventanas)	Cemetery/elite residence/ceremonial and civic center/craft production	Early Horizon, Middle–Late Horizon
Sapame	Cemetery/ceremonial and civic center	Middle–Late Horizon
Huaca Julupe	Cemetery/residence/metallurgical production	Middle–Late Horizon
Huaca del Pueblo Batan Grande	Residence/craft production	Late Early Intermediate Period–Late Horizon
Cerro Huaringa	Metallurgical production	Middle Horizon? Late Intermediate–Late Horizon
Cerro Sajino	Metallurgical production	Middle Horizon? Late Intermediate–Late Horizon
Tambo Real	Administrative center/residence/craft production	Early–Late Horizon
Pampa Grande	Residence/craft production/Moche V capital	Middle Horizon–Late Intermediate

posts, and other primary context features found among at least forty-two occupational surfaces (Fig. 4; Appendix).

Rapidly expanding data from ongoing research in the Sican Precinct effectively complement these chronologies. The precinct is a 1,000 m (north–south) by 1,600 m (east–west) T-shaped area, roughly 12–13 km to the west of HPBG, defined by some dozen monumental adobe constructions of inferred religious and administrative functions (Fig. 5). Added to insights gained from the contrasting perspectives of core vs. perimeter and elite vs. populace areas is the emerging picture provided by nearby metallurgical centers with associated agricultural fields and residential settlements.

Overall, data from these sites combine to provide an effective diachronic examination of cultural continuities and discontinuities in the Lambayeque region during the Middle to Late Horizon.

CHRONOLOGICAL CONSIDERATIONS

My primary interest is in the time period ca. A.D. 550–1350, although comments and data pertinent to dates as late as A.D. 1532 are also presented. Usage of the terms Middle and Late Horizons and Late Intermediate period in this paper follows strictly chronological definitions (Rowe 1962; Table 1). Other than those historically derived for the Late Horizon, absolute dates

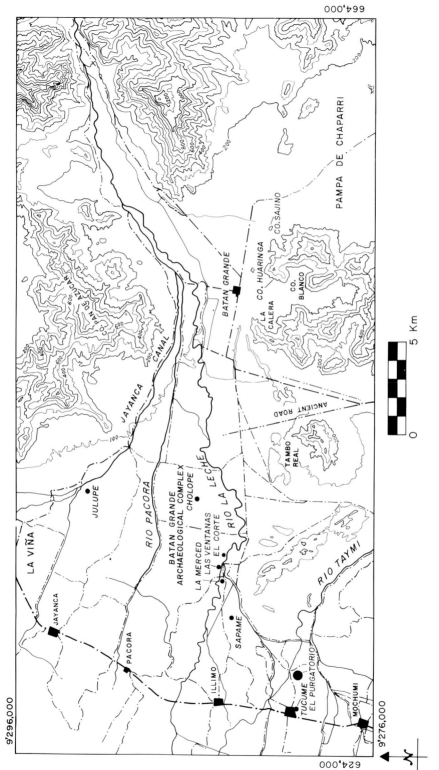

Fig. 3   Map showing the Batan Grande Archaeological Complex and some of its nearby major sites.

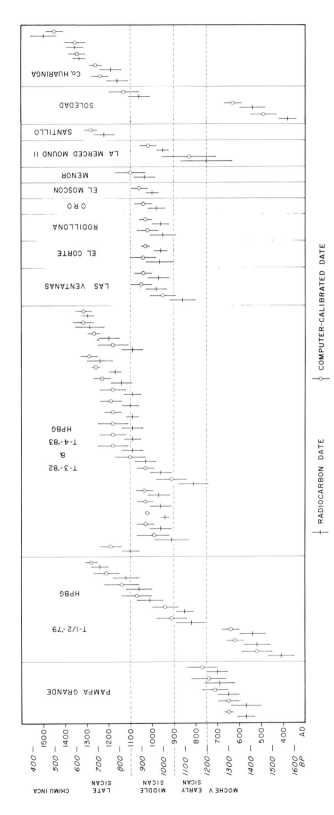

Fig. 4   Graphic representation of radiocarbon and calibrated dates available for sites in the Lambayeque and Leche Valleys. Note the dates for the site of Huaca del Pueblo Batan Grande serve as the backbone of the regional chronology, and the tight cluster of dates around A.D. 1050–1100 for the monumental architectural sites in the Poma district of Batan Grande.

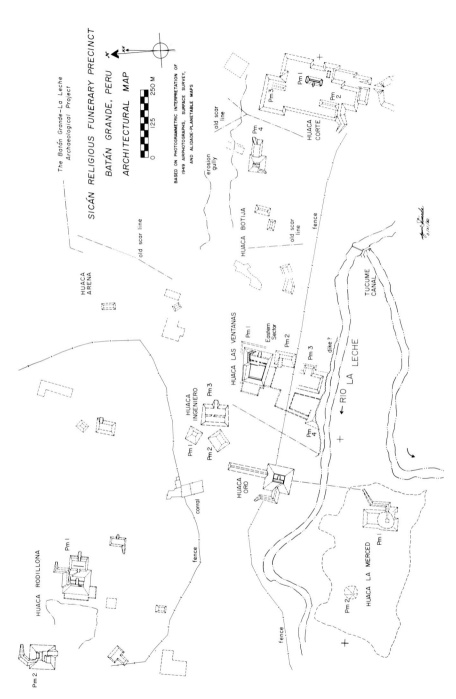

The Batán Grande–La Leche
Archaeological Project

SICÁN RELIGIOUS FUNERARY PRECINCT

BATÁN GRANDE, PERU
ARCHITECTURAL MAP

BASED ON PHOTOGRAMMETRIC INTERPRETATION OF
1949 AIRPHOTOGRAPHS, SURFACE SURVEY,
AND ALIDADE-PLANETABLE MAPS

0   125   250 M

old scar line

erosion gully

old scar line

HUACA ARENA

HUACA BOTIJA

fence

old scar line

HUACA CORTE

Pm 1

Pm 3

Pm 2

Pm 4

HUACA RODILLONA

Pm I

Pm 2

fence

corral

fence

HUACA INGENIERO

Pm 3

Pm 2

HUACA ORO

HUACA LAS VENTANAS

Pm I

Eastern Sector

Pm 2

Pm 3

Pm 4

dike ?

RIO LA LECHE

TUCUME CANAL

HUACA LA MERCED

Pm 1

Pm 2

Fig. 5   Architectural reconstruction map of the Sican Precinct within the Batan Grande Archaeological Complex.

are based on calibrated "calendrical" dates derived from more than 50 radio-carbon determinations for sites in the Batan Grande region summarized in the Appendix. For various reasons,[2] I feel we can place considerable confi-dence in these dates in regard to both precision/accuracy and association with the archaeological phenomena to be dated.

There are a few major gaps in the levels and sites thus far dated. Although the dates indicate a hiatus between about A.D. 700 and 900, in reality, there are floors and artifacts spanning this period at the site of HPBG. It is evident that the span between about A.D. 900 and 1100 is the one best dated, a fact that reflects the primary focus of the Sican Archaeological Project and corre-spondence to an era of numerous monumental constructions and large-scale metallurgical production that left behind an abundant supply of wood and charcoal for dating.

On the other hand, the span of about A.D. 1100–1250 is quite problemati-cal. It is important that, with the exception of HPBG, most dates falling

---

[2] Some years ago, the confusing array of "competing" calibration curves led some archaeolo-gists to insist on exclusive use of uncalibrated radiocarbon dates (5568 half-life radiocarbon age BP minus 1950, represented by lower case bc/ad dates). However, due to variation in the amount of atmospheric carbon isotopes, radiocarbon years are not a uniform measure of time. Conversion of radiocarbon dates to "calendrical" dates is not linear; the exclusive use of radiocar-bon dates deters meaningful chronological comparisons (Hoopes 1988). However, with the recent recommendation of the Twelfth International Radiocarbon Conference that high preci-sion (decadal) calibration tables be established as the international standard (Pearson and Stuiver 1986; Stuiver and Pearson 1986), and ready availability of computer calibration software (e.g., Stuiver and Reimer 1986), we should concurrently utilize more meaningful calibrated dates (represented as B.C./A.D. years). Thus, the calibrated dates in the Appendix are based on the high precision data of Pearson and Stuiver (1986) and Stuiver and Pearson (1986), and the calibration algorithm of Steven Robinson of the U.S. Geological Survey in Menlo Park, Califor-nia (Herbert Haas, personal communication, October 1986). It should be noted that some of the calibrated dates in the Appendix are the averages of multiple intersections with the standard calibration curves and thus have a wide span separating the minimum and maximum dates of the 2 sigmas or 95 percent confidence interval. Surprisingly, for the amount of archaeological fieldwork carried out on the North Coast, there are few sets of radiocarbon dates that are not problematical in respect to the nature, stratigraphic position, and context of samples, and/or association with events to be dated. This situation is further complicated by the uncritical and inconsistent use and presentation of radiocarbon dates and associated information in the litera-ture. The Appendix presents characterizations of the samples used and the resultant dates, as well as critical evaluations of discrepancies between expected and observed dates. I urge other researchers to provide the same range of data and critical assessment for their radiocarbon dates.

In regard to these issues, it is important to note that all but a few radiocarbon dates in the Appendix were derived from high quality lump charcoal (as opposed to problematic "aggre-gate samples") and other organic samples from clearly defined primary contexts. Most radiocar-bon dates from three deep trenches at HPBG are consistent with their stratigraphic positions and associated artifacts, though some are clearly unacceptable as the accompanying comments attest (Appendix). Most samples dated at the Radiocarbon Laboratory, Southern Methodist University (SMU) were counted twice and at times thrice. Care was taken to use only the outermost portions and in some cases, bark, of samples, so that we may speak confidently of cutting dates. Good interlaboratory comparison of the SMU dates assures there are no gross or systematic errors. Similarly, excellent results in replicability tests conducted at the SMU labora-tory give us confidence in the technical consistency.

then come from sites that have thus far not yielded any date or artifact belonging to the preceding two-hundred-year era. In other words, there was at least one significant shift in the regional settlement pattern sometime around A.D. 1100.

The character and timing of major events that have been radiocarbon dated (e.g., the initiation of a series of monumental constructions and intense bronze smelting, and the conflagration and subsequent abandonment of the constructions) match well with the significant quantitative and qualitative changes in material culture discussed in this paper. These changes, in turn, form the basis of a tripartite division of the Sican culture (Table 1; Early: A.D. 700–900, Middle: A.D. 900–1100, and Late: A.D. 1100–1350[?]). A comparison of the resultant cultural chronology for the Batan Grande region with that of the broader Lambayeque region presented in papers by Alan Kolata (this volume) and Michael Moseley (this volume) shows some major differences.

The Early Sican period begins about A.D. 700 with the demise of the Moche V hegemony, which had been centered at Pampa Grande.[3] Middle Sican starts around A.D. 900, roughly coinciding in time with initiation of monumental constructions in the Sican Precinct and intense arsenical copper production at HPBG. The onset of Middle Sican is also signaled by the formalization of a syncretized iconography as it attains its own distinct configuration and meaning.

The end of the Middle Sican period, about A.D. 1100, is marked by a widespread fire that thoroughly burned the principal constructions of Huacas El Corte, Las Ventanas, Rodillona, and El Moscon (also known as the Colorada or El Horno), and the concurrent abandonment of much of the Sican Precinct. In Late Sican, El Purgatorio seems to have supplanted the Sican Precinct as a (if not the) dominant political and religious center in the Lambayeque Valley Complex.

The bipartition of the Late Sican period into subphases A (A.D. 1100–1250?) and B (A.D. 1250?–1350?) is based on a preliminary, unfinished analysis of changes observed in the style, technique, and form of funerary ceramics in stratigraphically ordered burials excavated at HPBG.

The earliest date for Imperial Chimu intrusion into the HPBG sequence, however, can be established rather precisely because its ceramics appear for the first time in a refuse deposit two layers above an earthen floor with a storage pit containing a well-preserved cache of *Campomanesia latifolia* fruits. Seeds and pods together, and seeds alone were separately radiocarbon-dated to highly consistent and precise dates of 650 ± 30 BP and 660 ± 70 BP,

---

[3] The radiocarbon dates presented in the Appendix form the basis for placing the end of Moche V culture in the Lambayeque region at ca. A.D. 700. In a recent volume, Christopher Donnan (1986: 22) places the end of the Moche occupation at Pacatnamu around (or even after) ca. A.D. 900 without offering any supportive evidence. I see no reason to accept this date.

respectively. These fruits are likely to have been gathered sometime during the year preceding abandonment of the cache.

This inference is independently supported by a radiocarbon date of 590 ± 40 BP from a smelting furnace in Sector III, a large-scale smelting area of Cerro Huaringa (also known as Cerro de los Cementerios), that is believed to date to the Late Sican B–Imperial Chimu transition on the basis of associated ceramics. Thus, the Imperial Chimu intrusion into Batan Grande may be tentatively set sometime after A.D. 1350. James Nolan (n.d.: 327–330) suggests a date of around A.D. 1400 or later as the date of Imperial Chimu expansion into the Lambayeque Valley. A radiocarbon date of 450 ± 60 BP for an arsenical copper smelting workshop at Cerro Huaringa associated with both Provincial Inca and Chimu-Inca ceramics supports the conventional historically derived date for Inca domination of this area starting around A.D. 1460–1470.

Finally, we should note here a significant discordance between part of this chronological scheme and the dates traditionally assigned to various stylistic phases within the Middle Horizon (e.g., Menzel 1964, 1969, 1977; Rowe 1962). Middle Sican ceramics have been assigned stylistically to Middle Horizon Epoch 3 with corresponding dates of about A.D. 720–810 (e.g., see the chronological chart in Menzel 1977: 88), whereas numerous radiocarbon dates for floors, constructions, and a burial clearly associated with diagnostic Middle Sican ceramics argue for a time span of around A.D. 900–1100. The importance of analytical separation of time and style must be kept in mind.

CERAMICS AND ICONOGRAPHY

Moche V and Early Sican

On the basis of stylistic comparison with funerary vessels and other artifacts from the sites of Pachacamac and Chimu Capac on the central and north-central coasts, respectively (e.g., Menzel 1968, 1977; see also Schmidt 1929), Early Sican ceramics can be assigned to Middle Horizon Epoch 2. It is a phase about which we know entirely too little on the North Coast. Although many sites are inferred to have Middle Horizon 2 components, the number of sites with a demonstrated presence of this component is quite small.

In the Batan Grande region, diagnostic Early Sican sherds have been excavated thus far only at HPBG, Huacas El Corte, La Merced, and Las Ventanas. HPBG has yielded the only primary-context Early Sican ceramics. The emergence of the characteristic Early Sican finely burnished, deep black, and mottled black ware sherds from levels immediately overlying those of Moche V some 4.5 to 5.0 m below the surface coincides with the first appearance of *paleteada* (paddle-decorated ware; Fig. 6) and Sican

Fig. 6   Photo showing the earliest *paleteada* sherds (central and left-hand pieces) recovered from an immediately post-Moche V context in T-1/2 at the site of Huaca del Pueblo Batan Grande. The right-hand piece is a Moche V grooved ceramic that shows the same design element as the central *paleteada* fragment.

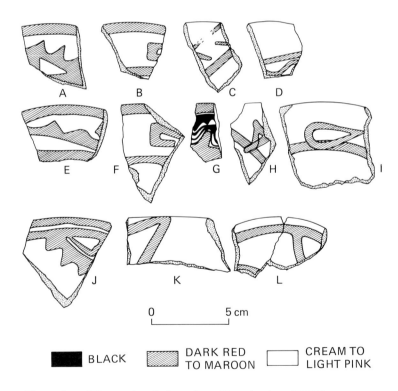

Fig. 7   Examples of Sican painted plates from Trench 1/2 at HPBG.

Fig. 8   At left, a large fragment of a two-tier blackware bottle with an opposing pair of seated felines decorating the upper tier excavated from immediately post-Moche V context in Trench 1/2 at HPBG. Compare it to the vessel in the Brüning Museum collection, at right.

painted plates with low annular bases (Fig. 7; Shimada 1982; Shimada et al. 1981; Shimada and Elera 1983).

Early Sican blackware vessels in the Brüning Museum in Lambayeque and those excavated at the site of HPBG are two-tier globular jars (Fig. 8) and globular bottles with low single spouts, round loop handles on shoulders close to the base of the spout, and flat or slightly rounded bottoms (Figs. 9, 10; see fig. 95 in Menzel 1977: 120).

The single-spout bottles often bear the same face seen at the base of the spout on the effigy vessel illustrated in Figure 9. Where facial details are carefully executed and preserved (Fig. 10), it is apparent that the face represents a peculiar blend of human and raptorial bird features. The "nose" seems to be a pointed, hooked avian beak, and there is no indication of a bilabial human mouth. Two merging lines create crescent-shaped eyes. At the same time, the ears have enlarged lobes, each with one round hole in the center for ornamentation. The eyes and at times the central line of the nose are represented either by shallow polished incisions or appliqued pieces that have been shaped and burnished. The face is clearly demarcated on the top and bottom and, except for the hooked beak, seems more two-dimensional

Fig. 9 Blackware single-spout globular bottle that accompanied Burial V excavated some 5 m below the surface in Trench 1/2 at HPBG.

Fig. 10 Blackware single-spout globular bottles (Brüning Museum collection) with an anthropomorphic-avian-like face at the base of the spout.

than that shown in Figure 9. These avian facial features are very similar to the mythical "eagle" of the prestigious Pachacamac style of Middle Horizon 2 (Menzel 1968).

A good indication of Huari-derived iconographic influence is seen in a largely reconstructable black two-tier globular bottle showing a pair of seated four-legged low-relief animals facing each other within a rectangular panel (Fig. 8). The vessel form is highly reminiscent of Middle Horizon 2 Viñaque (Ocucaje, Ica) and Atarco (Nasca) vessels on the South Coast (Shimada and Elera 1983; also cf. Menzel 1977, fig. 95). The animals are likely to be the "Moon Animals" of the North Coast tradition. They are quite similar to those carved on a wooden staff excavated at the Templo de Idolo (also known as the Huaca Pintada or Temple of Pachacamac) in Pachacamac and stylistically dated to Middle Horizon 2 (Fig. 11; see Bueno 1982: 39; Jiménez 1985: 47, photo 4; unnumbered photo in Paredes 1985: 79).[4]

Huari influence on local ceramics is already notable during the Moche V period. The new vessel forms that have been excavated at Pampa Grande show strong affinity in Huari-derived vessels in areas to the south (Shimada 1982: 168). In this regard, it is important to note the presence of a Moche-Huari syncretic frieze at Huaca La Mayanga (part of the broader Huaca Facho; Bonavia 1974; Donnan 1972) and Huari style (Robles Moqo) Middle Horizon 1B ceramics at Facho. The latter include a vessel representing a man wearing a nose ring and a vertical-striped garment with dotted bands holding a Spondylus shell and another small ceremonial vessel depicting the "Sacrificer," a winged spirit animal with pronounced feline features and projecting nose.

Seen from this long-term, broader perspective, Early Sican blackware forms, iconography, and manufacturing techniques already combine those of the Huari (Middle Horizon 1 and 2) and earlier Moche, and well may have been introduced through avenues and/or mechanisms already established with areas farther south during Moche V or even late Moche IV-B times.[5]

[4] The deep black color and highly burnished nature of the Early Sican and the succeeding Middle Sican blackwares are reminiscent of the rare small bowls with thin walls of hard fine paste found in elite architectural settings at Moche V Pampa Grande (Shimada 1982, fig. 13). The more common grayish reduced ware "lids," plates, and double-tier short-neck jars found in various areas of Moche V Pampa Grande (Shimada 1982:167–168, figs. 13, 14) do not show the fine paste, care, and technical mastery of the small bowls. The grayware may well have been "poor man's" imitations of the fine blackware. The inspiration for the Moche V blackware may have come from earlier Cupisnique blackware vessels.

[5] We cannot ignore the fact that Moche V ceramics show considerable intervalley variability in iconography and form, in addition to the differences in blackwares already noted. Double-stirrup-spout bottles with "monkeys" perched at the juncture of the stirrups and spouts, as well as depiction of the "Funerary Scene" done in traditional bichrome fine-line painting, seem to occur much more frequently at a few midvalley sites (e.g., San Jose de Moro) in Jequetepeque than in the remainder of the Moche V heartland. This particular regionalism may well be related to long-term contact the valley had with the adjacent Cajamarca culture and its role as a major traffic route.

Fig. 11 Middle Horizon 2A style decoration on the wooden idol found at the Templo del Idolo at Pachacamac (redrawn after Jiménez Borja 1985: 47, foto 4). Compare with Fig. 8.

What may be local in origin aesthetically and technically is the newly emergent *paleteada* ceramics. Stratigraphically, the oldest *paleteada* sherd at HPBG replicates in form the geometric, incised design of a body sherd found on the underlying Moche V floor (Fig. 6). This supports the traditional contention that *paleteada* ware began in the Middle Horizon somewhere between Lambayeque and Piura (e.g., Collier 1959; Kroeber and Muelle 1942; Lanning 1963; Schaedel 1979; see also Richardson et al., this volume). The *paleteada* samples derived from the stratified deposits at HPBG show that, in spite of technical stability and continuity to this day, certain attributes of *paleteada* designs are chronologically (and perhaps culturally) significant (see below).

Middle Horizon Epoch 2B is critical to our discussion of the cultural continuities and discontinuities that preceded the formalization of the Middle Sican style and iconography and the associated cultural florescence during Epoch 3. Dorothy Menzel (1977: 106–107, figs. 50–52, 54) illustrates double-spouted bottles from the sites of Moche and Chimu Capac that are all dated stylistically to Middle Horizon 2B. These bottles are characterized by long, tapering spouts connected by a wide flat or ovoid bridge (with or without decoration) to a squat body with a flat base. Often the bridge is decorated with a fully modeled human head wearing a highland style "four-cornered cap" (Menzel 1977: 106, fig. 52; see Fig. 12).

Fig. 12 The bridge of a "Provincial Huari" double-spout bottle decorated with a human head wearing a four-cornered cap. It was looted from the site of San Jose de Moro (Moro Viejo) in Jequetepeque (private collection).

Fig. 13   Double-spout blackware bottle with elaborately decorated bridge (Amano Museum collection). Compare with figures on the bridge shown in Figs. 9 and 10.

A complete blackware double-spout bottle with a low ring base at the Amano Museum in Lima (Fig. 13) is crucial in demonstrating Early–Middle Sican iconographic continuity. Decorating the bridge top is the head of an individual with an Early Sican bird-like face (cf. Figs. 9–10) who wears a four-cornered cap. He is flanked on each side by reclining humanoid figures whose raised heads have mask-like flat faces and wear semicircular head-dresses. Significantly, these flanking figures are a basic and ubiquitous component of the Middle Sican ceramic iconography described later. They flank the principal Middle Sican image of the "Sican Lord." In addition, the long narrow spouts that somewhat straighten at the distal ends and the low ring base are features that appear early in the morphological trends seen among funerary vessels from stratigraphically ordered Sican burials. This basic double-spout vessel form persists well into Middle and Late Sican times, when it appears with a pedestal base and spouts showing more accentuated straightening at the distal ends.

Thus, iconographically and morphologically, this double-spout bottle seems to be transitional between Early and Middle Sican (Middle Horizon 2B–3). Though we cannot conclusively verify the possibility that the local antecedent Early Sican avian-humanoid creature evolved into the "Sican Lord," the hallmark of Middle Sican art (see below), it is argued here that the avian–human duality is a critical feature of the Sican Lord. This iconographic linkage must be accounted for by proponents of the view that Middle Sican iconography is intrusive and that the Sican Lord represents Naymlap.

Middle Sican

The single most salient feature of Middle Sican iconography gleaned from the Lambayeque region sample is a ubiquitous anthropomorphic figure whom we choose to call the "Sican Lord." I shall describe the figure in some detail here because of its dominant position in Middle Sican art and its hypothesized identity as the legendary Naymlap. Its abrupt disappearance in the Late Sican period also has important ramifications for some of the central issues of this volume.

The Sican Lord is characterized by a wide, flat, mask-like, semicircular face and all or most of the following details (Figs. 14, 15): (a) "comma-" or "almond-shaped" eyes with upward pointing outer corners, (b) below the eyes, paired vertical lines or "bands" containing regularly spaced dots, (c) pointed ears often with concentric lines on the upper portion and pierced round lobes from which tiered triangular earrings hang, (d) a pointed or hooked beak-like "nose," (e) a closed mouth (at times with parallel lines perpendicularly closing it) or, rarely, a partially open mouth showing saw-like lower and upper teeth (fangs rarely ever shown). In addition, the figure may also wear (f) a wide "collar" in low relief and (g) a large, elaborate fan-shaped headdress. The latter may have been composed mostly of multicolored bird feathers judging by its depiction in murals and ceramic artifacts (Carcedo and Shimada 1985).[6] On single-spout ceramic bottles the Sican Lord figures show single or multi-tiered headbands with small contiguous spikes. Many of these incised features on ceramics are executed in thin, shallow, polished indentations termed *Sican grooves* (Cleland and Shimada n.d.a). The grooves are already apparent on some of the inferred Middle Horizon 2B vessels described earlier.

The Sican Lord has been variously identified as "Naymlap" (Alva and Alva 1984; Kauffmann 1983), "bird-man," "personification of the moon" (Carrión ·1940), "Chimu God" (Menzel 1977), and "Tin Woodsman" (Scheele and Patterson 1966). Alfred Kroeber (1926, 1930, 1944; also Bennett 1939) re-

[6] Miniature *tumbaga* figurines on a Middle Sican litter at the Museo de Oro, Lima, still have feather remnants adhering to their faces and headdresses (Carcedo and Shimada 1985).

Fig. 14 Typical Middle Sican single-spout blackware bottle with Sican Lord image flanked by pair of "dragon-like" heads (Brüning Museum collection).

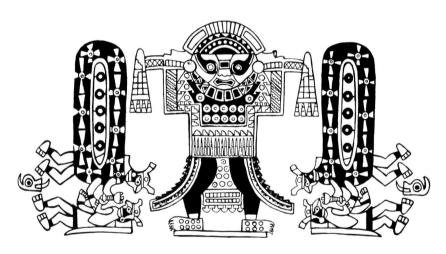

Fig. 15 A Sican Lord image from Huaca Pintada (redrawn after Carrión 1940: 585, fig. 17).

Fig. 16   A Middle Sican *tumi* showing a seated, winged
Sican Lord (Museo Oro del Peru, Lima, object 2443). Photograph courtesy of the Royal Ontario Museum.

Fig. 17   Sherds showing the Sican Lord image as *paleteada* designs. The large piece was excavated from the south sector of Huaca Las Ventanas, while the two small fragments were recovered from Huaca La Botija.

ferred to these widespread ceramic vessels as "rotund figure jars." Here the term *Sican Lord* is formally adopted. The designation "bird-man" is meant to emphasize the fact that the Sican Lord is at times shown with "wings," beak-like hooked nose (and no accompanying mouth), and talon-like feet (Fig. 16).

We regard the Sican Lord as the hallmark of Middle Sican iconography. The face and/or figure literally saturates Sican art and is replicated many times in a given mural, textile, ceramic, or metal vessel (see examples in Carcedo and Shimada 1985). The Sican Lord face is, in fact, one of numerous short-lived "logographic" or "semasiographic" paddle-designs that decorated the bodies of relatively large utilitarian vessels and serves as an effective Middle Sican temporal marker (Fig. 17).

The Sican Lord image is highly distinct and can be readily recognized regardless of the medium of expression. At the same time, there are significant variations in the position and the range of iconographic features in different media and contexts. For example, avian features such as wings are found on the Sican Lord's back on gold and/or silver "ceremonial *tumi* knives" (Carcedo and Shimada 1985, Carrión 1940) and on the central figure in murals (e.g., those at Huacas Oro [Florián 1951; Kosok 1965] and Pintada [Carrión 1940; Schaedel 1978a]), but rarely and less explicitly in ceramics (see Menzel 1977: 116, fig. 81A). Talon-like feet are found only on the standing Sican Lord who is the focus of the mural. Rebeca Carrión (1940) interpreted the winged Sican Lord as a part of his metamorphosis (nocturnal bird) representing the "personification of the moon."

Hind views of the Sican Lord, including details of the back of his dress and headdress are found only on gold and/or silver *tumis* (see Carcedo and Shimada 1985: 71, fig. 13). In sharp contrast, Sican Lord representations on ceramics are two dimensional, usually lacking any detail on the back. Together with many *tumbaga* beakers that are, in reality, disguised rattles (Carcedo and Shimada 1985: 73), these *tumis* were probably used in public rituals.

In other words, the elaborate polychrome murals and precious metal objects that were publicly displayed set the aesthetic standards of the Middle Sican art emulated by ceramics and other media. In this sense, the widely found "mask faces" (e.g., *paleteada* designs and actual masks made of arsenical copper, gilt copper, or *tumbaga*) with "comma-shaped eyes" and other diagnostics can be interpreted as a practical means for bestowing the supernatural and sacrosanct qualities of the Sican Lord upon the users and owners. This view is supported by the fact that figurines actually wearing "Sican Lord masks" (those standing under the portals of the so-called Chimu Litter at the Museo de Oro del Perú in Lima [MOP-4055/6] and one on a *tumbaga* earspool at the Hamburgisches Museum für Völkerkunde [28.147:11]) have ordinary human faces.

We are only now beginning to appreciate the extent and possible meaning of Middle Sican iconographic and stylistic variation. Consider the variations in the faces, headdresses, "wings," and clothing seen among the six principal full-frontal figures in a polychrome frieze at the site of Ucupe (Alva and Alva 1984). Even greater variation is seen among the eighteen figures standing inside six "temples" on a "Chimu Litter" (Carcedo and Shimada 1985: 68–69, figs. 7, 8). Even such a critical feature of Middle Sican iconography as upturned eyes is not strictly standardized or unique; they are seen on late Moche "mythical" personages (see McClelland, this volume), and an impressive Middle Sican gravelot containing more than two hundred gold and silver objects includes Sican Lord representations that vary a good deal in eye details (Carcedo and Shimada 1985: 63, fig. 2). The comma-shaped eyes of the Sican Lord may be used in depictions of his attendants to denote their similarly mythical or divine qualities; however, these secondary figures may be distinguished by their smaller size, less elaborate clothing and headdress, and facial features. As noted earlier, avian characteristics such as wings and talons distinguish the centrally placed and disproportionately large representations of the Sican Lord in friezes at Huacas Oro and Pintada (Fig. 15).

The Sican Lord assumes one of several basic positions, including (a) cross-legged and seated, (b) standing alone holding an object(s) in his hands, (c) a standing figure or just the head accompanied by an opposing pair of secondary figure(s), animals and/or humans or, rarely, portals encasing the Sican Lord face, and (d) seated on a "raft" supported by an opposing pair of auxiliary stretched out figures. The first two positions are seen mostly on gold and/or silver *tumis*. The first and the last positions are also seen in Moche art. In respect to the solitary, standing position, there is a good deal of variation, including the Sican Lord holding a Spondylus shell with both hands or a *tumi* in one hand and a round, unidentified object in the other.

The standing figure, or just the head accompanied by auxiliary figures, is most common, particularly on single-spout ceramic bottles with strap handles. In ceramic representations, the Sican Lord head is often flanked on either side (apparently fixed loci) by an opposing pair of auxiliary figures including the stretched out ("swimming") figures described earlier.[7] These representations may be shorthand versions of rare, but more elaborate scenes of "swimming men" accompanying a raft carrying the seated Sican Lord, much like painted and modeled Moche scenes (e.g., Urteaga 1919: 90, fig. 9; Donnan 1978: 93, fig. 146). Federico Kauffmann (1983: 500) describes these swimming men as Naymlap's children.

Fine Middle Sican ceramics are most commonly highly burnished black and brown wares, although some sites yield highly burnished gray vessels. During the latter portion of the Middle Sican stylistic evolution we see Sican Lord bottles with a cream-colored wash and dark red and fugitive black painted designs. Middle Sican iconography and style are sufficiently distinct and standardized, however, for ready identification wherever they occur and whatever the medium of expression.

The preceding characterization of Middle Sican iconography and style is based on our excavated materials and private and public collections in the Lambayeque region. Specimens from outside Lambayeque manifest certain stylistic and technical variation. For example, Middle Sican reduced-ware single-spout face-neck bottles attributed to cemeteries around San Pedro de Lloc in the Jequetepeque Valley to the south are a well-burnished gray rather than having the typical black exterior finish.

Blackware face-neck bottles from the Upper Piura Valley to the north use ground shell or other calcareous materials as temper in contrast to sand in the southern specimens. In addition, details and forms of many local bottles differ from the corresponding features found in the Lambayeque

---

[7] In many cases, these "swimming men" are replaced by an opposing pair of fox-like animals and in rare cases the Sican Lord is depicted with a pair of standing female figures with long hair loose down their backs. Also rare is the Sican Lord head represented alone without accompanying animal or human figures. The Sican Lord head or figure may also appear with just one "swimming" man, bird, or fish positioned midway atop the straphandle. A pair of secondary figures, facing each other, whether men, "dragons," "foxes," frogs, birds, or monkeys may appear without any Sican Lord representation. Identical opposing pairs of monkeys have been found flanking the spout bases of Moche V double-stirrup jars and may be prototypic.

specimens. For example, Piura bottles often have spherical to oblong bodies rather than Lambayeque's more oblate or squat forms. Sometimes, the spout is noticeably inclined toward the back rather than nearly vertical as on the Lambayeque specimens. The Sicán Lord face at the base of the spout on Piura bottles, though clearly recognizable with all the diagnostic features, often has an exaggerated width-height ratio. These and other differences (Cleland and Shimada n.d.a) indicate the persistence of local technical and stylistic traditions in spite of the adoption in toto of Middle Sicán iconography.

The organization of production and the differential value and prestige attached to products may be a key to observed iconographic and stylistic variation. Labor-intensive and relatively large *tumbaga* objects having many details, colors, moveable parts, sound effects, and even three-dimensionality (Carcedo and Shimada 1985: 67) were likely to have been individually handcrafted by master artisans for specific individuals and/or special events, unlike standardized mold-made blackware bottles for the "faceless masses." Large polychrome murals for public viewing were also able to show details that could not be shown on relatively small blackware bottles. In addition to considerations of skill, labor investment, and size constraints, *tumbaga* objects and murals with their elite association and public settings are expected to be the "pace setters" or holders of the "aesthetic standards" and trends of the society (Cleland and Shimada n.d.a). Though rare, the presence of (a) unusually large and carefully made blackware bottles and (b) utilitarian vessels paddle-stamp decorated with the Sicán Lord face or seated feline much like the "Moon Animal" may mean that, altogether, there were four qualitatively distinct classes of ideologically charged objects produced in Middle Sicán society (Cleland and Shimura n.d.b).

In addition to our rapidly expanding knowledge of largely synchronic variability in the Middle Sicán art and ceramics described above, we now have a good understanding of diachronic changes in widespread single-spout pedestaled blackware bottles. Recent computer-assisted analysis of bottle body-part ratios, including those from the gravelots of six excavated and salvaged burials, and ceramics recovered from well-defined stratigraphic positions at HPBG, has allowed us to test and refine the original three-phase Sicán bottle seriation I proposed some years ago (Shimada 1985b: 366, fig. 16.3). Figure 18 shows the refined five-phase seriation.[8] In general, earlier vessels are characterized by simple scenes with a small number of auxiliary figures. In the beginning, the Sicán Lord has minimal facial detail and typically lacks headdress and ear ornaments. Over time, the complexity of incised facial features, accompanying ornamentation, and number of auxiliary figures increases; in essence, the image becomes increas-

---

[8] See Cleland and Shimada (n.d.b) for the positive test results and refinement process.

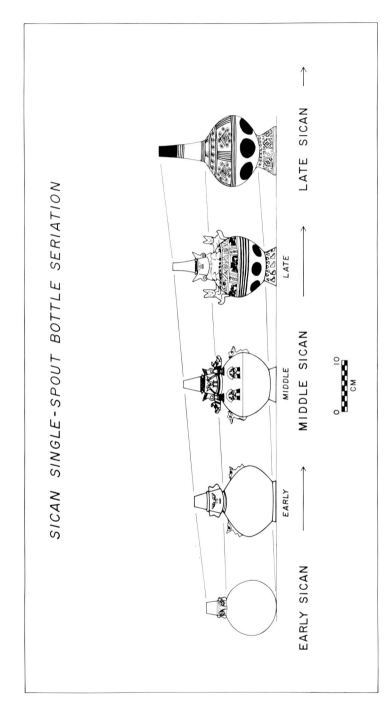

Fig. 18 Five-phase seriation of Middle Sican blackware single-spout bottles. The vessel at the extreme left represents the earliest phase.

ingly "Gothic." Concomitantly, we note an increase in height of the spout and pedestal base, as well as roundness of the vessel chamber.

In contrast to our expanding understanding of Middle Sican ceramic art, stylistic analysis of various polychrome murals found in the study area have produced a confusing picture regarding their date and cultural affiliation. One mural at Huaca Pintada (near the Pan American Highway west of the Sican Precinct) showing a poorly preserved central figure with clawed feet and "eleven impaneled processional figures and assorted elements" has been characterized as Moche V (Middle Horizon 1A or B) or immediately post-Moche by Schaedel (1978a: 35). He also sees stylistic and iconographic links to the personage depicted in the mural atop Huaca Oro (or Loro) within the Sican Precinct (ibid.; see Bonavia 1985: 119, fig. 82). Duccio Bonavia (1985: 109) attributes the Huaca Pintada mural to Middle Horizon 2A or perhaps 2B and considers the Pintada-Oro linkage tenuous. The Huaca Oro fresco was not well documented (Bonavia 1985: 118–122). Architectural analysis, however, has shown that the pyramid body was constructed in one episode with diagnostic Middle Sican techniques and features (see below). A radiocarbon date indicates that the Huaca Oro pyramid construction and thus, by inference, the fresco date to Middle Sican.

There is said to have been a second Huaca Pintada mural (Fig. 15) showing a large standing figure, perhaps 2.8 m high, with clawed feet and wearing elaborate headdress and garb.[9] Bonavia (1985: 117) characterizes it as "stylistically an epigonal of the Middle Horizon, one of those elements transitional to the Lambayeque style."

At Chornancap a polychrome mural showing a procession of human and anthropomorphic birds, many of whom carry trophy heads, was found decorating the inner walls of a large open courtyard at the north base of the main two-tiered platform mound with a central ramp (Donnan 1984, this volume; cf. Bonavia 1985). Although difficult to place chronologically or stylistically, Donnan (1984: 35) feels that some iconographic elements suggest the "Early Chimu" style, dating to between A.D. 750 and 900. These human and bird figures are associated with an animal head having a long, upcurving tongue and long, ear-like projections pointing forward. Pairs of similar heads often flank the Sican Lord head on Middle Sican bottles.

Bonavia questions this linkage, noting that "the simple fact that an element appears in a given style is not enough to establish a relationship" (1985: 132). Citing the absence of Moche influence and predominance of Huari

---

[9] Based in part on his interview with an eyewitness to the original discovery of the Huaca Pintada mural and his cross-checking of various relevant early reports, Richard Schaedel (personal communication, June 1988; also see Schaedel 1978a) insists that, to date, only one mural has been found at the site. The claim for the existence of a second mural (Bonavia 1985: 116–117) is based on a Carrión (1940) drawing, which, Schaedel (1978a) notes, though perhaps reasonable, is nonetheless a reconstruction.

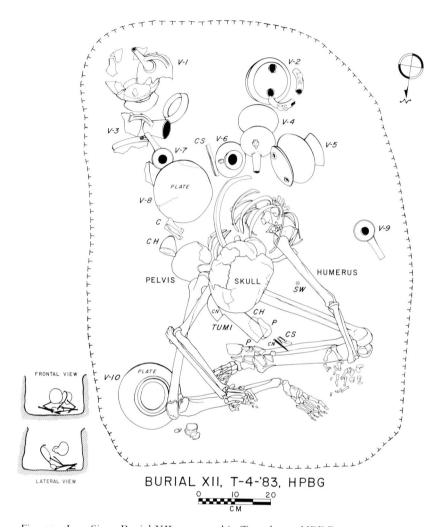

Fig. 19   Late Sican Burial XII excavated in Trench 4 at HPBG.

features, he (1985: 133–134) characterizes the mural at Chornancap as foreign (north-central coast in origin?) to the North Coast and not related to Middle Sican. Instead he attributes it to Larco's [Kosok 1959] Huari Norteño B (Table 1) of Middle Horizon 4.

This characterization is important because stylistically the mural would be later (instead of earlier if we accept Early Chimu attribution) than Middle Sican (Middle Horizon 4) and would raise the distinct possibility that "intrusion" at Chornancap occurred after the demise of the Middle Sican polity.

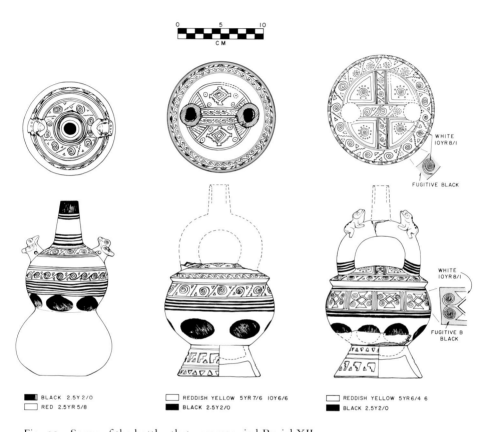

Fig. 20   Some of the bottles that accompanied Burial XII.

However, as we will see later, the Chornancap pyramid manifests specific architectural features diagnostic of Middle Sican.

Late Sican

Continuities and discontinuities between Middle and Late Sican iconography and style are most dramatically illustrated in vessels from the gravelot of a seated adult excavated at HPBG (Figs. 19, 20). Most notable in the well-made ceramics is the nearly total absence of the Sican Lord, in spite of the continuing presence of auxiliary creatures such as pairs of opposing toads or birds such as flank the Sican Lord head in Middle Sican single-spout bottles.

LATE SICAN BOTTLES FROM BURIAL 13, CERRO HUARINGA

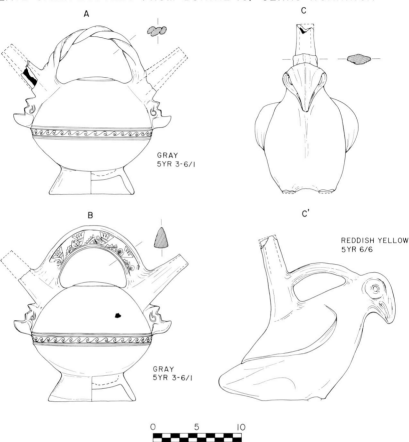

Fig. 21 Late Sican bottles from Burial XIII excavated in Sector I of Cerro Huaringa. Note that this and Fig. 20 show no representation of the Sican Lord.

Although vessel form shows definite continuation of the trend toward higher spout and pedestal (fretted or champlevé) and more spherical body observed during the Middle Sican, the Sican Lord that earlier saturated this iconography is hardly seen. In addition, stirrup-spout and double-spout bottle forms that are quite rare in the Middle Sican period are represented by various funerary vessels from HPBG and Cerro Huaringa (Fig. 21). Further, the Middle Sican straphandle is replaced with one that gives the impression of two parallel coils bonded together (figure-eight cross section; Fig. 21). Sican grooves are replaced with fugitive black line decoration consisting of series of spirals, diamonds, circles, or triangles with central dots and step motifs located within partitioned decorative zones on the body, shoulder, neck, and handles.

In general, the Late Sican iconography gleaned from these gravelot vessels and others similar or identical in form in private and public collections is largely devoid of what can be identified as ideologically charged motifs and themes. In some cases a pair of highly conventionalized heads of "dragon" monsters with little facial detail decorates the vessel body (Fig. 21). The impression is that the once-pervasive Middle Sican iconography and associated ideology have been lost or purged of their cultural significance.

Concurrently, we note the disappearance of Middle Sican painted (popularly known as "Coastal Cajamarca") plates where simple geometric or highly stylized creatures were painted on the interior surfaces with thick maroon paint against a cream background. Undecorated plates with low ring bases, however, persist during the phase tentatively identified as Late Sican A. Paddle designs are geometric in nature, having lost the earlier "logographics."

Ceramics from HPBG for the Late Sican B and later periods are still largely unanalyzed. At this point, Late Sican B is tentatively recognized on the basis of extended (as opposed to seated) burials with the head to the south, which are associated with zoomorphic blackware bottles and jars that have outflaring necks and large press-molded designs on the body. The earlier Late Sican A stirrup-spout bottles with high pedestal champlevé bases and geometric decorations in fugitive black and white against light brown background seem to disappear.

ARCHITECTURE AND SETTLEMENT PATTERN

A diachronic examination of regional architecture and settlement patterns offers independent corroboration and additional insights into the cultural continuities and discontinuities just elucidated. A number of persistent features and techniques of northern North Coast monumental pyramidal architecture are noteworthy during much of the 1,000-year period (ca. A.D. 550–1532) under discussion here (Cavallaro and Shimada 1988; Shimada and Cavallaro 1986, n.d.). These features include: (a) wooden posts set in rectangular adobe boxes ca. 1 m to a side, filled with clean sand or a sand-and-gravel mixture presumably to provide a sound (perhaps anti-seismic) footing for elaborate mound top colonnades; (b) what A. L. Kroeber (1926: 13) called "chamber and fill," whereby room-like quadrilateral spaces created by adobe walls were filled with a variety of materials such as camelid dung, sand, gravel, and/or even large sherds, for rapid erection of monumental pyramids and platforms; (c) logs several meters in length horizontally placed at various levels of the pyramid, from near the base to the top, presumably for structural purposes and perhaps to protect adobes at the terrace edges (Kroeber 1930: 61, 78; cf. Willey 1953: 163–164) or to minimize subsidence of fill; and lastly

(d) adobe bricks, varying proportions of which were marked with relatively simple geometric and representational designs (see below for details).

These features and techniques are not static; they manifest changes that provide some important insights into the issues at hand. They will be examined in sections to follow within the broader contexts of regional settlement patterns.

Moche V

From various settlement pattern surveys and dispersed excavations, we can glean some generalizations about the nature and extent of Moche V occupation and control on the northern North Coast: it was short-lived but intense and continuous from the coast to the necks of the Jequetepeque and Zaña Valleys, though in the former there may have been pockets of Middle Cajamarca settlers, and in the Lambayeque and Leche Valleys it took an appearance of a wedge driven in through the midvalley (up to the valley neck) along the so-called "Inca North-South Trunk Road" (Kosok 1965: 144). This road linked sites such as Sipan-Collique and Patapo that could have easily controlled the north-south traffic and intervalley canals of Antiguo Taymi and Collique (Fig. 2). Moche V political dominance and territorial control east of this wedge probably did not extend too much beyond Cerro Boro near the modern town of Pomalca. The presence of Moche V face-neck and double-tiered jars as far coastward as Reque and El Purgatorio suggests Moche V influence may have covered much of the lower Lambayeque Valley.

The best-documented Moche V example of the above constellation of architectural features is the Huaca Fortaleza pyramid (also known as La Capilla, Huaca Grande, or Iglesia) at the capital site Pampa Grande at the neck of the Lambayeque Valley (Haas 1985; Shimada and Cavallaro 1986, n.d.). The terraced pyramid has basal dimensions of approximately 270 m by 185 m, and a height of about 50 m. A 290-m long straight ramp provides access to the first terrace. A hierarchical terrace complex at the east end of the first terrace, in turn, controlled access to the second terrace and the steep ramp to the main body of the pyramid, which occupies some three-quarters of the total pyramidal volume. The pyramid seems to have been built in two phases. Evidence for the first phase includes a "floor" of fired rectangular tiles (ca. 50 × 35 × 3 cm thick) in frontal portions of the main body. The second phase accounts for more than two-thirds of the total pyramidal volume and is built of contiguous, free-standing sand-filled square adobe chambers roughly 4 m per side. The resultant grid of chambers was stabilized and strengthened by solid adobe-mortar, segmented (1.5 m wide and 1.0 m thick) "exterior walls" (Shimada n.d.c). Logs embedded in the frontal portions of the main body may have contributed to overall structural soundness.

The pyramid top and first terrace, as well as three platforms northeast of the pyramid had major roofs supported by columns set in adobe boxes filled with sand (Anders 1981; Haas 1985). Some of the columnar boxes at the pyramid contained partial or whole juvenile/neonatal camelids and/or articulated human extremities (Haas 1985; M. Shimada and I. Shimada 1981).

In regard to the variability and distribution of Moche V marked bricks in the corporate architecture thus far sampled at Pampa Grande (Hans Knapp, personal communication, 1988), the picture is quite complex (Shimada n.d.c.). Within each 6-m segment of the south perimeter wall of Deer House (Compound 14) there is one-to-one correspondence among brick mold, soil, and mark, much like the pattern observed at Huaca del Sol and Huaca de la Luna at Moche (Hastings and Moseley 1975). However, within Huaca Fortaleza, each constituent vertical exterior wall segment, as well as the bonded walls of each filled chamber, are built of bricks of varying size, shape, and soil in notable contrast to the above-mentioned. Unfortunately, we do not yet have pertinent information on marked bricks in these walls. A 6-m segment of the south perimeter wall of nearby Spondylus House (Compound 15) was built of heterogeneous bricks bearing at least ten distinct marks (Fig. 22).[10] On the other hand, the standardized, specialized adobe rooms of the formal storage facilities within tightly controlled central areas of the site were built in segments using only unmarked, homogeneous bricks.

Overall, these architectural features suggest that traditional Moche socioeconomic organization (e.g., labor and resource management) underwent significant transformations during the Moche V period (Shimada n.d.a, n.d.c), concurring in general with the picture presented in our earlier discussion of Moche V ceramics. The Inca *mit'a*-like labor tax model applicable for the Huaca del Sol and Huaca de la Luna construction (Moseley 1975) needs to be modified to incorporate such features as task differentiation (e.g., fill transport, clay mortar preparation, and brick placement), stockpiling of bricks under a central authority, specialized fulltime builders (as opposed to generalized, conscripted labor force), and task-specific production of bricks (Shimada n.d.c).

Early Sican

At present, no adobe or large-scale "corporate" construction can be assigned definitely to the Early Sican period; however, the Huaca La Merced pyramid in the Sican Precinct merits attention. In 1983 torrential El Niño rains caused floodwaters from the Tucume Canal to bisect the pyramid. The resultant profile was impressive; the bulk of the pyramid's volume was sand

---

[10] Hans Knapp (personal communication, February 1988) identified a total of thirty-nine marks among eight sampling loci in the central portion of the site.

ARRANGEMENT OF MARKED AND UNMARKED ADOBE BRICKS
IN A SINGLE CONSTRUCTION SEGMENT,
SOUTH WALL, COMPOUND 15,
MOCHE V PAMPA GRANDE

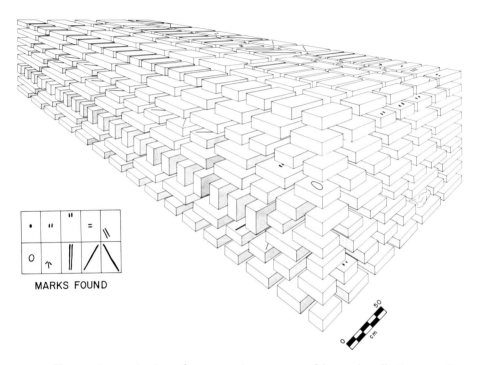

MARKS FOUND

Fig. 22   Isometric view of a construction segment of the south wall, Compound 15, Pampa Grande. Note the mixing of bricks of different size, form, and marks. Adapted from an original drawing by Hans Knapp.

fill partitioned by a series of somewhat irregularly placed intersecting one-adobe wide mortarless walls. It is unlikely that these walls were strong enough to retain the sand fill securely or permanently. The sloping, adobe-mortar exterior walls (some 6.5 m near the bottom to ca. 5 m near the preserved top) still seen on the western base, however, served as primary retention walls. The stacked adobes may have served as footings or boundaries of "chambers" during the sand filling task.

The pyramid overlies a refuse layer and a floor associated with Moche V (perhaps IV-B as well) sherds. Of partricular interest were the ceramics associated with two partially disturbed burials salvaged from the western base of the pyramid. The burials were stratigraphically contemporaneous with a late modification (Elera n.d.) and contained two bottles: an inferred late Early Sican (Middle Horizon 2B?) copper-covered double-spout bottle and an early Middle Sican single-spout bottle with low ring base.

An examination of chunks of mortared adobes that had fallen from the pyramid after the flood revealed a considerable variability in shape and size and in horizontal and vertical placement. Very few of these, however, were marked; of some fifty whole flat rectangular bricks I examined, only four bear what appear to be simple, intentional marks.

Although it is difficult to determine how representative this small sample is, it is clear that the degree of shape and size variability and the low percentage (if any at all) of marking differs from both the Moche V and Middle Sican norms. This fact suggests that the first phase of Huaca La Merced pyramidal history may date La Merced to the late Early Sican period.

Some 260 m west of the La Merced pyramid lies the smaller Mound II, which had been bisected by a looters' bulldozer, leaving behind a 6-m high, 30-m long profile with well-preserved superimposed constructions and a minimum of twenty-five associated, plastered floors that together may span a thousand years between the late Early Intermediate period and Late Horizon (Fig. 23). Some Early Sican blackware sherds were recovered from the bulldozer's backdirt.

The excavation revealed two superimposed platforms occupying the middle portion of the profile and a local evolution of adobe-lined columnar sockets. The upper platform had two parallel rows of regularly spaced, sand-filled square adobe columnar "sockets." Although radiocarbon dating of two preserved wooden columns from these boxes yielded one Early Sican and one Middle Sican date (Appendix), the architectural features and associated ceramics favor an Early Sican date. Between the upper and lower platforms was a compacted clay-silt layer with Moche V and Early Sican ceramics. The lower platform featured regularly spaced, crude circular adobe-lined columnar sockets of suspected Early Sican date.

Overall, during the Early Sican period, both ceramic/iconographic and architectural data point to (a) strong foreign influence (Huari and Middle Cajamarca), (b) political disarray after the demise of the Moche V state based at Pampa Grande, and (c) the concomitant absence of any notable political centralization, perhaps until the final portion of this period.

Middle Sican

The Middle Sican settlement pattern is still not well known due in part to the incomplete nature of settlement surveys undertaken thus far in the study area. Available survey data tend to focus on middle and upper valley areas and ceramics. Though we have precisely defined Middle Sican diagnostics, many (e.g., logographic *paleteada* designs, marked flat adobe bricks, arseni-

Fig. 23   Architectural superposition revealed in the west profile of a bulldozer cut through Mound II, Huaca La Merced. White tags mark plastered floors. Note the different adobe forms.

cal copper) were only recently identified after the surveys were carried out or are difficult to apply without excavation or laboratory analysis.

At the same time, excavations at HPBG have clearly shown that diagnostic blackware bottles with the Sican Lord image are not confined to funerary contexts, but also occur in habitational and craft workshops. Overall, a tentative characterization of the Middle Sican settlement pattern can be presented using this and other diagnostics.

Within the La Leche Valley, Middle Sican *paleteada* and blackware ceramics are most common in the central sector and decrease as one moves inland and coastward. Whether the Motupe Valley immediately to the north came under the Middle Sican religious polity's control or influence is still uncertain. The extensive cultivation of fields around the site of Apurlec linked to the Antigua Jayanca canal (north bank of the La Leche Valley) seems to date from the Late Sican period onward (Shimada 1982). In the Lambayeque Valley, evidence for Middle Sican occupation is found from near the seaport of San Jose (Middle Sican burial excavated by Bennett [1939]) to the inland sites of Santa Rosa near Lambayeque (Schaffield n.d.), Patapo, Sipan-Collique, Saltur, Pampa Grande, and up to Carniche Alto near Chongoyape. At the key lower valley sites of Chotuna and El Mirador (near Eten), I have recorded Middle Sican blackware bottle fragments and "logographic" *paleteada* sherds. At Pampa Grande, Middle Sican ceramics are associated with a complex of small mounds and room blocks (Shimada 1985a, n.d.), and a recent salvage excavation there revealed *tuyeres* (ceramic blowtube tips) and other remains of copper metalworking (Victor Pimentel, personal communication, July 1985). To the south, Middle Sican ceramics are found in the Rinconada de Collique, which links the Lambayeque and Zaña Valleys, as well as at various lower (e.g., Ucupe) and middle valley sites (e.g., Pampa de Chumbenique, Cerro Corbacho) up to about Oyotun. In the Jequetepeque Valley, their distribution seems quite spotty, but they have been found in the looted area east of the City Wall of Pacatnamu, at San Jose de Moro and Cañoncillo adjacent to the Huaca Tecapa (Eling n.d.). In addition, I collected Middle Sican single-spout bottle fragments from looted cemeteries between San Pedro de Lloc and Cañoncillo. Whole bottles, attributed to these cemeteries, in a private local collection are well burnished, but are gray rather than the typical blackware. Middle Sican control in Jequetepeque appears to have been limited or tenuous.

In general, the closer to Batan Grande, the more ubiquitous Middle Sican diagnostics become. Along the east-west axis, they occur from the Pacific Coast to the lower *yunga*/valley necks. This general settlement pattern resembles that of Moche V.

Hardly any of the aforementioned sites can be described as "fortified" or "defensive." We have no definite weapons or depictions of battle scenes in Middle Sican art. This situation is probably related to the basic character of the Middle Sican polity. We have characterized it as a Vatican-like religious polity that promoted ideological and social unity and economic growth. Economic growth appears to have been accomplished by patronage of craft production and establishment of trade partners and secondary shrines and temples.

The constellation of Middle Sican architectural features is perhaps most evident among the major pyramids within the Sican Precinct in Batan Grande, the inferred Middle Sican political and religious capital (Fig. 5), and we will examine them in some detail below.

Columnar Construction. The T-shaped Huaca El Corte pyramid, which occupies the east end of the Sican Precinct, was originally constructed as a platform some 4 m high made up of a lattice of filled chambers. A series of subsequent modifications and additions culminated with a colonnade of forty-eight painted columns atop the elongated pyramid with a backdrop wall. This wall was ornamented with polychrome murals running north-south along the pyramid's east edge (Shimada 1981, 1985a, 1986). The colonnade consisted of four rows of twelve painted columns (ca. 3.7 m apart north-south and 2.0–2.3 m east-west) set on tabular stone bases in roughly 1 m², sand-filled boxes made of marked adobes. After the boxes were sealed

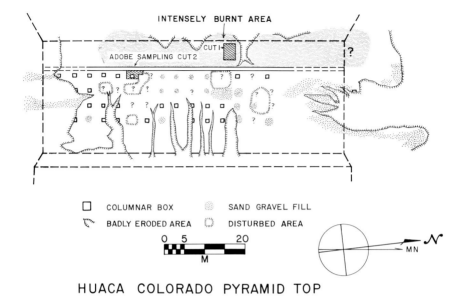

COLUMNAR BOX   SAND GRAVEL FILL

BADLY ERODED AREA   DISTURBED AREA

0 5   20

M

HUACA COLORADO PYRAMID TOP

Fig. 24   Colonnade atop the Huaca El Moscon (also known as Huaca Colorada) pyramid.

with clay that matched the floor, the columns were carefully wrapped with cord, which was then covered with clay to produce a square form with rounded corners. The elaborately painted colonnade and back wall occupied much of the available space atop the pyramid, creating dramatic visual impact upon those who ascended the short central western ramp.

Essentially, the same columnar construction was present at the now largely destroyed Mound 2, Huaca El Corte, some 100 m southwest of the principal mound just described. The principal pyramid of Huaca Las Ventanas, which lies 1 km west of Huaca El Corte and is perfectly aligned with it, also shows vestiges of similar construction on its south terrace.

Numerous columns on the terraced tops of the Huacas El Moscon (Fig. 24) and Rodillona pyramids (Fig. 18a, b) are similarly set in marked adobe boxes about 1 m to a side. At El Moscon, a minimum of four rows of at least fifteen regularly spaced (ca. 3.5 m apart) columns occupied much of the highest terrace. This terrace stands 12 m high above the pyramid base and measures about 80 m long and 40 m wide. At Rodillona, at least three rows of an estimated 20 columns regularly spaced (2.0–2.2 m apart on both axes) ran along the best-preserved western portion of the over 45 m high pyramid. Although badly eroded by the 1983 El Niño rains, vestiges of enough columnar boxes are visible on the sides of erosion gullies to suggest there were originally some fifteen rows of twenty columns each. The columns either supported a single massive roof or, more likely, a series of partially overlapping roofs that together covered the pyramid top.

The column boxes at these two *huacas* were filled with a white sand/reddish limestone gravel mixture (typically 1 m deep). The boxes often had a tabular stone placed on the solid clay mortar bottom. The column box seal atop the fill probably corresponded to a plastered layer. The alternating layers of marked adobe bricks and clay mortar (overall, some 50–60 cm thick) that overlie the fill of the boxes situated along the western edge of Huaca Rodillona's top are believed to have provided a solid foundation for the floor of the now-eroded highest terrace.

Seven partially or fully excavated column boxes at Huaca Rodillona reveal a distinct pattern. Box contents alternate between unmodified Spondylus shells with some thirty to fifty bundles of I-shaped arsenical copper "foil" wrapped in coarse plain cotton cloth and the same plus a dedicatory human burial (Fig. 25). Each bundle has two small copper foil sheets (2.0–2.5 cm wide × 8.0–9.5 cm long × 0.02–0.07 mm thick, and weighing 0.5–0.8 g). An examination of badly eroded columnar boxes at the Huaca El Moscon pyramid suggests that at least some of them also received offerings of copper foil bundles.

Chamber and Fill Construction. An examination of deep cuts and tunnels made by large-scale looting (Huacas El Corte, Las Ventanas, and Oro) or torrential rains and associated floods (Huacas Las Ventanas, Rodillona, La Merced, and El Moscon) has shown that all pyramids in the Sican Precinct feature the chamber-and-fill construction. Other monumental pyramids in the Lambayeque region also show this technique. The body of the Chotuna pyramid is well-preserved due to the adobe constructions built atop the pyramid during Chimu occupation (Bruce n.d.), but the original construction format is chamber and fill. Hans Horkheimer (1944: 41) describes the pyramid as having been built of series of adobe brick "chimneys" filled with earth, and notes that many component adobe bricks were marked. This was confirmed by my own observations made inside a large looters' tunnel that had been dug into the side of the pyramid.

One crucial aspect of the Middle Sican chamber-fill construction technique is that sets of contiguous chambers forming "tiers" or horizontal lattices were built in single episodes; constituent walls do not exhibit the segmentation seen in earlier Moche pyramids. Even if the layout of adobe bricks at a given wall corner presents the appearance of being an abutment, the thick clay mortar between two layers of bricks is continuously laid. The use of large amounts of wet clay mortar and continuously bonded construction meant that a good deal of the preparation for pyramidal construction had to take place near or at the actual construction site and that a premium was placed on a unified, large-scale, single-episode construction effort. A large labor force had to be mobilized and closely supervised, in contrast

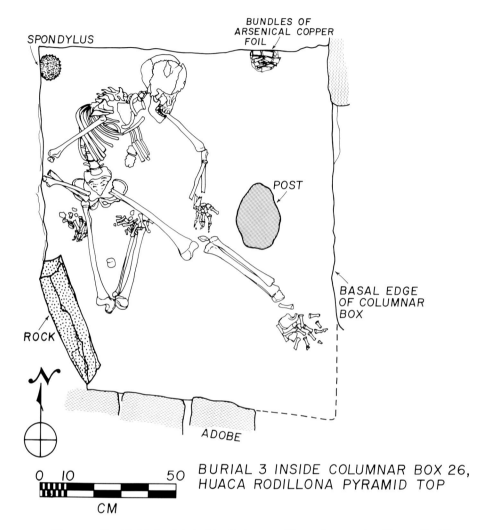

SPONDYLUS

BUNDLES OF
ARSENICAL COPPER
FOIL

POST

BASAL EDGE
OF COLUMNAR
BOX

ROCK

N

ADOBE

0   10   50

CM

BURIAL 3 INSIDE COLUMNAR BOX 26,
HUACA RODILLONA PYRAMID TOP

Fig. 25 Sacrificial burial inside Columnar Box 26 atop the Huaca Rodillona pyramid.

with the Moche segmentary construction approach. This construction format assured a greater overall structural strength to the resultant lattice. Further details and variability in this construction format are described elsewhere (Cavallaro and Shimada 1988; Shimada and Cavallaro 1986, n.d.).

Marked Adobe Bricks. Variability in size, form, and marking of Middle Sican adobe bricks has been carefully documented at the Huacas El Moscon, El Corte, La Merced (Mounds I and II), Las Ventanas, and Rodillona pyramids and their auxiliary structures. Some one thousand whole, flat- and slightly convex-topped rectangular bricks examined at eight sampling loci at Huacas Las Ventanas and El Corte revealed that (a) the overwhelming percentage (85–95 percent) has one of more than seventy distinct marks that are simply geometric or in some cases representational or "logographic" in nature, (b) horizontal and vertical distributions of marked adobes in most sampling loci show no statistically significant clustering (at times, several adobes of the same mold and mark may appear in a small horizontal and/or vertical cluster of two to three layers), (c) there is no one-to-one correspondence between a given mark and adobe brick mold (bricks from the same mold may bear different marks, and, conversely, the same mark appears on adobes from different molds), and (d) the volumetric ratio of alternating layers of bricks and mud mortar approximates 1:1; thick mortar serves as an effective buffer in a given layer for adobes of variable size and shape (Cavallaro and Shimada 1988; Shimada and Cavallaro 1986, n.d.).

Huaca Eten (Taco or Mirador) near Eten in lower Lambayeque and the earliest monumental constructions at Huaca Chotuna (Fig. 26; Bruce n.d.; see Donnan [Chotuna], this volume) are all constructed of tabular rectangular bricks with the four features described previously (Shimada and Cavallaro 1986, n.d.). Though no qualitative analysis has yet been carried out, the flat rectangular adobes in the walls of the small Ucupe temple (with impressive Middle Sican polychrome murals) recently excavated by Alva and Alva (1984) also seem to have the same four major characteristics just described.

The one model that effectively accounts for these features sees marks found on Middle Sican bricks as identifying "sponsors," who donated bricks appropriately marked with their symbols as a token of religious devotion or as a means of achieving and/or maintaining social status and prestige (Cavallaro and Shimada 1988; Shimada 1985a).

A hypothesis was developed that the aforementioned features, together with chamber-fill and encased columnar formats found in corporate adobe architecture, were diagnostic of Middle Sican date and cultural affiliation. The hypothesis was confirmed by subsequent tests at Huacas El Moscon and Rodillona. More than two hundred whole adobes (flat to slightly convex) recorded at each of two sampling loci at each pyramid showed the same four features previously noted (Fig. 27). Eight-five and eighty-four distinct marks were recorded among the sampled bricks at Huacas El Moscon and Rodillona, respectively. The percentage of marking for all loci was somewhat more than 90 percent (Fig. 26). Sixteen marks are shared by bricks examined at the Huacas Las Ventanas and El Moscon pyramids. An equal number is shared by the Huacas Las Ventanas and Rodillona bricks examined thus far. El Moscon and Rodillona share twenty-three marks.

Three wood samples from the Rodillona and El Moscon pyramids have all been dated to about A.D. 1020–1060 (see Fig. 4 and Appendix) confirm-

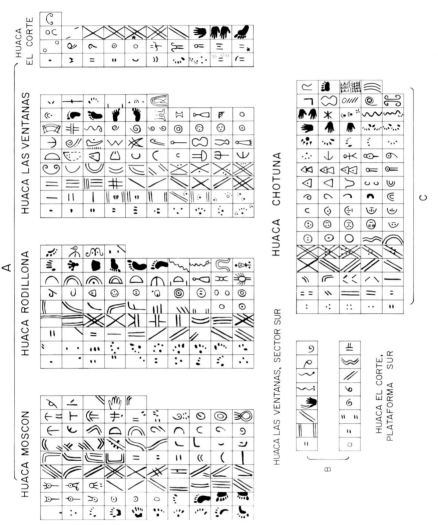

Fig. 26 Marks found on flat, rectangular Middle Sican bricks at the Sican Precinct (A) and (B), and in the basal portion of the perimeter walls of the Artisans' Quadrangle, Huaca Chotuna and the pyramid at Chornancap (C). Item C is based on field notes taken by Susan Bruce.

344

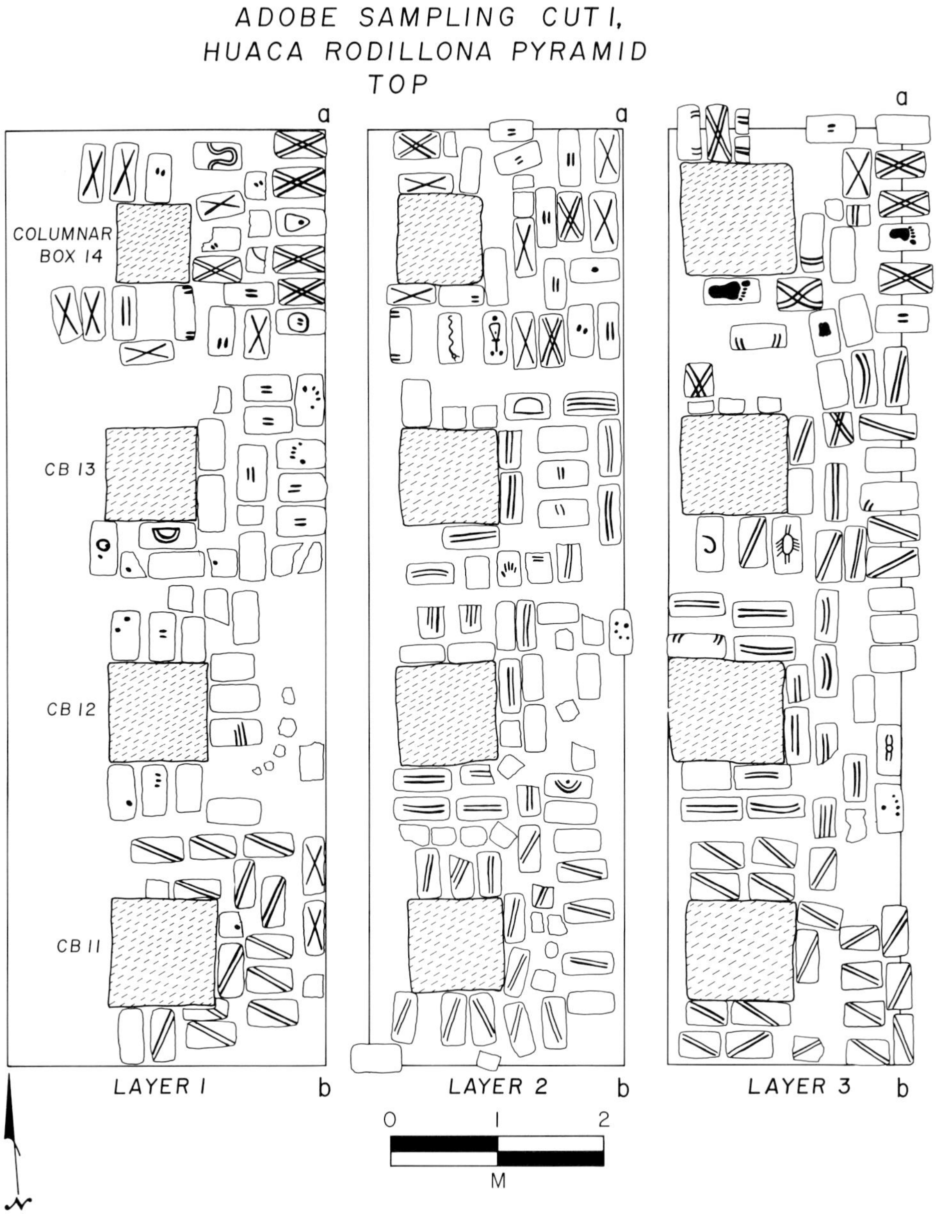

ADOBE SAMPLING CUT I,
HUACA RODILLONA PYRAMID
TOP

COLUMNAR
BOX 14

CB 13

CB 12

CB 11

LAYER 1   b

a

LAYER 2   b

a

LAYER 3   b

a

0   1   2
M

Fig. 27   Horizontal and vertical distributions of marked adobes found in Cut 1 atop the Huaca Rodillona pyramid. Although clustered placements of certain marks suggest a segmentary construction, the thick clay mortar between layers of adobes was continuously laid without any segmentation. Note the careful sorting of identically marked, but differently sized adobes.

ing a Middle Sican date and suggesting these pyramids may be somewhat later (perhaps about fifty years?) than the Huacas El Corte and Las Ventanas. Though minor, this inferred temporal difference is supported by the adobe seriation discussed later. The main body of the Rodillona pyramid seems to have been built in a single episode, while the El Moscon pyramid shows evidence of some reconstruction after a major fire.

The preceding discussion shows that, in addition to the use of the same kinds of marked adobes, many, if not most of the documented or inferred Middle Sican monumental constructions in and outside of Batan Grande have the persistent T-shaped configuration (inset or overlying central ramps): for example, Huacas El Corte and El Moscon in Batan Grande, Huaca Susy at Chotuna, Huaca Chornancap (Bruce n.d.), and Huaca Eten (Middendorf 1894: 418; Kroeber 1930: 92, pl. xxx). The T-shape mound at Huaca Miguelito near Cerro Guitarras in the Zaña Valley, Huaca Las Estacas (Kroeber 1930, pl. xxx-1; Kosok 1965: 123, figs. 12, 13) and Huaca Teodora south of Mocupe in the Jequetepeque Valley (Kosok 1965: 141–142, figs. 4–7) should be examined for adobe and other Middle Sican architectural features.

Overall, during the Middle Sican period we see a definite resurgence of monumental religious structures and a formalization of certain labor organizational practices first seen during Moche V times. Undoubtedly, these trends went hand in hand with the emergence of a distinct iconography and new corporate image. This regional cultural flowering, however, was relatively short-lived. Implications of the abruptness and broad range of major cultural changes that define the onset of the Late Sican will be discussed later.

Late Sican

Sometime around A.D. 1050–1100, much of the Sican Precinct was abandoned, marking the end of the Middle Sican period. An extensive, intense conflagration took place within the Precinct near the time of its abandonment and may have actually caused it. Abandonment was followed by a general westward shift in the loci of large-scale public constructions. The Huaca del Pueblo Tucume pyramid and the some dozen monumental, truncated adobe pyramids of El Purgatorio that surround the spike-like Cerro La Raya (Fig. 28; see also photos and sketch map in Schaedel 1951b) situated at the strategic juncture of the La Leche and Lambayeque Valleys all lie west of the Sican Precinct (Shimada et al. 1981; Shimada and Cavallaro 1986, n.d.; cf. Trimborn 1979). Various superimposed tiers of adobe chambers with loose fill form the cores of these pyramids. On the heavily eroded top of the gigantic Huaca Larga pyramid (460 m long, 120 m wide and 25 m high), one sees the remains of encased columns: tabular basal stones, cascades of sand and gravel mixtures, and outlines of adobe boxes. Whether this particular

Fig. 28   An aerial view of the site of El Purgatorio (SAN Proyecto 159-'68, neg. 41).

columnar construction characterizes all pyramids at El Purgatorio remains to be seen. Likewise, no systematic examination of constituent adobe bricks has been carried out to date. We can say, however, that at least some of the walls atop and around the base of the Huaca Larga pyramid are built of "low loaf" or "high loaf" types of bricks similar to those documented at Huaca Chotuna by Susan Bruce (n.d.; see also Donnan [Chotuna], this volume, and Kroeber 1930: 94) and at HPBG in levels ceramically dated to Late Sican A and later.

Within the La Leche Valley proper, with the exception of Huaca Santillo (or Soltillo), there are no adequately dated constructions matching the scale of the El Purgatorio and Sican Precinct pyramids for either Late Sican A or B. Erosion of an enormous looters' pit that removed perhaps a third of the Santillo pyramid suggests the chamber-and-fill format was used there. Unfortunately, the pyramid has not been examined in sufficient detail to comment on the other architectural features being considered.

At HPBG, Late Sican A adobe constructions are relatively small and, with one notable exception (Shimada n.d.c), built of unmarked bricks that are somewhat convex on the top, resembling what Bruce (n.d.) calls "low loaf" type (Fig. 29). By Late Sican B, the adobe top is more noticeably convex, and a few scattered marked bricks without any apparent meaningful distribu-

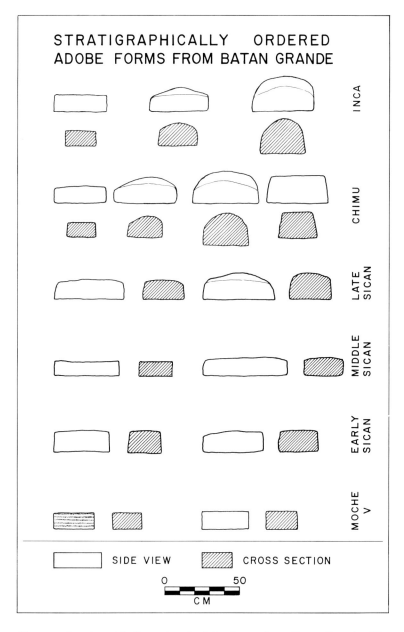

Fig. 29 Stratigraphically ordered adobe forms from Batan Grande. The relevant information is derived from HPBG and Huaca La Merced, Mound II. Note the coexistence of different forms.

tion are found. However, in most cases only the lowest one or two courses remain, and the overall sample size is small. The adobes of a terrace immediately overlying an early Late Sican floor atop a major T-shaped platform overlooking Sector III, Cerro Huaringa (Epstein and Shimada 1984), show no markings and are only slightly convex.

It should be clearly remembered that the architectural considerations thus far have focused on monumental adobe pyramidal ("temple" type) constructions. The apparent paucity of Late Sican (perhaps Early Sican as well) corporate architecture, in this sense, cannot be taken at its face value without a parallel examination of other types of constructions and settlements. Of particular importance are the extensive terraced hillside settlements that Schaedel (1951a, 1966a,b) has designated as "urban lay centers." These centers occupied locations strategic to control of productive resources such as metallurgical centers (e.g., Cerro La Calera), fertile lands (e.g., Cerro Corbacho in the middle of the Zaña Valley), and intravalley and intervalley canals and roads (e.g., Patapo and Saltur on the north and south banks in the Lambayeque Valley). Unfortunately, impressive multilevel platforms built against the slopes at these sites have not been studied thoroughly for their construction techniques, materials, and features or for their behavioral and organizational significance.

Cerro La Calera has been studied to some extent in relation to our ongoing investigations of Sican metallurgy. The site appears to have been an integral part of what I call "Southern La Leche Agro-Industrial Complex" (Fig. 3).

The Complex during the Late Sican era seems to have encompassed (a) a residential zone stretching from the east and west bases and walled ridge tops of Cerro La Calera to the west base of Cerro Cabeza de Leon and on to the north and east bases of Cerro Tambo Real, (b) inferred Pre-Hispanic lime kilns that exploited the high-quality limestone of Cerro La Calera, (c) the metallurgical centers of Cerros Huaringa and Sajino (Epstein and Shimada 1984; Shimada et al. 1982, 1983), (d) mines at Cerros Blanco, Mellizo, and Barranco Colorado (Shimada 1985b), and (e) portions of about 20 km² of planned cultivation fields in Pampa de Chaparri irrigated by the Raca Rumi I and II canals (Shimada 1982), as well as small fields east of Cerro La Calera and west of the site of Tambo Real.

Contemporaneous with the above Complex, a series of residential settlements, a major copper mine (Cerro Pan de Azucar) and a metallurgical complex (Huaca Julupe-Cerro Jotoro [Epstein and Shimada 1984]), may have been linked functionally with the agricultural production in and around Apurlec to form the Northern La Leche Agro-Industrial Complex along the north margin of the La Leche Valley. A major ancient road links these two agro-industrial complexes (on a straight line between the Tambo Real and La Viña sites). There is a distinct possibility that these two complexes were the economic bases of the two powerful late Pre-Hispanic ethnic polities of Tucume (southern) and Jayanca (northern) often mentioned in ethnohistorical sources (e.g., Espinoza Soriano 1975; Netherly 1984, n.d.; Ramírez 1981, 1985, and this volume).

Chimu Domination

In general, intensive settlement surveys and/or excavation programs carried out thus far (e.g., Bennett 1939; Eling n.d.; Kosok 1959, 1965; Netherly n.d.; Nolan n.d.; Ravines 1982a; Schaedel 1951a, b, 1966 a, b; Shimada 1982, n.d.; Shimada et al. 1981) clearly attest to an extensive and intensive Imperial Chimu occupation of the Lambayeque Valley Complex, including the entire Batan Grande region (see both Netherly and Ramírez, this volume).

The brief span of Imperial Chimu domination of the study area saw a good deal of non-pyramidal adobe and masonry construction activity (both modifications of the extant Late Sican structures, as well as building new ones) at HPBG, Cerros Huaringa and Sajino, and elsewhere throughout the Lambayeque Valley Complex. At HPBG, a series of interlinked rooms was built and remodeled with variously shaped bricks (flat rectangular, low and high loaf, and a few trapezoidal) but most commonly high-loaf adobes (Fig. 29). Imperial Chimu reduced ware vessels are some of the most widespread and common ceramics found throughout much of the Complex. Following the pattern set during the Late Sican era, locations crucial to control of productive resources (e.g., Cerros Guitarras, Corbacho, Songoy, and Culpon in the Zaña Valley, Saltur, Sipan-Collique, La Puntilla, Patapo, and Tres Picos in the Lambayeque Valley, and Cerros Huaringa and La Calera and Tambo Real in the La Leche Valley [see Fig. 2]) show abundant Chimu ceramics associated with well-preserved masonry constructions (e.g., free-standing formal rectangular compounds, U-shaped *audiencias*) whose layouts seem to have been established during if not long before (even Moche V) Late Sican.

Within the Lambayeque Valley Complex, many Chimu sites continued to be occupied after the Inca conquest, often resulting in mixing of Imperial Chimu and Chimu-Inca ceramics on the surface. The problem of differentiating Imperial Chimu and Inca period constructions without clear stratigraphic evidence or diagnostic architectural features (e.g., *audiencias, trapezoidal niches*) should be clearly kept in mind here. At the same time, the Chimu also built atop earlier, local ceremonial adobe structures, for example, at the Huaca Chotuna pyramid, presumably to capitalize on established reputation and prestige, as well as to symbolize dominance.

At Huaca La Merced Mound II, we have a highly instructive case of an adobe construction from what we believe to be the Imperial Chimu period. Just below the surface of the highest preserved portion of the bisected mound

Fig. 30　Inferred Chimu construction atop Mound II, Huaca La Merced, showing contrasting pattern of adobe brick marking. Only one of the tall loaf bricks seen in the upper portion of the photo is marked, while all well-preserved low loaf bricks in the photograph bear the same mark.

(Fig. 23) we encountered a corridor (Phase 2 construction) that had been intentionally blocked and filled, presumably to provide a foundation for an inferred Late Horizon (after A.D. 1460–70) construction (Phase 1 construction).

The two parallel walls that define this corridor display sharply contrasting brick features, although both articulate with the single plastered floor, implying contemporaneity. The wider north wall was overwhelmingly built with low loaf bricks (201 out of 217 whole bricks), some 80 percent of which carried one mark. These marks were poorly executed, and a few bricks actually may have carried other marks. The remaining sixteen were unmarked tall loaf bricks.

The south wall was erected nearly exclusively of tall loaf bricks that were unmarked with the one definite and two possible exceptions (Fig. 30). Three low loaf bricks were noted among the 212 complete bricks recorded.

This contrasting, contemporaneous situation raises a serious question concerning the validity of straightforward seriation based on the convexity or relative height of brick cross-section profiles (as detailed in the following section). It also seems to cast doubt on the applicability of the "sponsor" and other models considered most plausible for the Middle Sican marked adobe data and associated construction labor organization (Cavallaro and Shimada 1988; cf. Shimada and Cavallaro n.d.). However, the north wall is appreciably wider than the south wall (90 vs. 70 cm), which does not run the full length of the mound's upper structure. Perhaps the north wall was an exterior or crucial boundary wall, while the south wall was simply an internal division wall. Also, it may be that La Merced Mound II experienced adobe production and wall construction under both direct state supervision (in this case the Chimu Kingdom) and local ethnic lords or special interest groups such as "guilds" of craftsmen and artisans (Shimada and Cavallaro n.d.). Such a division could be the cause of the two brick types used in a single-phase building.

With state involvement we envision standardized adobe production and construction by conscripted labor forces. We did not identify any vertical seam that might have marked the standardized unit of a task assigned to such a labor group in either of two excavated walls built exclusively with tall loaf bricks. However, the presence of one marked brick in each wall is quite intriguing and not unlike the Moche pattern. The contemporaneous walls built with marked low loaf bricks, on the other hand, may be seen as retention of a time-honored, local tradition dating back to the Middle Sican era.

It should be noted that the preceding inferences are untested. One crucial fact casts serious doubt on these inferences: both the low and tall loaf bricks in question were handmade. The various explanatory models discussed previously, such as sponsor or labor tax, define brick production and labor organization by recognizing the patterned relationships among various features pertaining to mold-made bricks. We cannot readily apply these models to handmade bricks.

Furthermore, we do not know the extent to which the Chimu state adobe production and use seen at Chan Chan (Kolata 1982, n.d., and this volume) was replicated in our study area. Faithful replication of Chimu state architecture such as *audiencias* has been noted at regional administrative centers such as Farfan and Manchan in the Jequetepeque and Casma Valleys, respectively (Keatinge and Conrad 1983; Mackey and Klymyshyn 1981). Can we, however, expect the same situation outside of such centers, particularly in the Lambayeque region with its notable local socio-political developments that preceded Chimu domination. Even at Manchan, Carol Mackey and A. M. Ulana Klymyshyn (1981) note the presence and use of marked adobe bricks that cannot be accounted for with the Chan Chan model. It should be kept in mind that at Chan Chan, in notable contrast to the Mound II situation, corporate architecture used a segmentary format and mold-made unmarked "tall" and "square-ended" bricks that may have been supplied by the state.

Insights gained from various studies of state-local interaction (including our own diachronic study of copper alloy production in Batan Grande, which encompassed Chimu and Inca domination [e.g., Epstein and Shimada 1984; see also Netherly 1984, n.d.; Schaedel 1978b]) suggest that wholesale imposition of new institutions and technologies is unlikely in areas with indigenous state-level socio-political integration. This "indirect" rule approach is more likely to be found in peripheral or recently conquered areas. Time-honored, local technologies and infrastructures of productive activities are commonly retained and coexist with certain notable introductions that serve as effective reminders of the new socio-political order.

Inca Domination

Recently, it has been shown archaeologically that Inca control of the Lambayeque region was much more extensive and tighter than typically assumed (cf. Epstein and Shimada 1984; Netherly n.d.; Nolan n.d.; Schaedel 1978b, 1985b; Shimada et al. 1981; see also both Netherly and Ramírez, this volume). Cuzco Inca polychrome sherds have been recovered at Cerro Jotoro in Batan Grande and Cerro Saltur in the Lambayeque Valley, while Provincial Inca, as well as Chimu-Inca ceramics occur in abundance at the regional administrative centers of Tambo Real and La Viña (and to a lesser degree at Apurlec and El Purgatorio), and at the metallurgical centers of Cerros Huaringa and Sajino.

The distribution and quantity of Chimu-Inca, Imperial Inca, and Provincial Inca ceramics are likely to have been closely related to several features: (a) productivity of the "Southern and Northern La Leche Agro-Industrial Complex" described earlier, (b) the main intake for the intervalley Antigua Jayanca canal that brought much of the water to Apurlec (a site with some 40 km² of well-ordered cultivation fields and associated irrigation canals) (Shimada 1982), and (c) convergence of the two main coastal roads (one each through the middle and lower valleys [Schaedel 1978b]). The agro-industrial complexes are believed to have been controlled by the Jayanca and Tucume *curacazgos,* perhaps seated at Apurlec and El Purgatorio, respectively (see Ramírez, this volume).

During the brief period of Inca control of the study area, the Southern La Leche Agro-Industrial Complex seems to have been expanded by the addition of a ceramic production area (attested to by a large pile of wasters near the northeast base of Cerro Tambo Real [Shimada n.d.b]). Expansion of cultivation fields in Pampa de Chaparri up to the maximum of some 20 km² may have occurred under Chimu, rather than Inca, control (Shimada 1982). It is apparent that regional metallurgical production was significantly increased during Imperial Chimu domination and that same level (if not higher) was maintained during the period of Inca control.

One of the major future research tasks elucidated by the previous discussion is archaeological testing of the hypothesis that these two agro-industrial complexes formed the economic and demographic foundations for the two powerful *curacazgos* of Tucume and Jayanca.

We have seen that certain constellations of architectural features and their distinctive qualitative and quantitative properties are culturally and chronologically specific. In general, architectural features can be explored further in elucidating the historical validity of Naymlap and the Lambayeque dynasty or Taycanamo and Imperial Chimu expansion. For example, in respect to the Naymlap legend, we need to establish whether the Chornancap pyramid was built using the chamber-and-fill format. The Chornancap pyramid gives an impression of being solid adobe. Given the long tradition and widespread use of the chamber-and-fill technique in the northern North Coast, the solid adobe construction would be anomalous and may be construed as intrusive.

The need to clarify the chronological value of adobe brick form (as well as its spatial parameters) is amply illustrated by the discussion that followed the 1985 conference at Dumbarton Oaks (compare Donnan [Chotuna], this volume, with Kolata, this volume, for the respective dating of Huaca El Dragon based on iconography and adobe brick seriation, respectively). Relevant data are available to shed some new light on this topic.

Perhaps the stratigraphy at HPBG provides the best single data source for the long-term evolution of local adobe bricks. Speaking in general terms, the gradual increase over time in the convexity of the top surfaces of adobe bricks from flat to low loaf and eventually to high loaf is one evident trend as seen in Figure 29. The stratigraphic position, as well as the associated ceramics and radiocarbon dates, argue that slightly convex adobe bricks begin to appear relatively late in Middle Sican times (ca. A.D. 1050?) and coexist with the flat type for sometime. The slightly convex form predominates by early Late Sican A (ca. A.D. 1100?). The subsequent increase in convexity brings the medium-to-high loaf adobes into existence during Chimu domination sometime after A.D. 1350.

Loaf bricks are readily identifiable in cross-sectional profiles. They have rectangular bases, upon which additional mud-based mixture is hand-shaped to create mounds of different heights. Although Middle Sican flat rectangular bricks in the Sican Precinct have a mean height of approximately 10 cm, low and tall loaf bricks, for example, at Huaca La Merced Mound II, have mean heights of about 13 and 17 cm, respectively. With increased height, mean and overall variability in length are notably reduced for loaf bricks. Concurrently, the mud mortar-adobe brick volumetric ratio decreases from a Middle Sican high that approached 1:1 to a low of around 2:3 for tall loaf bricks.

Data from other sites in and outside of Bátan Grande confirm and refine this general trend. Though more punctuated in the nature of observed changes in brick form in comparison with the picture from HPBG, superimposed constructions at Huaca La Merced Mound II (Fig. 23) essentially show the same trend in increasing convexity. Here, readily notable changes in adobe form coincide with major changes in construction features, configuration, and techniques, as well as in the composition of associated ceramics.

Based on her examination of adobe bricks at the Huaca Chotuna-Chornancap Complex in the lower Lambayeque Valley, Susan Bruce (n.d.) independently reached the same conclusion regarding diachronic trends of adobe brick form. On the basis of a "height-to-width ratio," she established a typology that basically consists of flat rectangular, loaf, and tall loaf bricks. Using data on stratigraphic position and reuse of adobes, as well as wall abutment patterns, Bruce seriated these types in order of decreasing age from flat to loaf to tall loaf. Flat rectangular bricks are subdivided into A and B types with the former having an even top surface and the higher frequency of marks. Bricks at the Huaca El Corte and Las Ventanas pyramids in Batan Grande belong to Bruce's subtype A. Subtype B, on the other hand, is only slightly convex, much like bricks found mixed with the flat-topped examples at the Huaca El Moscon and Rodillona pyramids. At Huaca Chotuna, subtype B bricks are described as having a "lower incidence" of marking than those of subtype A; at Huacas El Moscon and Rodillona, B-type bricks are almost always marked.

Interestingly, Bruce (n.d.) reports that, although these subtypes may represent successive phases of construction that preceded low loaf adobes, attempts to order them chronologically have not been successful. This difficulty arises from a crucial fact that is evident in Figure 29 and already discussed in respect to the Huaca La Merced Mound II excavation: various adobe forms coexist in time and space.[11] There is notable continuity and stability in the tabular rectangular bricks from Moche V to Inca times. In fact, for the relatively short spans of Chimu and Inca dominations of Batan Grande, the HPBG stratigraphy shows the coexistence of various adobe forms. The absence of the trapezoidal form in Inca times may well be a function of small sample size. At the Huacas El Moscon and Rodillona pyramids in the Sican Precinct, flat tabular adobe bricks are found thoroughly mixed with those that have very slightly convex upper surfaces. This variation in form does not readily lend itself to a simple typology because it is essentially continuous.

The preceding discussion clearly shows the serious limitations of relative chronologies and cultural identification based on adobe form. Before we can

---

[11] Since this paper was first written in 1985, Donald McClelland (1986) has independently documented the coexistence of differently formed bricks at Pacatnamu.

contemplate the use of adobe form as a temporal or cultural diagnostic, the representativeness of a given brick sample must be assessed in regard to local and imposed patterns for a specific time period. Even a stratigraphic cut that shows, for example, low loaf bricks overlying tabular bricks cannot by itself be considered sufficient evidence for identifying two different cultures or periods, due to the notable longevity of the tabular to slightly convex rectangular brick. A large representative sample is required.

At the same time, trapezoidal and tall loaf forms seem to have some diagnostic value in indicating a Late Intermediate–Late Horizon date and/or Chimu-Inca affiliation at least in the Lambayeque region (cf. Kolata 1982, n.d.; McClelland 1986).

DISCUSSION

This paper has presented much information on northern North Coast prehistory and numerous observations on archaeological verification of the Naymlap legend. Key observations and supportive evidence are briefly recapitulated in the following sections under topical headings with discussion of their relevance to the specific test implications that were detailed at the onset of this paper, as well as to the broader issues addressed in this volume.

Chronological Issues

There is a confusing array of cultural chronologies in our study area, many of which employ the same terms (e.g., Lambayeque) in spite of major differences in spatial and temporal parameters, methodologies used (e.g., stylistic or morphological seriation of looted funerary vessels, frequency seriation of surface-collected ceramics), and the resultant data base. All previous chronologies lack stratigraphic or other independent verification and suffer from imposition of exogenous perspectives and criteria (Chicama and Moche Valleys). The situation is complicated by the fact that these terms carry different absolute dates. Table 1 is an attempt to interrelate various chronologies in and outside of the study area with our stratigraphic and radiocarbon chronology.

Although the number and technical control of radiocarbon dates has risen significantly since various compilations of available dates were made some years ago (e.g., Ravines 1982b; Watson 1986), too often they are used uncritically. Furthermore, all dates should not be considered as having the same level of technical and interpretive reliability. Specific justifications for the level of confidence placed in our radiocarbon dates for Batan Grande were described above (note 2). It is urged that archaeological publications of radiocarbon dates include detailed commentaries not only of the nature (e.g., aggregate vs. lump charcoal) and context of samples (e.g., primary vs. secondary) used, but also of their "expected" dates and "interpreted cultural significance."

We have seen a rather general increase in convexity of top surface of adobe form over time for the study area and time periods concerned here. Furthermore, a set of specific qualities of marked flat to slightly convex rectangular bricks was found to be diagnostic of Middle Sican date and cultural affiliation. At the same time, adobe-form chronologies have serious drawbacks, particularly when applied to large areas and small samples or small scale (local, low level) constructions, even if stratified, because of the coexistence of bricks of different forms and because of the idiosyncracies of regional brick traditions. To be of any value, brick typologies and seriations must be developed on the basis of large samples derived from various sites of different characters and periods. We cannot expect a typology and seriation based on samples from a state capital to be applicable to samples from local settlements away from the core region.

We have also seen a confusing array of stylistic dating of murals (e.g, those at Huacas Oro, Pintada, and Chornancap) found in the study area. Not only are these dates not internally consistent, they do not match well with generally consistent radiocarbon dates and architectural seriation. Before we can place any confidence in stylistic dates, they must achieve greater objectivity and internal consistency. Similarly, any attempt at interregional extrapolation of stylistic dates (e.g., between the Moche and Lambayeque Valleys) must clearly keep in mind that stylistic contemporaneity is classificatory and not absolute. To say that two artistic expressions are of the same stylistic date is not adequate for detailed assessment of the sequential or cause-effect relationships being considered in this volume.

Chronologies in and outside the study area, overall, are still not precise and reliable enough to judge some of the critical test implications and views being considered here. For example, the Chotuna-Chornancap Complex should produce the earliest example of site-unit intrusion. The earliest "intrusive" features seem to appear in the mural of Chornancap. Unfortunately, the stylistic or chronological placement of the mural remains quite problematical (e.g., Middle Horizon Epoch 2 vs. 4), as we have seen previously. Although there seems to be definite iconographic and stylistic coherence and continuity among the murals found at Huacas Pintada, Oro, El Corte, and Ucupe, the Chornancap mural appears to have been dictated by different artistic canons (Bonavia 1985; Donnan 1984). If it is "Early Chimu" in style dating to between A.D. 750 and 900 as Donnan suspects, what was its cultural relationship with the Early and Middle Sican occupations defined in Batan Grande? How are the corresponding absolute dates (A.D. 750–900) for the "Early Chimu" in the lower Lambayeque Valley derived? Are they independently derived or extrapolated from the tenuous Moche Valley sequence? I do not see a reliable set of radiocarbon dates to support this dating. Further, adobe constructions associated with the Chornancap mural show a diagnostic set of Middle Sican features (as do the earliest major constructions at Chotuna). How can we resolve this notable chronological discrepancy? Are we dealing with an archaic revival of an earlier style (see Moseley, this volume)? We still have a long way to go in dealing with this critical test implication.

Even if the mural is Early Sican in style, available dates do not allow us to determine where the relevant evidence first appeared: at Chornancap or in Batan Grande or elsewhere in the still largely unexplored study area. We need to search more thoroughly for Early Chimu or Early Sican (or even earlier) occupation in the nonmonumental and ceremonial zone at Chornancap and at other sites in the study area.

If the mural indeed represents a culture distinct from the Sican tradition, we face numerous major questions: do we see the prototype or isomorph on the Guayas or Manabi coasts in Ecuador (or conversely south of Lambayeque such as at Huaca El Dragon in the Moche Valley [Schaedel 1966c] or in the Huarmey Valley [Bonavia 1985: 134])? Is it of the same time period as Middle Sican? If two distinct cultures coexisted in the Lambayeque region, what happened to them? Did the collapse of the Middle Sican polity about A.D. 1100 allow the ascent of a Naymlap-derived polity or did the latter cause the former? Are the changes noted at the onset of the Late Sican era, in reality, changes attendant to the observed political ascendancy?

Kosok (1959, 1965) envisioned such a coexistence until the lower Lambayeque polity centered at Chotuna expanded at the expense of middle and upper valley polities centered at Colluz, Mirador, and other sites. However, this scenario is difficult to support given the notable presence of Middle Sican ceramics and architecture at the sites of Chotuna and Mirador.

Cultural Continuities

There has been a strong tendency to emphasize the "distinctiveness" of the Middle Sican iconography and style in the literature. Its impressive coast-wide distribution and seemingly invariable and ubiquitous representation of the Sican Lord in diverse media and techniques of artistic expression have contributed to the emergence and persistence of this impression. Also important to understanding this perception is the seemingly abrupt emergence of the Sican Lord, which some argue represents the legendary arrival of Naymlap. The legend and the perception have effectively reinforced each other.

The basic flaw of logic here is that the critical question of local and preceding traditions is not adequately considered; that is, does the Middle Sican culture represent an autochthonous development out of the preceding Early Sican or some other local culture? Even if Naymlap was an exogenous (Ecuadoran or south of Lambayeque?) elite who somehow successfully imposed himself as the new leader of the local population, the nature of the local culture and responses begs our attention. How was it accomplished? What extant local conditions permitted it to happen? What are the short- and long-term local responses to the arrival and subsequent assimilation?

Much of the Early Sican period appears to have been a time when prestigious Huari-derived styles and iconographies were highly esteemed and locally imitated. However, the present study has shown that the Early Sican art, which had adopted Moche and Huari elements, formed an integral part of (if it was not ancestral to) the Middle Sican iconography and style. The latter seems to have been formalized sometime during the Middle Horizon 2B–3 transition with its own configuration and meaning. Architectural and ceramic evidence from Huaca La Merced and the aforementioned double-spout vessel in the Museo Amano are particularly illuminating in this regard.

I suggest that during this critical, but brief (perhaps a generation or two) period when the Huari polity collapsed (and the Pachacamac and Cajamarca polities were accordingly disrupted), there was an attempt to create a distinct ideology and associated iconography through selective integration of earlier Moche and Huari features into a new overall configuration and value system (Shimada 1985a, n.d.d). These earlier features are particularly prominent in Middle Sican iconography (Menzel 1977; Shimada n.d.d; Zevallos Quiñones 1971). Dorothy Menzel (1977: 61–62), for example, argues that the Sican Lord represents syncretism of the polytheistic concept of "Moche Lords" with the single male Huari deity. At the same time, we should keep in mind that continuity in form between Moche and Huari, on one hand, and Middle Sican features, on the other, does not imply continuity in meaning. Nonetheless, syncretism would have been an effective means of providing some cultural continuities while imbuing them with new ideas, institutions, and priorities.

In fact, as an alternative to the hypohesis of Naymlap's arrival as the initiating mechanism of the Middle Sican culture and polity, we may consider a revitalization or messianic movement (Shimada 1985a, n.d.d; Wallace 1956, 1966; also Ossio 1973), which seems effectively to account for the cultural conditions that prevailed during the Early Sican period and interrelated changes during the Middle Sican era. Here, following the functional and processual perspective offered by Anthony Wallace (1956, 1966), the revitalization movement is conceived of as a specific culture change phenomenon, not a gradual incremental progression, and is characterized by a deliberate, organized effort by members of a given society under stress to establish a new social and moral order that is "more satisfying." The new order is created by removing dissonant features and combining those that were selected into a new identity or configuration with new overall significance. The participants successfully innovate not only discrete, isolated items and features, but a new cultural system. The movement is preconditioned by the coexistence of mutually contradictory beliefs and customs, a circumstance often found in societies burdened by such serious internal problems as factionalism and natural disasters, or conversely, impinged upon over prolonged periods by various cultures that are often politically more powerful.

The rallying focus or catalyst of the revitalization movement is a prophet or some charismatic leader, a local culture hero. Such an individual, with the aid of disciples, within a matter of one or two generations, forces dogmatic rejection of various tangible and intangible aspects of the extant society and culture, and at the same time forces a synthesis of selected features. As a result, the individual may command devotion long after his or her death and may be transformed into an icon.

What we observe in our study area during the Middle Horizon are, in fact, prolonged foreign domination or influence (Middle Cajamarca, Huari, and, perhaps, Pachacamac), rapid changes (Middle Horizon 2B–3) based on synthesis of selected extant and/or earlier features, and their far-ranging impact. Earlier traditions of arsenical copper production and marking of adobe bricks continued from Moche times to Middle Sicán in form, but on a different scale and usage and/or with new meaning. Middle Sicán art became the highly visible symbol of a new identity. Data from Batán Grande have shown that a constellation of major material, behavioral, organizational, and ideological features emerged at roughly the same time, about A.D. 900. Though we cannot specify whether we are dealing with synchronic, systemic changes or a string of cause-effect relationships, this temporal coincidence seems quite significant.

In these respects, the legendary Naymlap may be interpreted as the local leader who initiated the changes that culminated in the Middle Sicán cultural florescence and was thus accorded semi-divine status and a distant mythical origin. The resultant flowering was characterized by, among others, large-scale arsenical copper production, a resurgence of monumental religious structures, unprecedented accumulation of sumptuary goods, and inferred trade with coastal Ecuador (Shimada 1985a,b, 1987a; see Cordy-Collins, this volume).[12]

Clarification of the Early–Middle Sicán relationship has a long way to go. Our sample of Early Sicán ceramics and other material evidence at present is too limited to resolve satisfactorily the questions at hand. The limited material and understanding of the Early Sicán culture we have at the present are, I

---

[12] At the same time, when we consider evidence for the local development of arsenical copper smelting technology and production, we see that the earliest set of smelting furnaces, dating to ca. A.D. 900–950 at HPBG, was already quite well-developed (Shimada 1987b). We have no firm evidence of earlier metallurgical activities at this or any other site in Batán Grande thus far. Are they yet to be found in the study area, or was the arsenical copper technology introduced from elsewhere? We should bear in mind that Moche metallurgists already utilized small quantities of arsenical copper (Lechtman 1979).

suspect, a function of Early Sican materials having been buried deep by the extensive and intensive constructions of the succeeding Middle Sican culture and of inadequate knowledge of their diagnostic features. It is encouraging, however, that the sample size is steadily increasing.

Early–Middle Sican architectural continuities are still poorly understood. Available evidence suggests, however, that the concepts of chamber-fill and encased-columnar construction continued uninterrupted from Moche V through at least the end of the Late Sican period. How these concepts are implemented vary from one period to the next. For example, during the Middle Sican period we see that adobe chambers are built as bounded lattice, unlike the juxtaposed set at Moche V Huaca Fortaleza.

In their pioneering study carried out at the Huacas El Sol and La Luna at the site of Moche, Charles Hastings and Michael Moseley (1975) noted that the tradition of marking bricks began in early Moche III times. Marked Moche bricks have been found in various areas of Moche III presence, near and far, such as the Viru, Santa, and Lambayeque Valleys (Shimada, n.d.a; Shimada and Cavallaro n.d.). In the Lambayeque region the tradition persisted until the Inca conquest (ca. A.D. 1460–70). However, various features of Middle Sican marked bricks imply a careful coordination among numerous adobe makers, construction workers, and supervisory personnel at various levels and locations, much more so than that associated with the Moche adobe marking pattern and segmentary construction (Cavallaro and Shimada 1988, Shimada and Cavallaro 1986, n.d.). As noted above, we are speaking of a reconceptualization of the earlier Moche tradition of marking bricks.

Once again, however, the paucity of relevant data from the Early Sican period and the imprecise character of our archaeological chronology hamper us from being conclusive about whether the seemingly abrupt appearance of the complex Middle Sican pattern of production and use of marked adobe bricks was indigenous or introduced from elsewhere. Examination of bricks used at Huaca La Mayanga with the Moche-Huari syncretic mural, for example, would be helpful. Similarly, Huaca Miguelito in the Zaña Valley, and Huacas Las Estacas and Teodora in the Jequetepeque Valley deserve our attention. The Mirador platform near Eten, the Chotuna-Chornancap Complex, the Sican Precinct, and the Ucupe mound near the mouth of the Zaña River all have platform mounds with a short, straight central ramp (Kosok 1959; 1965: 141–142, 178), and all share at least some of the architectural features under consideration. Kosok suspects that the minor variation seen among these T-shaped platforms reflects temporal differences and that Huaca Miguelito in the Zaña Valley was the prototype for the remainder. This opinion implies that the principal mound at Chornancap postdates Huaca Miguelito and that the T-shaped platform is a Lambayeque development. Such a sequence would cast serious doubt on the exogenous origin of Naymlap.

Cultural Discontinuities

Without doubt the two most apparent and significant cultural discontinuities are the systematic burning of corporate architecture and the attendant abandonent of, first, the Moche V ceremonial city of Pampa Grande around A.D. 700 (Shimada n.d.a) and, later, the Sican Precinct ca. A.D. 1050–1100. The latter is believed to have been causally linked to a major, coterminous iconographic and/or architectural change noted at Chotuna and HPBG, and extensive water damage observed in the Moche Valley (Nials et al. 1979a,b; Moseley 1987, and this volume; Moseley et al. 1981; cf. Wells 1987), at Pacatnamu (Donnan 1986: 22), Chotuna (Donnan [Chotuna], this volume), and Batan Grande (Craig and Shimada 1986; see below).

Radiocarbon dates for the cutting of the locally available hardwood logs used in major pyramidal and auxiliary constructions in the Sican Precinct suggest that the latest round of construction before the fire and abandonment occurred around A.D. 1050. The exact date of the fire is not as yet established. For the time being, the date of A.D. 1100 is used as the ending date of the Middle Sican on the assumption that the fire occurred within fifty years of the cutting date. This date is quite reasonable considering the independent set of radiocarbon dates obtained for the site of HPBG which, as detailed, showed a marked shift in ceramics about A.D. 1100.

The extent of the fire can be gauged, for example, by the fact that an area of at least 40 × 60 m in the south sector of Huaca Las Ventanas shows a thick layer (up to 50–60 cm) of thoroughly burnt roof and other architectural remains. Adobe-mortar walls were fired to the point of being friable and flaky. The hardwood posts in the middle of these walls were thoroughly carbonized. Perhaps the most dramatic illustration comes from the Huaca El Moscon pyramid. The fire along a roughly 5-m wide portion of the western edge of the pyramid was so intense that it completely baked and discolored adobe bricks and clay mortar down to at least 2 m below the top adobe layer. In fact, there are indications that the discoloration may reach some 3 m below. The pattern and extent of discoloration suggest that a large quantity of fuel was piled against the western face of the pyramid and set on fire (thus the alternative name of the pyramid, El Horno).

We will probably never know whether the fires at various huacas in the Precinct occurred at the same moment in time. At least for Huacas El Corte and Las Ventanas we have evidence that suggests the fires occurred close to their abandonment. Architectural remains preserved by the fire show that it occurred when the architecture (e.g., cane and cord of roofs and painted plaster) was still in excellent condition. We can be reasonably sure that the fire was intentional, not only from the abnormally intense heat damage, but also from the discontinuous and highly selective (pyramid tops in all but one case) contemporaneous locations where evidence occurs. What brought about this destruction is still not clear, though a severe drought of over thirty years' duration starting around A.D. 1020 is likely to have contributed to it (Schaaf et al. n.d.; Thompson et al. 1985). Within the past 1,500 years, there has been only one other drought of comparable severity and duration, a thirty-two-year drought between A.D. 562 and 594 (Schaaf n.d.: 63; ibid.) that undoubtedly contributed to the Moche IV-V transition.

It is argued that the above destruction in the Sican Precinct and Middle and Late Sican cultural discontinuities are effects of the same processes. The temporal coincidence is definite. The highly selective destruction of the pyramids and associated compounds, and little evidence of their repairs or reoccupation, point to a concerted effort to remove the extant political and religious leadership. In contrast, at HPBG away from the inferred Middle Sican capital, we see no physical destruction, but ceramics no longer bear the Sican Lord image.

The inferred contemporaneous constructions at the Chotuna-Chornancap Complex manifest no evidence of an abrupt and violent end such as seen in the Sican Precinct (Donnan [Chotuna], this volume). This difference should be remembered in assessing the Naymlap legend.

It is apparent, however, that the destruction and abandonment of the Sican Precinct was accompanied close in time by the rather abrupt, nearly complete disappearance of the prestigious Sican Lord images that were so ubiquitous during the Middle Sican era and the initiation of monumental construction at El Purgatorio. Large-scale copper alloy production also seems to begin at Cerro Huaringa (and possibly Cerro Sajino) at this time, early in the Late Sican A period. Thus, the Middle-Late Sican transition was marked by significant changes in the ideology and iconography and the settlement pattern/power seat in the La Leche Valley (and perhaps elsewhere in the Lambayeque Valley Complex). The destruction by fire and associated cultural changes are notable for their magnitude and breadth. In this respect, they may be interpreted as the material manifestations of problems associated with Fempellec, a descendant of Naymlap who, as the story goes, unsuccessfully tried to move the sacred idol of the Naymlap dynasty and was enticed by the Devil (Table 2; see Donnan [Naymlap], this volume). But the material evidence of destruction comes from the Sican Precinct and not the Chotuna-Chornancap Complex. Further, if we accept the above scenario, how do we explain the "distinct" character of the Chornancap mural?

The Legendary Thirty-day Rain and Flood?

I have referred to major flood damage previously. Before ending this discussion, let me briefly consider archaeological verification of the thirty days of rain and floods described in the Naymlap legend. Exposed on both banks of the present La Leche River course (before the 1984–85 road construction) are remains of adobe constructions that were once parts of Huaca Oro. In fact, the 1925 flood of the river washed out Middle Sican burials rich in gold objects from these banks next to Huaca Oro (Valcárcel 1937). Before the 1983–84 flood of the river and Tucume Canal (which carries water from the river directly to the area around El Purgatorio; Figs. 3, 5), there were still vestiges of an adobe mound called Huaca Abeja at the inferred southeast corner of the T-shaped Sican Precinct (see Shimada et al. 1981: 413, 431, figs. 8, 32).

Further, a geomorphological and hydrological study by A. Craig (Shimada et al. 1981: 431) indicated that the Tucume Canal is actually an ancient channel of the La Leche River, and that sometime in the past, most likely during a major flood, the river crevassed from the original southwestward channel and began flowing westward along the new (present) channel. During the 1983 El Niño intrusion, attendant torrential rains swelled the river to the point that it shifted its course back to the ancient channel (Tucume Canal). It appears, then, that the force and volume of the ancient flood that caused the earlier shift matched that of the 1983–84 flow. Considering that the Huaca Oro pyramid construction is dated around A.D. 1050, it is likely that this ancient flood postdates its construction; however, we do not know how closely in time. Data from the excavation of a room with a flagstone floor in the nearby south sector of Huaca Las Ventanas help to date that flood more precisely. The excavation revealed a silt-sand laminated layer full of small, evenly distributed chunks of charcoal covering a large part of the somewhat tilted floor. That charcoal is believed to have resulted from the conflagration at the end of the Middle Sican period, about A.D. 1050–1100. It was apparently sorted, transported, and deposited by flood water, which suggests that the flood in question occurred close in time to A.D. 1100.

This conclusion corroborates findings from analysis of deep-core samples drilled from the Quelccaya ice cap at the northern edge of the Tititica Basin (Cerveny et al. 1987; Thompson et al. 1984, 1985). Local and pan-Andean meteorological studies indicate that, though the Peruvian highlands stretch across 15° of latitude, the meteorology of the entire region is governed by the southeast tradewinds and annual southward and northward migrations of this equatorial trough (Schaaf n.d.: 39). Based on his climatological study of the northern highlands above the Chicama Valley, W. E. Howell (1954: 41) concluded that the "local pattern of rainfall is determined mostly by local orography but its occurrence or non-occurrence is governed by air-mass characteristics associated with the large scale weather situation." This conclusion is also supported by the pan-Andean climatological study by A. M. Johnson (1976) and others. Overall, the 1,500-year precipitation record from Quelccaya can be used directly to reconstruct the history of north highland precipitation and thus major fluctuations in water availability on the ancient North Coast (Schaaf n.d.: 55; Schaaf et al. n.d.). Similar extrapolation, however, is not possible for Chile and Ecuador, which are under different climatic regimes.

The precipitation records point to a major El Niño around A.D. 1050 within the span of the prolonged (thirty-one-year long), severe drought referred to earlier. Just as the El Niño that occurred during the thirty-two-year drought in the late sixth century is suspected to have had a particularly strong impact over much of the North Coast (e.g., soil erosion) due to the prevailing hyperaridity, the El Niño around A.D. 1050 probably wrought similar havoc over a wide area.

At the same time, there were many suspected El Niño events over the span of the Quelccaya record. Given the imprecise nature of archaeological dating, archaeologists should guard against the temptation to juggle their dates to fit the precisely dated (down to the year) "El Niños" in the Quelccaya sequence or others that are imprecisely dated by archaeological means.

Elsewhere we described a massive flood deposit (more than 1 m thick) recorded along the 5 km Poma Canal, which cuts through the Sican Precinct linking the La Leche and Pacora Rivers (Craig and Shimada 1986; Shimada et al. 1981: 43). Middle to late Middle Sican burials interred in the deposit indicate that the flood responsible for this massive deposit occurred sometime before an estimated date of A.D. 1050. In other words, the inferred flood that severed Huaca Oro constructions is distinct and postdates the one responsible for this massive deposit.[13]

The only water-deposited silt-sand layer (up to 30 cm thick and containing some charcoal bits and sherds) found at HPBG overlies the Moche V levels. At Pampa Grande we found Moche V rooms filled with more than 1 m of water-deposited sand that preserved intact 1-m high storage jars in situ (Craig and Shimada 1986; Shimada n.d.a). The first phase constructions of Mound II, Huaca Soledad (north of the Sican Precinct—with an associated date of about A.D. 650—also show extensive water damage. On the basis of the preceding data, we may argue that there was a major flood about A.D. 700 that affected an extensive portion of the Lambayeque Valley Complex.

In fact, a major flood close in time to A.D. 700 raises the possibility that the Naymlap legend may correspond to Moche V settlement and related changes (cf. Donnan 1978: 101; Means 1931: 54–56). Consider curious coincidences between the end of Moche V Pampa Grande and Middle Sican occupation of the Sican Precinct. Both manifest large-scale, intentional burn-

---

[13] The date of this massive deposit was erroneously interpreted in a recent article by Moseley (1987: 9).

ing of corporate architecture and abandonment close in time with major flooding. Could recurrent events have been forged into myth?

Also, it is worth considering the unknown duration of the interregnum following the thirty-day rains and resultant flood described in the Naymlap legend as well as the notion of the founder of a given ethnic group arriving by raft. A high-status individual aboard a raft is a recurrent Andean theme depicted in both Moche and Middle Sican art (see Zuidema, this volume). One may argue that the legend describes the arrival at Pampa Grande of a fleeing king and his entourage from Moche and their establishment of a new capital at Pampa Grande—omitting the fact that the area was preconditioned by a preceding conquest (i.e., Moche I–III presence [Shimada n.d.a]). Though suggestive, this scenario cannot account for the location and name of the Temple of Chot.

It is likely that there were at least two separate floods, one dating close to A.D. 700 and another close to A.D. 1100. Although the legendary thirty-day rains and resultant flood may correspond to one of these two, it should be remembered that, as yet, we cannot be certain of the validity of Naymlap or the timing of his arrival and that not all major floods leave archaeologically recognizable deposits.

Archaeology–History Concordance

In addition to various discrepancies and concordances between archaeology and history already noted earlier, let me identify a few others here. Various scholars since the days of Brüning have identified the site of Chotuna as the location of the legendary Temple of Chot mentioned in the Naymlap legend (e.g., Brüning 1922; Kosok 1965; Kroeber 1930; Means 1917; Rondón n.d.; Trimborn 1979). The legend relates that the temple was built on the bank of a major river near its mouth. As mentioned previously, our geomorphological and hydrological study suggests that the site of Chornancap, rather than Chotuna, fits the historical description (Shimada et al. 1981: 434). While the T-shaped mound of Chornancap is situated on a river, Chotuna bears no relationship to any significant surface drainage. An extensive sand sheet that began moving inland sometime in the past blocked the surface flow of water downstream to Chornancap (see Shimada et al. 1981: 434, fig. 33).

In regard to the chronological issues surrounding Chimu and Inca domination of the study area, archaeological dates from Batan Grande provide strong support to historical reconstruction (e.g., Rowe 1945, 1948). The Chimu intrusion appears to have occurred sometime after A.D. 1350, while that of the Inca took place sometime around A.D. 1450.

Though space limitation does not allow a detailed discussion, it should be clearly noted that archaeological evidence from the study area provides some independent support for late Pre-Hispanic maritime trade linking Chincha, Lambayeque, and coastal Ecuador suggested by Colonial documents (Rostworowski 1970, 1975; see also Salomon 1986, 1987). Trade was apparently managed by specialists (*mercaderes*) who utilized copper as a standard medium of exchange. Among the valued goods obtained from coastal Ecuador were Spondylus shells and *chaquiras* (shell and stone beads).

We have already noted a surge in the amount of Spondylus shell used by the Middle Sican culture, including an estimated four hundred whole Spondylus shells interred with an estimated two hundred human sacrifices and two thousand bundles of arsenical copper foil at the Huaca Rodillon pyramid. The shells are also frequently and prominently depicted in Middle Sican art, including their collection by divers discussed by Alana Cordy-Collins in this volume.

The strongest support for trade, however, comes from the significant degree of overlap in intrinsic and extrinsic qualities of the *naipes* and *moneda hacha*—the inferred primitive currencies—found in contemporaneous Lambayeque and upper Piura, on the one hand, and Tumbez to south coastal Ecuador, on the other (Shimada 1985a,b, 1987a; Fig. 31). Both "currencies" share internal standardization of size, form, material, and manufacturing techniques, in addition to portability, durability, and the established functional and ideological value of copper (Holm 1975: 2–3). The beginning of

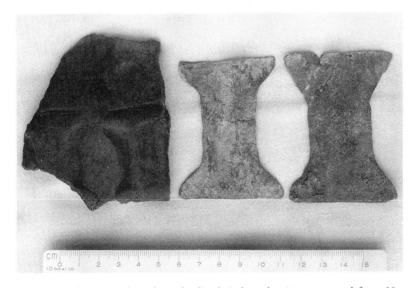

Fig. 31   At right, examples of standardized, I-shaped *naipes* recovered from Huaca Menor, Sican Precinct and, at left, a sherd decorated with a *naipe* motif excavated in the southern sector, Huaca Las Ventanas, suggesting the significance of *naipes* in the Sican heartland.

large-scale production and use can be securely dated to Middle Sican in respect to the *naipe,* while *moneda hacha* has been conventionally assigned much more imprecisely to the florescence of the Huancavilca-Manteño and Milagro-Quevedo cultures sometime after A.D. 800–900 (e.g., Holm 1966/7, 1972, 1982; Meggers 1966). Olaf Holm (1966/7: 140–141; 1975: 9–10; see also Estrada 1961; Pedersen 1976) has suggested that *moneda hacha* was possibly imported to coastal Ecuador from northern Peru because there are neither local copper deposits nor evidence of copper smelting.

Naipes, typically stacked or formed into bundles, have been reported as funerary offerings in Lambayeque (from Huacas El Corte, Menor, Las Ventanas, and La Merced, all in the Sican Precinct, and from San Jose and Sipan [Bennett 1939; Pedersen 1976; Shimada 1985a,b, 1987a; Wassén 1973]) and upper Piura (from the east base of Cerro Vicus, Huaca Carbonel, Nor-Peru and Batanes to Encantada near the city of Chulacanas). Though the number of excavated burials with *naipes* in Lambayeque is thus far limited (three), as one would expect, the total number of *naipes* and/or their size/shape categories seems to correlate well with tomb size and the overall range, quality, and quantity of funerary goods. This pattern of differential accumulation also holds for Ecuadoran *moneda hacha* (see, e.g., Holm 1966/7, 1975; Meggers 1966).

Moneda hacha is described as having been cut out of pure copper sheets. The *naipe,* on the other hand, is cut from hammered sheets of arsenical copper (typically 2–5 percent arsenic) locally smelted in Batan Grande using essentially local ores and fuels (Shimada 1985a,b, 1987a). *Naipes* from upper Piura await compositional analysis, but other "copper" objects of Middle Sican style recovered in this area have been determined to be arsenical copper (Noemi Vilela E., personal communication, August 1988). Future compositional analyses of *moneda hacha* that take this into account, I suspect, will show that at least some specimens are made of arsenical copper. Trace element signatures in these specimens may allow us to verify the trade hypothesis.

In addition to the above compositional analysis, one feature that requires further clarification is the frequency and context in which *naipe*-like I-shaped (as opposed to typical T-shaped) *moneda hacha* occurs on coastal Ecuador. We know only that T-shaped specimens are not known south of Tumbez (Minato 1960) and that I-shaped pieces occur occasionally on coastal Ecuador. The two bodies of data should help determine whether we are dealing with one unified trade network linking coastal Ecuador and northern Peru or two smaller, partially overlapping networks centered perhaps in the Guayas Basin and Lambayeque regions.

In essence, the proposed Middle Sican trade with coastal Ecuador would represent a local antecedent of the ethnohistorically described late Pre-Hispanic status traders of Chincha-Lambayeque in coastal Peru. That the *naipe* is spatially and chronologically confined to sites in the Lambayeque and upper Piura areas is significant. However, the bundles of narrow, elongated arsenical copper foil often found in Late Sican and Sican-Chimu burials may not only be later versions of the Middle Sican *naipe,* but also have a wider distribution.

Overall, the preceding discussion shows that our study area distinguishes itself from the southern half of the North Coast, not only in regard to architectural features and associated labor organization, but also in its interaction with neighboring areas, particularly the north highlands and coastal Ecuador. In fact, the list of distinct cultural features is much more extensive and includes, among others, arsenical copper metallurgy, Middle Sican shaft tombs, and the preeminence of pyramidal religious structures (Shimada n.d. a; Shimada and Cavallaro 1986, n.d.).[14] Historical sources give us some general indications of the cultural subdivisions on the North Coast, but it is archaeology that offers specifics, time depth, and explanations of possible underlying reasons.

CONCLUSIONS

This has not been an easy paper to write given (a) the complexity and number of issues involved, (b) my ambivalence as to the feasibility and worthiness of the proposed archaeological verification of legends, and (c) the diversity and quantity of archaeological data acquired over the past fourteen years, that, at the same time, are uneven in quantity and quality for different topics and time periods, if not seemingly contradictory at times. The basic thrust of this paper has been twofold: to present as much specific data as possible on an area and for time periods that have long merited our attention but have not received it, and to consider contextually and processually cultural continuities and discontinuities. Though the available data have been examined primarily with the testing of the Naymlap legend in mind, there are ample data that are valuable in dealing with the Chimu and Inca domination of the study area.

In spite of various limitations, this paper can help to clarify various matters:

1) It is quite evident that the chronological issues being examined in this volume require better regional chronologies and a critical use of radiocarbon dates. In addition, limitations of stylistic dating have become quite evident.

2) Archaeological verification of the legendary accounts of Naymlap's or Taycanamo's arrival is meaningful only if the "before" and "after" pictures of regional conditions and processes are concurrently investigated at both

[14] This list contains a number of features, such as "primitive currencies" and shaft tombs, that are shared by contemporaneous cultures in coastal Ecuador (see Estrada 1961). These shared features, together with notable emphasis on Spondylus and the reference to balsa-wood rafts, would make coastal Ecuador (e.g., Guayas coast and basin) a logical location to study in seeking the provenance of Naymlap.

the point of origin and destination. We need to clarify the general cultural conditions surrounding such events and their long-term effects, not just to identify "trait intrusion" or "site-unit intrusion" or similar characteristics at two locations that presumably represent the point of origin and the destination. Even if we were able to show the historicity of Naymlap, what is his cultural significance? What general conditions would have allowed a group of exogenous elite to establish itself readily in a new locale? How would such a process be archaeologically manifested? Do the ceramic and iconographic changes and continuities noted here faithfully reflect the sort of cultural changes described in the Naymlap legend? Further, post hoc historical descriptions may reduce what is in essence a diachronic process to a series of discrete events, giving an illusion of ready archaeological identification. It is my distinct impression that historians may have unrealistic expectations and images of archaeologists' capability in detecting and dating specific historical events. The "Pompeii" phenomenon is extremely rare.

In recent years an ethnohistorical component has become a standard feature of any major archaeological project in the Andes. However, far from approximating the ideal of interdisciplinary research, the role of collaborating historians and ethnohistorians has been limited to research hypothesis formulation and/or searching for ethnohistorical analogies to observed or inferred archaeological phenomena. Though ethnohistorical data are commonly used in locating late Pre-Hispanic sites, long-term, problem-specific joint fieldwork (not just day trips) has been quite rare. Active fieldwork collaboration, in addition to various scholastic benefits, would most likely reduce the misguided confidence and expectations that some historians and ethnohistorians have in archaeology. The converse is likely to be true as well.

3) There is some tantalizing correspondence between archaeological data, on the one hand, and historical accounts of Naymlap, as well as the Chimu and Inca domination of the study area, on the other. There are, at the same time, serious discrepancies between them, particularly in regard to the inferred timing of Naymlap's arrival (onset of Moche V, Early, Middle, or Late Sican?) and his exogenous origin (north-central coast of Peru, Guayas Basin of south coastal Ecuador, or simply upstream of the Lambayeque River?). We cannot claim to have verified or refuted the Naymlap legend. There are enough ambiguities in both archaeological and historical records to entice us into endless speculation and pigeon-holing. In general, this volume reaffirms what we have known for quite some time, that productive collaboration between archaeology and history requires a thorough understanding of one's own methodological and substantive limitations. The numerous comments that have appeared in print on the role of ethnographic analogy in archaeology are certainly applicable here.

4) One area for which we have a clear picture is future tasks. For example,

we need to improve our understanding of Early and Late Sican settlement patterns, ceramic and absolute chronologies, and cultural dynamics. The nature of Early-Middle Sican cultural linkage could not be adequately determined with the presently available data. One scenario that merits further investigation is that the inferred Naymlap-related culture may be coterminous with, but distinct from, the Middle Sican culture. Related to this is the task of elucidating the broader significance of the observed Middle-Late Sican iconographic and settlement pattern-architectural changes—are they in any way related to the ascendancy of the Naymlap-related culture? Concurrently, we must define the occupational history at Chornancap better.

Though largely ignored in this volume, we must consider the northern coastal situation in close coordination with developments in the adjacent northern highlands. The ebb and flow of Moche and Sican polities are inversely mirrored in the distribution and technical and stylistic coherence of Cajamarca-style ceramics (Shimada 1987b, n.d.a; Terada and Matsumoto 1985). In other words, coastal developments were sometimes stimulated and other times constrained by activities of adjacent highland peer polities (see Renfrew 1986). Lowland-highland interaction is one area for productive future collaboration between archaeologists and ethnohistorians, and specific research issues and directions have already been elucidated (e.g., Ramírez 1985; Rostworowski 1985; Schaedel 1985b).

Possible correspondence between the legendary thirty-day flood and geological and archaeological evidence of a flood sometime around A.D. 1100 was discussed in this and other papers in this volume. It is interesting that other significant changes seem to occur around A.D. 1100, notably the conflagration closely followed by the abandonment of the Sican Precinct and the disappearance of the Sican Lord images. Related to these changes is the possibility that Taycanamo, the founder of the Chimu Kingdom from the north, came from the Lambayeque region at the time of the Middle Sican collapse about A.D. 1100 seeking refuge and an opportunity to re-establish his political base (see Kosok 1965: 180). This is yet another possibility deserving scrutiny by archaeologists and ethnohistorians.

APPENDIX. ANNOTATED TABLE OF RADIOCARBON DATES FOR THE LAMBAYEQUE REGION

Context and Material	Lab No.	Radiocarbon Age (BP ± 1δ; ad)	Calibrated Date
Pampa Grande			
burnt cane, roof of Spondylus workshop, rectangular compound (Unit 15)	SMU-682	1380 ± 40 BP; ad 570 f	A.D. 650 ± 20

Unless the cane was reused or lasted for a few generations (a definite possibility), the difference between this and other dates for Moche V occupation at Pampa Grande and elsewhere (Batan Grande, Galindo) seems a bit wide.

Context and Material	Lab No.	Radiocarbon Age (BP ± 1δ; ad)	Calibrated Date
carbonized corn kernels in an urn placed in the floor of Structure 43, Unit 45, Sector H	A-1705	1380 ± 70 BP; ad 570	A.D. 650 ± 50

Though maize is a C-4 plant, no C-12/C-13 fractionation correction has been measured for this sample. A corrected date may be somewhat younger and closer to the cotton dates.

Context and Material	Lab No.	Radiocarbon Age (BP ± 1δ; ad)	Calibrated Date
charred cotton, floor of elite compound ("Deer House"; Unit 14)	SMU-399	1300 ± 60 BP; ad 650	A.D. 710 ± 60

This cotton seems to represent a single harvest in the process of being carded. This sample should yield a very precise date to help us pinpoint the termination of Moche V occupation at the site.

Context and Material	Lab No.	Radiocarbon Age (BP ± 1δ; ad)	Calibrated Date
burnt wooden post atop platform mound (Huaca 18), Sector H	A-1704	1280 ± 70 BP; ad 690	A.D. 740 ± 80
charred cotton, floor of burnt platform mound in rectangular enclosure (Unit 16)	SMU-644	1250 ± 50 BP; ad 700	A.D. 770 ± 70

The comment for SMU-399 applies here. In this regard, a difference of some 50 radiocarbon years between SMU-399 and 644 dates seems too wide. Squatter occupation is unlikely considering the absence of any supporting stratigraphic and artifactual data and widespread burning of formal settings.

Overall, these dates are all reasonable. We may interpret the SMU-399 and 644 dates derived from an inferred "single harvest" of cotton as indicating the end of Moche V occupation at the site, while other dates may indicate how early Moche V occupation may date back.

Batan Grande Sites

Huaca del Pueblo Batan Grande Trench 1/2-'79

charcoal from firepit near the sterile sand, Stratum XII, Level N — SMU-873 — 1540 ± 60 BP; ad 410 — A.D. 520 ± 70

This sample, more than 5 m below the present-day mound top, provides an approximate date for the initiation of human occupation at the site.

charcoal from firepit in the sandy Stratum XII, Level D/E — SMU-901 — 1430 ± 60 BP; ad 520 f — A.D. 620 ± 40

charcoal from buried, discolored, and sooted vessel near the top of Stratum XII — SMU-876 — 1410 ± 60 BP; ad 540 — A.D. 640 ± 40

Moche Phase V sherds, including a large figurine fragment, were recovered from the floor, as well as in the overlying sandy deposit. This date compares reasonably well with the Moche V dates from Pampa Grande.

charcoal from firepit, Stratum XI, Level D — SMU-1066 — 1130 ± 70 BP; ad 820 f — A.D. 910 ± 70

Associated with Sican blackware decorated with burnished "goose skin" dots, Sican Painted Plates ("Coastal Cajamarca"), and paleteada (paddle-decorated) wares. Roughly marks the transition from Early to Middle Sican.

charcoal from firepit, Stratum XI Level A — SMU-899 — 1100 ± 40 BP; ad 850 f — A.D. 940 ± 60

Middle Sican burnished blackware with the diagnostic Sican Lord images defined by burnished incisions now coexists with the Sican Painted Plates ("Coastal Cajamarca") and paleteada (paddle-decorated) wares.

charcoal from firepit, Stratum IX — SMU-875 — 940 ± 60 BP; ad 1010 — A.D. 1070 ± 70

Near the beginning of the Middle Sican occupation.

charcoal from firepit, Stratum VIII — SMU-1068 — 890 ± 60 BP; ad 1060 f — A.D. 1140 ± 80

Transition to Late Sican. Diagnostic Middle Sican blackware and Sican Painted Plates essentially disappear, though paleteada ware continues.

charcoal from a firepit, Stratum VI-A — SMU-900 — 830 ± 60 BP; ad 1120 f — A.D. 1210 ± 60

Late Sican

charcoal from firepit, Stratum IV — SMU-902 — 710 ± 40 BP; ad 1240 f — A.D. 1280 ± 30

Overall, these dates for T-1/2-'79 are highly consistent with the stratigraphy and associated ceramics.

Huaca del Pueblo Batan Grande Trenches 3-'82 and 4-'83

charcoal from a "firepit" on Floor 6, Rm 41, T-4-'83	SMU-1745	990 ± 50 BP; ad 960 fp	A.D. 1030 ± 35
charred wooden post bottom found intruding into Floor 5, Room 40, T-4-'83	SMU-1324	1010 ± 20 BP; ad 940 f	A.D. 1020 ± 10

The above two dates should be seen in light of SMU-1322, which is based on a sample from an intrusive post with clear point of origin. SMU-1324 is also an intrusive sample and likely to have been part of a Middle Sican construction. Its point of origin appears to be immediately below Furnace Set 4 (SMU-1312).

Both Floor 6, Room 41 and Floor 5, Room 40 (adjacent rooms and nearly coterminous stratigraphically) yielded Moche V ceramics. SMU-1745 sample was dated in order to provide independent verification of the Moche V date. Though we identified the charcoal cluster that yielded this sample as a "firepit," given the resultant date and two similar dates from two "intrusive" samples from nearby locations, we now suspect that SMU-1745 is also intrusive—that is, that the charcoal is likely to have been the preserved portion of a Middle Sican wooden post whose tip had been fire-hardened.

charcoal from hearth (Feature 154), Floor 5, Room 38, T-4-'83	SMU-1320	850 ± 40 BP; ad 1100 f	A.D. 1190 ± 50

In light of dates from stratigraphically lower and higher positions, this date seems *too young* by nearly 200–250 years to be acceptable. This is by far the most problematical date.

charcoal from buried inverted urn (annealing brazier? Feature 135), Floor 9, Room 33, T-4-'83	SMU-1328	1040 ± 80 BP; ad 910 f	A.D. 990 ± 80

This date seems reasonable for its stratigraphic position.

charcoal from a firepit immediately below Smelter 14, Furnace Set 4, T-4-'83—may be mixed with ash and soil	SMU-1312	990 ± 50 BP; ad 960 f	A.D. 1030 ± 40

In light of SMU-1314 and SMU-1746 dates obtained from samples derived from somewhat higher stratigraphic locations, this SMU-1312 date was expected to be somewhat older.

charcoal from a firepit immediately below Smelter 8, Furnace Set 2, Floor 1, Rm 38, T-4-'83	SMU-1746	980 ± 50 BP; ad 970 f	A.D. 1035 ± 40
charcoal and humates from Smelter 6, Furnace Set 2, T-4-'83	SMU-1326	1140 ± 70 BP; ad 810 f	A.D. 910 ± 70
charcoal from the trough of Furnace Set 2, Floor 6, Room 34, T-4-'83	SMU-1314	990 ± 50 BP; ad 960 f	A.D. 1030 ± 40

The sample contexts for SMU-1314 and SMU-1746 argue that their dates should be quite close, with the latter being somewhat older. In this sense, the closeness of these dates is quite reasonable. At the same time, the preceding conclusion automatically brings the SMU-1326 date into question. It may be up to 100 years *too old*. Its problematical nature may be explained by the fact it was obtained from a very small, heterogeneous sample.

charcoal from a burnt wooden post (Feature 166) intruding from above (from slightly above Furnace Set 2?) into Floor 3, Room 40, T-4-'83   SMU-1322   920 ± 50 BP; ad 1030 f   A.D. 1100 ± 70

charcoal from Smelter 2, Furnace Set 1, Floor 28 (Feature 59) between Levels 22 and 23, T-3-'8   SMU-1175   860 ± 50 BP; ad 1090 f   A.D. 1180 ± 70

In light of dates from stratigraphically higher and lower (in particular other dates derived from charcoal associated with earlier smelters) positions, the preceding date seems *too young* by 50–100 years.

charcoal from an inverted urn (annealing brazier? Feature 117), Floor 4, Room 31, T-4-'83   SMU-1313   856 ± 40 BP; ad 1094   A.D. 1172 ± 73

Seems a bit too young (50 years?) for its stratigraphic position and in respect to the following two dates.

charcoal from the hearth in Feature 113, Floor 7, Room 27, T-4-'83   SMU-1315   860 ± 50 BP; ad 1090 f   A.D. 1180 ± 70

burnt wooden post (Feature 111), Floor 7, Room 29, T-4-'83   SMU-1321   860 ± 30 BP; ad 1090 f   A.D. 1180 ± 40

The two preceding dates are reasonable in that the contexts from which the samples were drawn are stratigraphically quite close to each other. There is some doubt as to the original stratigraphic position of the post for SMU-1321.

charcoal from a burnt post (Feature 106), Floor 5, Room 29, T-4-'83   SMU-1744   850 ± 40 BP; ad 1100 fp   A.D. 1190 ± 50

Stratigraphically this sample context is just above that of SMU-1321 and should be slightly younger. Though they are reverse of the stratigraphic order, they are close to each other.

charcoal from an inverted urn (annealing brazier? Feature 117), Floor 4, Room 31, T-4-'83   SMU-1313   860 ± 40 BP; ad 1090 f   A.D. 1180 ± 60

charcoal from a hearth (Feature 53), Floor 22, Level 16L, T-3-'82   SMU-1209   810 ± 50 BP; ad 1140 f   A.D. 1230 ± 40

charcoal from the hearth at the corner of Walls 37 and 42, Floor 22, Room 13, T-3-'82   SMU-1743   780 ± 28 BP; ad 1170 fp   A.D. 1260 ± 20

charcoal from a thoroughly burnt small square-shaped   SMU-1176   710 ± 60 BP; ad 1240 f   A.D. 1290 ± 40 oven-like room (Feature 49, Room 14), Floor 21, Level 16, T-3-'83

The last three dates, though internally consistent, seem somewhat young for their stratigraphic positions. We suspect that this situation stems from a prolonged use of these floors and hearths.

charcoal from a firepit (Feature 32), Floor 19, Room 10, T-3-'82	SMU-1183	860 ± 50 BP; ad 1090 f	A.D. 1180 ± 70

The preceding date is *too old* (by about 100 or more years?) for its stratigraphic position given that stratigraphically higher SMU-1176, -1209, and -1743 dates are considerably younger.

charcoal from a firepit (Feature 27), Quad. 13, Room 7, T-3-'82	SMU-1329	750 ± 50 BP; ad 1200 f	A.D. 1270 ± 30
seeds from pods (*Campomanesia latif*) preserved in a storage pit (Feature 7), Floor 14, Quad. 27, T-3-'82	SMU-1341	660 ± 70 BP; ad 1290 f	A.D. 1320 ± 50
seeds and pods (*Campomanesia latif*) preserved in a storage pit (Feature 7), Floor 14, Quad. 27, T-3	SMU-1334	650 ± 30 BP; ad 1300 f	A.D. 1320 ± 40

The last two dates (SMU-1334 and SMU-1341) are excellent indications of the technical precision and control of the SMU dates. Two samples (seeds vs. seeds and pods) that are likely to represent single-season harvest yielded two nearly identical dates. Chimu ceramics make their first appearance at this site just a few floors higher. Thus these two dates together help bracket the earliest possible date of Imperial Chimu intrusion into the Batan Grande region as ca. A.D. 1350.

Overall, the dates from T-1/2-'79 are most reasonable in regard to their agreement with stratigraphic positions of the samples and associated ceramics. T-3-'82 and T-4-'83 dates have some internal problems, in particular SMU-1183, -1328, and -1745.

However, two sets of dates from T-1/2-'79, on the one hand, and stratigraphically linked T-3-'82 and T-4-'83, on the other, dovetail effectively to cover much of the thousand-year long Pre-Hispanic occupation of the site. With some half a dozen exceptions, the dates are generally consistent with the stratigraphic positions of samples used.

Huaca Las Ventanas

charcoal from firepit on the floor that immediately underlies the buried Wall 1, Eastern Sector	Beta-3403	1090 ± 60 BP; ad 860	A.D. 950 ± 60

Wall 1 is believed to represent part of a Middle Sican Phase 1 construction at Huaca Las Ventanas. The wall defined the eastern perimeter of the monumental sector. The wall, over 3.5 m in height and having the identical orientation as the principal pyramid, was completely but carefully buried when the pyramid was later enlarged. To the south of Wall 1 is another buried wall that is stratigraphically lower and has a slightly different orientation. This may be an Early Sican construction. This date is reasonable in light of Early Sican and early Middle Sican dates from other sites.

| log buried in the clay mortar foundation underlying constructions in the south sector | SMU-1070 | 970 ± 50 BP; ad 980 f | A.D. 1050 ± 50 |
| burnt roof, adobe enclosure overlying the clay mortar foundation (SMU-1070) | Beta-3402 | 980 ± 50 BP; ad 970 | A.D. 1040 ± 40 |

The above two dates, though essentially contemporaneous, are reversed in terms of their stratigraphic positions. The roof from which the sample for Beta-3402 was derived was built upon the foundation that contained the log that supplied the sample for SMU-1070. Archaeologically, one would expect perhaps 50 years difference between them. The observed (admittedly minor) discrepancy may be a problem of comparing two dates generated by two different laboratories.

| aggregate charcoal sample from a charcoal layer that covered Floor 4 (flagstone floor), Room 1, Excavation Area 1, south sector | SMU-1820 | 910 ± 30 BP; ad 1040 | A.D. 1120 ± 50 |

The charcoal layer was partially mixed with and covered by water-laid silt and sand.

Huaca El Corte

| charcoal from burnt roof atop Platform Mound 1 | Beta-1802 | 985 ± 65 BP; ad 965 | A.D. 1040 ± 60 |
| charcoal from burnt roof of a structure at the east base of Platform Mound 1 | SMU-1622 | 990 ± 30 BP; ad 960 fp | A.D. 1030 ± 20 |

These two dates are quite reasonable in respect to each other and other Middle Sican monumental constructions. The two constructions that yielded the samples are only 20 m apart and form parts of a single architectural complex. We suspect that they were burnt down within ca. 50 years of the construction.

| charcoal derived from a "pre-Chavin" burial, cemetery | TK-30 | 2880 ± 100 BP; bc 930★ | 1080 ± 140 B.C. |

Not much can be said about the nature and exact context of the sample. This is a sample submitted by Jorge Zevallos Quiñones (not illustrated in Fig. 4).

Huaca Rodillona

| charcoal from a partially burnt wooden post atop the pyramid | Beta-13933 | 1000 ± 60 BP; ad 950 | A.D. 1020 ± 50 |
| horizontally laid log at the south base of the pyramid | SMU-1625 | 990 ± 40 BP; ad 960 fp | A.D. 1030 ± 30 |

These two dates are consistent with our reconstruction of a rapid, single-episode construction of the pyramid using the efficient chamber-fill technique. The log at the base gave an appropriately earlier (though minor) date.

Huaca Oro

| horizontally laid log at the northwest base of the pyramid | SMU-1330 | 970 ± 40 BP; ad 980 f | A.D. 1040 ± 40 |

The sample represents the outer portion of a well-preserved log. It should give an approximate date for cutting of the tree and, by extension, the date of the construction activity that formed the presently observable pyramid form. It is a reasonable date given the Middle Sican mural that once existed atop the pyramid.

Huaca El Moscon

| charcoal from a burnt column atop the pyramid | SMU-1623 | 950 ± 30 BP; ad 1000 fp | A.D. 1060 ± 40 |

This date is also quite reasonable considering various architectural/constructional similarities we see with other Middle Sican pyramids that have yielded essentially contemporaneous dates. Adobe brick and ceramic seriations both support this conclusion.

Huaca Menor

| wooden bow from gravelot of looted shaft tomb | GrN-5474 | 915 ± 50 BP; ad 1035 | A.D. 1100 ± 70 |

Not much can be said about the sample used, but the resultant date is reasonable given that the associated Middle Sican ceramic vessel and other grave offerings are stylistically late Middle Sican.

Huaca La Merced, Mound II

| bark from a wooden post inside an adobe columnar box (No. 3), Platform 1 | SMU-1818 | 1180 ± 105 BP; ad 770 | A.D. 840 ± 120 |
| outer portion of a wooden post inside Box 6, Platform 1 | SMU-1819 | 1040 ± 30 BP; ad 910 | A.D. 990 ± 30 |

These two samples were taken from two contiguous posts of the same platform. Architectural features and associated ceramics suggest that the platform may date to the Early–Middle Sican transition. At the same time, the presence of two disturbed dedicatory burials and a broken clay layer sealing the sand fill of the platform argues that this platform has a complex history.

Huaca Santillo

| charcoal from a burnt area, platform south of the pyramid | SMU-1184 | 730 ± 50 BP; ad 1220 f | A.D. 1280 ± 30 |

At present, this is the only Late Sican monumental construction that has been radiocarbon dated. Considering that the sample was derived from a floor that is both underlain and overlain by additional plastered floors, the site must have a reasonably long occupational history. Surface collected ceramics and the presence of low loaf adobe bricks argues that this is a reasonable date.

Huaca Soledad

| charcoal from a firepit, Test Pit 3, Cut A, Southern Cemetery | SMU-897 | 1570 ± 40 BP; ad 380 f | A.D. 490 ± 60 |

Reasonable considering that it dates a feature that is stratigraphically pre-Moche IV intrusion and is associated with "Gallinazo-like" face-neck jar fragments.

| charcoal from "protective organic layer" covering Phase I construction, Mound II | SMU-833 | 1410 ± 60 BP; ad 540 | A.D. 630 ± 40 |

Reasonable date as the few diagnostic (also the latest) ceramics recovered from the "protective organic layer" are well-burnished blackware bowls highly reminiscent of those found in Moche V Pampa Grande elite settings.

| wood from plastered/painted column, Phase III construction, Mound II | SMU-903 | 890 ± 50 BP; ad 1060 f | A.D. 1130 ± 70 |

Difficult to assess the reasonableness of this date as the associated architecture, floor, and fill are remarkably devoid of any datable materials and features. The string of wall niches and centrally placed platform and attendant backwall probably once had elaborate murals much like those found at the nearby Huacas La Mayanga and Pintada.

Cerro Huaringa

charcoal from firepit below Floor 11, Excavation Area I, Sector III — Beta-5671 — 790 ± 50 BP; ad 1160 — A.D. 1240 ± 40

Dates the beginning of smelting activity in Sector III of this site. Significantly, this date roughly dovetails with the disappearance of evidence of smelting activity at nearby Huaca del Pueblo Batan Grande.

charcoal from a firepit dug into sterile zone, top of T-shaped platform, Sector III — Beta 5672 — 760 ± 50 BP; ad 1190 — A.D. 1260 ± 30

The firepit may have been an offering made at the time when this major T-shaped platform that overlooks an area of the concentrated bronze smelting was built. Its contemporaneity with Beta-5671 is significant in that the latter dates the beginning of the smelting workshop in the area below the platform.

charcoal from a large cache of charcoal on Floor 15, T-1-'83, Sector III — SMU-1822 — 650 ± 30 BP; ad 1300 — A.D. 1320 ± 40

The date seems reasonable given that the cache is stratigraphically intermediate between the contexts that yielded Beta-5671 and SMU-1161.

charcoal from smelting furnace, Excavation Area I, Sector III — SMU-1161 — 590 ± 40 BP; ad 1360 f — A.D. 1360 ± 50

Seems reasonable in that the sample was derived from a furnace that was built in a level associated with some Chimu ceramics. As the smelting workshops often had compacted earthen floors and were the setting for constant movement, there may well have been some mixing of ceramics. However, above this level, the amount and variability of Chimu ceramics increase notably. The date is also in general agreement with SMU-1334 and -1341 which set the maximum early end of Chimu intrusion at Huaca del Pueblo Batan Grande.

charcoal from smelting furnace, Excavation Area I, Sector III — Beta-2591 — 450 ± 60 BP; ad 1500 — A.D. 1450 ± 40

Quite reasonable given that this and associated furnaces were found with Chimu-Inca ceramics. The date agrees well with the historically derived date of Inca intrusion into this area ca. A.D. 1460–1470.

Sites outside of Batan Grande

Tucume/El Purgatorio★★

horizontal log, east wall of the Huaca El Mirador pyramid	Bonn-1141	660 ± 60 BP; ad 1290	A.D. 1320 ± 50
charcoal from the burnt surface atop the Huaca El Mirador pyramid, 55–60 cm below surface	Bonn-1142	680 ± 50 BP; ad 1270	A.D. 1300 ± 40
horizontal log (4th tier from the bottom), north wall of the Huaca de las Estacas pyramid	Bonn-1143	940 ± 50 BP; ad 1010	A.D. 1070 ± 60
horizontal log from the middle of the east wall of the Huaca Larga pyramid	Bonn-1144	690 ± 50 BP; ad 1260	A.D. 1300 ± 40
wood post atop the Huaca Grande (Huaca del Pueblo Tucume) pyramid	Bonn-1955	790 ± 70 BP; ad 1160	A.D. 1240 ± 60
wood post atop the Huaca Grande (Huaca del Pueblo Tucume) pyramid	Bonn-1956	900 ± 70 BP; ad 1050	A.D. 1130 ± 90

These dates are taken from H. Trimborn's 1979 publication. Bonn-1955 and Bonn-1956 come from the same general setting (pyramid top) that would be expected to be coterminous. A difference of 100 years is disturbing. The sample for Bonn-1956 may have been derived from a recycled log. Consideration of the sample contexts for Bonn-1141 and Bonn-1142 suggests that the pyramid of Huaca El Mirador was rapidly erected, much like the Middle Sican pyramid of Huaca Rodillona. Overall, with the exception of the Bonn-1143 date for the Huaca de las Estacas pyramid, these dates indicate that at least the presently observable portions of the pyramids at the site of El Purgatorio were constructed during the Late Sican period.

Chotuna

wood, south border, middle level of the pyramid	Bonn-1957	720 ± 70 BP; ad 1230★★	A.D. 1280 ± 50
wood, south border, middle level of the pyramid	Bonn-1958	590 ± 70 BP; ad 1360★★	A.D. 1360 ± 60

As with a number of other dates reported by Trimborn, these two dates, though coming from the same general setting (south border) that would be expected to be coterminous, show a major discrepancy. A difference of 80 years is disturbing. For the time being, we may consider that these dates suggest at least the presently observable portions of the Chotuna pyramid were constructed during the Late Sican or Early Chimu periods.

charcoal from hearth in plastered floor coterminous with low loaf adobe perimeter wall of Room 10, Arti-sans Quadrangle	UCR-1477	820 ± 75 BP; ad 1130***	A.D. 1225 ± 55
charcoal from hearth in plastered floor coterminous with high loaf adobe perimeter wall of Room 3, Arti-sans Quadrangle	UCR-1478	690 ± 90 BP; ad 1260***	A.D. 1281 ± 20
charcoal from hearth in plastered floor coterminous with high loaf adobe perimeter wall of Room 28, Arti-sans Quadrangle	UCR-1479	720 ± 85 BP; ad 1230***	A.D. 1275 ± 30

Rooms 3 and 28 are stratigraphically on the same level and are immediately above Room 10. In general, these dates are in good agreement with those Batan Grande dates associated with the same types of adobe bricks.

Chornancap

charcoal from hearth in strata immediately below the first course of low loaf bricks at the northwest corner of the Huaca	UCR-1476	920 ± 80 BP; ad 1030***	A.D. 1100 ± 70

f = C-13/C-12 fractionation computed.
p = preliminary dates.
* Date reported by Jorge Zevallos Q.
** Dates taken from Trimborn 1979.
*** Dates reported by C. B. Donnan.
All calibrations except those of Chornancap and Chotuna were computer-generated at the Radiocarbon Laboratory, Institute for the Study of Earth and Man, Southern Methodist University on the basis of the Belfast Laboratory's results on Irish Oak chronologies. The calibration program used here was designed and written by Steven Robinson of the USGS Radiocarbon Laboratory in Menlo Park, California. The calibrated dates for Chornancap and Chotuna are based on the 20-year calibration curve published by Stuiver and Pearson 1986.

BIBLIOGRAPHY

ALVA A., WALTER, and SUSANA MENESES DE ALVA
  1984   Los murales de Ucupe en el valle de Zaña, norte del Perú. *Beiträge zur Allgemeinen und Vergleichenden Archäologie* 5 (1983): 335–360. Deutsches Archäologisches Institut, Bonn.

ANDERS, MARTHA B.
  1981   Investigation of State Storage Facilities in Pampa Grande, Peru. *Journal of Field Archaeology* 8: 391–404.

BENNETT, WENDELL C.
  1939   *Archaeology of the North Coast of Peru.* Anthropological Papers of the American Museum of Natural History 37 (1). New York.

BONAVIA, DUCCIO
  1974   *Ricchata Quellccani. Pinturas murales prehispánicas.* Banco Industrial del Perú, Lima.
  1985   *Mural Painting in Ancient Peru* (Patricia J. Lyon, trans. and ed.). Indiana University Press, Bloomington.

BRUCE, SUSAN LEE
  n.d.   Adobe Seriation: The Site Reconstruction of Chotuna-Chornancap, Peru. M.A. thesis, Department of Anthropology, University of California, Los Angeles, 1982.

BRÜNING, ENRIQUE (HEINRICH)
  1922   *Estudios monográficos del Departamento de Lambayeque, Tomo 1: Lambayeque.* Dionisio Mendoz, Chiclayo.

BUENO MENDOZA, ALBERTO
  1982   El antiguo valle de Pachacamac: Espacio, tiempo y cultura. *Boletín de Lima* 4 (24): 1–53.

CABELLO BALBOA, MIGUEL
  [1586] *Miscelánea antártica.* Instituto de Etnología, Universidad Nacional
  1951   Mayor de San Marcos, Lima.

CARCEDO, PALOMA, and IZUMI SHIMADA
  1985   Behind the Golden Mask: Sicán Gold Artifacts from Batán Grande, Peru. In *Art of Precolumbian Gold: Jan Mitchell Collection* (Julie Jones, ed.): 60–75. Weidenfeld & Nicolson, London.

CARRIÓN, REBECA
  1940   La luna y su personificación ornitomórfa en el arte Chimu. *Actas y Trabajos Científicos del 27 Congreso Internacional de Americanistas* 1: 571–587.

CAVALLARO, RAFFAEL, and IZUMI SHIMADA
  1988   Some Thoughts on Sicán Marked Adobes and Labor Organization. *American Antiquity* 53: 75–101.

CERVENY, R. S., B. R. SKEETER, and K. F. DEWEY
  1987   A Preliminary Investigation of a Relationship between South American Snow Cover and the Southern Oscillation. *Monthly Weather Review* 115: 620–623.

CLELAND, KATHRYN M., and IZUMI SHIMADA
    n.d.a   Sicán Bottles: Marking Time in the Peruvian Bronze Age. Unpublished manuscript, 1987.
    n.d.b   *Paleteada* Ceramics from Batán Grande: New Data and Thoughts on Chronology, Form, Function, and Production. Paper presented at the Fifth Northeast Conference of Andean Archaeology and Ethnohistory, Ithaca, New York, November 1986.

COLLIER, DONALD
    1959   Pottery Stamping and Molding on the North Coast of Peru. *Actas del 33 Congreso Internacional de Americanistas* 2: 421–431.

CRAIG, ALAN K., and IZUMI SHIMADA
    1986   El Niño Flood Deposits at Batán Grande, Northern Peru. *Geoarchaeology* 1: 29–38.

DONNAN, CHRISTOPHER B.
    1972   Moche-Huari Murals from Northern Peru. *Archaeology* 25(2): 85–95.
    1978   *Moche Art of Peru.* Museum of Cultural History, University of California, Los Angeles.
    1984   Ancient Murals from Chornancap, Peru. *Archaeology* 37(3): 32–37.
    1986   Introduction. In *The Pacatnamú Papers,* Volume 1 (Christopher B. Donnan and Guillermo A. Cock, eds.): 19–26. Museum of Cultural History, University of California, Los Angeles.

ELERA, CARLOS G.
    n.d.   Caracteristicas e implicaciones culturales en dos tumbas disturbadas de Huaca La Merced, complejo arqueológico de Batán Grande, Lambayeque, costa norte del Perú. Report submitted to the Instituto Nacional de Cultura, Lima, 1984.

ELING, HERBERT J.
    n.d.   The Role of Irrigation Networks in Emerging Societal Complexity during Late Prehispanic Times, Jequetepeque Valley, North Coast, Peru. Ph.D. dissertation, Department of Anthropology, University of Texas, Austin, 1987.

EPSTEIN, STEPHEN M., and IZUMI SHIMADA
    1984   Metalurgia de Sicán: Una reconstrucción de la producción de la aleación de cobre en el Cerro de los Cementerios, Perú. *Beiträge zur Allgemeinen und Vergleichenden Archäologie* 5 (1983): 379–430. Bonn.

ESPINOZA SORIANO, WALDEMAR
    1975   El valle de Jayanca y el reino de los Mochica, siglos XV y XVI. *Bulletin de l'Institut Français d'Etudes Andines* 4(3–4): 243–274. Lima.

ESTRADA, EMILIO
    1961   Correlaciones entre la arqueología de la costa del Ecuador y Perú. *Humanitas* 2(2): 31–61. Quito.

FLORIÁN, MARIO
    1951   *Un icono mural en Batán Grande.* Imprenta Amauta, Lima.

HAAS, JONATHAN
    1985   Excavations on Huaca Grande: An Initial View of the Elite at Pampa Grande, Peru. *Journal of Field Archaeology* 12: 391–409.

HASTINGS, C. M., and M. E. MOSELEY
    1975   The Adobes of Huaca del Sol and Huaca de la Luna. *American Antiquity* 40: 196–203.

HODDER, IAN
    1978   Simple Correlations between Material Culture and Society: A Review. In *The Spatial Organization of Culture* (I. R. Hodder, ed.): 3–24. University of Pittsburgh, Pittsburgh.
    1979   Economic and Social Stress and Material Culture Patterning. *American Antiquity* 44: 446–454.

HOLM, OLAF
    1966/7 Money Axes from Ecuador. *Folk* 8–9: 135–143. Copenhagen.
    1975   Monedas primitivas del Ecuador prehistórico. *La Pieza* 3. Casa de la Cultura Ecuatoriana, Guayaquil.
    1982   *Cultura Milagro-Quevedo*. Museo Antropológico y Pinacoteca del Banco Central del Ecuador, Guayaquil.

HOOPES, JOHN W.
    1988   *Early Ceramics and the Origins of Village Life in Lower Central America*. University Microfilms, Ann Arbor.

HORKHEIMER, HANS
    1944   *Vistas arqueológicas del noroeste del Perú*. Instituto Arqueológico de la Universidad Nacional de Trujillo. Librería y Imprenta Moreno, Trujillo.

HOWELL, W. E.
    1954   Local Weather of the Chicama Valley (Peru). *Archiv für Meteorologie, Geophysik, und Bioklimatologie,* Serie B, 5: 41–51.

JIMÉNEZ BORJA, ARTURO
    1985   Pachacamac. *Boletín de Lima* 7 (38): 40–54.

JOHNSON, A. M.
    1976   The Climate of Peru, Bolivia and Ecuador. In *Climates of Central and South America* (W. Schwerdtfeger, ed.): 147–201. World Survey of Climatology 12.

KAUFFMANN DOIG, FEDERICO
    1983   *Manual de arqueología peruana*. Peisa, Lima.

KEATINGE, RICHARD W., and GEOFFREY W. CONRAD
    1983   Imperialist Expansion in Peruvian Prehistory: Chimu Administration of a Conquered Territory. *Journal of Field Archaeology* 10(3): 255–283.

KOLATA, ALAN L.
    1982   Chronology and Settlement Growth at Chan Chan. In *Chan Chan: Andean Desert City* (Michael E. Moseley and Kent C. Day, eds.): 67–85. University of New Mexico, Albuquerque.
    n.d.   Chan Chan: The Form of the City in Time. Ph.D. dissertation, Department of Anthropology, Harvard University, 1978.

KOSOK, PAUL

1959   El valle de Lambayeque. *Actas y Trabajos del II Congreso Nacional de Historia del Perú (época pre-hispánica)* 1: 69–76. Lima.

1965   *Life, Land and Water in Ancient Peru.* Long Island University, New York.

KROEBER, ALFRED L.

1926   *Archaeological Explorations in Peru, Part I: Ancient Pottery from Trujillo.* Field Museum of Natural History, Anthropology Memoirs 2(1). Chicago.

1930   *Archaeological Explorations in Peru, Part II: The Northern Coast.* Field Museum of Natural History, Anthropology Memoirs 2(2). Chicago.

1944   *Peruvian Archaeology in 1942.* Viking Fund Publications in Anthropology 4. The Viking Fund, New York.

KROEBER, ALFRED L., and JORGE C. MUELLE

1942   Cerámica paleteada de Lambayeque. *Revista del Museo Nacional* 11: 1–24. Lima.

LANNING, EDWARD P.

1963   *A Ceramic Sequence for the Piura and Chira Coast, North Peru.* University of California Publications in American Archaeology and Ethnology 46(2): 135–284. Berkeley.

LECHTMAN, HEATHER N.

1979   Issues in Andean Metallurgy. In *Pre-Columbian Metallurgy of South America* (Elizabeth P. Benson, ed.): 1–40. Dumbarton Oaks, Washington, D.C.

MACKEY, CAROL J., and ALEXANDRA M. ULANA KLYMYSHYN

1981   Construction and Labor Organization in the Chimu Empire. *Ñawpa Pacha* 19: 99–114.

McCLELLAND, DONALD

1986   Brick Seriation at Pacatnamú. In *The Pacatnamú Papers,* Volume 1 (Christopher B. Donnan and Guillermo A. Cock, eds.): 27–46. Museum of Cultural History, University of California, Los Angeles.

MEANS, PHILIP A.

1917   A Survey of Ancient Peruvian Art. *Transactions of the Connecticut Academy of Arts and Sciences* 21: 315–442. New Haven.

1931   *Ancient Civilizations of the Andes.* Charles Scribner's Sons, New York.

MEGGERS, BETTY J.

1966   *Ecuador.* Praeger, New York.

MENZEL, DOROTHY

1964   Style and Time in the Middle Horizon. *Ñawpa Pacha* 2: 1–106. Berkeley.

1968   *La cultura Wari.* Compañía de Seguros y Reaseguros Peruano-Suiza, Lima.

1969   New Data on the Huari Empire in Middle Horizon Epoch 2A. *Ñawpa Pacha* 6: 47–114.

1977   *The Archaeology of Ancient Peru and the Work of Max Uhle.* R. H. Lowie Museum of Anthropology, University of California, Berkeley.

MIDDENDORF, E. W.
    1894   *Peru II: Das Küstenland von Peru.* Robert Oppenheim, Berlin.
MINATO, H.
    1960   Chemical Analysis of Copper and Bronze Wares. In *Andes 1: Report of the Tokyo University Scientific Expedition to the Andes in 1958* (E. Ishida, ed.): 516–517. Bijutsu-shuppansha, Tokyo.
MOSELEY, MICHAEL E.
    1975   Prehistoric Principles of Labor Organization in the Moche Valley, Peru. *American Antiquity* 40: 191–196.
    1982   Introduction, Human Exploitation and Organization on the North Andean Coast. In *Chan Chan: Andean Desert City* (Michael E. Moseley and Kent C. Day, eds.): 1–24. University of New Mexico, Albuquerque.
    1987   Punctuated Equilibrium: Searching the Ancient Record for El Niño. *The Quarterly Review of Archaeology* 8(3): 7–10.
MOSELEY, M. E., and ERIC DEEDS
    1982   The Land in Front of Chan Chan: Agrarian Expansion, Reform, and Collapse in the Moche Valley. In *Chan Chan: Andean Desert City* (Michael E. Moseley and Kent C. Day, eds.): 25–53. University of New Mexico, Albuquerque.
MOSELEY, M. E., R. A. FELDMAN, and C. R. ORTLOFF
    1981   Living with Crisis: Human Perception of Process and Time. In *Biotic Crises in Ecological and Evolutionary Times* (Mathew Nitiecki, ed.): 231–267. Academic Press, New York.
NETHERLY, PATRICIA
    1984   The Management of Late Andean Irrigation Systems on the North Coast of Peru. *American Antiquity* 49: 227–254.
    n.d.   *Local Level Lords on the North Coast of Peru.* Ph.D. dissertation, Department of Anthropology, Cornell University, 1978.
NIALS, FRED L., ERIC E. DEEDS, MICHAEL E. MOSELEY, SHELIA G. POZORSKI,
THOMAS G. POZORSKI, and ROBERT A. FELDMAN
    1979a,b   El Niño: The Catastrophic Flooding of Coastal Peru. *Field Museum of Natural History Bulletin* 50 (7): 4–14 (Part I); 50 (8): 4–10 (Part II). Chicago.
NOLAN, JAMES L.
    n.d.   Pre-Hispanic Irrigation and Polity in the Lambayeque Sphere, Peru. Ph.D. dissertation, Columbia University, 1981.
OSSIO, JUAN
    1973   *Ideología mesiánica del mundo andino.* Instituto de Estudios Peruanos, Lima.
PAREDES, PONCIANO
    1985   La Huaca Pintada o el Templo de Pachacamac. *Boletín de Lima* 7(41): 70–84. Lima.
PAREDES, PONCIANO, and RÉGULO FRANCO
    1987   Pachacamac: Las Pirámides con rampa. Cronología y función. *Gaceta Arqueológica Andina* 4 (13): 5–7. Lima.

PEARSON, GORDON W., and MINZE STUIVER

    1986   High-Precision Calibration of the Radiocarbon Time Scale, 500–2500 B.C. *Radiocarbon* 28(2B): 839–862.

PEDERSEN, ASBJORN

    1976   El ajuar funerario de la tumba de la Huaca Menore de Batán Grande, Lambayeque, Perú. *Actas del 41 Congreso Internacional de Americanistas* 2: 60–73. Mexico City.

PORTUGAL VIZCARRA, JOSÉ A.

    1966   *Influencia de Proyecto Tinajones.* Editorial Huascarán, Lima.

RAMÍREZ, SUSAN

    1981   La organización económica de la Costa Norte: Un análisis preliminar del período prehispánico tardio. In *Etnohistoría y antropología andina* (A. Castelli, M. Koth de Paredes, and M. Mould de Pease, eds.): 281–297. Instituto de Estudios Peruanos, Lima.

    1985   Social Frontiers and the Territorial Base of *Curacazgos.* In *Andean Ecology and Civilization* (S. Masuda, Izumi Shimada, and Craig Morris, eds.): 423–442. University of Tokyo, Tokyo.

RAVINES, ROGGER

    1982a   *Arqueología del valle medio del Jequetepeque.* Instituto Nacional de Cultura, Lima.

    1982b   *Panorama de la arqueología andina.* Instituto de Estudios Peruanos, Lima.

REICHLEN, HENRY, and PAULE REICHLEN

    1949   Recherches archéologiques dan les Andes de Cajamarca. *Journal de la Société des Américanistes* 38: 137–174.

RENFREW, COLIN

    1986   Introduction. In *Peer Polity Interaction and Sociopolitical Change* (Colin Renfrew and John F. Cherry, eds.): 1–18. Cambridge University Press, Cambridge.

RONDÓN SALAS, JORGE

    1966   Ferreñafe prehispánico. *Ferruñap* 3 (25): 7–15.

    n.d.   Paleoclima de Lambayeque. Paper presented at the 39th International Congress of Americanists, Lima, 1970.

ROSTWOROWSKI DE DIEZ CANSECO, MARÍA

    1970   Mercaderes del valle de Chincha en la época prehispánica: Un documento y unos comentarios. *Revista Española de Antropología Americana* 5: 135–178. Madrid.

    1975   Pescadores, artesanos y mercaderes costeños en el Perú prehispánico. *Revista del Museo Nacional* 41: 311–349. Lima.

    1985   Patronyms with the Consonant F in the *Guarangas* of Cajamarca. In *Andean Ecology and Civilization* (Shozo Masuda, Izumi Shimada, and Craig Morris, eds.): 401–421. University of Tokyo, Tokyo.

ROWE, JOHN H.

    1945   Absolute Chronology in the Andean Area. *American Antiquity* 10: 265–284.

    1948   The Kingdom of Chimor. *Acta Americana* 6(1–2): 26–59.

1962   Stages and Periods in Archaeological Interpretation. *Southwestern Journal of Anthropology* 18: 1–27.

SALOMON, FRANK
1986   Vertical Politics on the Inka Frontier. In *Anthropological History of Andean Polities* (J.V. Murra, N. Wachtel, and J. Revel, eds.): 89–117. Cambridge University Press, Cambridge.
1987   A North Andean Status Trader Complex under Inka Rule. *Ethnohistory* 34: 63–77.

SCHAAF, CRYSTAL BARKER
n.d.   Establishment and Demise of Moche V: Assessment of the Climatic Impact. M.A. thesis, Extension School, Harvard University, 1988.

SCHAAF, C. B., IZUMI SHIMADA, LONNIE G. THOMPSON, and E. MOSLEY-THOMPSON
n.d.   Climatic and Cultural Changes in Ancient Peru. Unpublished manuscript.

SCHAEDEL, RICHARD P.
1951a   Major Ceremonial and Population Centers in Northern Peru. *Civilization of Ancient America, Selected Papers of 29th International Congress of Americanists* (Sol Tax, ed.): 232–243. Chicago.
1951b   The Lost Cities of Peru. *Scientific American* 185: 18–23.
1966a   Incipient Urbanization and Secularization in Tiahuanacoid Peru. *American Antiquity* 31: 338–344.
1966b   Urban Growth and Ekistics on the Peruvian Coast. *Proceedings of the 36th International Congress of Americanists* 2: 531–539.
1966c   The Huaca "El Dragón." *Journal de la Société des Américanistes* 55(2): 383–496.
1972   The City and the Origin of the State in America. *Actas y Memorias del 39 Congreso Internacional de Americanistas* 2: 15–33.
1978a   The Huaca Pintada of Illimo. *Archaeology* 31(1): 27–37.
1978b   Early State of the Incas. In *The Early State* (H. Claessen and P. Shalnik, eds.): 289–320. Mouton, The Hague.
1979   The Confluence of the Pressed Ware and Paddle Ware Traditions in Coastal Peru. In *Festschrift für Hermann Trimborn* (Roswith Hartmann and Udo Oberem, eds.): 231–239. Amerikanistische Studien II, Haus Völker und Kulturen, Anthropos-Institut, St. Augustin.
1985a   The Transition from Chiefdom to State in Northern Peru. In *Development and Decline: The Evolution of Sociopolitical Organization* (Henri J. M. Claessen, Pieter van de Velde, and M. Estellie Smith, eds.): 156–169. Bergin and Garvey, South Hadley, Mass.
1985b   Coast-Highland Interrelationships and Ethnic Groups in Northern Peru (500 B.C.–A.D. 1980). In *Andean Ecology and Civilization* (Shozo Masuda, Izumi Shimada, and Craig Morris, eds): 443–473. University of Tokyo Press, Tokyo.

SCHAFFIELD, BRIAN A.
n.d.   Prehispanic Corporate Architecture and Labor Organization on the North Coast of Peru. B.S. thesis, Department of Anthropology, Harvard University, 1985.

SCHEELE, H., and T. C. PATTERSON
  1966 A Preliminary Seriation of the Chimu Pottery Style. *Ñawpa Pacha* 4: 15–30.
SCHMIDT, MAX
  1929 *Kunst und Kultur von Peru.* Propyläen-Verlag, Berlin.
SHIMADA, IZUMI
  1981 Temple of Time: The Ancient Burial and Religious Center of Batán Grande, Peru. *Archaeology* 34(5): 37–44.
  1982 Horizontal Archipelago and Coast-Highland Interaction in North Peru. In *El hombre y su ambiente en los Andes centrales* (Luís Millones and Hiroyasu Tomoeda, eds.): 137–210. Senri Ethnological Studies 10. National Museum of Ethnology, Osaka.
  1985a La cultura Sicán: Una caracterización arqueológica. In *Presencia histórica de Lambayeque* (Eric Mendoza, ed.): 76–133. Editorial y Imprenta DESA, S.A., Lima.
  1985b Perception, Procurement and Management of Resources: Archaeological Perspective. In *Andean Ecology and Civilization* (Shozo Masuda, Izumi Shimada, and Craig Morris, eds.): 357–400. University of Tokyo Press, Tokyo.
  1986 Batán Grande and Cosmological Unity in the Andes. In *Andean Archaeology: Papers in Memory of Clifford Evans* (R. Matos and S. Turpin, eds.): 163–188. U.C.L.A. Institute of Archaeology, Los Angeles.
  1987a Horizontal and Vertical Dimensions of Prehistoric States in North Peru. In *The Origins and Development of the Andean State* (J. Haas, S. Pozorski, and T. Pozorski, eds.): 130–144. Cambridge University Press, Cambridge.
  1987b Aspectos tecnológicos y productivos de la metalurgia Sicán, costa norte del Perú. *Gaceta Arqueológica Andina* 4 (13): 15–21. Lima.
  n.d. Socioeconomic Organization at Moche V Pampa Grande, Peru. Ph.D. dissertation, Department of Anthropology, University of Arizona, 1977.
  n.d.a *The Mochica City-State of Pampa Grande.* University of Texas Press, Austin. (Forthcoming)
  n.d.b Behind the Golden Mask: The Research Problems and Preliminary Results of the Batán Grande-La Leche Valley Archaeological Project. Paper presented at the 44th Annual Meeting of the Society for American Archaeology, Vancouver, May 1979.
  n.d.c Organizational Significance of Marked Bricks and Associated Construction Features on the North Peruvian Coast. Paper presented at the 46th International Congress of Americanists, Amsterdam, July 1988.
  n.d.d The Formation of the Middle Sicán Polity: The Highland Connection and Revitalization Movement. Paper presented at the 48th Annual Meeting of the Society for American Archaeology, Pittsburgh, April 1983.
SHIMADA, IZUMI, and RAFFAEL CAVALLARO
  1986 Monumental Adobe Architecture of the Late Pre-Hispanic Northern North Coast of Peru. *Journal de la Société des Américanistes* 71: 41–78.

      n.d.   Monumental Adobe Architecture of the Late Pre-Hispanic Northern North Coast of Peru: A Holistic Perspective. In *La tecnología en el mundo andino* 2 (H. N. Lechtman and A. M. Soldi, eds.), Universidad Nacional Autónoma de México, Mexico. (Forthcoming)

SHIMADA, IZUMI, et al.
      1981   The Batán Grande-La Leche Archaeological Project: The First Two Seasons. *Journal of Field Archaeology* 8: 405–446.

SHIMADA, IZUMI, and CARLOS G. ELERA
      1983   Batán Grande y la complejidad cultural emergente en nor-Peru durante el Horizonte Medio: Datos y modelos. *Boletín del Museo Nacional* 8: 41–47. Lima.

SHIMADA, IZUMI, STEPHEN M. EPSTEIN, and ALAN F. CRAIG
      1982   Batán Grande: A Prehistoric Metallurgical Center in Peru. *Science* 216: 952–959.
      1983   The Metallurgical Process in Ancient North Peru. *Archaeology* 36(5): 38–45.

SHIMADA, MELODY J., and IZUMI SHIMADA
      1981   Explotación y manejo de los recursos naturales en Pampa Grande, sitio Moche V: Significado del análisis orgánico. *Revista del Museo Nacional* 45: 19–73. Lima.

STUIVER, MINZE, and GORDON W. PEARSON
      1986   High-Precision Calibration of the Radiocarbon Time Scale, A.D. 1950–500 B.C. *Radiocarbon* 28(2B): 805–838.

STUIVER, MINZE, and P. J. REIMER
      1986   A Computer Program for Radiocarbon Age Calibration. *Radiocarbon* 28(2B): 1022–1030.

TERADA, KAZUO, and RYOZO MATSUMOTO
      1985   Sobre la cronología de la tradición Cajamarca. In *Historia de Cajamarca 1. Arqueología* (F. Silva S., W. Espinoza S., and R. Ravines, eds.): 67–92. Instituto Nacional de Cultura, Cajamarca and Corporación de Desarrollo de Cajamarca, Cajamarca.

THOMPSON, L. G., E. MOSLEY-THOMPSON, J. F. BOLZAN, and B. R. KOCI
      1985   A 1500-Year Record of Tropical Precipitation in Ice Cores from the Quelccaya Ice Cap, Peru. *Science* 229: 971–973.

THOMPSON, L. G., E. MOSLEY-THOMPSON, and B. MORALES ARNO
      1984   El Niño-Southern Oscillation Events Recorded in the Stratigraphy of the Tropical Quelccaya Ice Cap, Peru. *Science* 203: 50–53.

TRIMBORN, HERMANN
      1979   *El reino de Lambayeque en el antiguo Perú*. Collectanea Instituti Anthropos 19. Haus Völker und Kulturen–Anthropos Institut, St. Augustin.

URTEAGA, HORACIO H.
      1919   *El Perú, bocetos históricos: Estudios arqueológicos, tradicionales é histórico-críticos*. Casa Editora E. Rosay, Lima.

VALCARCEL, LUIS E.
  1937 Un valioso hallazgo arqueológico en el Perú: Informe sobre los hallazgos en los yacimientos arqueológicos de La Merced, La Ventana y
        otros del Distrito de Illimo, Lambayeque. *Revista del Museo Nacional*
        6(1): 164–168. Lima.

WALLACE, ANTHONY F. C.
  1956 Revitalization Movements: Some Theoretical Considerations for Their
        Comparative Study. *American Anthropologist* 58: 264–281.
  1966 *Religion: An Anthropological View*. Random House, New York.

WASSÉN, S. HENRY
  1973 A Problematic Metal Object from Northern Peru. *Göteborgs Etnografiska Museum Arstryck* 1972: 29–33. Göteborg.

WATSON, RICHARD
  1986 C_{14} and Cultural Chronology on the North Coast of Peru: Implications
        for a Regional Chronology. In *Andean Archaeology: Papers in Memory of
        Clifford Evans* (R. Matos and S. Turpin, eds.): 83–129. U.C.L.A. Institute of Archaeology, Los Angeles.

WELLS, LISA E.
  1987 An Alluvial Record of El Niño Events from Northern Coastal Peru.
        Journal of Geophysical Research 92 (C13): 14463–14470.

WILLEY, GORDON R.
  1953 *Prehistoric Settlement Patterns in the Virú Valley, Northern Peru*. Bureau of
        American Ethnology, Bulletin 155. Smithsonian Institution, Washington, D.C.

WILLEY, GORDON R., and DONALD W. LATHRAP
  1956 An Archaeological Classification of Culture Contact Situations. In
        Seminars in Archaeology, 1955 (Robert Wauchope, ed.):1–30. Memoirs
        of the Society for American Archaeology 11.

ZEVALLOS QUIÑONES, JORGE
  1971 *Cerámica de la cultura "Lambayeque"* (*Lambayeque I*). Universidad Nacional de Trujillo, Trujillo.

Fonga Sigde, Shell Purveyor to the Chimu Kings

ALANA CORDY-COLLINS

UNIVERSITY OF SAN DIEGO AND SAN DIEGO MUSEUM OF MAN

INTRODUCTION

THE ACCOUNT OF LORD NAYMLAP'S ARRIVAL in the Lambayeque Valley forms the basis for the following investigative essay. Miguel Cabello Balboa ([1586] 1951) and Fr. Justo Rubiños y Andrade ([1782] 1936) tell of this great lord's landing on the shores of Lambayeque along with a host of courtiers. Among that number was a certain Fonga Sigde. It is my purpose here to investigate this particular individual by comparing details concerning him in the reports by Cabello Balboa and Rubiños y Andrade with archaeological and iconographic data from the North Coast of Peru.

HISTORY AND ARCHAEOLOGY

Although the accounts of Naymlap's dynasty provide provocative data about the prehistory of the North Coast (see Donnan [Naymlap], this volume, for a summary of the story), some doubt exists concerning their veracity. In fact, John H. Rowe concluded that the story of Naymlap was "pure legend" and that to try assigning his dynasty to an archaeological time frame was futile (1948: 38–39). A similar view held by R. Tom Zuidema (this volume) is that the Naymlap story is not historical at all, but a structural statement. Nonetheless, the preceding papers by Christopher Donnan and Izumi Shimada provide some very interesting correlations with the Naymlap account. Chotuna, excavated by Donnan, and Batan Grande, excavated by Shimada, show a remarkable consistency of events with each other and with the historic account. Although the archaeological evidence

I extend my appreciation to the many individuals and institutions whose help has contributed to the writing of this essay. I am indebted especially to Iris Engstrand, Carol Mackey, Daniel Sandweiss, Izumi Shimada, and María-Isabel Silva who generously allowed me access to their unpublished material. The development of ideas presented herein has benefited greatly from comments by Janet Berlo, Christopher Donnan, and Donna McClelland. Colin McEwan is due a special note of thanks for providing some of the early impetus for this project.

from these excavations in the Lambayeque Valley does not substantiate the Naymlap story unequivocally, neither does it negate the account. Ultimately, both Donnan and Shimada express doubt that archaeology can be used successfully to test dynastic questions such as the Naymlap legend. However, I think it can be shown that archaeology, when it is augmented with techniques from other disciplines, *can* support some specific aspects of the legend. The investigation presented in this essay follows such an interdisciplinary approach.

NAYMLAP'S COURTIERS

While other investigators have tended to concentrate on the question of the documents' overall credibility, I think it is profitable to look more closely at individuals reported in the two chronicles. Naymlap is said to have brought with him wives, numerous concubines, and forty retainers. Among those retainers, there were eight named nobles, each with specific administrative duties (cf. Netherly n.d.: 303, 307). It is important to point out that the roles these individuals are said to have played within Naymlap's court are ones that indeed would have been performed by prehistoric North Coast courtiers. Therefore, it is worth reviewing who these eight lords were and what services they performed.

Pita Zofi was the conch-shell trumpeter, and Ninacola was the litter and throne master. Xam Muchec provided the royal face paint, while Ollopcopoc presided over the monarch's bath. Occhocalo prepared his meals, and Ninagintue saw to his drink. Llapchillulli was his clothier who produced the royal wardrobe of feather garments. Fonga Sigde scattered seashell dust where his lord was to walk. With the possible exception of a royal bath steward, each of these roles finds analogy in the archaeological, art historical, or independent ethnohistorical record. Shell trumpeters appear in the art (Donnan 1978: fig. 241) and are referred to in the chronicles (Salomon 1983: 418). We know that important lords in Pre-Columbian times were borne on litters; indeed, this was one of the rights the Spanish Conquerors withdrew from the indigenous North Coast lords (Netherly n.d.: 173). Furthermore, regal individuals are portrayed in the art with elaborately painted faces (cf. Alva and Alva 1985), and elite burials have been found with the interred's face painted red (Donnan and Mackey 1978: 180). Ethnohistoric sources identify royal providers of both food and drink (Netherly n.d.: 304). In addition, magnificent feathered garments—which must have been created for a wealthy clientele—were produced on the North Coast during the Chimu Empire (Rowe 1984). The foregoing documentation makes it quite clear that some group of individuals performed these various royal tasks and duties—we have the tangible evidence. Therefore, although I will not argue that those specifically named individuals originated these royal roles, I see no reason to doubt that the roles existed.

Fig. 1   Open valves of *Spondylus princeps.*

Carried a step further, though, logically there had to have been a point at which time these royal offices were begun. I must admit, it is conceivable that a person named Pita Zofi and his supposed cohorts instituted those official roles, but I find that scenario somewhat unlikely. Given what seems to be the Chimu penchant for truncating history (see various authors, this volume), I suspect that names such as Pita Zofi may derive from later office holders. Over time, it is likely that these names became titles of office. Hence, it would be completely appropriate to speak of the Pita Zofi, meaning anyone who held the office of conch trumpeter.

Although the question of who bestowed his name upon a particular office may be moot, the question of when that office was begun is not entirely outside our grasp. I specifically refer to the office of the shell dust purveyor, the Fonga Sigde. This officer's sole role, if we are to interpret the ethnohistory literally, was to scatter seashell dust in his sovereign's path. This seemingly inconsequential task has considerable import, however, if the shells whose dust was scattered are identified as Spondylus (Fig. 1), the thorny oyster that has a 4,000-year history of veneration in Peru (Davidson n.d.: vii; Paulsen 1974: 597). Most scholars are in accord with this identification because both archaeological and ethnohistorical data attest to the unique prestige value accorded this crimson-colored shell (Conrad 1982: 104; Davidson n.d.: 32; Netherly n.d.: 303).

Though the ritual importance of Spondylus in Peru spanned millennia, the shell was not used in large numbers until the Late Intermediate period. This evolution from limited to massive Spondylus use is directly attributed to the office of Fonga Sigde.

SPONDYLUS USE IN ANCIENT PERU

Spondylus shells and their depictions were relatively rare during the Initial period and Early Horizon era, were practically unknown in the Early Intermediate period, and began to make an appearance in increased numbers only during the Middle Horizon (Cordy-Collins n.d.a; Shimada n.d.: chs. 6 and 8). This situation changed dramatically with the florescence of the Kingdom of Chimor. The Chimu elite utilized the shell in unprecedented quantity: at Chan Chan all royal burials were accompanied by tremendous offerings of the shell—whole, cut, and pulverized as dust (Conrad 1982: 99; Pozorski 1979: 134). At the ruins of Site H in the Moche Valley a cache of hundreds of whole and cut Spondylus was found cascading down the summit of Cerro Blanco (Uhle n.d.). Imposing caches of Spondylus also have been found at Huaca El Dragon in the Moche Valley (Schaedel 1966: 434, 436) and at Manchan in Casma, where a cache of Spondylus was found prepared and buried like a high-status interment (Carol J. Mackey, personal communication, 1983). The enormous utilization of Spondylus shells by the Chimu elite is most notable for two reasons: first, it contrasts with the shell's extreme scarcity during earlier periods; and second, the shell is not native to the cold Peruvian coastal waters, but must be imported. The nearest source of Spondylus is coastal Ecuador. Therefore, a management importation and distribution system would have been necessary to handle effectively the vast amounts of the shell demanded by the Chimu aristocracy. I believe that such a system of Spondylus management was developed by the office of Fonga Sigde in the Lambayeque dynasty and later was co-opted by the Chimu imperium. The Fonga Sigde officer was a good deal more than a simple "preparer of the way" (Rowe 1948: 47). To bring Spondylus shells up from their beds 25 m deep off the Ecuadoran coast, either Peruvian divers would have to have been trained, or negotiations with experienced Ecuadoran divers would have been necessary. Given the long history of Spondylus collection in Ecuador, the latter explanation seems more likely. And we can be sure that the Ecuadoran divers would not have given their goods away: some barter agreement would have to have been arranged. Next, the shells would have to have been transported to a storage facility. Furthermore, somewhere in this chain of events, the shells would have to have been processed. Only then could the Fonga Sigde literally "roll out the red carpet." In the following analysis I will marshal iconographic, archaeological, and ethnohistorical evidence that not only can illustrate this process, but can demonstrate its temporal point of origin.

Iconographic Evidence

Thirteen examples of Middle Sican (Classic Lambayeque) art illustrate divers collecting Spondylus shells.[1] Although varying in detail, each situation manifests a distinct set of features: there is a diving platform with divers below, each with a cord tied around his waist. The upper ends of the cords are held by individuals on the platform. The number and sizes of the shells depicted vary from a single large one on the platform deck to several small ones throughout the scene. Spondylus shells are frequently and consistently depicted in Middle Sican art, which facilitates their identification in diving scenes. Artists chose the most salient features of the shells—their spiky projections—to characterize the mollusks. Detailed Spondylus depictions reveal a rounded triangular shape covered with raised elements (these can be simple lines, rectangles, or more amorphous forms, depending on the medium used, e.g., repoussé gold vs. embroidered textile). More general renditions of the shell illustrate the same overall shape, but with a serrated upper portion to represent the spikes. The ensuing iconographic discussion serves to document the methods of Spondylus procurement as recorded by the ancient Peruvians.

To date, only one depiction of Spondylus procurement has been discussed in the literature: a silver earspool in the collection of the Museum of the American Indian, New York (Fig. 2). Although this artifact has been published several times, attention has focused mainly on whether or not the object attached to the boat is a sail (Dockstader 1967: 149; Lothrop 1932: 239). This "sail" in fact may be a cloth or thatch roof, designed to afford protection from the intense sun on the Ecuadoran coast, or it may be a composite sail and roof. In the scene, a boat apparently made of balsa logs (*Ochroma*) seats two individuals who hold lines attached to the waists of two other people below the boat, that is, in the water. These latter individuals are actively involved in gathering Spondylus shells. Each holds one, while more shells are shown above them. In addition, there is a small object attached to their belts that may be a diving weight. Divers harvesting the deep Spondylus beds would have needed to descend to them as quickly as possible because of limited air supply. Thus, a weight—probably of stone—would have been very useful. It is an interesting coincidence that Jorge Marcos and Presley Norton interpreted as diving weights a number of oblong stones found amid Spondylus shells in their excavation on Ecuador's La Plata Island (Marcos and Norton 1981: 148–149).

A second metal earspool depicts an almost identical scene, although it is

---

[1] Since this article was written, I have located five additional representations of Spondylus diving. One appears on a tapestry in Lima's Museo Amano. The other four are in metal, two pieces in the Moises Saenz collection in Mexico City (Treviño de Saenz 1946–47: 117, 173), a third in the Museo de Oro in Lima (Tushingham 1976: fig. 230), and the final example is in the Museo Rafael Larco Herrera in Lima.

Fig. 2   Silver earspool with repoussé design of Spondylus shell diving. Photograph courtesy of the Heye Foundation, Museum of the American Indian.

Fig. 3   Middle Sican period metal earspool with a Spondylus diving motif (after Antze 1930: fig. 10).

more impressionistically rendered than is the first example (Fig. 3). Here, the boat is not tapered but appears as a straight bar; however, other details are comparable: birds perch above the roof, two people appear in the boat holding Spondylus shells, and lines are attached to the waists of two people in the water who collect more Spondylus shells. Additional shells are interspersed along the lines.

Two gold ornaments in Lambayeque's Museo Brüning constitute the third and fourth examples of diving for Spondylus shells (Fig. 4). Perhaps because of the open-work format, the scene is simplified further: the boat is again a straight bar, and a single Spondylus shell is shown on the deck. Two people on board again hold lines tied to the waists of divers below. The divers hold implements that may have been used to pry the shellfish away from the rocks to which they attach themselves. An object very similar in size and shape was found by Max Uhle amid the Spondylus shells at Site H (Fig. 5).

Spondylus diving is depicted yet again on a gold earspool in the Museo de Oro in Lima (Fig. 6). Here, as in the preceding two examples, the boat is a bar, and two people appear on the deck holding the life lines of the two divers in the water. A feature unique to this representation is that conch shells are shown alongside the Spondylus, apparently being gathered as well. These latter are two univalve shells of the sort the Pita Zofi may have used as trumpets. They appear directly beneath each diver's head.

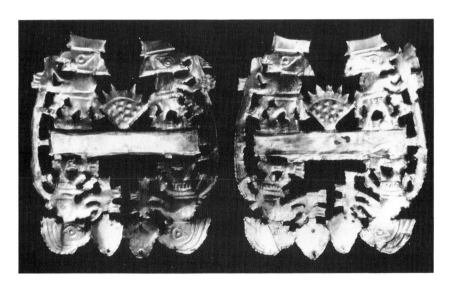

Fig. 4 Pair of Middle Sican gold ornaments with Spondylus procurement scene.

Fig. 5 Wooden implement found with Spondylus shells at Site H, Moche Valley. Photographs courtesy of the Lowie Museum of Anthropology, University of California, Berkeley.

Fig. 6 Middle Sican gold earspool with a scene of Spondylus and conch shell diving.

Fig. 7   Middle Sican metal earspool bearing a simplified Spondylus shell diving scene (after Antze 1930: fig. 15).

Another metal earspool pertinent to the discussion carries a much simplified version of shell diving and really is identifiable only because of the consistency of motifs in the preceding examples. As is the case in Figure 3, this specimen is available only in the form of a drawing, and its complete accuracy is questionable (Fig. 7).[2] Here it appears that a single central figure has completely replaced the boat and its two occupants. Nonetheless, he holds a Spondylus shell in one hand and a line in the other, albeit attached to a smaller figure's neck rather than to his waist. (This could be an error in the drawing.)

A pair of silver earspools in the Metropolitan Museum of Art, New York, illustrates yet another variant of the activity (Fig. 8). Like the preceding example, no boat is present; two shell-collecting divers in the water, their diving lines held by two individuals above, imply the existence of a raft or a platform. The ninth example, a single gold earspool in a private collection, is not available for publication. However, its details accord well with those in the foregoing examples. A raft or platform with up-tapering ends supports three individuals. Two of these people hold the life lines of divers in the water, while the third sits within an enclosure surmounted by a furled

[2] The drawings reproduced here in Figures 3, 7, and 13 are from a 1930 publication (Antze 1930) in which they were said to be in Hamburg's Museum für Völkerkunde. As of 1984, however, two of the pieces could not be located and are believed to have been lost during World War II. The third piece is so badly corroded that its details are less clear now than they were in 1930 (Wolfgang Haberland, personal communication, 1984).

Fig. 8   Pair of silver earspools with simplified Spondylus procurement designs in repoussé. The Metropolitan Museum of Art, lent by Jane Costello Goldberg from the collection of Arnold I. Goldberg, 1978. Photograph courtesy of the Metropolitan Museum of Art.

roof shade or sail. Four birds flank it and the raft. Three Spondylus shells are gathered by the divers, and more shells appear as a decorative motif around the rim of the earspool.

On a textile in San Diego's Museum of Man, the diving motif is repeated ten times (Figs. 9, 10). The form of the figures is not exactly comparable to the preceding specimens mainly because of the geometric constraints imposed by weaving. Its technique of manufacture places its point of origin on the North Coast (Susan L. Bruce, personal communication, 1983). The motif in each case is identical: a raft shown as a straight bar, with what is either a sun shade support or a mast, carries two people on deck who reach toward a line attached to the divers below. Spondylus shells appear throughout the scene.

The eleventh example of Spondylus diving occurs on a silver open-work cylinder in the Museo Brüning (Figs. 11, 12). The motif appears twice and consists of a central frontal figure standing on a bar below which Spondylus shells are shown. The upper tier of his crescent headdress is likewise ornamented with Spondylus shells. The figure holds a line in each hand, which connects to a profile diver on each side. Two more flanking divers are attached to the shells on each standing figure's headdress. Sea birds hover in front of these upper figures.

Detailed Spondylus procurement is illustrated in elaborate inlaid designs in the center of both sides of a wooden bowl in Lima's Museo Nacional de Antropología y Arqueología. Details of the boat (with a cabin), the line holders on board, the divers below, and the Spondylus representations are executed principally in shell inlay—much of it Spondylus mosaic (Fig. 13).

Fig. 9 Tapestry-weave textile with repeated Spondylus diving scenes.

Fig. 10 Detail of a single scene from the textile in Fig. 9.

Fig. 11 *left* Middle Sican silver cylinder showing Spondylus diving activity.

Fig. 12 *above* Roll-out drawing of the cylinder in Fig. 11 showing the complete Spondylus scene.

The preceding group of Spondylus diving depictions is expanded by five additional pieces of metalwork showing aspects of the motif. Two matched silver disks in the Museo de Oro (only one is illustrated in Figure 14) are divided into four registers, each depicting some form of aquatic activity. In the first register out from the center a group of individuals appears holding a long, undulating line. These people probably are shell divers because they are associated with numerous Spondylus shells interspersed along the line they carry.[3] Next, the finial of a metal spatula is formed by a seated figure bedecked with Spondylus shells (Fig. 15). This figure wears an object on the back of his belt similar in shape to the objects on the belts of the divers in Figure 2. As suggested, these probably represent stone diving weights. The conjunction of shells and weights suggests that the spatula finial depicts a Spondylus diver. Two gold earspools inlaid with turquoise each illustrate four individuals who hold Spondylus shells and are surrounded by more of them. One of the pair is located in the Museo de Oro, while its mate is housed in Dumbarton Oaks in Washington, D.C. (Fig. 16). This pair is interesting because the individuals do not seem to be divers; no diving lines are shown, and their costume is different from clothing shown in diving

[3] The other three registers carry complementary acquatic iconography. The register outside the Spondylus divers is filled with anthropomorphic waves and the outermost one contains tule boats. Both iconographies are similar to those discussed by McClelland (this volume).

Fig. 13   Interior (*top*) and exterior view of wooden bowl with a Spondylus scene in shell and stone mosaic inlay.

Fig. 14   One of a pair of Middle Sican silver repoussé disks in the Museo de Oro, Lima. Spondylus divers appear in the third register holding a diving line. Spondylus shells are scattered throughout the register. Photograph courtesy of the American Museum of Natural History.

scenes. Therefore, these earspools may depict some other aspect of Spondylus procurement.

Fortunately, the provenance of five of the Spondylus diving scenes is known (Figs. 3,4,7,11,15). These are now either in the Museo Brüning or the Museum für Völkerkunde. All were collected by Heinrich (Enrique) Brüning at Cerro Sapame in the Poma District of Batan Grande. In addition, three of the pieces in the Museo de Oro collection (Figs, 6,14), according to Shimada (1981: 405), originated in Batan Grande as well. All these objects are stylistically Middle Sican, or Classic Lambayeque, and, therefore, must date to A.D. 900–1100 (Shimada, this volume). The provenance

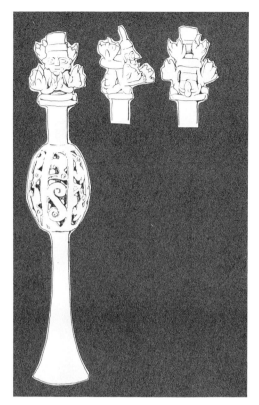

Fig. 15   Three views of a Middle Sican spatula depicting a Spondylus shell diver at the top (after Antze 1930: figs. 109, 109a, 109b).

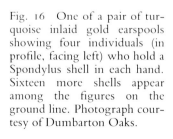

Fig. 16   One of a pair of turquoise inlaid gold earspools showing four individuals (in profile, facing left) who hold a Spondylus shell in each hand. Sixteen more shells appear among the figures on the ground line. Photograph courtesy of Dumbarton Oaks.

of the remaining diving scenes is uncertain, but judging by either their style or iconographic consistency (or both), these artifacts also are probably Middle Sican from Batan Grande.

The foregoing iconographic documents make it quite clear that Spondylus diving was a standardized activity represented in North Coast Peruvian art by A.D. 900–1100. Equally clear is that Sican artisans recorded the activity, not the Moche Valley Chimu nor the Manteño of southern Ecuador (there are no known depictions of Spondylus diving in either style). Because, however, Spondylus procurement has an ancient history in Ecuador, extending back long before A.D. 900, it seems likely that the divers portrayed in the art were Ecuadoran. Nonetheless, as a caveat, we should bear in mind that the distinction in the Lambayeque Valley between what is intrinsically Peruvian as opposed to Ecuadoran is not well understood prior to the area's incorporation into the Chimu Empire at around A.D. 1350–1370. This cultural blurring will be discussed in the next section.

Archaeological Evidence

During the Early Intermediate period on the North Coast (and seemingly everywhere else in Peru as well), Spondylus shells were extremely rare. By Middle Horizon 2, however, the shells began to appear in the Lambayeque Valley. Excavations at the Moche V site of Pampa Grande revealed a small quantity of ritually interred shells and at least one Spondylus workshop (Shimada n.d.: chs. 6 and 8).[4] Apparently, although Moche V peoples in the Lambayeque Valley began to import the shells in earnest, it was not until the Middle Sican era that the process of Spondylus diving came to be represented in art. This discovery is important because it demonstrates that what became an obsession for the Imperial Chimu—amassing Spondylus treasure—began among a more northern people in a more distant era. Although some Spondylus shells have been found in the most sumptuous of early Moche royal tombs, they are of an aberrant character and do not correspond to the type known from the Middle Horizon onward. Apparently, the Moche V polity of about A.D. 700 established a contact with Ecuador that, by A.D. 900 or so, allowed the Middle Sican craftsfolk to learn precisely how the shells were gathered. Although the transition (or continuation) from Moche V to Middle Sican culture still is clouded (see Shimada, this volume), it is clear that sometime between A.D. 700 and 900 Spondylus importation from Ecuador was begun in earnest. We can refer to the organization that facilitated such importation as the Office of Fonga Sigde.

---

[4] A small number of Spondylus shell beads have been found in a late Moche V room of burned offerings at Pacatnamu in the Jequetepeque Valley, somewhat to the south (Cordy-Collins n.d.b).

Ethnohistorical Record

We know that the Spondylus-producing coast of Ecuador was controlled in the late prehistoric period by the kingdom of Salangone (or Çalangone, see Norton 1986; also Çalangome, see Silva n.d.). It has been argued that Salangone was a monarchy whose wealth was based on sea trade (Norton 1986) and whose ventures extended as far south as Chincha in Peru. This far southern trade is indicated by mention of the specific sort of sea craft used by the Ecuadorans, a balsa-log raft (Rostworowski 1977: 181).

Bartolomé Ruiz, pilot and navigator for Francisco Pizarro's ships, stopped such a log raft under sail to its home port. It was laden with trade goods, including what are identifiably Spondylus shells (Samano [1527] 1844). It is in this enterprise that the cultural blurring mentioned earlier is most evident. Although ethnohistoric boat references can be confusing,[5] there is firm evi-

---

[5] Unfortunately, many authors use the terms *balsa* and *caballito* (for reed boat) interchangeably, a situation that continues to hamper analysis. Strictly speaking, a balsa is a craft made of balsa-wood logs, while a *caballito* is a craft made of bundled reeds. An example of the confusion can be appreciated in the following: "The balsa or raft made of bundles of reeds lashed together has a wide distribution in the New World . . ." (Lothrop 1932: 238).

Fig. 17   Colonial period illustration of balsa raft in Guayaquil. Original in the Museo Naval, Madrid. Photograph courtesy of Iris Engstrand.

Fig. 18 Colonial period illustration of a balsa raft sailing past the old city of Guayaquil. Original in the Museo Naval, Madrid. Photograph courtesy of Iris Engstrand.

Fig. 19 Colonial period illustration of a balsa raft sailing past a Spanish galleon near the mouth of the Río Guayaquil. Original in the Museo Naval, Madrid. Photograph courtesy of Iris Engstrand.

dence that the balsa raft was in use from Ecuador as far south as the Lambayeque Valley, but never beyond that region (Edwards 1965: 107).

The form of the craft illustrated in the Sicán artifacts discussed previously corresponds quite well to descriptions and illustrations of balsa rafts employed in the fifteenth through the seventeenth centuries by these southern

Fig. 20   Colonial period woodcut illustrating Ecuadoran balsa rafts (both with and without sail) (after Speilbergen 1906).

Ecuadorans/northern Peruvians. The shape of most is flat and blunt nosed (Figs. 17–19), but some were pointed in front, with the central log longer than the rest and each of the side logs progressively shorter (Fig. 20D). Therefore, what looks like a tapered boat in Fig. 2, actually may be a representation of the flat raft, distorted to fit the round earspool better. The large trading raft encountered by Ruiz is described as having a cabin, and cabins are shown on the rafts in Figures 17 through 19. The wooden bowl illustrated in Figure 13 shows a very similar structure as well. Ruiz states that the craft he encountered was under full sail. The vessels shown in Figures 17–19 and 20D are all shown under sail. Thus, the "pole" on the rafts in Figures 9 and 10 probably is a mast. My speculation that the apparatus shown in Figures 2 and 3 is a sunshade may not be too far from the mark. The engraving in Figure 17 illustrates a cabin whose sides and roof seem to be cloth draped over a cabin framework. Consistently, the ethnohistoric evidence parallels the iconographic documents, but the caveat remains: based on log-raft use alone, we cannot distinguish ancient south-coast Ecuadorans from far-north coast Peruvians (see also Richardson et al., this volume).

DISCUSSION

All data lead to the conclusion that the Lambayeque Valley aristocracy from Moche V to Middle Sican times valued the bright crimson Spondylus shell just as had their ancestors; however, they were in a position which their ancestors were not and would have envied: they had acquired access to the coveted commodity by developing an organization to import it—the Office of Fonga Sigde. What we do not know is how this change came about, how a trading arrangement was made with the shell-procuring Ecuadorans. We do not know the antiquity of the kingdom of Salangone, which, by the sixteenth century, had monopolized Spondylus importation. Its roots may have extended far enough back in time to have made it contemporary with the Middle Horizon era. If so, it is not difficult to envision a formal trading arrangement whereby Spondylus shells were exchanged for Lambayeque goods—perhaps copper (as suggested by Rostworowski 1970: 153 and Shimada, this volume). Why Spondylus shells were so highly prized by the ancient Peruvians is not really understood,[6] but given that they were prized, anyone who could have made them available and in quantity must have commanded both respect and power.

In this regard, it is thought-provoking to consider the revitalization movement hypothesis suggested by Shimada (this volume). He notes that a charismatic leader is often the catalyst for a dramatic new cultural order, such as seems to be apparent with the ascendancy of the Middle Sican society. He suggests that the Naymlap legend may eulogize, not an outsider arriving from afar, but a local heroic lord. Although any number of occurrences might have given rise to the perception of a figure as charismatic or heroic, certainly opening up the Spondylus shell trade must be counted as one. While this venture obviously began in Moche V times, it does not preclude the feat being accorded to an individual of a later era. It has been shown repeatedly in this volume that Pre-Columbian "historiographers" commonly manipulated real history (Conrad; Moseley; T. Topic; Zuidema). And it could be that a Middle Sican lord took credit for the Spondylus accomplishment by commissioning the very artifacts we have been examining. Shimada points out that an artifactual hallmark of the Middle Sican period is the ubiquitous representation of the Sican Lord, who is sometimes shown holding a Spondylus shell. In the present sample, Figure 12 shows the Sican Lord dominating the shell diving scene. Indeed, following Shimada's suggestion that Naymlap might have been a local hero, his purported arrival in Lambayeque on balsa rafts could signify a triumphant return from a successful northern venture to acquire Spondylus shells.

Although such speculations must remain just that, someone or some group did develop a conduit whereby this treasured commodity began to flow successfully into northern Peru in ever-increasing numbers. Whether

---

[6] Daniel Sandweiss (n.d.) suggests that during some prolonged El Niño conditions, live Spondylus will migrate south to Peru along with the warm current. Because the unusually warm waters spell death for the indigenous cold-water Peruvian fish, ancient Peruvians may have seen the Ecuadoran shellfish as both omnipotent and a harbinger of doom for the native sea life. In similar reasoning, Luís Lumbreras, concurring with Jorge Marcos, has argued that the arrival of the Spondylus on the Peruvian coast during El Niños would have been looked upon as more than just the death knell for sea life, but as a supernatural omen of the widespread disruption, destruction, and decimation of all life—particularly human (1987).

this success can be attributed to someone called Fonga Sigde or Naymlap, or to somebody else, probably we shall never know for certain, yet the documents that have been reviewed in this paper—the art, the archaeological data, and the ethnohistorical record—leave no doubt that a formal means of importing Spondylus shells from Ecuador had been accomplished by Middle Sican times. I suggest that such a formal means was an official conduit, which, for convenience, we may call the Office of Fonga Sigde, an office that *someone* established in ancient Lambayeque.

CONCLUSIONS

I have suggested that the Naymlap story in its entirety may not be a fabrication (as concluded by Rowe 1948), nor simply a structural statement (as argued by Zuidema, this volume). I have pointed out that, of the eight courtiers named in the ethnohistory, at least seven could have existed. The logic of my argument is that the goods or expertise they reportedly controlled are not mythical; all are well within the northern Peruvian prehistoric cultural tradition. I chose one courtier specifically, Fonga Sigde, who was referred to merely as a scatterer of seashell dust in the royal pathway. I have tried to show, first, that the shell from which the dust was prepared—Spondylus—had become both treasure and wealth by Imperial Chimu times, but that it only began to appear on the North Coast in Moche V times, and its retrieval was not artistically represented until the Middle Sican period. Second, I have stressed that, because it was treasure, Spondylus would not have made its way casually onto the North Coast; it was imported by an organized effort that became the formal court office of Fonga Sigde.

This summary leads me to speculate why the artistic documents portraying Spondylus procurement exist at all. Each depiction is rendered in a costly medium: gold, silver, tapestry, or Spondylus-inlaid wood. Not everyone in Sican society would have had access to these goods. In fact, it is not improbable that these Spondylus diving representations were owned by the very people who controlled the importation of the actual shells, either the Fonga Sigde or the Sican Lord himself. Thus, the function of these depictions would have been to underscore the noble's position as controller of the ritual commodity by conspicuously displaying representations of its procurement. Furthermore, as I have already suggested, the first appearance of Spondylus collection in Middle Sican art may have been an attempt on the part of a Sican lord to claim credit for the trade arrangement itself. Above all, I would point out that if these seashells had not been venerated in ancient Peru, if Spondylus had not been ground into dust and placed in the royal tombs of Chimor, then it would be a great deal easier to believe that Fonga

Alana Cordy-Collins

Sigde was a mythical character. But Spondylus shells were accorded the status of treasure, and they were interred with kings.[7]

[7] C. Donnan ([Naymlap], this volume) has made a similar argument for Chotuna as Naymlap's palace.

BIBLIOGRAPHY

ALVA, WALTER L.
1988 Discovering the New World's Richest Unlooted Tomb. *National Geographic* 174(4): 510–549.

ALVA, WALTER L., and SUSANA MENESES DE ALVA
1985 Los murales de Ucupe en el valle de Zaña, norte del Perú. *Beiträge zur Allgemeinen und Vergleichenden Archäologie* 5(1983): 335–360. Deutsches Archäologisches Institut, Bonn.

ANTZE, GUSTAV
1930 *Metallarbeiten aus dem nordlichen Peru*. Ein Beitrag zur Kenntnis ihrer Formen. Museum für Völkerkunde, Hamburg.

CABELLO BALBOA, MIGUEL
[1586] *Miscelánea antártica: Una historia del Perú antiguo.*
1951 Universidad Nacional Mayor de San Marcos, Lima.

CONRAD, GEOFFREY W.
1982 The Burial Platforms of Chan Chan: Some Social and Political Implications. In *Chan Chan: Andean Desert City* (Michael E. Moseley and Kent C. Day, eds.): 87–118. University of New Mexico Press, Albuquerque.

CORDY-COLLINS, ALANA
n.d.a Mega-Niños, Spondylus Shells, and the Chimor-Salangone Connection. *Boletín del Museo de Arte Precolumbino*. Museo Chileno de Arte Precolumbino, Santiago. (Forthcoming)
n.d.b Burnt Offerings. Paper presented at the Institute for Andean Studies Annual Meeting, Berkeley, 1985.

DAVIDSON, JUDITH R.
n.d. The Spondylus Shell in Chimu Iconography. M.A. thesis, Department of Anthropology, California State University, Northridge, 1980.

DOCKSTADER, FREDERICK J.
1967 *Indian Art in South America*. New York Graphic Society, Greenwich.

DONNAN, CHRISTOPHER B.
1978 *Moche Art of Peru*. Museum of Cultural History. University of California, Los Angeles.

DONNAN, CHRISTOPHER B., and CAROL J. MACKEY
    1978   *Ancient Burial Patterns of the Moche Valley, Peru.* University of Texas Press, Austin.

EDWARDS, CLINTON R.
    1965   *Aboriginal Watercraft of the Pacific Coast of South America.* Ibero-Americana 47. University of California Press, Berkeley.

HEYERDAHL, THOR, and ARNE SKJOLSROLD
    1956   *Archaeological Evidence of Pre-Spanish Visits to the Galapagos Islands.* Society for American Archaeological Memoirs (12).

KEEN, A. MYRA
    1971   *Sea Shells of Tropical West America,* 2nd. ed. Stanford University Press, Stanford.

KROEBER, ALFRED L.
  1924–27 *The Uhle Pottery Collections from Moche.* University of California Publications in American Archaeology and Ethnology, 21 (A.L. Kroeber and R. Lowie, eds.). University of California Press, Berkeley.

LOTHROP, SAMUEL K.
    1932   Aboriginal Navigation off the West Coast of South America. *Journal of the Royal Anthropological Institute* 62: 229–256, plates 15–21. London.

LUMBRERAS, LUÍS G.
    1987   Childe and the Urban Revolution: The Andean Experience. In *Studies in the Neolithic and Urban Revolutions: The V. Gordon Childe Colloquium, Mexico 1986* (Linda Manzanilla, ed.): 327–344. BAR International Series 349, London.

MARCOS, JORGE G.
  1977–78 Cruising to Acapulco and Back with the Thorny Oyster Set: A Model for a Lineal Exchange System. *Journal of the Steward Anthropological Society* 9(1–2): 99–132. Urbana.

MARCOS, JORGE G., and PRESLEY NORTON
    1981   Interpretación sobre arqueología de la Isla de La Plata. *Miscelánea Antropológica Ecuatoriana. Boletín de los Museos del Banco Central del Ecuador* 1: 136–154.

NETHERLY, PATRICIA J.
    1984   The Management of Late Andean Irrigation Systems on the North Coast of Peru. *American Antiquity* 49(2): 227–254.
    n.d.   Local Level Lords on the North Coast of Peru. Ph.D. dissertation, Department of Anthropology, Cornell University, 1977.

NORTON, PRESLEY
    1986   El señorio de Salangone y la liga de mercaderes. *Miscelánea Antropológica Ecuatoriana. Boletín de los Museos del Banco Central del Ecuador* 6. Simposio de 45 Congreso Internacional de Americanistas, Universidad de los Andes, 17 Julio 1985. Bogotá, Colombia (José Alcina Franch and Segundo E. Moreno Yánex, eds.): 131–144.

n.d.　El señorio de Çalangone y la liga de mercaderes/The Kingdom of Çalangone and the League of Merchants: The Spondylus-Balsa Wood Cartel. Mimeographed.

NORTON, PRESLEY, RICHARD LUNNIS, and NIGEL NAYLING

1983　Excavaciones en Salango, Provincia de Manabí, Ecuador. *Cambio y Continuidad en Salango:* 9–72. Museo Arqueológico del Banco del Pacifico, Guayaquil.

OLSSON, A. A.

1961　*Molluscs of the Eastern Pacific, Particularly from the Southern Half of the Panamic-Pacific Faunal Province (Panama to Peru): Panamic-Pacific Pelecypoda.* Paleontological Research Institution, Ithaca.

PAULSEN, ALISON C.

1974　The Thorny Oyster and the Voice of God: Spondylus and Strombus in Andean Prehistory. *American Antiquity* 29(4): 597–607.

POZORSKI, THOMAS

1979　The Las Avispas Burial Platform at Chan Chan, Peru. *Annals of the Carnegie Museum* 48. Carnegie Museum of Natural History, Pittsburgh.

ROSTWOROWSKI DE DIEZ CANSECO, MARÍA

1970　Mercaderes del valle de Chincha en la época prehispánica: Un documento y unos comentarios. *Revista Española Antropologia Americana* 5: 135–178.

1975　Pescadores, artesanos, y mercaderes costeños en el Perú prehispanico. *Revista del Museo Nacional* 41: 311–339. Lima.

1977　Coastal Fishermen, Merchants, and Artisans in Pre-Hispanic Peru. *The Sea in the Pre-Columbian World* (Elizabeth P. Benson, ed.): 167–188. Dumbarton Oaks, Washington, D.C.

ROWE, ANN POLLARD

1984　*Costumes and Featherwork of the Lords of Chimor: Textiles from Peru's North Coast.* The Textile Museum, Washington, D.C.

ROWE, JOHN HOWLAND

1948　The Kingdom of Chimor. *Acta Americana* 6(1): 226–259.

RUBIÑOS Y ANDRADE, JUSTO MODESTO DE

[1782]　Succesión cronológica: ó serie historial de los curas de Mórrope,
1936　y Pacora en la Provincia de Lambayeque de Obispado de Truxillo del Perú. . . . In "Un manuscrito interesante . . ." (Carlos A. Romero, ed.). *Revista Histórica* 10(3): 289–363. Lima.

SALOMON, FRANK

1983　Shamanism and Politics in Late-Colonial Ecuador. *American Ethnologist* 10(3): 413–428.

SAMANO, JUAN DE

[1527]　Relación de los primeros descubrimientos de Francisco Pizarro y Diego
1844　de Almagro. *Colección de Documentos Inéditos para la Historia de España,* 5: 193–201. Madrid.

SANDWEISS, DANIEL H.

n.d. Choromytilus Chorus: Possible Precursor to Spondylus in Ancient Andean Ritual. Unpublished manuscript.

SCHAEDEL, RICHARD P.

1966 The Huaca El Dragón. *Journal de la Société des Américanistes* 55(2): 383–496.

SHIMADA, IZUMI

1981 The Batan Grande-La Leche Archaeological Project: The First Two Seasons. *Journal of Field Archaeology* 8: 405–446.

n.d. *The Mochica City-State of Pampa Grande*. University of Texas Press, Austin. (Forthcoming)

SILVA, MARÍA ISABEL

n.d. Agricultural and Fishing Communities of Coastal Ecuador: Ethnohistorical Evidence for Pre-Columbian Economic, Social, and Political Organization. Paper presented at the American Society for Ethnohistory, 1984, Albuquerque.

SPIELBERGEN, JORIS VAN

1906 *The East and West Indian Mirror, Being an Account of Joris van Spielbergen's Voyage Round the World [1614–1617] and the Australian Navigations of Jacob Le Maire* (J.A.J. de Villiers, trans., introd.). Hakluyt Society (18), London.

TREVIÑO DE SAENZ, MELINDA

1946–47 *Peru: Colección del Profesor Moises Saenz: Joyas, telas, cerámica*. Ministeria Justicia Instrucción, Culto y Beneficencia. Mexico.

TUSHINGHAM, A. D., et al.

1976 *Gold for the Gods*. Royal Ontario Museum, Ontario.

UHLE, MAX

n.d. Field Notes for Site H, Moche Valley, Peru. Microfilm. University of California, Berkeley.

The Northern Frontier of the Kingdom of Chimor: The Piura, Chira, and Tumbez Valleys

JAMES B. RICHARDSON III

CARNEGIE MUSEUM OF NATURAL HISTORY AND UNIVERSITY OF PITTSBURGH

MARK A. McCONAUGHY

PENNSYLVANIA STATE MUSEUM

ALLISON HEAPS DE PEÑA

UNIVERSITY OF PITTSBURGH

ELENA B. DÉCIMA ZAMECNIK

UNIVERSITY OF PITTSBURGH

INTRODUCTION

WHEN FRANCISCO PIZARRO entered the Chira Valley on May 25, 1532, he encountered a culture called the Tallanes (Pizarro [1571] 1921: 70; Zárate [1555] 1944: 31). Even with the presence of the Imperial Chimu and later the Inca in extreme northwest Peru, the Tallanes maintained their distinctiveness. Studies of surviving word lists from the Piura and Chira Valleys conclude that the Tallanes spoke a language unrelated to Yunga, the language of the Kingdom of Chimor (Rabinowitz 1983: 247).

This cultural distinctiveness of the region north of the Sechura Desert to the Ecuadoran border will be the focus of this paper. The presence in the Peruvian Departments of Piura and Tumbez of the Kingdom of Chimor

We wish to thank the personnel of the International Petroleum Company, Belco Petroleum Company, and Petro Peru who have given their time and support to our research efforts in the Piura and Chira Valleys. We also want to thank Robert L. Stuckenrath of the Radiation Biology Laboratory of the Smithsonian Institution and Dennis Coleman of the Radiocarbon Laboratory of the Illinois State Geological Survey for providing many of the radiocarbon dates on the ceramic period complexes. We wish to dedicate this paper to the memory of Edward P. Lanning, who laid the foundations for all subsequent research in northwest Peru.

and the evidence of cultural contact between Peru and Ecuador will be discussed.

THE ENVIRONMENTAL PARAMETERS

The Sechura Desert is some 90–150 km wide, separating the Lambayeque region from extreme northwest Peru. The geography of far northern Peru is quite different from that south of the Sechura Desert. The region north of the Sechura Desert to the Ecuadoran border is an environmental zone of transition between the tropical rainfall regime of Ecuador and the region of intense aridity that characterizes the Peruvian coast (Fig. 1).

A major coastal mountain range, the Amotape, parallels the coast from the Chira River to Tumbez. A series of three raised Pleistocene marine floors (Mancora, Talara, and Lobitos Tablazos) begins north of the Illescus Peninsula and reaches a height of 300 m at El Alto (Bosworth 1922).

This rugged terrain of extensive deserts, *tablazos,* and mountains is cut by three river valleys: the Piura, Chira, and Tumbez. The Piura Valley has the largest amount of land under irrigation of any coastal Peruvian valley, and it can be divided into an upper and a lower section with the city of Piura as the dividing point. The upper Piura Valley runs for 130 km, paralleling the foothills of the western Cordillera, and is partially within the annual rainfall zone. This stable water supply permits a large area of the upper Piura Valley to be irrigated and cultivated. The Chira is the third largest river in Peru in terms of water discharge, but ranks only seventh in the extent of land under irrigation. It cuts through the *tablazos* and is deeply entrenched. Only the narrow upper portion of the river is within the annual rainfall zone. There are three dry valleys (Pariñas, Mancora, and Bocapan) between the Chira and Tumbez Valleys, which have water flow only during El Niño periods. The Tumbez River receives annual rainfall and has the second highest water discharge of any Peruvian river, but due to geological factors its irrigated zone is small (Robinson 1964).

FAR NORTH COAST CULTURAL PHASES

The Imperial Chimu presence north of the Lambayeque Valley has received little attention in the literature; however, surveys in the 1970s have provided extensive evidence of Chimu influence in extreme northwestern Peru.[1] In the following discussion, settlement pattern data, analysis of surface ceramic collections, and radiocarbon dates are used to compare the

---

[1] J. Richardson surveyed from Cabo Blanco south to Colan; M. McConaughy focused on the Paita Peninsula south to Bayovar, A. Heaps de Peña concentrated on the Chira Valley, and E. Décima Zamecnik worked in the upper Piura Valley.

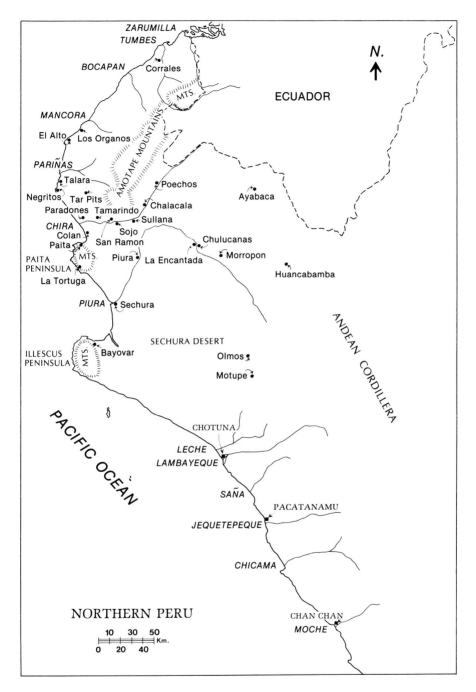

Fig. 1   Map of northern Peru showing the modern towns and archaeological sites mentioned in the text. Drawing by Nancy Perkins.

Chimu occupation of the Departments of Piura and Tumbez to those of the preceding cultural periods.

The survey data presented herein build upon David A. Kelley's (1971) and Edward P. Lanning's (1963) pioneering surveys in the Piura and Chira Valleys.[2] Only limited excavations have been conducted in extreme northern Peru; thus, the interpretations in this paper should be used with caution until more extensive research is completed in this relatively unknown region. In the lower Piura Valley, Ross T. Christensen (n.d.) excavated the late Sechura and Piura Phase site of Chusis. In the upper Piura Valley, Hans D. Disselhoff (1971) excavated seven Vicus tombs, and Jean Guffroy, Peter Kaulicke, and K. Makowski Hanuba (Guffroy 1987; Shimada and Shimada 1987–88: 15–22) are conducting excavations at Formative, Vicus, and Tallan (Piura) Phase sites. Mercedes Cárdenas Martín (1976, 1978) tested a series of Preceramic through Piura Phase sites along the Illescus Peninsula coast south to Reventazon. To date, no excavations have been carried out in the Chira Valley. In the Tumbez Valley Seiichi Izumi and Kazuo Terada (1966) established three ceramic phases through excavation.

Lanning (1963) proposed four chronologically significant ceramic styles based upon surface collections made by Ynez Haase. From suspected oldest to youngest, these were called Negritos, Paita, Sechura, and Piura. James B. Richardson III (1983) demonstrated that Negritos pottery was actually a utilitarian jar form of Sechura ware and that, therefore, Negritos can no longer be considered a valid pottery type. The other three ceramic styles and their chronological placement were confirmed by Richardson's (1983) investigations along the Chira beach ridges. The surveys conducted by Allison Heaps de Peña (n.d., Richardson and Heaps de Peña n.d.) and Mark A. McConaughy (n.d.) further corroborate this sequence and spatially have extended the known distribution of Paita, Sechura, and Piura pottery styles from Bayovar on the Illescus Peninsula, north to Los Organos. Radiocarbon dates correlated with these three pottery styles were used in conjunction with settlement pattern data to define chronological phases for Quebrada Pariñas, the Chira, and lower Piura River Valleys (Fig. 2).

The upper Piura River Valley presents a different ceramic chronology and settlement pattern. The earliest known ceramic period is Encantada, followed by Vicus, then Piura (Décima Zamecnik n.d.) (see Fig. 2). The Tumbez River Valley also presents a different ceramic sequence beginning with San Juan, followed by Pechiche, Garbanzal, and Tallan (Piura) (Izumi and Terada 1966) (Fig. 2).

---

[2] See J. Richardson (1977, n.d.) for a bibliography of research in the Departments of Piura and Tumbez.

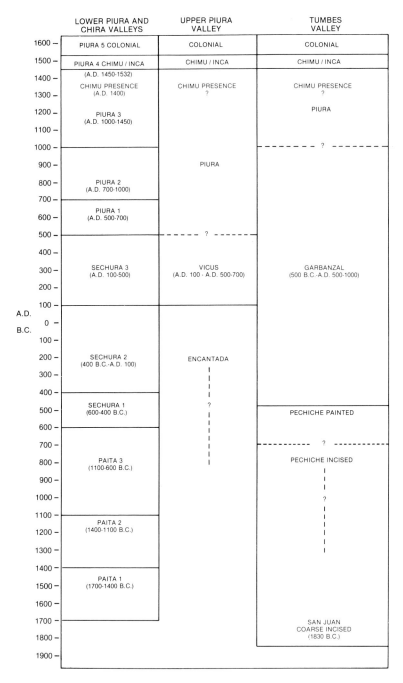

	LOWER PIURA AND CHIRA VALLEYS	UPPER PIURA VALLEY	TUMBES VALLEY
1600 —	PIURA 5 COLONIAL	COLONIAL	COLONIAL
1500 —	PIURA 4 CHIMU / INCA	CHIMU / INCA	CHIMU / INCA
1400 —	(A.D. 1450-1532)	CHIMU PRESENCE ?	CHIMU PRESENCE ?
1300 —	CHIMU PRESENCE (A.D. 1400)		
1200 —	PIURA 3 (A.D. 1000-1450)		PIURA
1100 —			
1000 —			------- ? -------
900 —		PIURA	
800 —	PIURA 2 (A.D. 700-1000)		
700 —	PIURA 1 (A.D. 500-700)		
600 —			
500 —		----- ? ------	
400 —			
300 —	SECHURA 3 (A.D. 100-500)	VICUS (A.D. 100 - A.D. 500-700)	GARBANZAL (500 B.C.-A.D. 500-1000)
200 —			
100 —			
A.D. 0 —			
B.C. 100 —			
200 —	SECHURA 2 (400 B.C.-A.D. 100)	ENCANTADA	
300 —			
400 —			
500 —	SECHURA 1 (600-400 B.C.)	?	PECHICHE PAINTED
600 —			
700 —			------- ? -------
800 —	PAITA 3 (1100-600 B.C.)		PECHICHE INCISED
900 —			
1000 —			?
1100 —			
1200 —	PAITA 2 (1400-1100 B.C.)		
1300 —			
1400 —			
1500 —	PAITA 1 (1700-1400 B.C.)		
1600 —			
1700 —			SAN JUAN COARSE INCISED (1830 B.C.)
1800 —			
1900 —			

Fig. 2   Chronological chart of the ceramic phases in the Piura, Chira, and Tumbez Valleys. Drawing by Nancy Perkins.

Based on changes in ceramic and settlement pattern data, the Piura Phase has been divided into five subphases: four prehistoric and one historic (Fig. 2). They are as follows: Phase 1, A.D. 500–700; Phase 2, A.D. 700–1000; Phase 3, A.D. 1000–1450; Phase 4, A.D. 1450–1532; and Phase 5, post-A.D. 1532 and representing the Colonial period.

Piura Phase ceramics are characterized by mold-manufactured forms, paddle stamping as a major decorative element, and reduction-fired blackware. Mold-made ceramics are reported from Moche contexts in the Moche Valley, and, thus, mass production techniques for pottery manufacture may have been introduced into northwestern Peru from the south (Donnan and Mackey 1978: 55). As far as can be ascertained, the earlier Sechura and Vicus peoples did not produce any mold-made ceramics. In fact, mold-made pottery does not appear until Piura Phase 3 in extreme northwestern Peru. The antecedents of paddle stamping first appear during the Middle Chimu period (A.D. 900–1100) in the Moche River Valley, along with the use of burnishing and a high frequency of reduction-fired blackware (Donnan and Mackey 1978: 289). In the Lambayeque Valley paddle stamping and blackware are dated to Early Sican times (A.D. 700–900) (Shimada, this volume). On the basis of current evidence, paddle stamping is present by A.D. 700 and blackware by A.D. 1000 in the Piura-Chira area (Richardson n.d.).

Many elements from the earlier Sechura Phase ceramics carry through to Piura Phase 1, indicating local cultural continuity. These ceramic elements include the use of white paint, applique decorations, and production of several jar forms. However, Piura Phase 1 potters appear to have applied white paint carelessly to their vessels; whereas the Sechura Phase potters were more exacting. New elements, not present in Sechura Phase ceramics, were added to the Piura Phase 1 ceramic complex. These include rolled vessel rims and loop handles on jars. These elements continue into Piura Phase 2 when paddle-stamped decorations appear for the first time.

Blackware and mold-made forms first appear in Piura Phase 3. Phase 3 ceramics have been found at the Bayovar site south of the Piura River mouth, and blackware specimens found at this site are referred to as Lambayeque ware by Cárdenas Martín (1978: 14–45), who also recovered a Chimu stirrup spout associated with paddle-stamped pottery at a site in Quebrada Nunura in the northern part of the Illescus Peninsula (1978: 13–14, 39, 49). Paddle-stamped pottery and burnished blackware have been recovered from Chira beach ridge 2 (Richardson 1983: 273) and from PPR-6, a large shell midden near Parachique.

It is during Piura Phase 3 that evidence for the Imperial Chimu presence appears in the Piura-Chira area. Piura Phase 3 sites are located throughout far northwestern Peru to Tumbez where Piura pottery is found at the Garbanzal site (Ishida et al. 1960: 119, 123, 424–425) and at San Pedro de los Incas at Corrales (Ishida et al. 1960: 123, 145, pl. 62: 7–10, 16). The end date for Garbanzal has not been conclusively established, but four radiocarbon dates indicate that Garbanzal ends between A.D. 1060 and 1145. However, Izumi and Terada (1966: 71) believe these dates are contaminated by later carbon, and they place Garbanzal between 500 B.C. and A.D. 500. Another possibility is that the succeeding Piura Phase may not have reached Tumbez until late in its spread from the Piura-Chira area and that the four dates for the end of Garbanzal are correct. In all collections from Piura Phase 3 sites from the Piura and Chira Valleys, Chimu vessels are represented (Lothrop 1948: 62–64; Means 1931: 179–183; Scott 1895: 14).

Piura Phase 4 begins with the Inca domination of the region and ends with the Spanish Conquest in A.D. 1532. Inca ceramics are found at the former Piura Phase 3 centers of Monte Lima (PV9-70), San Ramon (PV9-71), and Chalacala (PV9-54) in the Chira River Valley, and at San Pedro de los Incas at Corrales in the Tumbez River Valley.

Piura Phase 5, the Colonial period, is represented at PV7-14 in upper Quebrada Pariñas where Spanish olive oil vessels and associated Piura Phase 5 paddle-stamped pottery date to A.D. 1740 (Richardson n.d.).

PIURA PHASE SETTLEMENT PATTERNS

During the preceding Sechura Phase (600 B.C.–A.D. 500, Fig. 2) populations of extreme northwestern Peru apparently were divided into fishing or agricultural specialists. Fishing hamlets or villages of five to twenty houses were located along the coast of the Paita Peninsula and at the mouth of Quebrada Pariñas. An inland agricultural population is represented by two large Sechura Phase villages located north of Quebrada Pariñas and by a small cluster of Sechura Phase houses in the central Chira Valley. The largest recorded Sechura Phase agricultural site was the seventy-five-room PV7-18 situated in Quebrada Honda, a tributary of Quebrada Pariñas.

Part-time shellfish collecting was conducted along the Chira and Piura beach ridges by Sechura Phase peoples. Chira beach ridges 3–5 are continuous middens testifying to the Sechura Phase people's heavy exploitation of shellfish. Small U-shaped features, representing short-term lean-to dwellings or windbreaks, were built by the shellfish collectors.

No Sechura Phase ceremonial centers have been located or recognized. Evidence is also lacking for the development of polities or other forms of integrated political organization in the Chira and lower Piura River Valleys during the Sechura Phase.

Conversely, the Encantada and Vicus Phase populations were developing some form of more complex political organization in the upper Piura Valley. This may be due to the fact that the upper Piura Valley had a 130-km long floodplain and seasonal rainfall that provided the Vicus populations with a greater agricultural potential than many other coastal valleys. This, coupled with the interaction of the Vicus with the Moche state to the south, may partially explain why the upper Piura Valley reached a higher level of complexity prior to the Piura Phase than did the lower Piura, Chira, and Tumbez Valleys. Elena B. Décima Zamecnik's (n.d.) survey located a number of Encantada and Vicus Phase *huacas* and residential centers. The largest Vicus Phase *huaca* is a rectangular—88-m long, 44-m wide, 15-m tall—adobe pyramid (PV11-95) located near La Huaca, northeast of Chulucanas. There also is evidence for social ranking within the society based on differential quantities of precious or exotic grave goods placed with Vicus burials (Lechtman 1982). The Moche-like copper artifacts from Loma Negra conceivably could be from only one or two high-status tombs.

Piura Phase 1 and 2 settlement patterns contrast greatly with those of the preceding Sechura and Vicus Phases. Evidence for inland farming villages, *huacas,* residential centers, and large cemeteries has not been documented during Piura Phase 1 or 2. Fishing hamlets or villages dating to Piura Phase 1 and 2 were apparently confined to the Piura and Chira coasts and the Illescus Peninsula. There were no Piura fishing villages established along the Paita Peninsula, which was favored by Sechura Phase fishermen. However, part-time shellfish collecting along the Paita coastline and Piura River beach ridges intensified during Piura Phases 1 and 2. A series of large Piura Phase shell mounds extends from the mouth of the Chira River south to Parachique. The last Piura River beach ridge also has a series of large shell mounds strung out south of, through, and north of the village of San Pedro. Chira beach ridge 3 also provides evidence of having been utilized extensively by early Piura Phase peoples.

The evidence for part-time shellfish collecting along the Piura and Chira River beach ridges during Piura Phases 1 and 2 suggests there were inland farming villages that were destroyed or masked by Piura Phase 3 and later settlements in these valleys. Thus the contrast between the Sechura Phase and early Piura Phase settlement patterns might not be as great as it now appears. Also, if some of the Piura Phase 3 and 4 centers described later were first established during Piura Phase 1 or 2, something that cannot be determined from survey work, then contrasts with the Vicus Phase would not be as apparent.

It is during late Piura Phase 3 that centers consisting of a particular type of large adobe *huacas* and associated walled compounds appear in the Chira River Valley. There are five major and a number of lesser centers currently recorded from the Chira Valley and one major one from the Piura Valley.

At Paredones, just east of San Felipe de Vichayal and 20 km inland from the mouth of the Chira River, there are three *huacas,* several rectangular enclosures, and a twenty-five room Inca storage facility on the *tablazo* above the center. The Paredones complex was first recorded by Samuel Scott (1895: 9–10) who reported that these *huacas* were constructed of circular to oval tall adobes with rounded tops (hereafter referred to as circular adobes) and had two or three terraces (see also Ishida et al. 1960: 129, 426, 427, figs. 1–2).

Our studies of the Paredones complex (PV9-9) distinguished three *huacas* built of circular adobes. The largest was built with two terraced levels, but the terraced form of the other two *huacas* described by Scott (1895: 9–10) could not be confirmed by our investigations because modern dwellings were constructed on top of them. The circular adobes were usually set upright in layers, but occasionally some were set upside down and all were cemented with mortar (Fig. 3). Blackware and paddle-stamped pottery were recovered eroding from throughout the adobe construction layers, and these sherds indicate that the *huacas* were built during Piura Phase 3.

The largest center in the Chira River Valley is located 15 km upstream from Paredones, just east of the town of Tamarindo. This site was first reported by Scott (1895: 19–20) and is in an area known as Monte Lima (PV9-70). The site complex consists of at least six *huacas,* various rectangular platforms, compounds, and cemeteries, and a large fortress covering more than a km² (Figs. 4–5). The Monte Lima complex is partially situated upon the top of an eroded one-km long remnant of the Talara Tablazo. The remainder of the complex is on a terrace bordering the Chira floodplain. On top of the western end of the *tablazo* ridge is a partially destroyed *huaca* and associated walled courtyards known as Huaca Reina. Directly to the west

Fig. 3 *Huaca* at Paredones in the lower Chira Valley showing construction with circular adobes. Photograph by James Richardson.

Fig. 4 Huaca Rica and associated compounds of the Monte Lima complex in the Chira Valley. Air photograph by Mark McConaughy.

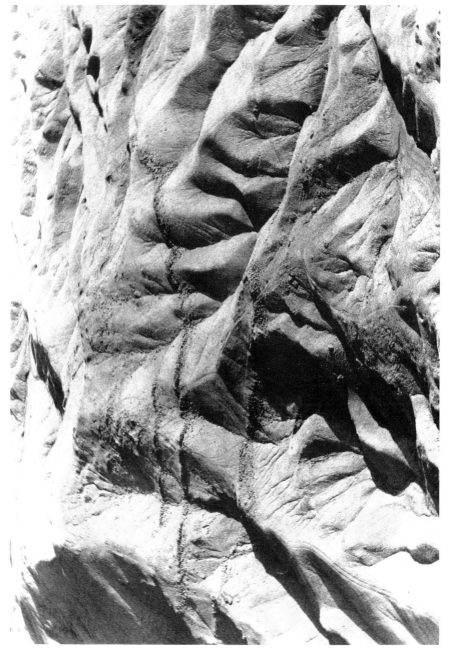

Fig. 5   Fortress at the east end of the Monte Lima complex in the Chira Valley. Photograph by Mark McConaughy.

Fig. 6 The San Ramon complex in the Chira Valley. Upper left: terraced *huaca* of circular adobes; lower left: large compound (circle in center is a modern well); upper right: a residential compound. Photograph by the Servicio Aerofotográfico Nacional, Lima.

and below Huaca Reina is Huaca Rey, and to the east and below Huaca Reina is Huaca Rica and a series of walled compounds. Huaca Rica is the largest *huaca* of the Monte Lima complex. All of these *huacas* were constructed of circular adobes. Two other platforms on the *tablazo* remnant, a separate residential compound, cemeteries, and some small *huacas* are also part of the Monte Lima complex. A large, 70-m high, fortified hill forms the eastern boundary of the Monte Lima complex. Three walls made of rough cut blocks of *tablazo* rock are laid in courses along the northeast side of the hill. Natural spurs on the hill act as bastions and were made into fortified rooms. The southern part of the hill is very steep and apparently did not warrant construction of defensive walls.

The San Ramon (PV9-71) center is located 10 km east of Monte Lima and was also first reported by Scott (1895: 18). It is composed of one *huaca* constructed of circular adobes, with three terraces and an attached walled compound, a detached walled residence compound, cemeteries, a series of smaller mounds, and irrigation canals (Fig. 6).

The fourth center is Chalacala (PV9-54) located in the upper Chira Valley on a large terrace and adjacent floodplain. Kelley (1971) noted twenty *huacas,* most of which are small mounds. However, the site is dominated by three large *huacas,* a series of walled compounds, and a large rectangular enclosure. Two of these *huacas* and associated attached walled compounds are situated on the terrace and display evidence of stone rubble construction (Fig. 7). The other large *huaca* is made of circular adobes and is located in the Chira River floodplain (Fig. 8). This *huaca* only produced specimens of Piura Phase 3 paddle-stamped pottery and blackware. The two stone rubble *huacas* have paddle-stamped pottery, blackware, and Inca sherds in their fill, indicating that they were later constructions built during Piura Phase 4. Chalacala is situated at the point where the Chira floodplain begins to narrow and where the Piura and Chira Rivers come to within 5 km of each other. Thus, Chalacala is in a position to have been able to control contact and communication between Chira and Piura River Valley populations and movements west of the Amotape Mountains to Tumbez.

The fifth center is the Sojo *huaca,* located on the south side of the Chira River and west of the modern town of Sullana. It is described by Philip A. Means (1931: 179–218) as having three terraces. Samuel K. Lothrop (1948: 59–60) indicated that the Sojo *huaca* was constructed with circular adobes, a point that was confirmed in 1987. Lothrop also recovered Piura Phase 3 paddle-stamped pottery and a blackware sherd from the *huaca* walls.

Narihuala is the largest Piura Phase *huaca* in the lower Piura River Valley (Ishida et al. 1960: 134, 135, 428; Kelley 1971: 15; Ramos de Cox 1973). The Japanese expedition reported that both circular and rectangular adobes were used in the construction of this *huaca.* They also recovered Piura Phase 3 paddle-stamped and blackware pottery from the *huaca* fill.

Fig. 7   Rubble *huaca* and associated walls at Chalacala in the upper Chira Valley.
Photograph by James Richardson.

There are seventy-eight recorded Piura Phase sites in the upper Piura
Valley (Décima Zamecnik n.d.). The largest Piura Phase 3 *huaca* (PV11-62)
is situated on Comite Carrasco Cooperative property, located east of the
modern town of La Matanza. Most of the Piura Phase sites are habitation
sites or, more rarely, *huacas;* however, two sites, located at the point where
the Piura River cuts through an extension of the Andean foothills, apparently were fortresses. The first of these fortresses is located on Cerro Santo
Tome (PV11-52), situated north of the modern Morropon bridge. Two
walls were built along the western flank of Cerro Santo Tome and two
rectangular structures were erected on its summit. These structures were
made from rough-cut stone blocks laid in courses that were cemented with a
mud mortar in some places. A major Pre-Hispanic road was situated to the
west and southwest of this fortress. A larger fortification (PV11-42) was
located near the village of Pabur Viejo, upriver from the first fortress
(PV11-52). It consists of four concentric walls built around the hill slopes
and a high oval wall enclosing a series of rectangular rooms on top of the hill
(Fig. 9). These structures were built of rough-cut stone set in courses. Piura
Phase 3 paddle-stamped pottery, blackware, and sherds of large storage jars

Fig. 8   Circular adobe *huaca* at Chalacala in the upper Chira Valley. Photograph by James Richardson.

were recovered from both fortress sites. There also is a large Piura Phase 3–4 urban center (PV11-74) located on the opposite side of the Piura River at the town of Piura Viejo, which has structures and walls made of rough-cut stone blocks. A ruined adobe Colonial church at the site testifies to its occupation into Piura Phase 5.

There is a *huaca* with attached walled compounds at San Pedro de los Incas at Corrales, south of the modern town of Tumbez (Ishida et al. 1960: 123, 425; Petersen 1962: 373–374, plan 3). This site is a Piura Phase 3 center. The structures were built of adobe, and although the adobe form has yet to be determined, it is suspected to be circular. There is evidence of a Piura Phase 4 presence here as well; a series of Inca compounds are situated on the terrace above the site.

Inca sherd concentrations have been found at Monte Lima, San Ramon, and Chalacala in the Chira River Valley, indicating that they continued to function as centers during Piura Phase 4. A series of Inca storerooms is located at Paredones in the lower Chira Valley. At Cerro Ñañañique, in the upper Piura Valley, a six-room walled rectangular construction is dated to the Inca period (Guffroy 1987: 14).

Fig. 9   Air photo of the Piura Phase fortress near Pabur Viejo in the upper Piura Valley. Photograph by the Servicio Aerofotográfico Nacional, Lima.

The only known purely Inca installation, however, is at the site of Ayapati in the highlands near the town of Ayabaca. Ayapati, with its cut stonework construction, might have been the Inca administrative center for the Andean portion of extreme northern Peru (Polía 1972, 1973).

THE CHIMU PRESENCE IN EXTREME NORTHWEST PERU

As mentioned above, it is during Piura Phase 3 that Imperial Chimu influence is seen in the Piura, Chira, and Tumbez Valleys for the first time. Its influence here can be examined and compared to the patterns of the overall growth of the Kingdom of Chimor. The development and expansion of the Kingdom of Chimor occurred in three stages (T. Topic, this volume). During the first stage (A.D. 900–1000/1050) consolidation of the Moche Valley was accomplished. After control of the Moche Valley was established, the first wave of expansion took place. Between A.D. 1130 and 1200 the region from the Chao to the Jequetepeque Valleys was brought into the Kingdom of Chimor. The second expansion incorporated the Nepeña and Casma Valleys by A.D. 1300; whereas the Lambayeque region's annexation is dated by various investigators to A.D. 1300–1350 (Kolata, this volume), A.D. 1370 (Donnan [Chotuna], this volume), or sometime after

A.D. 1350 and possibly as late as A.D. 1400 (Cavallaro and Shimada 1988: 79; Shimada, this volume).

There is one radiocarbon date from the Chira Valley that suggests the Kingdom of Chimor was influencing extreme northwest Peru by A.D. 1400. At Monte Lima, one of the compounds near Huaca Rica is dated to A.D. 1450 ± 85 (SI-3180), in association with Chimu blackware. In Tumbez, Chimu wares have been found at Garbanzal and at San Pedro de los Incas at Corrales (Ishida et al. 1960: 119, 123, 424–425).

We suggest that the influence of the Kingdom of Chimor on its frontier at Tumbez took place quite late. The Tallanes that Francisco Pizarro encountered are thought to have been the dominant culture in this region prior to the Chimu and Inca intrusions (Mejía Xesspe 1960: 206). As pointed out in the introduction to this paper, the populace encountered by the Spanish spoke a language unrelated to Yunga. This suggests that the Chimu presence was late, since there was not time for Yunga to have replaced the indigenous language.

Chimu influence did not stop at Tumbez; Chimu vessels have been recovered from sites on the islands of La Plata and La Puna in the Guayas Basin (Meggers 1966; Stothert n.d.) and possibly at Cerro Narrio, in the southern Andes of Ecuador (Collier and Murra 1943: 66).

There is a striking similarity between the Terminal Chimu (A.D. 1100/ 1150–1370) adobes at Pacatnamu and the circular adobes of the Piura and Chira Valleys. At Pacatnamu in the Jequetepeque Valley these late adobes are round, ellipsoidal, flat-based ovoid shapes (Ishida et al. 1960: 158; Mc-Clelland 1986: 29). The circular adobes in the Piura and Chira Valleys' *huacas*, although taller, are similar in form to those at Pacatnamu, but the architecture is very different. In the intervening area the *huacas* at Chotuna, Chornancap, and at Batan Grande in the Lambayeque Valley are built of rectangular tall or high loaf adobes (Donnan [Chotuna], this volume; Shimada, this volume). The evolution of adobe forms in the Lambayeque Valley is from rectangular to increasingly higher loaf shapes in the Chimu period (ibid.). This also holds true for the Moche Valley (Kolata 1982).

The adobe sequence has not been worked out for the Piura, Chira, and Tumbez Valleys, but if it follows the same trend as in the Moche, Jequetepeque, and Lambayeque Valleys, the tall, circular, flat-based adobes of extreme northwest Peru would be late in the Piura sequence.

This speculation is strengthened by the fact that the A.D. 1310 Cerro Huaco site in the Pariñas Valley is constructed of rectangular adobes, and the Monte Lima compound in the Chira Valley, with its A.D. 1450 date, is made of circular adobes. Further support comes from the earlier Vicus *huacas* in the upper Piura Valley having been constructed of rectangular adobes (Décima Zamecnik n.d.). There are also a number of Piura Phase rectangular adobe *huacas* reported for the Chira Valley at Cerro Mocho and

Hacienda San Jose east of San Ramon, and at Vistaflorida near Sullana (Ishida et al. 1960: 10, 128, 427) that may date to Piura Phase 1 or 2.

PRE-PIURA PHASE AFFINITIES

Until recently it was felt that Peruvian cultures south of the Sechura and Ecuadoran cultures had little cultural influence on the indigenous societies of far northwest Peru prior to the Piura Phase (Burger 1984a: 42–45). However, recent work in the Lambayeque, Cajamarca, Piura, and Chira regions has revealed evidence of Early Horizon influence in extreme northwest Peru.

Paita Phase 2 and 3 (1400–600 B.C.) vessels are decorated with incised panels of tear drops, circles with dots, and bowls with incised fret designs characteristic of Cupisnique designs. Similar influence is seen in specimens of Pechiche Incised ware (Izumi and Terada 1966: pls. 20b and 24a,b). A Cupisnique-style vessel from the Piura Valley is illustrated by Means (1931: fig. 79). The Rojo Grabado and Lineas Incisas Cortantes ceramics from Pacopampa, Cajamarca, are similar to the Paita 3 (1100–600 B.C.) and Sechura 1 wares (600–400 B.C.) (Fung Pineda 1975: 152, 180, 202, figs. 15 [1–10], 18 [8–14]). Pandanche B, near Pacopampa (Kaulicke 1975: figs. 12 and 15b), also has bowls and incised designs comparable to those of Paita Phases 2–3. The Bagua complex of the Utacubamba River in the northeastern Andes is considered (Shady and Rosas 1979: 126, figs. 21, 22, 24) to have affinities with Paita Phases 2 and 3 and to the Pacopampa-Pacopampa Phase at Pacopampa. Ceramics from Huaca Cholope at Batan Grande in the La Leche Valley are comparable to Paita 3, Sechura 1, and Encantada pottery (dated at 580 ± 65 B.C. [DIC-1386], Shimada 1982: 145–148). Jean Guffroy (1987: 21) has found Chavin elements in the Formative ceramics from Cerro Ñañañique in the upper Piura Valley. Izumi Shimada (1982: 148) has proposed that these Early Horizon cultures of the Lambayeque and Cajamarca areas are part of as yet undefined "Cupisnique Religious Tradition." This proposed tradition, dating as early as 1000–1200 B.C., can now be extended into extreme northwest Peru.

Paita also has similarities with the coastal Ecuadoran complexes. The Paita date range (1700–600 B.C.) overlaps with Valdivia 6 through 8, Machalilla, and Chorrera. The combed decorations and the carinated bowls of Paita Phases 1 and 2 are found in late Valdivia and Machalilla wares (Meggers, Evans, and Estrada 1965). Machalilla red-banded ware is similar to Paita Phase 2 and 3 red-lined decorations, and the predominant everted low-rimmed jar of Paita is also present in Late Valdivia and Machalilla. According to Peter Kaulicke (1981: 388), Pandanche A, near Cajamarca, has affinities with Valdivia 8 and Early Machalilla. Valdivia 8 is known from La Plata Island and Arenillas of southern Ecuador, and it now appears that late

Valdivia ceramic elements were spreading southward into the coastal and highland zones of northern Peru by 2000 B.C.

Sechura Phase ceramics of the Piura and Chira Valleys are similar to those of Jambeli in southern Ecuador (Estrada, Meggers, and Evans 1964), Garbanzal from the Tumbez Valley (Izumi and Terada 1966), and Vicus in the upper Piura Valley (Lumbreras 1979). Sechura, Vicus, Garbanzal, and Jambeli are considered to be regional expressions of a white-on-red and negative-painted ceramic tradition. Vicus appears to originate after A.D. 100 and lasts until about A.D. 500–700 (Richardson n.d.).

Interaction with groups from south of the Sechura Desert intensified during the Vicus Phase. A strong Moche trading presence in the upper Piura River Valley is suggested by a wide range of Vicus-Moche vessel forms and metal remains recovered from Vicus sites (Lechtman 1982; Lumbreras 1979: 118–119; Richardson n.d.; Schaedel 1985: 449; Shimada 1982: 152–153, and this volume). It is noteworthy that during Sechura Phases 2 and 3, there is evidence of copper smelting at PV7-18 in Quebrada Honda and possibly at PV10-33 on the Paita Peninsula. Metallurgy is one of the major hallmarks of Moche and Vicus cultures and may have spread from the upper Piura Valley to the lower Piura Valley north to Quebrada Honda. However, during these phases, the southern interaction with the far North Coast appears to have been the result of trade rather than of Moche conquest.

EXTREME NORTHWEST PERU: BARRIER OR FILTER?

Extreme northwest Peru consistently has been thought to be a barrier to significant cultural interaction between cultures south of the Sechura Desert and Ecuador (e.g., Burger 1984a: 33; Parsons and Hastings 1988: 197). Nonetheless, there is increasing evidence that the area north of the Sechura Desert in Peru was influenced by cultures and events both south of the Sechura Desert and north of Tumbez before the Chimu presence in this region.

The town of Sechura in lower Piura Valley was historically a focus of commercial raft movements to Lima. The Piura Phase sites at Colan and from the mouth of the Piura River south to Bayovar contain some of the largest shell middens known from Peru for this period. Piura populations at these sites may well have participated in the maritime traffic from Ecuador to Peru south of the Sechura Desert that passed along the Piura coast.

The development of exchange networks between Mesoamerica and Ecuador began as early as 6000 B.C. when the Vegas peoples of the Santa Elena Peninsula were practicing similar burial patterns to those at Cerro Mangote in Panama (Stothert 1985). Contact between Ecuador and Peru begins as early as the Preceramic period and is indicated by the presence of a few fragments of Spondylus shell from La Paloma (Quilter n.d.: 65) and Aspero (Feldman n.d.: 162). The Valdivia motif on the Huaca Prieta gourd (Lathrap et al. 1975: 29) further substantiates contacts with Ecuador by 2500 B.C. During the Peruvian ceramic periods Spondylus was a major medium of exchange for the maritime merchants of Ecuador, who also traded with Mesoamerica and Peru (Fonseca and Richardson 1978; Marcos 1977/78; Marcos and Norton 1982). Spondylus and Strombus fragments are also found at Early Horizon sites in Peru (Burger 1984a: 49; 1984b: 257).

There is increasing evidence of Spondylus use by the Moche people in the Lambayeque and Moche Valleys (Donnan 1986; Shimada 1982: 164–165; T. Topic 1982: 273). In Middle Sican times (A.D. 900–1100) there were Spondylus workshops and the production of copper double-T shaped ingots (*naipes*). Izumi Shimada (1985: 386) feels that the *naipes* were used as a medium of exchange with Ecuadoran merchants. Certainly Spondylus must have been one category of goods traded for by the Sican peoples (see Cordy-Collins, this volume). Spondylus is present in even greater quantities during the Late Intermediate period from many Chimu sites throughout the kingdom. Spondylus has been recovered from Cerro Vicus in the upper Piura Valley, but it is uncertain to what phase the Spondylus dates (Shimada and Shimada 1987-88: 21). Although Richard Burger (1984a: 51–53) does not take into consideration maritime trade, seaborne commerce was certainly a major factor in the exchange of commodities between Ecuador and Peru. Llama caravans may also have brought the precious shell commodity into Peru. There is ample evidence of ocean-going watercraft in Peru from Moche and later periods based on ceramic depictions, models, and actual raft parts (Engel 1983: 129, 142; Fonseca and Richardson 1978). There is also abundant evidence of the great cargo rafts plying the coasts of Peru and Ecuador during the Colonial period (Cordy-Collins, this volume; Edwards 1965; Fonseca and Richardson 1978).

The late Pre-Hispanic maritime merchant center of Chincha was engaged in far-flung commerce by land and sea, as far north as Ecuador (Rostworowski 1977: 181; Sandweiss n.d.). During the same time period, the island of Puna was the center of a major maritime trading power in Ecuador (Stothert n.d.). The people of Puna exchanged such items as salt for precious metals and other commodities through long-distance trade. The existence of maritime trade had its roots in the Preceramic period, and it might have been more extensive than the current evidence suggests. For example, the archaeological evidence for the thousands of eighteenth-century U.S. whaling voyages along the Peruvian coast is almost nonexistent. Without a written record of this maritime traffic, it would not be known (Richardson and Décima Zamecnik 1977).

This implied maritime commerce further lends support to the accounts that Taycanamo, legendary founder of the Imperial Chimu dynasty, might have come from extreme northern Peru (Conrad, this volume). The Naymlap legend, which indicates that a lord and his court arrived in the

Lambayeque Valley on balsa rafts, also implies that transport of armies by sea for conquest purposes was part of a northern coastal military strategy. Alana Cordy-Collins (this volume) argues that Fonga Sigde, the shell purveyor in the Naymlap legend, is most probably a real figure whose office controlled the procurement of Spondylus from Ecuador.

CONCLUSIONS

Except for the ubiquitous paddle-marked and burnished blackware pottery found throughout the Kingdom of Chimor, the ceramic indicators of either Sican or Imperial Chimu influence are rarely present in the surface collections from the Piura, Chira, and Tumbez Valleys. In collections of whole vessels from extreme northwest Peru there are Sican and Chimu vessels, but their provenance is not always satisfactorily documented.

In documenting the expansion of the Kingdom of Chimor, most investigators rely upon architectural forms and brick sequences to identify the presence of the Imperial Chimu. From the data at hand, it is not possible to ascertain whether the Kingdom of Chimor dominated or simply brought extreme northwest Peru into their sphere of influence. Present architectural evidence indicates that the kingdom did not dominate the region, but rather integrated with the polities holding control over the Piura, Chira, and Tumbez Valleys sometime after A.D. 1400. The architecture of the Piura Phase 3 sites are dissimilar to Imperial Chimu administrative centers such as Manchan, Chan Chan, and Farfan. In addition, they are unlike and not of the magnitude of the great centers located immediately south of the Sechura Desert, such as Pacatnamu and the Batan Grande complex. Although Piura Phase rectangular adobe *huacas* in the Chira Valley have not been dated, the circular adobe *huacas* and associated structures are clearly late phenomena and date to around A.D. 1400–1450.

Extreme northwest Peru maintained its distinctiveness to the time of Spanish contact and, although the region seems to have felt pressure from the Imperial Chimu, the Kingdom of Chimor did not control this region as it did its domains south of the Sechura Desert.

As has been demonstrated, far northwest Peru was never a barrier to cultural transmission from Ecuador or Peru south of the Sechura Desert. Maritime trade between Ecuador and Peru was initiated as early as the late Preceramic period and continued and increased through time when major maritime trading centers emerged in Peru and Ecuador. The Piura, Chira, and Tumbez areas constitute a crucial link in the long-term and intensive interaction between Peru and Ecuador, and, thus, it is essential that future researchers turn their attention to this relatively unknown quarter of Peru.

Admittedly, our interpretations are founded on a data base that is smaller than we would like, but we hope that our discussion is suggestive of the macro-cultural trends that prevailed in the far North Coast during the ceramic periods.

BIBLIOGRAPHY

BOSWORTH, THOMAS O.
  1922 *Geology of the Tertiary and Quaternary Periods in the North-West Part of Peru.* Macmillan and Co., New York.

BURGER, RICHARD L.
  1984a Archaeological Areas and Prehistoric Frontiers: The Case of Formative Peru and Ecuador. In *Social and Economic Organization in the Prehispanic Andes* (David I. Bowman, Richard L. Burger, and Mario A. Rivera, eds.): 33–71. British Archaeological Reports International Series 194. London.
  1984b *The Prehistoric Occupation of Chavín de Huántar, Peru.* University of California Publications in Anthropology 14. University of California Press, Berkeley.

CÁRDENAS MARTÍN, MERCEDES
  1976 Informe preliminar numero uno del trabajo de campo en Piura (Bajo Piura, Sechura e Illescus), Febrero de 1976. *Seminario de Arqueología, Instituto Riva-Aguero, Pontificia Universidad Católica del Perú,* Lima.
  1978 *Columna cronológica para el desierto de Sechura-Piura.* Seminario de Arqueología, Instituto Riva-Aquero, Pontificia Universidad Católica del Perú, vol. 2, Lima.

CAVALLARO, RAFFAEL, and IZUMI SHIMADA
  1988 Some Thoughts on Sicán Marked Adobes and Labor Organization. *American Antiquity* 53: 75–101.

CHRISTENSEN, ROSS TAYLOR
  n.d. *An Archaeological Study of the Illescas-Jubones Coast of Northern Peru and Southern Ecuador.* Ph.D. dissertation, Department of Anthropology, University of Arizona, 1956.

COLLIER, DONALD, and JOHN V. MURRA
  1943 *Survey and Excavations in Southern Ecuador.* Anthropological Series, Field Museum of Natural History 35, publication 528. Chicago.

DÉCIMA ZAMECNIK, ELENA B.
  n.d. Report on an Archaeological Survey Conducted in the Upper Piura in 1977. Submitted to the Instituto Nacional Cultural, Lima, 1977.

DISSELHOFF, HANS D.
  1971 *Vicús, eine neu entdeckte altperuanische Kultur.* Monumenta Americana 8. Berlin.

DONNAN, CHRISTOPHER B.
1986   Introduction. In *The Pacatnamu Papers, Volume 1* (Christopher B. Donnan and Guillermo A. Cock, eds.): 19–26. Museum of Cultural History, University of California, Los Angeles.

DONNAN, CHRISTOPHER B., and CAROL J. MACKEY
1978   *Ancient Burial Patterns of the Moche Valley, Peru.* University of Texas Press, Austin.

EDWARDS, CLINTON R.
1965   *Aboriginal Watercraft on the Pacific Coast of South America.* Ibero-Americana 47. University of California Press, Berkeley, California.

ENGEL, FRÉDÉRIC-ANDRÉ
1983   Notes on Pre-Columbian Fishhooks and Other Fishing Devices in the Cold Waters of Southern America. In *Prehistoric Andean Ecology, Man, Settlement and Environment in the Andes: Stone Typology* (Frédéric-André Engel, ed.): 129–160. Department of Anthropology, Hunter College, City University of New York, Humanities Press, New York.

ESTRADA, EMILIO, BETTY J. MEGGERS, and CLIFFORD EVANS
1964   The Jambeli Culture of South Coastal Ecuador. *Proceedings of the United States National Museum* 115: 483–558. Washington, D.C.

FELDMAN, ROBERT A.
n.d.   Aspero, Peru: Architecture, Subsistence Economy, and Other Artifacts of a Preceramic Maritime Chiefdom. Ph.D. dissertation, Department of Anthropology, Harvard University, 1980.

FONSECA Z., OSCAR, and JAMES B. RICHARDSON III
1978   South American and Mayan Cultural Contacts at the Las Huacas Site, Costa Rica. *Annals of the Carnegie Museum* 47 (13): 299–317.

FUNG PINEDA, ROSA
1975   Excavaciones en Pacopampa, Cajamarca. *Revista del Museo Nacional* 41: 129–207. Lima.

GUFFROY, JEAN
1987   *Informe sobre las investigaciones arqueológicas realizadas en 1987, en El Cerro Ñañañigue (Departamento de Piura-Perú).* Misión Arqueológica del Alto-Piura Convenio Orstom-PUC, Lima.

HEAPS DE PEÑA, ALLISON
n.d.   Report on an Archaeological Survey of the Chira River Valley. Submitted to Instituto Nacional Cultural, 1977.

ISHIDA, EIICHIRO, et al.
1960   *Andes: The Report of the University of Tokyo Scientific Expedition to the Andes in 1958.* Kadokawa Publishing Company, Tokyo.

IZUMI, SEIICHI, and KAZUO TERADA (eds.)
1966   *Andes 3: Excavations at Pechiche and Garbanzal, Tumbes Valley, Peru.* Kadokawa Publishing Company, Tokyo.

KAULICKE, PETER

> 1975   *Pandanche: Un caso del formativo en los Andes de Cajamarca.* Seminario de Historia Rural Andina, Lima.
> 1981   Keramik der Frühen Initialperiode aus Pandanche, Dpto. Cajamarca, Peru. *Beiträge zur Allgemeinen und Vergleichenden Archäologie* 3: 363–389, Munich.

KELLEY, DAVID H.

> 1971   Reconocimientos arqueológicos en la costa norte del Perú. *Arqueología y Sociedad* 5: 1–15. Publicación Trimestral del Museo de Arqueología y Etnología de la Universidad Nacional Mayor de San Marcos, Lima.

KOLATA, ALAN

> 1982   Chronology and Settlement Growth at Chan Chan. In *Chan Chan: Andean Desert City* (Michael E. Moseley and Kent C. Day, eds.): 67–85. University of New Mexico Press, Albuquerque.

LANNING, EDWARD

> 1963   *A Ceramic Sequence for the Piura and Chira Coast, North Peru.* University of California Publications in American Archaeology and Ethnology 46(2): 135–284. Berkeley.

LATHRAP, DONALD W., DONALD COLLIER, and HELEN CHANDRA

> 1975   *Ancient Ecuador: Culture, Clay and Creativity 3000–300 B.C.* Field Museum of Natural History, Chicago.

LECHTMAN, HEATHER N.

> 1982   New Perspectives on Moche Metallurgy: Techniques of Gilding Copper at Loma Negra, Northern Peru. *American Antiquity* 47: 3–30.

LOTHROP, SAMUEL K.

> 1948   Pariñas-Chira Archaeology: A Preliminary Report. In *A Reappraisal of Peruvian Archaeology* (Wendell C. Bennett, ed.): 53–64. Memoirs of the Society for American Archaeology 4.

LUMBRERAS, LUÍS G.

> 1979   *El arte y la vida Vicús.* Banco Popular del Perú, Lima.

MARCOS, JORGE G.

> 1977–78   Cruising to Acapulco and Back with the Thorny Oyster Set: A Model for a Lineal Exchange System. *Journal of the Steward Anthropological Society* 9 (1–2): 99–132. Urbana.

MARCOS, JORGE G., and PRESLEY NORTON (eds.)

> 1982   *Primer simposio de correlaciones antropológicas Andino-Mesoamericano.* Escuela Superior Politécnica del Litoral, Guayaquil.

McCLELLAND, DONALD H.

> 1986   Brick Seriation at Pacatnamu. In *The Pacatnamu Papers, Volume 1* (Christopher B. Donnan and Guillermo A. Cock, eds.): 27–46. Museum of Cultural History, University of California, Los Angeles.

McCONAUGHY, MARK A.

> n.d.   Prehistoria de la peninsula de Paita. Acuerdo No. 01/02, 06, 77, de la Comisión Técnica Calificadora de Proyectos Arqueológicas, 1977.

MEANS, PHILIP A.
    1931   *Ancient Civilizations of the Andes*. Charles Scribner's Sons, New York.
MEGGERS, BETTY J.
    1966   *Ecuador*. A. Praeger, New York.
MEGGERS, BETTY J., CLIFFORD EVANS, and EMILIO ESTRADA
    1965   Early Formative Period of Coastal Ecuador: The Valdivia and Macha-
            lilla Phases. *Smithsonian Contributions to Anthropology*, Vol. 1. Smithso-
            nian Institution, Washington, D.C.
MEJÍA XESSPE, TORIBIO
    1960   Algunos nuevos elementos de la civilización Recuay-Pasto en el ex-
            tremo norte del litoral peruano. In *Antiguo Perú, espacio y tiempo*
            (Ramiro Matos Mendieta, ed.): 205–217. Juan Mejía Baca, Lima.
PARSONS, JEFFREY R., and CHARLES M. HASTINGS
    1988   The Late Intermediate Period. In *Peruvian Prehistory* (Richard W.
            Keatinge, ed.): 190–229. Cambridge University Press, New York.
PETERSEN, GEORG
    1962   Las primeras operaciones militares de Francisco Pizarro en el Perú. In
            Actas y Trabajos de II Congreso Nacional de Historia del Perú 11: 359–383.
            Lima.
PIZARRO, PEDRO
    [1571] *Relation of the Discovery and Conquest of the Kingdoms of Peru* (1571). The
    1921   Cortes Society, New York.
POLÍA, MARIO
    1972   *Las ruinas de Aypate*. Colección Algarrobo 10, Universidad de Piura,
            Piura.
    1973   Investigaciones arqueológicas en la sierra de Piura. *Arqueología, Boletín
            del Seminario de Arqueología* 14, publicación no. 92: 35–84. Instituto
            Riva Aguero, Pontificia Universidad Católica del Perú, Lima.
QUILTER, JEFFREY
    n.d.   Paloma: Mortuary Practices and Social Organization of a Preceramic
            Village. Ph.D. dissertation, Department of Anthropology, University
            of California, Santa Barbara, 1981.
RABINOWITZ, JOEL
    1983   La Lengua Pescadora: The Lost Dialect of Chimu Fishermen. In *Investi-
            gations of the Andean Past: Papers of the First Annual Northeast Conference
            on Andean Archaeology and Ethnohistory* (Daniel H. Sandweiss, ed.):
            243–267. Latin American Studies Program, Cornell University, Ithaca.
RAMOS DE COX, JOSEFINA
    1973   Cuarto centros de interés etno-arqueológico en Piura. *Arqueología,
            Boletín del Seminario de Arqueología* 14, publicación no. 92: 4–7. Instituto
            Riva Aguero, Pontificia Universidad Católica del Perú, Lima.
RICHARDSON, JAMES B. III
    1977   A Bibliography of Archaeology, Pleistocene Geology and Ecology of
            the Departments of Piura and Tumbes, Peru. *Latin American Research
            Review* 12 (1): 122–137.

1983   The Chira Beach Ridges, Sea Level Change and the Origins of Maritime Economies on the Peruvian Coast. *Annals of the Carnegie Museum* 52(11): 265–276.

n.d.   The Chronology and Affiliations of the Ceramic Periods of the Departments of Piura and Tumbes, Northwest Peru. Paper presented at the 52nd Annual Meeting of the Society for American Archaeology, Toronto, May 1987.

RICHARDSON, JAMES B. III, and ALLISON HEAPS DE PEÑA

n.d.   The Emergence of the State in the Chira Region of Northwest Peru. Paper presented at the 39th Annual Meeting of the Society for American Archaeology, Washington, D.C., May 1974.

RICHARDSON, JAMES B. III, and ELENA B. DÉCIMA ZAMECNIK

1977   The Economic Impact of Martha's Vineyard Whalers on the Peruvian Port of Paita. *The Dukes County Intelligencer* 18: 67–93.

ROBINSON, DAVID A.

1964   *Peru in Four Dimensions.* American Studies Press, Lima.

ROSTWOROWSKI DE DIEZ CANSECO, MARÍA

1977   Coastal Fishermen, Merchants and Artisans in Pre-Hispanic Peru. In *The Sea in the Pre-Columbian World* (Elizabeth P. Benson, ed.): 167–186. Dumbarton Oaks, Washington, D.C.

SANDWEISS, DANIEL H.

n.d.   The Fishermen of Chincha: Occupational Specialization on the Late Prehispanic Andean Coast. Paper presented at the 50th Annual Meeting of the Society for American Archaeology, Denver, May 1985.

SCHAEDEL, RICHARD P.

1985   Coast-Highland Interrelationships and Ethnic Groups in Northern Peru (500 B.C.–A.D. 1980). In *Andean Ecology and Civilization* (Shozo Masuda, Izumi Shimada, and Craig Morris, eds.): 443–473. University of Tokyo Press, Tokyo.

SCOTT, SAMUEL MATTHEWSON

1895   The Huacos of Chira Valley, Peru. *American Anthropologist* 8: 8–22.

SHADY, RUTH, and HERMILIO ROSAS

1979   El complejo Bagua y el sistema de establecimientos en la sierra norte del Perú. *Ñawpa Pacha* 17: 109–142.

SHIMADA, IZUMI

1982   Horizontial Archipelago and Coast-Highland Interaction in North Peru. In *El hombre y su ambiente en los Andes centrales* (Luís Millones and Hiroyasu Tomoeda, eds): 185–257. Senri Ethnological Studies 10, National Museum of Ethnology, Osaka.

1985   Perception, Procurement and Management of Resources: Archaeological Perspective. In *Andean Ecology and Civilization* (Shozo Masuda, Izumi Shimada, and Craig Morris, eds.): 357–406. University of Tokyo Press, Tokyo.

SHIMADA, IZUMI, and RAFFAEL CAVALLARO

    1986   Monumental Adobe Architecture of the Late Pre-Hispanic Northern Coast of Peru. *Journal de la Société des Américanistes* 71: 41–78.

SHIMADA, IZUMI, and MELODY SHIMADA (eds.)

    1987–88   *WILLAY: Newsletter of the Andean Anthropological Research Group* 26/ 27. Department of Anthropology, Harvard University, Cambridge.

STOTHERT, KAREN E.

    1985   The Preceramic Las Vegas Culture of Coastal Ecuador. *American Antiquity* 50: 613–637.

    n.d.   Archaeological Survey and Settlement Pattern Study of La Puna Island, Guayas Province, Ecuador. National Science Foundation Proposal, 1986.

TOPIC, THERESA L.

    1982   The Early Intermediate Period and Its Legacy. In *Chan Chan: Andean Desert City* (Michael E. Moseley and Kent C. Day, eds.): 255–284. University of New Mexico Press, Albuquerque.

ZÁRATE, AGUSTÍN DE

    [1555]   *Historia del descubrimiento y conquista del Perú.* Reed, Lima.
    1944

Ethnohistorical Considerations about the Chimor

MARÍA ROSTWOROWSKI DE DIEZ CANSECO

INSTITUTO DE ESTUDIOS PERUANOS

THIS PAPER EXAMINES some aspects of government in the Kingdom of Chimor. Several of the themes dealt with here benefit from my ethnohistorical research over the past twenty-five years wherein I have used early Colonial documents to help understand the late Pre-Hispanic coastal polities.

POLITICAL STRUCTURES OF THE CHIMOR

For the Peruvian coast there is only fragmentary Pre-Hispanic political information in Colonial documents dating before the extensive reorganization of the Peruvian viceroyalty carried out by Viceroy Don Francisco de Toledo (1568–80). Nevertheless, that which has been found can be used to construct some hypotheses about the Chimor's political organization. One such source of information is a voluminous litigation spanning twelve years (1550–62), housed in the Archivo General de Indias in Seville. Testimonies of several witnesses provide information about the Pre-Hispanic political organization of Guaman, a small polity located in the Moche Valley. Ownership of this polity was disputed by two wealthy Spanish *encomenderos,* Melchor Verdugo and Rodrigo Lozano (AGI Justicia 398; Netherly, this volume; Rostworowski 1976).

In 1535 Melchor Verdugo was granted the *encomienda* of Cajamarca by Francisco Pizarro. It included the *cacique* Chiquiamanaque, lord of the town of Changuco in the Moche Valley (RAN 1942[1]: 13). Rodrigo Lozano was the *encomendero* of Guañape and Chao in 1542, when he was granted the polity of Guaman by the Governor, Licenciado Cristóbal Vaca de Castro.

Within Guaman there were two smaller polities, composed of only a few settlements, that probably represented the lower level of the Pre-Hispanic political structure. One was located on the right (north) bank of the Moche

I thank Guillermo A. Cock, Mary Doyle, and Patricia Netherly for translating this paper from the original Spanish, and I am grateful to Guillermo Cock and Mary Doyle for editing it prior to publication.

River and was bounded on the west by the Pacific Ocean. This was a polity of fishermen, with a main settlement called Chichi; at the time of the Spanish Conquest, the highest ranking lord was Guamonamo, later succeeded by Guaman. Another lord called Cipra ruled as a *segunda persona*—second in command (AGI Audiencia de Lima 118, 36v).

The second polity was called Chican or Chicamy, and its lands extended along the left (south) bank of the same river, from the sea to a place where the town of Changuco was located, above the "great *huaca*"—presumably, east of the Huacas El Sol and La Luna. Only two settlements made up this polity: the above-mentioned Changuco, and Xacon, a fishing settlement near the sea (Rostworowski 1976).

The lord of Changuco, Chiquiamanaque, is mentioned in the litigation as a hammock-bearer of the Chimu Capac, who at that time was known by the Spanish name, Don Martín. Being called a hammock-bearer suggests that the people of Changuco were retainers of the Chimu lords in Pre-Hispanic times, who provided them with specialized labor as their service (Rostworowski 1976).

The foregoing information about the Moche Valley allows one to infer that the Pre-Hispanic Chimu government system in that valley consisted of territorial divisions made up of small polities ruled by local lords. These lords ruled just a few settlements within a recognizable territory; in turn, the valley's lords were subjects of the ruling lord of the macro-ethnic group[1] (cf. Netherly, this volume).

WAS THERE DUALITY IN THE GOVERNMENT?

The existence of masculine political duality in the Pre-Hispanic and Colonial polities in various parts of the Andean area has been demonstrated by abundant information in early Colonial documentary sources (Rostworowski 1983; 114–174; 1988: 189–194). The question remains whether a similar system existed specifically in the Kingdom of Chimor; was this a characteristic of Chimor's socio-political organization? Evidence suggests that it was.

Dual lords existed in the Guaman polity. Moreover, in the witnesses' testimonies during the above-mentioned litigation, the early Colonial Chimu Capac, called Don Martín, is mentioned together with Don Francisco, his *segunda persona,* whose indigenous name was Chibianamo. The duality in the organizational system is related to the upper and lower moieties, as in the cases of the widespread concepts of Hanan and Hurin and the

---

[1] Because the Moche Valley was the center of power of the Chimu state during the Late Intermediate period, it could have been organized internally in a different fashion from the coastal valleys to the south and north. The size of the polities and their degree of integration seem to have been higher in the northern valleys: Chicama, Jequetepeque, and Lambayeque (see Cock n.d.; Netherly n.d.).

divisions into "right" and "left," as seen in the cases of Ichoq and Allauca. The Spanish translation for this duality principle was standardized with the terms *cacique principal* and *segunda persona*. In Quechua, the latter concept was expressed by the term *yanapak,* which means "helper" or "companion" (Jiménez de la Espada 1881–97, 2: 72).

It is very difficult to assess whether duality was imposed by the Inca when they conquered the region or whether it represents a local tradition. However, in 1551, in a litigation between Diego de Mora and Doña Francisca Pizarro (daughter of the conqueror), among the certificates of *encomienda* grants presented by her, there is one by which she was granted the "cacique of Chimo who is called Don Martín and whoever succeeds him with one thousand Indians" (AGI Justicia 398, 2v). In the same document the lord is called by his native name Sachoca. This name is different from the one mentioned by the *Relación Anónima* published by Rubén Vargas Ugarte (1936) where the lord of Chimor is called Don Martín, his Spanish name, and Cajaçimçim, his indigenous one. It is possible that Sachoca and Cajaçimçim were two different lords who took the same Spanish name, one the *cacique principal,* the other the *segunda persona* (Rostworowski 1983: 118–119).[2]

Although duality seems to have been a characteristic of the Late Horizon and Early Colonial times, there is not yet conclusive evidence that this was the case in the Late Intermediate period. Nevertheless, the consistency of the evidence found throughout northern Peru points toward the existence of a dual system during Chimu times.

INHERITANCE OF POWER

One of the characteristics of the succession of power among the lords of the North Coast was the inheritance from brother to brother, until that generation was exhausted, before passing to the following one (Rostworowski 1961; 1988: 139). This contrasts with the Inca practice of tending to choose the sister's son to succeed, a practice that favored incestuous marriage (Rostworowski 1983: 154–173). Besides these differences, in the Andean area the election of the "most able and sufficient" to succeed and exercise power prevailed as the principal rule, from the lesser ethnic group to the head of the macro-ethnic group. In Tahuantinsuyu the requirements to be "able" to govern brought about the replacement of many older *curacas* who were no longer able to carry out their duties. In the *Informaciones* (inquiries about the Andean Pre-Hispanic past, ordered by Viceroy Don Francisco de Toledo) there are many testimonies given by old *curacas* who

[2] Another avenue of research to investigate duality could be through archaeology. Perhaps the duality of the Chimor lords was expressed through some dual architectural structures found in Chan Chan, as indicated by Michael Moseley and Alan Kolata (this volume) in their analysis of the buildings of the city.

were forced to leave their posts because they were no longer "able" (Levillier 1940). For the same reason, minors were not allowed to assume power when a relative died. The Spanish changed the Andean practice and introduced the concept of regency and the rights of minors in accordance with European customs and law, something that produced endless litigation among the Colonial lords seeking to obtain positions, many of them referring to the customs and practices during "Inca times" as a way to legitimize their pretensions (Rostworowski 1988: 137–147).

HYDRAULIC POLICY AND COASTAL–HIGHLANDS RELATIONSHIPS

Analysis of the characteristics of irrigation in coastal valleys offers interesting information about each valley's autonomy and power, as well as relationships with neighbors in the highlands. Differences in the political evolution of each *yunga*[3] valley reflects that valley's own development and the degree of restrictions that may have been imposed by the highlanders (Rostworowski 1988: 276–282).

Because the documentary sources show important regional differences in the relationship between coastal and highland polities (fluctuations and changes through time and sometimes differences within the same valley), the information obtained for a particular river drainage cannot be applied to any other one. As an example, one can compare the strong control exercised by the highland polities over the South Coast during the Late Intermediate period with what happened in the Chimor state during the same time period. While in the south the presence of powerful polities located in the highlands extended their control into the coastal valleys, on the North Coast a strongly centralized Chimor state kept a far more balanced situation.

Some examples from the Central and South Coasts provide information on how power fluctuated over time as a consequence of changes in the control over the irrigation system.

The Collique Polity

The first case is the Collique (Collec) polity, located in the Chillon Valley near Lima. There, during the Late Intermediate period, the lords defended the polity from attack by the Canta highlanders by constructing a chain of fortresses through the valley. They also built a fortress-palace for the *curaca,* as well as high walls to surround an extension of agricultural lands that were irrigated by two springs. That defensive system allowed the lord of Collique to resist the highlanders' raids and attacks, and, with lands and

---

[3] Throughout the documentary sources *llanos* and *yunga* are terms used to refer to the coastal plains; *yunga* or *yungas* is also used as a generic denomination for the coastal inhabitants. In Quechua it means "warm lands," and it is applied also to the jungle lowlands. In this text the meaning of the term will be restricted to its coastal implications.

water, he could sustain a prolonged siege (AGI Justicia 413; Rostworowski 1977: 25–38).

The Canta lord laid claim to the lowlands belonging to the Collique polity on the basis that the water used by the *yungas* of Collique to irrigate their fields came from his highland polity. Such claims show the highlanders' attitude toward the coastal groups, as well as the people living in the middle valley range between the two. In the same Colonial document, it can be seen that the Canta lord was involved in another dispute over water rights with the Chacalla and the Quivi polities, because all three had the same sources of water. Nevertheless, in the case of a severe drought, highlanders and coastal people worked together to drain and use water from the *puna* lakes to satisfy the needs of all (AGI Justicia 413).

Lima and Lurin: The Pachacamac Polity

During the same period, the lower valleys of Lima and Lurin were unified under the hegemony of the religious center at Pachacamac, a polity that was also known as Ychma. Fear inspired by the powerful *yunga* god, who was worshiped in Pachacamac, may have been sufficient to keep in check the claims of the macro-ethnic group of Huarochiri.[4] As in the Chillon Valley, the middle parts of the Lima and Lurin Valleys were inhabited by *yungas* and highlanders. In Sisicaya,[5] in the Lurin Valley, the population was from the coast, but they were reported to be part of the *Chaucarima Guaranga*[6] from Huarochiri (Rostworowksi 1978: 112). The relationships between the highland and coastal groups seem to have been more peaceful, although the Inca conquest and its alliance with the *Yauyos*[7] highlanders is said to have contributed increased pressure from the highlanders. Nevertheless, the Lima and Lurin Valleys lacked defensive measures at the water intakes, understandable if the pressure exercised over them came not from the neighbors in the highlands, but from the Inca state centered in Cuzco.

In this region, a myth told to Francisco de Avila explains how the hero Llacsamisa taught the men how to use water from the lakes, measure its capacity, and interpret the signs of an increase in the volume of water, as well as to build dams to store water for the dry season. There, it is also mentioned that both highlanders and coastal people were involved in these tasks (Avila 1987 [1597?]: 453–487, esp. 473–481). The myth shows not

---

[4] Huarochiri is located in the highlands southeast of Lima. The wealth of the oral tradition collected by Francisco de Avila [1597?] has made this area well known. Karen Spalding (1984) has conducted ethnohistoric research there, covering the Inca and early Colonial periods.

[5] Sisicaya is a village that presumably pertained to the Huarochiri ethnic group.

[6] *Guarangas* were social as well as political divisions said to have been introduced by the Inca. Each comprised one thousand individuals or households, under the authority of a lord. The Chaucarima Guaranga was one of several of these groups found in Huarochiri.

[7] *Yauyos* is a region and the name of a Pre-Hispanic ethnic group. It is located southeast of Lima, just south of Huarochiri.

only the techniques of water management for irrigation, but also the preventive measures to avoid floods and avalanches during the rainy season. This information was corroborated by two Colonial inspections of the Yanacocha and Llacota lakes made in 1637 and 1648. The Spanish inspectors found evidence of the existence of a complete system of measures and indicators to determine the level of the water stored in those lakes, as well as the presence of people in charge of these duties (Rostworowski 1978: 117–122). Collaboration, instead of conflict, was a characteristic in these valleys.

The Cañete and Ica Valleys

The Guarco polity, in the modern Cañete Valley, provides a different situation from that of the Central Coast. Pressure from the highlands was avoided by the construction of fortresses and high walls and by the presence of a well-trained army. The topography of the valley helped the defensive system because the river flows toward the left (south) part of the valley, instead of flowing down the middle. The system proved its efficiency in the struggle against the Inca, which was lengthy and ended with a harsh punishment imposed on the population after their defeat by the Cuzqueños (Rostworowski 1981a; 1988: 278).

In the Ica Valley the *yunga* macro-ethnic group had controlled the water intakes in the highlands since the Late Intermediate period (Guillén 1963). Because they appeared to lack the defensive measures of the Guarco, at the time of the Inca conquest the lords of Ica did not offer resistance, thus avoiding Inca reprisals (Rostworowski 1988: 278).

The Lambayeque Valley

In 1540 Sebastián de la Gama made a tour of inspection (*Visita*) to Jayanca, in the Lambayeque area. De la Gama reports that the *cacique* of Jayanca stated that the lord of the Guambos in the highlands controlled both the river water at its source and its course to the coastal plains, demanding a "ransom" (compensation) for the use of water from the lord of Jayanca (Espinoza Soriano 1975: 271; Netherly n.d.; Ramírez, this volume). There are two important points in this statement. First, the control of water that irrigated the *yunga* valley was in the hands of a highland lord who claimed to be able to control its distribution at will. Second, the coastal lord was obliged to pay tribute or compensation to the highland lord for the use of the natural resource. It appears that the relationship was restricted at the level of the two lords, and that commoners were not involved in these dealings.

Also in the Lambayeque Valley, in 1566, two lords from Tucume complained to the *Visitador* Gregorio González de Cuenca about the excessive "tribute" they were required to pay to another lord for the use of water from a secondary canal, called Cuy (AGI Justicia 458, 2013r).[8] Both asked Cuenca to abolish the *yunga* custom and establish the Spanish custom of having pasture and water held as common property. In this case, the three lords involved appeared to be from the same ethnic group, but the two lesser-ranking nobles were obliged to pay a compensation for water use to the higher-ranked lord.

This case further clarifies the rights of access to water. It appears that the lord of the macro-ethnic *yunga* group charged a "payment" for the use of water to his lower-ranking lords; in turn, he compensated the highland lord for the water used by all his subjects, making this essentially a relationship between high-ranking lords.

Because the nature of this "tribute," "payment," or "compensation" is unknown, a comparison with a case in the Mala Valley, on the Central Coast, can provide further insights. There, when the lord of Mala needed a larger labor force to carry out certain tasks, such as a major cleaning of irrigation ditches or the draining of a fishing lagoon, he requested the help of the nearby lord of Coayllo, in the coastal Asia Valley, giving him in exchange the temporary use of certain agricultural lands as compensation for this help (Rostworowski 1981a). One wonders if this type of relationship existed between the lords of Jayanca and Guambos. (However, this coastal custom should not lead one to erroneous interpretations or hasty conclusions about the presence on the coast of highland enclaves or highland "archipelagos.")

If, indeed, these were the conditions on the North Coast under the Inca rule, the situation could have been different in earlier periods. The presence of *yungas* installed in the highlands of Cajamarca, in Celendin, Contumaza, Chota, Hualgayoc, and San Miguel well before the Inca conquest is recognized by means of linguistics and geographical names. Not only are certain names in these areas *yunga,* but the use of the sound *F* in patronyms verifies their presence here; *F* is a consonant found exclusively in the Yunga, or Mochica, language (Rostworowski 1985). These *yungas* seem to be different from the *mitmaq* transferred from the coast to this area in the highlands by the Inca, because the *mitmaq* were grouped in a special *guaranga* with members of the Quechua, Cañari, Guayacondo, and Colla groups.[9]

Richard Schaedel (1985) has suggested that these coastal people installed in the Cajamarca highlands formed independent polities from those located

---

[8] It is interesting to note that one of these lords was the *cacique principal* of the Cooks, and the other the *cacique principal* of the Deer Hunters, two groups of specialists. Both were, in turn, retainers of the lord of Tucume.

[9] This information is found in the *Visita* of Cajamarca ordered by Viceroy Toledo and carried out in two stages: the first in 1571–72, before the *reducción* (resettlement) of the indigenous population, the second in 1578; unfortunately information on this second stage is much more scanty than on the first.

on the coastal plains. Given the political structures observed in Chimor (like the aforementioned Changuco and Guaman), it is a reasonable supposition. However, no one has yet pursued the implications of such a suggestion, to assess the type of relationships that these groups would have maintained with their parent populations on the coast, or those they would have established with their highland counterparts.

The *yunga* presence in the highlands was probably a consequence of the need to control the water intakes of the canals for the hydraulic systems of the coast. It may have been a question of a preemptive conquest during the *yunga* apogee to insure the water supply for their irrigation canals and may have lasted until the Inca conquest of northern Peru, about A.D. 1470. It is very difficult to evaluate and date this process without archaeological investigation, but the construction of fortresses on the coast during the "Tomaval period" [within the Early Intermediate period] (Willey 1953) and late in the Late Intermediate period (J. Topic and T. Topic 1978; T. Topic, this volume) appears to suggest that there were two periods when the coastal polities were strong enough to advance toward the cis-Andean highlands and establish colonies there—during the Early and Late Intermediate periods. At the end of these periods they had to retreat and build fortifications because of the advance of the highland people at the very beginning of the Middle and Late Horizons. When the coastal people no longer controlled the neighboring highlands above their valleys, they maintained strategic fortifications to defend the entrance to their lands.[10]

A final comment about the importance of water on the North Coast of Peru has to do with the possible existence of a system of measuring cultivated lands according to their irrigation needs. In some early Colonial documents pertaining to the *Corregimientos*[11] of Zaña and Chiclayo, in the Lambayeque area, the Spanish word *asequia* (irrigation ditch) is used as a unit of measure for a cultivated area. Perhaps it is a translation of a Mochica word. As a unit of measure, it can be hypothesized that it was related to the volume of water necessary to irrigate a field in a given period of time. This

---

[10] During the Late Intermediate period two fortresses were built in the Moche Valley and a third in the Chao Valley, but the three show indications of brief use (Topic and Topic 1978; T. Topic, this volume). The two fortresses in the Moche Valley controlled access to the length of the valley, while two additional forts located upland in the narrow zone on either bank of the river defended the entrance to the valley via the highland route. It is possible that these structures were built against the imminent danger of the Inca advance, or perhaps as a defensive measure against the neighbors from Cajamarca, Huamachuco, and Conchucos. Nevertheless, the strategy used by the Inca, and the highlanders in general, was to cut off the water that descended from the highlands, a measure against which fortresses were not effective at all (Rostworowski 1953).

[11] *Corregimientos* were political and judiciary divisions (districts) introduced by the Colonial government for the first time during the 1560s on the North Coast of Peru, and applied throughout the viceroyalty in the 1570s. The *Corregimiento de Chiclayo* had jurisdiction over the entire Lambayeque and Olmos area, while that of Zaña included the Jequetepeque Valley.

idea was also present in the Quechua unit *tupu,* which is a unit of measure for area, length, and productivity (Rostworowski 1981b).

Revolt of the Chimu Capac

Inca historical narratives display a tendency to idealize the empire, describing it as an idyllic state. Nothing could be further from reality; frequent disturbances and uprisings in the provinces of Tahuantinsuyu have been used as a proof of the discontent felt by the ethnic lords against the Inca domination. The brief period of Inca expansion did not permit a consolidation of their territorial possessions, nor did it allow for the development of an awareness among the ethnic lords that they were part of the Inca state. Instead, the populations incorporated into the Inca state identified with their lands, *ayllu,* villages, and local or regional lords, a loyalty that made complete integration into the Inca state difficult.

The constant rebellions that shook the Inca empire illustrate the lack of integration and show that, in fact, peace was more apparent than real. Agustín de Zárate ([1555] 1944: 46) tells that the Chimu Capac, after Chimor's conquest by the Inca, rebelled against Tahuantinsuyu. The chronicler does not provide more details about the events beyond stating that the Inca prevailed and that the rebel was executed. Zárate also states that the coastal people thereafter were not allowed to carry arms. The rebellion of the Chimu Capac may have influenced the decision of the Inca not to integrate the coastal population into their armies. In the Huaura Valley, during the *Visita* ordered by Licenciado Don Pedro de la Gasca in 1549, the *curaca* was asked whether in former times he had supplied men to serve in the wars, and he replied that because they were *yungas,* they did not take part in the campaigns (Rostworowski 1978: 224).

A similar testimony is found in the *Visita* to Atico and Caraveli,[12] which was also carried out in 1549. The *curaca,* Chincha Pula, was asked if in Pre-Hispanic times men were sent to serve in the Inca army, and he replied in the negative. It seems that it was a general custom not to require labor service for war from the *yungas.* This information tends to confirm the lack of confidence shown by the Inca toward the coastal people (Galdos Rodríguez 1977).

The mistrust produced by the Chimu Capac's uprising had another consequence: the dispersal of many of his subjects as *mitmaq* to many places in Tahuantinsuyu. It was a common practice of the Inca state to send large contingents of people from one place to another for various purposes. When it was a case of rebellion or a large-scale war of conquest, the conquered local inhabitants were replaced by other populations. This is what happened

---

[12] Atico and Caraveli are valleys located on the South Coast of Peru, in the Department of Arequipa.

in Guarco, the Cañete polity, after its defeat by the Inca who proceeded then to remove the local population and in their place to establish *mitmaq* from Chincha on the south bank of the river. People from the neighboring Coayllo Valley occupied much of the rest of the Cañete Valley (Rostworowski 1981a).

Enforced resettlement of northern metalworkers, fishermen, and water management specialists is reported. The best known case is that of the metalworkers who were removed from their northern homeland and sent to Cuzco to make objects of gold and silver (Rowe 1948; J. Topic, this volume). There is also information of *ayllus* that came from Pachacamac, Chincha, Ica, and Huancavilca, who were sent to the Inca capital to manufacture gold and silver objects (Rostworowski 1977: 234–238);[13] but North Coast contributions to the development and improvement of fishing and irrigation techniques in the Late Horizon are almost unknown. Such contributions are suggested by a number of cases, however, some of which are as follows.

Huaura Valley. In the early Colonial period, there was an *ayllu* of people native to Trujillo who specialized in fishing and hunting marine birds, while on the list of *parcialidades* grouped in the *reducciones* ordered by Viceroy Toledo there is an *ayllu* in the Huaura Valley called Mochica, although it is not certain that it refers to the Trujillo natives (BN A 629 1583; BN B 1845 1697).

Chancay Valley. There is a long litigation initiated in 1549 between Captain Jerónimo de Aliaga and Ruy Barba Tinoco Cabeza de Vaca for the possession of the *cacique principal* Parpo and his subjects in the Chancay Valley, just south of Huaura. In the document, these people are called fishermen of Moche origin, coming from the Santa and Casma Valleys. They were placed in the Chancay Valley by the Inca in order to supply the sovereign with "fish and shellfish [machas]" when he traveled through the valley (Rostworowski 1978: 125–130).

Maranga. The 1549 *Visita* to Maranga, in the Rimac Valley, reports that one of the *ayllus* was called Moche *mitmaq* and the people were fishermen (Rostworowski 1978: 92–97).

Acari. Another group of Moche *mitmaq* were noted in the Acari Valley, on the South Coast of Peru. In the 1593 *Visita* of Acari there is an *ayllu* called Yaucalla Muchic (Pease 1973: 131–209; Rostworowski 1982). On a map published by the Sociedad Geográfica de Lima in 1921 and in Germán Stiglich's *Diccionario geográfico* (1922) there is a village called Mochica on the north bank of the river, between the towns of Yauca and Jaqui. Moreover,

---

[13] The massive exodus of *yunga* artisans should be kept in mind by those studying Inca metallurgy because although it is true that the artisans followed the artistic patterns imposed by their masters in accordance with local taste and tradition, they contributed their North Coast skills and technology.

on the map of the watershed of the Yauca River there are two canal intakes called Mochica Alta and Mochica Baja (ONERN 1975, 3: map 27). This information provides a basis for suggesting that the Moche *mitmaq* in the Acari region could have been sent there to build or improve irrigation canals. Even today, in valleys like Ica, there are important canals called "la Mochica."[14] Was hydraulic technology a specialization of the Moche, the name used in documents for the inhabitants of Chimor? What still remains of their ancient irrigation systems suggests this possibility.

SUMMARY AND CONCLUSIONS

On the basis of archival documentation it can be suggested that Chimor's political structure was composed of a number of polities scattered throughout the valleys under the domain and hegemony of the lord of Chan Chan. As in other Andean polities, and at least since the Inca conquest, duality was a characteristic of power and government. Power succession on the North Coast had certain characteristics: first, the choice of the most able and competent [sufficient] person for the office; second, the choice of one brother after another before passing the office on to the following generation.

A crucial aspect in the development of the *yunga* cultures was the development of hydraulic technology that gave rise to a whole system of water use and rights. This system had implications both in the relationships between inhabitants of the same valley, and between them and those from the neighboring highlands. This relationship between the coast and the highlands was complicated and complementary, for the highlanders claimed a number of rights because the water and rivers necessary for coastal irrigation originated in their territory.

When, at particular periods, the coastal polities were strong enough, their people controlled the canal intakes in the adjacent highlands and even created *yunga* polities in the cis-Andean region. When the coastal dwellers lost their power in the face of highland advance, they were forced to build fortresses and defensive walls to protect their irrigation canals and to guard their intakes. A third scenario occurred when the highlanders exercised total control over water resources, as during the Late Horizon and, perhaps, the Middle Horizon periods, when the coastal peoples seem to have been subordinated to the highland polities. These events did not occur at the same time

[14] A declaration made in 1606 by Don Alonso Chancor, a lord of the Moche Valley, provides information on a sale of lands called Messe, located at the base of the highlands. These fields were next to a lake "Mochica" that originated a canal also called "Mochica" (AGN Títulos de Propiedad, Cuaderno 159, 6). Further archival research would augment the information available on Mochica *mitmaq*. For instance, in the 1552 Real Cédula of land possession in Cuzco granted to Felipe Topa Yapanqui, Alonso Tito Atauche, and Doña Juana Marca Chimbo Coya by Carlos V and his mother Doña Juana, there is a detailed reference to the lands of these nobles. Among the many places named, there is a Chimor in Amaraes or Amparaes with twenty people classed as *yana* (retainers) (Rostworowski 1962).

in every valley, for the events are closely related to the evolution of the politics in both the coast and the highlands, as well as the balance maintained in their relationships. This fluctuating situation underscores the need to search out additional archival data as well as to intensify archaeological reconnaissance and excavation in the upper reaches of the coastal valleys to understand the variations of water use and rights in each of the North Coast valleys.

BIBLIOGRAPHY

AGI (ARCHIVO GENERAL DE INDIAS)
 Justicia 398, 1550–62
 Justicia 413, 1559
 Justicia 458, 1566
 Audiencia de Lima 118

AGN (ARCHIVO GENERAL DE LA NACIÓN, LIMA)
 Títulos de Propiedad, Cuaderno 159, 1606

ATLAS DEL PERÚ
 1921 *Atlas del Perú.* Cartographer Camilo Vallejos Z. Scale 1: 1,000,000. Lima: Sociedad Geográfica de Lima.

AVILA, FRANCISCO DE
 [1597?] *Ritos y tradiciones de Huarochirí* (Gerald Taylor, ed.). Biographical study
 1987 of Francisco de Avila by Antonio Acosta. Historia Andina 12. Instituto de Estudios Peruanos and Instituto Francés de Estudios Andinos, Lima.

BN (BIBLIOTECA NACIONAL DEL PERÚ)
 BN A 629, 1583
 BN B 1845, 1697

CARRERA, FERNANDO DE LA
 1644 *Arte de la lengua yunga de los valles del Obispado de Truxillo del Perú, con un confesionario y todas las Oraciones Christianas traducidas en la lengua y otras cosas.* J. Contreras, Lima.

COCK, GUILLERMO A.
 n.d. From the Powerful to the Powerless. The Jequetepeque Valley Lords in the 16th Century. M.A. thesis, Archaeology Program, University of California, Los Angeles, 1985.

ESPINOZA SORIANO, WALDEMAR
 1975 El valle de Jayanca y el reino de los Mochica, siglos XV y XVI. *Bulletin de l'Institut Français d'Etudes Andines* 4 (3–4): 243–274. Lima.

GALDOS RODRÍGUEZ, GUILLERMO
    1977   Visita a Atico y Caravelí (1549). *Revista del Archivo General de la Nación* 4–5: 55–80. Lima.

GUILLÉN Y GUILLÉN, EDMUNDO
    1963   Un documento para la historia social y económica de Ica (1594). *Revista del Archivo Nacional del Perú* 27. Lima.

JIMÉNEZ DE LA ESPADA, MARCOS
    1881–97   *Relaciones geográficas de Indias.* 4 vols. Ministerio de Fomento, Madrid.

LEVILLIER, ROBERTO
    1940   Informaciones de Toledo. In *Don Francisco de Toledo,* 2. Espasa-Calpe, Buenos Aires.

MURRA, JOHN V.
    1975   *Formaciones económicas y políticas del mundo andino.* Historia Andina 3. Instituto de Estudios Peruanos, Lima.

NETHERLY, PATRICIA J.
    n.d.   Local Level Lords on the North Coast of Peru. Ph.D. dissertation, Department of Anthropology, Cornell University, 1977.

ONERN (OFICINA NACIONAL DE EVALUACIÓN DE RECURSOS NATURALES)
    1975   *Inventario, evaluación y uso racional de la costa. Acarí, Yauca, Chala y Chaparra.* 3 vols. Lima.

PEASE, FRANKLIN (ed.)
    1973   Visita de Acarí. *Historia y Cultura* 7: 129–209. Lima.

RAN (REVISTA DEL ARCHIVO NACIONAL DEL PERÚ)
    1942   Algunas provisiones de Francisco Pizarro sobre encomiendas. Años 1534–1540. *Revista del Archivo Nacional del Perú* 15(1). Lima.

ROSTWOROWSKI DE DIEZ CANSECO, MARÍA
    1953   *Pachacútec Ynca Yupanqui.* Lima.
    1961   *Curacas y sucesiones. Costa Norte.* Imprenta Minerva, Lima.
    1962   Nuevos datos sobre la tenencia de tierras reales en el Incario. *Revista del Museo Nacional* 31: 130–164. Lima.
    1976   El Señorío de Changuco, Costa Norte. *Boletín del Instituto Francés de Estudios Andinos* 5 (1–2): 97–147. Lima.
    1977   *Etnía y sociedad: Costa peruana prehispánica.* Historia Andina 4. Instituto de Estudios Peruanos, Lima.
    1978   *Señoríos indígenas de Lima y Canta.* Historia Andina 7. Instituto de Estudios Peruanos, Lima.
    1981a   Guarco y Lunahuaná. Dos señoríos prehispánicos, costa sur central del Perú. *Revista del Museo Nacional* 44: 153–214. Lima.
    1981b   Mediciones y cómputos en el Antiguo Perú. In *La Tecnología en el Mundo Andino* 1 (Heather Lechtman and Ana María Soldi, eds.): 397–405. Universidad Nacional Autónoma de México, Mexico.
    1982   Comentarios a la visita de Acarí de 1593. *Histórica* 6(2): 227–254. Pontificia Universidad Católica del Perú, Lima.
    1983   *Estructuras andinas del poder. Ideología religiosa y política.* Historia Andina 10. Instituto de Estudios Peruanos, Lima.

1985 Patronyms with the Consonant F in the *Guarangas* of Cajamarca. In *Andean Ecology and Civilization: An Interdisciplinary Perspective on Andean Ecological Complementarity* (Shozo Masuda, Izumi Shimada, and Craig Morris, eds.): 401–421. University of Tokyo Press, Tokyo.

1988 *Historia del Tawantinsuyu.* Historia Andina 13. Instituto de Estudios Peruanos, Lima.

ROWE, JOHN H.
1948 The Kingdom of Chimor. *Acta Americana* 6(1–2): 26–59.

SCHAEDEL, RICHARD
1985 Discussion. In *Andean Ecology and Civilization: An Interdisciplinary Perspective on Andean Ecological Complementarity* (Shozo Mazuda, Izumi Shimada, and Craig Morris, eds.): 443–473. University of Tokyo Press, Tokyo.

SPALDING, KAREN
1984 *Haurochirí: An Andean Society under Inca and Spanish Rule.* Stanford University Press, Stanford.

STIGLICH, GERMÁN
1922 *Diccionario geográfico del Perú.* 2 vols. Imprenta Torres-Aguirre, Lima.

TOPIC, JOHN, and THERESA LANGE TOPIC
1978 Prehistoric Fortification Systems of Northern Perú. *Current Anthropology* 19(3): 618–619.

VARGAS UGARTE, RUBÉN
1936 La fecha de la fundación de Trujillo. *Revista Histórica* 10: 229–239. Lima.

WILLEY, GORDON R.
1953 *Prehistoric Settlement Patterns in the Virú Valley, Perú.* Bureau of American Ethnology, Bulletin 155. Smithsonian Institution, Washington, D.C.

ZÁRATE, AGUSTÍN DE
[1555] *Historia del descubrimiento y conquista del Perú.* Lima.
1944

Out of Many, One: The Organization of Rule in the North Coast Polities

PATRICIA J. NETHERLY

UNIVERSITY OF MASSACHUSETTS, AMHERST

WHAT KIND OF HISTORY IS ANDEAN HISTORY?

HISTORY AS WE KNOW IT is an artifact of Western culture. The scrupulous determination of cause and effect necessary for the creation of a truthful account of past events embodies particular concepts of time and causality. Although they work with material remains and their contexts instead of documents, archaeologists share these concepts with historians and rarely question them.

Concepts such as linear time—the ordering of events from the past, through the present, to the future—seem universal but, in fact, are not. In the Mediterranean world of Classical Antiquity as in the Andes, time was viewed as a series of repeating cycles or ages. Moreover, in the Andean view, the Western distinction between past and future is not made; time is present or nonpresent (Delran 1974). Regardless of their temporal scheme, the events that figure in a particular account must be selected and ordered. This imposes choices, for otherwise such accounts would be incomprehensible to the cultures from which they derive. The choices of Western historians are as culturally constrained as those of non-Western historiographers.

Thus, when working with early European records of Andean oral history, one must keep in mind both the cultural biases of the Western historian and the very different concepts and purposes to be found in what appear to be Andean historical accounts (Netherly 1988b). The aim of the sixteenth-century chroniclers was to inform their readers of the deeds of men who had lived in the past (J. Rowe 1948). The emphasis is on causal relations: who or what was responsible for a particular act or event. Genealogical accounts and king lists provided handy points of reference in such histories. The underlying assumption is that knowledge of past events will assist in understanding the present. In their initial encounter with the Andean world, the Spanish encountered societies whose standard of living, technology, and ability to mobilize human energy were in many respects far superior to their own. The chroniclers attempted to record and explain this greatness, its origins, and its destruction.

In contrast, Andean historiography concentrated on structural rather than causal relations, that is, relations between people or groups of people rather than processual relations between events. Among other things, the intent of Andean accounts is to define or redefine the social and political order. Different accounts serve to emphasize different aspects of the socio-political structure. Thus, because the Andean distinction is between present and non-present, distance from the present or *ego* (the person taken as a point of reference) can be expressed in terms of either the future or the past to define social distance or hierarchy. Persons or events closer to the present (or *ego*) outrank those farther away (Duviols 1979; Zuidema 1973, 1978, 1982). In this volume and elsewhere R. Tom Zuidema has shown how the kinship structure was used as a shorthand to express these temporal and social relationships.

Andean oral history must be used with these points in mind. A historical—in the Western sense—personage or event may be recorded, but this is incidental to the message embedded in the *form* of the account, which reaffirms, for example, the rights of a particular group or their place in the socio-political hierarchy. The form itself can vary according to the canons of Andean principles of hierarchy and kinship with the location of the person who is the point of reference. Things look one way if *ego* is a founding ancestor and quite another if the focus is on fifth-generation descendants (Zuidema 1977, this volume). This places real constraints on the Western use of Andean oral history, particularly the king lists provided by the European chroniclers (Duviols 1979; Zuidema, this volume). The interpretation of reworked Andean accounts as they appear in the Spanish narrative histories must be approached with caution (Netherly 1988b). Even where narratives of specific events appear to be included, as the founding of the Naymlap dynasty or the punishment of Fempellec (Cabello Balboa [1586] 1951: 327–328), their primary purpose is to make a structural statement, not to give a true account of events, as Zuidema demonstrates in his discussion in the following contribution. As the culture of the North Coast region comes to be better understood, it will be possible to use the oral history of the Andes to better advantage.

Spanish Colonial administrative and legal documents provide the other major sources of information for the writing of an Andean *ethnohistory,* if not history as we generally understand it. An ethnohistory in this context is a synchronic description of societies at the time of contact or immediately before, not the historical account of relations between non-Western and Western peoples. In the course of governing the complex societies of the Andes, the Spanish were obliged to acknowledge socio-political categories that were unknown in their own political tradition. This made possible an ethnological analysis of Chimu social organization and political structure independent of the intentionally historical narratives or the origin myths (Netherly 1984, n.d.a, n.d.b), which can be compared with similar information from other areas of the Andes. The results of these analyses also provide a structural framework for the analysis of Andean oral history in combination with information from contemporary ethnographic studies.

A review of what is known from these sources will give a fairly clear idea of middle levels of socio-political organization just before the European Conquest. These principles can then be used to achieve a better understanding of the Spanish version of the Chimu account of their rulers beginning with Taycanamo.

NORTH COAST POLITICAL ORGANIZATION AT THE REGIONAL LEVEL

The broad outline of socio-political organization at the regional or valley level in the immediate Pre-Spanish period has been established (Netherly 1984, n.d.a, n.d.b). This organization was built around the principles of hierarchy and duality that ordered the population into a ranked series of ever-larger, discrete, bounded groups, which are found throughout the Andean region. I have called the groups from the North Coast region by the Spanish term *parcialidades* because the Yunga word for these groups is not known. The difficulty encountered with the word *parcialidad,* which simply means "part of a whole," is that it was used in the documents for such groups at *different levels of organization* (see Fig. 1). In each instance it is necessary to establish the context or level in the hierarchy with which one is dealing. This task is complicated by the fact that high-ranking lords operated on several different levels simultaneously (Netherly 1984, n.d.a, n.d.b).

There are several features that characterize the North Coast variant of Andean socio-political organization. First, at every level the *parcialidades* or polities are grouped in pairs as ranked moieties, and the heads of these moieties are also grouped in ranked pairs at each level. Thus, when the relative ranking or hierarchy of the lords is known or can be inferred, the position of the groups they headed—and the socio-political organization—can be deduced. Such a system results in the nesting of allegiances and affords the highest-ranking lords direct access to human energy through groups at lower levels of organization that are directly subject to them, but not to all the energy available at these lower levels (see Fig. 1). In like fashion, it gave the higher-ranking lords access to the leadership and administrative skills of the lower-ranking lords subject to them (Netherly 1984, n.d.a, n.d.b).

A second characteristic of Andean political organization on the North Coast is that no ruler, not even the paramount, governed alone. While one ruler may have been paramount or highest ranking at any given level, his rule was limited by the fact that only a part of the lower levels of the polity were

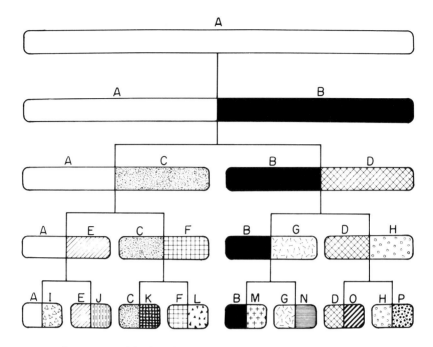

Fig. 1 Schematic model of Andean socio-political orgnization.

subject to him directly. The required presence of the lords of the other princi-pal sections of the polity acted as a check on unilateral action by a paramount lord (Netherly 1984, n.d.a, n.d.b). This conciliar political organization is one of the salient features of Andean government. Its efficiency for the mobiliza-tion of human energy is the reason for the success of the Andean states. The structure of this organization also explains how it was possible for large expansive states to grow so quickly and why lower-level political units did not disappear when the large empires broke apart. In like fashion Andean political structure indicates the lines of cleavage along which the large states could be subdivided without major social or political disruption.

Figure 1 offers a visual demonstration of the ordered complexity that characterizes Andean political structure as it is found on the North Coast. In this ideal schema, the higher-ranking moiety at each level is distinguished by color or pattern. The first or highest level represents the entire polity in abstract fashion, and only the paramount, "Lord A," is indicated. Level 2 shows the same polity as two ranked moieties with Lord A heading the higher-ranking first moiety (in white) and Lord B heading the second moi-ety (in black). At Level 3 the same moieties are shown divided into ranked moieties at a lower level, giving a total of four sections in the whole polity.

At this level Lord A heads only the higher-ranking submoiety, while Lord C heads the other subdivision. Lord B, head of the lower-ranking second moiety at the preceding level, here is lord of the higher-ranking subdivision of this moiety and Lord D heads the other section. The same principles can be seen in operation on Levels 4 and 5. On Level 4 there is a total of eight lords; Lord A and Lord B each rule only one section in eight, albeit the highest-ranking one in their respective moiety. By Level 5 there are a total of sixteen lords with only one section in sixteen controlled by Lords A and B, although these continue to be the highest ranking in each moiety at this level. This nesting gave the highest-ranking lords a power base at the lowest levels, but limited their freedom of action by requiring the consensus of lower-ranking lords for any concerted action by the entire polity. There are many references in the chronicles to paramount lords, including the Inca, taking the advice of their "council," which should be understood to include the lower-level lords (cf. Netherly 1984: 234, table 1). The drastic consequences that befell a lord who defied his "council" of co-rulers are discussed elsewhere (Netherly n.d.a, n.d.b; Cabello Balboa [1586] 1951: 327–328). Among these examples is the punishment of Fempellec, paramount lord of Lambayeque, which was ordered by the subordinate lords in council.

This system of political organization has been described for the polity of Chicama as it existed in the 1560s on the basis of Colonial administrative documents (Netherly 1984, n.d.a). The Chicama Valley had been subdivided under Inca rule into two polities: Chicama and Licapa (see Fig. 2, also Netherly 1984: 232, fig. 2). The early *encomienda* lists of the 1540s refer to Licapa simply as the polity of "Apocama" (Loredo 1958: 251). Use of the Quechua term *apu* or "great lord" indicates that this ruler was likely an Inca imposition. The segment *–cama,* which is not Quechua, may well be a corruption in transcription of the form *–namo,* which appears to have been an indigenous title among lords of the Chimu heartland, cf. Tayca*namo* (Netherly 1984: 232–233, n.d.a, n.d.b). The division of the valley into two polities was the result of the late Inca policy of dividing the large Chimu regional polities as noted in the Taycanamo genealogy of 1604 (Vargas Ugarte 1936: 232; Netherly 1988a, n.d.a).

There were two moieties in the polity of Chicama, which appears to have retained about two-thirds of the land and population of the Chicama Valley. The people and lands of the moiety headed by the paramount lord—the *cacique principal* in Colonial administrative parlance—were located on the north bank of the Chicama River. Those of the second, lower-ranking moiety were on the south bank. Each moiety was further subdivided into two and again into four parts, making a total of eight subsections under four principal sections, each subject to its own lord. These rulers regularly appeared before the Colonial authorities together. Sometimes only the two moiety heads were present; on other occasions they were joined by the

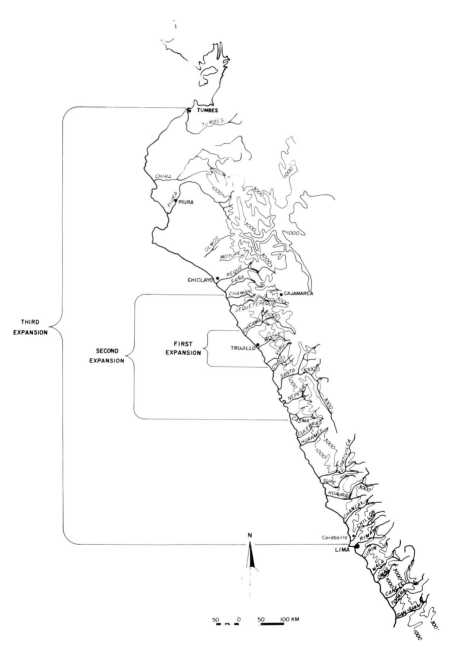

Fig. 2 The successive expansions of the Chimu state based on archaeological evidence.

466

second lords in each moiety, making a total of four rulers. In Chicama some eighteen other lords appear in the documentary record below the initial divisions into two, four, and eight sections (Netherly 1984, n.d.a, n.d.b). The presence of eighteen lords suggests that there may have been as many as six levels of organization under the Chimu when the population was probably larger than during the latter part of the Inca domination and certainly far greater than in the mid-sixteenth century.

Given the depopulation and social disorganization of Andean polities in the mid-sixteenth century, it is difficult to know exactly how these lords and their *parcialidades* were organized. While dual division appears to be almost universal in the Andes, other principles such as quadripartition and decimal organization, which were present on the North Coast of Peru, appear to come into play in diverse ways in different areas of the Andes. The classic description is that of Zuidema for Cuzco (1964; Wachtel 1966), which attempts to show the integration of tripartition, quadripartition, and decimal division into one system. Waldemar Espinoza Soriano (1967) has presented documentation that clearly establishes the presence of a system of ten decimally based *waranga* (units of one-thousand households) in Cajamarca. A number of scholars have reported on quadripartition for the southern Andes, among them Nathan Wachtel (1974) in his study of Chipaya, and Thérèse Bouysse-Cassagne (1978) for the Omasuyu region around Lake Titicaca. Javier Albó and his colleagues have reported a combination of tripartite and quadripartite systems into groupings of twelve (Albó et al. 1972). Quadripartite systems in the Central Andes have been studied by a number of scholars, among them José María Arguedas in his description of Puquio (1964), Marie-France Houdart-Morizot's study of Cuenca (1976), and Billie Jean Isbell's examination of Chuschi (1978). Patricia J. Netherly and Tom D. Dillehay (1986) have discussed this and other material with regard to establishing models to be tested in the archaeological record.

Finally, multilevel Andean systems incorporating duality, quadripartition, and decimal division at different levels of organization are coming to be recognized (Platt 1975; Zuidema 1964, this volume). Mentioned by Cabello Balboa ([1586] 1951: 327–329) as part of the Naymlap myth, this evidence has been discussed and evaluated for its application to Chimu organization (Netherly n.d.a: 307). Summarizing briefly, this argument notes that, because the counting systems of the North Coast appear to have been base ten (Carrera [1644] 1939: 82–84), a resolution with the pattern of dual division and further subdivision into four and eight parts appears to lie in the statement that Naymlap brought with him a total of *forty* principal retainers (Cabello Balboa [1586] 1951: 327). Such a number would permit twenty lords with their subject groups in each moiety, ten lords in each section of 1:4, and five lords in each division of 1:8. Additional lines of evidence for decimal division in the political organization of the North

Coast are discussed elsewhere (Netherly n.d.a: 158–161), but the present evidence is fragmentary at best.

The close association of *parcialidades,* the lands they occupied and tilled, and the canals that watered these lands is recorded repeatedly in Spanish Colonial legal and administrative documents. Using this material, it has been possible to demonstrate that the Pre-Hispanic irrigation system can be employed to locate moieties, sections, and even lower-level units (Netherly 1984, n.d.a). The organization of human groups across an irrigated landscape follows predictable rules or practices in the Andes, constrained in part by the technology of irrigation itself. Tracing the canals associated with the four principal sections of Chicama facilitated locating their core territories (Netherly 1984: 232, fig. 2). Claims to particular canals as well as irrigation regulations going back to the mid-sixteenth century and purporting to codify pre-European practice have been used to establish that the polity that included Lambayeque as one moiety and Cinto as the other irrigated with canals leading off from the main Taymi Canal (Netherly 1984: 240–242 and fig. 5; n.d.a).

The functions of the higher-ranking lords are also fairly well established, with the exception of their military role (Netherly n.d.a, n.d.b). The suppression of all military activity and the dismantling of all military organization in Chimor appears to have been the direct result of a major rebellion against Inca rule in the reign of Huayna Capac (Netherly 1988a). According to the Cuzco version of events as recounted by the Colonial administrator and chronicler, Agustín de Zárate, the rebellion was put down, the Chimu ruler killed, and arms forbidden to the people of Chimor ([1555] 1944: 46). The extreme "destructuration"—to use Nathan Wachtel's term (1977)—carried out by the Inca is particularly evident in the case of Chimor, the formal core of the Chimu state, which was reduced to a regional polity occupying only a part of the Moche Valley. Again, Figure 1 demonstrates how a polity could be thus downgraded without being destroyed.

Even under Inca domination, the higher-ranking lords exercised major functions in the mobilization of human energy, which was the principal source of wealth and power on the North Coast as elsewhere in the Andean region, for their own support and for the benefit of the lords above them. To this end the lords supervised, either directly or through their agents, many aspects of production and redistribution. These included both the primary productions of crops and exploitation of marine resources as well as secondary craft production. Artisans were grouped into *parcialidades* under lords and headmen who depended directly on the higher-ranking lords (Netherly n.d.a, n.d.b; Rostworowski 1975). This is one aspect of Chimu economic and political organization for which there is now archaeological confirmation (J. Topic 1982, n.d.; Donnan 1983; Shimada et al. 1982). The higher-ranking lords also appear to have been responsible for nonredistributive exchange, either through dependent *parcialidades* of exchange specialists, as in the Lambayeque region, or else directly through administered trade (Netherly n.d.a, n.d.b; Rostworowski 1975). Given the role of the lords in initiating and administering production, we would expect to find that in terms of the total economy, storage was probably decentralized down to fairly low organizational levels as a risk-reducing mechanism (Netherly n.d.a).

The other aspect of the lords' administrative role for which there is archaeological evidence is the supervision of labor services on large projects (Hastings and Moseley 1975; Moseley and Day 1982). The archaeological evidence is particularly valuable because of the confirmation it offers for Andean work patterns known from ethnographic descriptions of contemporary Andean groups.

The ritual importance of the regional lords is frequently overlooked. Nevertheless, religion and ritual were unquestionably motivating forces of great importance. Most economic activities required ritual participation by the lords or they would not have been carried out (Netherly n.d.a, n.d.b). Furthermore, the lords' position as living ancestors, as the link between the living and the dead, the present and the nonpresent, greatly enhanced their power (Conrad 1982; Netherly n.d.a, n.d.b; Zuidema 1973).

IMPLICATIONS FOR THE STUDY OF CHIMOR

The picture of North Coast political organization at the regional level just outlined has been pieced together from fragmentary evidence found in Spanish Colonial administrative and judicial records. It would not have been possible to draw a coherent picture if it were not for the description of various models of Andean socio-political structure from other areas of the Andean region that are described on the basis of much better ethnographic and ethnohistorical evidence than is available for the North Coast. It has been a question of finding the model that fits the information available and that is what is presented here. Although it was not possible to begin with the few surviving fragments of North Coast oral history, once the outline of the socio-political structure has been established these fragments become much more informative and understandable.

Using both ethnographic and ethnohistoric materials as sources of models, it has been possible to establish the patterns of settlement across the landscape, which appears to be an extension of the principles of socio-political organization (Netherly and Dillehay 1986). In Andean spatial organization at the regional level, rivers were found to act as median lines in an initial dual division. Dual patterning on each bank of the river confirms the higher ranking of upstream sites relative to those downstream, which is consistent with the ethnographic information (pp. 90–91, 108–109). Dual and quadripartite division within archaeological settlements as expressed in both site organization and architectural planning have been found to have surprising time depth, extending back to the Late Preceramic period on both the North and Central Coasts (pp. 92–94, 110–113). There are a number of different ways duality and quadripartition can be expressed, but once the principal modes or patterns are known, they are difficult to miss. Evidence for the physical expression of the socio-political organization has become so compelling that it has become necessary to look for it as a matter of course.

In the following sections the organizational implications of the Taycanamo genealogy, the remnant Chimor polity of the sixteenth century, the territorial divisions of the Chimu state, and the internal organization of Chan Chan will be considered. The assumption is made that the political organization of Chimor is not different in general outline from the dual and quadripartite organizations found at the regional level on the North Coast, nor is it different in principle from state-level organization found elsewhere in the Andes.

The Taycanamo Genealogy

There are three known accounts of dynastic origin for the North Coast of Peru: those of Eten (Liza 1967; Netherly n.d.a: 300–301, n.d.b), Lambayeque (Cabello Balboa [1586] 1951: 327–329), and Chimor (Vargas Ugarte 1936: 231–233). These three accounts share a number of formal characteristics suggesting that North Coast origin myths share certain themes.

The Eten myth was recorded earlier in this century by Jacinto Liza from old residents of Eten. It represents a popular oral history of Eten in which in ancient times a lord (*jefe*) and his people (men and their families) came from the north by sea on balsa rafts landing at a point on the south bank of the Reque River between the river and the Morro de Eten (a local landmark with a long Pre-Hispanic history) and spreading inland (see Fig. 2).

The Lambayeque myth, which is discussed at length in this volume, offers far more detail about the suite of wives and lords and their accouterments that Naymlap brought with him on balsa rafts from the north (Netherly n.d.a: 301–307, n.d.b). This myth goes on to describe the subsequent activities of the founder, who built a palace/ritual center and occupied himself in cult activities, leaving the expansion inland to his sons and followers.

In the Taycanamo account, which is incomplete, the initial details are missing; however, the recorder notes that the balsa wood rafts on which Taycanamo arrived are well known in the far north of Peru at Paita (at the mouth of the La Chira River) and Tumbez. The foreignness of Taycanamo is emphasized by the fact that he spoke a different language and had to learn the dialect of Yunga spoken in the Moche Valley (cf. Netherly n.d.a: 86–100). A great lord had ostensibly sent Taycanamo to govern. This was a form of validation of his rule, which was further strengthened by his use of yellow powders and familiar loincloths. The importance of the garments of the Chimu lords, particularly the loincloths with their elaborate front and back panels, is superbly documented in Ann Rowe's study of Chimu textiles (1984). The yellow powders (face and body paint) are also noted in the Naymlap account as part of the adornment of a great lord. Thus, it appears that in both form and content the Taycanamo oral history conforms to the canons of North Coast accounts of dynastic validation.

The account of territorial expansion as attributed to Taycanamo's descendants follows. His son, Guacricaur, won over lords and their subjects in the Moche Valley. His son Nañçenpinco (sic), in turn, conquered the head of the Moche Valley and the coast north to Pacasmayo (the Jequetepeque Valley) and south to Mayao (the Santa Valley) (see Fig. 2). Nañçenpinco is said to have been followed by seven unnamed descendants who were succeeded by Minchançaman. This ruler is attributed with the conquest of the coast as far north as Tumbez and as far south as Carabayllo in the Chillon Valley north of Lima. Minchançaman was also the Chimu ruler who was conquered by Topa Inca Yupanqui, carried off to Cuzco as a hostage, and married to a daughter of the Inca. The Inca ritual of subordination was completed with the installation of a son, Chumuncaur, by a (presumably secondary) wife from Huaura to rule in his father's stead, and his sending the required goods and women to Cuzco. The son of Chumuncaur, Guamanchumo, succeeded him and was followed in turn by his son, Ancocoyuch, during whose reign Huayna Capac initiated the break-up of the larger Chimu regional polities (Netherly 1988a, n.d.a; Rostworowski 1961). Ancocoyuch was succeeded by his brother Cajaçimçim, who reigned over a vastly reduced Chimor polity at the time of the arrival of the Spanish. Cajaçimçim was also known as Sachas Guaman, a Quechua title used by the Inca and by his baptismal name, Don Martín (Rostworowski 1976). There follow six Colonial descendants, but the account gives the names of only Don Antonio Chayhuac, *cacique principal* in 1604 at the time the oral history was recorded. It is possible to supply the names of three of the earlier Colonial lords, Don Christóbal and Don Rodrigo from the 1540s and 1550s and Don Pedro Oxa Guaman from the 1560s to the 1580s (AGI Justicia 338, in Rostworowski 1976; Netherly n.d.a).

Theresa Topic (this volume) offers a perceptive and sensible commentary on the Taycanamo account as history. As she notes, the rulers from Minchançaman onward are very likely historical. She also draws attention to the categorization implicit in this oral history.

The information given in the Taycanamo account is laid out schematically in Figure 3. Here, it is easier to visualize how the founding ancestor, Taycanamo, his son and grandson, who are drawn in black, are set off as the founder and builders of the core territory of the Chimu state. They are

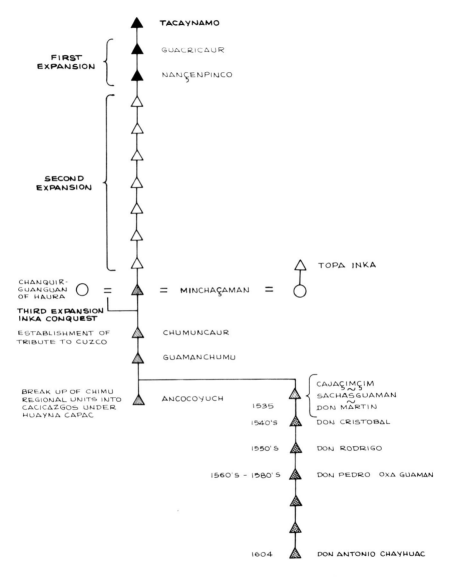

Fig. 3 The rulers of the Taycanamo oral history as given in the 1604 account.

separated from the more recent rulers by the interpolation of seven unnamed rulers who are collectively responsible for further territorial conquest. The five named protohistorical rulers follow. Only Minchançaman is
credited with the final expansion of the Chimu territory to Tumbez and

Carabayllo. This ruler and his successors who rule increasingly diminished polities under Inca domination are set off in hatchure from the nameless lords who precede them and the Colonial *caciques* who follow. The only example given for succession by brothers is the last two rulers in this group, Ancocoyuch and Cajaçimçim, although this form of succession was very common before the coming of the Spanish (Netherly n.d.a: 190–199, n.d.b).

There are a number of difficulties presented by the Taycanamo account as it has come down to us. From what is known of Andean political structure as presented through kinship models, the setting-off of Taycanamo and his immediate descendants is entirely consistent (Zuidema 1973, this volume). But who are the following seven nameless lords or what do they represent? If, as the papers by Carol Mackey and A. M. Ulana Klymyshyn (this volume) and Theresa Topic (this volume) suggest, the second expansion, that is, the major aggrandizement of the Chimu Empire, was a process lasting centuries and not a single event, then this perhaps explains the elision of the intervening rulers. However, in any case, seven rulers are insufficient to cover the span of time involved—at least three centuries.

The list is also incomplete if, as was unquestionably the case, the political structure at the highest level was dual. Given the pervasiveness of dual political structures in the entire Andean region and the evidence for surviving duality presented in the next sections, proof will have to be presented for any other kind of structure. Following the arguments presented for the Inca by Zuidema (1964, 1978, this volume) and Duviols (1979), these seven unnamed rulers may be seen as the lords of the second moiety complementary to both lines of succession (cf. Netherly n.d.a: 199; n.d.b).

This hypothesis is presented in Figure 4. The hiatus between Nañçenpinco and Minchançaman is shown, as are the last five named rulers. Together, if Taycanamo as founder of both moieties is excluded, there are seven named and seven unnamed lords. Thus, we must assume that in this account only the beginning and end of Chimu rule were considered relevant for the oral history (cf. Zuidema 1973, this volume), but violence is not done to one of the fundamental principles of Andean political structure. In conclusion, although there is implicit evidence in the Taycanamo account to support this interpretation, the model applied is based on evidence external to the account. It may also be noted that the organization of the expansion of Chimor in three stages in the genealogical account may reflect the sociopolitical reality indicated by the three major shifts in the style of the loincloths and tunics worn by the Chimu lords (A. Rowe 1984).

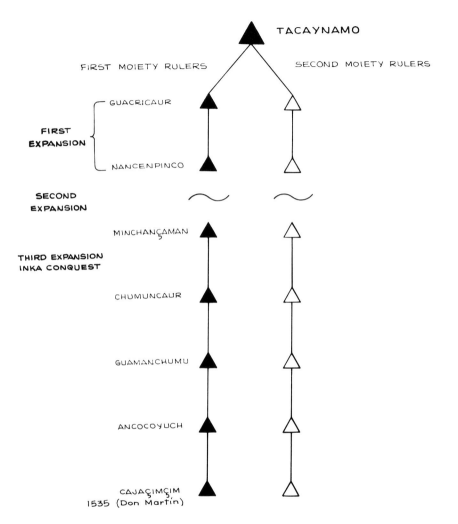

Fig. 4   The rulers of the Taycanamo oral history presented as a moiety system with Taycanamo as founder of both moieties.

The Remnant Chimor Polity in *1535*

While late sixteenth-century documents offer abundant evidence for dual and quadripartite organization in the Moche Valley, I have been reluctant to use this material as an argument for Chimu socio-political organization because of the very heavy impact of the Spanish Colonial regime in the Moche Valley where the city of Trujillo was the major Spanish center for the North Coast (Netherly n.d.a). However, through the kindness of John Murra we now have two of the earliest *encomienda* grants for the North Coast, and other early materials have come to light as well (AGI Justicia 1065; AGI Justicia 398 in Rostworowski 1976; Loredo 1958). These materials, if taken together with the evidence for the Chimu canals in the Moche Valley, permit more secure location of the principal socio-political divisions on the landscape.

The original grant of *encomienda* (found by Murra) of the "pueblo"of Manziz (or as it was called, the *repartimiento* of Chimor) to Martín de Estete was made by Pizarro on March 5, 1535. Three lords are mentioned: the *cacique principal* (an administrative title used by the Spanish throughout the Indies), Sachas Guaman (Cajaçimçim). Of his *principales* or subordinate lords, two are named: Yspilco, lord of the "pueblo" of Çabin (Sauin), and Çuyçuy (Suysuy), lord of the "pueblo" of Nasapac (AGI Justicia 1065).

In a grant made to Melchor Verdugo on the same day in the same place, Trujillo, he received half of Cajamarca and one *principal* or lord named Chicama Anaque who was lord of the "pueblo" of Chongueo, called Changuco in the litigation published by Rostworowski (Lee 1926: 1819; AGI Justicia 398 in Rostworowski 1976). The testimony in the litigation establishes beyond doubt that this lord was a *hamaquero* or hammock bearer, a service designation which, like the titles of the lords in the Naymlap oral history, indicates very high estate. He was a lord in his own right, with lands located on the south bank of the river above the "guaca grande" (modern Huaca del Sol). Apparently this grant was intended to provide Verdugo with labor service closer to Trujillo than his vast Cajamarca holdings.

In 1548 or 1549, the President of the Real Audiencia in Lima, Licenciado Pedro de La Gasca granted the *repartimiento* of Guaman to Rodrigo Lozano. In this grant the principal lord is given as Guaman and the *segunda persona* or head of the second moiety is called Cipra (AGI Lima 118: fol. 36r, in Rostworowski 1976: 103). The grant of Guaman does not appear in the *encomienda* lists drawn up in the 1540s by Diego de Mora for La Gasca, not even in the last of these dated Abril 6, 1548, and signed by Diego de Mora and Rodrigo Lozano among others (Loredo 1958: 251–258). Lozano had held the *encomienda* of Guañape (Viru Valley) and Chao (Chao Valley) since the 1530s, and this does appear in all the lists. The Guaman *repartimiento* had as its "pueblo" Chichi or Chuchi, which was located on the north bank of the Moche River near the sea (AGI Justicia 398 in Rostworowski 1976: 121–147). The location of Guaman can be fixed even more precisely, for these lands were watered by the canals from the *puquios* in the middle valley (ART Juan de Mata 1598: fols. 459v–461r; see Netherly n.d.a: 277, fig. VI.1; Ortloff et al. 1985: 70, fig. 1). This places the Guaman lands in a wedge-shaped area between the *puquios* on the east, the Moche River to the south, the Pacific Ocean to the west, and the lands watered by the Mochica Baja canal to the north (cf. Netherly 1984, 1988b: 263, fig. 9.3). This was a particularly favorable location, because the *puquio* canals, fed by upwellings of groundwater in the middle valley, the *puquios,* provided year-round irrigation (ibid.).

The litigation testimony already alluded to in the suit between Pedro Lozano, son and heir of Rodrigo, and Melchor Verdugo provides further information on the south bank of the Moche River. In addition to the polity headed by Chicama Anaque, located in the lower part of the valley, there was another lord, Don Alonso Chancon, who held land on the south bank to the east and upstream of Chicama Anaque. A second lord or *principal* is mentioned, Don Diego Tintomys, whom I believe to be Don Alonso's *segunda persona* or lord of the second moiety at that level (AGI Justicia 398 in Rostworowski 1976). This clarifies the situation on the south bank of the Moche River where there were two *parcialidades,* that of Don Alonso Chancon (in the early 1550s at the time of the litigation) and that of Chicama Anaque (in 1535). Since upstream locations tend to outrank those downstream (see Netherly and Dillehay 1986 for the argument), if we consider the south bank of the Moche River as a unit for the moment, we may assume an upstream/downstream moiety division that would leave the predecessor of Don Alonso Chancon or lord of the higher-ranking moiety division with the predecessor of Don Diego Tintomys as head of the second division within that moiety. Chicama Anaque was lord of the second moiety division on the south bank of the river. No lord is mentioned as his *segunda persona* in the litigation documents, but the testimony repeatedly states that there was a second "pueblo" or *parcialidad* called Xacon (Jacon) subject to him and located near the sea.

We can now place these socio-political units on the landscape using the canals (Netherly 1984). There were three canals on the south bank of the Moche River in Chimu times. The farthest upstream is the Orejas Canal (S3 in the designation used by Ortloff et al. 1985: 79, fig. 1). This canal may be associated with the lord of the first south bank moiety division, the predecessor of Don Alonso Chancon mentioned in the litigation testimony. The second section of the first moiety on the south side of the valley, the *parcialidad* of the predecessor of Don Diego Tintomys, may have used the Santo Domingo Canal (S2 in Ortloff et al. 1985). There is an area to the west of Cerro Orejas that has fairly high-status Chimu architecture and a fairly extensive Chimu settlement now largely buried under moving sand (M. E. Moseley, personal communication, 1984). There is an extensive Chimu settlement in the Quebrada Santo Domingo, which is also covered by sand. This area may be associated with the second section of the first south bank moiety. The whole area between Cerro Orejas and Cerro Ochupitur to the west is of great strategic importance. The strategic value of Cerro Orejas has been noted by T. Topic (this volume), and the Quebrada Santo Domingo-Quebrada

Ancados area to the west is the site of many important routes of communication to the south (M. E. Moseley, personal communication, 1978; Mujica in Rostworowski 1976: 112–120).

It would appear that both sections of the second south bank moiety, that of Chicama Anaque in 1535, irrigated with the canal now called *la general de Moche*. The testimony in the litigation of the early 1550s unhesitatingly placed the seat of the lord of Changuco just east of the huge pyramid called *la huaca grande* in the sixteenth century and now known as Huaca del Sol (Netherly n.d.a). Elías Mujica has discussed the possible archaeological location for Changuco and for Xacon, the subordinate *parcialidad* mentioned for this moiety in the litigation testimony (Rostworowski 1976: 112–120). The south side of the Moche River has not been so affected by the urban expansion of the city of Trujillo and would repay further study with these hypotheses in mind.

There was also a quadripartite division on the north bank of the Moche River. In 1535 three lords are mentioned in the *encomienda* grant of Chimor: Sachas Guaman (Cajaçimçim, later Don Martín), whose "pueblo" was Manziz and who was paramount and thus head of the first moiety division on the north bank as well as the first section of four. I make the assumption that Yspilco of Sauin, whose name follows that of Sachas Guaman, was the head of the lower-ranking moiety on the north bank. This would leave Suysuy (surely a title, for it appears repeatedly as the name of lords in the Chimu heartland from Licapa to Casma [Netherly n.d.a]), whose "pueblo" was Nasapac as lord of the second section of the second moiety (AGI Justicia 1065). The fourth lord was Guamannamo, head of the *parcialidad* of Guaman whom I would place as the lord of the second moiety of the first section, because of his obviously close relationship to Sachas Guaman, whose order to fill in for the missing Chicama Anaque with labor service to the latter's *encomendero*, Melchor Verdugo, was obeyed by Guamannamo (cf. Fig. 1; AGI Justicia 398 in Rostworowski 1976: 121–143). The Cipra mentioned in the grant of *encomienda* of Guaman to Rodrigo Lozano was unquestionably the head of the second moiety within the *parcialidad* of Guaman, but this brings us to a level of organization one step lower than the one just described (Rostworowski 1976: 103). The location of Guaman is secure. Very likely the first moiety irrigated with waters from the northern Puquio Canal and the second moiety used waters from the slightly smaller southern Puquio Canal (see Netherly n.d.a: 277, fig. VI.1; 1988b: 263, fig. 9.3).

There were three long canals on the north side of the Moche Valley that took water directly from the river: the Moro (the maximum level canal), the Vichansao, and the Mochica Canals. These are numbered N3, N2, and N1, respectively, in the recent studies of the Moche Valley canal system (Ortloff et al. 1982, 1983, 1985; see also Netherly 1988b: 263, fig. 9.3). Of these, the Moro, although the highest canal in Chimu times, watered the smallest area at the narrow neck of the valley (Ortloff et al. 1985: 79–80). The middle canal, the Vichansao, was a very large and long canal in Chimu times. The area watered in the upper and middle valley is relatively modest; however, at its distal end this canal fed the Huanchaco system to the north of Chan Chan and was probably the most significant canal in the valley for the period that it did so (pp. 80–82). The third canal is the Mochica, which today has two branches called the Mochica Alta and Mochica Baja. This canal has been in continuous use since Chimu times (pp. 82, 95, table 4) and waters the largest area of arable land in the valley. The lower Puquio Canals have already been noted.

These three canals unquestionably were associated with the three sections represented by the three lords in the 1535 *encomienda* grant. We may assume that in 1535 the principal lord, Cajaçimçim (Sachas Guaman), as lord of the highest-ranking moiety, and his section were associated with the Mochica canals. This is reinforced by the fact that the early Spanish *reducción* of Mansiche to the west of Trujillo represents the relocation of the "pueblo" of Manziz mentioned in the *encomienda* grant of 1535 and is watered by the Mochica canal (Netherly n.d.a). It may well be that in the past the principal lord of Chimor controlled the Vichansao. The abandonment of the lower part of this canal and the Huanchaco network fed by it would be sufficient justification for a reassignment. If Yspilco was the principal lord of the second section (1:2) of the north bank, then Suysuy would be the head of the second division within that section. I would therefore place Yspilco and his people in control of lands watered by the Vichansao and Suysuy's *parcialidad* on the lands watered by the Moro. Here I use the size of the area irrigated as a rough criterion for the rank of the group or section associated with it, despite the fact that the intakes of these canals are farther upstream than the intake of the Mochica canal. According to one Andean schema, this should accord them, and the groups associated with them, higher rank (Netherly and Dillehay 1986). This was, in fact, one of the considerations used in the ranking of the moiety sections on the south bank.

In the case of Chimor, however, there were unquestionably multiple rearrangements to accommodate the far more complex situation involving the middle levels of authority of the imperial rulers. This is particularly true for the irrigation system of the north bank. The system of political organization I am proposing for Chimor permits both movement upward and downward through the levels of organization, which must have been constantly redefined as the Chimu polity expanded and contracted.

The political structure of the remnant polity of Chimor, which occupied the Moche Valley in 1535, can now be described. The paramount lord, Sachas Guaman, was associated at all times with the lords of the following divisions. There was a primary dual division into two ranked moieties mediated by the Moche River (Netherly and Dillehay 1986), which placed the higher-ranking moiety on the north bank of the river under Cajaçimçim (Sachas Guaman) and the lower-ranking south bank moiety under the predecessor of Don Alonso Chancon. At the next, quadripartite, level of organization, the heads of the two ranked sections on the north bank would be Cajaçimçim (Sachas Guaman) and Yspilco. Those on the south bank would be the predecessor of Don Alonso Chancon and Chicama Anaque. At the third level of organization into eight divisions, we have a moiety division of the four divisions at the preceding level as follows: Guamannamo is the head of the second moiety division within the section headed by Cajaçimçim (Sachas Guaman); Suysuy stands in the same relation to Yspilco; on the south bank the second moiety of the section headed by the predecessor of Don Alonso Chancon is headed by the predecessor of Don Diego Tintomys; and presumably the lord of Xacon stood in the same relation to Chicama Anaque.

Once the Spanish granted away the lords of the south bank in separate *encomiendas* in 1535 (AGI Justicia 398 in Rostworowski 1976), the *repartimiento* of Chimor was confined to the north bank of the river. This means that the dual division and quadripartition manifest in the Spanish written record for Colonial Chimor correspond to levels two and three in Table 1.

The Territorial Division of Chimor

Any discussion of the territorial and hierarchical organization of the Chimu state before the Inca conquest involves certain assumptions and certain risks. The latter arise because there is no written evidence although less than a century separates the end of Chimu independence from the arrival of the Europeans. More significant is the elimination by the Inca of the upper-most levels of Chimu political organization, perhaps as many as four or five, leaving the local-level structures intact. The truly great lords were already a thing of the past, although the Spanish were dumbfounded by the wealth of those whom they saw in their diminished estate. More importantly, gone also with the top levels of organization were the administrative functions of a large, intact state.

The assumption made here is that the formal organization of the Chimu state did not differ from the dual and quadripartite organization described above for the regional polity of Chimor. In this, it resembles the Inca state, whose institutions were also modeled on and arose out of those found at lower levels of organization. I also assume that the Chimu state was one of a continuum of Andean states and that its formal organization reflects Andean concepts of political organization.

It is important, when considering pre-industrial states, to distinguish between state-level *functions,* such as administration, procurement of revenue, and direct production, and the *institutions* through which these were

TABLE 1. POLITICAL ORGANIZATION IN THE MOCHE VALLEY IN 1535

Level	First Moiety (North Bank)			Second Moiety (South Bank)		
1	Cajaçimçim (Sachas Guaman)			Predecessor of Don Alonso Chancon		
2	Cajaçimçim		Yspilco	Predecessor of Don Alonso Chancon		Chicama Anaque
3	Cajaçimçim	Guamannamo	Yspilco	Suysuy	Predecessor of Don Alonso Chancon	Predecessor of Don Diego Tintomys	Chicama Anaque	lord of Xacon

carried out. There never was a class of independent bureaucrats in the Chimu state similar to that which arose in the nation states of Western Europe. The functions of a pre-industrial state must have been carried out in the Chimu state by groups under their own lords whose function was administration, which depended directly upon one or another of the great lords in a fashion analogous to the position of artisans; or by members of the lords' lineages depending directly upon them for prestige, power, and maintenance; or by personal retainers of the lords drawn from the groups they ruled in the fashion of the highland *yana yanayayku,* "he who serves me exclusively"; or more probably a combination of all of the above (Netherly n.d.a, n.d.b). Such individuals might well count as great lords themselves. Without an understanding of the Andean concepts of state-level administration, we are not likely to identify the centers associated with such activities.

The territorial organization of the Chimu state can also be shown to conform to Andean principles of spatial organization (Netherly and Dillehay 1986). The dual and quadripartite organization of the Chimor polity in the Moche Valley has been demonstrated. In order to show how the larger Chimu state conformed to these principles, we must consider Andean modes of dual division and quadripartition. The four *suyu* of Tawantinsuyu, the Inca state, are laid out pie-fashion from a central point, the Cuzco Valley, where the river mediates the territorial division between Hanan and Hurin—the fundamental dual division. There is another way to divide Andean space into four parts longitudinally, which is described by Thérèse Bouysse-Cassagne in her study of Omasuyu in the Lake Titicaca region (1978). Here, the arrangement of the parts is linear rather than circular. A midline divides the whole territory into two ranked parts with a further subdivision in each half parallel to the midline. Within each larger half, there are, then, two ranked subdivisions; the one furthest from the original midline is hierarchically lower than the one adjacent to the midline. The two farther subdivisions are ranked between themselves by the relative position of their moiety.

Thus, in the case of Chimor, the Moche River divides the long, narrow imperial territory into a higher-ranking northern half analogous to the Hanan division of the highlands and a lower-ranking southern half similar to Hurin. Each half was divided in turn into two asymmetrical parts, with the higher-ranking one bordering the Moche River and the lower-ranking sections on the periphery. As the Chimu state expanded, the interior boundaries within the northern and southern divisions were constantly redefined. As both T. Topic (this volume) and Mackey and Klymyshyn (this volume) have indicated, this makes it very difficult to fix these internal boundaries or even establish contemporaneous northern and southern interior frontiers. Nevertheless, I feel confident that the ranking of the four territorial divi sions corresponded with the ranking of the four principal lords of the realm, including the highest-ranking: the Chimor Capac, as the Inca called him.

Thus, we may expect the paramount Chimu ruler to be associated with the highest-ranking northern section closest to the Moche River and can suppose that the midline separating this section from the lower-ranking northernmost section was shifted from Chicama to Pacasmayo to Zaña to the northern edge of the Lambayeque polity as the empire expanded northward. The other northern section would have been under the rule of the third-ranked lord of the four, second of course to the paramount in the northern division. The second-ranking lord of Chimor ruled the southern section bordering the Moche River, with the division between it and the peripheral southern section moving from Viru to Santa to Nepeña to Casma to Paramonga and finally, perhaps, to Huaura. This may explain the multiplicity of Chimu "administrative" centers and assist in their interpretation. The southern half of the southern division would have been ruled by the lowest-ranking of the four great lords of Chimor. Figure 2 shows how the internal boundaries would have to shift as the Chimu Empire expanded.

The Organization of Chan Chan

There should be evidence for the fundamental dual and quadripartite divisions of the Chimu state at its capital, Chan Chan. The complexity of the imperial organization, the size of the city, the historical remodeling it underwent, the nature of the archaeological evidence, and the paradigms of the scholars studying the city have all hindered an immediate understanding of the city.

The question of what physical expression the principles of duality and quadripartition, which are so pervasive in other areas of the political structure, may have had in the highly symbolic Chimu capital remains. We expect to see in the architecture and urban design some clue of these principles as they reflect the socio-political organization of the society. At first glance this does not appear to be the case. However, Kolata's analysis of the growth of the Chimu capital as based on the seriation of the adobe bricks used in the different construction phases offers some promising suggestions (Kolata, this volume). These are found in the ceremonial architecture, clearly quadripartite in the final urban plan of the city, and in the elite compounds or *ciudadelas,* the seats of the Chimu rulers, which are apparently clustered in their use through time (Kolata 1982, this volume).

Zuidema (this volume) warns, however, that the lords of the Hanan and Hurin moieties of Cuzco, the Inca and his co-ruler, were localized in only two areas of that city and lived successively in only two structures or palaces. There is no simple interpretation for the evidence from Chan Chan, which seems to me to be plagued both with gaps and by the large number of structures of different kinds at any given point in time.

In Kolata's figure 3 (this volume), the ceremonial and *ciudadela* structures known to be present during the first phase of the city, Chimu 1A, are shown. There is one large platform mound, Huaca Higo, and one large enclosure, Chayhuac. Inasmuch as many earlier structures were razed by the Chimu themselves to make way for later building, we do not know what else may have existed at this early date. However, one enclosure, one large ceremonial structure, is not incompatible with Andean structural patterns. We may speculate that Chayhuac was the seat of the paramount Chimu lord at this early stage and that Huaca Higo served as a cult center for the entire Chimu polity. The construction of Uhle in Early Chimu 1B times may suggest the beginning of dual expression; however, there seems to have been multiple contemporary occupation within Uhle itself. This raises the question of whether these early *ciudadelas* were not the seats of the co-rulers as well as the paramount. It would be tempting to see quadripartition in the cluster of *ciudadelas,* apparently all in use at about the same time. More significant, it seems to me, is the continued use of Huaca Higo and the appearance in Early Chimu 1C of Huaca Olvido (see Kolata, this volume: figs. 3–5). This clearly dual pattern in the ceremonial structures continues through Early Chimu 2 times (see Kolata, this volume: fig. 6).

During Middle Chimu times two new ceremonial structures come into use, Huaca Las Conchas and Huaca Obispo in association with the extremely large Gran Chimu complex. Gran Chimu is one complex that, because of its size and complexity, might suggest a concentration of the entire socio-political structure in one architectural scheme. The two ceremonial structures associated with it suggest an expression of duality (see Kolata, this volume: fig. 7).

The final phases of construction at Chan Chan during Late Chimu 1 and 2 suggest far more deliberate architectural and urban planning. The number of ceremonial structures is brought up to four with the addition of the Huaca Toledo, assuming that Huaca Higo continued as a cult center. The configuration of four must surely have been associated with a quadripartite socio-political structure and the four divisions of the Chimu territory (see Kolata, this volume: figs. 8 and 9). The final four *ciudadela* compounds may have been occupied as pairs. If used singly, these compounds then require us to examine the interior architecture anew. The reduction in the area devoted to storage at Chan Chan during the Late Chimu period (Kolata, this volume) may indicate that, in fact, three of the four co-rulers were resident elsewhere, presumably in regional capitals located in their respective territorial sections. Such regional capitals would have to be identified and correlated temporally to the late period. Storage could be dispersed regionally as a mechanism of risk reduction and logistic convenience. However, the logic of Andean political structures would suggest that the co-rulers were located in the capital.

The foregoing discussion has emphasized the evidence for Andean co-rule in the Chimu Empire, not only on the regional level, where it survived into the Spanish Colonial period, but also the projection of this form of organization to the highest levels of imperial organization. The justification for this lies in the mode of organization of other Andean state-level societies, particularly Tawantinsuyu and in the mechanisms by which Andean lords could move up and down the hierarchical scale, falling back in diminishment of their rule to lower-level polities.

By recasting the political model away from unitary rule toward the Andean variety of collegial rule, where no one individual could have power over the whole society, but rather had to negotiate the acquiescence of his co-rulers, heads of important sections of the society, more questions have been raised than have been answered. If the integration of ethnological models based on documentary and ethnographic information has opened new lines of research, the corroborating evidence must still come from the archaeological record.

BIBLIOGRAPHY

AGI (Archivo General de Indias), Seville
Justicia 1065
Justicia 398, fols. 1r–14v. In Rostworowski 1976: 121–147.

ALBÓ, JAVIER, and CIPCA personnel (Centro de Investigación y de Promoción del Campesinado)
1972   Dinámica en la estructura inter-comunitaria de Jesús de Machaca. *América Indígena* 32: 773–816. Mexico.

ARGUEDAS, JOSÉ MARÍA
1964   Puquio, una cultura en proceso de cambio. In *Estudios sobre la cultura actual del Perú* (Luis Valcarcel, ed.). Universidad Nacional Mayor de San Marcos, Lima.

ART (Archivo Regional de la Nación-Trujillo), Trujillo
Juan de Mata 1598, fols. 459v–462r.

BOUYSSE-CASSAGNE, THÉRÈSE
1978   L'espace aymara. *Annales: Economies, Sociétés, Civilisations* 33: 1057–1080. Paris.

CABELLO BALBOA, MIGUEL
[1586] *Miscelánea antártica.* Universidad Nacional Mayor de San Marcos,
1951 Lima.

CALANCHA, ANTONIO DE LA
1638 *Crónica moralizadora del Orden de San Agustín en el Perú con sucesos egenplares en esta monarquia.* Pedro Lacavalleria, Barcelona.

CARRERA, FERNANDO DE LA
[1644] *Arte de la lengua yunga.* Instituto de Antropología, Publicaciones Espe-
1939 ciales Numero 3. Universidad Nacional de Tucuman, Tucuman.

CONRAD, GEOFFREY W.
1982 The Burial Platforms of Chan Chan: Some Social and Political Implications. In *Chan Chan: Andean Desert City* (Michael E. Moseley and Kent C. Day, eds.): 87–117. University of New Mexico Press, Albuquerque.

DELRAN, GUIDO GERARDO
1974 El sentido de la historia: Una visión de los vencidos según tradiciones campesinas de Paucartambo (Cuzco, Perú). *Allpanchis* 6: 13–28. Cuzco.

DONNAN, CHRISTOPHER B.
1983 *Excavations at Chotuna.* Museum of Cultural History, Publications. University of California at Los Angeles, Los Angeles.

DUVIOLS, PIERRE
1979 La dinastia de los incas: ¿Monarquía o diarquía? *Journal de la Société des Américanistes* 66: 67–83.

ESPINOZA SORIANO, WALDEMAR
1967 El primer informe etnológico sobre Cajamarca, año de 1540. *Revista Peruana de Cultura* 11–12: 1–37. Lima.

HASTINGS, C. MANSFIELD, and MICHAEL E. MOSELEY
1975 The Adobes of Huaca del Sol and Huaca de la Luna. *American Antiquity* 40: 196–203.

HOUDART-MORIZOT, MARIE-FRANCE
1976 *Tradition et pouvoir a Cuenca, communauté andine.* Institut Français d'Etudes Andines, Travaux 15. Lima.

ISBELL, BILLIE JEAN
1978 *To Defend Ourselves.* University of Texas Press, Austin.

KOLATA, ALAN LOUIS
1982 Chronology and Settlement Growth at Chan Chan. In *Chan Chan: Andean Desert City* (Michael E. Moseley and Kent C. Day, eds.): 67–85. University of New Mexico Press, Albuquerque.

LEE, BERTRAM T.
1926 Encomenderos y encomiendas. *Revista del Archivo Nacional* 4. Lima.

LIZA, JACINTO A.
1967 *Historia de la aparición del Niño Jesús en el antiguo pueblo mochica de Eten en 1649.* Editorial Jacinto A. Liza, Chiclayo and Eten.

LOREDO, RAFAEL
1958 *Los repartos.* Lima.

MOSELEY, MICHAEL E., and KENT C. DAY, eds.
    1982   *Chan Chan: Andean Desert City.* University of New Mexico Press, Albuquerque.

MURRA, JOHN V.
    1962   An Archaeological 'Restudy' of an Andean Ethnohistorical Account. *American Antiquity* 28: 1–4.

MURRA, JOHN V., and CRAIG MORRIS
    1976   Dynastic Oral Tradition, Administrative Records and Archaeology in the Andes. *World Archaeology* 7(3): 269–279.

NETHERLY, PATRICIA J.
    1984   The Management of Late Andean Irrigation Systems on the North Coast of Peru. *American Antiquity* 49(2): 227–254.

    1988a Las fronteras inka con el reino de Chimor. In *La frontera del estado inca* (Tom D. Dillehay and Patricia J. Netherly, eds.): 105–129. BAR 442, Cambridge.

    1988b From Event to Process: The Recovery of Late Andean Organizational Structure by Means of Spanish Colonial Written Records. In *An Overview of Peruvian Prehistory* (Richard Keatinge, ed.): 257–278. Cambridge University Press, Cambridge.

    n.d.a. Local Level Lords on the North Coast of Peru. Ph.D. dissertation, Department of Anthropology, Cornell University, 1977.

    n.d.b. Lords and Ancestors. Manuscript in author's possession.

NETHERLY, PATRICIA J., and TOM D. DILLEHAY
    1986   Duality in Public Architecture in the Upper Zaña Valley, Northern Peru. In *Perspectives in Andean Prehistory and Protohistory* (Daniel H. Sandweiss and D. Peter Kvietok, eds.): 85–114. Latin American Studies Program, Cornell University, Ithaca.

ORTLOFF, CHARLES R., ROBERT A. FELDMAN, and MICHAEL E. MOSELEY
    1985   Hydraulic Engineering and Historical Aspects of the Pre-Columbian Intervalley Canal System of the Moche Valley, Peru. *Journal of Field Archaeology* 12: 77–98.

ORTLOFF, CHARLES R., MICHAEL E. MOSELEY, and ROBERT FELDMAN
    1982   Hydraulic Engineering Aspects of the Chimu Chicama-Moche Intervalley Canal. *American Antiquity* 47: 572–595.

    1983   The Chicama-Moche Intervalley Canal: Social Explanations and Physical Paradigms. *American Antiquity* 48: 375–389.

PLATT, TRISTAN
    1975   *Espejos y maíz.* Centro de Investigación y de Promoción del Campesinado, La Paz.

ROSTWOROWSKI DE DIEZ CANSECO, MARÍA
    1961   *Curacas y sucesiones:Costa norte.* Lima.

    1975   Pescadores, artesanos y mercaderes costeños en el Perú prehispánico. *Revista del Museo Nacional* 41: 311–349. Lima.

    1976   El señorío de Changuco, Costa Norte. *Bulletin de l'Institut Français d'Etudes Andines* 5 (1–2): 97–147. Lima.

ROWE, ANN POLLARD
    1984   *Costumes and Featherwork of the Lords of Chimor*. The Textile Museum, Washington, D.C.

ROWE, JOHN H.
    1948   The Kingdom of Chimor. *Acta Americana* 6: 26–59.

SHIMADA, IZUMI, STEPHEN EPSTEIN, and ALAN CRAIG
    1982   Batan Grande: A Prehistoric Metallurgical Center in Peru. *Science* 216: 952–959.

TOPIC, JOHN R.
    1982   Lower-Class Social and Economic Organization at Chan Chan. In *Chan Chan: Andean Desert City* (Michael E. Moseley and Kent C. Day, eds.): 145–176. University of New Mexico Press, Albuquerque.
    n.d.   The Lower Class at Chan Chan: A Qualitative Approach. Ph.D. dissertation, Department of Anthropology, Harvard University, 1977.

VARGAS UGARTE, RUBÉN,
    1936   La fecha de la fundación de Trujillo. *Revista Histórica* 10(1): 229–239. Lima.

WACHTEL, NATHAN
    1966   Structuralisme et histoire: À propos de l'organisation sociale de Cuzco. *Annales: Economies, Sociétés, Civilisations* 21: 71–94. Paris.
    1974   Le dualisme chipaya: Compte-rendu de mission. *Bulletin de l'Institut Français d'Etudes Andines* 3(3): 55–65. Lima
    1977   *The Vision of the Vanquished: The Spanish Conquest of Peru through Indian Eyes 1530–1570*. Harvester Press, Sussex.

ZÁRATE, AGUSTÍN DE
    [1555]   *Historia del descubrimiento y conquista del Perú*. Imprenta Miranda, Lima.
    1944

ZUIDEMA, R. TOM
    1964   *The Ceque System of Cuzco: The Social Organization of the Capital of the Inca*. Brill, Leiden.
    1973   Kinship and Ancestorcult in Three Peruvian Communities. *Bulletin de l'Institut Français d'Etudes Andines* 2: 16–33. Lima.
    1978   The Inca Kinship System. In *Andean Kinship and Marriage* (Ralph Bolton and Enrique Mayer, eds.): 240–281. American Anthropological Association, Washington, D.C.
    1982   Myth and History in Ancient Peru. In *The Logic of Culture: Advances in Structural Theory and Methods* (Ino Rossi et al., eds.). J. F. Bergin Publishers, Inc., New York.

Dynastic Structures in Andean Culture

R. TOM ZUIDEMA

UNIVERSITY OF ILLINOIS, URBANA

THIS PAPER IS CONCERNED with the interrelationships in Andean societies between dynastic structures and their bureaucratic use for spatial and temporal organization. Mentioning the word *dynasty* obliges us to think of historical chronology; but dynasty is also, and even more so, a problem of kinship and of a system of kin terms, of age classes and of systems of *mita* services regulated in terms of an annual calendar. Moreover, public and political thinking about the past in Andean societies was carried out by making use of mummies, bodies intended to resist genealogical time. These were dressed up and carried around for ritual and political use as needed in a given moment. The past was not conceived in terms of dated documents or well-preserved real genealogies enabling us to check one local genealogy against another, as with Maori genealogies in New Zealand, for example. Thus, our best empirical check on Pre-Spanish genealogies known from ethnohistorical documents in Peru is in terms of space, rank, and repetitive calendrical concepts.

I know of only five examples in the Andes of recorded dynastic genealogies. The data in all five examples are embedded in significant descriptions of cultural and social contexts, and all show important mutual parallels and contrasts. I will introduce the genealogies one by one, beginning with the two cases reported by Rodrigo Hernández Príncipe in 1622: one for the village of Allauca, near Choque Recuay in the Department of Ancash, and one for the village of Ocros in the upper reaches of the Huanchac River, a northern affluent to the Pativillca River on the western side of the Andes. The Ocros example introduces an important feature concerning the connection between the royal dynasty and political organization in Cuzco, which is the third example. As a fourth case, I will mention the myth of Naymlap, which describes a political concept close to that of Cuzco (Zuidema 1977). Both cases are examples of a political ideology that may have been common in the whole central Andes, examples to which I could add those of Allauca, already mentioned, and of Incaic Copacabana. (Probably the fact that we do know of these examples of political ideology, and of these four only, is just a case of historical accident.) Finally, the Chimu (or Taycanamo) dynasty is the fifth case of a dynastic genealogy recorded by a Spanish chronicler.

The village of Allauca was classified in Inca bureaucracy as one of the rank of a *pachaca,* a word translated as a "group of a hundred families." There were four *ayllus* (local groups), each with four male ancestors, who were designated as being either of a high ($\triangle$), middle ($\triangle$), or low ($\blacktriangle$) rank (Fig. 1) (Hernández Príncipe [1622]1923: 35–40; Zuidema 1973a). Moreover, the ancestors of both the first and third *ayllus* were considered to be the sons of eagles who had come from Lake Titicaca and who, in each *ayllu,* had become a *huaca principal.* People in the second and fourth *ayllus* claimed their descendence from two women who had come out of a lake that created all women and female llamas. Each of these two female ancestors also had become a *huaca principal,* each of its own *ayllu.* The genealogies report two generations in Pre-Hispanic times and two from after the Spanish Conquest. Thus, there are four generations between the "Creation of the World" and the ethnographic present of Hernández Príncipe's time. Clearly, some genealogical foreshortening occurred; it is the last and lowest lineage in the fourth *ayllu* that suggests where in the genealogies this happened. The ancestor here was called *sapan churi,* "single son," and he had four generations of descendants down to Spanish times (compared to only one in almost all other cases). The similar genealogical data of Choque Recuay are less complete, and I will not reproduce them here (Hernández Príncipe [1622]1923: 25–35; Zuidema 1973a). They reveal, however, that people in its last and fourth *ayllu* also were represented by a longer genealogy then those in the other *ayllus.* In their past, all *ayllus* of Choque Recuay had performed human sacrifices and Hernández Príncipe gives us a full list of the particular occurrences. The fourth *ayllu,* however, had not sent the victims elsewhere, as did the other *ayllus.* Its members, being potters, had offered their victims to the earth in the place where they lived. This was done in order to obtain good clay for their pots. On the basis of modern ethnographic parallels and data from Incaic Cuzco, I would argue that in the cases of Allauca and Choque Recuay it was not primarily the upper classes who were interested in divulging real or imputed genealogical knowledge about their ancestors, but the lower classes, those who had to labor with their own hands, working land they had inherited from their fathers. Today, local farmers and herders know exactly how a *chacra* (cultivated field) or a corral has come into their hands. Sometimes they are able to enumerate up to ten occurrences of change of hands.[1] These people are less concerned about their political connections than are local leaders, but they are more concerned about their roots.

The second example, that of Ocros, seems to confirm the one of Allauca (Fig. 2) (Hernández Príncipe [1622]1923: 50–64; Mariscotti 1970; Zuidema

---

[1] Personal fieldwork in the River Pampas area, Department of Ayacucho.

Ceremonial organization of the pachaca (village) of Allauca.

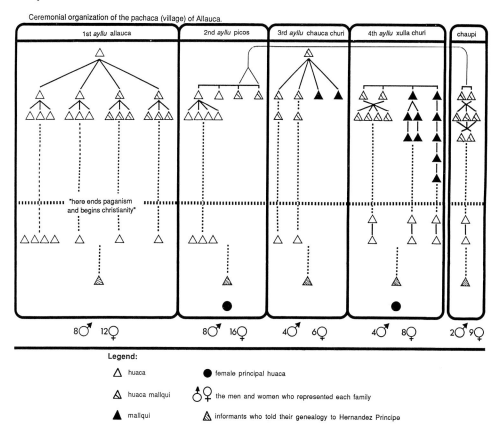

Legend:

△ huaca		● female principal huaca	
△ huaca mallqui	♂♀	the men and women who represented each family	
▲ mallqui	△	informants who told their genealogy to Hernandez Principe	

Fig. 1   The ceremonial organization of the *pachaca* (village) of Allauca (Hernández Príncipe [1622]1923; Zuidema 1973a).

1977–78). The genealogy concerns two towns from an organization of four. An ancestor who was equated with the Thundergod had four sons. They came as conquerors to the area. The *curacas* (lords) and nobility of the nearby town of Chilca descended from the first son, Parana, but their genealogy is not further continued. Those of Ocros descended from the second brother, Caha Yanac. The common people of the conquerors descended from the third and fourth brothers. We are not given the data on the conquered people who formed the third class of people. Caque Poma, a great-grandson of the second brother, had been, at some time in the past, *curaca* of Ocros, and we are given the names of all his sons and of one daughter. Otherwise, the list of his descendants as *curacas* down to the time of Hernández Príncipe is short. The lineages of the lower-class third and fourth brothers are much longer. We observe an opposition between a horizontal genealogical specification for the upper-class people against a vertical genealogical specification

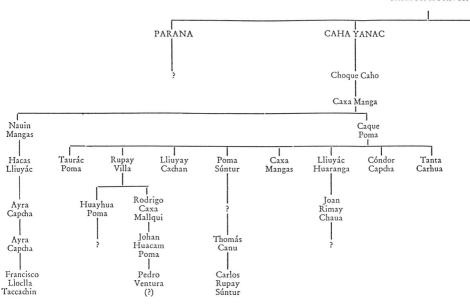

Fig. 2   The genealogy of the *curaca* Caque Poma in Ocros (Hernández Príncipe [1622]1923: 51–57; after Mariscotti 1970).

for those of the lower class; the observation made about the fourth *ayllus* in Allauca and Choque Recuay is supported by the case of Ocros.

The unique importance of Ocros for Andean studies in general and for a study of Cuzco in particular, however, concerns two other conclusions that can be drawn from Hernández Príncipe's data. We know of the Ocros genealogy because of a historical, political act—though recorded with mythological overtones—carried out by Caque Poma. This act is verifiable through archaeological methods. Caque Poma and the people of his village built an irrigation canal with the help of other neighboring villages. For that reason, the Inca king had elevated him in rank to the position of *curaca* over the other villages. On that occasion Caque Poma was allowed to sacrifice his own daughter. Caque Poma buried her alive in a shaft tomb on top of a mountain that had *collcas* (storehouses) to house the produce of the newly irrigated lands. Finally, because he had been elevated in rank, his own mummy had been placed in a new tomb, which was dedicated to him, together with the mummies of his descendants.

During three visits to the area, I discovered the mountain that had contained the shaft tomb of the daughter, and possibly the tomb of her father as well. (There are at that location in the old village of Ocros only four tombs

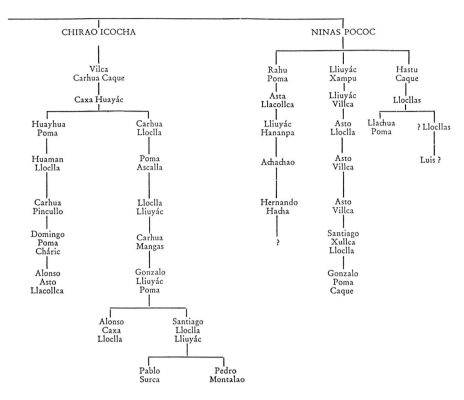

CHIRAO ICOCHA

Vilca
Carhua Caque

Caxa Huayác

Huayhua Poma — Carhua Lloclla

Huaman Lloclla — Poma Ascalla

Carhua Pincullo — Lloclla Lliuyác

Domingo Poma Cháric — Carhua Mangas

Alonso Asto Llacollca — Gonzalo Lliuyác Poma

Alonso Caxa Lloclla — Santiago Lloclla Lliuyác

Pablo Surca — Pedro Montalao

NINAS POCOC

Rahu Poma — Lliuyác Xampu — Hastu Caque

Asta Llacollca — Lliuyác Villca — Llocllas

Lliuyác Hananpa — Asto Lloclla — Llachua Poma — ? Llocllas

Achachao — Asto Villca — Luis ?

Hernando Hacha — Asto Villca

? — Santiago Xullca Lloclla

Gonzalo Poma Caque

such as the one described by Hernández Príncipe for Caque Poma.) I traced the canal and I located the place that Hernández Príncipe mentions as an archaeological site. Thus, our ethnohistorical data allow us to define the political unit governed by Caque Poma after being elevated in rank: that is, the villages that had helped in the construction of the canal and whose inhabitants worshiped the tomb of the girl. Hernández Príncipe reports that their *curacas* together had ceremonially drunk beer (*chicha*) made from corn grown on the newly irrigated lands. With such data available, we can ask the following questions: first, how did Caque Poma's family dominate and govern the three other villages from their own; and, second, when did these historical facts really occur? Hernández Príncipe mentions that the girl had visited Cuzco alive, but after she had been elected for sacrifice. He found her body, and he also found the mummies of Caque Poma and his descendants. From inspecting graves that had been undisturbed since the Spanish Conquest, he reconstructed the genealogy of Caque Poma's descendence. Theoretically speaking, we should be able to ask questions about chronology and to find out whether the events could have occurred in Incaic times or if the Incas just had availed themselves of an old story for their own political benefit. We are in a position to evaluate critically the genealogical tree as reported.

Coming now to the extremely complicated problem of Cuzco genealogy, I will outline the results of my recent re-evaluation of the issue (Zuidema 1964, 1977, 1986). First, however, I must explain some data concerning Inca social organization that influenced the genealogical problem. The valley of Cuzco was divided into two halves, Hanan, north of the Huatanay River, and Hurin, south of the river. It was also divided into four parts: Chinchaysuyu (I) and Antisuyu (III) in Hanan, and Collasuyu (II) and Cuntisuyu (IV) in Hurin. The city of Cuzco itself, where the king and his relatives lived, although it was part of and completely integrated into Chinchaysuyu (I), again was divided into a Hanan and a Hurin half. Thus, we have two moiety-type divisions: one that pertains to the whole valley and another solely to the city. Each *suyu* was divided into three distinct and localized administrative units. Of the total twelve units, one belonged to Hanan Cuzco and one to Hurin Cuzco; they were situated, together with their lands, above town in Chinchaysuyu (I). In the other ten units, Inca government had assigned fields (*chacras*), houses, and storehouses (*collcas*) to people coming from the outside whenever they had to carry out their *mita* obligations in the Cuzco Valley. In this way, the people of each unit were assigned their own service time of about a month, during which period they had to feed themselves with their own food, which they cultivated and stored on the lands given to them in the valley. The last two of these twelve units were, however, left to the autochthonous people of the valley, who remained there after being conquered by the Incas. The chronicler Juan de Betanzos ([1551]1987: 32, 57, 75) calls these "units" *chapa,* and describes them as sectors of land located perpendicularly to the river and the valley.[2] The practice of assigning *chacras* to visitors, so that they can sustain themselves with their own produce, still exists in the River Pampas area in the Department of Ayacucho.[3]

In accordance with Bentanzos's data, the chroniclers Bartolomé de las Casas ([1525–65]1957–58: 590–599) and Pedro Gutiérrez de Santa Clara ([1600?]1963–64: 435) tell us how the Inca king assigned administrators, probably one for each *chapa,* who were ranked according to their real or ascribed genealogical distance from the king himself. The data allow us to reconstruct which administrator received which *chapa* (Figs. 3, 4). The king himself and a close relative, one described as his father's son (Fs), retained Hanan and Hurin Cuzco, respectively, together with their supportive lands. The autochthonous people did not receive an administrator ranked as a royal relative. They were called the *cacacuzco,* "the wifegivers to (the Incas of) Cuzco," although the wives whom they did give were only secondary

---

[2] A similar, but far more elaborate description of such a system of land division was given in 1556 for the Valley of Cochabamba (Wachtel 1980–81).

[3] Personal field observations.

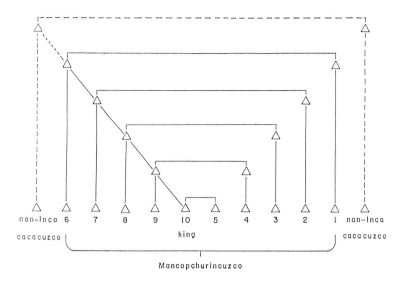

Fig. 3   The administrative model of Cuzco (Zuidema 1986: 37).

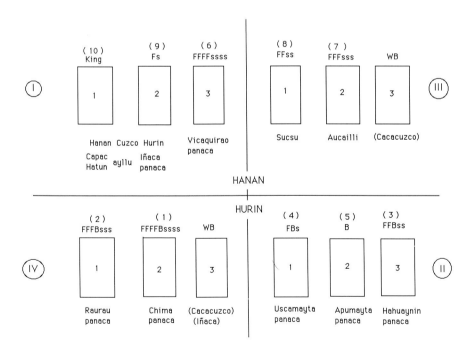

Fig. 4   The administration by the royal *panacas* in Cuzco of the ten *chapas* in the valley (Zuidema 1986: 27–34, 52) (F = father; W = wife; B = brother; s = son).

ones. The lands that they retained probably were distributed within the territory of the *chapas* of the Inca conquerors.[4] In conclusion, we note that this description of the administrative system explains explicitly and in detail what was mentioned in more general terms for Ocros also. In both examples, one group, which in Cuzco constitutes the royal family in Chinchaysuyu (I), dominates and governs three other similar groups, which in Cuzco are the other *suyus.*

How did the Spanish chroniclers, on the basis of this material and perhaps with the interested support of their Indian informants, come to reconstruct a Western type of dynasty? They did this at a time when Inca government had stopped functioning; when its genealogical way of ranking administrators had become frozen in time with respect to the last Pre-Hispanic king, Huayna Capac, and when Spaniards and Indians alike thought of the Incas in terms of a utopian past. We can arrive at an answer, considering first another description of the administrative system, given by Felipe Guaman Poma de Ayala, similar to the one of Las Casas and Gutiérrez.

Guaman Poma defines the ranks of the royal relatives not by way of ancestral linkages to the reigning king, but through a system of kin terms for his descendants (Fig. 5) (Guaman Poma [1615]1987: 288[290, 740, 754]; Zuidema 1977: 276–277; 1986). His description relates two important points. First, each king defined the ranks from his own point of view. Even if a newly elected king, he says, was a younger son of the former king, his older brothers would still be redefined by him as son, grandson, nephew, and so on. Second, a living brother could be called, for instance, great-great-grandson, because of his low status and not because of a real generational distance. Guaman Poma's model was a shorthand version of the one shown in Figure 6. The latter elucidates the ancestral model.

The people, defined in Guaman Poma's model as sister's children, *concha,* were not really what the term itself says. Betanzos, Guaman Poma, and others make abundantly clear that the *concha* were children of the king himself by secondary, especially non-Inca wives. They were second-class citizens, in the way the Spanish term *sobrino* was used in Colonial times and even today in some parts of Ecuador and Bolivia. In Inca society, however, with the exception of the king and the crown prince, everyone could be termed *concha* to refer to his lower status. Moreover, referring back to the ancestral version of the model, we can apply the term *panaca* (group of the descendants of a man's sister) to the descendants of each of the various royal ancestors. The so-called "sister" (*pana*), in fact, was a secondary wife, and her children were the *concha,* the so-called "sister's children." The *panacas* were the occupants of ten *chapas* as mentioned by Betanzos. On the basis of these ideas, we can reconstruct the

---

[4] A similar integration of autochthonous people into the political model can be suggested on the basis of the map made by Wachtel of the Incaic organization of the Valley of Cochabamba, mentioned in an earlier note.

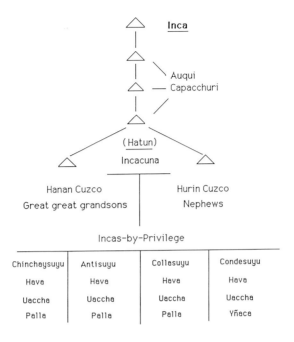

Fig. 5   Guaman Poma's descent model of ranks (Zuidema 1986: 35).

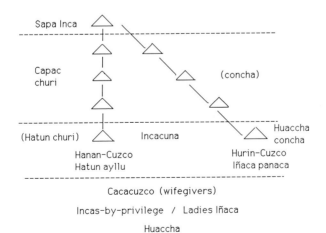

Fig. 6   The place of *Hatun ayllu* and *Iñaca panaca* in the organization of Cuzco.

Cuzco dynastic model. Figures 7 and 8 illustrate the two steps by which Spanish historiography arrived at that model (see also Duviols 1979: 67–83). Even when Pedro Sarmiento de Gamboa mentions how each king "founded" his own *panaca* (he is the first author to say so), we are now able to interpret the value of such a statement (Sarmiento [1572]1943: 134). The so-called "ancestors" were links in a ranking system who did not need to be historical kings at all. Even if such "kings" could have existed, still the dynastic model tells us something about their political ranking, but nothing about their chronological place in history.[5]

Later I shall return to other details of the Cuzco model, but I shall first consider the North Coast myth of Naymlap and his descendants as kings of Lambayeque in pre-Chimu times (Cabello Balboa [1586]1951: 327–330). Naymlap came from overseas with an idol of green stone. He founded a dynasty of twelve kings that ended similarly to the way it started: by way of water. Naymlap arrived from across the water and his dynasty ended because of rains. The last king also removed the green stone upon which the dynasty had been founded. After this dynasty's demise came the, apparently, more historical Chimu kings (the Taycanamo dynasty). The elements of greenness and water, mentioned at the beginning and the end of the dynasty, were used frequently in Andean cultures to represent primordial time. For example, the autochthonous people of Cuzco lived there from before the Flood and the Inca conquest; they grew green *coca* and green or red *aji* when the valley was still tropical (Betanzos[1551]1987: 20) and without seasons. Similar stories are known from elsewhere in the Andes; it is always the conquerors who cause the changes of seasons.

The Naymlap myth also says that his son had twelve sons; that each son was the founder of one of twelve towns; and that each of the twelve kings governed for twelve or fewer years. The number twelve is important, and a further detail about the dynasty of twelve kings makes it interesting to compare with the Cuzco dynasty. When Naymlap died, his people were told that he had flown away. His fellow conquerors went out to search for him, leaving the valley abandoned to its indigenous inhabitants. His son stayed behind and had twelve sons by twelve women, and these sons, in the

---

[5] The recently published, much longer version of the chronicle of Betanzos ([1551]1987: 99, 150) adds extremely important new material for elucidating the problem of the *panacas*. As it supports completely the reconstruction given here, I will mention some of the details. When Pachacuti Inca married the queen, he also received ten wives from the Incas in Hanan Cuzco, where the descendants of Inca mothers lived, and ten from the Incas in Hurin Cuzco, those with non-Inca mothers. They were called *Capac ayllu*. But those members who later married non-Inca wives had to adopt new surnames. Betanzos thus makes clear his awareness that all the *panacas* descended from Pachacuti Inca and not from earlier ancestors. Sarmiento was the first author to attach the name of *Capac ayllu* to the person of Topa Yupanqui and the names of the other families descending from Pachacuti Inca as *panacas* to the kings before Topa Yupanqui.

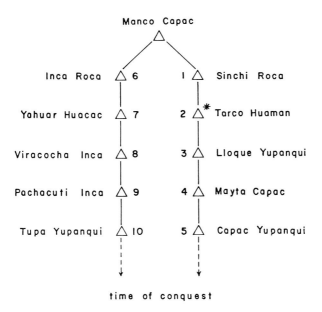

Fig. 7   The model of the double dynasty in Cuzco (Zuidema 1964: 52–54, 122–128).

Fig. 8   The model of the single dynasty in Cuzco.

next generation, became the founders of the twelve towns. Naymlap and his son lived in the time of the original inhabitants, and only the next ten kings are comparable to the ten "kings" in Cuzco.

Finally, Naymlap had forty servants, each with a professional specialization. In Cuzco the people who gave their *mita* service to Cuzco, people defined by Cristóbal de Molina as *mitimaes,* were classified, in terms of territorial extension, as belonging to forty different groups, and they also gave to Cuzco various specialists (Molina [1573]1943: 31–32; Zuidema 1977, 1985). The term *mitimae* or *mitmaq* in this case refers to a temporary displacement of people to a political center to which they are subject, and not to any kind of permanent displacement as the term normally is interpreted. A similar arrangement may have existed in the relationship between Naymlap and his forty servants.

I contend that Naymlap's story is a myth from beginning to end, but it tells us something important about a kind of political organization that was common knowledge at the time of the Spanish Conquest. Concluding this part of my discussion, I want to mention one other detail of the myth where I disagree with other interpretations. Fempellec, the last king, removed the green stone; he committed a sin by being seduced by a beautiful woman; thus he caused heavy rains for a month, followed by a drought for a year. Similar myths or stories are told in Cuzco and elsewhere. I see no immediate reason to connect it with an El Niño event, and less with a particular historical one (cf. Donnan and Moseley, who argue for such a conclusion, and Shimada, who doubts that a particular El Niño can be specified, this volume). The myth, first of all, refers to a recurring calendrical occurrence in a month of each year. On the basis of comparative data one cannot infer more from it.

We come now to the stories of the Chimu governors in Lambayeque told by Miguel Cabello Balboa, and of the dynasty of Chimu kings in Chan Chan (Rowe 1948). Little can be said as to whether these two Chimu genealogies' internal structures derive from myth or from established social patterns, either in Lambayeque or in Chan Chan. There is no internal reason to attach any value to the number of Chimu kings. Also, while once I had hoped that we could establish a connection between a concept of ten *ciudadelas* and the type of organization of ten *huarancas* (ten groups of 1,000 families each), so well known from northern Peru, especially from the region of Otuzco (Zuidema 1964: 16, 220), now this does not seem feasible. The *ciudadelas* were not all inhabited in overlapping times, and there seems to be no useful way to make a connection to a possible decimal organization.

Nonetheless, I do think that we can say something positive by making a comparison with Cuzco, though in a different way from that proposed by Geoffrey Conrad some years ago (Conrad 1981). First, let me dismiss certain misconceptions about Cuzco. I hope that it has become clear that the idea of *panacas* in their relationship to the organization of ten *chapas* has nothing to do with dynastic history or state formation; it simply is an administrative device to govern the valley of Cuzco in a manner similar to the way Ocros and other towns governed themselves. Secondly, I do not think that there were any royal palaces in the city of Cuzco belonging to successive kings, with each king building his own palace. There was a palace complex in Hanan Cuzco above the plaza of Haucaypata, used by all kings in general. There was also another palace complex in Hanan Cuzco, but below the plaza, used by the queens in general, which included the *acllahuasi,* "the house of the chosen women." Hurin Cuzco contained the Temple of the Sun and other buildings that were important for ritual use. There did exist buildings where individual mummies of so-called "royal ancestors" were kept, but these stood outside town and functioned in relation to the *chapa* lands. We do not know much about who lived on those lands, but clearly they were not occupied simply by descendants of former kings. Nonetheless, there is one feature about Cuzco's organization as a city that is of interest for comparison with the *ciudadelas* of Chan Chan.

I mentioned that Hanan Cuzco and Hurin Cuzco were recognized as two territorial units existing in combination with the ten *chapa* lands distributed over the valley. Guaman Poma and Betanzos report that the direct descendants of the kings and high nobility lived in Hanan Cuzco and that the descendants of non-Inca wives, called the "sister's children," lived in Hurin Cuzco. Although Sarmiento was the first chronicler to relate the concept of *panaca* to that of a single dynasty, nonetheless, he was still close to the original ethnohistorical sources. This allows us to discover where his data came from and how he reinterpreted them. When he mentions a *panaca,* called *Hatun ayllu* or *Iñaca panaca,* we can demonstrate the following (Figs. 5,6): "*Hatun ayllu*" is a shorthand version of the term—still used in early Colonial times—*Hatun Incacuna ayllu* (the numerous (*hatun*) descendants of the Incas who did not belong to Capac *ayllu* anymore). More in particular, *Hatun ayllu* were the descendants of the kings who, together with the high nobility, lived in Hanan Cuzco, while *Iñaca panaca* were the "sister's children" who, as descendants of non-Inca women called *iñaca,* lived in Hurin Cuzco (Sarmiento [1572]1943: 219–220; Zuidema 1986, n.d.).

Coming back to Chan Chan, Alan Kolata, William Conklin, and Patricia Netherly (this volume) have argued that one can distinguish between the two temporal sequences of *ciudadelas* and ceremonial platforms, an eastern and a western one. Would it be possible to define a pattern of two *ciudadelas,* an eastern and a western one, that functioned simultaneously and that we can compare to Hanan and Hurin Cuzco, respectively? More in particular, would it be possible to compare two *ciudadelas* to the two royal architectural complexes in Hanan Cuzco, of which the lower one was called Hatuncancha, "the large enclosure" (using the term *hatun,* "large, numerous," as in *Hatun ayllu*)? People of *Hatun ayllu* were administrators in the Hanan part of the valley of Cuzco, and those of *Iñaca panaca* administered its Hurin part. We can study the administrative connections among the city, the valley, and the forty groups of *mitimaes* who did their *mita* service in Cuzco. The similarity between the Cuzco and Lambayeque dynastic models and the possible similarity between the two-*cancha* model of Cuzco and the dual model of Chan Chan make me wonder if a Lambayeque "dynastic" model would not work also with reference to Chan Chan and the Moche Valley.

I shall conclude with an observation concerning chronological possibilities in the list of Chimu kings. The arguments made by Conrad (this volume) and by Michael Moseley and Kolata (n.d.) about the Chimu general Pacatnamu are convincing and lead me to think that we can search for other verifiable chronological information. The Chimu dynastic data might enable us to study certain problems that we can correlate to events that can be tested archaeologically, as I suggested for Ocros. Thus, the Chimu dynasty might be distinct from what I have concluded about the Inca and Lambayeque dynasties. I want to mention one item, however, which has been used for chronological arguments, but which to me seems to be more interesting for other reasons. John Rowe, in his article on the Kingdom of Chimor, analyzes the reference to king Minchançaman, conquered by the Inca king, or general, Topa Yupanqui, in relation to Cuzco data on Inca conquests by generals Capac Yupanqui, Topa Capac, and the future king Topa Inca Yupanqui (1948: 42–44). Rowe assigns specific dates to these conquests. All of them were said to have occurred, either in the time of Pachacuti Inca or of Topa Yupanqui, individuals who, in the single dynasty scenario were respectively the ninth and tenth kings. I shall consider the three Inca names and what they mean.

First, we observe that they are synonyms: Capac and Topa mean "royal," and the general Topa Capac combines both names. Second, all three persons are mentioned, though at different times, in connection with a river called Yanayacu or Yanamayu (the black water or river), near the Inca town of Vilcas Huaman. Documents allow us to identify this river with the River Vischongo, which passes the Inca ruins of Pomacocha and Vilcas Huaman. Capac Yupanqui was disobedient to his king at Yanayacu, and he was executed after his conquest of Cajamarca. Topa Capac is mentioned as a traitor and rebel because of an event happening at Yanayacu, and thus he was killed there by Topa Yupanqui (Sarmiento [1572]1943: 228–229; Zuidema 1967, 1973b). The term *yanayacu* (from which Sarmiento erroneously derives the name and institution of *yanacuna*), refers to a ritual called *yanayacu,* carried out at a river (Zuidema 1982: 130). The incidents near Vilcas Huaman refer to the River Yanayacu as a border to be crossed, or not to be crossed—a kind of Andean Rubicon. When we look at other regional documents from outside

Cuzco, for instance, those from Huarochiri or Chincha, it almost seems as if the names of Capac Yupanqui or Topa Yupanqui were the first or the only ones by which other peoples in Peru knew of the Incas. This is one reason I am suspicious of attaching too much historical value to a connection between a Topa Yupanqui and a Minchançaman.

Another reason for my suspicion is the following. We knew from José de Acosta ([1590]1954: 201) that there was not one king by the name Topa Yupanqui, but that there were two, and from Pedro Cieza de León ([1551]1967: chs. 49, 57) that there were also two generals of the name Capac Yupanqui, one being active before the other. Now, with the new and complete version of the chronicle of Betanzos, we know that there was a king Yamqui Yupanqui between Pachacuti Inca and Topa Yupanqui, also making conquests in northern Peru. With such an incertitude of the dynastic succession after Pachacuti Inca it is difficult to derive any definite idea of when the defeat of king Michançaman occurred.

SUMMARY

In this paper I compared five Pre-Hispanic Andean genealogies of which four at least had certain similarities to each other. The Cuzco dynasty as counted from Pachacuti Inca back in time had no historical value and its later history was compressed into a much shorter development of only two generations—those of Topa Yupanqui and Huayna Capac—than seems probable. A similar procedure was carried out in Allauca, Choque Recuay, and Ocros where also only two generations were recognized from before the Spanish Conquest. The Naymlap dynasty presented striking parallels with the Cuzco one in its connection to social organization. But it was placed as a totality before the time that the Lambayeque Valley was conquered by the Chimu. Given the parallels to Cuzco, we may detect two different elements in this mythical account: one, a reference to pre-Chimu times, and another to a local pattern of political organization as it might still have operated at the time of the Spanish Conquest.

I could not present any data that would support the veracity of Andean genealogies composed in Pre-Hispanic times. The example of Ocros comes closest to such an ideal situation. The chronicler wrote down a genealogy as he "observed" it; that is, he saw a ranked order of mummies in a grave, he received a first-hand indigenous interpretation of it, he placed the data in an archaeological and political context that was meaningful to his informants and to him, and it was a context that we, as archaeologists and ethno-historians, can verify in the field. A rich ethnohistorical documentation has now become available for this region of Peru (Duviols 1986), and it may become possible to tie its archaeological record into those of Cuzco and the North Coast.

BIBLIOGRAPHY

Acosta, José de
  [1590]   *Historia natural y moral de las Indias. Biblioteca de Autores Españoles 73,*
  1954   *Madrid.*

Betanzos, Juan de
  [1551]   *Suma y narración de los Incas.* Atlas, Madrid.
  1987

Cabello Balboa, Miguel
  [1586]   *Miscelánea antártica.* Instituto de Etnología, Universidad Mayor de San
  1951   Marcos. Lima.

Cieza de León, Pedro de
  [1551]   *El Señorío de los Incas.* Instituto de Estudios Peruanos, Lima.
  1967

Conrad, Geoffrey W.
  1981   Cultural Materialism, Split Inheritance, and the Expansion of Ancient
       Peruvian Empires. *American Antiquity* 46(1): 3–28.

Duviols, Pierre
  1979   La dinastía de los incas: ¿Monarquía o diarquía? *Journal de la Société des
       Américanistes* 66: 67–83.
  1986   *Cultura Andina y Represión. Procesos y Visitas de Idolatrias y Hechicerías.
       Cajatambo, Siglo XVII.* Archivos de Historia Andina 5. Cuzco. Centro
       de Estudios Rurales Andinos "Bartolomé de las Casas."

Guaman Poma de Ayala, Felipe
  [1615]   *Nueva crónica y buen gobierno.* Historia 16. Madrid.
  1987

Gutiérrez de Santa Clara, Pedro
  [1600?]   *Historia de las guerras civiles.* Biblioteca de Autores Españoles. Madrid.
  1963–64

Hernández Príncipe, Rodrigo
  [1622]   Mitología andina. *Inca,* vol. 1.
  1923

Las Casas, Bartolomé de
  [1525–65]   *Apologética histórica.* Biblioteca de Autores Españoles 106. Madrid.
  1957–58

Mariscotti, Ana María
  1970   Die Stellung des Gewittergottes in den regionalen Pantheen der Zen-
       tralanden. *Baessler-Archiv* 18: 427–436.

Molina, Cristóbal de
  [1573]   *Fábulas y ritos de los Incas.* D. Miranda, Lima.
  1943

MOSELEY, MICHAEL E., and ALAN L. KOLATA
    n.d.   Myth and History on the North Coast of Peru: Steps to an Archaeological Concordat. Paper prepared for the Dumbarton Oaks symposium The Northern Dynasties, October 1985.

ROWE, JOHN H.
    1948   The Kingdom of Chimor. *Acta Americana* 6(1–2): 26–59.

SARMIENTO DE GAMBOA, PEDRO
    [1572]   *Historia de los Incas.* Emecé, Buenos Aires.
    1943

WACHTEL, NATHAN
    1980–81   Les *Mitimas* de la vallée de Cochabamba. *Journal de la Société des Américanistes* 67: 297–324.

ZUIDEMA, R. TOM
    1964   *The Ceque System of Cuzco: The Social Organization of the Capital of the Inca.* E. J. Brill, Leiden.
    1967   El juego de los ayllus y del Amaru. *Journal de la Société des Américanistes* 56(1): 41–51.
    1973a   La parenté et le culte des ancêtres dans trois communautés péruviennes. Un compte-rendu de 1622 par Hernández Príncipe. *Signes et Langages des Amériques, Recherches Amérindiennes au Québec* 3(1,2): 129–145.
    1973b   La quadrature du cercle dans l'ancien Pérou. *Signes et Langages des Amériques, Recherches Amérindiennes au Québec* 3(1,2): 147–165.
    1977   The Inca Calendar. In *Native American Astronomy* (Anthony F. Aveni, ed.): 219–259. University of Texas Press, Austin.
    1977–78   Shafttombs and the Inca Empire. *Journal of the Steward Anthropological Society* 9(1,2): 133–178.
    1982   Review Article: El Primer Nueva Crónica y Buen Gobierno. *Latin American Linguistics* 6(2): 126–132.
    1985   L'organisation andine du savoir rituel en termes d'espace et de temps. *Techniques et Cultures* 6: 43–66.
    1986   *La Civilisation Inca au Cuzco.* Collège de France/Presses Universitaires de France, Paris.
    n.d.   The Role of Ladies Iñaca in an Inca Theory of Marriage and Alliance. Unpublished manuscript.

The Inca Conquest of the North Coast:
A Historian's View

SUSAN E. RAMÍREZ

DE PAUL UNIVERSITY

INTRODUCTION

GENERAL ACCOUNTS OF PERU before the Inca expansion describe disordered lands where savage and untaught natives feasted on human flesh, and where one polity warred on the other (Cieza de León 1864: 135). In some areas, like the valleys of the *yungas* (coastal plains), great tyrants arose who battled with their neighbors, conducted raids, and committed robberies and murders (pp. 135, 210). Such remarks were probably intentionally selected and exaggerated, first, to justify the Inca conquest, and second, to impress the early Spanish chroniclers.

Indeed, the Inca ideology of expansion promised the peoples incorporated into the empire peace, order, and a new state of well-being, that is, the benefits of imperial "civilization" (Cieza de León, 1864: 177). When Inca emissaries approached opposing lords to convince them to surrender without a fight, they reassuredly explained "that he [the king] wanted them as kinfolk and allies" (Cieza de León 1967: 52–53). The king wanted to establish and maintain order and justice and defend them from whoever would harm or make war on them (Santillán 1927: 14). In some instances, the propaganda promised that within his proposed confederation, all would be equal (Cieza de León 1967: 201–202).

Topa Inca Yapanqui, having heard of the fertility and grandeur of the North Coast, tried to gain domination with such promises. He sent his messengers with compliments and presents to the local lords begging them to accept him as a friend and companion, because he wanted to be an equal among them . . . and not make war on them if they wanted peace, and he would exchange some of his women and clothes for theirs . . . (Cieza de León 1967: 193). His message spread along the coast. Inhabitants heard that Topa Inca Yapanqui was not a bloody or cruel master and that he would only harm those who opposed him. They learned to praise the customs and the religion of the *Cuzqueños,* thinking that the nobles (*orejones*) were saints and that the Incas were divine, children of the sun (ibid.).

If the lords accepted these advances, like those of Tumbez[1] did for example (Cieza de León 1967: 193–194), they were fêted. They were rewarded with gifts of gold, silver, cloth, and women, and confirmed in their offices (pp. 54, 193). But those who refused subjugation, the Inca threatened by force of arms. Hernando de Santillán states that the Inca king cruelly victimized those who would not voluntarily obey him (1927: 15). The valiant king Chimu Capac, who ruled the coast from Huarmey to Tumbez (Cabello Balboa [1586] 1951: 317), resisted, and therefore the Inca troops fought and defeated the Chimu, terrorizing them in the process (ibid.: 319).

Regardless of how Inca rule was established, the aftermath of acceptance or rout, say these general accounts, was to impose "order and security in all the territory" (Cabello Balboa [1586] 1951: 332). Details varied by province or polity. In outline, the chroniclers say that the Inca appointed high-ranking *Cuzqueños* as governors (Cieza de León 1864: 177, 164), who were charged with overseeing the administration of the area and teaching the people "civilized" [meaning Inca] customs. Under Topa Inca Yapanqui, officials made a detailed accounting of the population and natural resources (Cabello Balboa [1586] 1951: 340). Miguel Cabello Balboa elaborates, saying

> He distributed the Domains (*Señoríos*) and Territories (*Cacicazgos*), giving each a name and the quantity of Indians that he considered advantageous, so that the Indians could rapidly contribute to the things that came up; and so he named *Guarangas* (that are like Thousands), others he made *Pachacas* that are Hundreds, and others decurions and with such an order no one was lazy. . . .[2] (ibid.:340)

As part of the same reorganization, lands and other resources were assigned to support the Incas, the state, and the religion (Cabello Balboa [1586] 1951: 346, 348; Cieza de León 1967: 222; Rostworowski 1966). Some people were moved out of the province and others were moved into it. If the people were hungry, the Inca provided food from the storehouses. The population was organized to construct roads, temples to the sun, and buildings for Inca administrators and to cultivate land to support the new as well as their traditional lords (Cabello Balboa [1586] 1951: 348; Cieza de León 1967: 188). The people were instructed to worship the sun, to learn Quechua, and to adopt Inca law. But local lords were allowed to maintain their traditional customs as long as these did not conflict with Inca law. With such changes, the Incas built a reputation for making sterile provinces

---

[1] I use the modern spelling for proper names of places, except in direct quotations.
[2] This quotation seems to support Catherine Julien's contention that the decimal system was imposed to exact labor tribute service (1982).

fertile and for being just and benevolent rulers (Anonymous [1583] 1925: 294; Cieza de León 1967: 52–55, 188, 191, 193–196; Melo [1582] 1925: 272; Santillán 1927: 18, 34–35). The Inca used this growing reputation as further propaganda to help subjugate and integrate new lands into the expanding domains.

The purpose of this rather long introductory review is to establish in outline form the Inca imperialistic ideology, policy, and procedure for incorporating polity after polity into a growing empire. These generalized claims will serve as a benchmark against which to document the impact of the Inca conquest in an area of the North Coast of Peru between modern-day Pacasmayo on the south and Motupe on the north. Before the Inca conquest, this area was part of the Chimu Empire, the most ancient and developed center of civilization in the central Andes and the largest and most organized political body to contest Inca suzerainty. Remarks will focus on three aspects of life affected by the Inca arrival: (a) population division, wrought by the chronicled imposition of the decimal system, (b) land tenure, and (c) exchange patterns. Throughout, local-level Colonial manuscripts from the sixteenth century that explicitly recall pre-Inca and Inca times in the North Coast valleys will be used to offset the chroniclers' macro-perspective and assess the extent to which Inca organization was accepted in the Chimu's provinces that were incorporated relatively late into the Cuzco imperial system. These suggest that the Inca Empire or model was not unaffected by local custom.

THE CASE FOR DECIMAL DIVISION

According to Cabello Balboa, Topa Inca Yapanqui conquered Chinchaysuyu, which included the area of the North Coast ([1586] 1951: 314, 319, 331) under discussion here. Returning from a successful campaign against the Chimu Capac, his armies passed through the lands irrigated by the Pacasmayo River and "disrupted all those valleys" (Cabello Balboa [1586] 1951: 319). On a return trip, his captains encountered resistance from Indians who lived in the Penachies mountains in the polity of Jayanca. For this, the *cacique* (*curaca* or paramount lord) of Jayanca was imprisoned and sent to Cuzco (Cabello Balboa [1586] 1951: 331). If chroniclers' accounts are to be believed, one of the changes these Incas introduced was the imposition of the decimal system, as the previous quotation (ibid.: 340) from Cabello Balboa attests (see also BM/Add. 13992, 411). But surviving Yunga vocabularies and grammars indicate that the pre-Inca numerical system of Chimor was already established on the basis of ten (Carrera [1644] 1939: 82–84; Harrington 1945: 29). Further, there is nothing in the archaeological record to suggest that the autonomous *yunga* system was anything other than decimal. The ten palace complexes at the Chimu capital of Chan Chan are possible archaeological support for a decimal structure (see Kolata; Netherly, this volume).

If decimal counting already existed on the North Coast, then the local record suggests that the Inca attempted to co-opt it and elaborate upon it by introducing a decimal nomenclature to parts of the hierarchy of noble titles. An indication of this is early Colonial testimony in a court case between Alonso Carrasco, *encomendero* (grantee of Indian labor) of Jayanca, and Alonso Pizarro de la Rua, *encomendero* of Pacora, over the disposition of four *principales* (lesser lords) and their Indians. Evidence in that case incorporated extracts from previous trials, including one between Francisco de Lovo and Diego de Gutiérrez, the previous *encomenderos*. In 1570, Alonso de Fuentes, an associate of Alonso Carrasco and resident manager of his properties and Indians in the valleys for more than fourteen years, declared that the word used to designate the local lord second-in-command was *conozeque* and that the word itself meant "lord of a thousand Indians" (AGI/J418, 1573, 209).

A check of the available literature on the Yunga (or Mochica) language confirms the translation. Augusto Orrego lists *cuno* as "thousand" and *cico* as "lord" (mister or *señor*) (Orrego 1958: 86, 92, respectively). A more direct translation comes from Jorge Zevallos Quiñones' *Un diccionario Castellano-Yunga* (1947: 182). There *cuno* means "thousand" and *ciec* means "mister or mistress" (*señor* or *señora*) (ibid.: 186; see also Harrington 1945: 27). These independent sources thus substantiate the translation of *conozeque* as lord of a thousand [Indians] (see also Carrera [1644] 1939: 69), and as a direct translation of *guaranga curaca,* mentioned by Felipe Guaman Poma de Ayala in his discussion of the highland decimal system (1980: 65 [65]).

Very little additional information is available on the *conozeque*. A witness in the Carrasco vs. Pizarro de la Rua case testified that the *conozeque* had been subject to the *cacique* of Jayanca before the Spanish invasion. He said that he heard the paramount chiefs of Tucume and Pacora and other Indians and *principales* say that in the time of the Inca and until the time that the Marques Francisco Pizarro distributed *encomiendas* (grants of Indians in trust to Spaniards), all the Indians and *principales* entrusted to the said Diego Gutiérrez had been subjects of the *curaca* of Jayanca, a man named Jayanque (AGI/J418, 1573, 320–321; see also 218, 459). Reports from the years 1536, 1541, and 1543 also show that there was a *conozeque* in Tucume, probably the same individual in each case (Table 1).

The naming practice of native officials changed during the first years after the Spanish Conquest. The change provides hints of the meaning of traditional names. The earliest Spanish observers who referred to Indians—lords and commoners alike—usually identified them by only one name. For instance, Jayanque is the only name cited for this individual who was the paramount lord of the Jayanca Valley. Similarly, *principales* Sican, Pacorapa,

TABLE 1. REFERENCES TO LORDS (*Ceques*) ON THE NORTH COAST,[1]
SIXTEENTH CENTURY

Name	Community	Date	Source
Pedro amas xeque	Cinto	1588	ASFL/Reg. 9, Ms. 7, 1585
D. Diego calance q[ue]	Chuspo	1563	ART/LC 29-III-1563
Martín calanceque	Ferreñafe	1549	AGI/E 502A, 43v-44
D. Felipe calanceq[ue]	Ferreñafe	1560	AGI/AL 133, 1560
D. Diego Senseq[ue]	Ferreñafe	1560	AGI/AL 133, 1560
D. Francisco Palarref Conçonçiq[ue]	Ferreñafe	1560	AGI/AL 133, 1560
Tuni çeq[ue]	Illimo	1566	AGI/J461, 1572
D. Pedro calanceq[ue]	Illimo[2]	1572	AGI/J460, 333v
calançeq[ue], calançeque	Jayanca	1540	Gama [1540] 1974: 217, 225
Conoseq[ue]	Jayanca	ca. 1540	AGI/J418, 1573, 256v, 270v
calansec[que]	Jayanca	ca. 1540	AGI/J418, 1573, 271
D. Joan ponon çec[3]	Jayanca	1566	AGI/J461, 1432
D. Joan pononçeque[3]	Jayanca	1566	AGI/J462, 1863
D. Juan principal de conosaque	Jayanca	1557	AGI/J418, 1573, 258
D. Joan cononçeque[3]	Jayanca	1560	ART/CoAG, 13-II-1565
D. Luis calançeq[ue]	Lambayeque	1566	AGI/J462, 1867
D. Luis calançeque	Lambayeque	1572	AGI/J460, 332v
D. Luis calançeque[4]	Lambayeque	1572	AGI/J457, 695v
D. xpoval calloçic[que]	Lambayeque	1572	AGI/J457, 714v
D. Gaspar purriseche	Tucume	1566	AGI/J462, 1863
D. Andrés Conanseque	Tucume	1566	AGI/J462, 1739 and 1863
D. Andrés Con nonseque	Tucume	1573	ART/CoO, 3-XII-1573
conoçique	Tucume	1536	AGI/E 502A, 7
calanseque	Tucume	1541	AGI/E 502A, 55
conoseque (sic çique)	Tucume	1541	ART/CoO, 13-VII-1570, 100v
locnoserque (el conoserque)	Tucume	1543	ART/Alvarez 28-IV-1543, 33
D. Andrés Connonse[que]	Tucume	1569	ART/CoO, 13-VII-1570, 130v
D. Lorenço Puri çeq[ue]	Tucume	1570	ART/CoO, 13-VII-1570, 166v
D. Andrés Cononceq[ue]	Tucume	1571	ART/CoO, 13-VII-1570, 190

[1] The *Visita* of Cajamarca also lists Indians with names ending in -*ceque:* van[von]ceque, colque ceque, tanta ceque (AGI/J1063, 3 and 7). Note, too, that with one exception (Chuspo), all these lords live north of the Lambayeque (Chancay) River. The names of lords in Pacasmayo share different suffixes. Does this indicate a linguistic or another type of boundary?

[2] Created from Tucume in 1540–41 (ART/CoO, 13-VII-1570 or AGI/E 502A, 9 and 40-43).

[3] Don Juan Pononçeque was identified as the *segunda persona* of the *cacique,* therefore, *pononseque* appears to be a transcription error in the above two cases.

[4] *Mandón de los hamaqueros* (lesser lord of the litter bearers).

Jotoro, Mocochomi, Minimisal, and Ferriñafee were all referred to by these single names.[3] Likewise, Spanish census takers referred to unbaptized Indian commoners as infidels and listed them by one indigenous name (Espinoza Soriano 1975; Gama [1540] 1974; Ramírez 1978; Zevallos Quiñones 1968).

By contrast, in other, usually later, documents some individual Indians, including indigenous lords, were identified by two or more names. For example, the name of the lord of the Jayanca fishermen was Enequisiquel Enenysal (AGI/J418, 1573, 326v–327). An earlier document, an *encomienda* grant of 1536, refers to eight named lords, two of whom had double names:

> the principal ferriñafee sino pullaqui and another whose name is chiclefee potapuc[e] who is lord of the town of potapuco [patapo ?] and another whose name is chuli and another who is called fipilco and another whose name is sindolufo and another who they call sanoco and another filipillo and another coxquefe with their Indians . . . (AGI/AL 201, 1633).

This suggests that, traditionally, important lords had two names, although the Spanish may have listed only one for lesser lords. This suggestion is supported by the fact that the lord of the Jayanca fishermen, Enequisyquil Enenysal (see below), was important enough to be carried in a litter by his subjects, a clear sign of high status and rank (Gama [1540] 1974: 225).

Over time, these traditional names were replaced by Spanish ones. For instance, early references to a *principal* of Jayanca call him Enequisiquil Enenysal or just Minimisal. Later, his successors were called Don Hernando Minimisal. Likewise, as noted above, in 1536 the lord of Tucume was referred to as *conozeque*. By 1566, his apparent successor adopted a compound name, Don Andrés Conan (or Con Non) Seque, who is described in various documents as a *principal,* a *segunda persona* (second person or second-in-command), and an *alcalde* (mayor) of the recently established Indian *cabildo* (town council) (Table 1).

This pattern is also seen in the names of commoners. The *Visita* (administrative inspection tour or census) of Ferreñafe published by Jorge Zevallos Quiñones in 1968 catches the Indians in transition. Some still use only one traditional name, while others have adopted hispanicized first names like: P[edr]o Yapacop, Ju[an] Cunol, and Al[ons]o Pecho (ibid.: 176, 178). Similarly, in a document regarding the disposition of lands of a lord of Lambayeque named only Calanseque, his heirs are recorded as Hernando Mezcon, Miguel Mynllon, and Francisco Quizquiz (ANCR/1586–1611, 9–V–1607).

[3] AGI/J418, 1573, 459–459v. Çicani (Çican, 1536; later, Sican) (AGI/J418, 1573, 201v, and 237–238v); Pacarapa (Pacorag, Pacorap, Pacallapa) (AGI/J418, 1573, 61v–62, 202v, and 217v); Jotoro (AGI/J418, 1573, 202v, and 217v); Mocochomi (AGI/E 502A, 55; J461, 1558; and J418, 1573, 330); Minimisal (AGI/J418, 1573, 52v); and Ferriñafee (AGI/E 502A, 40v–41v).

Clues to what the native names meant come from voluminous depositions presented in the court case cited earlier between Lovo and Gutiérrez, which involved several *principales* that both *encomenderos* claimed. The *principal* Minimisal, the lord of a group of fifty fishermen in 1540 (Gama [1540] 1974: 225), was one of these. According to the *encomendero* and others, confusion resulted from the fact that this lord was known by two different names, Minimisal[4] and Enequecheque.[5] The confusion was remedied by Gaspar Chiquina. Native of Jayanca and adult witness to the Spanish Conquest, he was a subject of the *principal* in question. He stated that the lord Enequis Yquil Enenysal was a subject to the paramount lord of the Jayanca Valley and the reason he had two names was because his proper name was Enequesequil [Enequechequel] and the name of the *señorío* or the territory of his jurisdiction was Nynymysal [or Minimisal]. He went on to say that Enequesequil's ancestors traditionally had taken as their surname the name of the domain (Minimisal) over which they ruled (AGI/J418, 1573, 326v– 327). Apten, a fisherman born in Tucume and a subject of the *principal* Mochumi (Mocochomi), corroborated Chiquina's explanation. He elaborated by saying that "Ynequececquil" was a name that Jayanca's *principal* had since he was a child (AGI/J418, 1573, 330v).

Alonso de Fuentes, the witness in the Lovo *vs.* Gutiérrez case, explained in sworn remarks recorded in 1563 that he personally had known three "*señores*" that had succeeded each other by inheritance in that domain and that "All three were called minimisal although they might have their own names like Don Hernando" (309v–310). Another witness, Gaspar de Morín, a Portuguese national who managed Gutiérrez' affairs for more than a decade and lived in the Valleys of Jayanca, Pacora, and Tucume, added (in 1563), even more clearly, that the name "minimisal" is the name of the *señorío* or domain. He continued by stating that whoever succeeds in that *señorío* is called by the name of the *señorío* even though he had his own personal name. Morín said he heard the chiefs of Jayanca and Pacora say that Nequesiquil was *principal* of Minimisal at the time that Pizarro distributed the Indians (AGI/J418, 1573, 322). These testimonies establish that lords took the names of the *señoríos* (loosely defined as *parcialidad* [subjects] and domain [309v; and Ramírez 1985]) at the time they took control.

This information helps us to understand the significance of the variety of names found in the sources. At the risk of over-generalizing, it seems that early references to individual lords at the *curaca* or *principal* level were by the name of the *señorío*. Thus, Minimisal and Sican, like Jayanque, appear alone. The references give no indication that either Minimisal, Sican, or Jayanque,

---

[4] Note that Minimisal contains *ni,* which in Yunga means sea or ocean (Zevallos Quiñones 1947: 182).

[5] Enequisqueel, Ynequiseque al, Enequi Siguel, Ynyquis Si Quil (AGI/J418, 1573, 297; see also 49; 298v–299v; and 301v).

as names, referred to rank or status in a hierarchical decimal system. The *segunda persona,* in contrast, was often referred to by his title or rank in a hierarchical, probably bureaucratic order, alone (Murra 1984: 81). As noted previously, a few years later, lords and individuals used compound names, perhaps in imitation of European practice. Most lords, it appears, used their given name and that of a *señorío.* Again, the obvious exception is the *segunda persona* who diverged from this rule and used a given name along with his rank in a decimal hierarchy.

Very occasionally, the rank modifies the given name and that of the *señorío,* such as Don Francisco Palarref Conoconciq[ue], who ruled in Ferreñafe (created from Tucume on February 2, 1536 [AGI/E 502A, 40–43]) (ART/CoO, 13-VII-1570). By analogy, Palarref would represent the name of a *señorío,* and *conozeque* would represent his status in a decimal ranking, based as it probably was originally, on the number of his subjects or size of the group. However, such complete references to lords are unusual.[6] They seem to have been quickly (by 1565–66) replaced with Spanish equivalents or substitutes for rank or *señorío,* such as Don Antonio Chumbi, *cacique principal* of Cinto in 1572; Don Juan Chiclayo *principal;* and Don Diego Zuche[i] *segunda persona* (AGI/J456, 399v; J460, 335; and P113, R. 8 [1565]).

Thus, these examples suggest that lords could take at least three names during any one lifetime, according to their capability, mobility, and position: a given name,[7] the name of the *principalazgo* or *señorío,* and, for a few who rose to high status or rank within the polity itself, a name reflecting a recognized position in a decimal-based system. The naming patterns and their meaning also suggest that the *conozeque* held a special status of prestige or authority that made the person prefer to be known by his decimal-based title rather than by *señorío* or *principalazgo,* perhaps because such designation enabled him to play a key or unique role in the life of the polity or recognized him as the named successor to the *curaca principal.*

To date, *conozeque* is the only term that clearly and unequivocally translates into a number associated with the traditional decimal hierarchy of the Inca (as presented by the chroniclers), although *-seque* appears in many of the names of other lords in early documents, as summarized and shown in Table 1. Calanseque, of all these, appears most frequently. The communities of Illimo, Lambayeque, Tucume, Jayanca, Chuspo, and Ferreñafe all had individuals using this designation. Tuni Ceque, as a name of a lord, appears only once, as the name of the father of Pedro Conchi, a *principal* of Illimo in 1566. If a complete decimal hierarchy had been imposed by the Inca, one would

---

[6] Other examples include Don Alonso Tayme Xuca, the *cacique principal* in 1558 of Cinto (Patapo) (AGI/J458, 2335); and Don Juan Tancun Mulasafu, a *principal* of Cinto (Patapo) and a landholder in 1566 and 1572 (AGI/J457, 26–27v; J460, 335; and J462, 1873).

[7] Cieza de León (1864: 280) suggests that Indians had at least two given names during their lifetime: one given in childhood and another given at puberty for adulthood.

TABLE 2. YUNGA PREFIXES AND THEIR MEANINGS

Prefix	Possible translations
amas, omas	[?]
calan, calo, callo	*kall*—*reir* [laugh] (Orrego 1958: 91)
purri, puri	*purri*—*pluma* [feather] (ZQ 1947: 185)
	purren—*plumas* [feathers]
	purr—*salado* [salty] (ZQ 1947: 186)
	pun, punic—*sombra* [shade] (ZQ 1947: 187)
sen	*sem*—*dulce, suave* [sweet, soft] (ZQ 1947: 179)
tuni	*tumi*—*lobo marino* [seal] (Orrego 1958: 85; ZQ 1947: 181) or *mucho* [a lot] (ZQ 1947: 183, 187)
	toni—*huaca* [temple, shrine] (Vargas Ugarte [1939] 1942: 476; Trimborn 1979: 69)
	tuni—*tiempo, universo* [time, universe] (Orrego 1958: 94; ZQ 1947: 187)

ZQ = Zevallos Quiñones

expect that the prefixes shown in Table 1 would translate into numbers. But, as Table 2 indicates, none of the prefixes, other than *cono,* translates as such in the available published work on the Yunga language.

Neither do the earliest Colonial census numbers suggest that the population was divided according to the decimal standard. Even dismissing the problematic and decimating effect of disease and the certainty that subjects had fled or been taken from the polity to serve the Spanish as carriers or servants (Vaca de Castro [1543]1943: 427–428, 465, 479) never to return, the 1540 *Visita* of Jayanca gives no clear indication that the society had been organized along decimal lines, either before or after the Inca. The *cacique* testified that he had 360 tribute-paying subjects, 118 *mitimaes* (outsiders or foreigners), plus an unknown number of Indians with a *principal* in Pabor (in modern Piura), and another number subject to a son. The total population directly under him, enumerated by the census taker, was 680.[8] A further ninety-eight persons were subjects of Facollapa(es), a second *principal* under the *cacique*'s command. According to my count, the *cacique*'s subjects numbered 933 (including twelve listed as absent, but not including 102 subject to the *principal,* Mulopa, who was not specifically identified with either the *cacique* or Facollapa).[9]

---

[8] Although, if one goes by the explicitly stated rules of counting and other information in the document, eight should not have been included because they really were subject to Facollapa.

[9] The 933 includes other groups of 27, 50, 16, and 70 enumerated separately, but said to be the *cacique*'s subjects.

The numbers of *principales* do not support the decimal division hypothesis either (Polo de Ondegardo 1917: 51; Santillán 1927: 16). In 1540 the *curaca* had eleven, specifically identified as subject to him, not counting the one in Pabor. Facollapa had five. Two other *principales* are mentioned by name and several others are referred to anonymously and not identified with either lord. The enumerator uses this "nonsensical census" (Mayer 1972) to estimate a total population of fewer than 4,000 individuals. But the census taker admits that "only divine revelation will make it possible to accurately verify the population in the said valley" (Gama [1540] 1974: 227).

Finally, the numbers of Indians under specific lords, though again problematic because of the disruptions caused by the Spanish presence, give no indication of originally being associated with a decimal system. A summary of these population figures is shown in Table 3. Note that lords with as few as twelve subjects and with as many as 180 all were called *principal,* making it nonsensical to assume that all the lords (e.g., *principales*) mentioned together in a document were, even originally, of the same status (see, e.g., AGI/J418, 1573, 314v; and E 502A, 54). Thus we lack linguistic and demographic evidence for the Inca imposition and local adaptation of a complete decimal hierarchy on the North Coast.

The other possible translations listed in Table 2, however, suggest alternative interpretations of the names of some lords. One would be that these names or titles refer to traditional lords: of feathers or featherwork (*puri seque*);[10] or of jesters or buffoons (*caloseque*).[11] *Tuniseque* may have referred to the lord of time or the universe, or a lord of the sky or astronomy. Or, if we accept *tuni* as equivalent of *tumi,* a Quechua term, and translate it after Cabello Balboa, *tumiseque* could have been the keeper of knives or arms.[12]

The legends of ancient Lambayeque suggest a correspondence between such lords and some of the members of Naymlap's retinue. Could these lords possibly be the successors of the specialists Naymlap brought with him? Could Naymlap's specialist in featherwork, Llapchillulli "purveyor or maker of feathered cloth" (Cabello Balboa [1586] 1951: 327; Rowe 1948: 37) antedate the traditional lords of specialist groups, like the *pintores* who still decorated cloth in early Colonial times? If *tumi* translates as knife and *tumiseque* is lord or the master maker of knives, was such a lord originally one of Naymlap's forty attendants and later head of a group that the early Spanish explorers called

---

[10] Recall that the legend of the founding of the Lambayeque kingdom mentions Llapchillulli, one of Naymlap's court attendants who made feathered cloth. After Naymlap's death, he supposedly led a group of followers inland to settle in Jayanca.

[11] This translation is problematic because in 1572 a *calanseque* had charge of a group of litter bearers (see later). Cieza de León (1864: 219) describes the buffoons and dancers who were always jesting while others played music and sang, who accompanied the coastal lords in ancient times.

[12] Cabello Balboa's translation of *tumi* is knife of stone ([1586] 1951: 269 and 506).

TABLE 3.   SUBJECT POPULATION OF LESSER LORDS,[1] North Coast,
Sixteenth Century

Lord	Date	Population	Source
(Illimo) yllame	1541	150 Indians *"de visitación"*	AGI/E 502A, 9
charanay	1541	60 Indians	"
estaninco	1541	90 Indians	"
mallupe	1574	65 married Indians	ART/CoO, 26-VIII-1573
(Jayanca) calançeque	1540	6 Indians	Gama [1540] 1974: 225
calana[ci]que	1540	13 Indians	"
mulenpe	ca. 1565	52 married Indians, 13 bachelors	ART/CoO 13-VII-1570
(Tucume) Don Fernando	1541	240 Indians	AGI/E 502A, 54
Samico[2]	1541	90 Indians	"
palseca refe	1541	20 Innkeeping Indians and 40 Indians	"
mocochomi	1541	100 Indians	AGI/E 502A, 55
calanseque	1541	140 Indians	"
lutuffe	1541	50 Indians	"
charan[2]	1541	60 Indians	"
fincala (talor effee)	1541	65 Indians	"
coxcafee	1541	50 Indians	"
Yllame[2]	1541	150 Indians	"
conoco	1541	180 Indians	AGI/E 502A, 55v
Don Hernando	ca. 1555	ca. 70 persons	ART/CoR, 3-VI-1564
Don Hernando efquip	1564	70 Indians	"
Don Diego mochumi	1566	12 subjects	AGI/J455, 1691

[1] *Principal,* unless otherwise noted.

[2] Also listed separately elsewhere in the same document as the Indians of the *encomienda* of Illimo. It is likely that these three hundred Indians were separated from Tucume to create another *encomienda.*

plateros (silver or metal smiths)? Our knowledge of the Yunga language and prehistory necessitates leaving these now as questions.

Another indication that the names of these lords—with the exception of *conozeque*—were traditional ones, not imposed relatively late by the Inca, is the fact that many survived as toponyms and as names of *parcialidades,* while other prefixes can be traced back to the mythical times of Naymlap. Calla (Calo, Callo), for example, appears in the legends of Naymlap as the founder of Tucume (Cabello Balboa [1586] 1951: 327–329; Rivero-Ayllon 1976: 28; Rowe 1948: 37). *Calan* appears as a toponym referring to lands associated with Lambayeque in 1611 and 1702 (ANCR/1586–1611, 23; ACMS, 1739–40). *Calannec* described lands belonging to Don Gonçalo Samico, *principal* of Illimo, lands that were irrigated by the water of the canal *trelo* or *tillo* (*til* ?) (AGI/J461, 1571v). Lands of the *cacique* of Lambayeque in 1566 were also called Callanec (AGI/J458, 2063v; and J461, 1551v). It should be added that *nech* in Yunga means river (AGI/J461, 1571v; Orrego 1958: 91; Zevallos Quiñones 1947: 186). Thus, perhaps *callanec* originally meant river belonging to Calla. It has been established elsewhere that control of the irrigation water defined land usage rights on the Pre-Hispanic coast of northern Peru (Netherly 1984: especially 239–240). Consequently, it might be assumed that the lands irrigated with the water in that river were used by Calla. Later, in 1712, Calanseque is recorded in titles as lands within the jurisdiction of the community of Lambayeque (ACMS/1813, 14v). A *hacienda* (large estate) near Jayanca, called Calasnique or Calesnique, existed between 1789 and 1800 (ANP/LC, 1789; 1800, 22–23; and 1793, 6). Such information could be used systematically to re-establish the extent and configuration of sixteenth-century *señoríos*.

An example of a title that survived as a *parcialidad* dates back to 1541. As Table 3 shows, a lord of Tucume, with one hundred forty Indians under him, was called a *calanseque*. In the seventeenth century, a *parcialidad* existed by that name in Ferreñafe (APF/Fábrica, 1633). And, in Lambayeque in 1572, Don Luis Calanseque was known to have been a *mandón*[13] of *los hamaqueros* (litter bearers) (AGI/J457, 695v). He, too, leaves his title to posterity as a *parcialidad* (AGI/AL 100 [1646]; ART/SC 1672). In fact, a manuscript from the second half of the eighteenth century refers to *calancec* as one of eleven *parcialidades* that existed in 1765 (ANCR/1765)[14] (Table 3).

With reference to the imposition of a decimal hierarchy on the North Coast, we may conclude that the Inca may have mandated the use of a decimal vocabulary. But, if so, it was imposed as a bureaucratic shorthand, as a means of signifying special rank,[15] and only at the upper levels of a polity's traditional hierarchy, perhaps to distinguish a lord with jurisdiction over more than one type of occupational specialist or *parcialidad*. There is no extant written evidence to indicate that it was actively used at the local level for actual administration, to calculate, for example, service obligations, as Catherine Julien argues (1982). Demographic records, including even the

[13] A lord of lesser jurisdiction and status than a *principal*.

[14] The same document states that before the Spanish Conquest, Lambayeque numbered a thousand Indians with one head. Although not referred to as such, this lord would have been a *conozeque*. Because of its late date, the information in this document needs independent verification.

[15] Or, it may signify category. The Quechua word *camoyoc* (a person capable of organizing or ordering) also appears on the coast before 1539 associated with officials subject to the paramount lord of Jayanca who were in charge of distributing irrigation water. Thus, *camoyoc* was introduced to designate a category of persons, between specialists and executives (managers or foremen), a usage that appears analogous to that of the term *conozeque* (AGI/J418, 1573, 465–466; Gama [1540] 1974: 227] transcribed as *campos* [sic]; Espinoza Soriano [1975: 271] transcribed the word more accurately as *camoyos;* Bruce Mannheim, personal communication, November 1985; Richard Schaedel, personal communication, November 1985; see also Falcón on the categories of *camoyoc* on the coast [1918: 149–51]).

earliest Colonial examples (dated 1536–40) are inconclusive and help little in further substantiating the decimal hypothesis, given the known disruptive effects of the Spanish invasion. If the Inca imposed more decimal nomenclature on the traditional lords they found ruling in the coastal valleys, few of these rankings survived as such even a generation after the Spanish Conquest. What survived were what appear to be the traditional names of the *señoríos,* either as toponyms[16] or *parcialidades.* Thus, Inca claims of reorganization, in this respect, may have consisted only of renaming certain existing social units. Even this, however, seems to have been partial and too late to have had any lasting effect (Murra 1984: 87; Salomon n.d.).

LORDS OF THE LAND

A second way the Inca king was supposed to have affected life on the North Coast was in the revamping of land tenure. By right of conquest, some chroniclers attest, the Inca assumed control, the eminent domain (*dominio directo*), over the lands of newly subjugated lords (AGI/AL 101). To keep the peace, the Inca established boundaries. Martín de Morúa elaborates, saying that boundary markers were placed between the four *suyus* or provinces. He also provides detail on the types of resources that were regulated, delegated, entrusted, and assigned to a *curaca*'s or *cacique*'s discretion. Fields, forestlands, all kinds of gold, silver, metal, and pigment mines, and even the islands of the sea near the coastline opposite towns were designated (1946: III-28, 231). This is confirmed by Guaman Poma de Ayala, who reiterates the great care that Incas like Topa Inca Yapanqui had in delineating the resources like pasturelands and rivers for fishing and collecting (1980: 1074 [1084]; see also Melo [1582] 1925: 272).

To guarantee these boundaries, according to an anonymous account entitled "Horden que el Ynga tubo en la governación del Piru," an Inca administrator (called a *micho*) lived in each principal town (*pueblo principal*). He "knew the markers and boundaries and limits of fields and irrigation ditches and water" and helped settle conflicting claims (BM/Add. 13992). The Inca established harsh penalties for those who did not respect the boundaries by entering or usurping the hunting grounds, fishing waters, forests, or mines of others, without special license or permission from the Inca (Morúa 1946: III-28, 231).

That this demarcation had been carried out on the North Coast is evident from both the chroniclers' accounts and various documents and petitions in the *residencia* (administrative review of office) of Dr. Gregorio Gonzalez de Cuenca, a Supreme Court judge who carried out an inspection tour of the North Coast in 1566. According to oral traditions written down by early

---

[16] Besides the toponyms mentioned previously, sixteenth-century lords, such as Çicani, Pacorap, Pucalá, Mochochumi, and many others, left their names as towns, *haciendas,* or geographical features that are still present or recalled today.

observers, the Inca or his agents and surveyors divided and marked a lord's domain when the coast was incorporated into the empire (between 1462 and 1470 [Rowe 1948: 40]). Guaman Poma de Ayala (1980: 852[866]) says that the Incas Topa Inca Yapanqui and Huayna Capac Inca and their surveyors, royal council, nobles, and judges established and placed boundaries and landmarks to separate the Indians of the highlands and the coastal plains so that they each would have jurisdiction and assigned authority. A more intimate testimonial is a 1566 petition brought before Dr. Cuenca by the *cacique* of Moro (a town in the modern valley of Pacasmayo), which asked that the lands held by him and his counterparts of Jequetepeque, Cherrepe, and Chepen be confirmed "according to the plan that the said paramount chiefs and old Indians of the said community made . . . in the time that the Inca divided them" (AGI/J458, 2041v–2042; on boundary markers see also Guaman Poma de Ayala 1980: 353 [355]).

Other local-level evidence strongly suggests, however, that the Inca's so-called reorganization was significantly tempered by the order prevalent under the Chimu. Evidence that the territorial domain of a *curaca* was indeed known and bounded comes from a viceregal decree, dated 6 December 1567, of Licenciado Lope de Castro, regarding the founding of the town of Santiago de Miraflores in the valley of Zaña. It locates the boundary between the valleys and—by extension—the lords of Pacasmayo and Zaña, "in the sand flats (*arenales*) that exist between the valley of Saña and the valley of pacasmayo . . . according to how the ancient Indians had divided them . . ." (ART/CoR, 30-VI-1576).

Archaeological evidence verifies the truth of these manuscript sources. Herbert H. Eling, Jr. (1977) studied the Talambo irrigation network in the Jequetepeque Valley. He provides a detailed account of the canals headed north and west toward the adjacent Zaña Valley. He argues that the water network could have reached the Zaña Valley, but did not because of cultural and political restrictions. He states that

> it is possible that some of the canals could reach the Zaña, if it had not been for cultural and political restrictions, and because of the fact that there were canals from the same Zaña that reached (came down) to the north shore of the Pampa of Cerro Colorado. (Eling 1977: 408)

In tracing the irrigation canals (see Fig. 1), he actually found the boundary markers, described above, that divided the water systems of the two valleys. He reports:

> Near the way station or inn (tambo) where the Zaña road starts, there is a series of stone piles or landmarks that go toward the southeast. . . . Although its extension could continue to the Valley

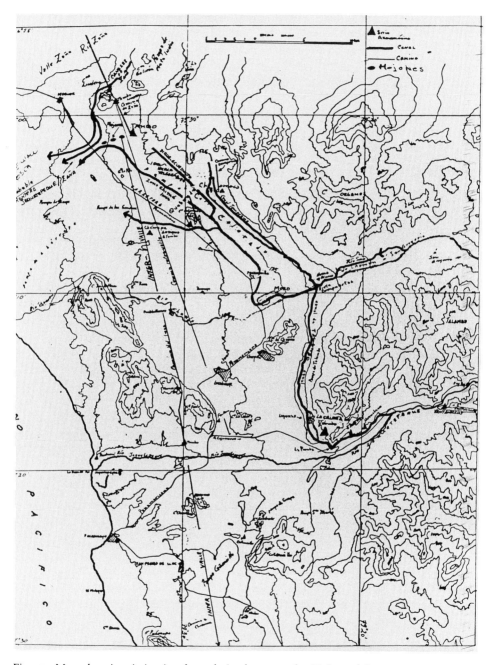

Fig. 1   Map showing irrigation boundaries between the Zaña and Jequetepeque Valleys (after Eling 1977).

of Zaña, the Jequetepeque canal finishes its route toward the north, after 12 kilometers, and turns toward the southeast, just where it finds the line of landmarks. The canal also is found with a series of canals that leave the Zaña . . . passing to the west of Cerro Lindero. These canals also turn toward the southeast to run parallel with the line of stone piles and the Jequetepeque canal. Both the Zaña and Jequetepeque canals, pass the Pampa de Chérrepe.

Now it is possible to see that the limit of the extension of Jequetepeque stays at the line of the tambo, the landmarks, the roads, and the canals. In a straight line, La Calera de Talambo, the principal control point, is 40 kilometers from this boundary, and more than 60 kilometers following the bed of the canal. All this indicates the hegemony of the Jequetepeque ends at this frontier and that of Zaña begins. (Eling 1977: 412)

Eling dates these canals to Chimu and Chimu-Inca times. Thus, the Inca probably only reconfirmed these already established boundaries following the pre-existing irrigation infrastructure at the time that he assumed control (Fig. 1).

Within these provincial boundaries, the Inca or his agent(s) supposedly demarcated individual parcels of land to various interests. After determining the needs of a community and delineating its territory, some land was assigned to support the religion and some to support state functions. Near Trujillo, there is evidence that this allocation took place. The members of the town council of the city assigned early settlers lands that had been worked for the Inca as early as 1551–52 and perhaps even earlier (ACT I: 11, 59, 75, 87–89 for 1551–52).[17] Manuscript sources mention and old army maps show such lands in the Jequetepeque Valley, as well[18] (Herbert Eling, personal communication, September 1985).

The Spanish town (*villa*) and later city of Zaña was established relatively late (1563), on lands acquired from the Indians of Mocupe (Angulo 1920: 281; Araujo 1957: 13–14). The Spanish assumed control of the northern bank; the Indians were relegated to the south (AFA/1.1, c. 19, 94v–95). Perhaps because of the late date of settlement, none of the land that was granted to the first Zaña settlers was specifically identified as having been plots used to support the Inca state or the sun. By then local *curacas* had begun appropriating such land for their own use (AGI/P189, R. 11, 1566; and ACT II: 3–7). Land titles from the study area show that Spaniards acquired land from *curacas* of the various valleys (Ramírez 1986: appendix 3), but again these acquisitions

---

[17] The first published minutes of the *cabildo* date from 1549.

[18] "Tierras del sol" (lands of the sun) are found on old army maps in several valleys (e.g., Jequetepeque and Chicama), marginal to the valley heartland and specifically to the north (Richard Schaedel, personal communication, November 1985).

are not identified as having been once the property of the Inca emperor or imperial institutions.[19] That such a distribution had taken place in these and other valleys of the coast is apparent from the 1540 testimony of the lords of Cajamarca, who specifically mentioned the Indians of the coastal communities of Pacasmayo, Zaña, Collique, Chuspo, Cinto (Patapo), and Tucume, who regularly delivered produce to storehouses in Cajamarca (Espinoza Soriano 1967: 35). The chroniclers Juan Polo de Ondegardo and Licenciado Falcón, among others, remind us that before the Spanish Conquest, the Inca received produce only from lands specifically set aside for his support, never from the lands meant to sustain community members themselves (Falcón 1918: 144; Polo de Ondegardo 1917: 53–55, 60, 64, 66; Guaman Poma de Ayala 1980: 353 [355]). So too, the religious establishment lived off the goods produced on land set aside for their maintenance. The goods being delivered to Cajamarca by these coastal community members, it follows, must have been produced on lands set aside for the state.

The actual management of these lands on the local level was left to the *curacas*. Although the often Cuzco-biased chroniclers give us the impression that the Inca was omnipotent and omnipresent, engaged in every detail of the subjugation and reorganization of an area, a close reading of Santillán suggests a more realistic scenario of how the "allocations" actually took place. Santillán, in telling how the Inca assumed control of the lands, also states that (a) all the land belonged to ("was the property of") the original peoples of the area, (b) upon conquest, the *curaca* took land away from the Indians to offer, probably ceremonially, to the Inca, and (c) it was the *curaca* who assigned service to the Inca to cultivate, harvest, and deliver the resulting produce, as was their custom (Santillán 1927: 44). Thus, it was the local *curaca*, who was responsible for managing the land on a year-to-year, day-to-day basis. He also assigned plots to individuals to sow and harvest for their own needs. Other lands were set aside to be worked communally to provide for the less fortunate members of society. Some commoners worked to produce for their local lords (ANCR/1586–1611; Santillán 1927: 17, 41).

Furthermore, the *curaca* was in charge of recruiting and directing the labor force that worked together to cultivate the lands of the state and the religious establishment. This, apparently, was a sign of submission. This practice was maintained on at least two levels of the ruling hierarchy. Below the level of paramount lord, *principales* organized workers to cultivate land set aside for the *curaca* as a sign of homage. In 1563, Alonso de Fuentes told the judge in the aforementioned court case between Lovo and Gutiérrez that seven years previously (in 1556) Don Francisco, who was the paramount

---

[19] Although logic argues that the first lands to have been acquired by the Spanish would have been lands belonging to imperial institutions rather than those used by provincial lords and their subjects.

lord of Jayanca, told him that he had four *principales* and the four each gave him (as early as 1540) a piece of land. Fuentes recalled that he had seen such a parcel of land, given to Don Francisco by his *principal* Neptur, under cultivation (AGI/J418, 1573, 311v–312).[20]

Again, as in the case of the division and the appropriation of the lands, the requirement of working them was not new. The custom of working a portion of the land in recognition of the suzerainty of a lord dated, according to Santillán, from the time when the various Indian groups of the coast were conquered and incorporated into the Kingdom of Chimor. He says:

> before [the Incas] . . . in each valley or province there was a para-
> mount lord, principal lord, and they had their principal nobles
> [*principales mandones*] subject to each paramount lord, and each of
> these valleys had war with its neighbor [*comarcano*], and for this
> reason there was no commerce or any communication among
> them; . . . and it was customary [*era uso*] that the subjects of the
> vanquished planted for the victor fields [*sementeras*] of corn and
> coca and chili pepper, and they gave him llamas (*ovejas* [*de la tierra*])
> and of everything they had, in recognition. And, in this way there
> were paramount lords that subjugated some valleys and provinces
> in particular, like the lord of the valley that now is called Truxillo,
> who was named Chimo Capac, and he became lord of most of the
> Yungas. (Santillán 1927: 12–13)

Under the Inca, the produce from such land was delivered to the *curaca,* at one level, or to Cajamarca, at the imperial level, for use or storage, instead of to the Chimu capital as presumably tribute would have been before the Inca gained control of the coast (Espinoza Soriano 1967: 35; Gama [1540] 1974). The Inca reoriented the tribute movement into the northern highlands, probably for the double purpose of feeding his garrison and armies that were either stationed there or poised for campaigns further north and of breaking the ties of local northern rulers to their former Chimu overlords.

In short, the Inca conquest of the coast meant that local communities alienated some land and provided labor service to support the imperial bureaucracy and infrastructure, but such allocations and service were long-established custom and pre-dated Cuzco hegemony. Management of the activities associated with the production and delivery of the resulting surplus remained decentralized, in the hands of local lords. Inca conquest, then, as far as land tenure goes, meant a reorientation of service. The Inca kings replaced the Chimu overlords. It is impossible to say, however, at this point, whether this represented a significant departure in the tribute

---

[20] The inescapable implication of this reference is that knowing which lord took lands from whom could help (a) re-establish the original indigenous hierarchy and (b) define the original prehistoric polities.

system or service burden, as contrasted with what it had been under the Chimu.

TRADE AS TRIBUTE

A third aspect of life of the North Coast *señoríos* that seems to have caught the attention of the Inca is the means of providing themselves with goods. Over the past few years, much debate has centered on the tribute or trade question. One well-known scholar emphasizes the overland tradition, where people of one community produce and move goods from one ecological tier to another, making it self-sufficient at least in basic foodstuffs and staples (Murra [1972] 1975). This model implies centralized control or management. Another scholar writes of the sea-faring tradition on the south Central Coast, where persons, whom the Spanish called "merchants," plied the ocean in rafts loaded with luxury goods.[21] According to this interpretation, this group of exchange specialists was apparently engaged in independent trade (Rostworowski 1970: 108, 115, 125, 138; 1975: 253–254; see Ramírez 1982 for an alternative view). Because so much already has been written about the subject, my treatment will be abbreviated and selective. Only those points crucial to the argument will be presented here. The classic literature, written by the chroniclers, gives conflicting stories on the topic. On the one hand, many do not mention commerce, markets, or merchants. Some generalize to say that Indians were not allowed to leave their communities (Morúa [1590] 1946: III-27, 229; Polo de Ondegardo 1917: 75; Santillán 1927: 78). Santillán, however, states that there was an exception or loophole to the general rule. Usually, tribute was not assessed on any good that was not locally available. The exception was an item produced with raw materials found in a nearby territory. Then, a person could obtain it in exchange for something else. The example Santillán gives is of a *cumbi* (a highland product) weaver (*oficial de cumbi*) in a valley where there was no wool. He would be allowed to obtain it in a neighboring valley in exchange for cotton or chili pepper (lowland products) (1927: 38).

This exception to the immobility rule may explain why some reference to trade is found in some chroniclers[22] (Betanzos [1551] 1987: 17, 111, 163, 189–190; Cabello Balboa, see below). It may also explain why "merchants" or exchange specialists are reported in some local, North Coast sources, as well (Ramírez 1982; Rostworowski 1975). Possibly the so-called merchants were moving goods from one area to another to gain access to materials needed for specialized work. Llama caravans loaded with goods (Shimada and Shimada 1985) or groups of bearers carrying products from one loca-

[21] María Rostworowski (1970: esp. 138) also mentions that they traveled overland to the Collao. See also Murra [1971] 1975.

[22] Juan de Betanzos ([1551] 1987: 189–190) provides evidence for state-sponsored trade and exchange that supports my argument in Ramírez 1982.

tion to another might have been called merchants by the early Spanish—before they had learned local indigenous languages and before the Indians had learned Spanish. As the latter learned Spanish, they would have equated that word with such individuals and their Spanish counterparts, and perpetuated its use, even though the Spanish word did not accurately convey the essence of the indigenous action.

Roswith Hartmann has cataloged the chroniclers who report seeing fairs and markets. Only a few of the exhaustive references of the article, however, explicitly refer to Pre-Columbian contexts for such gatherings. One that she cites is Garcilaso de la Vega, a relatively late and distant recorder of what he learned and saw as a child, and, therefore, a questionable source. According to Garcilaso, Pachacutec ordered that

> every month there be three fairs, one every nine days, so that the villagers and rural workers, having each spent eight days in their job (*oficio*), could come to the city, to the market, so that they could see and hear the things that the Inca or his Counsel had ordered; although later this same King wanted the markets to be held daily, like today . . .; and he ordered that the fairs be on holidays, so that they could be more famous. (1959, 2, bk. 6, ch. 35: 231, as cited by Hartmann 1971: 227)

A skeptical reader of this quotation might wonder whether again this relatively late observer may have been using "market" anachronistically and according to Spanish usage. It seems that the public gatherings were originally meant to convey news ("so that they could see and hear the things that the Inca or his Counsel had ordered . . ."), although reciprocal sharing or gift giving on such occasions might have occurred and might have been what such chroniclers observed. After the Spanish Conquest, with the division of the original communities into various *encomiendas,* the breakdown of the Pre-Hispanic system of reciprocity and redistribution, and restrictions placed on hospitality and travel, a market may have developed at these fairs, which Garcilaso and others may have projected back to the time of Inca rule (Betanzos [1551] 1987; Ramírez 1982, 1987).

Cabello Balboa, a second and more reliable writer that Hartmann cites (1971: 229), states, however, that certain Incas facilitated trade. He asserts that Topa Inca, for example, decreed that whoever wanted to be a merchant could wander freely throughout the land without being molested. The motivation behind this order was to find out the provenance of any gold, silver, or precious stones that might be offered in the fairs or markets that he also was interested in sponsoring (Cabello Balboa [1586] 1951: 349). This does not necessarily conflict or negate Garcilaso's statement. The Inca expansion was a continuing endeavor. Guaman Poma de Ayala discusses how Pachacuti Inca Yapanqui conquered part of the "coastal plains, yunga Indians"

(1980: 109 [109]). He may have turned ceremonial and festive occasions into fairs to which exchange specialists, perhaps from further north (Salomon n.d.), might have come. His successor, continuing the conquest in the north, may have liberalized travel restrictions to facilitate exchange and extended the practice of holding fairs in the territories he subjugated (Anonymous [1583] 1925: 289, 291; Guaman Poma 1980: 113 [111]; see also Cieza de León 1864: 217).

Both chroniclers agree that relatively late in Inca history, the Inca encountered organized exchange (perhaps as a consequence of their conquest of the coast) and, recognizing its importance, took measures to accommodate it. Thus, according to Cabello Balboa's account, freer movement was sanctioned, but only as a means to discover the sources of ores and precious stones, both materials held in high regard by the *Cuzqueños*. But in the long run, the mines would have been appropriated by the Inca, and ore, thereafter, would have been extracted by Inca order for his use (Ramírez n.d.a). The original purpose of these fairs would have been supplanted as centralized control was extended.

Polo de Ondegardo, writing in 1561, specifically mentioned exchange originating on the coast, and how it changed at the time of the Inca advance. In answer to a questionnaire, he states that under the Inca, value was not calculated in terms of money, because food was not purchased with gold or silver; although, he admits, there were cases of some coastal plains communities that exchanged (*rescatavan*) food that they took to the highlands for gold and silver. But, he continues, almost all the Indian elders conclude that this happened before the Incas conquered them, because afterward there were few such exchanges (*contrataciones*) and those exchanges (*permutaçiones*) that persisted involved cotton cloth for that of wool or fish for other foods. The former types of exchanges, he asserts, were carried out by *principales* because commoners exchanged (*rescatava*) only food for food and in small quantities. He concludes saying that there were different customs in different places that also changed from one era (Pre-Inca) to the next (Inca) (AGI/P188, R. 22, 8v–9). This, of course, clearly implies that some sort of commodity exchange, different from that previously practiced in the highlands, occurred between coastal and highland polities before the Inca conquest of the area.

On the North Coast, exchange with the highlands may have taken the form described by Polo de Ondegardo. Members of one North Coast polity could have exchanged one type of product (foodstuffs) for another (ores), although other mechanisms of procurement should not be ruled out (see Ramírez n.d.a: esp. fig. 1 and the attendant discussion for possible options; see also Craig n.d. and Rostworowski 1985). Oral tradition, written down and presented as evidence in a court case involving water, indicates that other such exchanges occurred regularly on the North Coast. In such transactions, one group provided food for access to water from another. The paramount lord of Jayanca claimed that his ancestors had "bought" (*compraron*) from the lord of Penachi "many years before the Spanish entered the realm," even "since the time of the founding of the town (*pueblo*) of Jayanca," the ravine (*quebrada*) of Chanchachala with presents (*presente[s]*) of salt, chili pepper, and pieces of cloth. He observed that this order of "tribute" persisted until the first visit by Dr. Cuenca in 1566 (ACMS/1654–1765, 7v–8; Brüning 1922–23, 3: 59; Ramírez n.d.b).

But returning to Polo de Ondegardo's 1561 remark, he indicates that after the Inca conquest such exchanges of metals for foodstuffs disappeared (although we know from the preceding example that the exchange of foodstuffs for water did not). Was this the point when Topa Inca Yapanqui declared there should be free travel and fairs as a means to discover and gain control of the sources of the metal and precious stones?

Was this part of a strategy (perhaps involving *mitimaes*) to make the coastal polities more self-sufficient? Primary sources often mention the Inca practice of relocating or resettling groups of subjects ("foreigners" or *mitimaes*) outside the domains of their original lords.[23] Gama mentions some two hundred Indians under a *principal* Labamy of Jayanca in 1540, who left the coast after the Inca conquest and still lived in the highlands of Guambos, and other subjects of the *curaca* in Pabor ([1540] 1974: 224–225). Petitions presented before Dr. Cuenca twenty-six years later speak of another two hundred *mitimaes* of the community of Moro (in modern Pacasmayo), who were in Cajamarca (AGI/J460, 457v). The *mitimaes* of Zaña are known to have been in Cajamarca in 1540 and to have lived in nine villages there in the 1560s (AGI/J460, 377v; Espinoza Soriano 1967: 35; Ramírez 1985: 427). And the list goes on (see Ramírez 1982: 126–127).

The problem with these *mitimaes* is that, although we know they existed, more often than not, we do not know what they were doing in the distant lands. Their mention in the 1540 inspection tour and census suggests that coastal Indians were in the highlands of Cajamarca and in Pabor to serve at the *tambos* or inns. Some were probably there to deliver goods from coastal lands, that is, temporarily, as suggested above (Espinoza Soriano 1967: 35). The *mitimaes* of Moro apparently lived there permanently and served their coastal lord until Dr. Cuenca's visit, when he ordered them to serve the *encomendero* of Cajamarca, Melchior Verdugo (AGI/J460, 457v). The full-time duties of the resident Zaña *mitimaes* in Cajamarca are unclear, but notarial records show that they sent cloth to the *curaca* on the coast as tribute in the 1560s (ART/Mata, 18-IV-1564). Many groups, in short, maintained contact and a relationship with their coastal lord.

These examples suggest that the Inca relocated some *mitimaes* perma-

---

[23] María Rostworowski (1985) thinks that coastal colonists lived in the highlands before the Inca conquest.

nently to relatively distant locations for other than garrison duty or to serve another lord, e.g., the potters of Collique (Espinoza Soriano 1969–70) or the metal workers (*plateros*) he took to Cuzco (Cieza de León 1967: 195). Perhaps instead some were moved to increase the self-sufficiency of their coastal counterparts, as was true of many in the southern highlands and in the highlands of Ecuador (Salomon 1986). If this were true, the movement of peoples and goods would have been managed by the lords.

Of significance here is, first, that limited types of exchange, characterized as barter (*"permutaciones," "presentes"*), survived or were permitted after the Inca conquest. The example that Polo de Ondegardo gives (i.e., cotton for wool), coincidently, supports what Santillán said about the exception or loophole to the immobility rule. And, second, this exchange was administered by the state, under the purview of the local lords (*"se hazia con los principales. . ."*).

The Inca must have realized that local lords would be valuable mediators and facilitators in an expanded procurement network. Cabello Balboa wrote that Topa Inca, after the conquest of Quito, invested a year or so of his life on a sea-faring voyage in the north to investigate the possibilities of the sea: "to see if the sea offered an enterprise with which to enhance his name and reputation on Earth" (Cabello Balboa [1586] 1951: 322). This trip and his stay there and exploration of the north suggest that he may have envisioned an even larger network that eventually would encompass the entire region.

These references suggest that the Inca realized the advantages of a type or scope of exchange that may have been unfamiliar to him, and, having investigated the possibilities, allowed certain individuals or groups to travel within the realms (perhaps on a concessionaire basis as hypothesized by Rostworowski for Chincha [1975]), and presumably under special protection and for his benefit. Indeed, on the eve of the Spanish Conquest, Juan de Betanzos tells us that Huayna Capac sent lords of Cuzco (*"señores de Cuzco"*) to obtain coca and chili pepper from the province of Chinchaysuyu. Betanzos characterizes the transactions as "purchases," but he undoubtedly meant barter and exchange. Parenthetically, this is another good example of the problems of translation in the early years and the imprecision of Spanish words used to describe similar, but different, indigenous relations (Betanzos [1551] 1987: 189–190). Also, Ann Rowe reports that procurement of colorful Amazonian bird feathers continued even after the Inca conquest of the coast, only later to be disrupted by the arrival and domination of the Spanish. Indeed, the archaeological record shows that Chimor-style artifacts, and particularly feathered cloth, were found over an even broader geographical range under Inca rule than before (Rowe 1984: 15–17, 33, 175, 179, 185–186).

It is important to emphasize that local lords administered the exchange and that the quantities involved were relatively small. Polo de Ondegardo states that the paramount lord sanctioned a few exchanges (*rescates*), but that in the end his subjects benefited from them. In most of the land, he continues, the chiefs did not try to acquire much more than could be used by his extended household. The exceptions were those who lived near Lima, Cuzco, and other cities who had adopted Spanish ways (AGI/P188, R. 22, 8v). This information supports the conclusion presented elsewhere that the "merchants" who traded within the confines of the North Coast region during Inca times were not "merchants" in the modern sense or *á la pochteca*[24] in that they were not engaged in trade for their own personal benefit (i.e., profit oriented), but, in fact, engaged in administered trade and, therefore, were retainers of their lords, albeit if also exchange specialists (Ramírez 1982; also Betanzos [1551] 1987: 189–190).

Polo de Ondegardo suggests later that the Indians were just learning to trade *á la española*. They began to understand the principle of private property as they learned how to buy and sell for gain (AGI/P188, R. 22, 10v). This may have been because of the limited knowledge commoners had of the world outside their own home communities, as suggested, when he says that the commoners did not engage in business (*negocio*) under the Inca, because they only understood how to obey the orders given to their *parcialidad*. Only the principal lords had a broader perspective (AGI/P188, R. 22, 18).

Moreover, contemporaries affirm that Indians were not engrossed in acquiring goods. Years later, they still showed little interest in working for the Spanish for gain, because their wants were limited.

> [If] the Indians would work for wages as shepherds or farm labor, they could earn their tribute . . .; [but] they reluctantly do so, even though the Spanish beg them to with silver; and they always say they are busy with their own work; unless there is an order or decree, they do not want to work, because they are not interested in acquiring goods beyond what they need for the present. (ANP/ DI, 1. 2, c. 26, 1580, 403v)

This evidence suggests that the Inca learned from his encounter with the coast. Perhaps, coastal customs and patterns of procurement were allowed to continue under some type of imperial control or regulation, a conclusion Murra (1984: 86–88) also favors, as a device to gain access to additional resources, like the mines. This implies that both paradigms, self-sufficiency and administered exchange, may have coexisted within the northern, re-

---

[24] The *pochteca* were a separate corporate group of long-distance merchants who traded for their own account, motivated by the profit motive in Aztec society. They served the state as spies, emissaries, and ambassadors and were accorded state protection and privileges in return.

cently conquered Inca domains in late Pre-Hispanic times.[25] The former was probably adequate to supply a community with basic foodstuffs. Scarce, exotic goods would have been the objective of the second. Long-distance exchange specialists, like those of Chincha, may have been affected and brought under Inca control, in return for access to or freedom to travel within the rest of the Inca territories, for example, the Collao. Local exchange was limited and remained the domain of the lords, if, indeed, it was effected by and transacted by their retainers. Trade, once affected by the centralizing tendency of the Inca, would have become, effectively, part of the tribute system.

CONCLUSIONS

This study attempts to assess the impact of the Inca conquest on the polities in an important region of the North Coast. Available local-level manuscript sources are used to determine the extent that the general Inca policy and pattern of provincial reorganization, as presented by the Cuzco-centered chroniclers, was followed. There is some truth to what the classic accounts say. Despite their relatively late conquest and brief presence, the Inca did change, in some respects, the political economy of the coast, but the change was generally quite shallow and not totally one way.

Linguistic evidence, although far from complete, now suggests several things. First, if traditional lords who were loyal were confirmed in their positions, at least for some there was some title changing, perhaps initially related to demographic reshuffling (although this is not proven by Colonial sources). Second, a complete decimal system, on the model presented in the classic literature, if ever present, disappeared within a generation or two of the Spanish arrival. This suggests that such imposed changes had been superficial and incomplete. Third, what persisted, in contrast, seems to have been the traditional names or titles of lords and *señoríos*. Many survive to this day as toponyms and *parcialidades,* despite the facts that the original hierarchy of officials and its categories collapsed (to *cacique principal* or *curaca, segunda persona, principal, mandón* and *mandoncillo* [little *mandón*]), and that social and ethnic distinctions were quickly lost. Fourth, with judicious use, the names of the lords, their position in the ruling hierarchical structure, and the identity of their *señoríos* could prove valuable leads in reconstructing spatial hierarchies and the jurisdictions or outlines of the original late Pre-Hispanic polities.

The Inca also affected land tenure by occupying land to support the growing imperial infrastructure and religious hierarchy. Provincial boundaries and customs seemed to have changed little, however, from what they

[25] Subsequent to presenting this paper, Frank Salomon called my attention to his article, "Vertical Politics on the Inka Frontier" (1986), in which he independently reached the same conclusion.

had been before the Inca conquest. Both before and after the Incas gained control, the vanquished relinquished lands to the victors and felt duty-bound to work them and make them produce. Under the Inca, day-to-day control and management of the land remained in the hands of the traditional local lords. They became the mediators and facilitators in the expanding system of tribute production and delivery.

Coastal exchange and procurement seems to have been a third area affected by Inca domination. The Inca apparently encountered different types of exchange on the coast. These transactions could have been between peoples of one polity living in different zones and, as likely, between peoples of two different polities. The Inca apparently allowed some of this interaction to continue and even facilitated exchange by liberalizing travel restrictions and turning ceremonial occasions into opportunities for barter and trade. The motivation behind this was the opportunity to gain control of the source of exotic goods (e.g., ores). The evidence strongly suggests that such concessions were intended to bring the exchange under imperial control. By gaining access to the sources of desired materials or goods, the Inca could control supply and channel production according to his criteria into his redistributive network. In this way, trade or exchange would become tribute. But, the fact that coastal ways of doing things survived, even in the short run or in the process of modification, was one way that the coastal people affected the thinking and practices of their highland overlords.

In general, then, one must conclude that the chroniclers' "macro-perspective" characterization of the Inca conquest and administration does not hold up well on the North Coast. This is probably because (a) the North Coast was subjected to the Inca's hegemony for a relatively short time, (b) the Inca Empire was not as effectively centralized as the chroniclers might suggest, especially in lately incorporated provinces distant from the Inca heartland, and (c) the Inca encountered a highly organized civilization with strongly entrenched customs that persisted and could not be changed overnight by mandate from above.

Manuscripts Cited

ACMS   Archivo del Señor Agusto Castillo Muro Sime, Lambayeque

ACT   Actas del Cabildo de Truxillo

AFA   Archivo del Fuero Agrário, Lima

AGI   Archivo General de las Indias, Seville

    AL   Audiencia de Lima

    E   Escribanía de Cámara

    J   Justicia

    P   Patronato

ANCR   Archivo Notarial de Carlos Rivadeneira
ANP   Archivo Nacional del Perú
   DI   Derecho Indígena
   LC   López de Cordova
APF   Fábrica Archivo Parrochial de Ferreñafe, Libro de Fábrica
ART   Archivo Regional de Trujillo (now Archivo Departamental de La Libertad)
   CoAg   Corregimiento, Asuntos de Gobierno
   CoO   Corregimiento, Ordinario
   CoR   Corregimiento, Residencia
   LC   López de Cordova
   Mata
   SC   Suárez del Corral
ASFL/Reg   Archivo de San Francisco de Lima, Registro
BM   British Museum, London

BIBLIOGRAPHY

ANONYMOUS
   [1583]   Relación anónima sobre el modo de gobernar de los Incas. In
   1925   *Gobernantes del Peru, Cartas y papeles, Siglo XVI* (Don Roberto Levillier, ed.) 9: 289–296. Sucesores de Rivadeneyra, Madrid.

ANGULO, DOMINGO
   1920   Fundación y población de la Villa de Zaña. *Revista del Archivo Nacional* [del Perú] 1 (2): 280–300.

ARAUJO, ALEJANDRO O.
   1957   *Reseña histórica de Saña.* Typescript, Eten, Perú.

BETANZOS, JUAN DE
   [1551]   *Suma y narración de los Incas.* Atlas, Madrid.
   1987

BRÜNING, ENRIQUE (HEINRICH)
   1922–23   *Estudios monográficos del Departamento de Lambayeque.* Dionisio Mendoza, Chiclayo.

CABELLO BALBOA, MIGUEL
   [1586]   *Miscelánea antártica.* Instituto de Etnología, Universidad Nacional
   1951   Mayor de San Marcos, Lima.

CARRERA, FERNANDO DE LA
   [1644]   *Arte de la lengua yunga.* Instituto de Antropologia, Publicaciones Espe-
   1939   ciales Numero 3. Universidad Nacional de Tucuman, Tucuman.

Susan E. Ramírez

Cieza de León, Pedro de
 1864   *The Travels of Pedro de Cieza de León*. Printed for the Hakluyt Society, New York.
 1967   *El señorío de los Incas*. Instituto de Estudios Peruanos, Lima.

Craig, Alan K.
 n.d.   Origins and Development of Andean Mining. In *Sican Metallurgy: Cultural and Technological Dimensions of Ancient Andean Metallurgy* (Izumi Shimada, ed.). Cambridge University Press, New York. (In press)

Eling, Jr., Herbert J.
 1977   Interpretaciones preliminares del sistema de riego antiguo de Talambo en el Valle de Jequetepeque, Perú. *III Congreso Peruano, El Hombre y la Cultura Andina (1977), Actas y Trabajos* (Ramiro Matos M., ed.) 2: 401–419. Lima.

Espinoza Soriano, Waldemar
 1967   El primer informe etnológico sobre Cajamarca de 1540. *Revista Peruana de Historia* 11–12: 1–37.
 1969–70 Los mitmas yungas de Collique en Cajamarca, Siglos XV, XVI y XVII. *Revista del Museo Nacional* [del Perú] 36: 9–57.
 1975   El valle de Jayanca y el reino de los Mochica, Siglos XV y XVI. *Bulletin de l'Institut Français d'Etudes Andines* 4 (3–4): 243–274. Lima.

Falcón, Licenciado
 1918   Representación hecha por el Licenciado Falcón en concilio provincial, sobre los daños y molestias que se hacen a los indios. In *Informaciones acerca de la religion y gobierno de los Incas*. Imprenta y Libreria San Marti, y Cía., Colección de libros y documentos referentes a la historia del Perú, 11: 133–176. Lima.

Gama, Sebastián de la
 [1540] Visita hecha en el Valle de Jayanca [Trujillo]. Historia y Cultura 8:
 1974   216–228.

Guaman Poma de Ayala, Felipe
 1980   *Nueva corónica y buen gobierno*. 3 vols. Siglo Veintiuno, Mexico.

Harrington, John P.
 1945   Yunka, Language of the Peruvian Coastal Culture. *International Journal of American Linguistics* 11 (1): 24–30.

Hartmann, Roswith
 1971   Mercados y ferías prehispánicos en el area andina. *Boletín de la Academia Nacional de Historia* 54 (118): 214–235.

Julien, Catherine J.
 1982   Inca Decimal Administration in the Lake Titicaca Region. *The Inca and Aztec States, 1400–1800* (George A. Collier, Renato I. Rosaldo, and John D. Wirth, eds.): 119–151. Academic Press, New York.

Mayer, Enrique
 1972   Censos insensatos: Evaluación de los censos campesinos en la historia de Tangor. In *Iñigo Ortiz de Zuñiga, Visita de la Provincia de Leon de*

Huánuco en 1562, 2: 341–365. Universidad Nacional Hermilio Valdizan, Facultad de Letras y Educación, Huánuco.

MELO, GARCÍA DE, et al.
    [1582]   Información . . . acerca de las costumbres que tenian los Incas del Perú,
    1925   antes de la conquista española. . . . In *Gobernantes del Perú, Cartas y papeles, Siglo XVI* (Roberto Levillier, ed.) 9: 268–296. Sucesores de Rivadeneyra, Madrid.

MORÚA, FRAY MARTÍN DE
    [1590]   *Historia del orígen y genealogía real de los Reyes Incas del Perú.* Consejo
    1946   Superior de Investigationes Científicas, Instituto Santo Toribio de Mogrovejo, Madrid.

MURRA, JOHN V.
    [1971]   El tráfico de mullu en la costa del Pacifico. In *Formaciones económicas y*
    1975   *politicas del mundo andino:* 255–268. Instituto de Estudios Peruanos, Lima.
    [1972]   El control vertical de un máximo de pisos ecológicos en la economia de
    1975   las sociedades andinas. In *Formaciones económicas y politicas del mundo andino:* 59–116. Instituto de Estudios Peruanos, Lima.
    1984   Andean Societies before 1532. In *The Cambridge History of Latin America* (Leslie Bethell, ed.) 1: 59–90. Cambridge University Press, New York.

NETHERLY, PATRICIA J.
    1984   The Management of Late Andean Irrigation Systems on the North Coast of Peru. *American Antiquity* 49 (2): 227–254.

ORREGO H., AUGUSTO
    1958   Palabras del mochica. *Revista del Museo Nacional* [del Perú] 27: 80–95.

POLO DE ONDEGARDO, JUAN
    1917   Del linage de los Ingas y como conquistaron. In *Colección de libros y documentos referentes a la historia del Perú* 4: 45–94. Sanmarti y Cía., Lima.

RAMÍREZ, SUSAN E.
    1978   Chérrepe en 1572: Un análisis de la Visita General del Virrey Francisco de Toledo. *Historia y Cultura* 11: 79–121. *Revista del Museo Nacional de Historia,* Lima.
    1982   Retainers of the Lords or Merchants: A Case of Mistaken Identity? In *El hombre y su ambiente en los Andes centrales* (Luís Millones and Hiroyasu Tomoeda, eds.): 123–136. Senri Ethnological Studies 10, National Museum of Ethnology, Osaka.
    1985   Social Frontiers and the Territorial Base of Curacazgos. In *Andean Ecology and Civilization* (Shozo Masuda, Izumi Shimada, and Craig Morris, eds.): 423–442. University of Tokyo Press, Tokyo.
    1986   *Provincial Patriarchs: Land Tenure and the Economics of Power in Colonial Peru.* University of New Mexico Press, Albuquerque.
    1987   The "Dueño de Indios": Thoughts on the Consequences of the Shifting Bases of Power of the "Curaca de los Viejos Antiguos" under the

Spanish in Sixteenth-Century Peru. *Hispanic American Historical Review* 67 (4): 575–610.

n.d.a   Ethnohistorical Dimensions of Mining and Metallurgy in Northern Peru: Sixteenth-Eighteenth Centuries. In *Sican Metallurgy: Cultural and Technological Dimensions of Ancient Andean Metallurgy* (Izumi Shimada, ed.). Cambridge University Press, New York. (In press)

n.d.b   'Myth' or 'Legend' as Fiction or Fact: A Historian's Assessment of the Traditions of North Coastal Peru. Paper presented at the IV International Symposium on Latin American Indian Literatures, Merida, Mexico, 1986.

RIVERO-AYLLON, TEODORO

1976   *Lambayeque, sol, flores y leyendas.* Gráfica Jacobs, S.A., Chiclayo.

ROSTWOROWSKI DE DIEZ CANSECO, MARÍA

1966   Las tierras reales y su mano de obra en el Tahuantinsuyu. *Proceedings, XXXVI Congreso Internacional de Americanistas* (1964) 2: 31–34. Seville.

1970   Mercaderes del valle de Chincha en la época prehispánica: Un documento y unos comentarios. In *Etnia y sociedad 1977:* 97–140. Instituto de Estudios Peruanos, Lima.

1975   Pescadores, artesanos y mercaderes costeños en el Perú prehispánico. In *Etnia y sociedad 1977:* 211–263. Instituto de Estudios Peruanos, Lima.

1985   Patronyms with the Consonant F in the *Guarangas* of Cajamarca. In *Andean Ecology and Civilization* (Shozo Masuda, Izumi Shimada, and Craig Morris, eds.): 401–421. University of Tokyo Press, Tokyo.

ROWE, ANN POLLARD

1984   *Costumes and Featherwork of the Lords of Chimor: Textiles from Peru's North Coast.* Textile Museum, Washington, D.C.

ROWE, JOHN H.

1948   The Kingdom of Chimor. *Acta Americana* 6 (1–2): 26–59.

SALOMON, FRANK

1986   Vertical Politics on the Inka Frontier. In *Anthropological History of Andean Polities* (John V. Murra, Nathan Wachtel, and Jacques Revel, eds.): 89–117. Cambridge University Press, Cambridge.

n.d.   *Ethnic Lords of Quito in the Age of the Incas: The Political Economy of North Andean Chiefdoms.* Ph.D. dissertation, Latin American Studies Program, Cornell University, Ithaca, 1978.

SANTILLÁN, HERNANDO DE

1927   Relación del origen, descendencia, politica y gobierno de los Incas. In *Colección de libros y documentos referentes a la historia del Perú* (Horacio H. Urteaga, ed.) 9 (second series): 1–124. Sanmarti y Cía., Lima.

SHIMADA, MELODY, and IZUMI SHIMADA

1985   Prehistoric Llama Breeding and Herding on the North Coast of Peru. *American Antiquity* 50 (1): 3–26.

TRIMBORN, HERMANN

1979   *El reino de Lambayeque en el antiguo Perú.* Collectanea Instituti Anthropos 19. Haus Völker und Kulturen, Anthropos Institut, St. Augustin.

TRUJILLO, PERU

1969–70   *Actas del Cabildo de Trujillo, 1549–1604.* 3 vols. Lima.

VACA DE CASTRO, LICENCIADO CHRISTÓBAL

[1543]   Ordenanzas de tambos distancias de unos a otros, modo de cargar los
1943   indios y obligaciones. . . . *Revista Histórica* 3: 427–492.

VARGAS UGARTE, RUBÉN

[1939]   Los mochicas y el cacicazgo de Lambayeque. *27 Congreso Internacional*
1942   *de Americanistas (1939), Lima, Actas y trabajos científicos* 2: 475–482.

ZEVALLOS QUIÑONES, JORGE

1947   *Un diccionario Castellano-Yunga.* Ministerio de Educación Pública, Lima.
1968   La visita del pueblo de Ferreñafe (Lambayeque) en 1568. *Historia y
Cultura* 9: 155–178. Lima.

Index